PASS THE 66™

A PLAIN ENGLISH EXPLANATION TO HELP YOU PASS THE SERIES 66 EXAM

ROBERT M. WALKER

PASS THE 66™ - A PLAIN ENGLISH EXPLANATION TO HELP YOU PASS THE SERIES 66 EXAM

By Robert M. Walker

Revised Edition – January, 2017 – 3rd Edition

www.examzone.com

Pass the 66™, 2nd Edition ISBN-13   978-0-9831411-8-1

Library of Congress Control Number (LCCN) 2016900471

Publisher: Sure Fire Publications, LLC.® Chicago, IL. (Acquired by Examzone, Inc. August 2016)

Printed in the U.S.A.

Table of Contents

How to Use This Book 7

CHAPTER 1: Economic Factors & Business Information 9

Analytical Methods 15
Financial Ratios and Their Uses 16
Valuation Ratios 20
Time Value of Money 21
Descriptive Statistics and Risk Measurements 23

Now What? 28

CHAPTER 2: Investment Vehicle Characteristics 31

Insurance-Based Products 31
Annuities 31
Life Insurance 39

Types and Characteristics of Cash and Cash Equivalents 44
T-Bills 44
Bankers' Acceptances 45
Commercial Paper 45
Repurchase Agreements 46
Tax-Exempt Municipal Notes 47
Certificates of Deposit (CDS) 47
Fed Funds 49

Types and Characteristics of Fixed-Income Securities 49
Form of Registration 50
Quotes 51
Notation 52
Types of Maturities 52
Special Types of Bonds 53
Risks 55
Corporate Bonds 56
U.S. Government Securities 58
Agency Bonds 62
Foreign Bonds 63
CMOs 64
Asset-Backed Securities 65
Municipal Securities 66
Methods Used to Determine the Value of Fixed-Income Securities 71

Types and Characteristics of Equity Securities 77
Common Stock 77
Preferred Stock 88
Yield vs. Total Return 91
Methods Used to Evaluate Equity Securities 92

Types and Characteristics of Pooled Investments 98
Investment Companies 98
REITs 118
Private Funds 118

Alternative Investments _____ 120
    Limited Partnerships (DPPs) _____ 120
    Structured Products _____ 126

Other Assets _____ 128

Futures _____ 129
    Forwards _____ 131

Now What? _____ 136

CHAPTER 3: Client Investment Recommendations & Strategies _____ 138

Type of Client _____ 138
    Sole Proprietor _____ 138
    Partnerships _____ 138
    LLC (Limited Liability Company) _____ 140
    Corporations _____ 141

Client Profile _____ 143
    Suitability _____ 146

Portfolio Management Strategies, Styles and Techniques _____ 156
    Strategies and Styles _____ 156
    Techniques _____ 161

Capital Market Theory _____ 163
    CAPM _____ 163
    Modern Portfolio Theory _____ 163
    Efficient Market Hypothesis _____ 164
    Behavioral Finance _____ 165

Tax Considerations _____ 167
    Portfolio Income _____ 168
    Mutual Fund Taxation _____ 174
    Taxation of Annuities _____ 176
    Taxation of Life Insurance _____ 178
    Transferred Securities _____ 178
    AMT _____ 179
    Progressive and Regressive _____ 180
    Corporate Taxes _____ 180

Retirement Plans _____ 181
    Individual Plans _____ 182
    Employer-Based Plans _____ 184

ERISA Issues _____ 187
    Fiduciaries _____ 188
    Safe Harbor, 404(c) _____ 189
    Company Stock _____ 190

Special Types of Accounts _____ 191

Ownership and Estate Planning Techniques _____ 195
    Estates _____ 195
    Gifts _____ 196

Trusts _____ 198

Disclaiming an Inheritance _____ 202

Qualified Domestic Relations Order _____ 203

Account Ownership Techniques _____ 204

Trading Securities _____ **205**

First Market – NYSE, etc. _____ 206

Over-the-Counter _____ 209

Third Market _____ 210

Fourth Market _____ 210

Dark Pools, High-Frequency Trading _____ 211

Selling Short _____ 212

Bond Trading _____ 214

Types of Orders _____ 215

Margin _____ 217

Performance Measures _____ **223**

Holding Period and Annualized Return _____ 223

Yield and Total Return _____ 223

Inflation-Adjusted, Real Return _____ 225

After-Tax Return _____ 225

Tax-Equivalent Yield _____ 226

Risk-Adjusted Return _____ 226

Time- and Dollar-Weighted Return _____ 227

Expected Return _____ 227

Benchmarks _____ 228

Possible Calculations _____ 228

Now What? _____ **229**

CHAPTER 4: Laws, Regulations, and Guidelines, Including Prohibition on Unethical Business Practices _____ ***232***

RIAs, IARs, Broker-Dealers, and Agents _____ **232**

State and Federal Securities Acts _____ **234**

Uniform Securities Act _____ 234

Federal Securities Acts _____ 253

Regulation of RIAs and IARs _____ **260**

Investment Adviser Representatives _____ 262

Federal Covered Advisers _____ 263

Wrap-Fee Programs _____ 264

State Registration _____ 265

NSMIA _____ 268

Exempt Reporting Advisers _____ 269

SEC Release IA-1092 _____ 270

Regulation of Broker-Dealers and Agents _____ **272**

Registration Procedure _____ 273

Record Keeping Requirements _____ 274

Net Capital Requirements _____ 275

Renewals and Other Registration Specifics _____ 275

Exclusions and Exemptions for Persons _____ 276
    Not a Broker-Dealer _____ 278
    Not an Agent _____ 279
    Investment Adviser Exclusions _____ 281

Communication with Clients and Prospects _____ 285
    Disclosures _____ 285
    Unlawful Representations _____ 288
    Performance Guarantees _____ 289
    Client Contracts _____ 290
    Correspondence and Advertising _____ 291

Ethical Practices and Fiduciary Obligations _____ 301
    Compensation _____ 302
    Fraud _____ 303
    Custody of Client Assets _____ 306
    Conflicts of Interest _____ 308
    Client Confidentiality _____ 315
    Code of Ethics _____ 315
    NASAA Model Rule on Business Practices for Advisers _____ 317
    Business Practices for Broker-Dealers and Agents _____ 326
    Cybersecurity, Privacy, and Data Protection _____ 339
    Business Continuity Plans _____ 343

Now What? _____ 344

Glossary _____ 345

How to Use This Book

We're happy you chose Examzone to help you pass the Series 66 exam. Our Pass the 66 Textbook is written in Plain English so you can learn concepts and assimilate the material quickly and easily. We hope you take advantage of our full **Series 66 Success Program™**, complete with test prep materials for each step of the learning process.

The Learning Components of the **Series 66 Success Program™** can be found at http://www.examzone.com/series65 and include:

- Pass the 66™ Textbook
- Pass the 66™ DVD Lesson Set
- Pass the 66™ Online Training Videos
- Pass the 66™ Online Test-Taking Strategies Videos
- Pass the 66™ Online Practice Question Bank
- Pass the 66™ Go/No Go Exams

Our research has shown that students who follow the entire **Series 66 Success Program™** have considerably higher pass rates than those who use only one or two of the Learning Components. Our Success Program integrates each of the Learning Components on a chapter-by-chapter basis. The sequence starts with each textbook chapter, followed by the requisite Practice Exams and finishes with the videos and DVDs for that chapter. You can see this sequence outlined on the next page in the Study Plan for the **Series 66 Success Program™**.

Additionally, our Pass the 66™ Go/No Go Exams are designed to test your readiness for the Series 66 exam. We recommend you take the Go/No Go at least two weeks prior to your scheduled test date. If you score an 80% or above, we think you're ready to take the Series 66 exam.

All of the Success Program materials mentioned above are available for purchase at http://www.examzone.com/series66. Email us at support@examzone.com or call us toll free at 1-855-EXAM-CARE – 1 (855) 392-6227 with any questions.

Thanks for studying with Examzone, and good luck!

Estimated Time Commitments:

- 4-6 weeks of study (60 hours)
- 3-4 days per week
- 2-4 hours per day

Weekly Study Plan:

WEEK 1 Goals:	• Finish textbook through Chapter 1 • Take Chapter 1 quizzes in Online Practice Question Bank • Watch the DVD and/or Online Streaming Video Lessons 1 through 3 • Video Lessons: 1,Financial Reporting, 2, Quantitative Methods, 3, Investment Risks
WEEK 2 Goals:	• Finish textbook through Chapter 2 • Take Chapter 2 quizzes in Online Practice Question Bank • Watch the DVD and/or Online Streaming Video Lessons 4 through 10 • Video Lessons: 4, Equity Securities, 5, Debt Securities, 6, Bond Yields, 7, Cash Equivalents, 8, Derivatives, 9, Pooled Investment Vehicles, 10, Insurance Based Products
WEEK 3 Goals:	• Finish textbook through Chapter 3 • Take Chapter 3 quizzes in Online Practice Question Bank • Watch the DVD and/or Online Streaming Video Lessons 11 – 17 • Video Lessons: 11, Clients, 12, Portfolio Management, 13, Taxation, 14, Tax Advantaged Plans, 15, Trading Securities, 16, Margin Accounts, 17, Performance Measures
WEEK 4 Goals:	• Finish textbook through Chapter 4 • Take Chapter 4 quizzes in Online Practice Question Bank • Watch the DVD and/or Online Streaming Video Lessons 18 – 22 • Video Lessons: 18, USA Administration Of The Act, 19, USA Registration Of Persons, 20, Securities, 21 Business Prac BD And Agent, 22, Biz Prac RIA and IAR
WEEK 5 Goals:	• Watch All 8 Test-Taking Skills Online Videos • Review textbook, DVD and Streaming Video materials
WEEK 6 Goals:	• Take all Practice Exams (100 Questions) in Online Practice Question Bank • Take the Go / No Go exams and proceed according to recommendation • Schedule tutoring if you need extra help@ **www.examzone.com/tutoring**

CHAPTER 1: Economic Factors & Business Information

Many successful American businesses are privately owned. Five Guys Burgers & Fries and Toys 'R' Us, for example, are well-known companies, but we would have to estimate their revenue, expenses and profits since private companies don't report their financial results to the public. By comparison, if we want to know the revenue and net income after tax for Starbucks or Microsoft, we can go to the SEC's **EDGAR** site and pull up the company's most recent quarterly or annual reports.

It's not that Five Guys and Toys 'R' Us don't have income statements, balance sheets, and statements of cash flows. They don't publish their **financial statements**. Starbucks, Microsoft, and McDonald's, on the other hand, are reporting companies who must disclose all relevant information to the investing public, even to those who will never invest in their stock.

An issuer of securities can only pay the interest on their bonds if they have enough revenue to cover it. The preferred stockholders will only get paid if the profits are dependable, and the common stock will rise over the long term only if the profits at the company rise. The financial statements released by public companies disclose the company's revenue, expenses, and profits, as well as their financial condition and their cash flows. Each statement tells a different story about the same company.

Income Statement

The company's revenue and net income are disclosed on the **income statement**. We'll look at another financial statement called the **balance sheet** up ahead. For now let's point out the difference between the two statements, put out by the same company. The balance sheet is a snapshot of the company's financial strength right now, at some point in time. The income statement, on the other hand, shows the results of the company's operations over a period of time. So, if you want to see how solid a company's finances are, check the balance sheet. If you want to see how profitable a company's last fiscal year was, look at their income statement.

A public company had to register its securities offering with the SEC under the **Securities Act of 1933** when it went public. That same company is then a reporting company required to file quarterly and annual reports with the **SEC** under the **Securities Exchange Act of 1934,** as well as making these reports available to their shareholders. This allows the shareholders who invested in these public companies to see the financial condition (balance sheet) of their company and whether the sales and profits are increasing, decreasing, or flattening out (income statement). Because the issuer uploads the information to the SEC's EDGAR website, anyone with curiosity can see the details of the issuer's operations, not just current investors.

An income statement can also be referred to as a "statement of earnings" or "statement of operations," while the balance sheet is often referred to as the "statement of financial condition." Whatever we call it, although the reports are primarily for shareholders, this information is available to anyone who wants to see it.

That includes the company's competitors, which is another reason many companies stay private. For example, if Five Guys is in secret talks to acquire another fast food chain, they would rather keep that on the down-low as opposed to letting McDonald's see what they're thinking and maybe try to out-bid them. On the other hand, if McDonald's is planning to open a certain number of restaurants in Africa next year, they would have to let the whole world know about it either on their next scheduled filing or by releasing an 8K.

If you go to your favorite financial website or search for a company's "10-K" or "annual shareholder report," you can see the financial statements for companies such as Microsoft, Oracle, and Starbucks. For now, though, let's start small. Let's say you're an 11-year-old kid again, and you have launched a lemonade stand for the summer. Each glass of lemonade sells for $1, and the dollars you pull in through your business this summer are called **sales** or **revenue**. Turns out you sell 10,000 glasses of lemonade, so your revenue is exactly $10,000 over the summer. Revenue is the top line of the income statement.

In some businesses there are returns, refunds, and discounts. Retailers, for example, often report their **net revenue** or **net operating revenue,** which is their revenue after all the returns, refunds, and discounts have been accounted for.

Your lemonade stand didn't do any discounting or experience any returns, so your revenue is what it is. However, $10,000 in revenue is not the same thing as $10,000 of profit. That lemonade you sold was produced by a combination of the following ingredients: purified water, fresh lemons, lemon juice, sugar, and ice. Those are the goods you bought to make the product you sold, which is why the money you spent on them is called the **cost of goods sold** or **cost of revenue.** You also have to serve your product in recyclable cups, which cost $1,000, on top of the $2,000 paid for the ingredients. So, now your $10,000 in revenue is down to $7,000 after subtracting the $3,000 for "cost of goods sold."

And, we're not done subtracting yet. Like all businesses, you have operating expenses to cover. Operating expenses are the expenses not directly associated with the production of the company's products: office rent, administrative salaries, office supplies, entertainment costs, travel costs, etc. You have a handful of operating expenses with your lemonade stand, as well. While you worked the stand yourself most of the time, you also hired your sister to come up with some marketing plans. Her $500 of compensation represents an operating expense to you. There are other operating expenses, including the advertising you do by putting up signs at both ends of the block and running a classified ad in the local paper. Your advertising expense was $500 over the summer.

Operating expenses are often referred to as "SG&A" for **"selling, general, and administrative"** expenses. At a manufacturing company, the labor of the workers on the production floor would generally be part of cost of goods sold, since that labor goes directly into the cost of the finished product. The compensation to the so-called "white-collar workers" out in the cozy offices is part of "selling, general, and administrative" expenses. If you hired baristas to serve up the lemonade, their labor is part of cost of goods sold (aka, cost of revenue), while the compensation for your sister's marketing work is an operating expense, not directly related to producing and serving your product.

Even though you're just an 11-year-old kid, you decided not to slap a piece of cardboard on a stick with the words "Cold Lemonade – $1." Instead, you got the boy next door to build you a stand for $200, and that is a different type of expense. See, you're going to be in business for the next five years, and you'll be using that stand each summer. So, you subtract 1/5 of that $200 on your income statement each year. Instead of subtracting $200 all at once, you only subtract $40 to "depreciate" this vital piece of equipment. Even though you spent the money all up front, next year you will also subtract $40 as a **depreciation** expense on your income statement. You will do that five times until you have depreciated the cost of the stand to zero.

To depreciate an asset means to spread its cost over its estimated useful life. A manufacturing company would not expense a $10 million piece of equipment out on the shop floor the way they would expense the paper and toner used up in the office. The latter are consumed and expensed all at once while the equipment is slowly subtracted/written down on the income statement to spread the cost over its estimated useful life.

Tangible assets are depreciated, while intangible assets are written down using **amortization.** If a company is manufacturing a drug under a patent with a limited life, they will amortize the patent over time, as they would depreciate a plastic injection molding machine over several years. In either case, an asset's cost is being spread over its estimated useful life by taking a series of charges on the income statement through these non-cash expenses called either depreciation or amortization.

There are other assets subject to depreciation at your lemonade stand. You had to buy several large thermoses, a couple of blenders, a little money drawer, a calculator, and a copy of QuickBooks™. These fixed assets all work out to $300, which you depreciate over three years, subtracting another $100 this year.

We have accounted for cost of goods sold, operating expenses, and depreciation. But there are **interest** payments and **taxes** to account for before arriving at the company's **net income** or **net loss** for the reporting period. Your mom had to spot you some credit to buy your first batch of ingredients and, unfortunately, she charges you interest on the loan. On the plus side, you get to deduct that interest before figuring your taxable income, just as homeowners deduct the interest paid on their mortgages. So, you subtract the $20 of interest, and your taxable income is $5,840. Your taxes work out to $40, and after paying those, you have a **net profit**, or **net income after tax**, of $5,800.

Let's review your lemonade stand's results of operations over the summer:

Sales/Revenue	$10,000
Cost of Goods Sold	– $3,000
Operating Expenses	– $1,000
Depreciation, Amortization	– $140
OPERATING INCOME	$5,860
Interest Expense	– $20
PRE-TAX INCOME	$5,840

Taxes	– $40
NET INCOME after tax	$5,800

Statement of Cash Flows

Some subtractions on the income statement do not involve an outlay of cash. Depreciation and amortization spread an asset's historical cost over an estimated useful life, but no cash is being spent when we record the expense on the income statement.

Therefore, since there's a difference between an accounting entry called "depreciation" and actual cash being spent, analysts ignore intangible expenses like that when focusing on **cash flow**, which is how much cash is being generated (or consumed) by a company. One way to estimate cash flow is to take the net income from the income statement and then add back two non-cash charges: depreciation and amortization. Your lemonade stand doesn't have a lot of depreciation and amortization going on, but companies that invest in expensive factories, warehouses, and equipment can show quite different figures for net income on the one hand and cash flow from operations on the other. When they add back the depreciation that reduced their net income, their cash flow is a much higher amount.

But, there's no need to estimate, since in the corporation's 10-K, we also find a separate **statement of cash flows** that shows how much cash has been provided or used by the business over the reporting period. You might think that is the same thing as the net income on the income statement (statement of earnings), but that's not the case. The accrual method of accounting is most widely used, and it involves the company booking revenue/sales before any cash has been exchanged. The statement of cash flows eliminates this sort of distortion, as well as intangible expenses like depreciation/amortization. A good fundamental analyst knows that some companies have been known to book "profits" when they're really not generating enough cash to stay afloat.

The statement of cash flows is separated into three distinct ways in which a company can generate (or exhaust) cash: cash flows from operating activities, cash flows from investing activities, and cash flows from financing activities. **Cash flows from operating activities** are what that phrase sounds like: the company provided or exhausted this much cash through their core operations. For example, Starbucks generates most of its cash by operating thousands of successful coffee shops, but it can also generate cash through investing activities and through financing activities. Most shareholders in SBUX would probably care most about the cash the company generates through its operations. I mean, they're not an investment company or a finance company, right? Cash flow from operations shows us the net income from the income statement, adds back depreciation/amortization, and then records the changes in working capital (from the balance sheet). After dealing with the change in the line items under current assets and current liabilities (working capital), the company can then calculate and report the net cash provided/used by operating activities.

Cash flow from investing activities indicates how much cash was used or generated, usually from investing in capital equipment, and to some extent buying and selling securities, e.g. U.S. Treasuries. Capital equipment ("capex") can be thought of as all the hard, tangible stuff that brick-and-mortar companies have to invest in to operate, stay afloat and maybe make a profit (buying a printing press, remodeling existing stores, building new stores, etc.). If a company is like MSFT or ORCL, they might go on a business buying binge, which is reflected in their cash used for acquisitions. Big increases in this number could indicate that the company is making strategic acquisitions of former competitors, or it could mean that they're generating too much of their returns by buying up smaller fish as opposed to operating successfully.

Cash flow from financing activities is the cash provided/used through basically any activity involving the shareholders (owners) or bondholders (creditors) of the company. If stock is issued, cash is generated, while if the company engages in share buyback programs, cash is used up. If a company issues bonds, cash is generated, while when it finally redeems or calls those bonds, cash is used up. Also, when the company pays dividends to shareholders, it's easy to see where that cash is ending up, right? Young, growing companies often issue stock to finance their operations. That may be fine, but new stock issues dilute the value of the existing shareholders' equity. More mature companies, with plenty of cash on hand, often buy back their shares to make each existing share more valuable. Either way, we could track these activities under this section of the statement of cash flows.

The terms "cash flows from investing activities" and "cash flows from financing activities" could be potentially confusing. Remember that if a company buys Government securities or shares of a public company on the open market, we'd see that under "cash flows from investing activities." And, if the company invests in a printing press, that's under cash flows from investing activities, too—no matter how much "sense" it might make to think of that as a "financing" activity. No, cash flow from financing activities includes the cash generated by issuing stocks or bonds and the cash flow exhausted buying back stock and/or retiring bonds. Would the test exploit this natural confusion? Anything's possible.

Balance Sheet

If you were applying for a loan, the lender would want to know two important things: how much money do you make, and what kind of collateral do you have? You could submit your statement of cash flow showing all your sources of income minus expenses. But the lender would also like to see what kind of **assets** you're holding minus your **liabilities**. Your lemonade stand might need to borrow money to expand someday. If so, the bank would want to see your balance sheet when you apply. The balance sheet reveals financial condition.

The basic formula for the balance sheet is expressed as:

Assets = Liabilities + Stockholders' Equity

or

Assets – Liabilities = Stockholders' Equity

Assets represent what a company owns. Liabilities represent what a company owes. You take what a company owns, subtract what it owes, and that's the **net worth** of the company. Another name for net worth is **stockholders' equity**, which implies that the stockholders are the owners of the company, so what we want to know is: what is that ownership worth?

Assets

Assets are divided into three types. The first type is **current assets**. Current assets represent cash and anything that could be converted to cash in the short-term: **cash & equivalents**, **accounts receivable**, and **inventory**. Cash is cash, and it's a good thing. "Equivalents" are money market instruments earning some interest, which is also a good thing. If they mature in the near term, commercial paper, bankers' acceptances, repurchase agreements, and T-Bills are considered "cash equivalents" here on the balance sheet.

From your profits at the lemonade stand, you wisely deposited $560 into a savings account at the end of the summer, as you know how important it is to have some cash on hand for expenses and investments into the business. File that under "cash." Accounts receivable is what customers owe the company. You were nice enough to sell lemonade on credit to two of your best friends over the summer, and they ran up a tab of $40 between them. You intend to be paid for those sales in the near-term, so you list that payment as an asset.

Inventory is the stuff the company makes and plans to sell just as soon as possible. When temperatures dropped suddenly and the cold rain started up in late August, you were left holding a rather large quantity of lemons, sugar, etc. You creatively made up as much lemonade as possible and turned it into popsicles. Next season, you intend to sell that inventory for $40, making the inventory a current asset.

The second type of assets, **fixed assets,** include office buildings, factories, equipment, furniture, etc. This is the stuff a company uses as opposed to putting directly into its finished products. Fixed assets could all be converted into cash, but this stuff was not purchased to be sold; it was purchased to generate revenue: printing presses, industrial control systems, fleet of delivery vans, etc. A large corporation would list the value of the real estate, as well as the value of the assembly line equipment, as well as the furniture and even the artwork hanging on the walls of the visitor lobby under fixed assets.

Then there are **intangible assets**. Intangible assets include patents, trademarks, and **goodwill**. When a company acquires another company, they usually pay more than just the value of the fixed assets. They're paying for the brand-identity, the customer base, etc. So, that excess paid above the hard, tangible value of assets you can touch and see is called "goodwill." Let's face it, your lemonade stand has no intangible assets at this point, but if you ever purchase the goodwill of a rival lemonade stand up the street, we would list that intangible asset here. Then, we would add all three types of assets and call the sum your **total assets**.

Liabilities

On the other side of the equation we find liabilities, which represent what a company owes. Anything that has to be paid out in the short term is a **current liability**. **Accounts payable**, **accrued wages**, and **accrued taxes** all represent bills the company has to pay currently, which is why they're called current liabilities. Your mom picked up a few batches of ingredients over the summer and put them on her credit card. Just as soon as she remembers doing so, you intend to pay her back the $60, listed under accounts payable. And, you owe your sister $100, which is listed under accrued wages.

The principal amount of a loan or a bond that has to be paid more than a year out is a **long-term liability**. You owe your mother $240 in principal, which is why it's listed under long-term liabilities. Add the current and the long-term liabilities together and you have **total liabilities** of $400.

Stockholders' Equity/Net Worth

Stockholders' Equity is sometimes called Shareholders' Equity or "net worth." Whatever we call it, remember that equity equals ownership, and the stockholders own a percentage of the company. What is that ownership worth at the time the balance sheet is printed? That's stockholders' equity. Companies place the total par value of their preferred stock under this heading. Common stock is assigned a par value of, say, $1, so if a company has 1,000,000 shares of common stock, they would list the par value as $1,000,000 and place it under stockholders' equity.

If investors bought the stock in the IPO at $11, that represents a surplus of $10 above the par value, so the company would list **paid-in surplus** of $10,000,000, as well. And then any earnings that have been retained are listed as **retained earnings**. Why did you only retain $600 this year? Because you're smart enough to know that a business that involves little capital equipment, little financing, and few recurring costs can afford to pay out big distributions to the owners. As the sole owner, you cut yourself a $5,200 dividend check on September 1st and smiled all the way to and from the bank.

Footnotes

In a company's quarterly and annual shareholder reports the financial statements are accompanied by **footnotes** that help clarify the numbers. For example, what does the company mean by "equivalents" in its "cash and equivalents" line item—debt securities with six months to maturity? Three months? When does a company recognize "revenue"? Is it when the company ships pies to a distributor, or only when someone has paid for the product? Also, unusual revenue events or charges need to be explained so that investors don't get the wrong idea about their long-term impact.

Whenever the numbers in a financial statement require further clarification, the footnotes section is used to provide it. A **10-K** or **annual shareholder report,** for example, presents the consolidated financial statements and then follows up with "notes to consolidated financial statements" that help clarify all the numbers presented from the balance sheet, income statement, and statement of cash flow.

Analytical Methods

This section explores many mathematical concepts and formulae. While both are important, the test is generally more concerned that you can recognize and work with a concept as opposed to leaning over your calculator and pushing buttons. Then again, there are calculations on the exam, which is why we write out the formulae and use them in our online practice questions.

 Just be prepared to deal with the information in this section from many different angles at the testing center. You might calculate a stock's price-to-earnings ratio. Or, you might choose which answer best describes the price-to-earnings ratio. Or, you might be asked which type of investor would care about the price-to-earnings ratio. Or, you might not see "price-to-earnings ratio" in your batch of questions at all.

So, there is really no reason to cover a white board or make a stack of flash cards with all the formulae we look at in this section and elsewhere in the book. Your time would be better spent reading the textbook and then doing the online exercises and practice questions.

Financial Ratios and Their Uses

Let's take a look at your lemonade stand's results in terms of various financial ratios pulled from your income statement and balance sheet. For a start-up lemonade stand $10,000 of revenue is impressive. But, your $10,000 of sales was immediately reduced by the $3,000 of cost of goods sold that went into producing the lemonade. The $7,000 that we are left with at this point represents your company's **gross profit.**

$$\text{Gross Profit} = \text{Revenue} - \text{Cost of Goods Sold}$$

To figure your **gross margin of profit,** or **gross margin,** we would divide that $7,000 by the $10,000 of revenue to arrive at a gross margin of 70%.

$$\text{Gross Margin} = \text{Gross Profit} / \text{Revenue}$$

If a company's cost of goods sold are too high, they have no hope of covering all the other expenses further down the income statement. A restaurant that sells a $5 hamburger with cost of goods sold of $4.50 will not survive, for example, yet if that same company could make a $5 hamburger for just $1.25, they might.

After cost of goods sold, we subtract the operating expenses and depreciation, and arrive at the **operating profit** or **operating earnings.** Some analysts call this line of the income statement **operating income** but whatever we call it, your lemonade stand had $5,860 at this point. If we divide that back into the revenue of $10,000, we see that your **operating margin** is 58.6%

$$\text{Operating Margin} = \text{Operating Income} / \text{Revenue}$$

As you're starting to see, this industry uses a lot of different terms for the same thing. Even though we used three names (operating earnings, operating income, and operating profit) so far, there is yet another name for "operating profit," called "**EBIT,**" or "earnings before interest and taxes." EBIT is a company's revenue minus all expenses other than interest and taxes. From the income statement, EBIT is the line we arrive at once we've taken revenue and subtracted cost of goods sold plus all operating expenses.

Companies that issue bonds must cover the interest payments, so bond analysts often compare the EBIT to the annual interest expense to arrive at the "**times interest earned.**" If a company has $3 million in "EBIT" and $1 million in interest payments to cover, their "times interest earned" is 3-to-1. In other words, the interest expense is earned three times over, which represents a cushion to the bondholders.

Similar calculations derived from the income statement include "EBT," which is "earnings before taxes," and EBITDA, which stands for "earnings before interest, taxes, depreciation, and amortization." EBITDA takes revenue and subtracts the cost of goods sold plus the basic operating expenses of running the business. It leaves off the fancier subtractions for interest, taxes, depreciation and amortization. Analysts often consider EBITDA for companies with a lot of fixed assets subject to depreciation. Such companies may show a net loss on their income statement due largely to depreciation and financing connected to those fixed assets, but when viewed through EBITDA may look more impressive.

For example, although a consulting firm might be able to show a profit the first year or two, a manufacturing company might have to invest so much in their property and equipment that profits are five years into the future. Looking at the company's EBITDA, however, analysts might see that the company is generating some rather impressive amounts of cash even while reporting a net loss on the income statement.

So, finally, we're at the bottom line. Net income, net income after tax, and net profit all mean the same thing. It is an amount of money, the $5,800 shown on the bottom line of your income statement. When we take that amount on the bottom line and compare it to the revenue on the top line, we arrive at the company's **net profit margin** or just **net margin**. If your lemonade stand shows net income of $5,800 on the bottom line, we divide that by the revenue on the top line of $10,000 to arrive at a 58% net margin.

Net Profit Margin = Net Income / Revenue

Lucky for you, your lemonade stand has no shareholders making claims on your profits of $5,800. To understand how it works at public companies, though, let's pretend you do have shareholders in your lemonade stand. You reported net income of $5,800. If you had raised your capital by issuing stock, you would have been issuing "shares," right?

Well, time to share. Who gets dividends first? Preferred stockholders. If you pay a preferred dividend of $800, that leaves exactly $5,000 of **earnings available to common**. If your company has $5,000 in earnings available to common with 1,000 shares of common stock outstanding, that represents $5 of **earnings per-share (EPS)**. Each share of stock is attached to $5 of profit, in other words.

Earnings per-share = Earnings Available to Common / Shares Outstanding

We could apply a more stringent test that assumes all convertible securities (bonds, preferred stock, or warrants) are turned into common stock all at once. When these investors convert to common stock, your $5,000 in earnings would end up being divided among more shares. If your company ended up with 1,250 shares outstanding after conversion, your **diluted earnings per-share** would be only $4.

Now that we have our earnings per-share, we can also see how much gets paid out in dividends. Not surprisingly, we call this the **dividend payout ratio**. This takes the annual dividends paid and divides it by the earnings per-share (EPS). Your company has earnings-per-share (EPS) of $5. If you paid out $1 in common dividends, you paid out 20% of your earnings, which is called your "dividend payout ratio."

Dividend Payout = Annual Dividend / Earnings per-share

As we saw earlier, the income statement shows the sales, expenses, and profit or loss over a reporting period. The question, "Did we make our numbers this quarter?" would typically be answered with a quick look at the income statement over the financial quarter.

The balance sheet reveals the financial condition of the company, and there are many important ratios pulled from this statement. Bondholders are concerned about a company's **asset coverage** of the bonds and the safety of their promised income stream. We looked at the safety of income on the income statement. Now let's see how the balance sheet reveals the asset coverage of the bonds.

Current assets represent what a company owns. Current liabilities represent what a company owes. Hopefully, the company owns more than it owes. If not, it has a "burn rate" showing how quickly it could go bankrupt. Fundamental analysts take current assets and subtract current liabilities to measure **working capital** (sometimes called "net working capital"). This is a measure of how able a company is to finance current operations.

We're talking about short-term **liquidity** here. When a company's short-term liabilities exceed its current assets, that company is in great danger of getting behind in payments to suppliers and interest payments to creditors. On the other hand, if a company's current assets exceed its current liabilities, this company is in a strong position to fund current operations, just as your lemonade operation would be if you had $1,000 in total bills and $4,000 in the bank.

Working Capital = Current Assets − Current Liabilities

Your lemonade stand shows current assets of $640 and current liabilities of $160. Your working capital is, therefore, the difference of $480. Working capital is an amount of money. Analysts also express current assets and current liabilities as a ratio, known as the **current ratio**. Instead of subtracting $160 from $640, we would say that $640, divided by (over) $160, gives you a current ratio of 4 to 1. Basically, for every $1 of short-term debt, you have $4 of liquid assets to cover it. Not bad.

Current Ratio = Current Assets / Current Liabilities

Inventory is a current asset along with accounts receivable and cash & equivalents. But, inventory is not always a liquid asset. When we subtract inventory from current assets, we arrive at our **quick assets.** Quick assets include assets easily converted to cash: cash and marketable securities plus accounts receivable.

Looking at the quick assets of a company, analysts apply a more stringent test, known as the **quick ratio** or the **acid test**. The "i" in the words "quick" and "acid" reminds us that "i̲nventory" is subtracted from current assets before we compare them to current liabilities. Why do that? Those frozen lemonade pops you made might go bad in storage, or might not strike your customers' fancy next summer. So, in case you didn't sell your inventory, what would your short-term financial condition look like then? We would deduct the $40 of inventory from your $640 of current assets first, and then compare that $600 to the $160 of current liabilities. At this point we would see a ratio of 3.75 to 1 for your quick ratio. For every $1 of short-term debt, you have $3.75 to cover it, even if the inventory completely spoils.

Quick Ratio = (Current Assets − Inventory) / Current Liabilities

Worth just $40, we can safely say that your lemonade stand has little inventory, but many manufacturing companies, car dealers, and supermarkets live and die by how effectively they manage their inventory. To measure this effectiveness analysts look at a company's **inventory turnover ratio**. This formula provides a link between the income statement and the balance sheet. To calculate it, we take the cost of goods sold from the income statement and divide that amount by the average inventory over the period. It is a ratio because it shows how many "times" inventory is turned over during the reporting period. If the turnover rate is too slow, that company is not deploying its capital effectively.

Current ratio, quick ratio, the acid test, and working capital measure short-term liquidity. A company's ability to meet current interest payments is reflected from a look at these concerns. The company's ability to repay the principal and avoid bankruptcy is reflected through a longer-term look at the balance sheet. For a picture of the company's long-term financial condition analysts calculate the **debt-to-equity ratio**. The debt-to-equity ratio shows us how leveraged the company is. It gives analysts an idea as to how much money was raised through borrowing/leverage compared to the money raised by selling ownership/equity stakes. The formula is:

Debt-to-Equity Ratio = Total Liabilities / Shareholders' Equity

The higher the ratio, the more leveraged the company is. Another formula that is frequently used for the same purpose is called the **debt ratio**, which compares the total debt of the company to its total assets. Again, the higher this number/ratio, the more leveraged the company is. The formula is:

Debt Ratio = Total Liabilities / Total Assets

another ratio that shows bondholders the risk of default is the **bond ratio**. This formula shows the percentage of the company's capitalization that comes from the issuance of bonds with maturities greater than one year. To calculate the bond ratio analysts take the value of the company's long-term debt and divide that by the long-term debt plus shareholder's equity. This shows what percentage the bonds make of the company's total capitalization. Except for utility companies, a bond ratio above 33% is generally considered a high amount of leverage.

We looked at "book value per-share" for common stock. Similarly, analysts often calculate an issuer's net asset value per bond to see how much in tangible assets is associated with each bond issued. To calculate this number, we take the net tangible assets of the company (not goodwill and other intangible assets) and divide that by the number of bonds issued by the company.

In a later chapter we'll see that ratings agencies including Moody's Investor Services and S&P use the concerns discussed above when assigning a credit rating to an issue of debt securities.

Bondholders are concerned about solvency and long-term liquidity. Shareholders are concerned about profitability, which is measured in many ways. Analysts call the hard, tangible asset value associated with a share of common stock the **book value per-share**. To calculate it, they take the stockholders' equity minus the preferred shares, divided by the shares outstanding. Value investors love to buy stocks trading at low multiples to book value. If they can buy the stock at or below book value, even better.

Book Value per-share = Stockholder's Equity / Shares Outstanding

To judge how effectively a company generates profits from its shareholders' investment into the company analysts calculate the company's **return on equity**. The return on equity (ROE) shows how much in profits each dollar of common stockholder's equity generates for the company. As with many measures of a company's financial health, this one combines a line from the income statement with a line from the balance sheet. The formula is:

Return on Equity = Net Income / Stockholders' Equity

Usually, "return on equity" relates only to common stock. Therefore, the preferred dividend is excluded from net income before comparing what's left to shareholder's equity. For more precision, some analysts use the term "return on common equity" to clarify that preferred stock is not being considered for this calculation.

Your lemonade stand has little inventory, but many manufacturing companies, car dealers, and supermarkets live and die by how effectively they manage their inventory. To measure this effectiveness analysts look at a company's **inventory turnover ratio**. This formula provides a link between the income statement and the balance sheet. To calculate it, we take the cost of goods sold from the income statement and divide that amount by the average inventory over the period. It is a ratio because it shows how many "times" inventory is turned over during the reporting period. If the turnover rate is too slow, that company is not deploying its capital effectively.

Valuation Ratios

Publicly traded stocks trade at various "multiples" such as the **price-to-earnings ratio**. The P/E ratio compares the market price of the stock to the earnings per-share. Growth stocks trade at high P/E ratios, while those trading at low P/E ratios are considered value stocks. The test could say that the P/E ratio shows the enthusiasm investors have for the company's profits, as reflected in the market price for their stock.

P/E = Market Price / Earnings per-share

Earnings are the bottom line of the income statement, which means they can be manipulated through creative accounting to some extent without necessarily being misleading. For this reason, many analysts prefer using **price-to-sales**. Sales/revenue is the first number reported on the income statement and is, therefore, probably the most reliable figure presented. Or, if the issuer is not yet profitable, there would be no earnings and, therefore, no "e" to compare to the "p." Price-to-sales compares the stock's market price to the revenue per-share.

Price-to-Sales = Market Price / Revenue per-share

If the issuer is not yet profitable, analysts typically focus on price-to-sales as well as **price-to-cash**. The price-to-cash ratio compares the stock's market price to the operating cash flow per-share.

Price-to-Cash = Market Price / Cash Flow per-share

If the issuer is not yet profitable, price-to-sales and price-to-cash are most instructive. For profitable companies, the price-to-earnings and **price-to-book** ratios are most instructive. As we saw, the book value is calculated from the issuer's balance sheet, sometimes considered a hypothetical liquidating value that indicates the tangible assets propping up a stock's value. A stock's price-to-book ratio is the market price compared to the book value per-share. If the ratio is high, we are looking at a growth stock. If the ratio is considered low, we are looking at a value stock.

Price-to-Book = Market Price / Book Value per-share

Time Value of Money

The **time value of money** means that a dollar can always earn some rate of interest in a savings account, CD, or T-Bill, so any amount of money is worth more the sooner it is received. We're about to look at **future value** and **present value**, where we will see that money earning 5% year after year grows magically into a large pile of cash due to "compounded returns" and the more frequently the principal compounds, the better. For now, let's just look at what happens in one year.

If you invest $100 today at 5% interest, you will have $105 in one year. We call that $105 the future value of the $100. It is calculated by multiplying $100 by 1.05. The number 1.05 represents that you will end up with 105% of what you started with—the $100 plus 5%. On the other hand, $100 received one year from now is worth only $95.24 today. Instead of multiplying $100 by 1.05 to calculate its future value, divide the $100 by 1.05 to find its present value. $100 divided by 1.05 = $95.24. In other words, if you invest $95.24 at 5% for one year, you'll end up with $100 at the end of the year. You can double-check that by taking $95.24 times 1.05 and getting back to $100. If the exam makes you calculate either future value or present value, I recommend double-checking your math.

Future Value

Of course, it's hard to get excited over the fact that $100 invested at 5% for one year takes the investment all the way up to $105. But, if you're patient and leave it in there a few years, it can grow quite nicely, even at just 5%. To see how large the investment would become, multiply $100 by 1.05, then multiply that by 1.05, and so on for every year you leave it in the account. These are **compound returns**, and through the magic of **compound interest** we see that $100 times 1.05 leaves us with $105 after year one. If we multiply that by 1.05, we have $110.25 after year two. Multiply that by 1.05, and we have $115.76 after year three, $121.55 after year four, and $127.62 after year five. So, the future value of $100 invested for five years at 5% compounded interest is $127.62. If that doesn't impress you, add zeros to your initial investment: $10,000 becomes $12,762 after five years, or $100,000 becomes $127,628 after five years, and so on.

The exam could say that a company's profits are $1 per-share—if they grow 7% per year for 5 years, what will the earnings per-share be at the end of the period? Just multiply the $1 by 1.07 five times in a row to get your answer. Or, the 25-cent dividend compounds at 6% for five years, and so on.

The formula for future value can be expressed a few different ways. One way is:

$$FV = Principal \times (1 + r)^t$$

Math is a language, and that is just the mathematical way to represent what we were doing by multiplying an investment by 1.05 for 5% or 1.10 for 10%, and so on. In this formula, "r" means "rate of return" and "t" means "time." Remember, our returns are compounded. So if you get 10% the first year, you'll have more money earning 10% the next year, and so on. Even if it's the same 10% rate of return, it's always 10% of a bigger number. So, if we expect to get 10% each year over a 5-year period, we would say that the FV (future value) of a dollar invested today will be $1 x (1.10)5. 1.10 is just the "1" plus 10%. The investment will multiply itself by 1.10 five times in a row. And remember that the "5" doesn't mean to multiply by 5. It means to multiply the 1.10 by itself five times. The exponent "5" means "to the fifth power."

So what we're doing in our example is multiplying our invested dollar by 1.10 five times in a row. The dollar would be worth $1.61 at the end of five years, and you can add as many zeroes as your client is willing to invest. $100,000 now would be worth $161,000 then (give or take). One million now equals about $1.61 million five years later.

Another way the formula can be written is:

$$Pn = PO \, (1 + r)^n$$

"Pn" now stands for the future value of the investment. The little "n" is the number of years the portfolio will be compounding. P0 is the original investment or original amount. So, it's the same idea and formula expressed differently.

We just looked at a magical portfolio that compounds conveniently once per year, right on schedule. Well, if we had an investment that compounded more frequently—every six months, every quarter, or every month—that would be known as a "really good thing." The more frequently an investment compounds, the better that is for the investor.

When an investor buys a bond paying 5%, he receives 5% *simple* interest. That means the issuer pays 5% of the same $1,000 principal each year. If a corporate bond paid compound interest, it would work like our compounded returns above. In that case, a 5% bond would pay (but doesn't) $50 the first year, but then 5% of $1,050 the next year, and 5% of $1,102.50 the next, and so on. Which would be great, but the reality is that the issuer pays 5% simple interest on a bond. If you hold a bond for five years paying 5% simple interest, you get your $1,000 back plus total interest payments of $250.

So, compound interest pays interest on the principal plus the accumulated interest on that principal, while simple interest pays a rate applied only to the principal. Bank CDs pay compounded rates of interest. Unfortunately, the rates of interest are so low and the terms so short that one barely notices a difference between simple and compound interest on those safe-money products. So, where would an investor find a 5% compounded rate of return? There might not be any security guaranteeing that rate, but a diversified bond portfolio could easily return that much or more over the investor's holding period through reinvestments of interest payments.

Present Value

Future value answers this question: if I invest this much money and get this rate of return for this period of time, what will my money be worth in the future? **Present value** answers this question: if I need this much money in the future and can get this rate of return for this period, how much money do I have to put in now, in the present? Maybe you need a certain amount of money to put your child through college. Given a rate of return, how much do you need to invest today to get there? That's present value. I already sneaked it in when I said that $100 received in one year is worth only $95.24 today, since I could invest $95.24 right now at 5% and turn it into $100 in just one year.

The formula for Present Value is:

$$PV = FV / (1 + r)^t$$

So, for Future Value, we said that $100,000 invested today at 10% would be worth $161,000 in five years. What if your client said she needed exactly $190,000 in five years—how much must she invest at 10% to get there? Start with $190,000 and divide by 1.10 five times in a row. The investor needs to put in $117,975 in the present to end up with $190,000 at the end of her holding period. Not that we should tell her to expect 10% compounded returns for five years; just illustrating how these formulas work for the exam.

Internal Rate of Return and Net Present Value

Whenever a business is considering the opportunity to invest in a new call center, 3D printer, or other cash-generating asset, they first need to determine whether the investment will produce enough cash to not just cover the cost of borrowing the capital, but also to make a profit. In other words, they need to calculate the **Net Present Value (NPV)** of the expected cash flows for the project. To do this, they "discount" the cash flows by a required rate of return called the **internal rate of return**. Internal rate of return can be defined as "the discount rate that makes the net present value of the cash flows equal to zero." That sounds fancy, but it really just means that the investment will look attractive if it can generate any positive cash flow above our required rate of return.

Think of net present value (NPV) as the difference—positive or negative—between the present values of an investment's cash inflows and its cash outflows. If the net present value is negative, the project should be rejected as not financially feasible. A negative NPV means that it costs more to borrow the money than it's worth given the cash flows expected from the investment/project. If the net present value is positive, on the other hand, the investment may be attractive, since the cash inflows outweigh the outflows/costs associated with generating it.

Descriptive Statistics and Risk Measurements

Many people think of risk as the chance of losing money, but risk is generally defined in terms of the fluctuations of value an investment experiences. The words "unpredictable" and "risky" basically mean the same thing from this viewpoint. During the accumulation phase of our retirement savings plan, we can withstand some of these fluctuations. But, once we retire, if we are liquidating shares of mutual funds to meet living expenses, we can get hurt during bear markets for stocks or bonds. If one month the account is worth $300,000 and the next only $265,000, a retiree could burn through her investments quickly just by making scheduled sales and withdrawals.

I'm not saying that younger people should shrug off large fluctuations in value, either. I would think that at age 23 watching an investment drop by, say, $5,000 could also be alarming, considering how many hours most 23-year-olds have to work to make five grand. In a panic, such an investor might pull out of the securities markets entirely and never reach his retirement goal because he was talked into more volatility than he could handle on an emotional and psychological level.

Risk can be measured through descriptive statistics including both measures of central tendency such as the mean, median, and mode, and measures of variability or dispersion, such as standard deviation.

Measures of Central Tendency

Measures of central tendency provide a summary of a set of data and give investors an idea of what a typical return might be for a stock, bond, or mutual fund investment. The **mode** is the most common number in the set of data—maybe the portfolio returns 2% frequently, and that becomes the mode.

The **median** is the halfway point or "middle value," meaning that half the numbers are below this number, and half the numbers are above.

Then there is the **mean**, which is the average of the numbers. You may have read about the "average annual income" in your area and also the "median income." Those two numbers are not the same thing. The average annual income is figured by adding up everybody's income and dividing by that number of people. The median income tells us where the middle point of all the incomes is, where half are below and half above this number. If we want the average net worth of Bill Gates, Warren Buffet and a normal human being we might total up $80 billion for Bill Gates, plus $65 billion for Warren Buffet, plus $500,000 for the normal human being, divided by three. The average or mean financial net worth is $48.3 billion. On the other hand, the half-way point or median is the middle number, $65 billion.

Another name for "mean" is "arithmetic mean." This is not the same as the "geometric mean."

If we calculated an arithmetic mean, we would be figuring a simple average that could be misleading. For example, if an investor put $10,000 into a brokerage account and had the following returns, what would the account be worth at the end of the third year?

Year 1: −10%

Year 2: −20%

Year 3: +30%

If we take a simple "arithmetic mean" or average of −10, −20, and +30%, it might seem that the account should be back at $10,000. That is because the arithmetic mean does not account for the effects of compounded returns. For compounded returns each year's return is dependent on the one before it.

So, rather than trying to take the simple average of -10, -20 and 30, we can avoid misleading the investor by using a finance calculator to calculate the geometric mean. The geometric mean reveals that the account is worth only $9,360. When the value dropped 10%, the account value dropped to $9,000. When it lost 20%, it dropped to $7,200. If that account rises 30%, we're only back to $9,360.

To avoid misleading investors about their returns the geometric mean should always be used. The only time the arithmetic mean is accurate is when the account experiences no volatility, which is just about never in my experience.

Measures of Dispersion

Measures of central tendency indicate what typically happens. On the other hand, when we discuss **standard deviation**, we look at how much variability there is among an investment's returns. Through the perspective of standard deviation, an investment whose results are all over the road is risky, whether the surprises are on the plus or the minus side.

A piece of data that resides far from the central tendency of a set of numbers is called an outlier. If an investment has had an unusually high or low return in one year, that will skew the mean much more than it will the mode or median. In a set of results where there is an outlier, statisticians prefer to use the median over the other two m-words. When there are no outliers, the arithmetic mean is the best measure of central tendency.

Let's say the returns for a portfolio the past 9 years were: 5, 6, 5, 7, 6, 8, 9, 15, 5. The mode is the most common value of 5. The median is 6 because there are four values above and below that number. The mean is just the average of the nine numbers, 7.33%. And the returns are all positive because it's just an example.

Standard Deviation

Measures of central tendency give us an idea of what the typical returns have been for an investment, while a measure of dispersion tells us how far away from that average an investment's returns can be.

Standard deviation measures how much an investment deviates from its average return. Or, we could say that standard deviation measures the dispersion of a data set from its arithmetic mean. However we define it, standard deviation is understood in percentage terms, so a standard deviation of 5 means the investment typically deviates 5 percentage points above and below its average return. If the average return is 10% and the standard deviation is 5, the likely range of return outcomes is from 5% to 15%.

More accurately, that's what happens within "one standard deviation," which tells us what happens about 2/3 (68%) of the time. What happens about 95% of the time? Those returns lie within "two standard deviations." So, if the average return is 10 and the standard deviation is 5, two-thirds of the time the returns are within 5% and 15% (–5 and +5 from the mean); about 95% of the time the returns are within 0 and 20% (–10 and +10 from the mean). And, in virtually all cases (99.7% of the time), the returns in our data set will be within three standard deviations, which would put virtually all of our annual returns within –5% on the low end and 25% on the high end. What about that other .3%? What happens there? Well, those are the years that can really smart, which is why prudent investors don't trust their computer models too much.

As always, the exam can test a concept from many angles, so if you get a test question showing a table of numbers, understand that the set of numbers that hover more closely together is showing you a lower standard deviation. In other words, if the monthly returns for one stock were 3%, 5%, and 6%, that would represent a much lower standard deviation—less volatility—than a stock whose returns were –4%, 7%, and 17%. If a mutual fund gained 1% each month, its standard deviation would be zero, since every month it did the same thing—went up by 1%. Maybe you're wondering what the fund's standard deviation would be if it steadily lost 1% each month. Also zero. So, while it's nice to have a low standard deviation, this is not to be confused with making money.

The exam may ask you to identify which portfolio is the riskiest and/or has the highest standard deviation in a way that lets you eyeball your way to the answer. That's what we're hoping. Maybe it will say that one portfolio had a high return of 8% and a low of –10%, while another had a high of 4% and a low of –8%. Obviously, the second one has a lower standard deviation. It didn't go up as high or down as low. Similarly, an equity income mutual fund usually doesn't go up or down as much as a growth fund, so its standard deviation is lower, regardless of which fund has a higher total return. Another name for this simplified form of standard deviation is **range**.

Just in case the exam expects you to know the math behind standard deviation, here goes. If our portfolio had a high of 8% and a low of –10%, what was the average or the mean return? Just take –10 plus 8 divided by two to get the average. The average or mean is –1%. If you're more of a visual person, imagine moving 9 spaces from either –10 or 8 on an imaginary number line—where do you end up?

Negative one percent. As we said, we now look at how far the returns were from that average. Positive 8% is 9 away from –1% and –10% is also 9 away from –1%. Since it's math, we now square both of those numbers. 9 squared = 81 and 9 squared = 81. We add those two 81s to get 162. Then, we divide 162 by (n–1) where "n" equals the number of values in our little data set. Since there are only two numbers, we divide 162 by (2–1), which is, of course, just 162. In case that wasn't enough steps, we now have to hit the little square root button on the calculator, and our answer is approximately 12.73. Yes standard deviation is also defined as "the square root of variance." So, 12.73 is the standard deviation of this portfolio. A portfolio with a standard deviation of, say, 9.2, then, is considered less risky.

Sharpe Ratio

The **Sharpe ratio** uses standard deviation to determine if an investor is getting enough return for the risk he's taking. The exam might say the Sharpe ratio measures the excess return per unit of risk. Mathematically, it is the actual return you get minus the "riskless rate of return," divided by the standard deviation.

Seriously. So, the Sharpe ratio measures **risk-adjusted returns**. And, the higher the number, the better. Also, the **riskless rate of return** we use as a comparison to what we're getting is the yield on 3-month T-Bills. So, if an investment gets a 10% return when the yield on 3-month T-Bills was 5%, we're down to 5% of excess return. If the standard deviation is 5, we would divide 5 by 5 for a Sharpe ratio of 1.

Notice how if the standard deviation had been 10, that Sharpe ratio would have been a lower number. Which is bad. The higher the Sharpe ratio, the better the investor is being compensated for the risk he's taking. That could be confusing—a high standard deviation is a red flag, but a high Sharpe ratio is a good thing.

Beta

If you click on the overview of a stock at your favorite financial website, chances are you'll see the **beta**, which is an investment's tendency to go up and down compared to the overall market. We use the S&P 500 as the measure of the overall market and then track how much the stock or portfolio moved compared to that index. So a beta of "1" means a security moves exactly in step with the overall market (S&P 500). A beta of more than 1 implies that the stock is more volatile than the overall market, while a beta of less than 1 implies that the stock is less volatile than the overall market.

A stock with a beta of more than 1 will out-perform the market when stock prices rise but under-perform the market when stock prices fall. Or, we could reverse that if the beta were less than 1, right? A stock with a low beta could be said to "under-perform a bull market and out-perform a bear market."

Alpha

If the expected return is 8%, but we only get a 6% return, we call that "negative alpha." The portfolio manager didn't do as well as expected. However, if the portfolio manager took a portfolio with an expected return of 8% and got a 10% return, that excess return could be referred to as "positive alpha." Portfolio managers who get excess returns or show positive alpha are said to be adding value with their money management skills. Those who consistently show "negative alpha" are eventually shown the door. I often see hedge funds described in terms of "alpha-driven" results, meaning that this portfolio's performance is almost entirely dependent on the skills of the portfolio manager, not on the movement of the overall market.

Like the Sharpe ratio, alpha measures performance on a risk-adjusted basis. Another way to define **alpha** is to say that it measures an investment's performance compared to a benchmark beyond what is predicted by beta.

The exam could have you figure alpha based on beta. For example, let's say an investment has a return of 8% and a beta of 1.5. The benchmark is the S&P 500, which was up 6% over the period. Because 8% is higher than 6%, this was a good investment, right? Well, a beta of 1.5 implies a volatility that is 50% greater than the benchmark. If the benchmark returned 6%, the beta of 1.5 implies that the returns should have been 9%. Because the return was only 8%, the alpha is -1, which means the investment was not good on a risk-adjusted basis.

R-Squared

R-squared is a statistical measurement that tries to explain how much of a portfolio's movement is explained by the movement in the benchmark index. For a fixed-income portfolio, T-Bills can serve as a benchmark. For stocks, the S&P 500 provides a useful benchmark. The values are from 0 to 100. If the R-squared value is 100, that means that 100% of the movement is explained by the movement of the benchmark index. A lower value (under 75, say) would indicate that the portfolio does not move in line with the index. Since index funds are so cheap to own, some investors don't like to pay for active portfolio management if the portfolio acts just like an index. So a lower R-squared value could be viewed as a sign that the portfolio manager is not just playing golf, mirroring an index, and charging unnecessary fees for active management.

Correlation

Alpha takes the volatility of an investment and compares its risk-adjusted performance to the benchmark that the investment most closely matches. Beta measures systematic risk, showing how much a security or portfolio moves compared to the overall market.

Correlation, on the other hand, shows how closely related—or unrelated—two investments are. The **correlation coefficient** between two investments ranges from 1 to -1. A positive correlation of 1 would indicate that two securities move in lock-step with each other. A negative correlation means that two securities move in opposite directions, with a coefficient of -1 meaning they move by the same amount but, again, in different directions. A correlation of zero means what it sounds like—there is zero correlation between two things. A correlation coefficient of .3 implies that two securities move in the same direction sharing a correlation of 30%. If one security rises 10%, the other rises 3%. A correlation coefficient of -.4 means that if one security rises 10%, the other one drops 4%.

The importance of correlation is that if a portfolio's securities are strongly and positively correlated, then when things go bad for one stock, they tend to go bad for the whole portfolio. If there is a slightly negative correlation among the securities in the portfolio, on the other hand, then when one part zigs, the other zags. Modern Portfolio Theory, with its efficient frontier approach, proposes that investors should seek portfolios with slightly negative correlations for this reason. The benefit of diversification is that investors can keep high expected return among assets that do not have a strong expected return correlation.

As with alpha and beta, there is no reason to assume that if two securities historically show a correlation of, say, .4 that they will continue to do so. Using statistical measures such as these merely provides a guide of likely outcomes.

Now What?

Reading a textbook takes time and effort. Unfortunately, it is only one important step in your learning process. The next important step is working with practice questions.

First up, we present simple questions designed to help you review and recall what you just read. When you work through these online review exercises, it is important that you do so with the textbook closed—no peeking!

The questions in the online review exercises generally have just two answer choices. They are designed to help you recall and review what you just read and move it into long-term memory. Please wait until you're completely done with the online review exercises before opening the textbook again.

After taking the online review exercises and skimming the textbook chapter, walk away from it for at least 20 minutes—sleeping on it is ideal. Either way, after this mandatory break, come back and take both chapter review quizzes, again with the textbook closed. There is a "mastery score" for each quiz in our Pass the 66 Online Practice Question Bank, and it is usually higher than the passing score at the testing center. That's okay—you need to shoot for higher than a 73% in practice to get at least that score on your license exam.

Chances are your scores on the first few chapter review quizzes will be on the low side, with steady improvement after that. Excellent—that's what we're shooting for. We're hoping that each online review exercise will help prepare you for the chapter review quizzes, and that the act of taking the chapter review quizzes will improve your general test taking skills.

The Series 66 requires you to know a lot of information and to be able to work with it from many angles. Students who report that they saw questions they'd never seen before on their Series 66 might as well report that the sky is blue and grass is generally green. NASAA pays testing companies big money to make sure that the questions you see on your test are not the same ones you've seen over and over again in practice.

That is why we have to help you both learn the information indicated on the exam outline and also improve your ability to take any question they throw at you on Exam Day, recognize what it's talking about, and quickly break it down in your favor. The trick there is to understand that the same concept can be presented in strikingly different ways.

For example, from the information in this textbook chapter you could see something like this:

If an economist says that the yield curve has inverted, which of the following is currently happening?
A. Prices of short-term debt securities are higher than those of intermediate and long-term debt securities.
B. Yields on short-term debt securities are higher than those of intermediate and long-term debt securities
C. Yields are equal across all maturities
D. Credit quality overall is deteriorating
EXPLANATION: as soon as the term yield curve comes to mind, we tend to imagine something being higher than something else. Choice A says that something is higher than something else, so it must be the right answer. Right? Let's see what else can be eliminated, first. If the yield curve is inverted, Choice C is eliminated. Choice C is a flat curve, so we discard that one. Yield curves have nothing to do with credit quality--those are yield or credit spreads--so we eliminate Choice D. Now, back to price versus yield. If the yields on short-term debt securities are higher than other maturities, it is because their prices are lower. Eliminate Answer Choice A, leaving us with . . .
ANSWER: B

The challenging questions on the exam are not interested in seeing what you memorized. Rather, they typically make the test taker feel disoriented at first, until he finally sees what is being asked. Rather than trying to quickly answer a test question from recall, successful test takers use what they know to eliminate the three incorrect answers. The incorrect answers are not always glaringly wrong, either. They simply do not answer what is being asked. Whatever the reason, the priority is to eliminate answer choices rather than trying to rush toward what seems the right answer.

With that in mind, let's try another one:

A public company includes three financial statements in a 10K report. To which of the following should an investor turn for the result of operations (sales & profits) over the reporting period?
A. The balance sheet
B. The income statement

C. The operations report

D. The statement of cash flows

EXPLANATION: the tests we took in college often only required us to be familiar with a term and quickly choose it. Unfortunately, on this exam there are too many synonyms for each term for that to be reliable. Often, the answer choice that is unfamiliar ends up being correct. Often, familiar phrases are used to mislead us. In this question, the writer knows that balance sheet is a much more familiar term than income statement. For that reason, many test takers will choose the answer, unconsciously ending a painful stimulus. If he does that often enough over 100 exam questions, we can imagine how the exam candidate will simply delay his pain until the end when he turns in his results. The balance sheet is not the right answer here, so we eliminate Choice A. The question stem used the term "operations." We see an answer choice called the operations report. That has to be right, right?

Wrong. It's fictitious. It's not something you were supposed to have memorized. It's just that right here, at the exam center, you are expected to know that this answer choice doesn't work. Eliminate Choice C. The statement of cash flows shows the result of operations. Maybe that makes it the right answer? What if we compare it to Choice B-- the income statement? Does the income statement have revenue on the top line and net income after tax on the bottom? Yes. So, if we pick Choice D here rather than eliminating it, we're going to end up like that test taker trading immediate pain for deferred pain at the end of the exam. Eliminate Choice D, leaving us with . . .

ANSWER: B

We have a lot of practice questions for you in our Pass the 66 Online Practice Question Bank. But, should you get through them all, we encourage you to write variations of our questions. Take a question on the income statement, for example, and make it more about the balance sheet or statement of cash flows. We'll worry about that later, since you already have a lot of homework to do. But recent educational research has shown that students who write their own questions learn more for the long-term than those using any other method of study. The same research also shows that students learn more from doing practice questions than they do from reading textbooks.

So, let's get you started on learning through practice questions. First, do the online review exercises for this chapter, closed-book. After at least a 20-minute break take the chapter review quizzes online. If you have time to study, watch the related training video lessons, and then move onto the next chapter in the textbook.

CHAPTER 2: Investment Vehicle Characteristics

Securities investors do not avoid risk. Rather, they determine which risks they can take and substitute those for the ones they can't. If an investor avoids default risk by purchasing Treasury Bonds, he trades that risk for purchasing power, interest rate, and reinvestment risk. If he needs to protect against purchasing power risk by buying common stock, he trades that one for market risk, business risk, and legislative risk.

Investing in securities is like playing offense in football. Whether we run the ball by buying bonds or throw passes by purchasing common stock, we know that we will get hurt a few times before we finally reach the goal line.

Therefore, before playing offense with their money most investors first lay down some protection. Step one is usually to establish a rainy-day fund at the local bank. Step two is to talk to your insurance agent. To protect your family against a sudden loss of income your agent may discuss disability, long-term care, and life insurance products.

To protect against running out of income in retirement your agent may discuss annuities.

Insurance-Based Products

Annuities

An **annuity** is an investment sold by an insurance company that either promises a minimum rate of return to the investor or allows the investor to allocate payments to various funds that invest in the stock and bond markets. These products offer regular payments for the rest of the annuitant's life, but owners of annuities can instead take money out as lump sums or random withdrawals on the back end. Annuities are part of the retirement plans of many individuals, and they can either be part of the "safe-money" piece or can provide exposure to the stock and bond markets.

The three main types of annuities are fixed, indexed, and variable.

Fixed annuities

A **fixed annuity** promises a minimum rate of return to the investor in exchange for one big payment into the contract or several periodic **purchase payments**. The purchase payments are allocated to the insurance company's **general account,** so the rate of return is "guaranteed." But, that just means it's backed by the claims-paying ability of the insurance company's general account. So before turning over your money to an insurance company, expecting them to pay it back to you slowly, you might want to check their **AM Best** rating and their history of paying claims.

In a fixed annuity the insurance/annuity company bears all the investment risk. This product is suitable for someone who wants a "safe money" investment that is more dependable than anything in the stock or bond markets, something that promises to make dependable payments for the rest of his life, no matter how long he ends up living. The fixed annuity offers peace of mind if not a high rate of return.

Indexed Annuities

A special type of fixed annuity is the **equity-indexed annuity** or just **indexed annuity**. With this product the investor receives a guaranteed minimum rate of return when the stock market has a bad year. But, he/she receives a higher rate of return when an index—usually the S&P 500—has a good year. Do they receive the full upside, as if they owned an S&P 500 index fund? No, and that should be made clear by the sales representative. The contract is also not credited with the dividends associated with the S&P 500, and those dividends can easily be worth 2 or 3% of the index's total return for the year.

Equity indexed annuities have a **participation rate**. A participation rate of 70% means that the contract gets credited with 70% of the increase in the S&P 500. If the index goes up 10%, the contract makes 7% . . . unless that amount is higher than the annual **cap**.

Yes, these contracts also have a cap placed on the maximum increase for any year, regardless of what the stock market does. So with a participation rate of 70% and a cap of 6%, what happens if the S&P goes up 20%? Although 70% of that is 14%, if you're capped at 6%, then 6% is all the contract value will rise that year. As you can see, indexed annuities are really about the downside protection, which is why a securities license is not required to sell fixed annuities, equity-indexed or otherwise.

Variable Annuities

A **variable annuity** doesn't promise a rate of return, which is what they mean by a "variable" annuity—the return varies. Since investors are investing in accounts of their choosing, maybe they'll end up doing better than the modest rate that the fixed annuity guarantees. In a variable annuity the annuitant bears the investment risk rather than having the insurance company promise a certain rate of return. In exchange for bearing the risks we've looked at in the stock and bond markets, the variable annuitant gets the opportunity to do much better than he would have in a fixed annuity, protecting his purchasing power from the ravages of inflation.

Could he do worse? Sure, but if he wants a guarantee, he buys a fixed annuity where the insurance company guarantees a certain rate of return. Now he lives with purchasing power risk, because if the annuity promises 2%, that's not going to be sufficient with inflation rising at 4%. If he wants to protect his purchasing power by investing in the stock market, he buys a variable annuity, but now he takes on all the investment risks we've discussed.

Variable annuities use mutual fund-type accounts as their investment options, but we don't call variable annuities "mutual funds." We call the investment options **subaccounts**. Salespeople must go out of their way to avoid confusing customers into thinking an annuity *is* a mutual fund. It is not a mutual fund. Mutual funds aren't subject to early withdrawal penalties from the issuer or the IRS. Mutual funds don't offer a death benefit or add expenses to cover it. Also, mutual funds are not tax-deferred accounts. A mutual fund held in a taxable account will subject investors to taxation every year. The dividend and capital gains distributions are taxable, and if the investor redeems shares for a gain, that's also taxable for the year it occurs. This tax burden reduces the principal in the account each year, which is a major drag on long-term returns. A variable annuity, however, is really a retirement plan where we get to keep all the dividends and capital gains in the account, adding to our principal, and compounding our returns.

In a deferred annuity the annuitant defers taxation until he takes the money out, which is usually at retirement. The money grows much faster when it's not being taxed for 10, 20, maybe even 30 years, but every dance reaches the point where we have to pay the fiddler. It's been a fun dance, for sure, but the reality is that we will pay ordinary income tax rates on the earnings we have been shielding from the IRS all these years—if and when we decide to get our own hands on the money. Ordinary income rates, remember. If the individual is in the 35% marginal tax bracket, the gains coming out of the annuity are taxed at that rate.

Features of Annuities

An annuity comes with a **mortality guarantee**, which means that once it goes into the pay-out phase, the annuitant will receive monthly payments as long as he is alive (a mortal). Of course, the fixed annuity states what the check will be worth at a minimum, while the variable annuity—well, it varies, people. In the variable annuity, the annuitant will receive a check each month, but it could be mighty meager if the markets aren't doing well.

A fixed annuity is an insurance product providing peace of mind and tax deferral. A variable annuity functions like a mutual fund investment that grows tax-deferred and offers some peace of mind. But, whether it's fixed or variable, the insurance company offers a **death benefit** that promises to pay a beneficiary at least the amount of money invested by the annuitant during his life—period. In a regular old mutual fund investment, we could put in $80,000 and when you we the investment could be worth $30,000, which is all our heirs would inherit. In a variable annuity (not just a *fixed* annuity), the death benefit would pay out the $80,000. And, if the value of your investment was more than the $80,000 cost basis, the heirs would receive the $90,000 or whatever the account was worth. Note that in the variable annuity, this death benefit is only in effect while the annuitant is deferring any payments from the contract. As we'll see, once we flip the switch to receive payments in a variable annuity, well, anything can happen.

Insurance companies sell peace of mind. Both the mortality guarantee and the death benefit help a lot of investors sleep better. Pretty tough to put a price tag on that. For maximum peace of mind, individuals should buy a fixed or indexed annuity. For some peace of mind and the chance to invest in the stock and bond markets, individuals should consider a variable annuity. A variable annuity offers the investment choices from a family of mutual funds (growth, value, high-yield bonds, etc.), the tax deferral from an IRA or 401(k) plan, plus a death benefit similar to a life insurance policy. A fixed annuity—or indexed annuity—offers the tax deferral, the death benefit, and a dependable stream of minimum payments, even if the annuitant lives to 100.

Interestingly, an annuity gives the insurance company a different kind of "mortality risk." In a life insurance policy, their risk is that someone will put in $10,000 and die the next year, forcing the company to pay out hundreds of thousands, maybe a million. In an annuity, their mortality risk is that the annuitant will end up living to 115. The insurance company makes a mortality guarantee, which promises to pay the annuitant each month for the rest of her life. But, they cover their risk with a fee, called a mortality risk fee.

An insurance company has the risk that their expenses will rise. They promise to keep expenses level, but they charge an expense risk fee to cover their risk. In fact, usually the two are combined and referred to as a "**mortality and expense risk fee**," or "M & E" for those in a hurry. Variable annuities use mutual fund–type accounts as investment vehicles, but they add charges in excess of what those mutual funds charge investors. The guarantees offered in the annuity contract can easily add an extra 1%-1.5% to annual expenses, which can really add up over 20 or 30 years.

A special feature is sometimes called a "rider," or a "bonus." Although these features can benefit the annuitant, they can also confuse him. For example, a deferred variable annuity can come with an "income guarantee," but that is all that is guaranteed. With this enhancement the insurance company guarantees an annual income stream that can be withdrawn starting a certain number of years into the future. This guaranteed income is not based on the investment performance of the subaccounts but, rather, on the claims-paying ability of the insurance company. Understand that even though the income stream does not depend on the account balance, the account balance can definitely drop due to poor investment performance.

So, is the investor guaranteed against a loss of principal? No. He's not even guaranteed a certain account balance. The investor is promised an income stream that can be withdrawn in a few years. The overview for a guaranteed deferred variable annuity that I'm looking at online includes this statement, "Guaranteed lifetime income that cannot be reduced due to market performance." The footnotes at the bottom of the page, however, point out that, "The contract value is subject to market fluctuations and investment risk so that, when withdrawn, it may be worth more or less than its original value."

And, how "guaranteed" is the income stream? As the footnotes also state, "Guarantees apply to certain insurance and annuity products and are subject to product terms, exclusions and limitations and the insurer's claims-paying ability and financial strength."

With a **bonus annuity** the annuity company may offer to enhance the buyer's premium by contributing an additional 1 to 5% of what he/she puts in. Of course, this comes with a price. First, there are fees attached and, second, the surrender period is longer. Third, if the investor surrenders the contract early, the bonus disappears. Remember that an investor is penalized by the annuity company with a "surrender charge" if they pull all their money out early. For bonus annuities that period where the investor could get penalized is longer.

Bonus annuities are not suitable for everyone. Variable annuities in general are not good for short-term investment goals, since the surrender charge is applied during the first 7 years or so. Should you switch a customer into a bonus annuity? Maybe. But, remember, even though the annuitant can avoid taxes through a 1035 exchange, when she exchanges the annuity, her surrender period starts all over again. And, yes, FINRA will bust you if it looks like you did the switch just to make a nice commission, forcing the investor to start the surrender period all over again. In general, investors should maximize their 401(k) and other retirement plans before considering annuities. Annuities are ideal for those who have maxed out those plans, since the annuity allows investors to contribute as much as they would like.

Variable annuities come with a **free-look period**, which is generally a minimum of 10 business days. If the consumer decides he or she doesn't want to keep the product, he or she can cancel without losing any premiums or surrender charges to the company. For fixed annuities, consumers have the same free look period their state requires of insurance policies.

Just like owners of mutual fund shares, owners of variable annuities get to vote their units on important decisions such as:

- Electing the Board of Managers
- Changing the Investment Objectives, Policies
- Ratifying the Independent Auditor/Accounting Firm

Purchasing Annuities

The categories of fixed, indexed, and variable annuities refer to the way payments are calculated on the way out. In terms of buying annuities the two major types are "immediate" and "deferred." These terms refer to how soon the contract holder wants to begin receiving payments—now, or later? These are retirement plans, remember, so you do need to be 59½ to avoid penalties. Therefore, some customers might want or need to wait 20 or 30 years before receiving payments. If so, they purchase a deferred annuity.

The tax deferral is nice, but if the individual is already, say, 68, she may want to retire now and start receiving payments immediately. As you can probably guess, we call that an immediate annuity. While there are immediate *variable* annuities, it is more common to buy the fixed *immediate* annuity. Why? The whole point of buying an immediate annuity is to know that—no matter what happens to social security and your 401(k) account—there is a solid insurance company contractually obligated to make a payment of at least X amount for as long as you live. An immediate *variable* annuity would work out well only if the investments did—while there is some minimal payment guaranteed, it is meager.

An immediate fixed annuity does not offer a high rate of return, but it does provide peace of mind to investors in retirement. Many financial planners would suggest that at least some of their customers' retirement money be in a fixed immediate annuity—maybe just enough to provide a monthly payment covering monthly expenses. Figuring withdrawal rates from retirement accounts is tricky, so having a payment of X amount from a solid insurance company could smooth out the bumps.

Customers can buy annuities either with one big payment or several smaller payments. The first method is called "single premium" or "single payment." The second method is called "periodic payment." If an investor has a large amount of money, she can put it in an annuity, where it can grow tax-deferred. If she's putting in a big single purchase payment, she can choose either to wait (defer) or to begin receiving annuity payments immediately. She has to be 59½ years old to annuitize, but if she's old enough, she can begin the pay-out phase immediately. That's called a **single-payment immediate annuity**. Maybe she's only 42, though, and wants to let the money grow another 20 years before taking it out. That's called a **single-payment deferred annuity** (SPDA).

Many investors put money into the annuity during the accumulation phase (pay-in) gradually, over time. That's called "periodic payment," and if they aren't done paying in yet, you can bet the insurance company isn't going to start paying out. So, if you're talking about a "periodic payment" plan, the only way to do it is through a **periodic *deferred* annuity**. There is no such thing as a "Periodic Immediate Annuity" since no insurance company I'm aware of would let me start sending in $100 a month while they go ahead and start sending me $110.

To review, then, there are three methods of purchasing annuities:

- Single-Payment Deferred Annuity
- Periodic-Payment Deferred Annuity
- Single-Payment Immediate Annuity

Again, understand that variable annuities use mutual funds (called subaccounts) as the investment vehicles in the plan. But, annuities add both features and extra expenses for the investor on top of all the investment-related expenses. Tax deferral is nice. So are the death benefit and the annuity payment that goes on as long as the individual lives. But, that stuff also adds maybe 1.0–1.5% per year in expenses to the investor. You can either slide that fact past your investor or fully disclose it. Depends on whether you want your name up on FINRA's website or not.

Receiving Payments (Settlement Options)

Some investors make periodic purchase payments into the contract while others make just one big purchase payment. Either way, when the individual gets ready to annuitize the contract, he tells the insurance company which payout option he's choosing. And, he is not able to change this decision—he makes the decision and that's that. Essentially, what's going on at this point in the contract is that the individual is about to make a bet with the insurance company as to how long he will end up living.

Seriously.

Same thing for a variable annuity, but it's probably not as surprising on the variable side. But, either way, if the individual throws the switch to receive payments and chooses **life only** or **straight life** he'll typically receive the largest monthly payout. Why? Because the insurance company sets those payments and the insurance company knows better than he does when he's going to die. Not the exact day or the exact method, of course, but they can estimate it with amazing precision. Since the insurance/annuity company only has to make payments for as long as he lives, the payments are typically the largest for a "life only" or "straight life" annuity settlement option. How does the individual win the "bet"? By living longer than the actuarial tables would predict. Not a bad motivation for exercising and eating right, huh? If this option seems too risky, the individual can choose a "unit refund life annuity." This way he is guaranteed a certain number of payments even if he does get hit by the proverbial bus. If he dies before receiving them, his beneficiary receives the balance of payments.

So, does the annuitant have family or a charity she wants to be sure receives the balance of her payments? If not, why not go with the life only/straight life option—tell the insurance company to pay her as much as possible for as long as she lives. If she dies—well, what does she care if State Farm or Northwestern Mutual comes out ahead? If she does have family, friends, or a charity that she'd like to name as a beneficiary, she can choose a **period certain** settlement option. In that case, the insurance company has to do what the name implies—make payments for a certain period of time. To either her or the named beneficiaries. For older investors, this option typically leads to a lower monthly payment, since the insurance company will now be on the hook for several years even if the annuitant conveniently expires early. If it's a 20-year period certain payout, the payments have to be made to the beneficiary for the rest of that period, even if the annuitant dies after the first month or two.

The annuitant could also choose **life with period certain**, and now we'd have a complicated either-or scenario with the insurance company. With this option the company will make payments for the greater of his life *or* a certain period of time, such as 20 years. If he dies after 2 years, the company makes payments to his beneficiary for the rest of the term. And if he lives longer than 20 years, they just keep on making payments until he finally expires. Please read that sentence again, because it seems that no one ever believes me when I say that if the annuitant chooses a 20-year life-with-period-certain settlement option and inconveniently lives 23 years, the insurance company makes payments for 23 years. When he dies, no more payments.

Finally, the **joint with last survivor** option would typically provide the smallest monthly check because the company is obligated to make payments as long as either the annuitant or the survivors are alive. The contract can be set up to pay the annuitant while he's alive and then pay the beneficiaries until the last beneficiary expires. Or, it can start paying the annuitant *and* the beneficiary until both have finally, you know. Covering two persons' mortality risks (the risk that they'll live an inconveniently long time) is an expensive proposition to the insurance company, so these monthly checks are typically smaller than either period certain or life-only settlement options.

Variable Annuities: Accumulation and Annuity Units

There are only two phases of an annuity—the **accumulation period** and the **annuity period**. An individual making periodic payments into the contract, or one who made one big purchase payment and is now just deferring the payout phase, is in the accumulation phase, holding **accumulation units**. When he throws the switch to start receiving payments, the insurance company will convert those accumulation units to **annuity units**.

In a fixed annuity, the annuitant knows the minimum monthly payment he can expect. A variable annuity, on the other hand, pays out the fluctuating value of those annuity units. And, although the value of annuity units fluctuates in a variable annuity during the payout phase, the *number* of those annuity units is fixed. To calculate the first payment for a variable annuity, the insurance company uses the following:

- Age of the annuitant
- Account value
- Gender
- Settlement option

Remember that health is not a factor—there are no medical exams required when determining the payout. This is also why an annuity cannot suddenly be turned into a life insurance policy, even though it can work in the other direction, as we'll discuss elsewhere.

As we said, once the number of annuity units has been determined, we say that the number of annuity units is fixed. So, for example, maybe every month he'll be paid the value of 100 annuity units.

Trouble is, he has no idea how big that monthly check is going to be, since nobody knows what 100 **annuity units** will be worth month-to-month, just like nobody knows what mutual fund shares will be worth month-to-month. So, how much is an annuity unit worth each month? All depends on the investment performance of the separate account compared to the expectations of its performance.

Seriously. If the separate account returns are better than the assumed rate, the units increase in value. If the account returns are exactly as expected, the unit value stays the same. And if the account returns are lower than expected, the unit value drops from the month before. It's all based on the **Assumed Interest Rate (AIR)** that the annuitant and annuity company agree to use.

If the **AIR** is 5%, that means the separate account investments are expected to grow each month at an annualized rate of 5%. If the account gets a 6% annualized rate of return one month, the individual's check gets bigger. If the account gets the anticipated 5% return next month, that's the same as AIR and the check will stay the same. And if the account gets only a 4% return the following month, the check will go down.

Don't let the exam trick you on this concept. If the AIR is 5%, here is how it could work:

Actual Return:	5%	7%	6%	5%	4%
Check:	$1,020	$1,035	$1,045	$1,045	$1,030

When the account gets a 7% return, the account gets much bigger. So when it gets only a 6% return the following month, that's 6% of a bigger account, and is 1% more than we expected to get. So, just compare the actual return with the AIR. If the actual return is bigger, so is the monthly check. If it's smaller, so is the monthly check. If the actual return is the same as the AIR, the check stays the same.

The Separate vs. General Account

An insurance company is one of the finest business models ever conceived. See, no one person can take the risk of dying at age 32 and leaving the family with an unpaid mortgage, a bunch of other bills, and a sudden loss of income, not to mention the maybe $15,000 it takes just for a funeral these days. But, an insurance company can take the risk that a certain number of individuals will die prematurely by insuring a large number of individuals and then using the precise laws of probability over large numbers that tell them how many individuals will die each year with only a small margin of error. Once they've taken the insurance premiums that individuals pay, they then invest what's left after covering expenses and invest it wisely in the real estate, fixed-income, and stock markets. They have just as much data on these markets, so they can use the laws of probability again to figure out that if they take this much risk here, they can count on earning this much return over here within only a small margin of error.

And, of course, most insurance companies not run by Warren Buffet are conservative investors. That's what allows them to crunch numbers and know with reasonable certainty they will never have to pay so many death benefits in one year that their investments are totally wiped out. This conservative investment account that guarantees the payout on whole life, term life, and fixed annuities is called the **general account**. In other words, the general account is for the insurance company's investments. Typically, it is comprised mostly of investment-grade corporate bonds.

Many insurance companies also create an account that is separate from the general account and, believe it or not, the industry calls it the **separate account**. It's really a mutual fund family that offers tax deferral, but we don't call it a mutual fund, even though it's also covered by and registered under the same Investment Company Act of 1940. The Investment Company Act of 1940 defines a separate account like so:

```
"Separate account" means an account established and maintained by
an insurance company pursuant to the laws of any State or
territory of the United States, or of Canada or any province
thereof, under which income, gains and losses, whether or not
realized, from assets allocated to such account, are, in
accordance with the applicable contract, credited to or charged
against such account without regard to other income, gains, or
losses of the insurance company.
```

When the **purchase payments** are invested in the general account, they are guaranteed a certain rate of return—whole life, fixed annuity. When the purchase payments are invested in the separate account, welcome to the stock and bond markets, where anything can happen.

From the perspective of the nice couple sitting across from a registered representative at the table, it all looks pretty much the same. He was talking about the Platinum Equity Income Fund a few minutes ago—now that he has switched to his variable annuity spiel, they're seeing the same Platinum Equity Income Fund.

It is the same fund, but if we buy it within a variable annuity contract, we call it a **subaccount**.

There are good reasons to avoid calling subaccounts "mutual funds." If the investor thinks he's in a "mutual fund," he might think he can take out his money whenever he wants. He also might not realize that he's paying an extra 1.0–1.5% a year to place the annuity wrapper around the "mutual fund" investments. So, be careful with the language out there, people.

Life Insurance

I've always felt it rude to die without insurance and leave family and friends footing the bill for my funeral. That's why I "rent" insurance coverage through something called **term life insurance**. It's cheap, but it's only good for a certain term—maybe it's a 5-, 10-, or 20-year term. The individual pays premiums in exchange for a guaranteed **death benefit** payable to a **beneficiary** if **the insured** dies during that period. If the insured does not die during that period, the policy expires. If the **policyholder** wants to renew, he can, but he's older now and more costly to insure. In other words, his premiums will go up, even though the death benefit will stay the same, because he's older and more likely to have some medical condition that raises his rates, too, or even that prevents him from being offered the insurance at all.

So, as with all products, there are pluses and minuses. Term insurance is cheap and offers nice protection, but it does not build any cash value and has to be renewed at higher and higher rates, just like renting an apartment.

Now would be a good time to note the language used in insurance:

- **Policyholder**: the owner of the policy, responsible for paying premiums
- **Insured**: the person whose life is insured by the policy, usually the policyholder
- **Beneficiary**: the party that receives the death benefit upon death of the insured
- **Death benefit**: the amount payable to the beneficiary upon death of the insured, minus any unpaid premiums or loan balances
- **Cash value**: a value in the policy account that can be partially withdrawn or borrowed against

So, let's say that Joe Smith buys an insurance policy with a $100,000 death benefit payable to his wife. He's the policyholder and the insured. If he dies, the death benefit of $100,000 is paid to the beneficiary, his wife. As we'll see, most insurance also builds up cash value, which can be withdrawn or borrowed while Joe is alive (note that term insurance does not build up this cash value, which is also why it's relatively cheap insurance).

Permanent vs. Temporary Insurance

As with housing, some people prefer to rent insurance for a term, and some prefer to buy it. Some feel that if you're going to be putting money aside, you might as well end up with something to show for it, so they purchase permanent insurance. The most common type of permanent insurance is called **whole life insurance**. The premiums are much higher than on the term insurance you sort of "rent," but insurance companies will guarantee a minimum **cash value**, and you can also pretty well plan for an even better cash value than that. This way it works to protect your beneficiaries if you die unexpectedly and also acts as a savings vehicle where the cash value grows tax-deferred. Maybe at age 55 you decide to borrow $50,000 of the cash value for whatever reason. Could come in really handy, yes?

So, term is cheap, but it builds no cash value. And, to keep it going, the policy owner usually has to pay more for the same benefit. Reminds me of how I spent five years paying "cheap" rent to a landlord. It was definitely lower than a mortgage payment would have been on a similar-sized house. But at the end of this 5-year term, I had turned over $40,000 to the landlord and was left with nothing but the opportunity to renew my lease at a higher rate. I covered myself with a roof for five years, and at the end of the five years I owned absolutely no part of that roof.

Whole life insurance is more like buying the house, which is exactly what I did after five years of renting. I had to come up with a down payment, and my monthly mortgage jumped by $200 above the monthly rent. The upside is that at the end of five years, I'll have some equity in the house that I can tap into for a loan maybe. Just like with a whole life policy, I'll be getting at least something back for all those payments I've made over the years. And the time will come when the full value is all paid up and mine.

So, whole life insurance involves premiums that are higher than those for term life insurance, but you end up with something even if you stop paying into the policy. There is a guaranteed cash value, whereas term leaves you with nothing. The death benefit is guaranteed, too, so whole life insurance is a popular product for people who want to protect their families and also use the policy as a savings vehicle, where all that increase in cash value grows tax-deferred.

If the exam asks which type of customer should purchase term insurance, look for a young, single parent, maybe, or someone who absolutely has to protect the kids from a sudden loss of income and wants to do it as cheaply as possible.

Since some customers crave flexibility, the industry bent over backwards to come up with a flexible form of permanent insurance called **universal life insurance**. Think "flexibility" when you see the words "universal life insurance." The death benefit and, therefore, the premiums can be adjusted by the customer. They can be increased to buy more coverage or decreased to back off on the coverage and save some money. If the cash value is sufficient, premiums can stop being paid by the customer and start being covered by the cash value. The cash value grows at a minimum, guaranteed rate, just like on traditional whole life polices, and if the general account does well, the cash value goes up from there. As mentioned, at some point the policyholder may decide to withdraw part of the cash value, or may usually borrow up to 90% of it.

Variable Policies

So, whether it's term, traditional whole life, or universal life insurance, we're talking strictly about insurance products. Death benefits and cash values are guaranteed by the insurance company, who invests the net premiums into their general account. Once they start attaching cash value and death benefits to the ups and downs of a separate account, however, they have created a new product that is both an insurance policy and a security. Opens a whole new market for the company, but it also means that those who sell them need both an insurance and a securities license.

Whole life and term life insurance policies tell customers exactly how much they will pay out upon death. So, in term and whole life policies, the investment risk is borne by the insurance company.

Well, with variable insurance products, the death benefit—as well as the cash value—fluctuates just like it does in a variable annuity. That's what they mean by "variable." It all varies, based on the investment performance of the separate account. The separate account, as we discussed under variable annuities, is made up of subaccounts. The investor chooses from these quasi-mutual funds that are trying to meet different investment objectives: growth, long-term bonds, short-term Treasuries, etc. He can even choose to invest some of the premiums into a fixed account, just to play it safe, and he can switch between the subaccounts as his investment needs change without a tax problem. This stuff all grows tax-deferred, remember.

The cash value is tied to account performance, period. So if the test question says that the separate account grew, it doesn't matter by how much. The cash value increases when the separate account increases. But death benefit is tied to actual performance versus AIR, just like an annuity unit in a variable annuity. So if the AIR is 6% and the account gets a 4% return, the cash value will increase due to the positive return, but the death benefit will decrease since the account returned less than AIR.

Variable Life Insurance (VLI) policies pay out the cash value/surrender value whenever the policyholder cashes in the policy. But, there's no way to know what the value might be at the time of surrender far into the future. If the subaccounts have performed well, the cash value might be better than expected. But if the market has been brutal, the cash value could go all the way to zero.

A minimum or fixed death benefit is guaranteed, however. Some refer to it as the "floor." No matter what the market does, the insurance company guarantees a minimum death benefit that could only be reduced or depleted by failure to pay premiums or taking out loans against the policy. Remember that any guaranteed payments are covered by the insurance company's general account. So, the minimum death benefit is guaranteed, and the policyholder also has the chance of enjoying an increased death benefit, depending on how well the subaccounts do. As we said, that's tied to AIR, so if the market is kind, the death benefit increases, but if the market is unkind, it could, theoretically, drag the death benefit all the way to the floor.

As with variable annuities, after the money's been allocated to the subaccounts of the separate account, the insurance company charges regular fees, just like they do in variable annuities:

- mortality risk fee
- expense risk fee (or "Mortality & Expense Risk Fee)
- investment management fees

The value of the subaccounts and, therefore, the cash value are calculated daily. The death benefit is calculated annually. If the separate account has several below-AIR months, it will take several above-AIR months after that before the customer's death benefit starts to increase.

Remember that flexibility we discussed that separates traditional whole life from universal life? Well, it probably isn't too surprising that someone eventually married that benefit to variable life to get **Variable Universal Life Insurance**. With VUL we have the death benefit and cash value tied to the separate account (variable), plus we have the flexible premium thing (universal) going on. Regular old variable life is called "scheduled premium." That means the insurance company puts your premium payments on a schedule, and you better stick to it. Variable Universal or Universal Variable Life policies are funded as "flexible premium." That means the customer may or may not have to send in a check. With a VUL policy, the customer has to maintain enough cash value and death benefit to keep the policy in force. If the separate account rocks, no money has to roll in from the customer. If the separate account rolls over and dies, look out. Since that's a little scary, some VULs come with minimum guaranteed death benefits.

The advantages of variable life over whole life insurance include the ability to invest some of the premiums into the stock market, which has historically enjoyed relatively high average returns and done well at beating inflation. A robust investment market can increase the cash value and death benefit, often faster than the rate of inflation. A traditional whole life policy, on the other hand, that promised to pay $50,000 when it was purchased in 1974 represented a lot of money then. But if it pays that $50,000 out in 2019, the $50,000 doesn't go far, due to inflation.

When selling variable insurance policies, the agent must remember that these are insurance policies first and foremost. He can discuss the benefits of investing in the subaccounts, but he can't present these insurance policies primarily as investment vehicles. Primarily, they're to be sold for the death benefit. They also offer the opportunity to invest in the subaccounts, but they're not to be pitched primarily as investment vehicles.

Four federal acts are involved with variable life insurance and variable annuities. The Securities Act of 1933 covers variable life insurance (and annuities). These products must be registered with the SEC and sold with a prospectus. Even though the company that issues these contracts is an insurance company, the subdivision that sells the securities products has to be a broker-dealer registered under the Securities Exchange Act of 1934. The separate account is defined as an investment company under the Investment Company Act of 1940 and is either registered as a UIT or an Open-End Fund as defined under that act. The "money manager" or "investment adviser" has to register under the Investment Advisers Act of 1940.

And, at the state level, both securities and insurance regulators are watching these products and those who sell them.

Policy Loans

Variable policies make 75% of the cash value available to the customer as a loan after three years. Guess what—they charge interest on that loan, just as they do on a whole life policy. If the loan is not repaid, that reduces both the cash value and the death benefit of the policy. And, if the customer takes out a big loan and then the separate account tanks, he'll have to put some money back in to bring the cash value back to a sufficient level, or risk having the policy lapse. Don't worry, though. Some people take out a loan with absolutely no intention of repaying it. They don't need as much death benefit at this point, so why not have some fun with the money right now?

Settlement Options for Insurance Policies

The policyholder can choose from many options concerning the method of payment to the beneficiary. These are called "settlement options." The "lump-sum" method is self-explanatory. "Fixed-period" means that the insurance company will invest the proceeds of the policy into an interest-bearing account and then make equal payments at regular intervals for a fixed period. The payments include principal and interest. How much are the payments? That depends on the size of the principal, the interest rate earned by the insurance company, and the length of time involved in this fixed period.

The "fixed-amount" settlement option has the insurance company invest the proceeds from the policy and pay the beneficiary a fixed amount of money at regular intervals until both the principal and interest are gone. The amount received is fixed, but the period over which the beneficiary receives payments varies.

So, for "fixed-period" versus "fixed-amount," the decision comes down to this: do you want to receive an uncertain amount of money for a fixed period, or do you want to receive a fixed amount of money for an uncertain period? Do you want to be paid something like $25,000 for exactly three years (fixed-period)? Or, would you prefer being paid exactly $25,000 for about three years (fixed-amount)?

In a "life-income" settlement option, the proceeds are annuitized. That means the insurance company provides the beneficiary with a guaranteed income for the rest of his/her life. Just like with annuities, the beneficiary's age expectancy is considered to determine the monthly payout, along with the size of the death benefit and the type of payout selected.

There is also an "interest-only" settlement option, whereby the insurance company keeps the proceeds from the policy and invests them, promising the beneficiary a guaranteed minimum rate of interest. The beneficiary might get more than the minimum, or not, and may receive the payments annually, semiannually, quarterly, or monthly. He/she also has the right to withdraw all the principal, or to change settlement options.

Types and Characteristics of Cash and Cash Equivalents

The first line of a corporation's balance sheet is "cash and equivalents," listed under current assets. Businesses can use cash and equivalents as a buffer against bad times or to make strategic acquisitions. When a business invests its excess cash in short-term interest-bearing securities, they are investing in **money market securities** as opposed to long-term bonds.

Debt securities maturing in greater than one year are sometimes called funded debt. Money market securities, on the other hand, are debt securities maturing in one year or less. They are considered safe, liquid investments that hold a steady value over the short-term. The exam may refer to money market securities as "cash equivalents" because, basically, they are just as good as cash. Better actually, because unlike cash hidden in a coffee can, money market instruments are earning interest. It's not necessarily a high rate of interest, but at least we are putting our cash to work and not risking it in the stock market, where anything can happen, or even the bond market, where interest rates could rise and knock down the value of our holdings.

Of course, the problem with investing too much money into cash equivalents is that we will miss the big growth opportunities that arise when the stock or bond markets experience bull markets. That, as we have seen, is called opportunity cost. Also, these investments do not keep pace with inflation, leaving the investor with purchasing power risk.

T-Bills

The rate of return on a short-term U.S. Treasury Bill is considered the "riskless rate of return" for certain calculations we'll look at later. There is little time for interest rates or inflation to do any damage to a T-Bill. And, the issuer guarantees it against default.

That's right, the interest and principal are guaranteed, and the U.S. Treasury has never defaulted. So, if you don't need to withdraw a certain amount of money for several months or longer, you can buy the 3-month or 6-month T-Bill and usually earn higher yields than you'd earn in a savings account. There are no fees to buy T-Bills if you buy them directly through www.treasurydirect.gov.

Bank CDs usually yield about the same as T-Bills, but the bank's FDIC insurance stops at $250,000 per account. T-Bills, on the other hand, are guaranteed no matter how large the denomination. Any given Monday T-Bills are available by auction through the website mentioned above from as small as $100 par value to as large as $5 million. No matter how big the bill, it's guaranteed by the U.S. Treasury.

Bankers' Acceptances

A **bankers' acceptance** is a short-term credit investment created by a non-financial company and guaranteed by a bank as to payment. "BAs" are traded at discounts to face value in the secondary market. These instruments are commonly used in international transactions, and the exam might associate them with "importing and exporting." As with a T-Bill, bankers' acceptances are so short-term that it would make no sense to send interest checks to the buyer. Instead, these short-term debt securities are purchased at a discount from their face value. The difference between what we pay and what we receive is the interest income.

The "BA" or "bankers' acceptance" is backed both by a bank's full faith and credit and the goods being purchased by the importer. This is how the BA is created. First, a computer manufacturer in California imports computer parts from a Japanese company but is not ready to pay just yet. So, the California company issues a "time draft" to the Japanese company, which is really a post-dated check that is good on a future date and backed up by their bank's line of credit. The Japanese company can now sit on this time draft until the due date and receive the full amount. Or, they can cash it immediately at their bank at a slight discount. If they do the latter, the Japanese bank would then have a "bankers' acceptance" guaranteed by the American company's bank and the computer parts purchased by the American importer. The Japanese bank can either wait until the due date or sell it on the secondary market at a discount.

Commercial Paper

Commercial paper is typically used by companies as a source of working capital, receivables financing, and other short-term financing needs. To build major items such as an $800 million factory, a company generally issues long-term bonds (funded debt), and pays the lenders back slowly. But if Microsoft needs a mere $50 million for a few months, they would probably prefer to borrow it short-term at the lowest possible interest rate.

If so, they issue **commercial paper** with a $50 million face amount, selling it to a **money market mutual fund** for, say, $49.8 million. Again, the difference between the discounted price and the face amount *is* the interest earned by the investor. Commercial paper is generally issued only by corporations with high credit ratings from S&P, Moody's, or Fitch. Unfortunately, each of the three ratings agencies uses different nomenclature, so I have decided not to tell you about the P-1 down to P-3 ratings issued by Moody's, let alone the A1 down to A3 ratings issued by S&P or the F1 down to F3 ratings issued by Fitch. Do know that a rating below any of those "3's" is considered speculative commercial paper and would, therefore, not be found in the typical money market mutual fund portfolio.

Commercial paper could be described as an unsecured promissory note, as opposed to the repurchase agreements up ahead, which provide collateral to the lender. Some large corporations issue their commercial paper directly to investors, which may be mutual funds, pension funds, etc. The industry calls this "directly placed commercial paper." When corporations use commercial paper dealers to sell to the investor, the industry refers to this as "dealer-placed commercial paper."

Large financial institutions borrow money at low interest rates over the short term by taking money and paying whatever a savings account or CD currently offers. They then lend that money out to someone else long-term at a higher interest rate. If they're able to borrow at a lower rate than they lend it at to someone else, they're fine.

But this business model also puts them at risk in terms of fluctuating interest rates. Think of the flat and inverted yield curves we looked at, or even a positive yield curve with only a tiny difference between short-term and long-term interest rates. These interest rate environments are no good for bankers. If they suddenly have to pay high interest rates to borrow short-term while they're earning lower and lower rates when they lend the money out long-term, that's got to hurt.

To shield themselves from interest-rate risk over the short-term, large financial institutions engage in **repurchase agreements** and **reverse repurchase agreements**. Basically, one party buys a certain amount of the other party's fixed-income securities today and then sells them back at a set price in the near future. The difference between what the buyer pays at the start of the transaction and what they receive at the end of the agreement is their rate of return, expressed as a percentage per year. This rate is called the "repo rate." The repo rate is not set by any regulatory body but rather through negotiations between buyers and sellers in these arrangements.

Even though these agreements are structured as a purchase and a sale, they function more like a short-term loan. The buyer is really lending money short-term to the seller, and the loan is collateralized by the securities being purchased and held for, perhaps, 30 days. The risk is low, since even if the other party could not repurchase the securities, chances are the securities would be worth about what the buyer just paid for them. But that is not the same thing as a risk-free investment, so, no, repurchase agreements are not risk-free even though they are safe due to the collateral involved. Their main risk is **counterparty risk** because collateral is protection, not a 100% guarantee against loss.

So, a "repo" reduces the buyer's credit risk, and if the securities purchased are liquid, this also reduces their liquidity risk. Provided the assets are liquid, the buyer can either sell them or even refinance at any time during the life of a repo by selling or "repoing" the assets to a third party. If he got that fancy, the buyer would subsequently have to buy the same type of collateral back to return it to his counterparty at the end of the repo. This right of use on the collateral reduces the liquidity risk that the buyer takes by lending to the seller at the start of the transaction. And, because lending through a repurchase agreement exposes the buyer to lower credit and liquidity risk, repo rates are typically lower than unsecured money market rates—commercial paper, for example.

For the party of the transaction doing the selling to raise the cash, this is a repurchase agreement. To the party on the other side, who starts out as the buyer, the agreement is known as a reverse repurchase agreement. Although part of the money market, repurchase agreements (repos) are more of a private arrangement than a security that gets bought and sold. There is no active secondary market for these transactions. The interest rates are established through negotiations between the two parties to the transaction.

46

Most repurchase agreements have fixed terms. In the U.S., the majority are done on an overnight basis, with virtually all of them short-term. Then, there are repurchase agreements without fixed terms, called "open repos." With this on-demand agreement, the open repo can be terminated on any day in the future by either party, provided they give notice before an agreed daily deadline. Until an open repo is terminated, it automatically rolls over each day.

Tax-Exempt Municipal Notes

We'll look at municipal securities in a moment, but for now just know that cities, counties, and school districts, etc., can borrow money long-term by issuing bonds, and they can borrow short-term by issuing anticipation notes. For example, property taxes are collected twice a year. If the city wants some of that money now, they can issue a **tax anticipation note**, or TAN. If it's backed by revenues—from sewer and water services, for example—it's a **revenue anticipation note**, or RAN. If the note is backed by both taxes and revenues, they call it a **tax and revenue anticipation note**, or TRAN. Through a **bond anticipation note** or BAN the issuer borrows money now and backs it with part of the money they're going to borrow when they issue more bonds.

Seriously.

The interest paid on these municipal notes is lower than the nominal rates paid on a corporation's commercial paper, but that's okay—the interest paid is also tax-exempt at the federal level. So, if an investor or an institution is looking for safety, liquidity, and dependable, tax-exempt interest over the short-term, they purchase these anticipation notes directly or through a tax-exempt money market mutual fund.

Certificates of Deposit (CDS)

To earn a higher interest rate than what their bank offers on savings or checking accounts, many bank customers put relatively large amounts of money into **certificates of deposit** or **CDs**. These are long-term deposits that pay higher rates of interest if the depositor agrees to leave the funds untouched during a certain time frame. CDs are typically offered in terms of three or six months, and as long as one, two, three or five years. Those are typical terms, but savers can find certificates of deposit with terms as short as seven days or as long as 10 years. Obviously, the bank would have to entice someone with a higher rate to get him to agree to leave a large deposit untouched for 10 years. And, a saver, on the other hand, could not expect a high rate of return when locking up funds for a mere seven days. Investors agree not to withdraw funds until the CD matures, which is why CDs usually offer higher yields than a regular savings account. As with any fixed-income investment, rates typically increase with the length of deposit terms.

Deposits in bank CDs are backed by the Federal Deposit Insurance Corporation for up to $250,000 per depositor and ownership category, per insured bank. Bank CDs are insured by the FDIC just like other bank deposits, so this is about as safe as "safe money" gets. As you might imagine, the yields on these government-insured deposits are also rather modest. Then again, for the liquid part of one's portfolio, bank CDs are often perfect.

The drawbacks include the fact that they are long-term deposits, not as liquid as a savings account or a money market mutual fund. If the individual wants her money out now to cover a roof replacement, she will be penalized and probably lose all or most of the interest she was going to make. Bank CDs are not bonds to be traded on the secondary market. CDs don't do much to protect purchasing power, either, but they are great at maintaining an investor's needs for liquidity and capital preservation. The rates offered on certificates of deposit can change every week.

A $250,000 investment is equally safe in a T-Bill or a bank CD. Above that amount, the T-Bill is safer. And, either way, T-Bills are securities that can be bought and sold any day the securities markets are open, while CDs, on the other hand, are commitments to keep money on deposit for a specified length of time.

Brokered CDS

As opposed to just walking into a local bank and accepting the yields they're currently offering on their certificates of deposit, investors who purchase brokered CDs open their portfolio up to yields offered by banks across the country. A brokered CD account would also provide liquidity for the investor since he could ask the broker/registered representative to sell the CD on the secondary market as opposed to taking an early withdrawal penalty from a bank. Assuming the CDs are all FDIC insured (up to $250,000), investors can put a substantial amount of money into brokered CD accounts and receive FDIC insurance on each individual certificate of deposit in the portfolio. All without opening accounts at dozens of different banks to avoid exceeding the $250,000 FDIC coverage. Of course, there are fees, and this works much like brokered mortgages—the interest rate you receive is less favorable after the broker takes his cut.

Although most CDs are short-term, there are also long-term certificates of deposit with maturities as long as 10 years. Although brokered CDs can be a great option for many investors, some investors have been shafted by brokers who put them into 10-year CDs which then led to large losses when the investors needed their cash. As one might imagine, these long-term CDs may have limited or even no liquidity and investors can lose money by selling these things on the secondary market. Also, the interest payments on long-term CDs are often complex and explained in fine print few investors understand. Broker-dealers and registered representatives selling these long-term CDs need to be sure that investors understand how these products differ from traditional bank CDs and must disclose all potential risks. Higher yields on the one hand, but the secondary market for the products might not be as liquid as one would hope. Suddenly, rather than sacrificing the interest on a bank CD, the individual could lose principal. I don't know about you, but "losing money" and "CDs" really don't go together in my mind. The regulators tend to have similar difficulty squaring the two notions.

Negotiable/Jumbo CDS

Some investors step outside the realm of FDIC insurance and purchase **jumbo** or **negotiable CDs**. The denominations here are often several millions of dollars. Therefore, jumbo CDs are usually not insured by the FDIC but are, rather, backed by the issuing bank. That makes their yields higher. Also, if you've ever pulled out of a bank CD early, you know how painful that can be. With a jumbo CD you have a negotiable security you can sell to someone else. That's what the word "negotiable" means—tradable. If you have one of those archaic things known as a "checkbook," you'll notice your checks are "non-negotiable." They're just bank drafts—not tradable or marketable instruments. Well, a "negotiable CD" is a tradable, marketable instrument as opposed to just a long-term deposit at a bank.

Banks typically lend out more money than they take in through deposits. In fact, it might be a ratio of $10 of lending for every $1 taken in from deposits. To keep the banks from going belly-up when the borrowers can't repay the loans, the Federal Reserve Board requires their member banks to maintain a minimum amount of their deposits in reserve. Like, in case someone wants her money this afternoon at the teller window in Conshohocken, Pennsylvania. If a bank in Conshohocken is a few million dollars short of meeting their reserve requirement, they might borrow excess funds from a bank in Pittsburgh or Poughkeepsie at the **fed funds rate**. The fed funds rate is the interest rate that banks charge other banks for overnight loans. The rate fluctuates daily and is considered an indicator of interest rate trends in general. For example, if the fed funds rate rises, it's likely that the prime rate that banks charge their most creditworthy corporate borrowers will also rise soon. As will rates charged on mortgages, car loans, and unsecured personal loans.

Types and Characteristics of Fixed-Income Securities

Insurance-based products provide financial protection. Investments in money market securities provide a rainy-day fund that earns interest and can be tapped in an emergency without having to sell at a loss. To earn higher rates of return investors purchase longer-term debt securities, provided they have a long enough time horizon. If the time horizon is 10 years, an investor would expect to receive a higher yield on a T-Note compared to purchasing and repurchasing T-bills over that period. After all, the yield curve is typically a normal or positive curve.

Businesses borrow money short-term by issuing money market securities. To borrow from investors over the long-term companies issue fixed-income securities that are usually called **bonds**. As we saw when looking at the balance sheet, businesses sell stock to some investors and bonds to others, forming their **capital structure**. Equity investors are owners; bond investors are loaners. Loaners are creditors who must be paid their interest and principal on time but don't get a vote in corporate management decisions. Owners don't have to be paid anything, but their potential reward is much bigger than those who buy the company's bonds.

For the issuing company there are advantages and disadvantages to both types of financing. Equity financing gives the business breathing room since there are no interest payments to meet. But, equity investors take a share of profits, have a voice in corporate matters, and never go away. Debt financing adds the burden of interest payments that could force the company into bankruptcy. However, if the company can meet the interest and principal payments, eventually the bondholders are paid off, never making a claim on the company's profits.

Corporate bonds are debt securities representing loans from investors to a corporation. Investors buy the bonds, and the corporation then pays them interest on the loan until the principal amount is returned with the last interest payment at the end of the term. The bonds are liquid, meaning that the lenders can sell the bonds to other investors if they need to convert to cash.

What separates them from, say, a money market mutual fund, then? Bond prices rise and fall based on many factors we discussed under investment risks. Even though a T-Bond is guaranteed against default, its market price could drop. If so, the investor would liquidate at a loss. The goal of a money market mutual fund is to maintain a stable share price of $1 so investors can liquidate without taking a loss.

Again, though, to earn a higher rate of return investors move into longer-term fixed-income securities.

A corporation issuing bonds is using **leverage**. A leveraged company has financed operations by issuing debt securities or taking out long-term bank loans. On the balance sheet, the par value of the bonds is listed under long-term liabilities. And, on the income statement the interest payments are recorded as an expense. Interest is, after all, the "I" in those EBIT, EBITDA, etc. abbreviations we looked at. So, an analyst assigning a bond rating spends much time with an issuer's financial statements to see if the issuer will have trouble making regular interest payments and returning the principal at maturity.

A bond has a specific value known as the **par value** or **principal** amount. Since it's printed on the face of the certificate, it is also called the **face amount** of the bond. Bonds usually have a par value of $1,000 and, occasionally, $5,000. This is the amount an investor will receive with the last interest payment from the issuer. Up to that point, the investor has only been receiving interest payments against the money he loaned to the corporation by purchasing their bond certificates.

The bond certificate has "$1,000" or whatever the par value is printed on the face, along with the interest rate the issuer will pay the investor e year. This interest rate could be referred to as the **coupon rate** or **nominal yield**. The interest rate a bondholder receives is a stated, known thing. That's a big difference from common stock, where investors own a piece of a company's profits and hope that company becomes more profitable all the time. On the other hand, if they buy a 5% bond, investors receive 5% of the par value ($1,000) every year, which is $50 per year per bond. In other words, if he owns $1,000,000 par value of a bond with a 5% nominal yield, the bondholder's interest income is $50,000 a year.

Form of Registration

A **bond certificate** is a paper or electronic document stating the details of the bond:

- issuer's name
- par value or face amount
- interest rate
- maturity date
- call date (if any)

There are four different forms that a bond can take in terms of the certificate itself. In the olden days, bonds were issued as **bearer bonds,** which meant that whoever had possession of the bond was assumed to be the owner. No owner name at all on the certificate. The bond certificate said "pay to the bearer," so whoever presented the bond at maturity received the principal. To receive the interest, investors holding bearer bonds used to clip coupons attached to the bond certificate every six months. There was no name on the interest coupon, either, so the IRS had no way of tracking the principal or the interest income. Bonds haven't been issued in bearer form since the early 1980s. That doesn't mean they don't exist. A few are out there in safe-deposit boxes surely.

Bonds also used to be **registered as to principal only**. That meant that we had a name on the bond certificate—the person who would receive the principal amount at maturity. But, again, we had the unnamed interest coupons. Therefore, only the principal was registered, thus the name "registered as to principal only."

In the early 1980s issuers started registering both pieces of the **debt service**. Ever since, the issuer has registered the name of the owner [principal] and automatically cuts a check every six months for the interest. We call these bonds fully registered, because both pieces of the debt service (interest, principal) are registered.

Book entry/journal entry bonds are also fully registered. It's just that it's done on computer, rather than on paper. The investor keeps the trade confirmation as proof of ownership, but the issuer's paying agent has an owner name on computer, and automatically pays interest checks to the registered owner. Book entry/journal entry is how virtually all securities are issued these days. But, since bonds often have 30-year maturities, there are investors out there with bond certificates in their possession.

Quotes

Bonds are quoted either in terms of their price, or their yield. Since the coupon rate or nominal yield doesn't change, if you give me the price, I can figure the yield. And, if you give me the yield, I can figure the price.

If we're talking about a bond's price, we're talking about bond points. A bond point is worth $10. So, if a bond is selling at "98," that means it's selling for 98 bond points. With each point worth $10, a bond selling for 98 bond points is trading for $980. A bond trading at 102 is selling for $1,020. Although fractions have been eliminated from stock and options pricing, they are alive in the world of bond pricing.

If a bond point is worth $10, how much is 1/2 a bond point worth? Five dollars. A quarter-point is worth $2.50. An eighth is $1.25. Therefore, if you see a bond priced at 102 3/8, how much does the bond cost in dollars and cents? The "102" puts the price at $1,020, and 3/8 of $10 is $3.75. So, a bond trading at 102 3/8 costs $1,023.75.

$$102 (\$1,020) + 3/8 (\$3.75) = \$1,023.75$$

Corporate and municipal bonds can be quoted in halves, quarters, and eighths. T-Notes and T-Bonds split the $10 into 32 parts, with each 32nd worth $.3125.

Not all bond prices are given in fractions these days, however. Often the price is a decimal indicating the percentage of par value one would pay to purchase the bond. For example, a bond that last traded at "97.65" traded for $976.50 per bond. Or, if a bond is trading at a price of $102.475, buyers pay $1,024.75 per bond, or 102.475% of the bond's face value. The exam could ask what the total cost is if the investor buys 10 bonds, or 100 bonds. For the bond trading at "97.65" 10 bonds would cost the investor $9,765 and 100 bonds would cost $97,650.

If we're talking about **basis points**, we're talking about a bond's yield. Yield to maturity, to be exact. If I say that a bond with an 8% coupon just traded on a 7.92 **basis**, I'm saying the price went up above par, pushing the yield to maturity down to 7.92%. In other words, the price pushed the yield to maturity to a certain percentage, or number of "basis points." A basis point is the smallest increment of change in a bond's yield. When the media talks about the Fed easing interest rates by fifty basis points, they're talking about 1/2 of 1 percent.

We would write 1% as .01, right? Well, basis points use a 4-digit display system, so .01 is written as:

.0 1 0 0

Then, we read that figure as "100 basis points." Two percent is 200 basis points. One-half of one percent is written as .0050 or "50 basis points." So, a bond trading at a 7.92 basis means that the YTM is 7.92% or 792 basis points.

An easy way to work with basis points is to remember that all the single-digit percentages are expressed in hundreds. 400 basis points means 4%. Anything less than 100 basis points is less than 1%. So, 30 basis points is only .3 of 1%.

When we look at mutual funds, we'll see that the fund's operating expenses are expressed as basis points so that the investment adviser's management fee could be .35% or 35 basis points per year of the fund's assets. The 12b-1 fees that agents earn on mutual fund sales are typically 25 basis points or .25% per year—also known as ¼ of 1%.

Notation

The exam might ask what the following means:

10M XYZ 8s debentures of '25, callable @103 in '18

Believe it or not, "10M" means $10,000 par value or 10 bonds. XYZ is the issuing corporation, and they pay "8s" or 8% in interest each year. The little "s" means you get the $80 in two semi-annual payments of $40 each. Remember that—a test question might ask how much the investor receives at maturity on this bond. The answer is $1,040. Remember that interest is always paid retroactively, meaning for the previous 6 months. So, when the bond matures, you get your final interest payment (for the previous 6 months) plus the principal/par value of $1,000. This investor owns 10 bonds, so she would receive $10,400 at maturity in 2025.

Assuming we make it that far. As we see above, if interest rates drop in 2018, the issuer can buy back the bonds for $1,030 each, end of story. That's what "callable at 103 in '18" means.

Types of Maturities

If an issuer issues bonds that all mature on the same date in the future, we call this a **term maturity**. On the other hand, if the bonds are issued all at once but then mature gradually over time, we call this a **serial maturity**. Municipal bonds are often issued as serial maturities. In this case, the municipality floats, say, a $50,000,000 issue in which a portion of the bonds will mature each year over, say, 20 years. The longer out the maturity, the higher the yield offered to those investors, and the lower the yield offered on the bonds coming due in just a year or two.

In a **balloon maturity,** some of the bonds issued come due in the near-term, while most of the principal is paid off all at once, usually at the final maturity date. The term "balloon maturity" only applies to bond issues not backed up with a sinking fund, which means such issues can put an issuer's cash flow under severe stress.

Zero Coupon, Step-Up Bonds

We saw that reinvestment risk is avoided by purchasing bonds that do not make regular interest payments to the investor. Such bonds are called **zero coupons**. Each year the investor's cost basis is accreted, but all interest income is delayed until the bond matures at a higher face amount than the investor paid. Because the value of the bond increases as opposed to the issuer paying interest, a zero coupon is also known as a **capital appreciation bond.**

Corporate and U.S. Government zero coupon bonds are taxable annually to the investor even though interest income is not received until maturity. Because there is no current cash flow, the market price of a zero coupon is more volatile than a bond with a similar term to maturity that pays interest.

A step-up bond makes higher interest payments in the future compared to the initial payment. Investors might receive a lower-than-current rate on the first payment, but in exchange for that, they might end up receiving higher payments going forward. Usually, the coupon rate resets annually, but after the call protection period has passed, the issuer also has the right to call the bonds. Some **step-up bonds** reset the coupon payment just once; most re-set it at regular intervals. If an investor is concerned that rates will rise in the future, a step-up bond may be suitable, as it would allow her to capture higher coupon payments should that happen.

Callable, Put-able, and Convertible

If a bond issue is **callable,** the issuer has the right to buy the bonds back for a stated price as of a certain date or on a series of dates. A bond might be callable starting in the year 2025 at 104, meaning that in the year 2025 the issuer can retire the debt by giving each bondholder $1,040 per bond plus any accrued interest. If the next call date is in 2027, maybe the issuer only has to pay 102 at that point, and so on. The terms of the call provisions are spelled out in the contract known as the bond **indenture.**

Why do issuers call bonds? When interest rates drop, bond issuers realize their current debt could be replaced with cheaper debt. If interest rates fall to 6%, they reason, let's issue new debt at 6% and use part of the proceeds to retire the debt we're currently paying 8% on. Maybe they have to pay a slight premium to par when retiring the bond early, but the issuer comes out ahead by refinancing a large amount of debt at a lower interest rate. The premium price of "104" or "102" just barely compensates the bondholders for having to give up their bonds early and go forward at a lower yield to their investment accounts.

Replacing one bond issue with another is called **refunding**. It tends to happen when interest rates fall. It allows the issuer to replace high-interest-rate debt with lower-interest-rate debt.

But, what can the bondholders do with the proceeds of the call? Reinvest them. At what rate? A lower rate. This is a form of reinvestment risk, but it could also be referred to as call risk. Whatever we call it, the fact is upon reinvestment, the bondholders will get a lower rate of return, since interest rates have now fallen.

And, what happens to bond prices as rates decline? They go up, only they stop going up the day the issuer announces that the bonds will be called, meaning the bondholder doesn't get the full appreciation in price he would have otherwise gotten.

So, since the bondholder takes on this call risk, callable bonds yield more than non-callable bonds. As always, if we want something good from the corporation, they take something away.

If a bond is callable, the issuer reserves the right to buy it back at a stated price as of a certain date or series of dates. On the other hand, if a bond is "put-able," this put feature gives the owner of the bond the right to sell the bond back to the issuer per the terms stated in the indenture. As with call dates, the indenture often spells out a series of dates on which the investor may sell the bonds. A "put-able" bond protects investors from interest rate risk. If interest rates rise, other investors will be holding bonds with depressed market prices while the owner of a put-able bond can sell his bond for the price stated in the indenture.

Both corporations and municipalities issue callable and put-able bonds. On the other hand, only corporations issue **convertible bonds**, as these bonds are convertible into shares of common stock. As with convertible preferred stock, the issuer offers some potential upside to fixed-income investors. What's the catch? The yield offered is lower.

For a convertible bond the investor applies the par value toward purchasing the company's stock at a pre-determined price. When a convertible bond is issued, it is given a conversion price. If the conversion price is $40, this means that the bond is convertible into common stock at $40. In other words, the investor can use the par value of her bond towards the purchase of the company's common stock at a set price of $40. If the par value is $1,000, she applies that $1,000 toward the purchase of stock at $40 per-share. When doing so, how many shares would she be able to buy?

25 shares. So, how much is this bond worth at any given moment? It's worth whatever 25 shares of the common stock are worth at that moment, give or take. Investors take the par value of the convertible bond and divide it by the conversion price to find out how many shares of common stock the bond could be converted into.

In this case, it's 25 shares, since $1,000 would go exactly that far when purchasing stock priced at $40 a share.

Par/Conversion price = # common shares

1,000/40 = 25 shares

As we will see with convertible preferred stock, another name for the 25:1 relationship here is conversion ratio.

Going forward then, how much is the bond worth? That depends—how much are 25 shares of the common stock currently worth? Since the bond could always be converted into 25 shares, it should be worth whatever 25 shares of the common stock are worth—give or take. When the bond trades for exactly what the 25 shares are worth, we call this relationship **parity**, which means "same" or "equal." Since one's price depends on the other, the two should have a price that is near "parity."

If the common stock started to trade above $40 in our example, the bond should trade for 25 times that amount. If the stock rises to $50, the convertible bond is worth $1,250 or more. If not, an investor would have an "arbitrage opportunity." That means he could buy the bonds for less than the underlying stock is worth. If the stock rose to $50, but for some reason, one could buy the bonds for just $1,200, this is an arbitrage opportunity where an alert trader could pay just $1,200 for $1,250 worth of stock.

What usually happens is the holder of a convertible bond experiences an increased market price if the underlying stock rises. The bondholder does not have to convert to profit. Rather, he can just sell his bond for a capital gain.

Unfortunately, most convertible bonds give the issuer the right to force investors to convert rather than wait for the stock price to rise even further. For that reason, most convertible bonds do not offer unlimited upside. Then again, these **hybrid securities** offer some downside protection to the investor holding a bond while also offering some upside to him by tying the value to the price of the common stock. The issuer benefits by issuing the bonds at a lower coupon rate than they would otherwise have to pay.

Common stockholders will see their equity diluted when convertible bonds are converted to shares of stock. That's why a company's EPS is often followed by its "diluted EPS" to factor in the earnings-per-share that would have been reported if all convertibles converted to the underlying common stock. While the interest payment to those bondholders would go away, unfortunately they would be getting a share of the net income of the company going forward. Looking at the most recent annual report for Starbucks, I noted yesterday that EPS was $1.84, while diluted EPS was just $1.82.

Risks

Let's do a quick review of the risks that bond investors face:

> `Credit/default risk`: the risk that the issuer will miss interest payments or be unable to return the principal to investors.

> `Interest rate risk`: the risk that interest rates will rise, knocking bond market prices down. This is most severe on longer-term bonds.

> `Purchasing power risk`: the risk that inflation will erode the value of the coupon/interest payment to the investor.

> `Call risk`: the risk that when interest rates drop, issuers will buy back/redeem their bonds early. This forces bond investors to reinvest at lower rates going forward when they buy new bonds with the proceeds of the call. Not all bonds are callable, but those that are have this risk.

> `Prepayment risk`: call risk for mortgage-backed securities.

Reinvestment risk: refers to the fact that e six months a fixed-income investor will reinvest interest payments into new bonds; when she does so, she will reinvest at lower rates if interest rates/yields have dropped compared to the stated interest rate on the existing bond in her portfolio.

Market risk: the risk that investors will panic and send bond prices downward.

Corporate Bonds

As the SEC explains in a notice to investors, "Companies use the proceeds from bond sales for a wide variety of purposes, including buying new equipment, investing in research and development, buying back their own stock, paying shareholder dividends, refinancing debt, and financing mergers and acquisitions."

As the SEC mentions, companies might even borrow money to buy back equity. A test question could ask about that in terms of how it would affect the issuer's balance sheet. If an issuer is trading debt for equity, they are using leverage, which is reflected in a higher debt-to-equity ratio. Whatever the earnings are going forward, by retiring equity the issuer could help boost the earnings per-share of the common stock, which is good news for the shareholders.

A default on a municipal bond is a rare thing, but many corporations end up unable to pay the interest on their bonds—or return the principal at maturity—and thereby go into default, which is always bad news for the bondholders. To protect bondholders from this, Congress passed the **Trust Indenture Act of 1939**. Under this act if a corporation wants to sell $5,000,000 or more worth of bonds that mature in longer than one year, they must do it under a contract or indenture with a trustee, who will enforce the terms of the indenture to the benefit of the bondholders. In other words, if the issuer defaults, the trustee can move to forcibly sell off the assets of the company so that bondholders can recover some of their money. The trustee is typically a large bank.

As we'll see, there are also federal bankruptcy laws that provide protections to both the issuers and investors of bonds.

A corporate bond pays a fixed rate of interest to the investor, and that bond interest must be paid, unlike a dividend on stock that is paid only if the board of directors declares it. We'll see that a bondholder doesn't suffer as much price volatility as a stock investor. But, unlike the owner of common stock, bondholders don't vote on corporate matters. The only time bondholders get to vote is if the corporation goes into bankruptcy. Creditors will be offered various scenarios by the corporation, and the bondholders will get to vote on these terms. In other words, the only time bondholders get to vote is when they wish they didn't have to.

Since bankruptcy is a concern, corporations often secure the bonds by pledging specific assets like airplanes, government securities, or real estate. These bonds secured by specific collateral are called **secured bonds.** The issuer of a secured bond pledges title of the assets to the trustee, who might end up selling them off if the issuer gets behind on its interest payments. Investors who buy bonds attached to specific collateral are secured creditors, the most likely creditors to get paid should the company become insolvent. If the collateral used is real estate, we call it a **mortgage bond.** If the collateral is securities, we call it a **collateral trust certificate**. And if the collateral is equipment, such as airplanes or railroad cars, we call it an **equipment trust certificate**. Since these bonds are usually the most secure bonds issued by the company, they offer the lowest coupon payment, too. Remember, if you take a small risk, you usually only get a small reward.

Most corporate bonds are backed by a promise known as the "full faith and credit" of the issuer. That's why we might want to see what S&P and Moody's say about an issuer's full faith and credit. If the credit is AAA, we won't be offered a large coupon payment. But if the issuer is rated right at the cut-off point of BBB (Baa for Moody's), then we demand a higher interest rate in exchange for buying bonds from an issuer just one notch above junk status. Regardless of the rating, if we buy a bond backed by the full faith and credit of an issuer, we are buying a **debenture**.

Debenture holders are general creditors with claims below those of the secured bondholders. In a bankruptcy, debenture holders must compete with all other unsecured creditors of the company, e.g., suppliers with unpaid invoices. Therefore, debentures pay a higher coupon than secured bonds, since they carry more risk.

Some bonds are **guaranteed bonds,** which means a party other than the issuer has promised to pay interest, principal, or both if the issuer of the bonds cannot. Often a parent company will guarantee the bonds issued by one of its smaller subsidiaries to improve the credit rating. A "guaranteed bond" does not imply the investor is guaranteed against loss. Outside of bank products backed by the FDIC, investors should never expect to be guaranteed against all investment risk. Being guaranteed against default is as good as it gets.

Subordinated debentures have a claim below debentures. Since these bonds are riskier, they pay a higher coupon than debentures.

Beneath all creditors, stockholders make their claims on the company's assets. Preferred stockholders get preference, and common stock is always last in line. Common stock represents the lowest claim on a company's assets, which is why it is called the most "junior" security issued by a company.

Priority of Claims

If a company becomes unable to pay its suppliers, employees, bondholders, etc., it files a petition for bankruptcy protection either under "Chapter 7" or "Chapter 11" of the federal bankruptcy laws. Under Chapter 11 the company could convince creditors to write off some of the debt or extend the terms of the debt they are currently unable to service. Or, in some cases the entity is completely re-organized under Chapter 11 and former creditors will typically become shareholders of the newly reorganized entity. The business entity often keeps functioning to the best of its abilities and is placed under a trusteeship as a company that is now a "debtor in possession." While the entity struggles along, the U.S. trustee oversees things, demanding that the debtor in possession file regular reports on the operations of the business. The U.S. trustee also appoints a creditors' committee whose role involves consulting with the debtor in possession on administration of the case, investigating the debtor's conduct and operation of the business, and participating in formulating a plan of reorganization. The creditors' committee ordinarily consists of unsecured creditors who hold the seven largest unsecured claims against the debtor.

Under Chapter 7 assets of the company are liquidated by a court-appointed trustee and paid out according to the priority of claims. A liquidation under Chapter 7 is done according to the "absolute priority rule." When the court-appointed trustee liquidates assets, the parties who are owed money would be paid according to the following order or priority:

1. Administrative expenses of the bankruptcy itself
2. Taxes, rents, wages, and benefits
3. Unsecured creditors, including suppliers and bondholders/lenders
4. Equity investors: preferred stock, common stock

As we saw, secured bondholders have a claim on specific assets, so they are outside the priority ordering. They can seize the assets or their value based on the indenture for their secured bonds. This is why a secured bondholder often gets paid, even when other creditors receive nothing. If secured creditors receive collateral that is insufficient to satisfy their claim, their excess claim becomes another claim by unsecured creditors.

Also, remember that an **income bond** only pays income if the company has income. It's usually issued by a company coming out of bankruptcy and usually offers a high coupon to compensate for the uncertainty of the interest payment. The idea here is that the re-organized company will get some breathing room from the creditors and maybe this breathing room will help it get its act together and start paying interest on its "income" or "adjustment" bonds." A potential trick question could try to confuse you into thinking that an "income investor" with a low risk tolerance should buy an "income bond."

No—only a bond investor with a high appetite for risk and little need for liquidity should do so.

Sinking Fund

Bonds pay interest-only until the end of the term. Since the issuing corporation must return the principal value of the bond at some point, they usually establish what's known as a **sinking fund**. If you held your interest-only mortgage 30 years, maybe your spouse would one day have to gently remind you, "Now, remember to add the $300,000 to this month's interest check, honey. Time to pay the principal back." Since that's how corporations pay back the principal, they set some money aside in escrow, which means they park it in safe, dependable U.S. Treasury securities. With this sinking fund established, the company would be able to return the principal or complete a "call." Having this money set aside can only help the rating by S&P and Moody's, too.

Some bonds—especially municipal bonds—are escrowed to maturity, which means the funds needed to retire that bond issue are already parked in a safe, interest-bearing account holding Treasury securities. Having the debt service covered by a verifiable escrow account tends to make such bond ratings AAA and easy to sell on the secondary market.

As we saw, a balloon maturity is a bond issue without a sinking fund and where most of the principal comes due at the end of the term.

U.S. Government Securities

 The rate of default on high-yield corporate bonds has ranged in recent years from about 1% to 13%. On the other hand, the rate of default on U.S. Treasury securities has ranged from 0% to 0%, going all the way back to when Alexander Hamilton first issued them in the late 1700s. If you buy a bill, note, or bond issued by the United States Treasury, you eliminate default risk. You're going to get your interest and principal for sure. You just aren't going to get rich in the process. In fact, you usually need to be rich already to get excited about U.S. Government debt.

These fixed-income securities are for capital preservation. Working people need to save up for retirement through common stock or equity mutual funds. The less daring will save up by investing through corporate bonds or bond mutual funds. But if one already has millions of dollars, the goal might become preserving that capital as opposed to risking it trying to get bigger returns. If you sell your company for $10 million, for example, you might put $2 million into T-Bonds. If they yield 5%, that's $100,000 in interest income going forward, after all, with no risk to the principal.

U.S. Treasury securities are virtually free of default risk. They carry most of the other risks that corporate bondholders face, but default risk is eliminated. Therefore, if an investor compares the yield on, say, a 10-year Treasury Note to the yield on a 10-year corporate bond, the higher yield offered on the corporate bond indicates the market's perceived default risk. If the Treasury Note yields 3.0% while the 10-year corporate bond yields 4.5%, the **risk premium** demanded by investors is that difference of 1.5%. To take on default risk, investors require that much more yield.

As I write this, 1.5% happens to be exactly the risk premium investors are demanding to buy the lowest investment-grade rating (BBB/Baa). To buy the first level of junk a risk premium of 2.7% over U. S. Treasuries is currently required.

U.S. Government debt is safe and, therefore, low-yielding. T-Bills, T-Notes, T-Bonds, STRIPS, and TIPS are all securities that can be traded on the secondary market, what we call "negotiable" securities. I-Bonds, on the other hand, are not negotiable, meaning they can't be traded/sold to other investors.

T-Bills

T-Bills pay back the face amount, and investors try to buy them for the steepest discount possible on the front end. If the T-Bill pays out $1,000, investors would rather buy it for $950 than $965, right? In the first case, they earn $50 interest, in the second, only $35. That's why the BID looks higher than the ASK for T-Bills trading on the secondary market. The bid is the discount that buyers are trying to get; the asked price is the discount the sellers are willing to give up.

So, the quote might look like this:

BID	ASK
1.0%	.75%

In other words, the buyers want a 1% discount; the sellers are only willing to give up a .75% discount from the par value.

For a newly-issued T-Bill investors are able to purchase the security for less than the face amount they will receive in as little as 4 weeks or as long as 52 weeks. The U.S. Treasury operates a website that allows investors to purchase Treasury securities. The following explanation is from their website at www.treasurydirect.gov and reflects how low interest rates were at the time they published it:

For example, if a $1,000 26-week bill sells at auction for a 0.145% discount rate, the purchase price would be $999.27, a discount of $0.73.

In any case, T-Bills mature in one year or less (4 weeks, 13 weeks, 26 weeks, 52 weeks), so there are no coupon payments. Rather, the difference between the discounted purchase price and the face amount is the investor's interest on the short-term loan to the federal government. T-Bills are offered in minimum denominations of $100 and, like all Treasuries, T-Bills are issued in book entry/journal entry form. The maturities available change from time to time. Currently (as you can see at www.treasurydirect.gov) the available maturities are 4 weeks, 3 months, 6 months, 12 months, and the extremely short-term "cash management bills."

That website, by the way, offers an overview of bills, notes, bonds, etc. T-Bills are auctioned every Monday by the Federal Reserve Board. The big institutions put in "competitive tenders," trying to buy the bills for the lowest possible price. Small investors put in a "non-competitive" tender that will be filled. Institutions will probably get a better price on T-Bills today, but they also might not get their bid filled at all.

T-Notes, T-Bonds

T-Bills are ideal for the short-term, but investors may get tired of receiving low yields, and yields that tend to fluctuate each time they buy a new T-Bill. If the investor wants to receive interest payments for a few years and at a higher rate of interest, he will purchase T-Notes and T-Bonds instead. T-Notes are offered with 2- to 10-year maturities. T-Bonds mature in 30 years.

Both make semi-annual interest payments, and are both quoted in 32nds. A quote of 98.16 means $980 plus 16/32nds. A 32nd is worth thirty-one-and-a-quarter-pennies or $.3125. So, a T-Bond quoted at 98.16 is priced at $980 plus 16 times $.3125 ($5); a total of $985. A T-Bond quoted at 102.20 is trading for $1,020 plus 20 times $.3125 ($6.25); a total of $1,026.25.

The exam might ask you to calculate the **spread** on a quote for a T-Note or T-Bond. If a market maker says their bid is 98.16 while their offer is 98.20, the difference or "spread" between the prices is whatever 4 times $.3125 turns out to be on the calculator provided at the testing center. The spread in this example is $1.25 per bond or note. The question might then have you multiply that amount by the number of bonds or notes involved in the quote.

While corporate and municipal bonds are often callable just a few years after issue, 30-year T-Bonds are callable only in their last five years. The T-Bonds issued with super-high coupon rates back in 1983, for example, were not called until 2008.

The Treasury Department also takes T-Notes and T-Bonds and "strips" them into their various interest and principal components. Once they strip the securities into components, they sell interest-only or principal-only zero coupon bonds to investors. We call these STRIPS, an acronym that stands for the "separate trading of registered interest and principal of securities." If an investor needs to send kids to college, needs to have an exact amount of money available on a future date, and wants to avoid having to reinvest interest payments, put him into STRIPS. This way, he'll pay a known amount and receive a known amount on a future date, allowing him to lock into a yield long-term. He won't get rich, necessarily, but he won't lose the kids' college fund, either.

STRIPS present a peculiar tax problem called "phantom tax exposure." Even though interest income is not received until the STRIP matures, the investor pays tax on the amount of annual interest that has been added to the value of the security each year. A test question, might, therefore, point out that a STRIP or other taxable zero coupon forces investors to pay tax annually even though interest is received only at maturity.

Treasury Receipts

Broker-dealers sell zero coupons backed up by U.S. Treasury securities and call them **treasury receipts**. For both receipts and STRIPS, remember that they are purchased at a discount and mature at the face value. And remember that the STRIPS are guaranteed by Uncle Sam, while a Treasury Receipt is not.

TIPS

The Treasury Inflation-Protected Securities adjust for inflation, meaning that if inflation rises, investors receive more money, and when it falls, they receive less. Inflation is measured through the Consumer Price Index (CPI), which tracks the basic things that consumers buy.

If prices in general are rising (CPI is positive), the principal amount of the TIPS is adjusted upwards. That's a little surprising, since some readers would assume the principal amount/par value would stay the same, with the coupon rate adjusting. No. That would probably make too much sense to ever fly in Washington, DC. In any case, if the (fixed) coupon rate on the security is 3%, suddenly the investor could be receiving 3% of, say, $1030 to reflect inflation/rising consumer prices.

If the economy is experiencing falling prices (the CPI is negative), the principal amount of the TIPS could be lower than $1,000 when calculating the semi-annual interest payment. Even if the principal amount used to calculate an interest payment could be less than $1,000, the TIPS will pay out the $1,000 face amount at maturity, period. So, there is no default risk and no purchasing power/inflation risk on a TIPS. Basically, if you can find a safer security than a TIPS, please buy it.

Just don't expect to get much of a yield for your money.

An investor purchases an inflation-protected Treasury note (TIPS) with a coupon rate of 3%. Inflation in the first year is 4%. Therefore:
   A. The coupon payment becomes $31.20
   B. The principal becomes $1,030
   C. The coupon payment becomes $40

D. The principal amount becomes $1,070

Answer: A. The rate of inflation is 4%, so the principal becomes 4% larger. Multiply the principal of $1,000 by 1.04 to get the new principal amount of $1,040. Then multiply that principal by 3%, and the new annual coupon rate is $31.20.

I-Bonds

Like all the other Government Securities above, TIPS are "negotiable securities," meaning you can sell them to other investors on the secondary market. I-bonds, on the other hand, are "non-negotiable," meaning there is no secondary market for them. An investor buys the I-bond from the U.S. Government and can only sell it by redeeming it to the U.S. Government for payment. In other words, they're not securities; they're merely "savings bonds." An I-bond is a savings bond issued by the U.S. Treasury, which means it's safe and also exempt from state and local income taxes.

An I-bond pays a guaranteed rate that is fixed but also pays more interest income when inflation rises. The semi-annual inflation rate announced in May is the change between the CPI (inflation) figures from the preceding September and March; the inflation rate announced in November is the change between the CPI figures from the preceding March and September. So, since they adjust the interest income to levels of inflation, there's no default risk and no real purchasing power risk, either. There are also tax advantages.

First, the interest isn't paid out; it's added to the value of the bond. You can, therefore, defer the taxes until you cash in the bond. And, if you use the proceeds for qualified education costs in the same calendar year that you redeem the bonds, the interest is tax-free. The investor does not even have to declare that the I-bonds will be used for educational purposes when she buys them. If she uses the proceeds in the same year she redeems the bonds—and meets the other requirements of the Education Savings Bond Program—the interest is tax-free.

Agency Bonds

Agency bonds or **agency issues** are debt securities issued by either Government Sponsored Enterprises (GSEs) or Federal Government agencies which may issue or guarantee these bonds. GSEs are usually federally-chartered but privately-owned corporations such as FNMA (Federal National Mortgage Association) and FHLMC (Federal Home Loan Mortgage Corporation). Government agencies include the Small Business Administration, GNMA (Government National Mortgage Association), and the FHA (Federal Housing Authority). A key difference here is that securities issued by GSEs are not direct obligations of the US Government, while those issued or guaranteed by GNMA (Ginnie Mae), the SBA, and the FHA are guaranteed against default just like T-Bills, T-Notes, and T-Bonds.

Agency securities tend to promote a public purpose. For example, FNMA and FHLMC purchase mortgages from lenders, which encourages lenders to make more loans and increase home ownership. Similarly, the Federal Farm Credit Banks provide assistance to the agricultural sector, while the Small Business Administration provides assistance to small businesses.

Fannie Mae (FNMA) and Freddie Mac (FHLMC) are public companies with common stock, unlike GNMA. While the US Government has provided financial assistance to these entities, it has not guaranteed their debt securities or preferred stock issues, let alone their common stock. So, while investing in Ginnie Mae involves no credit or default risk, this is not the case with Fannie and Freddie.

According to Ginnie Mae's website (www.ginniemae.gov), "At Ginnie Mae, we help make affordable housing a reality for millions of low- and moderate-income households across America by channeling global capital into the nation's housing markets. Specifically, the Ginnie Mae guaranty allows mortgage lenders to obtain a better price for their mortgage loans in the secondary mortgage market. The lenders can then use the proceeds to make new mortgage loans available. Ginnie Mae does not buy or sell loans or issue mortgage-backed securities (MBS). What Ginnie Mae does is guarantee investors the timely payment of principal and interest on mortgage-backed securities backed by federally insured or guaranteed loans — mainly loans insured by the Federal Housing Administration (FHA) or guaranteed by the Department of Veterans Affairs (VA). Ginnie Mae securities are the only MBS to carry the full faith and credit guaranty of the United States government, which means that even in difficult times, an investment in Ginnie Mae mortgage-backed securities is one of the safest an investor can make."

A minimum investment of $25,000 is required for GNMA mortgage-backed securities. Investors receive monthly interest and principal payments from a pool of mortgages. When will the mortgages in the pool be paid off? That is an uncertainty. If interest rates drop, the mortgages will be repaid sooner than expected, which we call prepayment risk. If interest rates go the other way, it will take longer than expected for the homeowners to pay off the mortgages, which we call extension risk. GNMA, FNMA, and FHLMC mortgage-backed securities all carry this risk, which we mentioned earlier.

GNMA is backed by the full faith and credit of the US Government. Still, the yields are typically higher than what one would receive on a Treasury security of a similar term due to prepayment and extension risk. Interest rates on mortgage securities from FNMA and FHLMC are also higher than on Treasury and higher than corporate bonds to reflect the compensation for the uncertainty of their maturity as well as their higher credit risk. While FNMA and FHLMC buy mortgages and issue mortgage-backed securities, GNMA adds her guaranty to mortgage-backed securities that have already been issued. FNMA and FHLMC do guarantee payment to investors, but, again, neither is the federal government, and both charge fees to provide the guarantee.

From an informative document put out by the Federal Reserve Bank of New York, I see that "The agencies use a variety of methods to distribute their securities including allocation to dealers, competitive dealer bidding, direct sales to investors, and sales to investors through dealers. A common distribution method for agency securities is to allocate them among members of a selling group or syndicate of dealers. The syndicate provides market and trading information to the issuing agency before and during the allocation, and may support secondary trading in the issue after allocation. In compensation for their services, the syndicate members retain a percentage of the proceeds from the sold securities."

Foreign Bonds

Some investors choose to purchase bonds issued outside the U.S., which typically offer higher yields. Does that imply that international investing is riskier? Absolutely. If the investor wants absolute safety, he sacrifices yield. If he wants high yield, he sacrifices safety. Investing in foreign bonds is risky, but there is a big difference between a developed market and an emerging market. In general, the following countries enjoy securities markets and economies that are considered developed: U.S., Canada, European Union countries, Australia, New Zealand, and Japan. Emerging markets would include everyone else, though South Korea and Singapore are much more advanced than China, India, and other "emerging" nations. If we purchase bonds issued and traded in emerging markets, we are investing in regions characterized by low per capita incomes, primitive securities markets, and/or economies that are not fully industrialized. In other words, there is a promising future, but it inconveniently hasn't shown up yet.

Whether the foreign market is considered developed or emerging, investors must deal with currency risk. If the bond pays interest and principal in yen or bot, the bondholder must convert that to U.S. dollars; if the dollar is strong, they receive fewer dollars. Luckily, not all foreign bonds pay interest and principal in foreign currencies. The exam might bring up the difference between "U.S. Pay Bonds" and "Foreign Pay Bonds." If a bond pays in U.S. dollars, currency risk is eliminated, but if it pays in another currency (foreign pay bond), then an American investor, obviously, does have currency exchange risk.

Types of "U.S. Pay Bonds" include "Eurodollar bonds," which are issued and traded outside the U.S. but are denominated in U.S. dollars. Another type is called the "Yankee bond," which allows foreign issuers to borrow money in the U.S. marketplace. Eurodollar bonds are not registered with the SEC and cannot be sold to U.S. investors until a certain number of days after being issued. Yankee bonds, on the other hand, are registered with the SEC.

The governments of emerging markets issue **Brady bonds**. Brady bonds are typically collateralized by U.S. Treasury securities, making these debt securities much safer than they seem on the surface.

CMOs

CMOs or **collateralized mortgage obligations** are inherently complex products. Generally, a financial institution takes either a pool of mortgages or a pool of mortgage-backed securities issued by GNMA, FNMA, or FHLMC and creates a CMO. The CMO offers various classes of bonds called **tranches**. The tranches are bonds that offer different rates of interest, repayment schedules, and levels of priority for principal repayment. Investors can choose the yield, maturity structure, and risk level that best suits them. Let's look at a simple example of a "plain vanilla" CMO product. The investors in the CMO are divided up into three tranches: A, B, and C. Each tranche differs in the order that it receives principal payments, but it receives monthly interest payments until it is completely paid off. Class A investors are paid out the principal first with prepayments and repayments until they are paid off. Then class B investors are paid off, followed by class C investors. In a situation like this, class A investors bear most of the prepayment risk, while class C investors bear the least.

As with other mortgage-backed securities, investors never know if they'll get their money back sooner [rates fall] or later [rates rise]. The risk of receiving principal sooner than expected is called prepayment risk, which is associated with falling interest rates. The risk of receiving principal later than expected is called extension risk, and is associated with rising interest rates. As the SEC explains, "CMOs are often highly sensitive to changes in interest rates and any resulting change in the rate at which homeowners sell their properties, refinance, or otherwise pre-pay their loans. Investors in these securities may not only be subjected to this prepayment risk, but also exposed to significant market and liquidity risks."

Two specific types of CMOs are called **PACs** and **TACs**. A "PAC" is a **planned amortization class**, while a "TAC" is a **targeted amortization class**. Since there is a "plan" with the PAC, the exam might say that it protects the investor more against prepayment and extension risk. A TAC does offer some protection against prepayment risk but not extension risk. In either case, there is a "support class" created to protect against prepayments—if the principal is repaid more quickly than expected, it goes into a support class. For the PAC, if interest rates rise and principal is being repaid more slowly, money will be transferred from the support class to protect that PAC owner against extension risk. This would not happen for the owner of a TAC.

The exam might bring up the methods of estimating prepayment rates on CMOs. One method is called the "average life" method in which CMOs are compared to other types of fixed-income securities, with an average maturity calculated for each tranche. The "PSA model" estimates the speed of prepayments against a benchmark. If the "PSA" is 100, that means that prepayment rates will remain stable. If the PSA is greater than 100, prepayments are expected to speed up. If the PSA is less than 100, prepayments are expected to slow down.

Beyond the PAC and TAC, the exam might mention the Z-tranche, which is basically a zero-coupon bond inside the CMO that returns principal (and, therefore, accrued interest) only after all the other tranches have been paid off/retired. And, there are "principal only" and "interest only" securities which are pretty much what they sound like. The principal and the interest are separated so that principal-only investors are concerned with how quickly they receive the principal—the *faster* the better. Interest-only investors enjoy a higher yield when prepayments slow down and a lower yield when prepayments speed up. That is because interest payments are based on the remaining principal amount on the loans—as that principal declines, so does the amount of interest paid by homeowners and received by the interest-only investors in the CMO. The faster that principal declines, the lower the yield to the investor; the longer it takes homeowners to pay off the principal, the *higher* the yield to the investor.

CMOs are not extremely liquid and are often too complex to be suitable for many investors. Registered representatives should get the customer's signature on a suitability statement when selling these products. A term that is used interchangeably with CMO is **REMIC**, which stands for a Real Estate Mortgage Investment Conduit. As defined at www.investingbonds.com, both CMOs and REMICs "are multiclass securities which allow cash flows to be directed so that different classes of securities with different maturities and coupons can be created. They may be collateralized by raw mortgage loans as well as already-securitized pools of loans."

Asset-Backed Securities

Asset-backed securities (ABS), are bonds or notes backed by financial assets. Typically, these assets consist of receivables other than mortgage loans, such as credit card receivables, auto loans, manufactured-housing contracts, and home-equity loans. Asset-backed securities differ from most other bonds because their credit quality comes from sources other than the originator of the underlying assets. Financial institutions that originate loans turn them into marketable securities through a process known as securitization. These institutions sell pools of loans to a special-purpose vehicle (SPV), whose purpose is to buy the assets to securitize them. The SPV then sells them to a trust. The trust repackages the loans as interest-bearing securities and issues them. The securities, which are sold to investors by the investment banks that underwrite them, are "credit-enhanced" with one or more forms of extra protection—whether internal, external or both.

Most asset-backed securities are rated AAA/Aaa. Because they are secured by collateral and come with credit enhancements, investors can receive a safe investment that yields more than Treasury securities. In fact, the yields are more in line with corporate bonds and mortgage-backed securities with similar terms to maturity and credit quality.

The most interesting asset-backed securities that I know of were the "Bowie Bonds" sold by now-deceased glam rocker David Bowie. For an upfront payment, the bondholders received around 7% interest, backed by the royalties earned annually by the artist--around $1 million at the time of issuance. Interestingly, soon after issuance, the royalties dropped due to illegal downloading of music; however, the holders of the bonds received all their interest and their principal at maturity.

CDOs

Another product divided into tranches is the CDO or **Collateralized Debt Obligation.** A CDO is a structured asset-backed security paying cash flows to investors in a predetermined sequence, based on how much cash flow is collected from the package of assets owned. While a CMO focuses on mortgages, a CDO is a security that repackages individual fixed-income assets into a product that can be divided up and sold in pieces on the secondary market. The assets being packaged (mortgages, corporate bonds, corporate loans, automobile loans or credit card debt) serve as collateral for investors, thus the name "collateralized debt obligation."

The senior tranches in a CDO are safer than the junior tranches because they have first claim on the collateral in case of a default and because they have a higher claim on any interest payments. Therefore, the senior tranches receive higher credit ratings and pay lower yields to investors than the junior tranches. The most junior tranche is called the "equity tranche," which receives only residual cash flows after the more senior tranches have been paid by the prescribed formula.

Municipal Securities

Across the street from our office used to sit an old brick industrial building that was supposed to be turned into a major condominium and townhouse development back before the bottom fell out of the real estate market. Unfortunately, the developers borrowed $15 million but pre-sold only one condominium, sending the property into foreclosure.

So, the park district, whose land sits next to the foreclosed property, wanted to tear down the outdated structure for their operations. The park district needed $6 million to acquire and develop the property and, therefore, raised that amount by issuing **municipal bonds**. In a recent election, a majority of Forest Parkers voted to allow the park district to raise property taxes slightly to create the funds needed to pay off a $6 million bond issue to be used to better the community.

The bonds have already been issued, and the building has been torn down with part of the $6 million worth of **general obligation** bonds sold to finance the project. The bonds pay investors tax-exempt interest at the federal level. Illinois residents also escape state income tax on the bond interest.

For me, all it took to see the connection between this municipal securities section and the so-called "real world" was to walk 15 steps to the front window and see that the building pictured below has now been torn down and carted away brick-by-brick, all because a municipal taxing authority borrowed money by issuing bonds.

There are two main types of municipal bonds: **general obligation** and **revenue**. General obligation bonds are safer than revenue bonds because they are backed by the municipality's ability to collect and raise taxes from various sources. However, some states are considered safer issuers than others, and the same goes for counties, school districts, port authorities, etc. Revenue bonds are only as safe as the revenue source tied to the bonds.

To make the bonds more marketable and keep interest payments as low as possible, many municipal bonds come with a credit enhancement from an insurance company who insures against default. Remember that if interest rates rise, bond prices drop. That is not what is covered here. The insurance policies cover interest and principal payments, not market or interest rate risk. Examples of municipal bond insurance (or assurance) companies include AMBAC and MBIA.

Because some municipal bonds are insured and some are not, bond ratings agencies including Moody's and S&P typically indicate whether a rating is "pure" or "insured." A "pure" rating is based on the credit quality of the issuer only, while an "insured" rating implies the credit quality is based on the insurance policy backing the bonds against default.

General Obligation Bonds

The phrase **general obligation** means that the municipality is legally obligated to pay the debt service on the bonds issued. GOs are backed by the full faith and credit of the municipality. Where does a municipality get the money they'll need to pay off the bonds? If necessary, they'll dip into all the sources of general revenue available to a city or state or park district, like sales taxes, income taxes, parking fees, property taxes, fishing licenses, marriage licenses, whatever. And, if they have to, they'll even raise taxes to pay the debt service on a general obligation bond.

General obligation bonds are backed by the full taxing power of the issuer, and that's why GOs require **voter approval**. As I said, Forest Parkers first had to approve a $6 million bond issue before the park district could do the borrowing and back up the loan with their increased property taxes.

States get most of their revenue from sales and income taxes, while local governments rely on property taxes. Since local governments (cities, park districts, school districts) get much of their revenue from property taxes, a GO bond is associated with property taxes, called **ad valorem**. That phrase means that the property tax rises or falls "as to value" of the property.

A municipality might assess property at 50% of its market value. So, a home with a market value of $400,000 would have an **assessed value** of only half that, or $200,000. A homeowner takes the assessed value of his home and multiplies it by a rate known as the **millage rate** to find his tax bill. If the millage rate is "9 mills," that means we multiply the assessed value of $200,000 by .009 to get a tax bill of $1,800. That $1,800 goes to support many different overlapping municipalities, for example: water district, park district, school district, library & museum district, village government, and county government.

Some municipalities limit the number of mills that can be levied against property. If so, they might end up issuing **limited tax bonds**, which means there are limits on the taxes that can be used to pay the debt service. Maybe property tax rates can only go so high to pay the debt service on a GO, or maybe only certain taxes can be used but not others. School districts are often limited as to how high property taxes can go to support their bonds, while other governmental units have no such limits. So if you see limited tax bonds, associate the term with GOs.

Whenever the issuer's full faith and credit backs the bonds, we refer to the bonds as "general obligations." There is a peculiar type of municipal bond that is backed by that full faith and credit but also by the revenues generated at the facility being built with the bond proceeds. These bonds are called **double-barreled bonds.**

For example, a hospital is something all residents of a municipality benefit from, which is why the county or state might put its full faith and credit behind the bond issue. However, hospitals also generate revenues, which can be used to pay debt service. In this case, the issuer has two sources of revenue to pay debt service, which is why we call it a double-barreled bond. Anything backed by the issuer's full faith and credit as well as revenues is called a double-barreled bond. Since the full faith and credit of the issuer backs the issue, we consider this a GO.

Revenue Bonds
Rather than putting the full faith and credit of the issuer behind it, a revenue bond identifies a specific source of revenue, and only that revenue can be used to pay the interest and principal on the bonds. Have you ever driven on a toll way or paid a toll to cross a bridge? What did you drop in the basket? A **user fee**. That money you put in the toll basket helped to pay the debt service on the revenue bond issued to build the toll way or toll bridge. If money problems arise, the issuer won't raise property taxes. They'll raise the user fees.

You don't like the higher tolls? Use the freeway. But, homeowners aren't affected one way or another since their property taxes cannot be used to pay off revenue bonds. Facilities that could generate enough revenue to pay off the bonds include airports, convention centers, golf courses, and sports stadiums. The Queens Ballpark or Citi Field, where the New York Mets play their home games, was built with the proceeds of a revenue bond. As I see from Bloomberg, "The Mets sold $613 million municipal bonds in 2006 backed by payments in lieu of property taxes, lease revenue and installment payments to finance the construction of Citi Field. The team also issued $82.3 million of insured debt in 2009, the year the 42,000-seat ballpark opened in Queens."

Unfortunately, the revenues a few years ago were significantly lower than what the consultants predicted. As you can imagine, that caused the bonds' rating to drop. At the time of this writing, however, with attendance up 20% last season, the revenues have improved just enough to boost the credit rating to one notch above junk. As you can see, revenue bonds are only as strong as the revenues being generated by the facility. When the revenues are tied to the success and popularity of a baseball team, it is not surprising that the credit rating could be upgraded and downgraded many times before maturity.

Since we don't have property tax on the table, the municipal government doesn't need any type of voter approval to issue a revenue bond. So we don't associate "voter approval" with a revenue bond. That belongs under the "GO" heading.

There are other ways that a municipality could identify specific sources of revenue for a bond issue. For example, if the residents of a county wanted their roads paved, the county could add a special tax on gasoline throughout the county and let motorists pay for the new roads each time they fill up their tanks. This **special tax** is used to pay the debt service on the revenue bonds, which are issued to raise the money required to pave the roads. That's an example of a **special tax bond,** a type of revenue bond. Any tax that is not a property or sales tax is considered a special tax, including special taxes on business licenses, excise taxes, and taxes on gasoline, tobacco, hotel/motel, bottled water, and alcohol. The exam might even refer to these as "sin taxes."

There are also **special assessment bonds**. Say that a wealthy subdivision in your community experiences problems with their sidewalks. The concrete is chipped, threatening the property values of the homes in the exclusive subdivision. The residents want the municipality to fix the sidewalks. The municipality says, okay, if you pay a special assessment on your property, since you're the only ones who'll benefit from this improvement. That special assessment will be the revenue used to pay the debt service on a special assessment bond, which is issued to raise the money to fix the sidewalks.

See how it works? They identify a future source of revenue, like tolls, ticket sales, or special taxes on gasoline. Then, since they need all that money right now, they issue debt securities against this new source of revenue they're creating. They take the proceeds from selling the debt securities and get the project built. Then those revenues they identified come in, and they use them to pay the interest and, eventually, the principal due to investors who bought the bonds.

Cities like Chicago and New York have public housing projects, which are under HUD, a unit of the federal government. Municipalities issue **PHA (Public Housing Authority)** or **NHA (New Housing Authority) bonds** to raise money for housing projects. The debt service is backed by the rental payments, which are in turn backed by contributions from Uncle Sam. PHAs and NHAs are considered the safest revenue bond because of this guaranteed contribution from the federal government. Sometimes they are referred to as "Section 8" bonds because something needs at least three names in this business. Note that they are not double-barreled bonds, because it's not the issuer's full faith and credit backing the things.

Industrial Development Revenue bonds are used to build or acquire facilities that a municipal government will then lease to a corporation. These **IDRs** carry the same credit rating as the corporation occupying the facility. The issuing municipality does not back the debt service in any way. Again, the debt service will be paid only from lease payments made by a corporation, so it's the corporation that backs the debt service. As you know, corporations have been known to go belly-up occasionally. If they're the ones backing up the debt service, you can imagine what happens when they themselves no longer have any assets behind them.

And if it happens, the issuer won't be there to bail out the bondholders. While revenue bonds are only serviced by specific sources of revenue, a **moral obligation bond** provides for the possibility of the issuer going to the legislature and convincing them to honor the "moral obligation" to pay off the debt service. This is a moral obligation, not a legal one, and it would take legislative action to get the money authorized.

Callable Bonds

A bond has a maturity date that represents the date when the issuer will pay the last interest check and the principal. At that point, it's all over—the debt has been paid in full, just like when you pay off your car, student loan, house, etc. This can be referred to as "maturity" or **redemption**. As we saw earlier, many bonds are repurchased by the issuer at a set price if interest rates drop. So, a bond might not make it to the maturity date because it might be called early. Either way, the debt would have been retired by the issuer.

Municipal bonds are frequently callable by the issuer. Refunding a current issue of bonds allows municipalities to finance their debt at lower rates going forward. Or, there could be a covenant in the bond indenture for the current issue that is burdensome, motivating the issuer to start over. An optional redemption gives the issuer the option to refinance/refund their debt as of a certain date at a stated price, or over a series of prices and associated call dates. Some bonds are issued with mandatory call provisions requiring the issuer to call a certain amount of the issue based on a schedule or on having enough money to do so in the sinking fund.

When issuers redeem callable bonds before the stated maturity date, they may call the entire issue or just part of it. For obvious reasons, the call provisions can, therefore, be referred to as in-whole redemptions or partial redemptions. The refunding is sometimes done through a direct exchange by bondholders of the existing bonds for the new issue. Usually, though, the issuer sells new bonds to pay off the existing issue.

When **refunding** an issue of bonds, issuers either perform a **current refunding** or an **advance refunding**. If the issuer uses the proceeds of the "refunding bonds" to promptly call (within 90 days) the "prior issue," we refer to this as a current refunding. On the other hand, when the issuer places some of the proceeds of the refunding issue in an escrow account to cover the debt service on the outstanding issue, we refer to this as an advance refunding. Because an escrow account is, literally, money in the bank, the prior issue whose debt service is now covered by the escrow deposit is not required to be included on the issuer's debt statement. Do we just take the issuer's word that the U.S. Treasury securities held in the escrow account are sufficient to cover the debt service on the prior issue?

No. Rather, an independent CPA issues a "verification report" verifying that the yield on the escrow deposit will be sufficient to pay off the outstanding or refunded issue of bonds. Because of the certainty surrounding a refunded issue of bonds, these bonds are typically rated AAA and are among the safest of all municipal bonds on the market. Because of their inherent safety, refunded bonds are also liquid.

The typical advance refunding is performed by placing proceeds from the sale of the refunding issue in an escrow account holding Treasury securities, with only the escrow account used to cover the debt service on the prior issue of bonds. In a "crossover refunding" the promised revenue stream backing the prior issue continues to be used to meet debt service until the bonds are called with proceeds from the escrow account.

Paying off a debt is sometimes referred to as a debt being "defeased." Therefore, the exam could refer to the refunding bonds as being issued to "defease" the prior issue of outstanding bonds.

Refunding bonds are not tax-exempt. Municipalities, in other words, can borrow money on the cheap for infrastructure, but if they could issue tax-exempt refunding issues, some governmental entities would do nothing but issue refunding bonds in a never-ending attempt to maximize their budgets.

Methods Used to Determine the Value of Fixed-Income Securities

Investors purchase U.S. Treasury securities to eliminate credit risk. Unfortunately, because interest rates fluctuate, U.S. Treasury securities are just as exposed to interest rate and reinvestment risk as are corporate and municipal bonds.

Bonds are issued with a fixed interest rate. If the bond is an 8% bond, it will always be an 8% bond, and it will always pay 8% of the par value every year no matter who owns it at the time or how much she paid for it. For purposes of illustration, the par value is $1,000. 8% of $1,000 is $80 per year to the bondholder in interest income, split into two payments of $40 semiannually. With $1,000,000 in 8% bonds the investor would receive $80,000 a year in interest income.

Bonds are fixed-income securities. If it's a 5% bond, it pays $50 a year per $1,000 of par value. If it's a 13% bond, it pays $130 a year, which is an extremely high rate of interest.

So, if a bond pays a nominal yield of 8%, it will always pay 8% of par or $80 per $1,000 per year. Therefore, whenever interest rates change, they change the bond's market price—what it could sell for if the investor chose to sell it. When rates on new bonds go up, the existing bond's price drops. When rates go down, the existing bond's price rises.

Yields and Rates are the same thing. Bond Prices move in the other direction, which is called an **inverse relationship**, like this:

| INTEREST RATES | ↑ | BOND PRICES | ↓ | YIELDS | ↑ |
| INTEREST RATES | ↓ | BOND PRICES | ↑ | YIELDS | ↓ |

A test question could relate the Federal Reserve's actions to the bond market. For example, if the Fed is tightening credit, bond yields rise and bond market prices drop. If the Fed is stimulating the economy, yields drop and bond market prices rise. As with everything else in the economy, monetary policy creates winners and losers. People taking out mortgages win when the Fed pushes down interest rates, but fixed-income investors in retirement will have trouble making ends meet, for example.

Discount Bonds

Par value is what is returned to the bondholder at maturity and what the coupon rate is multiplied against. But, bonds are not bank deposits. Rather, they are securities that trade on a secondary market. Among other factors, a bond's market price fluctuates in response to changes in interest rates. If a bondholder has a bond that pays a nominal yield of 8%, what is the bond worth when interest rates in general climb to 10%? Not as much. If you had something that paid you 8%, when you knew you could be receiving more like 10%, how would you feel about the bond?

Not too good. But, when interest rates fall to 6%, suddenly that 8% bond looks good, right?

Current Yield

When we take a bond's market price into consideration, we're looking at **current yield**. Current yield (CY) takes the annual interest paid by the bond and divides it by what an investor would have to pay for the bond.

Current Yield = Annual Interest divided by Market Price

So, let's say that after an investor buys an 8% bond, interest rates rise, knocking down the market price to just $800. What is the current yield if that happens?

$80/$800 gives us a current yield of 10%.

Did the bond's market price just drop, or did its current yield rise? Those are two ways of saying the same thing. So, yes, it did.

"Yield" answers the question, "How much do I get every year compared to what I pay to get it?" So, if interest rates go up to 10%, suddenly this bond that pays only 8% isn't worth as much. The only motivation for buying this 8% bond is if an investor could get it at a **discount**. And, if she can get the $80 that the bond pays in annual interest for just $800, isn't she really getting 10% on her money? That's why we say her current yield is equal to 10%, higher than the nominal yield that never, ever changes.

Rates and yields up, price down. Rates are what new bonds pay. Yields are what existing bonds offer, after we factor in their market price.

A **discount bond** is a bond trading below par value. When you see a current yield higher than the coupon rate of the bond, you're looking at a discount bond. An 8% bond with a 10% current yield, for example, must be a discount bond. An 8% bond with a 6% current yield would *not* be a discount bond. As we'll see in a minute, it would, in fact, be a "premium bond."

Yield to Maturity

Yield to maturity (YTM) is the return an investor gets if she holds the bond all the way to maturity. It is sometimes called basis and represents the only yield that really matters to an investor. It factors in all the coupon payments and the difference between the market price paid for the bond and the par value received if the investor is holding at maturity. At maturity, an investor receives the par value, which is $1,000. If the investor puts down only $800 to buy the bond and receives $1,000 when the bond matures, doesn't she receive more at maturity than she paid?

She does, and that's why her yield to maturity is even higher than her current yield. She gets all the coupon payments, plus an extra $200 when the bond matures. If you see a yield-to-maturity that is higher than the coupon rate or the current yield, you're looking at a discount bond. For example, a 4% nominal yield trading at a 5.50 basis or yield to maturity is a discount bond.

Yield to Call

Like homeowners, sometimes issuers get tired of making interest payments that seem too high. That's why many bonds are issued as callable, meaning that after a certain period the issuer can buy the bonds back from investors at a stated price. A bond that matures in 10 or 20 years is often callable in just 5 years. If a bond is trading at a discount, rates have risen. Therefore, it is extremely unlikely that such a bond would be called. But, if it were called, the investor would make his gain faster than if he had to wait until maturity. That's why **yield to call** (YTC) is the highest of all for a discount bond.

Premium Bonds

So, that is what happens when interest rates rise. What happens when interest rates fall? Bond prices rise. If you owned this 8% bond and saw that interest rates had just fallen to 6%, how would you feel about your bond?

Pretty good. After all, it pays 2% more than new debt is paying. Do you want to sell it? Not really. But you might sell it if investors were willing to pay you a **premium**.

Current Yield

So, bond investors would have just pushed the price of the bond up as interest rates went down. Maybe your bond is worth $1,200 on the secondary market now. Dividing our $80 of annual interest by the $1,200 another investor would have to pay for the bond gives us a current yield of just 6.7%. That's lower than the coupon rate.

So, wait, did the price of this bond just rise, or did its current yield drop?

Yes, and yes.

When you see a coupon of 8% and current yield of 6.7% (or anything lower than that 8% printed on the bond), you're looking at a **premium bond**. A discount bond trades below the par value, while a premium bond trades above the par value.

The nominal yield of the bond doesn't change. Therefore, the only way to push a yield lower than the nominal yield stated on the bond is to have an investor pay more than par for the bond. Similarly, the only way to push the yield higher than the nominal yield stated on the bond is to have an investor pay less than par for the bond.

Yield to Maturity

If you sell your bond, you obviously don't care about the next investor's yield. But, when this investor's bond matures, how much does she get back from the issuer? Only $1,000. So, she put down $1,200 and will only get back $1,000 at maturity. Her Yield to Maturity (YTM) goes down below both the nominal and current yields.

Yield to Call

Remember when we decided that a person who buys a bond at a discount wants the bond to return the principal amount sooner rather than later? Well, if you pay more than the par value for a bond, you're going to lose money when the bond returns your principal, no matter when that happens. So, if you're going to lose money, you want to lose it slowly to increase your yield. That's why a person who purchases a bond at a premium will have a lower yield to call than yield to maturity. He's going to lose money in either case, so he'd prefer to lose it over 10 or 20 years (maturity) rather than just 5 years (call).

So, yield to call is the lowest yield for a bond purchased at a premium. And, if there are successive call dates, the earliest call date will produce the worst or lowest yield to the investor.

Disclosing Yield on Customer Confirmations

When a customer purchases a bond, the broker-dealer sends her a **trade confirmation** no later than the settlement date. And, on this trade confirmation the firm must disclose either the YTM or the YTC. Should they disclose the best possible yield or the worst possible yield?

Always prepare the customer for the worst or most conservative yield, so there are no bad surprises, right? Okay, for a discount bond, which yield is lower, YTM or YTC? YTM. That's what the firm would disclose to a customer who purchases a bond at a discount.

For a premium bond, which yield is lower?

Yield to Call. So, that's what the firm would disclose to a customer who purchases a bond at a premium. The exam might call this calculation "yield to worst," by the way or even "YTW." The worst yield the investor can receive is the one based on the earliest call date.

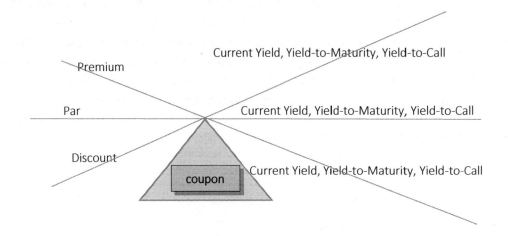

Duration

Duration measures the interest rate sensitivity of a bond, predicting how a small change in interest rates would affect the bond's market price. The longer/higher a bond's duration, the more sensitive it is to a change in interest rates. So, when interest rates go up, they push the prices of bonds with long/high durations down much more than those with lower durations.

Another way of talking about duration is to say that at some point all the coupon payments received by an investor will represent what the investor paid for the bond. If you pay par for a 30-year bond paying $40 a year, it would take you 25 years to receive $1,000 in the form of interest/coupon payments, right? So, the duration could be expressed as 25 years. A bond with a high duration is more susceptible to a rise in interest rates.

To express that mathematically, we could see how much the bond's price would decline if rates rose 1%. Just multiply the 20 (duration) by 1% to get an expected 20% decline in the bond's price should rates rise by just 1 point. That's volatile. If the bond paid a higher coupon, you'd get your original investment back sooner, knocking down the duration and making the bond's price less sensitive to interest rates.

Remember, the lower the coupon and the longer the maturity, the higher/greater the duration. And the greater the duration, the more susceptible the bond's price is to interest rate spikes.

For interest-paying bonds, the duration is always less than the years to maturity. But, for zero-coupon bonds, the duration *is* the maturity.

A common definition used for duration is "the weighted average of a bond's cash flows." As the formula shows, each cash flow is weighted by the amount of time the investor has to wait for the payment. For example, the first interest payment is multiplied by .5 and the next by 1.0 to represent that it takes ½ year to receive the first cash flow and one full year to receive the second. The principal payment is multiplied by the number of years it takes to receive it, and if it's a zero-coupon bond, all the cash flow is multiplied by the number of years to maturity.

Credit Ratings

There's nothing worse than lending some corporation a few million dollars and then finding out they are not going to pay you back. This is known as a "default," and it's the worst thing that can happen to a bond investment.

How likely is it that a bond will go into default? It isn't going to happen on a United States Treasury security. It might happen on some municipal securities. But when you get into the category of corporate bonds, you see that it happens more than you'd like. Luckily, Moody's, S&P, and Fitch all assign bond ratings designed to help investors gauge the likelihood of default. Remember that this is *all* that the bond rating agencies are talking about—the risk of default. They aren't making any recommendations with these ratings. The highest quality issuers have AAA/Aaa (S&P/Moody's) ratings. The **investment grade** issues go from AAA/Aaa down to BBB/Baa. And below that, we're looking at high-yield or junk bonds.

Standard & Poor's (& Fitch)	Moody's
AAA	Aaa
AA	Aa
A	A
BBB	Baa

BELOW THIS IS JUNK, NON-INVESTMENT GRADE, HIGH-YIELD, SPECULATIVE

BB	Ba
B	B
C	Caa

There is also a "D" rating indicating the bond is already in default. Only the savviest and most aggressive bond traders would likely trade a bond rated "D" or anything below "B" for that matter.

So, credit quality is the highest on the AAA/Aaa-rated bonds. As credit quality drops, you take on more default risk, so you expect to be compensated for the added risk through a higher yield. High yield and low quality go hand in hand, just as low yield and high quality do. How does a bond become "high yield" or "junk"? That means that a new issue of low-rated bonds would have to offer high coupon rates to get an investor interested in lending the money, and existing bonds would trade at lower and lower prices as people get more and more nervous about a possible default. As the price drops, the yield…increases.

It's not just interest rates that can push down a bond's market price. When S&P, Moody's, or Fitch downgrade an issuer's credit rating, the market price of those bonds will drop, increasing their yield.

How often do bonds default? To put it in perspective, here is the recent history of default rates on high-yield corporate bonds: the default rate in 2009 reached 13.7% before declining to 1.3% in 2010, as the economy began to recover, due in part to government initiatives and a general improvement in credit trends. Note this amount is significantly lower than the 16.4% default rate that occurred during the last financial downturn in 2002 (www.naic.org).

I noticed that the rate of default for investment-grade bonds was not even mentioned—it's that low. I also discovered that the main investment of insurance companies last year was corporate bonds. Insurance companies, in other words, can issue bonds to finance their operations, and they can also invest in bonds issued by other corporations. Investment-grade corporate bonds appear to be an ideal place for insurance companies to invest the net premiums paid on products like fixed annuities. According to the website cited above, 92% of those corporate bonds held by insurance companies are investment-grade. For good reason, insurance companies are not interested in stretching for every last bit of yield when they may be forced to sell their investments after a hurricane or other disaster strikes. Junk bonds are harder to sell in a hurry for a good price, so the higher the credit quality on the bond the higher its liquidity.

Types and Characteristics of Equity Securities

Some investors seek income. They loan a corporation $100,000 and receive $4,000 a year in interest payments for 10 years. That 4% **yield** is nice, but at the end of the term, the investor will only receive $100,000, which will have lost purchasing power over 10 years due to inflation.

Other investors give up that steady income to reach for the risky and uncertain growth offered by the stock market. Rather than lending money to a corporation, these **equity** investors buy **common stock** in the company. This way, if the company becomes more valuable, so do the shares of common stock the investor holds.

Common Stock

While bondholders represent an expense on the income statement, common stock represents a claim on what is left after the company meets all their expenses. Common stock is all about the profits generated by the company. Unlike with bonds and preferred stock, common stock does not give the investor a stated rate of return. If shareholders receive 64 cents per-share of common stock as a dividend this year, they might or might not receive that much next year. In fact, the company might stop paying dividends if it hits a rough patch, and some companies—like Berkshire Hathaway—never pay dividends.

As a prospectus for a stock mutual fund would make clear, both the income produced by common stock and the market value of the stock itself are unpredictable. Therefore, common stock investors should only invest the money they could afford to lose.

Frank & Emma's Fruit Pies

To illustrate how common stock works let's consider the story of Frank & Emma's Fruit Pies. For fifty years this mom-and-pop baked goods maker in Maywood, Illinois made a modest profit on as much as $10 million in annual revenue. But, by the time the company hit that milestone Founder

Frank Kaminski and his wife Emma were in their 60s and getting tired of the daily grind. When some "private equity" investors from Chicago offered to buy them out, it did not take long for both to accept the deal.

Since then the private equity investors have installed their own business managers, who have helped to find new markets for the fruit pies while slashing costs. Now that sales are pushing $20 million annually, the private equity group is ready to do an initial public offering. To cash in on their investment, they will be offering through an underwriting syndicate up to 40% of the company for approximately $25 million. Frank & Emma's will use most of the proceeds to expand. The underwriters will keep 7% of the proceeds as their underwriting fee. And, investors buying the common stock will profit if the sales and earnings at Frank & Emma's Fruit Pies continue to rise. While investors could lose their money if the business fails, there is also no limit to what they could earn on their investment. Seventeen years ago I myself purchased shares of a little e-commerce company called Priceline for $21 a share. As I type this sentence, that stock now trades for just over $1,500 per-share.

Yeah, that's upside!

Common stockholders are owners of the corporation and vote at all annual and special meetings. The owner of common stock has the right to vote for any major issue that could affect his status as a proportional owner of the corporation. Things like stock splits, board of director elections, and changes of business objectives all require shareholder approval.

Owners of common stock typically have the right to vote on:

- Members of the board of directors
- Proposals affecting material aspects of the business
- Ratifying the auditors
- Mergers & Acquisitions
- Stock Splits
- Liquidation of the company

One thing shareholders never vote on is whether a dividend is paid and, if so, how much. Letting shareholders propose and vote on dividends is like letting your kids propose and approve their own allowance. Like parents, the board of directors decides if a dividend is to be declared from profits and, if so, how much the payment per-share will be. Dividends benefit the shareholder now, while the profits that are reinvested back into the business should eventually help to increase the value of the stock, benefiting the shareholder in the long run.

At the annual meeting votes are cast per-share, not per-shareholder. Therefore, a mutual fund holding 45 million shares of Wells Fargo has a lot more votes than a retail investor holding 300 shares at the Wells Fargo annual meeting. In fact, the retail investor's vote is almost meaningless compared to what the mutual fund might decide to do with their 45 million votes. Either way, all shares get to be voted. The Board of Directors tells shareholders in the proxy statement how the Board recommends that shareholders vote, making it easy for a shareholder to just indicate that he wants to vote that way. Some shareholders might even go so far as to read the proposals and make up their own minds.

Either way, if a shareholder owns 100 shares of common stock, he has 100 votes to cast in corporate elections. Let's say there are three seats up for election on the Board of Directors. There are two ways that the votes could be cast. Under **statutory voting**, he can only cast the number of shares he owns for any one seat. So, he could cast up to 100 votes for any one seat, representing a total of 300 votes for three seats. Under statutory voting abstaining on any of the seats up for election provides no benefit to the shareholder.

Under cumulative voting, however, he could take those 300 votes and split them up any way he wanted among the three candidates. He could even abstain on the other seats up for election and then cast all 300 votes for one candidate. That's why **cumulative voting** gives a benefit to the small/minority shareholders. In other words, if we can get a candidate on the slate who will look out for us small shareholders, we can all cast all of our votes for her.

Beyond voting, common stockholders have the right to inspect the corporation's financials through quarterly (10-Q) and annual (10-K) reports. Public companies have to file these reports with the SEC, but even a shareholder in a private company has this same right. Shareholders may also see the list of stockholders and the minutes of shareholder meetings.

Common stockholders have a **pre-emptive right** to maintain their percentage of ownership. This means if Frank & Emma's wants to raise money in the future by selling more common stock, existing shareholders must get a chance to buy their percentage of the upcoming issue. If not, their ownership would be diluted. Investors buying the stock on the secondary market up to a certain date would also receive rights to buy more shares from the additional offering. Rights offerings avoid **dilution of equity** by giving owners a chance to maintain their percentage of ownership, if they chose to.

Should a corporation claim bankruptcy protection and have to be liquidated, common stockholders get in line for their piece of the proceeds. Unfortunately, they are last in line. They are behind all the creditors, including bondholders, and also behind preferred stockholders.

But, at least they are in line, and if there are any residuals left, they get to make their claim on those assets, known as a **residual claim** on assets or "residual rights." Common stock is the most "junior" security, since all other securities represent senior claims on the company's assets.

Shareholders have **limited liability**, which means they are shielded from the debts of the company and lawsuits filed against it. Unlike a sole proprietor whose business is going sour, shareholders of a corporation would not be sued by creditors.

Common stock owners have a claim on earnings and dividends. As owners, they have a share of the profits or net income that we looked at on the income statement. Some of the profits are reinvested into the business, which tends to make the share price rise. Some of the profits might be paid to shareholders as dividends.

Dividends

Not all shareholders are looking for dividends. An investment in Berkshire Hathaway today, for example, would be made without the issuer stating any plans to pay dividends, ever. The only type of investor interested in this stock, then, is a growth investor.

But, there are growth & income investors and also equity-income investors for whom dividends are important. Dividends are a share of profits paid out to shareholders if and when the Board of Directors for the corporation votes to declare them. The day that the Board declares the dividend is known as the **declaration date**. The board decides when they'll pay the dividend, too, and we call that the **payable date**. The board also sets the deadline for being an owner of stock if you want this dividend, and we call that the **record date** because an investor has to be the owner of record as of that date to receive the dividend.

Now, since an investor has to be the owner of record as of the record date to receive the dividend, there will come a day when it's too late for investors to buy the stock and also get the dividend.

Why? Because stock transactions don't "settle" until the third business day following the **trade date**, which means you might put in your purchase order to buy 1,000 shares of Frank & Emma's on a Monday, but you aren't the official owner until that transaction settles on Thursday. Your broker-dealer has to send payment to their clearing agency, and the seller has to deliver the 1,000 shares before the transaction has settled. This process takes three business days for common stock and is known as **regular way settlement**, or "T + 3," where the "T" stands for <u>T</u>rade Date. Assuming there are no holidays, a trade taking place on Monday settles on Thursday, while a trade on Tuesday settles on Friday.

So, if an investor has to be the owner of record on the record date, and it takes three business days for the buyer to become the new owner, wouldn't she have to buy the stock at least three business days prior to the record date? Yes.

On the other hand, if she buys it just two business days before the record date, her trade won't settle in time. We call that day the **ex-date** or **ex-dividend date**. Starting on that day investors who buy the stock will not receive the dividend. On the ex-date, it's too late. Why? Because the trades won't settle in time, and the purchasers won't be the owners of record with the transfer agent as of the record date. If the trade takes place on or after the ex-date, the seller is entitled to the dividend. If the trade takes place before the ex-date, the buyer is entitled to the dividend.

The regulators set the ex-date, as a function of "regular way" or "T + 3" settlement. The ex-date is two business days before the record date.

Investors don't qualify for the dividend starting with the ex-dividend date; therefore, the amount of the dividend is taken out of the stock price when trading opens on the ex-date. If the dividend to be paid is 70 cents, and the stock is set to open at $20, it would open at $19.30 on the ex-date.

Let's take a look at how the process looks from a press release:

```
Equity Office declares first quarter common dividend

Mar 16, 2005-- Equity Office Properties Trust (EOP), a publicly
held office building owner and manager, has announced that its
Board of Trustees has declared a first quarter cash dividend in
the amount of $.50 per common share. The dividend will be paid on
Friday 15 April 2005, to common shareholders of record at the
close of business on Thursday 31 March 2005.
```

March 16th is the Declaration Date. The Payable Date is April 15th. The Record Date is Thursday, March 31st. The article doesn't mention the Ex-Date (because that's established by the exchange regulators), but we can figure that it must be Tuesday, March 29th. If you bought the stock on Tuesday, your trade wouldn't settle until Friday, April 1st, which means the seller's name would be on the list of shareholders at the close of business on Thursday, March 31st.

A dividend can be paid in the following ways:

- Cash
- Stock
- Shares of a subsidiary
- Product

A corporation files its articles of incorporation with the state where they are organized. These articles disclose the name and purpose of the business, its address, and how many shares of stock the corporation is authorized to issue, known as the **authorized** shares. If a public company is authorized to issue 1,000,000 shares of common stock, they will probably not sell all of them at once. When they first sell shares to the public during their IPO, the number they issue is known as **issued** shares. Let's say this corporation could issue 1 million, but they only issue 600,000 shares. If so, there would be 600,000 issued shares after the public offering. And, at that point, the **shares outstanding** would also be the 600,000 that were issued in the IPO.

For various reasons, the corporation might decide to buy back some of those shares that are out in the secondary market. These shares, which were issued but repurchased, are called **treasury stock**. Treasury stock has no voting rights and pays no dividends. The benefit to the shareholders who remain is that the value of their existing stock tends to rise when the company is reducing the number of shares on the secondary market. If this corporation had issued 600,000 shares and then purchased 200,000 for the treasury, they would have 400,000 shares outstanding.

600,000	Issued
-200,000	Treasury
400,000	Outstanding

When we look at a company's **earnings per-share,** or **EPS**, on the income statement, we only count the **outstanding shares**. That's why the company can boost its earnings per-share (EPS) by repurchasing their outstanding stock on the secondary market. Even if the company's total earnings stayed the same, the earnings per-share would rise if the company were reducing the number of outstanding shares. For example, if the company earned $1 million in net income, that is an earnings per-share of $1.67 when there were 600,000 shares outstanding. However, after the company buys back 200,000 shares for the treasury, that same $1 million profit would be $2.50 of earnings per-share. Right? Just like at a birthday party, with fewer guest showing up there is more cake for the rest of us.

Treasury stock doesn't vote, so the officers and directors of the company, who own large positions in the stock, end up with more influence during corporate elections after a large share buyback. Also note that the cash used buying back shares is reflected on the company's statement of cash flows under financing activities.

The articles of incorporation list the common stock as either having a minimal par value or having no par value at all. As we saw when examining the balance sheet, companies record the higher IPO price above par value as "paid-in surplus." While the specific par value of preferred stock and of bonds is important, the par value for common stock is not considered important to the investor.

Common stock is easy to transfer to another party. It can be sold, donated, gifted, or inherited. The issuer of the stock hires a financial institution to keep track of the transfers of ownership, and they're called the **transfer agent**. The transfer agent keeps the ownership records of the company's stock. They deal with issuing and validating stock and bond certificates, recording name changes when investors sell their certificates, and re-issuing lost, stolen, or destroyed certificates. If there's a problem with the ownership records of the security, contact the transfer agent. They can validate or re-issue certificates, for a fee, as the case may be.

The corporation hires another outside firm—typically a bank—and we refer to this bank as the **registrar**. The registrar audits/oversees the transfer agent, just to make sure there aren't more shares outstanding than the company is authorized to issue, and that all the ownership records are accurate.

With just one share of some stocks worth thousands—even hundreds of thousands—of dollars, I don't want the responsibility of protecting the certificates from damage or misplacement. I mean, I could get them re-issued by the transfer agent if I lost them, but that's a pain in the neck, and there are fees involved. So, rather than having the securities in my account shipped to me, I could have the broker-dealer holding my account transfer the securities into my name and then hold them in the firm's vault (transfer and hold). The firm would likely charge a fee to do that. So, what I do is what most  customers do these days. I have the broker-dealer hold the securities in street name. This means my broker-dealer is the named or "nominal owner" of the securities and I the customer am the "beneficial owner" of the securities.

As we're about to see, shareholders can now also use the direct registration method.

But, whatever the customer chooses, the fact is that most customers these days have never seen a stock or bond certificate because their broker-dealer holds them in street name and may have them on deposit at centralized "depositories" such as the **Depository Trust Company (DTC)**. From there, the securities are transferred through electronic entries only, which explains why many registered representatives have also never seen a stock or bond certificate. From the Depository Trust Company's website at www.dtc.org we see how things currently work:

> With the implementation of direct registration, investors have three securities ownership options:
>
> *Physical Certificates*: Certificates are registered and issued in the investor's name. The investor will receive all mailings directly from the issuer or its transfer agent, including dividend or interest payments, annual reports, and proxies.
>
> *Street Name Registration*: Securities are registered in the street name of the investor's broker-dealer. While no physical certificate will be issued to the investor, the broker-dealer will issue, at least quarterly, account statements of the investor's holdings. The broker-dealer will pay dividends or interest to the investor, as well as provide the investor with mailing material from the issuer or transfer agent.
>
> *Direct Registration*: This option allows the investor to be registered directly on the books of the transfer agent without the need of a physical certificate to evidence the security ownership. While the investor will not receive a physical certificate, he or

she will receive a statement of ownership and periodic (at least yearly) account statements. Dividend or interest payments, proxy materials, annual reports, etc., will be mailed from the issuer or its transfer agent.

If an investor holds paper stock certificates, he would have to sign them when selling or otherwise transferring them. He would sign the back of the certificate exactly as it is named on the front, and if the certificate is registered to two owners, both must sign the back. The process of signing a stock certificate to effect a transfer is called an endorsement. The owner of the certificate would also fill in his broker-dealer as the "attorney to transfer" so that only they can complete the transaction on his behalf.

Again, though, effecting these transfers is faster and easier for customers who use the street-name or direct registration method above, both of which would lead to electronic records as opposed to paper certificates.

Broker-dealers are not the only financial institutions holding securities and cash for investors. Banks also do this, especially for large institutional investors. We will explore options a bit later. For now, know that when an institutional investor has to prove ownership of a certain number of shares, the bank with custody of the account may issue what is known as an escrow receipt evidencing that a certain number of shares are in the bank's possession and control for the customer's account. A party who has sold call options, for example, must deliver the underlying shares if exercised. Therefore, the broker-dealer may require an escrow receipt (or escrow agreement), which is the document from the custodian bank showing that the shares are available for delivery if the account is assigned and forced to deliver the shares to the buyer of the call option.

We will look at calls and puts in some detail up ahead.

Stock Splits and Stock Dividends

Cash dividends are taxable because they involve a payment to the shareholder. Stock dividends, on the other hand, are not payments. Rather, investors end up with more shares in the company, with the shares worth less per-share. So, the big idea behind **stock splits** and **stock dividends** is that even when the investor ends up with more shares, the total value of his investment is unchanged. If he had 100 shares at $10 before, that was worth $1,000. No matter how many shares he has after the split or the stock dividend, the total value is just $1,000. So, when a corporation does a 2:1 stock split, the investor would have twice as many shares. What would the price per-share be?

Half as much. The investor has $1,000 worth of stock both before and after the split. He used to have 100 shares worth $10 each. Now he has 200 shares worth $5 each. $1,000 worth, either way. The test might want you to work with an uneven split, like a 5:2 ratio. This is where the company gives investors five shares for every two that they own. So, let's say the question tells you the investor holds 100 shares of ABC, which she purchased for $50 each. What happens after a 5:2 stock split? All we have to do is multiply the number of shares by 5 and then divide that by 2. So, 100 times 5 equals 500, and 500 divided by 2 shows us the investor will have 250 shares after the split. Her cost basis is a total of $5,000 (100 shares @50), so take that $5,000 total and divide it by the new number of shares, which is 250. Her new cost basis is 250 ABC @20.

It's important to keep an investor's cost basis so that capital gains can be reported accurately in the future. But that is all that really happened in both examples—the investor's cost basis changes along with the lowered per-share price of the stock.

A stock dividend works the same way in terms of more shares/lower price. If an investor receives a 20% stock dividend, that's 20% more shares of stock, but the total value of the investment is the same. It's just divided among more shares. So an investor with 200 shares of XYZ common stock @40 would have $8,000 of XYZ stock. If XYZ declared a 20% stock dividend, she would then have 240 shares. Her $8,000 would then be divided among 240 shares, with a per-share price of $33.33. Companies in a growth phase are more likely to pay stock dividends than more established companies, who are more likely to pay cash dividends compared to small, growing companies.

Either way, nothing really changes for the investor after a stock dividend or a stock split. The investor has more shares at a lower price, which means her cost basis in the stock changes. 100 shares @50 might become 125 shares @40. Just keep track of your cost basis so that when you sell someday you can tell the IRS how much of a capital gain or loss you realized on the stock. But whether you have 100 shares @50 or 125 shares @40, you've paid $5,000 for a certain percentage of ownership. And, we'll deal with concerns such as "cost basis" and "capital gains" later in the book.

A forward stock split means investors end up with more shares. A 2:1, 3:2, or 5:4 split is a forward split that pushes the share price down.

Sometimes companies have the opposite problem. Their share price is so low that institutional investors won't touch it. These entities usually won't buy a stock trading below $5, so if our company's stock is trading for $1, we might need to increase that price. One way to do it is to perform a reverse stock split.

If JoAnne owns 100 shares of ABCD @$1, we might find ABCD doing a reverse split of 1:10. That means for every 10 shares she owns now, she'll end up with only one really big share. She'll have 10 shares when it's all over. If the shares were trading for $1 before the split and everybody now has shares that are 10 times bigger, the share price becomes $10 a share. JoAnne now owns 10 ABCD @$10.

Shareholders vote on stock splits, whether forward (5:4, 2:1, 3:2) or reverse (1:7, 1:10, etc.). Shareholders do not vote on dividends, whether cash or stock.

Sometimes a public company performs a type of "divestiture" known as a spin-off in which shareholders receive shares of a subsidiary or division of the company. For example, when Abbott Labs decided to make their business unit Hospira a separate company, they performed a spin-off in which ABT shareholders like me received a certain number of shares of HSP, which has since traded and operated as a completely separate company. If a company wants to exit a business line to concentrate on other areas, a spin-off may be completed. Usually, there are no tax consequences when the shareholders merely receive the shares of the spin-off. Rather, they have a cost basis, and are taxed on a capital gain if and when they sold the shares someday for a profit.

I have received shares of stock through spin-offs. Like many investors, I have also received shares of stock through mergers & acquisitions. If a larger company offers to give, for example, .75 shares of their stock for each share investors currently hold of the target company, shareholders will end up with a completely different holding. When they receive cash in an acquisition, shareholders record a capital gain or loss. But, if they're receiving shares of one company when turning in shares of their existing holding, investors record their cost basis in the shares for now. Someday, when they transfer those shares through a sale or gift, the tax consequences will be realized.

Interestingly, after holding those Hospira shares a few years common stockholders like me then voted to be acquired for cash by Pfizer. All in all, it turned out to be a decent investment, if I do say so myself.

ADRs

American Depositary Receipts (ADRs) are receipts issued to American investors against shares of foreign stock held on deposit by a U.S. bank outside the U.S. ADRs allow American investors to easily diversify their portfolio with foreign investments that trade, clear and settle in the U.S. financial system and U.S. currency while giving foreign companies easier access to U.S. capital markets. The ADR investor buys a negotiable certificate called an American Depositary Receipt that represents a certain number of American Depositary Shares of a foreign corporation's stock. The shares are held in a U.S. bank in the foreign country, which issues a receipt to the investor in America. The custodian bank provides services including registration, compliance, dividend payments, communications, and recordkeeping. These fees are typically deducted from the gross dividends received by the ADR holders.

Or, if the issuer does not pay dividends, broker-dealers and banks cover the custody fees charged by depositary banks and then pass the charges on to their customers. ADRs file a registration statement called an F-6 which discloses information on the structure of the ADR including fees that may be charged to the ADR holders. Some ADRs grant voting rights to the investor; some do not.

If dividends are declared, they are declared in the foreign currency and then have to be converted into U.S. dollars. That is why ADR owners are subject to currency risk. Also, if the stock is worth a certain number of yen on the Japanese markets, that won't work out to as many U.S. dollars when our dollar is strong, although it would work out to more American dollars if our dollar is weak.

As the SEC explains in an investor bulletin, "Today, there are more than 2,000 ADRs available representing shares of companies located in more than 70 countries."

There are currently three levels of ADR trading, ranging from the more speculative issues trading over-the-counter to those, like Toyota, trading on the NYSE or NASDAQ. Level 1 ADRs trade over-the-counter. Level 2 ADRs trade on exchanges. Level 3 ADRs are part of a public offering that then trades on the NYSE or NASDAQ. In other words, some ADRs merely establish a trading presence in the U.S. while Level 3 ADRs also raise capital for the foreign issuer.

Subscription or Stock Rights

As we mentioned, one of the rights common stockholders enjoy is the right to maintain their proportionate ownership in the corporation. We call this a pre-emptive right because the existing shareholders get to say yes or no to their proportion of the new shares before the new shareholders get to buy them. Otherwise, if you owned 5% of the company, you'd end up owning less than 5% of it after they sold the new shares to everyone but you, called dilution of equity.

For each share owned, an investor receives what's known as a right. It works like a coupon, allowing the current shareholders to purchase the stock below the market price. If a stock is trading at $20, maybe the existing shareholders can take two rights plus $18 to buy a new share. Those rights act as coupons that give the current shareholders two dollars off the market price. So, the investors can use the rights, sell them, or let them expire.

Restricted Stock

The term **restricted stock** means the investor's ability to sell or transfer the stock is restricted because of a required holding period. Stock purchased in a private placement is restricted stock, restricted in terms of the investor's ability to sell it to another party. Officers and key employees may also receive restricted shares subject to a holding period as opposed to stock options that can be exercised right away. When purchasing restricted securities, investors typically receive a certificate with a legend stamped on it indicating that the securities may not be resold in the marketplace unless they are registered with the SEC or are exempt from the registration requirements.

The SEC does not want people acting like underwriters and funneling unregistered stock to the securities markets in a way that bypasses the Securities Act of 1933's concerns for full disclosure. **Rule 144** provides a safe harbor exemption for those who want to sell restricted stock without violating securities law. And, remember, though a registered representative will perhaps never own restricted stock, if he executes a sale for a customer who does, he could get in trouble if he doesn't know and follow the rules.

The first requirement for selling restricted stock is that the issuer must have been a reporting company under the Securities Exchange Act of 1934 for at least 90 days immediately before the sale. And, the issuer cannot have missed filing any of the 10Q or 10K reports they were required to file during the preceding 12 months. Without this requirement, worthless securities in companies no one knows anything about could be dumped onto the securities markets at great harm to investors.

So, first, the issuer must be someone about whom investors can receive material information. Even if the issuer is an insurance company or a company not subject to reporting (non-reporting company) under the Securities Exchange Act of 1934, the SEC requires that certain basic information on these issuers be available including information on the nature of its business, the identity of the officers and directors, and financial statements.

Otherwise, no sale.

Restricted stock is subject to a holding period. If the issuer is a reporting company subject to reporting requirements at least 90 days, purchasers must hold the securities a minimum of six months before reselling them. If the issuer is not a reporting company, the minimum holding period is one year.

Once the holding period is met a non-affiliate can sell his shares if he wants to. However, as the SEC explains, "Even if you have met the conditions of Rule 144, you can't sell your restricted securities to the public until you've gotten the legend removed from the certificate. Only a transfer agent can remove a restrictive legend. But the transfer agent won't remove the legend unless you've obtained the consent of the issuer—usually in the form of an opinion letter from the issuer's counsel—that the restrictive legend can be removed. Unless this happens, the transfer agent doesn't have the authority to remove the legend and permit execution of the trade in the marketplace. To begin the legend removal process, an investor should contact the company that issued the securities, or the transfer agent for the securities, to ask about the procedures for removing a legend. Removing the legend can be a complicated process requiring you to work with an attorney who specializes in securities law."

For **affiliates** of the company Rule 144 has further requirements, whether selling restricted or **control stock**. Restricted stock is unusual because of the way it was offered to investors. For control stock, on the other hand, it's the owner himself who triggers the requirements, not the securities. Control stock is held by people who can control the issuer or could harm the market price of the stock by dumping a large amount all at once. So, whether selling restricted or control stock, affiliates must file a **Form 144** with the SEC no later than at the time of the sale. The filing is good for 90 days. Also, if the transaction is not larger than 5,000 shares and $50,000, the sale can be made without filing a Form 144. Basically, a transaction that small does not make the regulators nervous, as it won't impact the price of the stock due to the low volume of shares traded.

Typically, affiliates sell large amounts of securities, but they must comply with the volume limits under Rule 144. For exchange-traded securities affiliates are allowed to sell the issuer's stock provided they sell no more than the greater of 1% of the outstanding shares or the average weekly trading volume over the four most recent weeks. If the company has 1 billion shares outstanding, the affiliate could sell whichever is greater over the next 90 days—10 million shares or the average weekly trading volume going back four weeks. For stocks that either don't trade or trade on the OTC Bulletin Board or Pink Quote, only the 1% figure is used.

That's the amount that can be sold. As for the method of sale the rule states, "If you are an affiliate, the sales must be handled in all respects as routine trading transactions, and brokers may not receive more than a normal commission. Neither the seller nor the broker can solicit orders to buy the securities."

Also, affiliates can never sell the company's stock short. And, although control stock is not subject to a holding period, an affiliate can't take a profit on their company's stock held less than 6 months. This is called a short-swing profit, which must be turned back over to the company with the gain being taxed by the IRS.

FINRA is concerned that agents and their firms sometimes help customers sell unregistered restricted securities, which violates federal securities law. In other words, if the customer does not conform to all the stipulations we just went over, but wants to just take his unregistered restricted shares and sell them, firms need to be sure they don't help him skirt securities law in this manner. FINRA alerts its member broker-dealers that some customers are companies trying to sell their shares illegally. If the customer deposits certificates representing a large block of thinly traded or low-priced securities, that's a red flag. If the share certificates refer to a company or customer name that has been changed or that does not match the name on the account, that's another red flag. If a customer with limited or no other assets under management at the firm receives an electronic transfer or journal transactions of large amounts of low-priced, unlisted securities, that's another red flag.

Broker-dealer firms need to do a reasonable inquiry to make sure that they are not helping people get around securities law. The SEC has said that "a dealer who offers to sell, or is asked to sell a substantial amount of securities must take whatever steps are necessary to be sure that this is a transaction not involving an issuer, person in a control relationship with an issuer, or an underwriter." For this purpose, it is not enough for him to accept "self-serving statements of his sellers and their counsel (attorneys) without reasonably exploring the possibility of contrary facts."

Rule 144's prohibitions on reselling restricted stock only apply to a sale to unsophisticated investors. **Rule 144a** allows the restricted securities that we just discussed to be re-sold to institutional investors including banks, insurance companies, broker-dealers, investment advisers, pension plans, and investment companies without meeting the usual registration requirements under the Securities Act of 1933. So, if an investor acquires restricted securities through a private placement, he/they can re-sell them to **qualified institutional buyers** such as those mentioned without destroying the exemption the issuer is claiming from the registration requirements. As usual, the regulators want to prevent the shares from being distributed in a general public offering without registration requirements being met. When the buyers are sophisticated institutions, the regulators can ease up.

This SEC rule also states that the seller needs to be reasonably certain that the buyers are qualified institutional buyers, which generally means that the institution invests on a discretionary basis at least $100 million, or is a registered broker-dealer, an investment company, a bank, or a federal covered investment adviser. To check that the buyers are qualified institutional buyers, the SEC says that the seller can rely on the buyer's most recent publicly available financial statements, or a certification from the CFO or other officer of the institution.

Preferred Stock

A common stock investor might receive dividends, but the dividend is not stated or promised going forward. In fact, the company may never pay a dividend on their common stock at all. Common stock investors are generally interested in growth or capital appreciation more than income. That means they want to buy the stock low and watch it increase in market price over time. On the other hand, income investors who want to buy stock would more likely buy **preferred stock** than common.

Preferred stock receives preferential treatment over common stock if the company has to be forcibly liquidated to pay creditors through a bankruptcy proceeding, and it always receives dividends before owners of common stock can be paid. Some investors refer to a preferred stock position in a private company as "first money out," because if there are distributions of profits, preferred stock gets theirs first.

And, unlike common stock, the preferred stock dividend is a stated percentage of par value. The par value for a preferred stock is assumed to be $100, though I think the test question would tell you what the par value is if it's required to answer the question. Whatever it is, the stated dividend is a percentage of the par value of the preferred stock. Six percent preferred stock would pay 6% of $100 per-share, or $6 per-share per year. Three percent preferred stock would pay a dividend of 3% of the par value each year.

We hope.

See, dividends have to be declared by the Board of Directors. Preferred stockholders aren't creditors. They're just proportional owners who like to receive dividends. If the board doesn't declare a dividend, do you know how much an owner of a 6% **straight preferred stock** would receive?

Nothing. However, if the investor owned **cumulative preferred stock**, the company would have to make up the missed dividend in future years before it could pay dividends to common stockholders. If the company missed the six dollars this year and wanted to pay a dividend to common shareholders next year, cumulative preferred stockholders would have to get their $12 first. Most preferred stock has this cumulative feature, and partial or skipped dividends are a rarity though always a possibility.

So far this 6% dividend works more like a maximum than a minimum. If an investor wants the chance to earn more than the stated 6%, he'd have to buy **participating preferred stock**, which would allow him to share in dividends above that rate, if the company has the money and decides to distribute it. Generally, if the issuer increases the dividend paid to common stockholders, they will also raise the dividend paid to participating preferred stockholders. A test question might say that participating preferred stock pays a dividend that is "fixed as to the minimum but not as to the maximum," while straight or cumulative preferred stock pays dividends that are "fixed both as to the minimum and the maximum."

Adjustable-rate preferred stock pays a rate of return that is tied to another rate, typically a U.S. Treasury security—T-Bill or T-Note, for example. If T-Bill rates rise, so does the rate paid on the adjustable-rate preferred stock, and vice versa. Because the rate adjusts, the price remains stable.

As with bonds, corporate issuers often get tired of paying preferred stockholders a high dividend rate when new investors would now accept a lower rate of interest. While most types of preferred stock go on for "perpetuity," **callable preferred stock** may be retired early at the issuer's discretion. If an investor had purchased 5.5% preferred stock a few years ago and then interest rates went down so that new investors would accept, say, 3%, the issuer would likely issue a new batch of 3% preferred stock to new investors and use some of the proceeds to retire the existing issue.

When investors bought the callable preferred stock, the call price and the first possible date were named. So, if rates go down at that point, the issuer might buy back the callable preferred stock, forcing shareholders to reinvest at lower rates. Because it can be retired early, callable preferred stock tends to pay the highest dividend rate of all types of preferred stock.

Preferred stock issued by a corporation does not derive its value from the market price of the common stock. Unlike preferred stock, common stock enjoys a share of the company's increased profits. Preferred stock, on the other hand, is just a fixed-income security constantly being re-compared to current interest rates. So, a 5% preferred stock—whether straight, cumulative, or callable—would not be expected to rise even if the market price of the issuer's common stock were to double or triple.

As always, there is an exception. But, there is only one type of preferred stock with a market price tied to the market price of the issuer's common stock. This type is known as **convertible preferred stock.** Unlike all other types of preferred stock, convertible preferred stock is not just a fixed-income security. This type lets an investor exchange one share of preferred stock for a certain number of the issuer's common shares. It works much like a warrant here, where the investor starts out on the fixed-income side, but also captures any upside on the common stock.

Say the convertible preferred stock is convertible into 10 shares of common stock. If so, the convertible preferred stock is usually worth whatever 10 shares of common stock are worth at a minimum. If the common stock rises, so does the convertible preferred stock it's tied to. If the common stock rises to $14, we would expect the convertible preferred stock to trade for at least $140. If it trades at exactly $140, it trades at **parity** to the common stock, the exam might say.

On another note, if a security has a fixed payment, the market compares that fixed payment to current interest rates. Current interest rates represent what investors could receive if they bought low-risk debt securities. If low-risk debt securities are paying 4%, and your preferred stock pays you a fixed 6%, how do you feel about your preferred stock? Pretty good, right, since it's paying a higher rate than current interest rates. If someone wanted to buy it, they'd have to pay a higher price. But, if interest rates shoot up to 10%, suddenly your 6% preferred stock doesn't look so great. In that case the market price would go down. Not the par value—par value is etched in stone. It's the market price that fluctuates.

Market prices adjust for interest rates: rates up/prices down, rates down/prices up. Well, as we mentioned, if the rate adjusts along with the T-Bill rate, the price doesn't need to move. But for other types of preferred stock, the price moves in the opposite direction of interest rates, just like bond prices. That's because the value is really determined by a comparison of the fixed rate of return to current interest rates.

But, if we add another variable, now the security's price isn't so sensitive to interest rates. Convertible preferred stock has a value tied to interest rates, like other preferred stock, but its value is also tied to the value of the common stock into which it can be exchanged or converted. If rates are up, preferred stock prices drop. But if you're holding a convertible preferred stock while the common stock is skyrocketing, the price of the preferred stock would skyrocket right along with it. Remember, it's worth a fixed number of common shares. If the value of the common stock goes up, so does the value of the convertible preferred stock it's tied to. So, convertible preferred stock is less sensitive to interest rates than other types of preferred stock.

For all other types of preferred stock the price has nothing to do with the price of the company's common stock, or even their increased profits. The exception there is convertible preferred stock, but all other types of preferred stock are fixed-income securities with market prices tied to credit quality and interest rates. Remember that unlike a bond, preferred stock generally does not have a **maturity date**, and unlike common stock, usually does not give the owner voting rights. Two specific cases where preferred stock *does* get to vote are: 1) the corporation defaults on the dividend payment a certain number of times and 2) the corporation wants to issue preferred stock of equal or senior status.

To review how common and preferred stock relate to each other, let's note the similarities and differences between the two.

SIMILARITIES	DIFFERENCES

SIMILARITIES	DIFFERENCES
dividends must be declared by the board of directors to be paid	preferred stock is a fixed-income security paying a stated rate of return
both are equity securities	preferred stock has a higher claim on dividends and on assets in a bankruptcy
	common stock has voting rights and pre-emptive rights

Yield vs. Total Return

There are only two ways to make money in equities. One, the stock price goes up, and, two, the stock pays a dividend. If I'm looking only for the share price to go up, I'm a "growth investor." If I'm solely interested in the dividends, I'm an "income investor." If I want both growth and income, guess what kind of investor I am?

Would you believe "growth and income"?

But, that's the only way to make money on stocks. You either sell the stock for more than you bought it someday, or the stock paid you dividends along the way. There is no third way to make money on common (or preferred) stock.

If you buy a stock at $10, and a year later it's worth $20, that's a capital appreciation of 100%. If a stock pays $2 in annual dividends and costs $200 on the open market, that's a yield of 1%. Yield shows how much an investor has to pay to receive how much in dividends.

Annual Dividend / Market Price = Dividend Yield

For **total return**, add the dividend received plus the capital growth/appreciation over the period. In other words, if you buy a stock for $10 and the market price rises to $12, you have $2 of capital appreciation. If the stock pays $1 in dividends, you're now "up $3" on a $10 investment.

That's a total return of "3 out of 10" or 30%. Or, sometimes the market price drops, dragging down total return. If an investor pays $10 for a stock and receives $1 in dividends, his total return is negative if the stock drops to $8, $7, or lower. If you invest $10, and the stock drops to $7, the $1 in dividends will improve that 30% drop to a negative 20% total return for the year.

Ouch. And that is not at all unusual for an investment in stocks or stock mutual funds.

Registered representatives must be careful when quoting yield or total return to investors. If a customer receives a 5% yield on a bond investment, a registered representative might want to talk only about that and ignore the fact that the market price is down, and the total return negative. The registered representative should give the customer the whole picture to avoid misleading her. Yield, remember, is always a positive number. Total return gives a more accurate picture of how the investment performed over the year.

Descriptive statistics and the related approaches we looked at search for patterns that can be exploited among securities and/or industry groups. That approach does not involve studying companies or following chart patterns, let alone performing detailed cash flow analysis on a securities issuer.

In this section we will look at traditional ways to value equity securities, all of which can be used to make a decision about a particular stock, as opposed to allocating a portfolio to 25% equities, 50% fixed-income, and 25% money market, for example, and then rebalancing along the way.

Fundamental Analysis

Fundamental analysis involves looking quantitatively at the financial statements we looked at as well as studying the company qualitatively in terms of its industry position, the skill of its management team, and the goodwill it has among customers and suppliers. The headlines about the company are important to fundamental analysts, as are the quarterly and year-end earnings figures. Fundamental analysts care about price-to-earnings and price-to-book ratios as well as revenue and net income.

In May 2009 I traveled to Omaha to listen to two successful fundamental analysts and investors named Warren Buffet and Charlie Munger. For over five hours the two men discussed the operations and performance of the companies they invest in while snacking on See's Candies and Dilly Bars. At one point Mr. Buffet said he had recently made a small investment in a company just by spending a half-hour studying their most recent 10K. Companies are often purchased or invested in based largely on the skill of the current owners and managers. Only fundamental analysts care about any of these things.

Top-down fundamental analysis starts by studying economic trends, and then considers which industry groups and then which issuers within those groups will be affected by the good or bad news up ahead. On the other hand, bottom-up fundamental analysis starts at the company level, what some refer to as the "granular level."

Technical Analysis

Either way, fundamental analysts look at the company who issued the common stock. **Technical analysis**, on the other hand, involves studying the behavior of the stock itself as it trades on the secondary market. Technical analysts don't want to hear about how a company's products have been selling or who the new CEO might be. They want to know how the shares of the company's stock have been trading in terms of market price and **volume** levels. Rather than studying companies, technical analysts study stock market data.

Charts and Patterns

Many people feel that in terms of stock prices, history tends to repeat itself. Therefore, many technical traders make decisions on whether to buy or sell by looking at charts of a stock's market price over a certain period of time. These days, **chartists** can review the price patterns over 200 days, 30 days, one day, five minutes, what have you. The idea is that by watching the chart pattern start to develop, the trader using charts can predict where the stock is headed next.

A popular type of chart is the candlestick chart. Each "candlestick" is a little vertical bar that indicates the opening price, the high price, the low price, and the closing price for the stock. At the left of the chart, we see what the "candle period" is, whether weekly, monthly, etc. Below the pricing information the chart also shows volume for the shares traded.

Reading the patterns that develop from such charts is part art and part science—just like fundamental analysis. The key is to find a **trendline,** defined as "local highs and local lows forming a straight line." In other words, a trendline allows us to step back from the trees to see the forest. Rather than obsessing over yesterday's high, low and close, a trendline shows us the bigger picture in terms of whether the price of the stock is generally moving upward, downward, or sideways. A basic premise of trendlines is that stock prices tend to bounce upward from a lower limit called **support** and also bounce downward off a higher limit called **resistance,** like this:

Resistance

Support

This means that whenever the stock goes up, it meets resistance, when all the sellers step in to depress the price, and whenever it falls, it finds support, where the buyers step in to bid the price back up again. A stock's arrival at the resistance threshold is often referred to as the market being **overbought,** and its fall to the support price is called an **oversold** market. A trader following charts might consistently try to buy close to support and sell as soon as it nears resistance. Or, maybe he waits until the stock breaks through resistance before buying it, reasoning that if it hits a **breakout** it will keep running up. Breakouts occurring on high volume—in either direction—are considered especially significant.

If the trendline's support and resistance lines run parallel, this pattern is referred to as a channel. If the parallel lines are going up, you're looking at a "channel up" pattern, and at a "channel down" pattern if the parallel lines are going down. If the lines are horizontal, the pattern is a "channel."

A trader using channel patterns tries to predict where the stock is about to go. If he sees a "channel up" pattern start to form, he's going to start buying the stock and probably ride it until he sees that things are about to turn around.

Parallel support and resistance lines form channel patterns. On the other hand, when the support and resistance lines start to converge, the pattern is called a wedge. A "rising wedge" pattern is considered a bearish signal. The rising wedge starts out wide at the bottom and then narrows as prices rise but the range gets smaller, with the lines squeezing together toward the top. A "falling wedge" pattern starts out wide at the top and then narrows as prices full with the range becoming smaller. A falling wedge is considered a bullish signal, a sign that the downtrend is about to turn the other way.

Insert graphics of channels and wedges.

Speaking of which, a **"head and shoulders"** price pattern on a chart also signals the reversal of a trend. A "head and shoulders" top pattern is characterized by a prior uptrend and then three distinct highs for the stock. A head and shoulders "top" indicates the bull trend is about to end, a **bearish** signal.

This is a head-and-shoulders top formation:

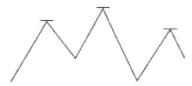

The stock makes a high represented as the left peak or "shoulder." It falls back and then really goes on a tear—the middle peak is called the "head." The stock then falls to the horizontal support line and makes one more big push. Unfortunately, the right shoulder is not as high as either the head or the left shoulder, which means the uptrend is about to end. So, when you see that right shoulder beginning to form, you're supposed to conclude that the stock price is headed for a big drop.

A head-and-shoulders top indicates the reversal of an uptrend and is a bearish indicator. A head-and-shoulders bottom or an **inverted head-and-shoulders** pattern, on the other hand, indicates the reversal of a downtrend and is a **bullish** indicator.

If a stock is trading in a narrow range between support and resistance, it is consolidating. A chart of a stock in **consolidation** appears to be moving sideways, like this:

The exam might talk about consolidation as the place where sophisticated investors (mutual funds, pension funds, etc.) are getting into or out of the stock. Since these institutional traders are presumed to be the experts, when we see them buying, it must mean the stock is going up, and when we see them selling, it must mean the stock is heading down. At this accumulation or distribution point, the price is, apparently, about to make a huge break on the up or down side. Consolidation and a "channel" pattern would be two ways of referring to the same phenomenon.

Other well-known chart patterns include the cup, the saucer, and the inverted saucer pattern. The cup pattern is a curved trendline. It usually starts to form just below resistance. The line curves downward as the closing prices drop, but then the line curves upward as prices rise. As the full curve is just about completed at the resistance line, many technical traders feel there is a high probability of a breakout. A cup pattern is formed over a few weeks. If the curve develops more slowly, chartists refer to the pattern as a "saucer" or a "rounding bottom." Either way, with a rounded bottom to its shape, this chart pattern indicates that the stock or index's level is about to rise. It is, in other words, a bullish indicator.

Well, as with the head-and-shoulders pattern, we could flip the saucer over and called it an "inverted saucer pattern." Here, with the curve flipped over, technical traders should conclude the stock's price is about to drop; the uptrend is about to end. Another name for this pattern is the "rounded top" pattern.

Whether it's an inverted or a regular-ole saucer pattern, the reason for the curve is a gradual shift from bearish-to-bullish or from bullish-to-bearish sentiment.

Advance-Decline Ratio

Technical analysts look to see how many stocks advance versus how many stocks decline. The name for this statistic is the **advance-decline ratio**. If advancers outnumber decliners by 2:1, that means that twice as many stocks finished up in market price as down that day. And if decliners outnumber advancers 2:1, that means that twice as many stocks went down that day as up. Maybe a technical analyst sees that advancers have outpaced decliners for several days and decides to go with the trend. Or, maybe he's a contrarian and figures that if advancers have been outpacing decliners consistently, that trend has to reverse itself soon because of other reasons. Again, notice how he's analyzing the overall movement of <u>stocks</u>, while the fundamental analyst focuses on the fundamentals of the <u>companies</u> underlying those stocks.

Volume

Volume is also of interest to the technical analyst. Volume indicates the total number of shares traded on, say, the NYSE, NASDAQ, or the regional exchanges in Chicago, Philadelphia, Boston, etc. Analysts expect stock prices to move on increasing volume. They would tend to place more significance on the fact that stock prices increased minutely on decreasing volume. Often, that situation is considered a reversal of a bullish trend, which is, of course, a bearish signal. It just means that the bull market is running out of steam—stock prices barely went up, and there was nowhere near as much trading going on.

Market momentum and sentiment

Market momentum is the ability of the market to sustain up or downswings in price. This concept combines both price changes and volume of trading. If a stock's price increases with large trading volumes, the momentum is much higher than if the share price rises on lower volume. The higher the momentum, the more likely the direction of the stock price will be sustained. Momentum is an "anticipatory indicator" used to predict price changes. Many technical analysts use stochastics to measure the momentum of stocks and stock indexes.

Market sentiment is a judgment of the mood or tone of a market. Markets are generally either bullish (going up) or bearish (going down). One way to gauge market sentiment is through the put/call ratio. We will look at puts and calls in depth in our chapter on Options. For now, understand that if an investor is worried about his stock dropping, he needs to "hedge" or protect his stock by buying puts. On the other hand, if he has bet against the market, he needs to hedge by purchasing calls. Therefore, technical analysts track the ratio of puts to calls and call this statistic the "put/call ratio" or "puts-to-calls." The ratio is > 1 if the volume of puts exceeds the volume for calls. When fewer puts are being traded than calls, the ratio is < 1. When the ratio is trading at relatively high levels, this is taken as an indication of bearish sentiment. Why? People must be worried about their stocks dropping, as evidenced by all the puts they've purchased to protect against that. When the ratio is trading at relatively low levels, this is taken as an indication of bullish sentiment.

Options are all about volatility. The more volatile/unpredictable a stock's price, the more one has to pay for options tied to that stock. Therefore, technical analysts are often interested in tracking option volatility. There are two types of volatility here—historical and implied. Historical volatility takes the daily price changes over a year for the underlying stock and finds the "standard deviation" showing if the stock is subject to wild price swings or, rather, trades more predictably. Implied volatility looks at the price of the options tied to a stock (or index of stocks) and determines what the market implies about the volatility of the stock up ahead.

Moving Average

A technical analyst looking at the put/call ratio would also factor in a **moving average** to make more sense of the information. A moving average replaces the oldest piece of data with the newest on a rolling basis. In baseball, if we say that someone is batting .286, that's over the whole season. A moving average would tell us how he's been hitting lately, and show graphically whether he's generally in a slump or on a hot streak. In other words, it would help us spot a trend. So, rather than focusing too hard on yesterday's or this week's closing price for a stock, we can use the moving average to see where the stock has been closing on average over the past so-many days.

The **200-day moving average** is probably the most commonly used. A technical analyst can track the 200-day moving average for a stock or for a index. He can also see what percentage of stocks have been closing above or below their 200-day moving average to get a feel for whether it's a bull or bear market. If a high percentage have been closing above their 200-day average, this is taken as a bullish indicator and vice versa for a low percentage.

Some technical traders assume that the movement of security index futures tied to the S&P 500, the Dow, etc., that happens before the market opens can predict the direction of the stock market. Therefore, if a customer has a large stock position to sell, he may be advised to wait until the market has opened and traded a while before placing a sell order, depending on the direction of the index futures. Most technical traders use the data on index futures to predict only the direction of the market in the short-term.

Theories

The technical analyst knows how smart he is. So much smarter than the small-time investor, in fact, that all he has to do is track what **odd-lot** investors are doing and bet the other way. If odd-lotters are buying, he sells. If odd-lotters are selling, he buys. Why? Because folks who can only afford an odd lot (<100 shares) of stock at a time always buy too high and sell too low. This is known as the **odd-lot theory**.

The **short interest theory** has to do with how many open short sales are out there. Now, as we'll see later, short sellers profit when a stock's price drops, but this theory also recognizes that short sellers eventually have to cover or buy back the shares that they borrowed to sell in the first place. So, if there are a lot of uncovered or "open" short positions out there, they might all suddenly be forced to buy the stock in a hurry. That would create buying pressure that could drive up the stock's price, which is why a large number of open short positions is a *bullish* indicator.

Discounted Cash Flow Analysis

We looked earlier at the net present value (NPV) of the anticipated cash flows from an investment in, say, a printing press or a new call center. This method is called **discounted cash flow analysis**. The basic question that this methodology tries to answer is, "how much cash can we generate from this investment adjusted for the time value of money?" Why adjust for the time value of money? Because, a company could always just park excess cash in a safe place and receive X amount on that cash; if they're going to, instead, aggressively invest that cash back into the business, they need to get a higher internal rate of return than what they could get parking the cash in T-Bills or bank CDs. If the company can't find any internal projects that provide a higher internal rate of return than what they can get in the securities markets, they might just invest their capital in the securities markets.

Of course, whether they're trying to calculate the cash flows generated by investing in, say, preferred stock of a public company or investing it internally into, say, a call center in Des Moines, Iowa, the company using discounted cash flow analysis always faces certain challenges:

- Small changes in inputs/assumptions can lead to large changes in results
- Estimating future cash flows is inherently imprecise

Dividend Discount

The **dividend discount model** is a way of valuing a common stock by using the dividends the investor predicts to receive in the future and then discounting them back to present value. If the value arrived at using this model is higher than the stock's current market price, the stock is thought to be undervalued and, therefore, a candidate for investment. The dividend discount model is considered the simplest method of valuing a common stock. The idea behind the model is that a common stock equals the present value of the expected dividends to be received. Of course, predicting dividends well into the future is no easy task, and if the company does not pay dividends, then this method can't be used.

FUNDAMENTAL ANALYSIS	TECHNICAL ANALYSIS
Financial Statements, e.g., balance sheet, income statement	Market Data
Revenue	Advance/Decline
Net Income	Moving Average
Profits, Profit Margins	Support/Resistance
Price-to-earnings, Price-to-book	52-week High/low
Working Capital	Price and Volume Levels
Qualitative judgments on the business	Market Sentiment, Momentum
Current Ratio, Quick Ratio	Short Interest
Debt-to-Equity or Debt Ratio	Charts, Patterns
Dividend Payout Ratio	Puts/Calls, Stochastics

Types and Characteristics of Pooled Investments

In the securities industry there are many ways to refer to the same thing. What some call a "pooled investment vehicle" others refer to as a "packaged product" or a "mutual fund." Whatever we call these investments, a **pooled investment** vehicle pools the capital of many investors together, with that capital then managed by a professional.

The best-known pooled investment vehicle is the mutual fund. While some investors buy shares of SBUX, many would prefer to own shares of a mutual fund that devotes a percent of the portfolio to SBUX and other large-cap stocks. Similarly, rather than putting $100,000 into one issuer's bonds, many investors prefer the diversification and professional management offered by a bond fund.

Investment Companies

A mutual fund is an investment portfolio managed by an investment adviser. Investors buy shares of the portfolio. The adviser uses the money from investors to invest in stocks and bonds that the shareholders in the fund share ownership in, mutually. When an investor sends in money, the portfolio gets bigger, but it also gets cut into more slices to accommodate the investment into the fund. The only way for the slices to get bigger is for the portfolio to become more valuable. The portfolio value rises when securities in the fund increase in value and when they pay income to the portfolio.

That is the same way it happens in any securities account. When the market values of the securities in the account drop, the account value is down for the day unless income is received that outweighs the drop in price. For example, if an account was worth $100,000 when the markets opened and then just $98,817 when the markets closed, the investor is down for the day. . . unless he happened to receive dividends and interest of more than that drop in market value of $1,183.

Now, couldn't an investor bypass the mutual fund and just buy whatever securities he chooses? Sure, but most people refuse to change the oil in their car. Why would they suddenly become do-it-yourselfers with their retirement accounts? It takes work to decide which stocks or bonds to purchase.

Also, if he only has $400 to invest, he can't take a meaningful position in any company's stock, and even if he tried, he would end up owning just one company's stock. Common stock can drop in a hurry, so we never put all our money in just one or two issues. Diversification protects against this unsystematic risk, and mutual funds own stocks and bonds from many different issuers, usually in different market sectors. Plus, the portfolio is run by professional investors called investment advisers.

Advantages of Mutual Funds

Advantages of investing through mutual funds vs. buying stocks and bonds directly include:

- Investment decisions made by a professional portfolio manager
- Ease of diversification
- Ability to liquidate a portion of the investment without losing diversification
- Simplified tax information
- Simplified record keeping
- Automatic reinvestments of capital gains and income distributions at **net asset value**

- Safekeeping of portfolio securities
- Ease of account inquiry

The first point is probably the main reason people buy mutual funds—they have no knowledge of stocks, bonds, taxation, etc., and they have even less interest in learning. Let a professional portfolio manager—often an entire team of portfolio managers—decide what to buy and when to buy or sell it. As we mentioned, it's tough to have your own diversified portfolio in individual stocks and bonds because a few hundred or thousand dollars will only buy a few shares of stock or a few bonds issued by just a few companies.

On the other hand, a mutual fund would usually hold stock in, say, 100 or more companies, and their bond portfolios are also diversified. Therefore, even with the smallest amount of money accepted by the fund, the investor is immediately diversified. This is called the "undivided interest concept," which means that $50 from a small investor owns a piece of all the securities in the portfolio, just as $1 million from a larger investor does.

Another bullet said, "Ability to liquidate a portion of the investment without losing diversification." That means if an investor owns 100 shares of IBM, MSFT, and GM, what is he going to do when he needs $5,000 to cover an emergency? If he sells a few shares of each, he'll pay three separate commissions. If he sells 100 shares of any one stock, his diversification is reduced. With a mutual fund, investors redeem a certain number of shares and remain just as diversified as they were before the sale. And, they can usually redeem shares without paying fees.

Mutual funds can diversify their holdings by:

- Industries
- Types of investment instruments
- Variety of securities issuers
- Geographic areas

If it's a stock fund, it is typically a growth fund, a value fund, an income fund, or some combination thereof. No matter what the objective, the fund usually buys stocks from issuers across many different industries. In a mutual fund prospectus there is typically a pie chart that shows what percentage of assets is devoted to an industry group. Maybe it's 3% in telecommunications, 10% retail, and 1.7% healthcare, etc. That way if it's a bad year for telecommunications or retail, the fund won't get hurt like a small investor who owns shares of only one telecom company and one retail company.

A bond fund can be diversified among investment interests. That means they buy debentures, secured bonds, convertible bonds, zero coupons, mortgage-backed securities, and even a few money market instruments to be on the safe side.

Even if the fund did not spread their investments across many different industries, they would purchase securities from a variety of issuers. If they like retail, they can buy stock in a variety of companies—Walmart, Target, Sears, Nordstrom, Home Depot, etc. And, since any geographic area could be hit by an economic slump, a tropical storm, or both, most funds spread their holdings among different geographic areas.

The Investment Company Act of 1940 defines a **diversified company** as:

> "Diversified company" means a management company which meets the
> following requirements: At least **75** per centum of the value of its
> total assets is represented by cash and cash items (including
> receivables), Government securities, securities of other
> investment companies, and other securities for the purposes of
> this calculation limited in respect of any one issuer to an amount
> not greater in value than **5** per centum of the value of the total
> assets of such management company and to not more than **10** per
> centum of the outstanding voting securities of such issuer.

So, how does the "Act of 1940" then define a **non-diversified company**?

> "Non-diversified company" means any management company other than
> a diversified company.

If the fund wants to promote itself as being diversified, it has to meet the definition above. For 75% of the fund's assets, no more than 5% of its assets are in any one company, and it doesn't own more than 10% of any company's outstanding shares.

If it doesn't want to abide by the definition, it must refer to itself as a "non-diversified fund." The term "management company" includes both open-end and closed-end funds. From there, each could be either diversified or non-diversified, leaving us with the following four types of management company:

- Diversified Open-End Fund
- Non-Diversified Open-End Fund
- Diversified Closed-End Fund
- Non-Diversified Closed-End Fund

Because closed-end funds use leverage, the most aggressive type above is the non-diversified closed-end fund. An example is found with the stock symbol KYN, of which I own a few shares.

I don't buy a lot of mutual funds, myself. That's because I like to own shares of companies of my own choosing and am willing to do a little homework. Unfortunately, I end up receiving proxy materials and annual reports from maybe 20 different companies, and keeping track of all the dividends I've received from the various sources is annoying. With a mutual fund, I'd get one **1099-DIV** showing all dividends and capital gains distributions, and I'd also get just one semi-annual report and one annual report from the fund.

Types of Funds

There are many types of open- and closed-end funds. Let's start with the most aggressive type, equity.

100

The primary focus of **equity funds** is to invest in common stock. Within equity funds, we find different objectives. **Growth funds** invest in companies likely to grow their profits faster than competitors and/or the overall stock market. These stocks usually trade at high p/e and price-to-book ratios.

Value funds, on the other hand, seek companies trading for less than the portfolio managers determine they're truly worth. These funds buy stock in established companies that are currently out of favor with investors. Since the share price is depressed, value stocks tend to have high dividend yields. Value funds are considered more conservative than growth funds.

What if he can't make up his mind between a growth fund and a value fund? There are funds that blend both styles of investing, and the industry calls these **blend funds**. In other words, no matter how creative the portfolio managers might get, they end up being either a growth fund, a value fund, or a blend of both styles.

If an investor's objective is to receive income from equities, an **equity income fund** may be suitable. These funds buy stocks that provide dependable dividend income. Receiving dividends tends to reduce the volatility of an investment, so equity income funds are lower risk than growth funds. They may also invest in debt securities to keep the yield consistent.

What if the investor can't decide between a mutual fund family's growth funds and its income funds? Chances are, he will choose their "growth and income fund." A growth and income fund buys stocks in companies expected to grow their profits and also in companies that pay dependable, respectable dividends. Since we've added the income component, growth and income funds have lower volatility than growth funds. Many allocate a percentage to fixed-income to assure a regular source of dividend distributions to the shareholders.

So, from highest to lowest volatility, we have growth, then growth & income, and then equity income funds. I have a catalog from a large mutual fund family that puts them in exactly that order, and even uses the color red for growth—as in, "Warning! This stuff can burn!" The bond funds and money market funds, on the other hand, use the colors blue and green.

Bond (Fixed-Income)

Stock is not for everyone. Even if an investor owns equity mutual funds, chances are he will put a percentage of his money into bond funds, as well. A rule-of-thumb is that whatever your age is, that's the percentage an investor should put into fixed-income. So, which type of fixed-income funds should the investor purchase? If the investor is not in a high tax bracket or is investing in an IRA, 401(k), etc., we'll recommend taxable bond funds—corporate and U.S. Government bonds.

The investor's time horizon determines if she should purchase short-term, intermediate-term, or long-term bond funds. Her risk tolerance determines if she needs the absolute safety of U.S. Treasury funds or is willing to reach for higher returns with high-yield funds. If the investor is in a taxable account and wants to earn interest exempt from federal income tax, her agent might put her into a tax-exempt bond fund, which purchases municipal bonds. If the investor is in a high-tax state such as Maryland,

Virginia, or California, she might want the "Tax-Exempt Fund of Maryland," Virginia, or California. Now, the dividends she receives will generally be exempt from both federal and state income taxes.

Whichever tax-exempt fund she chooses, the next question is, "How much of a yield does she want, and how much risk can she withstand?" Her answers determine how long the average duration of the fund, and whether to focus on high-yield or investment-grade bond funds.

Money Market

An investor's need for liquidity determines how much to place in **money market mutual funds**. There are both taxable and tax-exempt money market mutual funds. The **tax-exempt money market funds** buy short-term obligations of states, counties, cities, school districts, etc. They pay low rates of interest, but since it's tax-free, investors in high marginal tax brackets come out ahead.

The benefit of the money market mutual fund is its **stable value.** The money investors put here can be turned right back into the same amount of money without worrying, unlike the money in a bond or stock fund. Investors earn low returns but can often write checks against these accounts, which are treated like a sale of so-many shares times $1 each.

Another use for these funds is as a vehicle in which to sweep a brokerage customer's cash after a deposit, dividend, interest payment, or sale occurs. Money market mutual funds are a holding place for cash that is not ready to be either invested long-term or spent by the customer.

As the SEC explains, "Money market funds pay dividends that reflect prevailing short-term interest rates, are redeemable on demand, and, unlike other investment companies, seek to maintain a stable NAV, typically $1.00. This combination of principal stability, liquidity and payment of short-term yields has made money market funds popular cash management vehicles for both retail and institutional investors."

Some of these funds keep at least 99.5% of their portfolio in Treasury securities and are called government money market funds. The funds that hold municipal securities are tax-exempt money market funds. Those holding corporate debt securities are known as prime money market funds. These three types can be for retail or institutional investors.

Because of the financial crisis of 2008 the SEC wants to prevent future runs on money market funds during extraordinary situations. The problem is that if funds artificially maintain an NAV of $1 when their portfolio may suddenly not be worth that amount, there is a first-mover advantage for investors to hurry up and pull out. To prevent this the SEC now requires institutional prime and tax-exempt money market mutual funds to value their NAV at the actual market value of the securities--called floating the NAV. This way, there is a natural disincentive to run for the exits and end up receiving only, say, 97 cents on the dollar.

Also, except for government money market funds, both retail and institutional prime and tax-exempt funds can now impose both liquidity fees of up to 2% to discourage redemptions and even a temporary halt to redemptions if the situation is dire. If the board of directors for the fund decides the redemption gate is in the best interest of the shareholders, they can impose it for up to 10 business days. No more than one 10-day gate or halt could be imposed, however, in any 90-day period.

As with all funds, investors agree to pay operating expenses in exchange for the benefits provided by the investment product. Money market funds do not charge sales charges, but typically impose a 12b-1 fee of .25% as well as management fees and transfer agent fees, etc.

So, while money market mutual funds are a safe and liquid investment, their liquidity is not as automatic and across the board as it once was, especially outside of government money market funds.

Specialty Funds

Specialty/specialized funds focus their approach to investing. Some funds specialize in an industry, some in geographic regions, some in writing covered calls, etc. Investors can buy the Latin America, the Europe, or the Pacific Rim fund. They would then hope that those regions don't go into a major economic slump or suffer a natural disaster. See, when the fund concentrates heavily in an industry or geographic region, it generally takes on more volatility.

Most equity funds hold stocks in many different industries. On the other hand, there are **sector funds** that do exactly as their name implies—focus on industry sectors. If we buy a "growth fund," so far we have no idea which industries the so-called "growth companies" compete in. On the other hand, if we buy the Communications Fund, the Financial Services Fund, or the Healthcare Fund, we know which industry space the companies operate in. Concentrating in just one sector is the definition of aggressive investing. Investment results are unpredictable year by year. So, make sure the investor has a long anticipated holding period and high risk tolerance before recommending sector funds in a test question.

There are **asset allocation** funds for conservative investors. Rather than maintaining one's own mix of, say, 20% large cap value, 20% small cap growth, 40% high-yield bond, and 20% short-term Treasuries and constantly having to rebalance, investors can invest in an asset allocation fund that matches their goals. A similar type of fund is called a **balanced fund.** Here, the portfolio is always balanced between stocks and bonds and generally diversified among various types of each. There is not a set percentage for us to know here. Rather, the fund's prospectus would explain the parameters established by the board of directors.

A popular way to invest these days is through **age-based portfolios** or **lifecycle funds.** These funds shift the allocation from mostly-equity to mostly-fixed-income gradually as the investor gets closer and closer to his goal of retirement. Another name for these investments is **target funds.** If she plans to retire in or around 2050, for example, the individual would invest in the Target 2050 fund offered by a mutual fund family. The investments would be diversified, and that mix would become more conservative as we get closer and closer to the year 2050.

529 Savings Plans typically offer an age-based portfolio that is much more aggressive for kids 1-6 years old than those who are now 18 and in need of the funds. For example, the allocation for the youngsters might be 90% equity/10% fixed-income, while those 18 years old would be in a portfolio closer to 70% fixed-income/20% money market/10% equity.

Both international and **global funds** appeal to investors who want to participate in markets not confined to the U.S. The difference between the two is that an **international fund** invests in companies located

103

anywhere but the U.S., while a global fund would invest in companies located and doing business anywhere in the world, including the U.S. Remember that when investors move away from the U.S., they take on more political risk as well as currency exchange risk. For developed markets like Japan and Singapore, the political risk would be lower than in emerging markets such as Brazil and China. Both types of markets, however, would present currency exchange risk to U.S. investors.

Precious metals funds allow investors to speculate on the price of gold, silver, and copper, etc. by purchasing a portfolio usually of mining companies who extract these metals. Since a mine's costs are fixed, it only makes sense to open them for production when the price of what you're mining goes high enough to make it worth your while. Therefore, these funds typically hold stock in mining companies as opposed to holding precious metals themselves.

What if the investor does not believe that portfolio managers are likely to beat an index such as the S&P 500 with their active management over the long-term? He can buy an **index fund** that tracks an index as opposed to a fund trying to trade individual stocks. An index is an artificially grouped basket of stocks. Why are there 30 stocks in the Dow Jones Industrial Average, and why are the 30 stocks that are in there in there?

Because the company who put the index together says so. Same for the S&P 500. S&P decided that these 500 stocks make up an index, so there you have it. Investors buy index funds because there are no sales charges and low expenses. Since there's virtually no trading going on, the **management fees** should be—and typically are— low. So, for a no-brainer, low-cost option, investors can put their money into an index and expect to do about as well as that index.

Well-known indexes include the Dow Jones Industrial Average. The "Dow" is price-weighted, which means the stock price itself determines how much weighting the stock receives within the index. If a stock trades at $100, for example, its weighting is much higher than a stock trading at $11 per-share. The S&P 500, like most indexes, is market-cap-weighted. The share price of MSFT doesn't matter, but the fact that all of their outstanding shares are worth, say, $200 billion means MSFT could be weighted 20 times more heavily than other stocks within the index. Because the S&P 500 contains such a large percentage of the major stocks trading on the secondary market, its movement is considered to represent the movement of the overall stock market. We mentioned this when looking at beta, which measures how much one stock moves compared to the overall market, as measured by the S&P 500.

Note that neither the Dow nor the S&P 500 cares whether the stock trades on the NYSE or NASDAQ. It's the size of the company and the market cap that matter here. And, all 30 stocks within the Dow Jones Industrial Average would also be included with the 500 stocks in the S&P 500.

The most famous "Dow" is the **Dow Jones Industrial Average** (DJIA). But, there is also the Dow Jones Transportation Average and the Dow Jones Utility Average. Together, these three make up the Dow Composite, which provides what the publishers of the indices call a "blue-chip microcosm of the U.S. stock market."

As much as I hate to confuse you, the company that owns Standard & Poor's now owns the Dow Jones indices, too, so if you "google" it, you will find that the Dow Jones averages are now part of the "S&P Dow Jones Indices."

Another well-known market-cap-weighted index is the **NASDAQ 100**. This index represents the 100 largest non-financial company stocks, all trading on NASDAQ. Stocks such as Facebook, Google, Microsoft, and Amazon are found here.

A well-known small cap index is the **Russell 2,000**. There are also bond indices for bond investors who want to pay low management fees and engage in passive investing.

Open-end index funds are for long-term investors. If an investor wants to do as well as one of the indices above, this is where he goes. But, because it is an open-end fund, the shares must be redeemed, with everyone who redeems that day receiving the same NAV next calculated by the fund. In a few pages we'll see that Exchange-Traded Funds (ETFs) are another low-cost way to match the performance of a index, only these shares are traded throughout the day just as shares of MSFT or IBM are traded throughout the day. For a small investment of money, the open-end index funds are more cost-effective because the ETFs charge commissions. An investment of $100 into an ETF would be a bad move, even if the commission were just $9. That is like a self-imposed 9% front-end load! But, for investments of several thousands of dollars, the ETF is at least as cost-effective as its open-end cousin.

The other night I helped a friend review the investments in her 401(k) plan, and I was able to quickly point out that her "35 and up" fund was a fund made up of several other funds, all from the same company, with the allocation based on her anticipated retirement date. Since this fund was comprised of other funds, your industry went ahead and named the product a **fund of funds**. Funds of funds are usually associated with higher fees as opposed to picking just one or two of the funds within the group.

Comparisons

Once we decide that the investor wants to invest in a growth fund or a value fund, how do we go about comparing one growth or value fund to another? The mutual fund prospectus is a good place to start. In this disclosure document we find the fund's investment objectives and style. Do they focus on companies valued at $5 billion and above? $1 billion and below? Do they use fundamental analysis, poring over income statements and balance sheets, possibly meeting with senior management of the companies whose stock they hold? Or, do they rely more on technical analysis—charts, patterns, trendlines, and volume, etc.? Is a company's dividend payout important when selecting investments for the portfolio, or is the fund only looking at the growth potential? Is this a small cap, mid-cap, or large cap fund, and how does the fund define "small, mid, and large cap"?

There are also investment policies disclosed in the prospectus. Maybe the fund discloses here that it may invest up to 10% of its assets in securities of issuers outside the United States and Canada and not included in the S&P 500. Or, that they allow themselves to invest 20% of their assets in lower-quality debt securities rated below BB/Ba by S&P and Moody's, or even in debt securities no one has rated. If that sounds too risky for the investor, well, that's why we're disclosing it here in the prospectus.

The prospectus provides information on the party managing the portfolio. We call that party the **investment adviser** or the portfolio manager. Often, it's a team approach, so we can see the names of the individual portfolio counselors and how much experience they have doing this sort of thing. The prospectus I am looking at now has a team of eight stock and bond pickers, and their experience in the industry ranges from 18 to 40 years.

One of the most misunderstood aspects of mutual fund investing has to do with the fees and expenses. You'll often hear people say, "No, I don't pay any expenses on my mutual funds—they're all no-load." As we'll see in more detail later, whether the fund is "no load" or not, all funds charge **operating expenses**. Investors might not get a bill for their share of the expenses, but the fund takes out enough money from the portfolio to cover their expenses, whether this happens to be a "no load" fund or one that charges either front- or back-end sales charges. Sales charges are one thing; expenses are another. Not all funds have sales charges, but all funds have expenses.

In the prospectus the investor can see how much of her check is going toward the sales charge, and how much of the dollars she then invests will be taken as ongoing operating expenses. If two growth funds have similar 10-year track records but one has expenses of 1.5% while the other charges just .90%, this could certainly be the tiebreaker the investor is looking for. Expense ratios, in other words, are important factors when determining an investment into a mutual fund.

A mutual fund's **turnover ratio** tells us how actively the portfolio managers trade the portfolio securities. A turnover rate of 20 or 30% is considered a buy-and-hold strategy, while a turnover ratio greater than 100% indicates a fund that does a lot of buying and selling.

How well does the fund perform? The prospectus shows total return, usually as a bar chart and a table of numbers. Since I'm looking at a growth fund prospectus, the red bars are often long and pointing in both upward and downward directions. Over the past 10 years, the fund has gone up as high as 45% and down as much as 22% in any one year. As we said, investing in growth stocks requires a higher risk tolerance and a longer time horizon. There was a 3-year period here where the fund averaged returns of negative 9%.

That's why this would not be an account from which an investor should expect to make withdrawals. A growth fund is for an investor with a long time horizon, as these results make pretty clear. One could build up the account value over time in a growth fund but then shift some money out of that and into a money market mutual fund before taking withdrawals from the stable-value account.

What is total return? The point of buying a mutual fund share is that it might go up in value. The mutual fund will usually also pay out dividends from all those stocks and bonds they hold in the portfolio. And, at the end of the year if they took more profits than losses while trading their stocks and bonds, they distribute a capital gain to shareholders.

Total return takes all three of those things and compares it to where the fund started. If the fund started out with a "net asset value" or "NAV" of $10 and finished the year at $11 per-share, that's $1 of "capital appreciation." If the fund also paid a dividend of 50 cents per-share and a $1 capital gains distribution, we would add that $1.50 to the capital appreciation of $1 for a total of $2.50. Comparing that $2.50 to where we started—$10—gives us a total return of 25%.

How likely is it that a fund could have a total return of 25%? The prospectus I am looking at shows that the fund had positive total returns of 26%, 31%, and 45% during the first three years in the last 10-year period. So, naturally, it had a similar return the next three years, right? No, after that, it was anybody's guess: positive 7%, then negative 12%, followed by negative 22%. Which means the following year was probably even worse, right? No. The next year the fund had a total return of nearly 33% in a positive direction. Now we see why the prospectus says that "past results are not predictive of future results."

Most mutual funds are not short-term investments, especially not equity funds. Investors need a long time horizon, as the prospectus for this growth fund tells us on the first page. Nobody knows what will happen this year or next. We can show the returns over 1, 5, and 10 years and let investors be the judge. But no one can say which funds will go up this year, let alone which funds will go up the most.

Note that "total return" for a stock or bond is found the same way except that stocks and bonds lack that third component called a "capital gains distribution." For stocks and bonds, there is income (maybe), and then the security's market value either goes up or down. Those two amounts compared to the starting point equal the stock's or bond's total return.

The prospectus shows results after taxes have been figured in. Of course, this is a little tricky, as we see from the caveat in the prospectus on my desk:

```
Your actual after-tax returns depend on your individual tax
situation and likely will differ from the results shown below. In
addition, after-tax returns may not be relevant if you hold your
fund shares through a tax-deferred arrangement, such as a 401(k)
plan, IRA, or 529 Savings Plan.
```

Open-End Funds

Sales Charges vs. Expenses

Mutual funds are investment products, and it costs money to market these products to investors. To cover the costs of advertising and compensating sales people some open-end mutual funds charge **sales charges.** Unlike the ongoing operating expenses we'll look at, a sales charge is a one-time deduction taken out of an investor's investment into the fund.

Sales charges cover distribution expenses: printing and mailing sales literature, advertising the fund through magazines, radio, TV, and the internet, compensating sales people, etc.

If a mutual fund charges a maximum sales charge of 5.5%, that means that when the investor cuts her check, 5.5% of it goes to the distributor and the broker-dealer who sold her the fund. Only the other 94.5% goes into the mutual fund for investment purposes.

So, if the **net asset value (NAV)** is $9.45 but the **public offering price (POP)** is $10.00, the extra 55 cents is the sales charge. How big is that sales charge? It is exactly 5.5% of the investor's $10 check. The sales charge as a percentage equals:

(POP minus NAV) divided by the POP

If we plug our numbers into that formula, we see that $10 minus $9.45 is 55 cents. 55 cents divided by the POP of $10 equals 5.5%. Another way to refer to POP is the gross amount invested. NAV can also be referred to as the net amount invested, what is left after the front-end sales charge is deducted.

The fund is made up of perhaps 500 different stocks and bonds, all trading throughout the day. At the end of each day that the markets are open the fund recalculates the net asset value or NAV. Mutual funds use **forward pricing**, which means that when a customer puts in a purchase or redemption order at 10 AM, she won't know how many shares she'll buy or how many dollars she'll receive yet. Only when the NAV is next calculated are purchase and redemption orders processed.

If a mutual fund company were to allow certain large investors to see what the NAV is at about 4 p.m. Eastern and then receive the previous day's NAV, this is a violation known as late trading. As the SEC website explains, "Late trading refers to the practice of placing orders to buy or redeem mutual fund shares after the time as of which a mutual fund has calculated its net asset value (NAV), usually as of the close of trading at 4:00 p.m. Eastern Time, but receiving the price based on the prior NAV already determined as of that day. Late trading violates the federal securities laws concerning the price at which mutual fund shares must be bought or redeemed and defrauds innocent investors in those mutual funds by giving to the late trader an advantage not available to other investors. In , the late trader obtains an advantage – at the expense of the other shareholders of the mutual fund – when he learns of market moving information and is able to purchase or redeem mutual fund shares at prices set before the market moving information was released."

The NAV is the value of one share of the portfolio. The assets of the portfolio equal the value of the securities plus any cash they've generated, minus any liabilities. Where did the liabilities come from? The fund might borrow to handle redemptions because they don't always want to sell stocks and bonds to pay investors who are redeeming.

If the fund has $10,000,000 in assets and $550,000 in liabilities, the net assets of the fund are $9,450,000. If there are 1 million shares, the NAV per-share is $9.45. Investors will receive $9.45 per-share if they redeem their A-shares today, but they'll pay a POP higher than that if they're buying. Buyers of the B-shares will pay $9.45, but those redeeming/selling their shares will receive $9.45 per-share minus whatever percentage they leave behind to the contingent deferred sales charge.

A-, B- and C-shares

An open-end mutual fund that adds sales charges can take the sales charge from investors either when they buy or when they sell their shares of the fund. A-shares charge a **front-end load** when the investor acquires them. B-shares charge a **back-end load** when the investor sells them. For a B-share, the investor pays the NAV, but will leave a percentage behind when she sells. The percentage usually starts to decline in the second year, and after several years (6 to 8), the back-end load goes away completely. At that point, the B-shares are converted to A-shares.

B-shares are associated with **contingent deferred sales charges**. As the name implies, the sales charge is deferred until the investor sells, and the amount of the load is contingent upon when the investor sells. If the NAV is $10, the investor receives the $10, minus the percentage the fund keeps on the back end. So, if she sells 100 shares and there is a 2% back-end sales charge, she gets $1,000 minus $20, or $980 out the door.

Since the back-end or deferred sales charge eventually goes away, as long as the investor isn't going to sell her shares for, say, seven years, she should purchase B-shares, right?

Well, not exactly. While sales charges cover distribution costs, such costs are also covered by a **12b-1 fee**. Yes, a 12b-1 fee also covers distribution costs. You've heard of **no-load funds**, but you may not have gotten the whole story. A no-load fund can charge a 12b-1 fee, as long as it doesn't exceed .25% of the fund's assets. Every quarter, when they take money out to cover expenses, these no-load funds can also take an amount not to exceed 25 basis points—one-quarter of 1%.

But, while 12b-1 fees are associated with no-load funds, loaded funds also charge 12b-1 fees.

So, again, should the investor buy the A-share or the B-share? The choice has to do with the 12b-1 fee. The A-shares for the growth fund might charge a load as high as 5.5% on the front end, but the 12b-1 fee will often be .25%, while the B-shares will charge a 12b-1 fee of, say, 1.00%.

That complicates things. While the person who bought the B-shares is waiting for that contingent deferred sales charge schedule to hit zero, he's paying an extra .75% every year in expenses in this example. .75% times seven years is an extra 5.25%.

And, this 12b-1 fee is a percentage. As an investor's assets are growing over time, that .75% is also taking more money from him, even if it's a flat percentage.

As we'll soon see, 5.5% would probably be the maximum sales charge on the A-shares. If the investor puts in more money, she can reduce the sales charge to 3 or even 2%, which is why long-term investors with a large amount of money should almost always buy the A-shares. In fact, investors with $1 million or more will find that funds with sales charges waive those charges for investments of that size. Does that hurt the salesperson? No, the agent wants and earns most of the 12b-1 fee. The bigger the account value, the higher that fee.

Then, there are also **C-shares**, which usually don't charge an upfront load but do carry a 1% 12b-1 fee. The level 1% 12b-1 fee is the reason these are referred to as **"level load."** The level load shares are intended for shorter-term investments only.

So, which type of share should an investor buy? As a general guideline:

- Long-term investor with $50,000+ to invest – A-shares
- Long-term investor with small amount to invest – B-shares
- Short-term investor with up to $500,000 to invest – C-shares

The difference in expenses between A-shares on one hand and B- and C-shares on the other has to do with the 12b-1 fee. However, the 12b-1 fee is just one expense. The fund also charges a management fee to cover the cost of the investment adviser serving as portfolio manager. That fee is the same for all investors across the board and must be a separate line item. Management fees are not covered by any other charge. Rather, they must be clearly disclosed.

Other expenses cover transfer agent, custodial, legal and accounting services involved with running the fund. To see what the dollar amounts are investors can check the **statement of additional information** or **SAI**. For example, I just pulled up the SAI for the American Balanced Fund and saw that the investment adviser received $189 million managing the portfolio the previous year. The transfer agent, by comparison, received $74 million.

When we add the management fee, the 12b-1 fee, and the "other expenses" fee, we have the total operating expenses for the fund. Divide the total expenses by the assets of the fund, and we arrive at the fund's **expense ratio**. The expense ratio shows the administrative efficiency of the fund.

Both loaded and no-load open-end funds charge the following expenses, which are deducted from the fund's assets going forward:

- Management (investment advisory) fees
- Distribution fees
- Administrative service fees
- Transfer agent service fees
- Custodian fees
- Auditing and legal fees
- Shareholder reporting fees
- Registration statement and prospectus filing fees

Again, not all open-end funds have sales charges, but all open-end funds deduct operating expenses from portfolio income. Shareholders don't get a bill for the operating expenses, but whatever the fund takes out represents money that could have been paid to the shareholders in the form of dividends.

An open-end fund could be managed by an investment adviser, who then uses an outside distributor, transfer agent, etc. Management fees might be enough to interest the adviser to keep the fund open. At American Funds, on the other hand, the distributor, transfer agent, and investment adviser are all the same company. With over 50 different mutual funds all taking in fees from portfolio income it is not surprising that this company has grown since 1931 to be one of the biggest players in the industry.

Reducing the Sales Charge

Although A-shares charge a front-end load, investors can reduce that sales charge by employing various methods laid out in the prospectus.

Breakpoints

Breakpoints are quantity discounts. If the investor invests $1,000, he pays a higher sales charge than if he invests $100,000. For mutual funds, investors are rewarded with breakpoints. Let's say that the L & H Fund had the following sales charge schedule:

INVESTMENT	SALES CHARGE
<$50,000	5.5%
$50,000 – $99,999	5.0%
$100,000 – $149,999	4.0%
$150,000 – $199,999	3.0%

That means that an investor who buys $100,000 worth of the fund will pay a much lower sales charge than an investor who invests $20,000. In other words, less of her money will be deducted from her check when she invests. A breakpoint means that at this <u>point</u> the fund will give the shareholder this <u>break</u>. A lower sales charge means that an investor's money ends up buying more shares. For mutual funds, we don't pick the number of shares we want; we send in a certain amount of money and see how many shares our money buys us. With a lower sales charge, our money will buy us more shares. Keep in mind that fractional shares are common. For example, $1,000 would buy 12.5 shares if the POP were $80.

Breakpoints are available to individuals, husbands & wives, parents & minor child in a custodial account, corporations, partnerships, etc. So, if the mom puts in $30,000 and also puts in $20,000 for her minor child's UGMA account, that's a $50,000 investment in terms of achieving a breakpoint. The child cannot be an adult; he must be a minor. Corporations and other businesses qualify for breakpoints. About the only people who don't qualify for breakpoints are investment clubs.

Another important consideration for breakpoints is that a securities agent can never encourage an investor to invest a lower amount of money to keep him from obtaining a lower sales charge offered at the next breakpoint. That's called **breakpoint selling** and is a violation of FINRA rules. Likewise, if an agent fails to point out to an investor that a few more dollars invested would qualify for a breakpoint, that's just as bad as actively encouraging him to stay below the next breakpoint.

If a front-end-loaded fund has a breakpoint at $50,000, the registered representative should inform any investor who has even close to $50,000 to invest about that breakpoint. If the customer in the question has, say, $46,000, the agent must inform him about the breakpoint available for just $4,000 more.

Letter of Intent

What if the investor didn't have the $100,000 needed to qualify for that breakpoint? He could write a **letter of intent** explaining to the mutual fund our intention to invest $100,000 in the fund over the next 13 months. Now, as he sends in new money, say, $5,000 at a time, the fund applies the lower 4% sales charge, as if he'd already invested the full amount. The lower sales charge means he ends up buying more shares, right?

So, guess what the fund does? It holds those extra shares in a safe place, just in case he fails to invest that $100,000 he intended to. If he doesn't live up to his letter of intent, no big deal. He just doesn't get those extra shares. In other words, the higher sales charge applies to the money invested.

Also, that letter of intent could be backdated up to 90 calendar days to cover a previous purchase. If an investor bought $3,000 of the L & H fund on March 10, he might decide in early June that he should write a letter of intent to invest $50,000 over 13 months. He could backdate the letter to March 10 to include the previous investment and would then have 13 months from that date to invest the remaining $47,000.

If a test question says that one of your customers wants to invest today in a mutual fund with a front-end sales charge and is anticipating a large year-end bonus, make sure to inform the customer about the letter of intent (LOI) feature. That way he can approximate how much he'll be able to invest over the next 13 months and pay the lowest possible sales charge percentage.

Rights of Accumulation

If an investor's shares appreciate up to a breakpoint, the investor will receive a lower sales charge on additional purchases. In other words, when an investor is trying to reach a breakpoint, new money and account accumulation are counted the same way. So, if an investor's shares have appreciated to, say, $42,000 and the investor wanted to invest another $9,000, the entire purchase would qualify for the breakpoint that starts at $50,000. In other words, the $42,000 of value plus an additional $9,000 would take the investor past the $50,000 needed to qualify for the 5% sales charge.

This is known as **rights of accumulation**. Please note that this has nothing to do with a letter of intent. If you write a letter of intent to invest $100,000, you'll need to invest $100,000 of new dollars into the fund to get the breakpoint you're intending to get. Rights of accumulation means that you could save money on future purchases, based on the value of your account.

Combination Privilege

Most funds are part of a "family" of funds. Many of these fund families will let investors combine a purchase in their Income Fund with, say, their Index or Growth Fund to figure a breakpoint. They call this, cleverly, a **combination privilege**. So, if the individual invests $20,000 in the Income Fund and $30,000 in the Growth Fund, that's considered a $50,000 investment in the family of funds, and that's the number they'd use to figure the breakpoint.

Just trying to keep everybody in our happy family.

Conversion/Exchange Privilege

The fund might also offer a **conversion/exchange privilege**. This privilege allows investors to sell shares of, say, the L & H Growth Fund, to buy shares of the L & H Income Fund at the NAV, rather than the higher POP. If we didn't do that, the investor might get mad enough to leave our happy family, since there is no immediate benefit to his staying with us.

Remember, however, that buying the new shares at the NAV is nice for the investor, but the IRS considers the sale a taxable event. So if you get a test question on the tax treatment, tell the exam that a capital gain or loss is realized on the date of the sale.

Structure and Operation

The following parties do not work for free. Who pays their expenses? The shareholders of the fund do, ultimately, as the following parties are paid through the deduction of operating expenses against the assets of the fund. The higher the expenses, the lower the dividend distributions to the shareholders of the fund, and vice versa.

Board of Directors

A mutual fund has a **board of directors** that oversees operations and policies of the fund or family of funds. The board's responsibilities include:

- establish investment policy

- select and oversee the investment adviser, transfer agent, custodian
- establish dividends and capital gains policy
- approve 12b-1 plans

As with a public company, the shareholders of the fund elect and re-elect the board members. Shareholders also vote their shares to approve the investment adviser's contract and 12b-1 fees. Independent board members have no other connection to the mutual fund sponsor or investment adviser, while the other board members either currently or recently had such a connection.

Investment Adviser

Each fund has an **investment adviser**, whose job is to manage the fund portfolio according to its stated objectives. For example, Capital Research and Management Company is the investment adviser for the American Funds. The board of directors sets the policies for investing, but it is Capital Research and Management making each purchase and sale for the portfolio.

Shareholders and the board vote to hire and retain investment advisers, who are paid a percentage of the fund's net assets. That's why they try so hard. The more valuable the fund, the more they get paid. Their fee is typically the largest expense to a mutual fund. Investment advisers have to advise the fund (select the investments) in keeping with federal securities and tax law. They must also base their investment decisions on careful research of economic/financial trends. Since everything needs at least two names, the investment adviser is also called the "portfolio manager."

Custodian

The fund also keeps its securities and cash under the control of a **custodian**. Keeping track of all the dividends received from common and preferred stock held in the portfolio, interest payments from the bonds and money market instruments owned by the fund, purchases and sales, etc., is a big job, and the custodian performs it. The custodian is responsible for the payable/receivable functions involved when the portfolio buys and sells securities. That means they release the money and receive the securities purchased, and they accept the money and deliver the securities sold by the portfolio manager. When a security in the portfolio pays a dividend, the custodian receives it.

Transfer Agent

The **transfer agent** is the party that issues new shares to buyers and cancels shares that sellers redeem. Most of these shares are electronic files (book entry), but it takes a lot of work to issue and redeem them. While the custodian receives dividends and interest payments from the portfolio securities, it is the transfer agent that distributes income to the investors in the fund. The transfer agent acts as a customer service rep for the fund and often sends out those semi-annual and annual reports that investors have to receive. As we just saw, investors can purchase and redeem shares directly with the transfer agent. The transfer agent also handles name changes when, for example, mutual fund shares are re-titled in the name of the estate for a now deceased investor. Or, if a newly married couple now opens a joint account, etc.

Distributor

Funds are sponsored by broker-dealers acting as underwriters, who bear the costs of distributing the fund up front and are then compensated by the sales charge that they either earn themselves or split with the broker-dealers who make the sales. Underwriters (a.k.a. "wholesalers," **distributors**," or "sponsors") also prepare sales literature for the fund, since they're the ones who will be selling the shares, either directly to the public or through a network of broker-dealers. If a fund acts as its own distributor, it usually covers the distribution costs through a 12b-1 fee, as we mentioned. The fund can call itself "no load" as long as the 12b-1 fee does not exceed .25% of net assets. To call itself "100% no-load" the fund could have neither a sales charge nor a 12b-1 fee.

These are the methods of distribution for mutual fund shares:

- Fund/to underwriter/to dealer/to investor
- Fund/to underwriter/to investor
- Fund/to investor (no-load funds)

Shareholder Voting

Mutual fund shareholders get to vote their shares in matters of major importance:

- Changes in investment policies and objectives
- Approval of investment adviser contract
- Approval of changes in fees
- Election of board members
- Ratification of independent auditors (PricewaterhouseCoopers, KPMG, etc.)

Closed-End Funds

The third type of investment company defined by the Investment Company Act of 1940 is the **management company**, under which we find both open-end funds and closed-end funds. So far, we've been talking mostly about the open-end funds. Let's say a few words on the closed-end variety at this point.

The main difference between the two is that open-end fund companies continually issue and redeem shares. When an agent finds an investor for an open-end fund, the fund issues new shares to the investor, which is why he had to sell them with a prospectus. Open-end funds don't do an IPO and then force shareholders to trade the fixed number of shares back and forth. Rather, they issue new shares every time someone wants to buy them, and they let the shareholders sell back the shares when they are ready to redeem them.

On the other hand, closed-end funds do an initial offering, at which point there is a fixed number of outstanding shares. What if a shareholder wants to sell his closed-end fund this afternoon? He trades it the same way he trades any other share of stock. How much will he receive? Whatever a buyer is willing to pay. These things usually trade at a discount to their NAV, or at a premium. It just depends on the supply and demand for the shares, and since this is such a small part of the secondary market, the pricing is less than efficient.

Therefore, if the test question says that the NAV is $9.45 with the POP at $9.00, something's up, right? Investors can't buy an open-end fund at a discount. As we saw, the cheapest they can buy them is at the NAV. B-shares are sold at the NAV and so are "no load" funds. But, no way can a public investor buy open-end shares at a discount. Only dealers, who are members of FINRA, get to do that. So, if the fund shares are selling below NAV, they have to be closed-end fund shares.

However, that doesn't mean that closed-end funds always trade at a discount. If people really want the shares, they might pay a premium. We're not saying that closed-end funds always trade at a discount to their NAV. We're saying that only the closed-end fund could do that. Really, it's because only the closed-end fund shares are traded between investors. The fund figures the NAV at the end of the day, but the shares trade back and forth all through the day, and not always in the most liquid or efficient market.

And, since closed-end shares trade the same way that GE or MSFT shares trade, investors can both purchase them on margin and sell them short. As we discuss elsewhere, "selling short" involves borrowing shares from a broker-dealer and selling them, with the obligation to buy them back and replace them later. If the price falls, you buy low after you already sold high. If the price rises, you're in trouble.

Another difference between open- and closed-end funds is that an investor would purchase, say, 100 shares of the closed-end fund and pay whatever that costs. For an open-end fund, he would cut a check for, say, $1,000, and see how many shares he ends up with next time they figure the NAV. In almost all cases, he will receive "full and fractional shares" with an open-end fund, which means that $100 would turn into 12.5 shares if the POP were $8.00. That little "point-5" of a share is the fractional share. For a closed-end fund, he would either buy 12 shares or 13 shares, not 12.5

Open-end funds only issue common stock to investors. Closed-end funds, on the other hand, issue preferred shares and use other forms of leverage, usually through bank borrowings or issuing auction rate preferred shares. These funds attempt to earn higher returns through such leverage, but the use of leverage also increases risks.

The investment objectives between an open-end and a closed-end fund could be exactly the same. There are closed-end corporate bond funds, tax-exempt bond funds, aggressive growth funds, etc. Nuveen Investments (www.nuveen.com) is the largest issuer of closed-end municipal bond funds. Why would an investor want those versus the open-end variety? Well, what happens to yield when the price of the bond drops—it goes up, right? So, if he can buy someone's closed-end bond fund at a discount, he just goosed his yield a little bit. What about when he wants to sell his shares someday? Nobody knows.

The expenses for closed-end funds include:

- Management fees
- Interest expense on borrowings
- Shareholder servicing
- Custodial fees
- Trustee fees
- Professional fees
- Shareholder reporting expenses

- Stock exchange listing fees
- Investor relations expenses

Open-end funds would not have stock exchange listing fees, as their shares do not trade among investors on the secondary market.

Although it's true that closed-end funds have a fixed number of shares, investors in the fund are able to reinvest their distributions into more shares. And, there are rights offerings for closed-end funds if the board of directors decides to do an additional offering of shares. The difference is that with open-end funds new investors can buy shares that are created on-the-fly by the open-end investment company.

Unit Investment Trusts (UITs)

Management companies are one type of registered investment company. **Unit Investment Trusts** are another. The Investment Company Act of 1940 defines a Unit Investment Trust (UIT) as:

```
an investment company which (A) is organized under a trust
indenture, contract of custodianship or agency, or similar
instrument, (B) does not have a board of directors, and (C) issues
only redeemable securities, each of which represents an undivided
interest in a unit of specified securities; but does not include a
voting trust.
```

The main differences between management companies and UITs include the fact that UITs do not trade their portfolio, do not therefore have an investment adviser, and do not have a board of directors. A UIT is a "supervised, unmanaged investment company," because while the portfolio is supervised by a trustee, the securities in it are not traded by an investment adviser the way most management companies would actively manage their assets. Running the trust does involve fees for bookkeeping, trustee fees, administrative fees, etc., but—again—no management fees are charged. When the shares are purchased an upfront sales charge is often added, or a deferred sales charge is imposed if and when the unit holder redeems.

Similar to a closed-end fund, a finite number of shares are offered to investors on the primary market. But, unlike, a closed-end fund, unit investment trust interests are redeemable as opposed to having to be traded at prices based on supply and demand. Also, unlike both open- and closed-end funds, unit investment trusts have a termination date, which means they have a limited duration. On the termination date, everything is liquidated, unit holders are paid out, and that's that.

Face-Amount Certificates

The Investment Company Act of 1940 defines a **face-amount certificate** company as:

```
an investment company which is engaged or proposes to engage in
the business of issuing face-amount certificates of the
installment type, or which has been engaged in such business and
has any such certificate outstanding
```

Think of a face-amount certificate as a debt security in which the certificate is purchased at a discount and redeemed at a future date for the higher face amount. Or, if presented early, the investor will receive the "surrendered value" at that point in time.

ETFs

As its name implies, an **ETF** or **exchange-traded fund** is a fund that trades on an exchange, as opposed to being redeemed or sold back to the issuer.

An ETF is typically an index fund, so if an investor wants to do as well as a index, she can track that index by purchasing an exchange-traded fund (ETF). To track the S&P 500, she can buy the "Spider," which is so named because it is an "SPDR" or "Standard & Poor's Depository Receipt." Of course, we already saw that she could do that with an S&P 500 open-end index fund. But, that is an open-end fund that has to be redeemed. No matter what time of day, if we put in a redemption order, we all receive the same NAV at the next calculated price. So, if the S&P 500 drops 80 points in the morning and rises 150 points by mid-afternoon, there is no way for us to buy low and then sell high. ETFs facilitate "intra-day trading," which means that you can buy and sell these things as many times as you want throughout the day.

Unlike the open-end versions, these ETFs can be bought on margin and can be sold short by investors who are "bearish" on the overall market or a index. If an investor is bearish on technology stocks overall, the answer might be for him to sell the QQQ short, as it represents the NASDAQ 100, the 100 hundred largest non-financial company stocks trading on NASDAQ. If he's right, he'll profit as those stocks drop in price. Or, an investor mostly in large cap stocks could hedge his risk by selling shares of the Dow ETF (Diamonds) short. This way if the index rises, his stocks make money, and if the index drops his short sale makes money.

So, are the ETFs cheaper than the open-end index fund versions?

Depends how you do it. For a small amount of money the open-end mutual fund is a great option. For larger amounts of money, though, the ETF is typically cheaper, as the flat commission paid becomes a smaller and smaller percentage of the amount invested. In other words, if the commission is $10 either way, a purchase of $300 is a bad idea, while a purchase of $30,000 would make that $10 insignificant.

As with the open-end index funds, ETFs offer diversification. For a rather small amount of money, an investor can own a little piece of, say, 500 different stocks with the SPDR, or 100 stocks with the QQQ. It is also easy to implement asset allocation strategies with ETFs. An investor can find ETFs that track all kinds of different indexes (small cap, value, growth, blue chip, long-term bonds, etc.). If an investor wanted to be 80% long-term bonds and 20% small-cap stock, that goal could be achieved with just two low-cost ETFs. This point is not necessarily a comparison to the open-end index funds, which would offer the same advantage. Rather, it is a comparison to purchasing individual bonds or small cap stocks. To spread the risk among many bonds and small cap stocks, an investor would have to spend large sums of money. With an ETF (as with the open-end index funds) diversification can be achieved immediately with a much smaller investment.

An ETF such as the SPDR (SPY) or Mid-Cap SPDR (MDY) is appropriate for most investors with a time horizon and risk tolerance suitable for stock (equity) investing in general.

REITs

Investing in real estate has many advantages and disadvantages. The advantages are that property values often appreciate over time and that real estate provides diversification to a securities portfolio, since usually real estate and the stock market are not correlated. The disadvantages include the fact that real estate takes a lot of capital, and it isn't liquid. It often takes months or even years to get a property sold, or sold for a decent price, so the lack of liquidity keeps many investors from buying real estate, especially commercial real estate (shopping malls, skyscrapers, factories, etc.).

This is where publicly traded **REITs** come in. **A Real Estate Investment Trust** (REIT) is a company that owns a portfolio of properties and sells shares to investors. Investor can buy into REITs that own apartment buildings, office buildings, shopping centers, hotels, convention centers, self-storage units, timber—you name it. This way they can participate in real estate without having to be wealthy, and they can sell their shares as easily as selling shares of other publicly traded stock.

REITs are pooled investment vehicles that give the investor an ownership stake in a trust that owns real estate. They do not pass through losses (only real estate *partnerships* do that). REITS typically pay high dividend yields, but the dividend is taxed at ordinary income rates, not the kinder, gentler rate on qualified dividends that we will explore in the next chapter under Tax Considerations.

The type of REIT I just described is called an **Equity REIT**. A different type of REIT that provides financing for real estate projects as opposed to just buying up and managing properties. These are called **Mortgage REITs** and they provide financing as well as buy up mortgages and mortgage-backed securities. Some REITs do a little of both, and are called, fittingly, **Hybrid REITs**.

Private Funds

Investment company products are open to retail investors and can either be redeemed or traded whenever the markets are open. Publicly traded REITS are also open to retail investors, who do not have to sign net worth and risk acknowledgment statements the way they do for privately held REITS and the real estate limited partnerships we'll look at in a few pages. Private funds—including hedge funds, venture capital funds, and private equity funds—are also open only to sophisticated investors due to their risky investment strategies and relative lack of liquidity.

Hedge Funds

In general, **hedge funds** are only open to institutions and to individuals called **accredited investors**. An accredited investor has over $1 million in liquid net worth or makes > $200,000 per year. If it's a married couple, the assets held jointly count toward that $1 million figure, or the annual income needs to be > $300,000. The equity in the investor's primary residence is not counted toward the net worth minimum—we're talking about $1 million of net worth that could be invested.

Why does the investor need to meet net worth or income requirements? Because these hedge funds often use high-risk trading strategies including short selling, currency bets, and high levels of leverage, etc. If you're an average Joe and JoAnne, it wouldn't make sense to let you risk all of your investment capital on such high-risk investing. On the other hand, if you're a wealthy individual or an institution, chances are your hedge fund investment is just a percentage of the capital you invest. So, if you lose $1 million, chances are you have several more million where that came from.

A typical arrangement for a hedge fund is to have a limited number of investors form a private investment partnership. The fund typically charges 2% of assets as a management fee and extracts the first 20% of all capital gains. Then, they start thinking about their investors (we hope). Once you buy, there's a good chance you will not be able to sell your investment for at least one year. Rather than trying to beat an index such as the DJIA, hedge funds generally go for "absolute positive investment performance"—usually 8% or so—regardless of what the overall market is doing. In other words, hedge funds are designed to profit in *any* market environment, while index funds only work when the overall market—or the section of it represented by the index—is having a good year.

Now, although a **non-accredited purchaser** cannot invest directly in a hedge fund, there are mutual funds called **funds of hedge funds**, which she can invest in. As the name implies, these mutual funds would have investments in several different hedge funds. In most cases, the investor would not be able to redeem her investment, since hedge funds are illiquid (they don't trade among investors). Also, these investments would involve high expenses, since there would be the usual expenses of the mutual fund, on top of the high expenses of the hedge funds the mutual fund invests in.

The main testable points on hedge funds include:

- Designed to perform in any market environment
- Open to sophisticated, accredited investors with high net worth
- Illiquid—usually can't be sold for at least one year
- Employ riskier, more diverse strategies
- Charge high management fees and usually 20% of all gains
- Non-accredited purchasers can buy mutual funds that invest in hedge funds

Private Equity

Similar to a hedge fund, a **private equity fund** is structured as a limited partnership and is open only to sophisticated investors, as it is not liquid and generally takes on much greater risk than an open- or closed-end fund. As the name implies, private equity groups invest in securities that are not publicly traded. They often approach a company like Frank & Emma's Fruit Pies and cut a deal to buy all the common stock plus maybe a premium. After they appoint some better managers and board members, improve the profits at the acquired company, and get some good media buzz, maybe they then approach investment bankers to do an IPO so the owners can cash in as investors clamor for the stock. Private equity funds are typically set up for a period of time, maybe 10 years. After that, investors receive their money back from the general partner who set up the fund, plus—we hope—a profit.

The use of leverage is associated with private equity groups, whose acquisitions are often referred to as leveraged buyouts.

Venture Capital

Unlike private equity investors, **venture capital** firms typically focus on providing investments to early-stage companies, and rather than using leverage, VC firms typically use cash. Also, while private equity funds typically buy a company outright, venture capital funds typically make smaller investments in several companies in exchange for a minority stake.

 While private equity firms usually buy more mature companies, venture capitalists invest in much earlier-stage companies. Because most companies will fail, venture capital funds often invest smaller amounts in dozens of companies. The "VC" firms who invested early in companies such as Oracle, Microsoft, and Facebook realized mind boggling returns when those companies then offered shares to the public.

Uncovering the next grand-slam is the ultimate goal of a venture capitalist. Unfortunately, it's hard to see the future before it arrives.

Private equity investors buy a company that they expect to make more efficient and profitable, with— they hope— little risk of failure over the near-term. These investors plan to install new management and run the company for a while themselves. Venture capital investors, on the other hand, know that most of their investments will be losers; therefore, the returns are made on the handful of performers that survive and thrive. VC funds provide investment capital with a much more hands-off approach to running the companies in which they invest.

A private equity firm would purchase a company like the makers of Hostess snack cakes, fix it up, and then sell it. A venture capital firm would provide financing to an up-and-coming gluten-free snack cake maker who just did their first $1 million in revenue. And a hedge fund is more of a heavily traded portfolio of securities than a fund providing private investment capital to companies at various stages of their development.

Then again, the three terms (private equity, venture capital, and hedge funds) are subject to overlap. A hedge fund, for example, could end up buying a fast-food chain, although I would tend to think of that as "private equity." On the other hand, a private equity fund could provide capital to a less-mature enterprise, while a venture capital fund might occasionally purchase a young company outright.

Regardless, in all three cases the investors in the fund are taking on greater risk and are either institutions or accredited investors, with an investment adviser earning fees to manage the portfolio on their behalf.

Alternative Investments

Since mutual fund portfolios are open to retail investors, they can't focus on high-risk investment strategies. But, when the investors are all wealthy individuals and institutions, the regulators can relax a bit. Regulators, remember, provide necessary protection to investors, and sophisticated investors don't need so much protection to keep the playing field level. That's why such sophisticated investors can invest in the private funds we just looked at—private equity, venture capital, and hedge funds.

These investors can also invest in **direct participation programs**.

Limited Partnerships (DPPs)

A C-corporation is taxed as a business entity, with the owners then getting taxed on any dividend income that they distribute to themselves from the business's profits. C-corporations, in other words, lead to the double taxation of dividends for the owners.

On the other hand, in a direct participation program (**DPP**) the owners of the business take a share of the business entity's net income or net loss on their own personal income taxes. The partnership itself is not taxed. Rather, the partners are taxed on their share of the net income or net loss that flows through the business directly to them. Partnerships—like LLCs and S-corporations—are associated with **flow through** of net income/net loss to the owners.

Types of Programs

There are partnerships organized to perform all kinds of business, from movie making to sports teams, from construction projects to law firms. Broker-dealers often raise capital for their investment banking customers looking to form natural resource or real estate ventures through DPP offerings.

Oil & gas programs could involve exploring for natural resources, developing proven reserves, or buying an income/production program. **Exploratory programs** for oil and gas are the riskiest programs with the highest return potential as well. The act of exploring for oil is sometimes called "wildcatting," which provides a hint of the risk/reward nature.

Exploration generates **intangible drilling costs** or **IDCs**. As opposed to capitalized costs sunk into the oil rig and other equipment, intangible drilling costs are the costs/expenses that leave nothing to be recovered. IDCs include labor costs and the expense of the geological survey indicating there is—or should be—oil or natural gas down below. The IDCs in these programs are so high in the first few years that this type of program typically provides the most tax shelter to the investor, especially in the early years. Beyond IDCs, drilling programs take depreciation expenses on any equipment owned, which also may provide tax shelter to the LPs.

Sometimes DPPs drill for oil or gas in an area where these natural resources are already being extracted, with engineering studies confirming the existence of oil or natural gas below the ground. Such programs are called **developmental programs**. They're less risky than exploratory programs, but with a lower return potential. Some call these "step-out" programs, as if someone is starting at the existing well and stepping out so many paces before constructing another one. These programs also provide tax shelter through the intangible drilling costs we just looked at. And, there is depreciation on the expensive equipment if the partnership owns that equipment as opposed to leasing it.

The safest natural resources programs buy existing production and are called **income programs**. These investments provide immediate cash flow and are, therefore, the safest programs with the lowest potential reward. When I say they are "safe," I mean for a DPP. Even though income is expected, the prices of oil and natural gas are extremely volatile, making both the income and the investment's value difficult to estimate. And, as always, DPP investments are not liquid—there are no buyers standing ready should the investor wish to sell. The main tax advantage offered from these programs comes in the form of **depletion**. When oil or natural gas is sold, the partnership takes a charge/expense against their revenue, basically for depleting their assets. If the business entity owns the drilling equipment, depreciation may also provide tax shelter to the LPs.

In real estate, which is riskier, buying raw land or buying an apartment complex already filled with renters? **Raw land** is purely speculative and is, therefore, the riskiest type of real estate DPP. You buy parcels of land betting that an airport or industrial park will be built in the next few years. If you're right, the land appreciates in value. If not, it doesn't. And, you receive no income or tax benefits on raw land as you sit waiting for its value to go up. There is nothing to deplete, and land does not depreciate the way apartment buildings and oil rigs do.

New construction programs are aggressive programs, but once the projects are completed the townhouses or condominiums can be sold for capital gains. So they're safer than raw land and probably provide a lower reward potential. They also involve more costs, of course, as someone has to finance all that construction. For a construction program lasting several years, the LPs are likely to receive a share of net loss at the beginning, as the partnership sinks capital into building a townhouse community on the front end, hoping to sell enough units on the back end to turn a profit.

Existing properties DPPs are similar to income programs for oil. Here, the business is already up and running, with immediate cash flow. Investors can examine the financial statements and know what they're getting into, as opposed to an investment in raw land. Therefore, existing property DPPs offer lower risk and lower reward to investors. The tax shelter comes through depreciation of the buildings themselves as well as any maintenance equipment owned by the partnership.

Another common type of limited partnership is the **equipment leasing program.** These partnerships typically lease equipment that other companies do not want to own. For example, computers, transportation equipment, oil drilling and construction equipment, etc., might not be cost-effective for the users to own; therefore, it makes more sense to lease such equipment from an equipment leasing program. Tax benefits for equipment leasing would come largely through depreciation of the equipment.

Tax credits are the benefit for **government-assisted housing** programs. That means that if the partnership builds, acquires, or rehabs a government-assisted housing project, it will benefit from tax credits, and possibly from subsidy payments from the federal government. Or, a local government might provide tax credits to a partnership that does historic rehab or repurposing of former train stations or water pumping stations into shopping or restaurant districts, for example.

Either way, remember that a tax credit is always better than a tax deduction of an equal dollar amount. In fact, let's compare a $100,000 tax deduction to a $100,000 tax credit:

	$1,000,000	Income		$1,000,000	Income
-	$100,000	Deduction		x .30	30% tax rate
	$900,000	Net Income		$300,000	Tax
	x .30	30% tax rate	-	$100,000	CREDIT
	$270,000	Tax		$200,000	Tax

Notice how a deduction is subtracted from the top line—revenue. For a credit, you figure the amount of tax you were going to have to pay, and then apply the credit dollar-for-dollar against that amount.

Surprisingly, there is no requirement that a "DPP" has to be formed as a limited partnership. Here is how FINRA defines the term "direct participation program":

> *...a program which provides for flow-through tax consequences regardless of the structure of the legal entity or vehicle for distribution including, but not limited to, oil and gas programs, real estate programs, agricultural programs, cattle programs, condominium securities, Subchapter S corporate offerings and all other programs of a similar nature, regardless of the industry represented by the program, or any combination thereof.*

GPs and LPs

The owners who provide most of the capital to the business are the **limited partners (LPs)**. They are called "limited partners" because their liability is limited to their investment. If they invest $100,000, then $100,000 is all they can lose as passive investors in the partnership. Creditors can't come after the LPs for their personal assets if the business goes bankrupt. Lawsuits of all types could be filed against the partnership, but, again, the LPs would not have their personal assets at risk in such cases.

To maintain their limited liability status the limited partners need to stay out of day-to-day management of the business. Day-to-day management is left solely to the **general partner (GP)**. As manager, the GP can also be compensated for these managerial efforts through a salary. While the LPs provide most of the capital, the GP (general partner) must have at least a 1% financial interest in the partnership as well. The GP is granted the authority to acquire and sell property on behalf of the business and sign any documents on behalf of the business required to carry out its management. The GP has to keep accurate books and records and must provide annual financial statements to the LPs. Typically, the GP can also admit new limited partners at his discretion.

Unlike an LP, the general partner has unlimited liability. That is why the GP is often a corporation, providing the individual controlling the business protection for his or her personal assets. The general partner is also a fiduciary to the limited partners. That means the GP has to maintain a duty of loyalty and good faith to the investors trusting him to manage the business using their invested capital.

The GP's fiduciary responsibility to the limited partners means he must put the interests of the partnership ahead of his own interests or the interests of other businesses in which he is involved. The GP can't compete with the partnership through some other business venture and, therefore, can't charge some bogus "no compete" payment—since they can't compete in the first place. When the GP sells a building, piece of equipment, or the business itself, he/they must refrain from receiving economic gain at the expense of the limited partners. As with an investment adviser, if there are any conflicts of interest involved, these must be fully disclosed to the LPs. Note that the LPs have no such duty to refrain from owning businesses that compete with the partnership.

The GP could provide a loan to the business, but as a fiduciary to the LPs, he would have to disclose any conflicts of interest he might have. For example, if he's lending money to the partnership through a savings & loan institution that he controls or owns shares in, this potential conflict of interest that could end up clouding his judgment must be disclosed. On the one hand, he wants to help the business. On the other hand, he likes to help his own lending institution. That is an example of a conflict of interest that an honest GP will consider and disclose to the LPs rather than waiting for them to sue for breach of fiduciary duty.

Limited partners stay out of day-to-day management decisions, but because of **partnership democracy** they do get to vote on major issues like suing the GP or dissolving the partnership. Why would they sue the GP? Maybe the oil & gas program turns out to be a scam in which the sponsor is using partners' money to fund other businesses or a high-rolling lifestyle. Viewers of *American Greed* know that stranger things have happened in the world of investments.

If the exam asks if LPs can make loans to the partnership, the answer is yes. In other words, some of the capital LPs provide to the partnership can be through debt securities paying a reasonable rate of interest. If you're in business for yourself, you may have fronted some cash to your business and then had the business pay you a rate of interest on the "promissory note." Same idea here. Some partnerships might have investors providing capital in exchange for debt securities that later to convert to equity in the business. There are many ways to structure the financing of a DPP.

Documents

The General Partner is responsible for filing the **certificate of limited partnership** with the state where the entity is organized. This is a public document that provides only the most basic information, including the name and address of the partnership, the name and addresses of all the general partners as well as the registered agent who would accept any "service of process" should a lawsuit arise against the business. The GP signs and files this document with the state where the business is organized.

The **partnership agreement** is signed by all partners and is the foundation for the partnership. In this agreement we would find the following information:

- business purpose of the partnership
- effective date and term of operation (if termination date or event is stated)
- required capital commitments now and in future for GP and LP
- name and address of GP
- principal place of business for the partnership
- powers and limitations of the GP's authority
- allocation of profits and losses
- distributions of cash
- transfer of interests
- withdrawal, removal of a partner

Corporations are presumed to go on for perpetuity. A partnership is also assumed to live on indefinitely unless the partnership agreement establishes a date or triggering event for dissolution of the entity. For example, a new construction program may dissolve when the last townhouse has been sold. Or, if the GP dies, the business may dissolve according to the stipulations in the agreement.

While there are potential rewards to DPP investments, there are also plenty of risks involved. First, the business venture might strike out. Right across from our former offices in Forest Park, IL, we watched a large new construction program borrow $15 million and then go belly up when only one unit was sold. After spending untold sums sandblasting the original beams and posts, there must have been over 1,000 new windows installed in an old factory building, all of them eventually either broken by vandals, removed and sold for pennies-on-the-dollar, or smashed by the wrecking ball that eventually came. I'm thinking the partners in that program have made better investments.

Second, the IRS might determine that the partnership is an abusive tax shelter, set up to generate deductions through depreciation or depletion without ever intending to be economically viable. A DPP may be considered abusive if it's based on a false assumption or if the partnership overstated property values to take large depreciation deductions. If that happens, the IRS can suddenly disallow deductions that the partners previously claimed, causing investors to pay back taxes *plus* interest and penalties. If the IRS suspects the program was designed for tax losses without any intent to be run like a profitable business, they can go after everyone connected to the program with the full force of the IRS: audits, penalties, interest, seizure of assets, etc.

So, a registered representative must never recommend a DPP investment that has no chance of profitability based solely on the share of losses it will provide to the investor. When considering the economic viability of a direct participation program investment, a securities agent and his customer would consider:

- economic soundness of the program
- expertise of the general partner
- basic objectives of the program
- start-up costs

For example, if this is a real estate new construction program, has the General Partner already done a few successful programs like this, or is he doing his first big deal with the Limited Partners' money, therefore, at greater risk? If the price of oil and/or natural gas has plummeted, does it make sense to sink capital into start-up costs for an oil & gas exploration program?

Once economic viability of the business has been determined, the next consideration is tax benefits. If investors have **passive income**, they can use **passive losses** from DPPs to offset them for tax purposes. On the other hand, if they *do not* have passive income to offset, an agent may not recommend a program based on the tax shelter it provides, since they would not be able to benefit from that feature. And, some programs—including raw land—provide no tax benefits at all, regardless of the investor's tax situation.

The last thing a DPP investor should be in need of is liquidity because, basically, there isn't any. All investors must understand that a DPP investment is long-term and not liquid. A money market mutual fund investment is as liquid as one could find, while an investment in a DPP is on the other side of the liquidity spectrum. There are often estimates or target dates as to when LPs might be able to get some or all of their investment back, but these are only estimates.

As opposed to buying common stock or bonds issued by, say, GE, **structured products** are created and sold by financial intermediaries with terms that are mutually agreed upon by both parties.

We have looked at both bonds and ETFs in earlier sections. An **ETN (Exchange Traded Note)** has characteristics of both a bond and an ETF. An ETN is a type of unsecured debt security issued by a financial institution, e.g., Barclays Capital. This type of debt security differs from other types of bonds and notes because ETN returns are based upon the performance of an underlying benchmark minus fees. The benchmark could be a market index, a foreign currency, or commodities. No coupon payments are distributed during the investor's holding period and no principal protections exist. The issuer is borrowing the investor's money for a certain time frame, paying it all back (we hope) with interest at maturity, with the rate of interest dependent on the performance of the benchmark.

At maturity, the issuer pays the investor a sum of money based on the performance of the benchmark, investor fees, and the calculation explained in the prospectus for the ETN. During the holding period the value of the ETN fluctuates primarily based on two factors: the performance of the benchmark and the creditworthiness of the issuer. As with any bond, if the issuer's creditworthiness drops, so does the value of the security. ETNs can be traded on the secondary market, but, as with anything that can be traded on the secondary market, the price received could be less than what the investor paid. And, ETNs are generally not as liquid as stocks, bonds, and money market securities. The test might say that ETNs are subject to market risk, credit risk, and liquidity risk.

A big difference between ETNs and ETFs is that, while ETFs invest in securities that allow them to track the underlying benchmark, ETNs do not own what they are tracking.

OTC options are exotic options traded on the over-the-counter market, where participants can choose the characteristics of the options traded (offers flexibility).

HOLDRs are a financial product created by Merrill Lynch and traded daily on the American Stock Exchange that allows investors to buy and sell a basket of stocks in a sector, industry or other classification in a single transaction. The abbreviation stands for Holding Company Depository Receipt. There are currently 17 different HOLDRs currently trading on AMEX.

HOLDRs are often confused or lumped in with ETFs. As Think Advisor explains, "Essentially, a HOLDR is a static basket of stocks selected from a industry. As a result, HOLDRs do not track an underlying index like ETFs, and represent a rather narrow slice of an industry. Not only are HOLDRs completely unmanaged, their components almost never change. Furthermore, if a company is acquired and removed from a HOLDR, its stock is not replaced. This can result in even more concentration and added risk. In contrast, indexes that ETFs invest in can change and rebalance with some regularity, and generally contain more components. Such is the case with Barclay's 'iShares' and Vanguard's ETFs called 'VIPERs' (Vanguard Index Participation Equity Receipts), which collectively track Standard & Poor's and MSCI indexes." (http://www.thinkadvisor.com/2005/08/18/holdrs-vs-etfs-what-investors-should-know.

The term **leverage** sometimes refers to borrowed money but more generally refers to an investment promising higher returns on a percentage basis due to increased exposure to risk. For example, in a margin account the investor takes on the risk of borrowing money at a rate of interest, hoping to receive twice the returns he would have made on a percentage basis by being twice as exposed to the risks of the marketplace. With call options speculators can make much larger percentage gains than on the underlying stock and do so by putting down just a percentage of the stock's market price. On the other hand, options can lead to quick and painful losses when the speculator is on the wrong side of the market.

A **leveraged ETF** uses derivatives to increase the fund's exposure to the underlying index. Some funds are "2X," or exposed to the index in a way that will double the gains or losses. In other words, they are designed to go up or down 10% if the S&P 500 or other index goes up or down just 5%. Some funds are even "3X," designed to triple the exposure to the index and, therefore, triple the gains (or losses) to investors.

Leveraged funds are only for the short-term. In fact, the exposure is re-set e trading day and designed to capture the 2 or 3X returns for just that one day. The products are really designed for institutional and other sophisticated investors due to their complexity and amplified exposure to stock, bond, or commodities markets.

ETF shares can be sold short, as the shares trade throughout the day alongside shares of any public company you care to name. This allows investors to hedge their market risk by betting against the overall market with a percentage of their portfolio. If a trader thinks the S&P 500 will drop today, he can sell an ETF tracking the index short. If he's right, he'll make some money with that speculation, which will offset whatever he loses on his stock portfolio.

Inverse ETFs are designed to bet against an index, and most such funds do so at a 2 or 3X multiplier by using derivatives. This means that a leveraged inverse ETF is designed to move in the opposite direction of the index by a factor of 2 or 3. A 2X leveraged inverse fund is designed on a daily basis to, for example, rise 10% if the index drops 5%. Another name for a leveraged inverse fund is an "ultra-short fund." An example of a popular ultra-short fund is the *ProShares UltraShort S&P 500 ETF*, stock symbol SDS. As a helpful guide at the NASDAQ website explains, "Launched in July 2006, this fund seeks to deliver twice the inverse of the daily performance of the S&P 500 Index. With holdings of 500 securities, the fund has a certain tilt towards the technology sector with Apple Inc. (AAPL), Exxon Mobil (XOM) and General Electric (GE) as the top three firms. The product is largely concentrated in large cap firms with a 91% share, while the remainder goes to mid and small caps."

As tricky as an inverse and leveraged ETF might be, I would have to nominate the **viatical** or **life settlement** as the most alternative of all alternative investments. The investment vehicle is created when someone with a life insurance policy wants to receive most of the benefit right now while he's alive. If the policy has a $1 million death benefit, the viatical settlement would involve the buy-side purchasing the policy for more than its cash surrender value but at a discount to the $1 million death benefit. The third-party buyer then becomes the owner of the policy, paying any premiums due. Then, when the insured dies, the investor collects the full death benefit of $1 million.

But, wouldn't that imply that the sooner the insured dies the higher the investor's yield, and vice versa? Indeed. As I said—an extremely alternative approach to investing. A viatical settlement meets the definition of a security according to the state securities regulators. However, it is not liquid. If you purchase a viatical settlement, you may have to keep paying premiums, and you will only receive payment when the insured dies because there is no secondary market for these alternative investments. Unlike a bond investment, there is no annual return offered, and the actual return the investor receives is unpredictable since no one—except those relying on foul play—can accurately predict when someone is going to die.

The advantage is that this sort of investment would definitely provide diversification to the investor. And, since death benefits are not taxable, the gain made upon payout is tax-free.

Mortgages are pooled and sold to investors through Ginnie Mae and Fannie Mae securities. Life settlements are sometimes pooled into "death bonds." Here, investors buy shares of a diversified pool of life insurance policies. As with an individual life settlement, the investors will profit based on how long premiums must be paid on the policies versus how soon the death benefits in the pool are paid out to investors.

Other Assets

Shopping centers, office buildings, industrial centers, and apartments are all examples of real estate investment properties that take investors outside the world of securities. Historically, such investments have provided a hedge to a securities portfolio because the real estate market is not highly correlated with the stock and bond markets.

Real estate is not all upside, of course. It is often hard to sell an office building, or to sell it at an attractive price. In other words, it is illiquid. Also, rental property may require a management company or may require a major time commitment by the owner himself. And, unlike an investment in common stock, real estate investments often involve repairs, upgrades, insurance and many other expenses.

Bond investors face inflation risk. Therefore, some fixed-income investors hedge their risk by investing in gold, silver, and other **precious metals**. During inflationary periods or periods of financial uncertainty investors often bid up the price of such metals. Precious metals are used in coins, jewelry, and many varied industrial applications. The four main precious metals are gold, silver, platinum, and palladium.

There are several ways to invest in precious metals. Investors can buy bullion (bars of gold, silver, platinum, etc). Or, they can buy certain coins made of the four main precious metals. Some investors buy precious metals mutual funds that hold shares in mining companies. There are also ETFs that hold bullion in each of the four major precious metals. ETFs and mutual funds make it convenient to invest. Holding actual gold coins or bars of silver might be more fun. However, holding bullion or coins requires storage, security, and insurance.

Inflation makes it hard for consumers to keep up. It also means that commodity prices are high. Therefore, investors may add investments in cocoa, live cattle, or light, sweet crude oil to their portfolios to hedge their inflation or purchasing power risk.

To invest in **commodities** such as pork bellies, sugar, corn, and soybeans investors may open a commodity futures trading account or may purchase an Exchange Traded Note tied to the price of commodities. We will look at commodity futures contracts at the end of the next section.

Futures

The buyer of an options contract has the right to do something. On the other hand, a **futures contract** is a binding agreement between two parties that obligates the two sides to buy and sell something for a set price, with delivery occurring at a specified future date. In the world of commodities including corn, orange juice, and crude oil there is today's cash price—known as the spot price. And then, there is the futures price specifying what the commodity can be bought or sold for as of some future delivery date. Will the price of corn, orange juice or crude oil rise above or fall below that futures price by next December? That is why they open the markets for trading e day.

A grain farmer typically does not wait to harvest 1,000 acres of corn and soybeans in the fall and then see how much the cash or spot price might be at that point. With futures contracts the farmer can sell some corn and soybean futures to buyers who want to lock in a purchase price now for delivery, say, next November. The farmer, this way, can lock in a minimum price he'll receive for some of his corn and beans in case crop prices drop by the time he harvests them. And the buyers who need his corn and beans can lock in a maximum purchase price on what they need to buy in the near future.

Those who use futures to lock in purchase or sale prices related to their businesses are called hedgers. Those who use futures to bet on the near-term price movement of a commodity are called speculators. Common commodities traded include, corn, soybeans, crude oil, live cattle, sugar, and cocoa, to name just a few.

If a farmer is producing corn, and a cereal maker needs to buy corn, the farmer can sell some of his crop even before it's harvested, while the cereal maker can lock in a maximum price for corn set for delivery as of a certain month. In this case, the farmer producing the commodity is short, while the cereal producer is long in the futures contract.

Long positions profit when the price of the commodity rises, while short positions profit when the price of the commodity drops, just as they do with options and common stock. What the two sides are doing, then, is identifying their risk and betting that way. The cereal producer is hurt if the price of the commodities they need rises. Therefore, they bet that way and profit if their risk materializes. The farmer can't take the chance that all of his grain will be sold at depressed prices in the future; therefore, he sells some contracts now representing what could end up being the highest price for delivery the market sees for years. In other words, he'll be glad he sold the corn at $12 a bushel back then if it ends up being worth only $3.50 on the spot market by the time it's harvested.

Futures contracts are standardized by the exchange where they trade. That means that the quantity, the quality, and the delivery are all standard terms so that the prices of the commodities traded mean exactly the same thing to everyone in the market. For example, the quality specifications of each type of crude oil traded are standardized so that "light sweet crude" is the same no matter who produces it. As I write this, I see that the standard terms of coffee futures involve 37,500 pounds of coffee per contract with expiration months in March, May, July, September, and December. Corn futures contracts cover 5,000 bushels each, expressed as a price per-bushel with a minimum "tick size" of ¼ of 1 cent per bushel.

Most options contracts that are near- or in-the-money are closed out before expiration because the buyer of a call option that goes in the money, for example, doesn't want to come up with the cash to buy the stock at the strike price any more than the seller wants to go buy the stock and deliver it.

With futures, all buyers and sellers need to reverse/offset their contracts before expiration to avoid making or accepting delivery of grain, live cattle, or light sweet crude, etc. With futures both sides are obligated to perform the contract if they're holding at expiration. Of course, speculators and hedgers go through brokers, who remind their customers with open long or short positions to close them out before expiration, just as my broker-dealer does for everyone trading options. Even if a retail investor forgot to liquidate a contract to buy 400,000 pounds of live hogs, he would not see a semi-truck pull up to his front door the next day. Rather, he would receive a receipt good for 400,000 pounds of live hogs. Even the hedgers typically liquidate their futures contracts rather than taking delivery of corn, soybeans, etc.

These days the underlying instrument for futures contracts is not just the raw materials/commodities used to produce other products. Stock indexes, interest rates, currencies, and other financially based instruments are used to create **financial futures**. For example, rather than trading S&P 500 index options, a speculator could trade the S&P 500 futures contracts, e.g., the E-Mini S&P and the E-Mini NASDAQ-100. Or, he could speculate on interest rate movements or foreign currency values. There are even contracts for emissions credits, weather, and bandwith available.

As with all derivatives, futures are a "zero-sum game," meaning if one side makes $30,000 it's because the other side lost $30,000. The contracts are also sometimes called "wasting assets," along with options. That is somewhat different from common stock, where one investor can earn dividends over time and sell the stock to someone else, who might end up doing the same before passing it on to another investor. Also, futures give traders leverage, putting them at risk without having to put down much of their own money initially.

Remember that options, on the other hand, are paid in full. If you buy 3 ORCL Oct 40 calls @2, you must pay the full $600 upfront (3 times the $200 represented by the "@2").

Not so with futures. A futures contract is not something that you buy or sell, really. Rather, both sides agree to the daily margin settlement that will occur as the price of the commodity moves day by day. The futures exchange requires both parties to put up an initial amount of cash, called either margin or a good faith deposit—usually between 5 and 15% of the contract value. Then, since the futures price will change daily, the difference in the strike price and the daily futures price is settled daily also.

On the other hand, if you buy those ORCL Oct 40 calls for $2 a share, you don't lose anything right now if they start trading for, say, $1 a share. I mean, it stinks, but until the contract expires, it's just a "paper loss" when you're trading options. However, with futures the exchange will pull money out of one party's margin account and put it into the other's so that each party has the appropriate daily loss or profit. If the margin account goes below a certain value, a margin call is made and the account owner has to deposit more margin to keep the game going. This process of recalculating values daily is known as marking to market, just as it's called in a margin account for stocks and bonds.

When you buy an option, you can only lose what you pay. For example, no matter how far ORCL drops, you can only lose the $2-per-share premium. With a long futures position, however, you would continue to lose as the price of the commodity continues to drop.

As with options, the buyer would only pay the contract price—and the seller receive it—upon delivery. But, as with options, most futures contracts do not lead to delivery. Futures traders offset (reverse) their trades before settlement to avoid having to provide or accept delivery of the actual commodity itself. Maybe 1% of all contracts lead to delivery of the underlying commodity.

Forwards

A **forward** is like a futures contract in that it is a derivative that specifies a price for something for delivery at a specified future date. However, a forward is not traded on an exchange. Also, forward contracts are not standardized the way options and futures contracts are standardized by the exchanges on which they trade. On the options and futures exchanges, we find clearinghouses, which act as a buffer between every buyer and seller. I mean—how do you know for sure the other side can deliver 100,000 shares of ORCL or a million barrels of light sweet crude? You don't, but luckily the options and futures exchanges have all the buyers and sellers going through clearinghouses, which guarantee the performance of e contract, period.

So, forwards are side deals between two parties. How do you know the other side is good for the contract if there's no exchange enforcing margin requirements, settlement dates, and guaranteeing that all contracts are good?

That's the counterparty risk that forwards present to both sides of the contract. On a regulated exchange, options and futures traders do not have to worry about the financial strength of the other side of the contract. The advantage of trading in forwards is the flexibility they allow both sides of the contract—the expiration date, the size of the contract, the terms of the contract, etc., are up to the two parties as opposed to the standardized contracts available on the commodity futures and options exchanges. Some companies have a specific need for a type of derivative that may not be offered on the options or futures exchanges. If that is the case, they may want to structure a private derivative contract with another party called a "forward."

INVESTMENT VEHICE	FEATURES	RISKS	TAX IMPLICATIONS	LOW/MED/HIGH RISK
Common stock	Claim on earnings/dividends Voting rights Pre-emptive rights	Market Business Legislative	Dividends taxable Capital gains taxable	High

INVESTMENT VEHICE	FEATURES	RISKS	TAX IMPLICATIONS	LOW/MED/HIGH RISK
	Unlimited gain			
Preferred stock	Fixed-Income No voting rights No pre-emptive rights	Interest-rate risk Credit risk Reinvestment risk	Dividends taxable Capital gains taxable	Low-Med
ADRs	Common stock in foreign companies Purchased in US $s Traded on American markets	All risks of common stock PLUS, currency exchange risk	Dividends taxable Capital gains taxable Foreign Gov't could tax Investor receives credit for US taxes	High
REITs	Stock in operating real estate portfolio High dividend yields	All risks of common stock	Dividends are ordinary (not qualified) Capital gains taxable	High
Corporate Bonds	A loan to a corporation Receive interest-only, principal with last payment	Interest rate Credit Reinvestment Call Inflation	Interest taxable as ordinary income all three levels Capital gains taxable	Med

INVESTMENT VEHICE	FEATURES	RISKS	TAX IMPLICATIONS	LOW/MED/HIGH RISK
Municipal Bonds	A loan to a state, city, school district, park district, etc. Tax-exempt interest	Interest rate Credit Reinvestment Call Inflation Legislative	Interest exempt at federal and (maybe) state level Capital gains taxable	Low-Med
Treasuries	A loan to the US Government Guaranteed interest, principal	No credit risk All *other* risks to bondholders	Interest taxable at federal level Capital gains taxable all levels	Low
Zero Coupons	Bought at discount, mature at par No reinvestment risk	Interest Rate Credit Inflation Liquidity	Tax on annual accretion	Depends on issuer
Money Market Securities	Short-term debt securities High liquidity	Purchasing Power Risk/Inflation Risk	Taxable all levels (unless T-Bills or Muni)	Low
Mortgage-Backed Securities	Interests in a pool of mortgages Monthly income and principal	Prepayment Reinvestment Credit (not GNMA) Inflation	Taxable all levels	Low-Med

INVESTMENT VEHICE	FEATURES	RISKS	TAX IMPLICATIONS	LOW/MED/HIGH RISK
CMOs	Debt securities based on pools of mortgage-backed securities or mortgages	Complexity Illiquidity Interest Rate Reinvestment	Taxable at all levels	Med
Options	Derivatives based on stock, indexes, currencies, etc.	Capital risk	Gains/losses generally short-term	High
Non-qualified Variable Annuities	Insurance-and-Securities Product No limits on income or contributions	Risks to stock and bond investors, depending on subaccount choices	Tax-deferred earnings Earnings taxed as ordinary income No RMDs	Med-High depending on subaccount allocations
Fixed Annuities	Insurance Product No limits on income or contributions No RMDs	Purchasing Power Risk	Tax-deferred earnings Earnings taxed as ordinary income No RMDs	Low—obligation of insurance company
Variable Life Insurance	Cash Value and Death Benefit tied to subaccount performance Insurance-and-Securities Product	Risks to stock and bond investors depending on subaccount choices	Tax-deferred growth of cash value Death benefit not taxable to beneficiary	Med-High depending on subaccount choices
DPPs/Limited Partnerships	Tax Shelter	Depends on program	Tax Shelter if investor has	High

INVESTMENT VEHICE	FEATURES	RISKS	TAX IMPLICATIONS	LOW/MED/HIGH RISK
	Illiquid investments Net worth requirements	Legislative risk (tax code) Liquidity	passive income	
Unit Investment Trusts	Portfolio of preferred stock or bonds Non-managed Redeemable	Interest rate Credit Reinvestment Call Inflation	Distributions taxed as bond interest or preferred stock dividends	Medium-High
Exchange Traded Funds (typically)	Trade-able Non-Managed Purchased on Margin Sold Short Low Expenses	Depends on index	Tax-efficient	Depends on index
High-Yield/Junk Bonds	Credit quality of issuer in doubt High yields Capital Appreciation	All risks to bondholders Increased credit risk and volatility	Depends on issuer: corporate or municipal	Medium
Warrants	Right to buy issuer's stock at set price long-term Often attached to bond or preferred stock offering	Same risks as to holder of common stock Liquidity risk Time	Price-per-share added to cost basis when exercised to buy stock	High

Now What?

From this chapter the similarities and differences among common and preferred stock could provide a few exam questions. For example:

A true statement concerning preferred stock is that
   A. It is a fixed-income security, essentially the same as a corporate bond
   B. It is an equity security, with voting and preemptive rights
   C. It is both a fixed-income security and an equity security
   D. Its market price is tied to the market price of the issuer's common stock

EXPLANATION: as we saw in the chapter, preferred stock is unusual in that it is both a fixed-income security and an equity position. That right there is challenging for some folks, especially those who like things to fit into neat categories. In their minds, a security is either fixed-income or equity. And, in your industry, it is true that when folks say "fixed income," they typically mean bonds, just as they typically only mean common stock when they say they want to invest in "equities."

Oh well. Slowing down and thinking is what this test—and your job—is all about. Notice that part of Answer A is correct—preferred stock is a fixed-income security, but it is not just like a bond. A bond is a debt security whose interest has to be paid, while a preferred stock dividend has to be declared (or not) by the Board of Directors. Based on that, we can eliminate Choice A. Choice B is partly right—preferred stock is an equity security. However, it does not typically have the voting or preemptive rights enjoyed by the more junior common stock. Eliminate Choice B. Choice C looks tempting, but let's first see if we can prove Choice D to be wrong. What does the preferred stock's price have to do with the issuer's common stock? Nothing at all—not unless it happens to be convertible preferred stock, which is not the usual case. As a general rule, the two market prices are unrelated, so, yes, we can eliminate Answer Choice D, leaving us with the right answer

ANSWER: C

As always, that is just an example of what a test question could look like concerning common and preferred stock. The question would look different if presented like this:

The only accurate statement concerning preferred stock below is that:
   A. Preferred stock trades in sympathy with the issuer's common stock
   B. Preferred stock has a higher claim on the issuer's assets than either the common stock or subordinated debentures of that issuer
   C. Interest on preferred stock is typically paid semi-annually
   D. Convertible preferred stock is less interest-rate sensitive than either straight or cumulative preferred stock

EXPLANATION: your license exam is known to use some pretty fancy vocabulary such as "in sympathy" now and again. If you really don't know what it means, remember that you only have to find one true statement here. With three other answer choices, keep shopping and keep your cool. If you do know or can figure out what "in sympathy means," you know that Answer Choice A is saying exactly what Answer Choice D was saying in the previous question. And, either way we say it, it's incorrect—the issuer's preferred stock does not derive its market price from the common stock, as a general rule. Unless the question says we're looking at convertible preferred stock, there is no link between the market price of an issuer's preferred and common stock. So, we can eliminate Choice A. Answer Choice B starts out looking right but then takes a wrong turn by saying the claim is higher than that of a bondholder. That is false, so eliminate Choice B. Choice C is trying to sneak one past you. Is it paid semiannually, quarterly—wait, preferred stock doesn't receive interest at all! Preferred stock receives dividends as long as the Board declares them. Eliminate Answer C, and we're left with the only one that works,

ANSWER: D, convertible preferred stock is the exception, deriving its market value mostly from the price of the issuer's common stock. This makes interest rate moves less important to its market price.

What makes the Series 66 such a challenge is that there are so many ways it can cover any topic. And, this is just one of many topics in the chapter and on the exam outline. The trick is to learn as much detail as you can from the textbook and then take it to a higher level online with our Pass the 66 Online Practice Question Bank.

So, as always, it's time to do the online review exercises for this chapter. After a 20-minute minimum break, come back and take the chapter review quizzes. Focus on using what you know to eliminate three wrong answers to each question. After that, watch the training video lessons and move onto the next chapter in the textbook.

CHAPTER 3: Client Investment Recommendations & Strategies

Type of Client

Once you pass your exam and have your application accepted by the securities Administrator of your state, you can begin meeting with clients. Some of your clients will be human beings, and others will be businesses. Let's start with the **sole proprietor**, which is both a human being and a business.

Sole Proprietor

A handyman or a hair stylist typically pays for state and municipal licenses. Therefore, they might not want to also pay to set up a corporation or other business structure, which involves legal fees to attorneys and filing-and-renewal fees to the state. It might be tempting to just run the business as a sole proprietor. Unlike setting up a corporation or other business structure, setting up a sole proprietorship doesn't require much in terms of time and expense. The advantages of opening a business as a sole proprietorship include:

- Faster, easier, cheaper setup
- Easy tax preparation
- Income flows directly to the owner

The trouble with being in business as a sole proprietor is that the owner remains personally liable for the debts and lawsuits against the business. In other words, the owner and the business are the same

thing. If the sole proprietorship called Harry's Hot Dogs accidentally sells 1,000 tainted wieners that send sick people to the emergency room, Harry would have a hot mess on his hands. All the lawsuits would be filed against Harry personally.

Or, if Harry hits a slow patch, the creditors who used to spot him buns, hot dogs, and condiments are going to come after him personally for the unpaid bills. Even if he has insurance, once the insurance is exhausted, the angry parties move directly to Harry, not to a corporate structure that would have added a layer of defense. So, the disadvantages of owning a business as a sole proprietor include:

- Personal liability
- Harder to obtain loans or attract investment capital due to lower financial controls

Partnerships

Many business owners are renegades who don't play well with others. So they go into business for themselves and run everything as a sole proprietorship in which they control every aspect and answer to no one. We just looked at some pros and cons of that structure. Another approach is to take on partners. In a **partnership**, the income or net loss of the business flows through directly to the owners. The business entity itself is not taxed. The percentage of profits and losses flowing through to each of the owners is stated in the partnership agreement. Does the partnership create a separate entity that shields the owners from liabilities of the business? That depends on the type of partnership.

General Partnership

The main difference between general and limited partnerships involves liability. In a **general partnership** two or more persons own the business jointly and are subject to creditors and lawsuits personally, just like Harry of Harry's Hot Dogs. Unless otherwise stated in the agreement, the general partners control the business jointly, equally, with one vote each. Therefore, if three college friends want to open a restaurant and maintain 33.3% ownership each, a general partnership may be the way to go. However, all three are personally liable should someone get food poisoning at the restaurant, or trip over a loose piece of carpet, etc.

Either way, a general partnership is like a sole proprietorship with more than one owner. The owners agree to be in business together. They do not shield themselves personally from debts or liabilities of the business. But the income and expenses do flow through directly to the partners rather than being taxable to the business, and there are more people to split up the work load and hold each other accountable.

Limited Partnership

To form a **limited partnership**, there must be at least one **general partner** (GP), who has personal liability for debts and lawsuits associated with the business. But a limited partnership then has **limited partners** (LPs) who maintain **limited liability** status, meaning they can only lose what they invest into the business.

By "invest into the business," I mean the money they put in as well as any debts they personally guarantee. A debt that a limited partner signs his name to is called a **recourse note**, meaning that creditors have legal recourse to come after him for the amount he guaranteed personally. A **non-recourse note**, then, would mean that the creditors have no recourse to collect this debt out of the investor's personal assets beyond any collateral that might have been pledged.

Maybe a test question will ask what a limited partner's cost basis is equal to, with the right answer something like "it equals the capital he contributes initially plus the capital he agrees to contribute in the future."

To maintain the shield of protection limited partners must stay out of day-to-day management decisions. Nevertheless, the LPs do vote on the big issues of the partnership through **partnership democracy**. Partnership democracy is used to allow the LPs to have a voice on a limited number of items, such as:

- Dissolving the partnership
- Suing the GP for negligence, breach of fiduciary duty, and other major irritations
- Inspecting certain records

The LPs can get involved with the above without jeopardizing their limited liability status, but not much else.

The General Partner has a fiduciary relationship to the LPs, which means that the GP must put the LPs' needs first. In legal terms, the GP's fiduciary duty is "two-pronged," meaning he has a duty of loyalty and a duty of good faith. His duty of loyalty means he can't compete with the partnership. His duty of good faith means he must do whatever he can to run the business successfully and in accordance with the LPs' best interests. The GP can end up getting sued by the LPs if it becomes clear that he is not meeting his duty to the limited partners, through negligence or fraud.

Since the GP has unlimited liability, the general partner is often a corporation rather than a natural person (human being). The corporate structure, as we'll see, provides a layer of protection that would be lacking otherwise.

When the limited partnership is liquidated, the senior creditors are paid first, then the unsecured creditors. The next priority is the limited partners, with the general partner last in line.

The advantages of the limited partnership structure include:

- Flow-through of income and expenses directly to the partners
- Limited partners have limited liability

The disadvantages of the limited partnership structure include:

- General partner has unlimited liability
- Distribution of profits not as flexible as within an LLC

LLC (Limited Liability Company)

A **limited liability company** (LLC) is a type of business in which the owners are called "members" and the ones who also manage the business are called "managing members." In a minute, we will see that the S-corp. is limited to 100 shareholders, while the LLC has no limit on the number of members, who can be individuals, corporations, or even other LLCs.

The owners of an LLC are protected from the debts of and lawsuits against the company, including being sued for their own negligence in operating the business.

Advantages of setting up an LLC include:

- Limited liability
- More flexible profit distributions
- No minutes required
- Avoids double taxation of income

To be structured as an LLC rather than a corporation, the LLC needs to avoid two of four corporate attributes. That means it must avoid two of the following characteristics associated with corporations:

- Perpetual life
- Centralized management
- Limited liability
- Freely transferable assets

It's almost impossible to avoid the centralized management, since there must be managing members of the LLC. It's also tough to avoid limited liability as a limited liability company. So, how do they avoid the perpetual life and freely transferable assets associated with corporations? Unlike a corporation, an LLC has a limited life. For example, when the LLC is set up, perhaps it has a triggering event after which the business is dissolved—when the last townhouse is sold, or when any of the managing members dies, maybe. Or, there could be a fixed date upon which a private investment LLC dissolves, returning cash to the members.

Regarding the "freely transferable assets," the members agree they won't sell their interests except in accordance with a strict set of rules. For example, if a member wants to sell his interest to a stranger, the other members might have the right to buy the interest first to prevent that from happening. Such an agreement is often referred to as a "right of first refusal" clause.

The disadvantages of setting up an LLC include:

- Limited life
- Harder to attract financing
- More complexity than sole proprietorship

To set up a limited liability company, the business files its articles of organization with the Secretary of State (or similar office in the state) and pays the filing fees. The owners also typically draft and sign an **operating agreement**. Similar to corporate bylaws or partnership agreements, these operating agreements spell out important points about ownership, responsibilities, and profit distributions.

Corporations

The limited liability company provides protection to the owners against claims on their personal assets. Corporations do the same, although they require more work in terms of having meetings of shareholders and the board of directors and keeping the minutes of those meetings.

S-Corporations

The **S-Corporation (S-corp.)** offers protection against debts and lawsuits compared to running the business as a sole proprietor. The income and expenses pass directly to the owners, so it's like a partnership or limited liability company in that sense. It avoids being taxed as a business entity, even as it provides that separate legal structure known as a corporation for the protection of the owners' personal assets. The advantages of using the S-corporation structure include:

- No corporate tax
- Liability protection
- Write-offs

The disadvantages to the S-corp. include:

- One class of stock
- 100 shareholders maximum
- Corporate meetings and minutes required

If the business is hoping to attract venture capital, the VC firms will not like the S-corporation structure with its direct flow-through of income and expenses and the limit of 100 shareholders. Also, all stock has equal voting rights and claims on profits, tying the hands of the financiers. And, even if it is a good idea, many business owners hate having to hold an annual board of directors meeting and an annual shareholders meeting, especially if shareholders and board members are required to travel.

Oh well. If someone wants to create a business structure that offers protection against debts and lawsuits and avoids the double taxation of income, the S-corp. is an attractive option. To start an S-corp., the business files its articles of incorporation with the Secretary of State's office, usually by going through an attorney.

More details on S-corps include:

- The corporation can have no more than 100 shareholders with a husband and wife counting as one shareholder.
- Shareholders can be individuals, estates, and certain trusts.
- Shareholders must be American residents.
- The S-corp. must be a domestic company in any state.

C-Corporations

The **C-corporation (C-Corp.)** is the traditional corporate structure. When we were talking about common stock in General Electric, Microsoft, Oracle, etc., we were talking about C-corporations. This means that Microsoft is a separate legal entity that is taxed as a corporation. The profits do not flow directly through to shareholders. The corporation gets taxed on all those billions of dollars it makes year after year. Then, when the shareholders receive dividends on the stock, they are also taxed on that income. C-corporations also must hold annual shareholder and board of director meetings, and keep the minutes. Unlike S-corporations, there is no limit to the number of shareholders that may be authorized by the corporate charter.

TYPE	ADVANTAGES	DISADVANTAGES	TAXATION	PERSONAL LIABILITY
Sole proprietor	Fast, cheap setup No meetings	Personal liability	Personal income	Yes
General partnership	Flow-through of income, expenses	Personal liability	Flow-through to owners	Yes
Limited partnership	Flow-through of income, expenses	Must have one general partner, with unlimited liability	Flow-through to owners	Not for limited partners
LLC	Flow-through of income, expenses	Not good for attracting VC	Flow-through to owners	No, not even for negligence while running business

TYPE	ADVANTAGES	DISADVANTAGES	TAXATION	PERSONAL LIABILITY
S-corp.	Flow-through of income, expenses	Annual meetings Not good for attracting VC one class of stock	Flow-through to owners	No
C-corp.	Attracting capital	Double taxation of income Annual meetings	Taxed as business entity	No, not even for negligence while running business

Client Profile

A financial planner or a securities agent must gather key financial information about an investor before making investment recommendations:

- Income sources
- Current expenditures
- Discretionary income
- Assets
- Tax bracket

To determine how much the client can afford to invest, the investment professional looks at his income statement or statement of cash flow. A personal cash flow statement might look like this:

Monthly Income	
Salary	$7,000
Investment Income	$1,000
Other Income	$500
Total Monthly Income	$8,500

Monthly Expenditures	
Taxes	$2,000
Mortgage Payment	$2,000

Living Expenses	$2,000
Insurance Premiums	$300
Loan Payments	$200
Travel/Entertainment	$300
Other Expenses	$200
Total Monthly Expenses	$7,000
Monthly Capital for Investing	$1,500

The client has **discretionary income** or excess **cash flow** of $1,500. If he has a long time horizon of, say, 10+ years, the money could go into stock mutual funds investing for growth. If he has a lower tolerance for wide fluctuations of yearly performance, he might choose growth & income, equity income, or balanced funds. And, if his time horizon is shorter, he might stay out of the stock market entirely and invest, instead, in short- or intermediate-term bond funds.

Taxes are always a factor, too. If the client is in a high marginal tax bracket, we may want to recommend municipal bonds, which generally pay interest that is tax-exempt at the federal level. A high-tax-bracket client probably doesn't want to do much short-term trading, either, since any gain taken within a year is taxed at the short-term capital gains rate (which equals his marginal tax rate). He also might want to buy stocks that pay qualified dividends rather than REITs or royalty trusts, which will force him to pay his ordinary/marginal rate on the dividends.

Or, maybe he could put the REITs and royalty trusts into a retirement plan that allows the dividends to grow tax-deferred until withdrawn, when he is in a lower tax bracket. In other words, different clients require different recommendations and strategies.

Assets represent what someone owns, while liabilities represent what he owes. The difference between what someone owns and what he owes is his financial **net worth**. A client's assets include the value of his home, automobiles, personal possessions, investments, savings, and checking accounts. Liabilities include mortgages and other loan balances, credit-card balances, and, perhaps, debit balances in margin accounts.

A personal balance sheet might look like this:

Assets	
House	$400,000
Automobiles	$30,000
Personal possessions	$15,000
Stocks and Bonds	$100,000

Keogh Plan	$80,000
IRA	$20,000
Checking	$5,000
Savings Account	$5,000
Money Market	$5,000
Total Assets	$660,000

Liabilities	
Mortgage	$250,000
Auto Loans	$10,000
Credit Card Balances	$15,000
Total Liabilities	$275,000
Net Worth	$385,000

When we looked at corporate balance sheets in Chapter 1, we mentioned that analysts look only at a company's quick assets rather than including the hard-to-liquidate assets such as plant and equipment in some of their calculations. Similarly, since some assets are difficult to liquidate, we might exclude those items to calculate **liquid net worth**. Illiquid assets include real estate and private funds.

If a client has high total net worth but low liquid net worth, an investment adviser or securities agent might steer the client toward more liquid investments, like short-term debt versus a long-term zero coupon bond, or heavily traded stocks and bonds as opposed to something trading on the Non-Nasdaq OTC market.

By the way, if an investor takes $5,000 out of her savings account and pays down her mortgage or credit card debt by $5,000—how much does that increase her net worth?

Not at all. If he removes a $5,000 asset to remove a $5,000 liability, his net worth is unchanged. Net worth rises when asset values rise, and when assets provide income payments in the form of rent, interest, and dividends.

Even if the investor comes home tonight excited about a $10,000 raise, that is an item for the cash flow statement. If it ends up in a savings account, then it becomes an asset increasing financial net worth. On the other hand, if that increased income is spent on season tickets for a sports team or symphony, it was just money in and money out.

While gathering information on a client's assets, we are also uncovering his current securities holdings. Many investors have a large percentage of their portfolio tied up in one company's stock—their employer's. If a client has too much money concentrated in just one stock, an agent might advise him to sell some of that holding to diversify. Other clients will already be diversified, which is just as important to determine before recommending investments. If they already hold 20 large-cap stocks, we probably don't want to recommend that they put the rest of their discretionary income into Dow Jones Index funds, which is redundant.

Suitability

So, now that an agent or investment adviser representative has opened an account for a client, it is time to help her allocate her money to various investment vehicles. First, what are her **investment objectives**? Investment objectives include: capital preservation, income, growth & income, growth, and speculation. If the individual is in her 30s and setting up a retirement account, she probably needs growth to build up her financial net worth before reaching retirement age. If she's already in retirement, she probably needs income. If she's in her 50's and wants to retire in 10-12 years, she might be looking for both **growth & income,** which some firms consider one objective. An investment in a mutual fund by that name might be suitable, as might investments in blue chip or large-cap value stocks.

Some firms separate growth from **aggressive growth** as an investment objective. Some firms view growth as one objective that investors pursue with varying degrees of aggressiveness. Either way, aggressive growth investments include international funds, sector funds, and emerging market funds. For **speculation,** there are options and futures, and most investors should limit their exposure to these derivatives to a small % of their portfolio.

If they are saving for retirement, that generally means investors need **capital appreciation**. On the other hand, some investors already have capital and want to preserve it. This is called **capital preservation**. Investors can buy U.S. Treasury securities all on their own, without commissions. But, many chose instead to invest in U.S. Treasury mutual funds. Even though the fund is not guaranteed, the securities the fund owns are. So, it is an investment on the safer side of things, but while Treasury securities are guaranteed against default, a mutual fund is just a mutual fund.

Knowing the investor's objective is important, but that objective must be balanced with the investor's **time horizon**. In general, the longer the time horizon the more volatility the investor can withstand. If he has a three-year time horizon, he needs to stay almost completely out of the stock market and invest instead in high-quality bonds with short terms to maturity. If he's in for the long haul, on the other hand, who cares what happens this year? It's what happens over a 20- or 30-year period that matters.

With dividends reinvested, the S&P 500 has historically gained about 10% annually on average, which means the investment would double approximately every 7 years. Sure, the index can drop 30% one year and 20% the next, but we're not keeping score each year. It's where we go over the long haul that counts. A good way to see the real-world application of risk as it relates to time horizon is to pull out the prospectus for a growth fund and see if you can spot any two- or three-year periods where the bar charts are pointing the wrong way. Then compare those horrible short-term periods to the 10-year return, which is probably decent no matter which growth fund you're looking at. That's why the prospectus will remind folks that they "may lose money by investing in the fund" and that "the likelihood of loss is greater the shorter the holding period." See how important "time horizon" is?

Younger investors saving for retirement have a long time horizon, so they can withstand more ups and downs along the road. On the other hand, if the investor is 69 years old, he probably needs some income and not so much volatility. So the farther from retirement she is, the more likely your investor will be buying stock. The closer she gets to retirement, the less stock she needs and the more bonds/income investments she should be buying.

Many mutual fund companies take all the work out of retirement planning for investors by offering **target funds**. Here, the investor picks a mutual fund with a target date close to her own retirement date. If she's currently in her mid-40s, maybe she picks the Target 2040 Fund. If she's in her mid-60s, maybe it's the Target 2020 Fund. For the Target 2040, the fund is invested more in the stock market and less in the bond market than the Target 2020 fund. The fund automatically changes the allocation from mostly stock to mostly bonds as we get closer and closer to the target date. The same thing happens in an age-based portfolio used in a 529 Plan. When the child is a baby, the allocation is probably 90% growth, 10% fixed-income. As the child gets older, the portfolio gets more conservative, just as many readers have done over the years. Other names for target funds include **life-cycle funds** and **age-based portfolios.**

An investor might have the primary objective of growth or even aggressive growth. He might also have a time horizon of 10+ years. However, if he doesn't have the **risk tolerance** required of the stock market, his agent should keep him out of stocks. Remember that risk tolerance involves not only the financial resources, but also the psychological ability to sustain wide fluctuations in market value, as well as an occasional loss of principal.

The terms risk-averse, conservative, and low risk tolerance all mean the same thing—these investors cannot tolerate big market drops. They invest in fixed annuities, U.S. Treasuries, and investment-grade bonds. To invest in sector funds or emerging market funds the investor needs a high risk tolerance. Moderate risk tolerance would match up with balanced funds, equity income funds, and conservative bond funds.

Let's put the three factors together: investment objectives, time horizon, and risk tolerance. If we know that the investor in the suitability question seeks growth, we then need to know his time horizon and risk tolerance. If he's a 32-year-old in an IRA account, his time horizon is long-term. Unless he can't sleep at night knowing the account balance fluctuates, we would almost have to recommend growth funds. His risk tolerance would tell us whether to use small-cap, mid-cap, or large-cap growth funds—the higher the risk tolerance the smaller the "cap." Or, maybe we get even more aggressive with emerging market and sector funds.

If the investor is 60 years old and living on a defined benefit pension income, she might need to invest in common stock to protect her purchasing power. If so, her time horizon is long, but her risk tolerance is probably only moderate or moderate-low. So, we'd probably find a conservative stock fund—maybe a growth & income, equity income, or large-cap value fund.

If an investor seeks income primarily, we need to know her time horizon and risk tolerance. We don't buy bonds that mature beyond her anticipated holding period. If she has a 10-year time horizon, we need bonds that mature in 10 years or sooner. Buying 7-year bonds for someone with a 10-year holding period is not a problem, while going the other way is.

The investor's risk tolerance determines if we can maximize her income with high-yield bonds, or if we should be smart and buy investment-grade bond funds instead. If she needs tax-exempt income, we put some of her money into municipal bond funds. For capital preservation nothing beats U.S. Treasury or GNMA securities. Money market mutual funds are safe—though not guaranteed by the US Government or anyone else—but they pay low yields. Money market mutual funds are for people who want to not only preserve capital but also make frequent withdrawals from the account.

See, even though money is safer in a 30-year Treasury bond than in a money market mutual fund, the big difference is that the market price of a T-Bond fluctuates (rates up, price down), while the money market mutual fund stays at $1 per-share.

So if **liquidity** is a major concern, the money market mutual fund is better than T-Bonds, T-Notes, and even T-Bills, all of which have to be sold at whatever price. With the money market mutual fund investors can write checks, and the fund company will redeem the right number of shares to cover it.

Total liquidity. Then again, that total liquidity comes at a price. While there are no ongoing fees to hold Treasury Notes (and no commissions to buy them directly from the U.S. Treasury), money market mutual funds usually have annual expenses of about 75 basis points.

The questionnaire that the client fills out when opening an account with your firm will try to gauge what is more important—going for large returns or maintaining a stable principal? Earning a high level of income or making sure he gets his money back from the investment? Does he need to withdraw a large portion of his portfolio at a moment's notice? If so, put that portion in money market securities and short-term bonds.

Client Recommendations

To work with some of the preceding information let's look at 10 different case studies and see what we would recommend for each investor. As in the real world of investing, none of this is scientific. But, if we follow basic industry guidelines, we can match the questions on your exam closely enough to get you prepared.

Our first investor is a divorced 71-year-old man who recently sold a small landscaping business for $300,000 after capital gains taxes. Although he loved to work 12-hour days for decades, those days are behind him now. This customer does not trust the stock market and also remembers that his father lost a bunch of money in bonds back in the late '70s. This $300,000 is the money your customer plans to live on as a supplement to social security. His house has a mortgage balance of $25,000 and his living expenses are reasonable, although he will need a new automobile in the next few years and both a roof replacement and a new water heater for his 30-year-old house.

- INVESTMENT OBJECTIVES: capital preservation, income
- TIME HORIZON/LIQUIDITY: long-term, high liquidity needs
- RISK TOLERANCE: low

This investor is clearly not interested in risking a loss of his investment principal. If you make aggressive recommendations to him, it's not just a bad idea, but also a potential arbitration or civil court proceeding.

If capital preservation is the main objective, your recommendation has to address that first and foremost. Anything that conflicts with that goal is to be rejected. U.S. Treasury securities provide capital preservation, so we'll either buy them directly or through a mutual fund. Easy enough.

His next objective is income. Do U.S. Treasury securities provide income? Yes. Are they liquid? Yes, but if he anticipates frequent withdrawals from the account, we'd have to avoid long-term T-Bonds and stick to the more liquid 2-year U.S. Treasury Notes or even U.S. Treasury Bills, which have maturities of just a few weeks. Depending on the four answer choices in the suitability question, we might even end up choosing a money market mutual fund here. Why not? That's a safe place to park his money, it does provide income, and it is completely liquid.

What we can eliminate for this investor: equity funds, high-yield bond funds, municipal bond funds, and long-term bond funds. The municipal bond funds aren't risky, but if we see nothing about the investor's needs for tax-exempt income, we can't recommend them.

What we might recommend for this investor: T-Bills, short-term T-Notes, investment-grade bonds/bond funds with shorter maturities, money market mutual funds.

Our next investor is a 53-year-old school teacher who got a little too enthusiastic running half-marathons in her 40s and now lacks the energy to teach on her feet all day. She does not want to start taking withdrawals from her 403(b) account before age 59 but is ready to switch to part-time teaching now or perhaps even an administrative support position for the next 5–7 years, both of which would pay half or less of her current salary.

- INVESTMENT OBJECTIVES: income, capital preservation
- TIME HORIZON/LIQUIDITY: 5–7 years, moderate liquidity
- RISK TOLERANCE: moderate

This investor needs income, so I'm already thinking of bonds or bond mutual funds. Preferred stock might work, too, but my bias is with the bonds and bond funds. Remember that bond interest has to be paid while preferred stock dividends are paid if the board of directors declares them out of profits/net income. The investor's secondary objective is capital preservation, so I don't like junk bonds. I also don't see "capital appreciation" or growth as an objective, so why bring up stocks here? All we really have to do for this investor is recommend investment-grade bonds or bond funds that match her 5–7-year time horizon. So, if I see an intermediate-term investment-grade bond fund as an answer choice, I like that one. Right?

What we can eliminate for this investor: growth stock and growth stock funds, high-yield bonds, money market mutual funds (yields are too low given her moderate liquidity needs).

What we might recommend for this investor: intermediate-term investment-grade bonds and bond funds. A balanced fund would also work. Most balanced funds invest as if the investors are all conservative and in need of income, but they also invest a big % in the stock market. I don't see where this investor is telling us she needs to be in equities at all. Remember—it's her money. If she's happy in the bond market, and you're earning commissions or advisory fees, why stick your neck out? Make your case, but meeting the client's needs sometimes means doing what she wants to do regardless of what you would like her to do. Few parents can get their kids to do what they would like them to do—why would we expect adults we barely know to be totally compliant with our wishes?

Our third investor is the mother of our second investor, and is also a school teacher. Only this investor is a retired teacher. Her teacher's pension allows her to pay bills, but she also finds herself having to do without more often than she would like. Age 73, she remembers the rampant inflation of the 1970s and is afraid that her pension checks might not keep up with the price of groceries, gas, electric, clothing, etc.

- INVESTMENT OBJECTIVES: purchasing power protection
- TIME HORIZON/LIQUIDITY: long-term, moderate liquidity needs
- RISK TOLERANCE: moderate

Growth, capital appreciation, and purchasing power protection all mean the same thing, and they all point to the stock market. Don't all retirees need income investments? Not if they're already receiving a fixed income. A teacher's pension is a fixed income. And, like most fixed annuities, it may or may not keep up with the rising cost of living. So, we need to be in the stock market. And many of the stocks we like here are going to end up paying dividends. But, that is not necessarily what we're after. I mean, it's a good sign that a company can pay a dividend—means they earn regular profits. But, what we need here is growth or capital appreciation. And, we need to get it without getting too aggressive.

In other words, this is an easy recommendation. We want a diversified, professionally managed portfolio of large-cap stocks. Maybe the right answer choice will be something like "50% domestic large-cap stock fund, 50% international large-cap stock fund." That seems aggressive, but with her pension providing the fixed-income piece, this sort of allocation will address her purchasing power concerns without getting too crazy.

What we can eliminate for this investor: small cap funds, aggressive growth investments in general, bonds and bond funds, money market mutual funds.

What we might recommend for this investor: large cap growth stock or funds, blue chip stock or funds.

Our fourth investor is a 64-year-old man who retired last year with a modest pension benefit and a small Traditional IRA account that he does not want to touch until he's required to—at age 70½. This investor recently sold a five-bedroom house in an affluent neighborhood and bought a relatively inexpensive condominium near the shopping, restaurants, and theater district of the college town in which he was born and raised. He has been drawing down the proceeds of the sale (even after the purchase of the condo) and now has approximately $400,000 left to invest with you.

This investor is in excellent physical shape and plans to spend the next several years hiking the Appalachian Trail, kayaking the Boundary Waters, snorkeling in Costa Rica, etc. Since he has no plans to take a part-time job, the investor needs income to fund the travel he plans to do over the next several years. He does not need to make withdrawals of principal from this account, but he does plan to spend every dollar of income that he earns from whatever investments you and he choose. And, he knows that his living expenses will likely rise over time and he, therefore, needs his principal to keep up with the rising cost of living.

- INVESTMENT OBJECTIVES: high income, capital appreciation
- TIME HORIZON/LIQUIDITY: long-term, low liquidity needs
- RISK TOLERANCE: moderate-high

If this investor wants high income, we have to start in the bond market. Since his risk tolerance and time horizon are appropriate, we might recommend a high-yield bond fund. Chances are we don't want to pick individual "junk" or "high-yield" bonds, since each individual issue is somewhat susceptible to default; however, a well-managed and well-diversified mutual fund with a proven track record should be able to maximize the portfolio's income and minimize the rate of default. If the bonds mature at par, or at least rise in market value as the issuer's financial health improves, there will be capital appreciation.

Or, the exam question might give an allocation like this: 50% high-yield bonds, 50% stocks. That would work for me. Or, even 25% high-yield bonds, 25% investment-grade bonds, 50% stocks. If the best answer choice appeared to be "REITs," I could also live with that—they are known for high income and, as stocks, they do offer capital appreciation. However, that makes me nervous since REITs pay dividends, meaning the company has to make a profit to pay them. Bond interest, on the other hand, is a legal obligation that has to be paid just like your mortgage and credit card bills have to be paid.

Our fifth investor has a 13-year-old daughter who is an excellent student dreaming of one day attending Dartmouth, Yale, or Duke. This investor has a 529 Plan opened for her daughter's education, but so far only $10,000 has gone into the account, with the investments currently worth only $7,255.43 after some bad market years and the regular expenses of the plan. She knows she needs to build up the balance of the account but would be more comfortable reinvesting regular income checks from her investments as opposed to waiting for some promise of "capital appreciation" entirely. She has some confidence in the stock and bond markets. She also knows they are both unpredictable and should, therefore, never be used as a reserve or spending account.

- INVESTMENT OBJECTIVES: capital appreciation/growth, income
- TIME HORIZON/LIQUIDITY: 5–10 years, low liquidity needs
- RISK TOLERANCE: moderate

Since capital appreciation is the primary objective, we have to look at stocks or equity mutual funds for this investor. But, since she also has a secondary objective of income, we don't buy pure growth funds; we buy "growth & income" funds. Or, maybe the answer is something like "70% stocks, 30% bonds." A large-cap value fund is appropriate, also. In fact, there are many potential answer choices that could work for this investor—just make sure you put the capital appreciation first, and the income second.

What we can eliminate for this investor: bonds and bond funds, money market mutual funds.

What we might recommend for this investor: growth & income funds, stock index funds, blue chip equity funds. Equity income and balanced funds are pretty close as recommendations, but those funds would put income first, while a growth & income fund, believe it or not, puts growth first. An answer choice of "60% stock, 40% bonds" would also work. Again, there are many possible answers to an investor like this one. As always, weed out the answer choices that don't work first.

Our sixth investor is 59 years old and wants to retire at age 70. His Traditional IRA account is not well-funded and has not achieved much capital appreciation over the years. In fact, your team revealed that over the 30 years the account has been open, his contributions have equaled $50,000, with the account currently worth only $44,000. In other words, he has gotten a tax *deduction* on the contributions, but, so far, no tax *deferral.*

Oh well, customers will have a litany of complaints about their investment experience so far, but hindsight is 20/20. What matters now is the future. If the investor wants to retire in 10 years, with his account currently worth just $44,000, how can you help him? Does he have any real estate, annuities, or savings bonds to enhance his "net worth"? Unfortunately, no. Beyond a half dozen highly collectible electric guitars, the sum total of his "nest egg" is the $44,000 sitting in an IRA account. And, he has been seriously considering just taking out that money, buying a Harley, and touring the country until he runs out of gas, money, and gumption.

- INVESTMENT OBJECTIVES: capital appreciation/growth
- TIME HORIZON/LIQUIDITY: 10+ years, low liquidity needs
- RISK TOLERANCE: moderate

Before we worry about the investment vehicle first we need to convince this investor of the dire need to make his maximum IRA contribution each year until the IRS says he can't do it—which is only about 10 years away. Currently, he can contribute $6,500 a year as long as he has at least that much earned income. That number will likely rise a bit over the next 10 years, and your investment team needs to run some future value calculations to see how that amount of contributions plus a reasonable amount of growth can get him to an account large enough to help him in retirement. Frankly, though, I have my doubts—$44,000?

Anyway, once we get him on a regular monthly direct-deposit plan for his Traditional IRA account, we need to pick investment options. It seems clear that this investor will be in an equity fund, or a mix of equity funds. Also, these equity funds will be neither too aggressive nor too conservative for him. If I see an answer choice like "Mid-Cap Growth" or "Large Cap Growth," I'm tempted to choose it. An answer choice like "S&P 500 Index Fund" would also not be wrong. Basically, this guy is just a growth investor who doesn't want to get crazy chasing overvalued and overhyped stocks. Choosing a conservative stock fund makes me uneasy, too, since his account balance is going to be useless in retirement if it doesn't grow significantly through capital appreciation and regular contributions.

If the investor had a fixed annuity or a pension income to supplement this account, then we could be more aggressive with the stock picks. But, since we aren't finding any of that, we're in a tough spot. It's kind of like when you're late for an appointment: do you decide to speed or play it safe? If you speed and get by with it, you win. However, if you get caught speeding, you not only miss your goal of making the appointment, but also lose a bunch of money. Could you face this investor after talking him into some international aggressive growth fund that loses 70% of its value?

Me, neither. If the answer choices include mutual funds, we want growth funds that are neither too aggressive nor too conservative. If the choices are asset allocations, we might go with 80% stock, 20% bonds.

What we can eliminate for this investor: bonds and bond funds, money market mutual funds, aggressive growth investments (emerging markets, sector funds, etc.) small cap growth funds, conservative stock funds, balanced funds, equity income funds.

What we might recommend for this investor: large cap growth fund, blue chip equity fund, stock market index fund.

Our seventh investor is a 48-year-old woman who works in marketing for a successful mid-sized manufacturing company. Like most people her age, she has had to save for retirement mostly on her own. The company where she works offers a 401(k) plan, but they only match up to 5% of her salary, and her salary is only $53,000. Retirement seems a long way off, but she has a vague idea that she'd like to retire before she's 70. Her 401(k) plan balance is currently $127,000. She feels she cannot retire on less than $500,000, even if she makes a capital gain when selling her house and downsizing someday.

- INVESTMENT OBJECTIVES: capital appreciation/growth
- TIME HORIZON/LIQUIDITY: 20+ years, low liquidity needs
- RISK TOLERANCE: high

Again, even before we pick the investment vehicles, this investor should understand that regardless of how stingy her employer is her 401(k) account will allow her to contribute more than three times what she could contribute to a Traditional IRA account. Now, while she could definitely maximize her 401(k) contributions and also maximize her Traditional IRA with tax-deductible contributions, I don't see that she has that much money to sock away for retirement. She needs to make a reasonable contribution into her 401(k) account—as much as she can afford to.

As far as where to put those contributions, this investor will be in stocks or stock/equity mutual funds. This time, however, we want more aggressive investments. Small cap growth stocks or funds would be an ideal choice. Other correct recommendations might include sector funds, international funds, and global funds. Most stock index funds would also work—S&P Mid-Cap 400 or the Russell 2000, for example, would both be good answer choices.

What we can eliminate for this investor: bonds and bond funds, money market mutual funds, conservative stock funds, balanced funds, equity income funds.

What we might recommend for this investor: small cap growth stock/funds, stock index funds, sector funds, international funds.

Our eighth investor makes a lot of money, and has a lot of money. Then again, what's "a lot of money"? To me, $3 million of investable assets ought to do it, but for this investor there is, apparently, never enough. Since his late 20s he has been making at least six figures, and since his late 30s the thought of making a mere six figures has given him the willies. Then again, while his average income over any 10-year period has been pretty good, there always seem to be those 3- and even 5-year periods where the income drops much more than he admits to himself or his drinking buddies.

This investor is 57 years old and is not interested so much in retiring as in knowing that he could retire if he wants to. He has $1.5 million to invest with you. He has a small mortgage balance, two vacation properties, and approximately $100,000 in checking and savings that he is not interested in investing with you. His retirement accounts total about $900,000, and he plans to keep maximizing the SIMPLE-IRA he participates in as a salesman for a small software company. His father lived to age 93 and his grandfather to age 91. He does not plan to slow down or retire for at least 10 years.

- INVESTMENT OBJECTIVES: retirement income
- TIME HORIZON/LIQUIDITY: long-term, low liquidity needs
- RISK TOLERANCE: low

This investor seems like a prime candidate for a fixed annuity. If he already has close to $1 million in his retirement accounts, and plans to keep funding them a while, why not put $1.5 million into a fixed annuity that promises to pay a minimum amount each month once he throws the switch, no matter how long he lives? He's afraid that he never has enough money, and his father and grandfather lived long lives—I'd say he needs the annuity to assure he won't completely run out of money no matter how long he himself manages to live. If he were going to retire now, we'd choose an immediate annuity. Since he won't retire for at least 10 years, a deferred annuity works; he will not be hit with a surrender charge since he won't need to touch the money and there will also be no tax penalties that way.

If we saw statements about a fear of losing purchasing power/inflation, we might choose a variable annuity instead. That way, he could put some money in the stock market subaccounts and the rest in safer subaccounts, maybe. But with this investor's up-and-down income coupled with his fear of running out of money and his father's and grandfather's longevity, I think a question presenting this set of facts is crying out for a fixed annuity. Just make sure he keeps maximizing his other retirement options, and that he really doesn't need to touch the money for a while, and you can go ahead and recommend a deferred fixed or deferred indexed annuity. Knowing he'll get a minimum payment each month for the rest of his life will buy this investor a lot of sleep.

What we can eliminate for this investor: just about everything. I don't see a big need for current income or a huge need for capital appreciation/growth. He isn't complaining about high taxes, so we don't need to look at municipal bond funds or direct participation programs.

What we might recommend for this investor: fixed annuity or equity indexed annuity from an insurance company with a high claims-paying ability (AM Best Rating).

Investor Number Nine is a 75-year-old widow with a financial net worth of $5 million. Her income sources include rental income from a few real estate LLC interests she inherited from her husband, plus the IRA account now worth $1.2 million after she inherited and combined her husband's IRA with her own. She takes the required minimum distribution from the IRA each year, but that falls far short of funding her rather expensive lifestyle. Because she likes to shop, eat out, attend the theater, and decorate her townhouse, this investor needs income. However, since her annual income is close to $1 million, she ends up losing over 1/3 of that to the federal government and close to 5% to her state government. This investor is slightly concerned about a loss of purchasing power, though receiving income from her investments is clearly the main objective.

- INVESTMENT OBJECTIVES: tax-exempt income, purchasing power protection
- TIME HORIZON/LIQUIDITY: intermediate-to-long-term, low liquidity needs
- RISK TOLERANCE: low

Since she needs income that is tax-exempt, we will recommend municipal bonds. We can either buy them a la carte or as a packaged set. If she's truly in a high-tax state, there may be an open- or closed-end fund designed for residents of that state. For example, if she lives in Maryland, there will be municipal bond funds for residents of that state. The income dividends they generate would, therefore, be exempt from both federal and state income taxes for this investor. Now, to deal with her concern over inflation/loss of purchasing power, we can put a small percentage of her account into a conservative equity fund, possibly a low-cost S&P 500 Index fund.

What we can eliminate for this investor: aggressive investments, a large concentration in growth stocks/growth funds, taxable bonds (corporate or U.S. Treasury).

What we might recommend for this investor: municipal bonds primarily issued inside her state of residence or municipal bond funds designed for investors residing in her state.

Our tenth and final investor, a widow, has an annual income of $95,000, her mortgage is paid off, and she does not like to shop or eat out. She is 68 years old and lives comfortably on bond interest and dividend checks from a handful of stocks her husband picked decades ago. She works part-time, earning approximately $10,000 a year. She would like to continue to fund a tax-deferred account whose balance can pass directly to her only granddaughter upon her death.

- INVESTMENT OBJECTIVES: tax-deferral, estate planning
- TIME HORIZON/LIQUIDITY: long-term, low liquidity needs
- RISK TOLERANCE: moderate to high

It might seem strange to put her risk tolerance at "moderate to high," but why not?

She is already living comfortably on her investment income. She just wants to keep putting some money away that will grow tax-deferred for a rainy day, and whatever she doesn't spend in her lifetime will pass to her granddaughter. Stock funds within a Roth IRA are the answer here, most likely. The investor has earned income, enough to maximize her annual Roth IRA contribution. In a few years, she would have to stop putting money into a Traditional IRA, which is, again, why we're looking for a Roth IRA. The next-best answer would likely be an annuity. As with a Roth, she never has to take the money out, and can name the granddaughter the beneficiary of the account. Since the investor doesn't need to live on the Roth IRA, I don't mind the fact that if it's a new account, she needs to wait 5 years to make any withdrawals. As long as she doesn't need to touch the money for a bit longer, I can even live with the surrender period on a deferred annuity.

What we can eliminate for this investor: income investments, since she already has bond interest and cash dividends a-plenty. High-risk equities can be eliminated because nothing tells us she has an appetite for risk or is trying to keep up with purchasing power.

What we might recommend for this investor: equity funds within a Roth IRA, annuity.

Portfolio Management Strategies, Styles and Techniques

Strategies and Styles

To understand the difference between growth and value investments we first need to understand the following terms.

Valuation Ratios

When a fundamental analyst compares the market price of a stock to the earnings, cash flow or book value per-share, he is looking at a **valuation ratio**. Another name for a valuation ratio is a multiple. Whatever we call them, the following are comparisons between a stock's market price and some other number from one of the issuer's three financial statements.

Price-to-Earnings Ratio

When evaluating common stock, investors compare the price of the stock to the earnings per-share to see if the stock is attractively priced. This is called the price-to-earnings ratio. The higher the number, the more expensive the stock. A share of common stock is a share of the company's earnings. So, the question is, how much are people willing to pay for those earnings? If a stock trades for $25 on the secondary market when the earnings per-share = $1, the stock trades for 25 times the earnings, or a P/E ratio of 25:1.

The price-to-earnings ratio indicates how much investors value a company's profits as expressed through the market price of the stock. Are they willing to pay ten times the earnings? Twenty times the earnings? One hundred times the earnings? Stocks trading at high multiples are **growth stocks**, while those trading at low multiples are **value stocks**. Growth stocks involve more volatility than value stocks because the price is supported by enthusiasm rather than tangible measures such as book value.

Price-to-Book Ratio

We found the earnings of the company on the income statement. We can figure the **book value** on the balance sheet. If a company had to be liquidated, the equipment, factory, real estate, etc., would be sold at auction and the proceeds would be paid first to the creditors, then to the preferred stockholders. The amount that would be left for each share of common stock is the **book value per-share**. Think of this as the hard, tangible value of a share of common stock.

If the book value of a share of stock is $6, and the stock now trades for $30, it is trading at a **price-to-book ratio** of 5.

Price-to-Sales, Price-to-Cash Ratios

It isn't just that growth investors buy stocks trading at high price-to-earnings ratios. Many growth investors buy stocks in companies with no earnings at all. If the company has no earnings, it isn't worth talking about the P/E ratio. For a company with no earnings it is more practical to compare the market price of the stock to the sales the company makes (**price-to-sales**). Notice how this ties in with the income statement. Earnings represent the bottom line; sales represent the top line. Or, for companies not making a profit, many analysts pay closest attention to the price of the stock compared to the cash flow generated per-share. This is called, not surprisingly, **price-to-cash.**

So, if the company has net income and a strong balance sheet, fundamental analysts compare the stock price to the earnings and the book value. If the company is losing money as the sales and cash flow are growing, they can compare the market price to the sales or cash flow per-share.

Some analysts prefer using price-to-sales even if the company is profitable. As many famous companies have demonstrated, it is easy to manipulate earnings with creative accounting, but sales/revenue represents a number that is hard to fake. It is the top line of the income statement, remember, so it hasn't been filtered through all the subtractions for cost of goods sold, operating expenses, depreciation, amortization, or interest.

Growth Investing

Growth stocks trade at high P/E ratios. The higher the P/E ratio, the more speculative and volatile the stock. When a stock is trading at 35 or 50 times the earnings, every earnings announcement can move the stock's price dramatically.

A **growth investor** needs a long time horizon and the ability to withstand large fluctuations in the value of his investments. And he is not seeking dividend income if he is seeking capital appreciation/growth.

Value Investing

Value investors buy stocks trading at low price-to-earnings or price-to-book ratios. A value investor purchases stocks in out-of-favor corporations trading for less than they should be. For example, when GM's CEO is testifying before Congress over badly handled recalls, many traders will dump shares of GM, while value investors might decide to buy shares at currently depressed prices.

Value stocks would typically have higher dividend yields, especially if we compare large-cap value stocks to large-cap growth. Why? Large-cap companies are more likely to pay dividends to their shareholders now that their businesses are running relatively predictably. If their market price drops, suddenly the dividend yield will increase. The board of directors does not usually want to cut that dividend, so the decreasing market price will raise the dividend yield.

The word "growth" does not imply that value investors don't also want their investments to appreciate in value. It's just that growth investors buy expensive stocks expected to rise even more in the future, while value investors buy stocks of companies currently in trouble but worth more than the market realizes. If they were into real estate rather than common stock, growth investors would buy the new townhouses going up in the hot, new part of town, while value investors would buy foreclosed properties and rehab them for a profit.

Market Capitalization (Market Cap)

Market cap is an abbreviation for **market capitalization**. A company's market capitalization is their total number of outstanding shares times today's closing price. If the company has 100 million shares outstanding, their market capitalization is $1 billion if the stock closes at $10 per-share today. The number would, then, change each day the markets are open. In our example, if the stock closes down 50 cents tomorrow, the company's market cap would be reduced by $50 million.

There are small-cap, mid-cap, and large-cap stocks investors can choose from. The smaller the cap, the higher the risk-reward ratio.

Equity Style Box

We can now put growth and value together with market capitalization by looking at the Morningstar **equity style box.** This guide for investors places equity mutual funds in one of 9 boxes to indicate how aggressive the investment is. The most aggressive box is **small cap growth** while the least aggressive is **large cap value.**

In terms of style, growth is more aggressive than value. In terms of size, the lower the market capitalization the higher the volatility.

If a portfolio manager doesn't stick to just growth or value, that fund is called a **blend fund.** A blend fund sits between growth and value in terms of volatility.

Equity mutual funds fit somewhere in the following table or box of 9 cells developed in 1992 by Morningstar. The upper-left box is the least aggressive equity fund, while the lower-right box is the most aggressive.

Large Cap Value	Large Cap Blend	Large Cap Growth
Mid Cap Value	Mid Cap Blend	Mid Cap Growth
Small Cap Value	Small Cap Blend	Small Cap Growth

The center box--Mid Cap Blend--represents the core style of investing. Also, although not a separate style zone for the equity style box, the stocks that are smaller than small-cap are known as **micro cap.** These stocks frequently trade on the less liquid and less regulated OTC equities markets. Because of the small number of shares and the relative obscurity of the companies, these stock issues are more prone to manipulation.

We could find resources online that would set the cutoffs for small, mid, and large cap. But as Morningstar explains, "Large-cap stocks are those that together account for the top 70% of the capitalization of each style zone; mid-cap stocks represent the next 20%; and small-cap stocks represent the balance. The market caps that correspond to these breakpoints are flexible and may shift from month to month as the market changes."

Many people assume investors agree on the three market capitalization categories, but not exactly. The best we can do is see what S&P uses for their large, mid, and small cap indices. The S&P 500 is a large-cap index. To be included in the index a company must have a minimum market cap of $4 billion. To be included in the S&P SmallCap 600 a company must have a market cap between $300 million to $1.4 billion. And in the middle, the S&P MidCap 400 includes companies with a market cap of $1 billion to $4.4 billion.

You probably noticed that the mid-cap range overlaps both the high end of the small-cap range ($1.4 billion) and the low end of the large-cap range ($4 billion). That's how it works with all stock classification systems, turns out. Therefore, it is difficult to write a fair test question involving precise numbers, when S&P themselves don't use such rigid cutoffs. And, as always, the test is not that concerned with rote memorization. Reasoning skills are far more important than one's ability to commit a table of data to memory on this exam.

Active vs. Passive

Growth and value are terms that refer to types of stock as well as investment styles. The terms active and passive, on the other hand, refer only to types of investment styles. If you seek particular stocks (or bonds), you are an **active** manager. If you buy "growth" or "value" index funds, you are a **passive** manager. Is the investor actively determining that one security is more attractive than another? If so, that's active portfolio management. Now, who uses active management styles—fundamental or technical analysts?

Both. We could determine that ORCL is a better investment now than MSFT by looking at the fundamentals (balance sheet, income statement), or we could look at technical indicators including charts, the 200-day moving average, or short interest. Either way, if we are coming down on the side of one stock versus another, we are using active stock selection or active portfolio management.

A passive management style usually involves the use of indexes rather than trying to pick one investment over another. We could buy a growth index fund or a value index fund, which is choosing a style, but we would never try to pick one growth or value stock over another. Using this passive indexing strategy, we will pay lower expenses, because these funds aren't doing a lot of trading and, therefore, don't have to charge high management fees.

Income vs. Capital Appreciation

The terms "growth" and "value" have some overlap with the terms **income** and **capital appreciation**. Growth investors tend not to care about or receive dividend income, while value investors often receive a relatively high dividend yield. But growth and value are both mostly about capital appreciation. It's just that growth investors like to buy hot companies that will continue to grow, while value investors are drawn to companies currently in trouble but about to turn things around.

Income and capital appreciation could be called styles, but they are also investment objectives. Does the investor seek income, or is he interested in buying stocks that increase in market value? Income investors invest in bonds and preferred stock. Investors seeking capital appreciation invest in common stock.

As with many categories, these are not rigid. An investment in SBUX would involve income even though it trades as a growth stock, and growth is synonymous with capital appreciation. Some companies are successful and growing, like SBUX. They have the cash flow to cover a modest dividend, but their profits and share price may continue to rise well into the future.

Or not. Which is why SBUX is not an income investment, even if it pays a dividend. An income investor would not start with large-cap dividend paying companies. An income investor would allocate most of her assets to bonds and preferred stock.

The dividend income from common stock is associated with an investor who seeks both growth and income from a common stock investment. Such an investor is known as a growth-and-income investor, as one might expect.

But, an income investor has far better options among various bonds and preferred stock. Even though REITS offer extremely high dividend yields, an income investor should not be steered in that direction, since they are a form of common stock and, therefore, too risky for a pure income investor. A REIT is appropriate for a growth and income investor with a long time horizon who can withstand wide fluctuations in market value. Income investors don't expect to see wide fluctuations in the market values of their bonds and preferred stocks. On the other hand, any investor seeking capital appreciation has to live with the volatility that goes with it.

Asset Allocation

Asset allocation is a widely-accepted tenet of investing. Virtually no one 50 years old is 100% invested in equities, or even 100% in fixed-income. The rule of thumb has been that an investor should limit his equity exposure to 100 minus his age. If he's 47, he should have no more than 53% of his portfolio allocated to equities. These days, with age expectancies getting longer, some are now saying to increase the equity exposure to 120 minus the investor's age, which would give the 47-year-old a maximum of 73% for equities. Obviously, this rule of thumb is just a little bit arbitrary and unscientific, although it is based on a solid premise—portfolios that use asset allocation drive over the bumps in the markets much better than those concentrated too heavily on one asset class.

In general, investors in their 50s will have a little less than half their portfolio allocated to stock/equities and a little more than half devoted to fixed-income and money market/cash. Within those basic asset classes the equity portion could be divided by market cap and growth/value/blend, international vs. domestic, and industry sectors. The fixed-income piece could be divided by term to maturity, credit quality, taxable versus tax-exempt, and types of issuers.

For example, after an investor completes a questionnaire through a secure area of the firm's website, maybe the computer models return the following allocation:

- Equity – 40%
  - 20% Large-Cap Value
  - 20% Small-Cap Growth
- Fixed-Income – 50%
  - 20% High-Yield
  - 20% Investment-Grade, Taxable
  - 10% High-Yield, Tax-Exempt
- Cash – 10%

If we present that allocation as a full-color pie chart, you can imagine that most investors will begin to relax and feel that someone who knows what he is doing is about to take charge of their investments. And, of course, most investors will end up doing a whole lot better using a registered investment professional to allocate and manage their portfolio, as opposed to watching some guy on TV.

Whatever the asset allocation is the investor will tweak things from time to time to **rebalance** the portfolio back to its stated percentages. To maintain the strategic mix of asset classes the agent and the investor need to sell some of the assets that have appreciated to add to the ones that have gone down and now represent a smaller % of the portfolio.

Techniques

No matter how an investor arrives at the decision to invest in X, Y, or Z, he must manage those assets using various portfolio management techniques.

Buy and Hold

Whether I'm a growth, value, passive, or active manager, I could use **buy and hold** as a portfolio management technique. The buy and hold approach results in lower transaction costs, because the investor is not trading and generating commissions/markups. Rather, he is buying, and then holding.

Plus, he avoids getting taxed at short-term capital gains rates by selling infrequently and almost always for a long-term capital gain.

Diversification

Another accepted tenet of prudent investing is called **diversification**. As we see when discussing the Uniform Prudent Investor Act, a fiduciary is expected to diversify the assets of a trust, except in those rare cases where it is more beneficial and prudent not to. A diversified portfolio of stocks would not contain all technology or pharmaceutical companies, for example. If there were a number of oil company stocks, they would be diversified between domestic and international companies, producers of oil and refiners of oil. They would not all be small cap or large cap. A bond portfolio would not be all triple-A-rated or all junk, but would instead be diversified throughout different maturities, credit quality, and issuers that don't all come from the same industry.

Asset allocation and diversification are somewhat related. Where they differ is that asset allocation is a style that places percentages of capital into various types of stocks, bonds, and cash. Within those allocations, we use diversification to balance the risk of one investment with the characteristics of another. So, 20% large-cap growth, 20% mid-cap growth, 30% small-cap growth, and 30% long-term bond is an asset allocation. Drill down into the "20% large-cap growth" category, and the various companies owned would come from different industries to maintain diversification.

Also, diversification is not linked to asset allocation. An active stock picker using a growth style would tend to hold a diversified portfolio of stocks in companies from different industry sectors. The same is true of a value investor. That's what makes diversification a technique, while the others are considered strategies or styles. Whether I'm active or passive, growth or value, I'm almost certainly implementing the technique of diversification to reduce my risk.

We saw earlier that unsystematic risk can be reduced through diversification, while systematic risks cannot. In other words, investors reduce their legislative risk by purchasing securities issued by companies in different industry spaces. To reduce overall market risk—which is systematic—investors use options, futures, or ETFs to hedge. If the risk is that the overall market will drop, for example, investors can buy index put options, sell ETFs short, or purchase inverse ETFs designed to move opposite the overall market.

Sector Rotating

Some portfolio managers try to anticipate which sectors are about to rise and which are about to fall. The object then becomes to sell the sectors that are about to drop and buy the ones that are about to rise. Not surprisingly, this technique is called **sector rotating**. Deciding which sectors to "underweight" and which to "overweight" could be done through fundamental or technical analysis. If an industry space seems set for an expansion due to economic forces, that analyst is using fundamental analysis and probably top-down analysis, as well. Another trader may decide to sell pharmaceuticals when they are "overbought" and invest in telecommunications because they appear to be "oversold" at this point. That is technical analysis. Either way, the technique is known as sector rotating or sector rotation.

Dollar Cost Averaging

Investors often put a fixed dollar amount into securities on a regular schedule. Since stocks, bonds, and mutual funds fluctuate in price, investors using the **dollar cost averaging** technique end up buying fewer shares when they're expensive and more of their shares when they're temporarily (we hope) cheap. The test might point out that an investor's average cost is lower than the average share price…which is because of what I just said. To illustrate it clearly, though, we need a story problem. So here goes: Melody automatically invests $1,000 into a mutual fund each month. Over the past three months the Net Asset Value was $50, $40, and $25. Therefore, her average cost per-share is what amount?

We need to figure out how many shares she bought with her total dollars invested. She invested $3,000, so how many shares did she buy?

	SHARE PRICE	# OF SHARES
Jan: $1,000	$50	
Feb: $1,000	$40	
Mar: $1,000	$25	

In January, her $1,000 bought 20 shares. In February, her $1,000 bought 25 shares, and in March her $1,000 bought 40 shares. Therefore, her $3,000 in total acquired 85 shares. What is the average cost per-share? Whatever $3,000 divided by 85 shares equals—about $35.29.

I'm betting the question would also present the average share price as one of the false answers, because most people want to get through a question like this as fast as possible. The average cost is not $38.33. That would be the average of the three share prices, and that would only be relevant if the investor were buying, say, 100 shares of stock each month. But that is not what happens when dollar cost averaging. Here, it's not the number of shares that is fixed—it's the dollar amount. The number of shares acquired each time varies.

Investors often use the average-cost method to figure their cost basis when selling securities for capital gains/capital losses. The other methods are FIFO (First In First Out) and share identification.

Capital Market Theory

CAPM

The **Capital Asset Pricing Model** (CAPM) has something in common with the Sharpe ratio, but the two are used for different purposes. The Sharpe ratio calculates what already happened and calls it "risk-adjusted return," while CAPM calculates and predicts expected return based on some math we're about to look at.

Both concepts use the idea that an investor could put her money into a "riskless rate of return," so if she's going to put it into something risky instead, she demands a potential reward much larger than that riskless rate of return. That extra reward is known as a "risk premium."

The formula works like this. If the risk-free rate is 3%, the beta of the stock is 2, and the expected market return over the period is 10%, then the stock is expected to return 17%. To calculate that, you would take the risk-free rate and add that to the expected return minus that risk-free rate times the beta.

Even though the formula looks heavy, it does communicate a basic concept. The calculation is saying that the expected return on a stock is equal to the risk-free return an investor could get on 3-month T-Bills plus the potential return on the stock that is over and above the risk-free rate.

The numbers above are crunched like this: (3% + 2 (10% − 3%)). That's 3%, plus the sum of (20% minus 6%). 3% plus 14% equals the expected return of 17%. And, it shows that investors expect to be compensated both for the time value of money and the risk of investing in stocks.

Again, the Sharpe ratio and CAPM both incorporate the riskless rate of return. But CAPM calculates an expected return, while the Sharpe ratio adjusts actual returns for the risk the portfolio experienced. Notice how these approaches are purely mathematical, while fundamental analysis involves both a quantitative and qualitative examination of a company. A trader using CAPM and the Sharpe ratio is more interested in how a stock or a portfolio is behaving and is likely to behave in the future. Fundamental analysts are interested in determining which companies are likely to perform well in the future.

Modern Portfolio Theory

In the distant past, investors would consider the risk of any one security. **Modern Portfolio Theory,** on the other hand, looks at how an investment affects the risk/reward ratio of the entire portfolio. It also assumes that investors are risk-averse, no matter what they tell you. Since investors don't like risk, we could say that they would prefer to make, for example, 10% returns through the least risky path, or that, given a level of risk, they want the highest possible return. Using an entirely mathematical/statistical approach to investing, Modern Portfolio Theorists construct "optimal portfolios," which means that the investor is likely to get the highest possible return given the amount of volatility he is willing to bear.

If we reverse the words, we get **portfolio optimization,** which relates to a graph called an **efficient frontier.** What is considered key is the unique mix of securities in a portfolio. There are many portfolios that fall along this efficient frontier, so which one is better for the investor? It depends on the amount of volatility the investor can handle, and what potential return he thinks he will settle for. Portfolios are constructed of a percentage mix of equity, bonds, and cash, and these various mixes can, theoretically—based on historical data—determine the amount of risk, and the likely return.

Whichever risk-reward profile the investor chooses, we want the portfolio to lie along (not behind) the efficient frontier. The portfolios that lie on the lower left part of the curve are the most efficient for the low-risk–low-reward investors, while the portfolios that lie along the upper right part of the curve are the most efficient for the high-risk–high-reward investors.

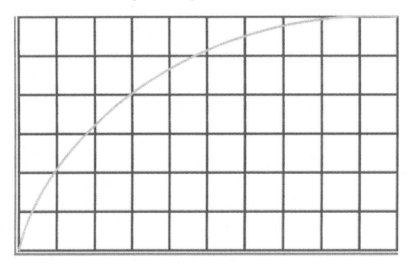

Modern Portfolio Theory is a mathematical approach to investment selection. It is interested in calculating the risk-reward nature of a portfolio by measuring expected returns, standard deviations, and correlations. Rather than thinking like a fundamental analyst that 1,000 shares of ORCL should rise next year when the company reports higher profits, Modern Portfolio Theory would, instead, calculate the likely return of a portfolio based on mathematical probabilities. Technical analysis would also be of no use to this crowd. Whether using financial statements or stock charts, to a modern portfolio theorist, either investor is actively and foolishly selecting securities.

Efficient Market Hypothesis

The **efficient market hypothesis** grew out of a Ph.D. dissertation by Eugene Fama. This school of thought assumes that at any given time in a liquid market all information about a security is already priced in, making the current market price an accurate estimate of any security's intrinsic value. Because all security prices accurately reflect their intrinsic value, attempts to outperform the overall market are based on luck rather than skill.

Efficient Market Hypothesis can be further broken down into three separate forms: weak, semi-strong, and strong. The **weak form** assumes that current stock prices fully reflect all currently available market information and contends that past price and volume data have no relationship with the future direction of security prices. It concludes that excess returns cannot be achieved using technical analysis.

The **semi-strong form** of efficient market hypothesis assumes that current stock prices adjust rapidly to the release of all new public information. It contends that security prices have factored in available market and non-market public information. It concludes that excess returns cannot be achieved using fundamental analysis, so all of that work we did in Chapter 1 on financial statements is a waste of time.

The **strong form** of efficient market hypothesis assumes that current stock prices fully reflect all public and private information. It contends that market, non-market and inside information is all factored into security prices and that no one has monopolistic access to relevant information. It assumes a perfect market and concludes that excess returns are impossible to achieve consistently. Even if an investor possessed material non-public information, it is of no benefit to him since even that is factored into stock prices.

All three forms suggest that trying to beat the overall market is not a realistic goal. Rather, investors should seek a reasonable rate of return given the risk they are willing to take.

Behavioral Finance

Proponents of the Efficient Market Hypothesis believe that prices for securities are the result of investors implementing the information available to them in a rational manner. This seems to hold true for most market situations over the long-term. However, to explain anomalies such as speculative bubbles **behavioral finance** concludes that irrational behavior on a massive scale is the culprit.

As an excellent guide to behavioral finance by Vanguard UK explains, "The behavioral biases discussed in this guide are ingrained aspects of human decision-making processes. Many of them have served us well as ways of coping with day-to-day choices. But, they may be unhelpful for achieving success in long-term activities such as investing."

One idea of behavioral finance is that investors make decisions based on an imprecise understanding of information rather than on a perfectly rational analysis of clear and irrefutable facts. Another is that the way a problem or question is framed or presented to an investor has a profound effect on his behavior. If you think of the 24-hour news cycle these days, it is not hard to understand how some investors get mistaken notions based on the volume of the pundits on their TV screens or the number of times a story is run. Such investors could end up selling investments that are not even related to the topic they're following on-screen based on the impression they get from the pundits on financial news shows.

Or, back when companies with a dot-com in their name were hot, investors got the idea that dot-com stocks would go up forever based on the enthusiasm of such pundits, all trying to advance their speaking and publishing careers. Another name for this phenomenon is framing. The way that information is framed or presented to investors has a profound impact on their decision making.

The term recency bias or the recency effect relates to the way many investors take the data and experience of the markets recently and extrapolate the situation into the future indefinitely. If stocks have risen 20% and then 28% two years in a row, many investors assume this is the new normal and end up investing heavily just before a bear market. Bloomberg takes a weekly survey of money managers' recommended weightings for stocks/bonds/cash and found that the highest stock weighting was recommended just after the peak of the Internet stock bubble, with the lowest stock weighting coming just after the lows of the financial crisis. This suggests that recency bias is alive and well, even among institutional investors.

On the other hand, the primacy bias or primacy effect occurs when the first information or experience is given more weighting than anything that comes later. A retail investor who experiences a big profit on his first options trade could end up chasing profits far into the future no matter how many losses he later racks up. This would suggest that his first experience with options was so strongly rewarded that subsequent losses are downplayed or ignored.

Another bias that affects decision making is overconfidence. Turns out we humans tend to overrate our abilities, including our ability to make decisions. For example, when asked to rate our driving abilities, virtually no one rates himself as below average, even though--by definition--50% of drivers are below average. Overconfident investors are likely to ignore the wisdom of diversification based on their belief that they can pick market sectors or individual stocks to overweight. These investors also tend to overrate the effect that their stock picking or sector rotating has on portfolio returns.

Such investors typically trade too often, as well, based on their belief that their skills are linked to market-beating results. However, as Professor Brad Barber and Terrence Odean found by studying the habits of U.S. retail investors, investors who were in the bottom 20% for portfolio turnover had an average annual portfolio return of 18.5%, while those in the top 20% for trading activity had an average annual return of just 11.4%. (Source: Brad Barber and Terrence Odean (1999) 'The courage of misguided convictions' Financial Analysts Journal, November/December, p. 50.)

On the other hand, the bias of loss aversion can be just as self-destructive. Research suggests that investors overweight a chance of loss by as much as 2-to-1 compared to a chance of gain. For example, when surveyed, investors required a 50/50 chance of either gaining $2,500 or losing just $1,000 to make the risk of loss worth taking.

However, when a loss occurs, many investors hang onto it indefinitely, assuming the stock price will eventually return to their "breakeven" point. You might assume that retail investors tend to take a profit only after holding it long-term due to the favorable tax treatment, while, on the other hand, cutting any losses rather quickly. In fact, the same professors mentioned above found that investors sell their winners quickly while hanging onto losing positions too long. Investors are, in fact, 50% more likely to sell a winning position than to lock in a loss. That implies that they are risk-averse when holding a winner and inexplicably risk-tolerant when holding a losing position.

Which, as with most of these biases, is not what one might expect. But, it does explain why the ability to recognize these biases of investing clients could reduce the negative effects of various human quirks in financial decision making.

Tax Considerations

Most of us pay income taxes at several different rates due to the graduated, progressive income tax system in the United States. At the time of this writing, there are seven tax brackets. For most taxpayers, the first $9,275 of income is taxed at 10%. The next dollars earned up to $37,650 are taxed at 15%. The next dollars up to $91,150 are taxed at 25%, and so on.

Notice that we don't pay 25% on all our income just because we reach that bracket. Rather, we pay 25% on the dollars we make above a certain amount. If the highest rate of tax applied is 25%, then 25% is the taxpayer's **marginal tax rate**. An exam question might define an investor's marginal rate as "the rate of tax paid on the last dollar of income earned."

Beyond the different tax brackets there are also different methods of filing income taxes, and these methods affect the rate of taxes paid. For example, a single filer is pushed into the 15% tax bracket and then the 25% bracket at a certain dollar amount, while a married couple filing jointly would get to make twice those amounts before being pushed into the 15% and then the 25% bracket.

On the other hand, if they choose "married-filing-separately," the dollar amounts are different. Turns out a married couple choosing to file separately can each earn as much as single filers, until we get to those middle tax brackets and, suddenly, they get pushed into the 28% and 33% brackets sooner than if they'd stayed unattached. The reasoning for this is that married couples share expenses and should, therefore, be pushed into higher marginal brackets at lower dollar amounts. Those who disagree with the notion refer to it as the "marriage penalty."

There is another method of filing called "head of household." If the test question says that your client is now raising two children orphaned when her sister was killed in a car crash, that individual should file as "head of household" versus "single filer." For a "head-of-household" filer, the dollar amounts of income allowed before being pushed into the next tax bracket are much higher compared to a single filer. For example, using this method the individual would not reach the 15% bracket until her adjusted gross income rose above $13,250, compared to just $9,275 for the other methods ($18,550 for married filing jointly).

For a more detailed look: https://www.irs.com/articles/projected-us-tax-rates-2016.

Whatever the marginal tax bracket, what we're talking about is **ordinary income**. Ordinary income includes wages, salaries, bonuses, commissions, some dividends, and bond interest. We'll talk later about investments held within retirement accounts, but for now, let's talk about the regular, old taxable brokerage account.

There are two types of taxes on investments:

- Taxes on income
- Taxes on capital gains

Let's start with income.

Bonds pay interest, and many stocks pay dividends. This income is a major part of a portfolio's total return. Unfortunately, it is also taxable.

Dividends

Let's say you buy 1,000 shares of GE for $30 per-share. Every three months you receive a quarterly dividend of 25 cents per-share, or $250. Believe it or not, it's only taxed at a maximum rate of 15% in most cases nowadays. Before the big change to the tax code, those dividends were taxed at ordinary  income rates. Many investors paying a 39% tax on dividends a few years ago are now paying no more than 15%. Imagine that. You're a wealthy individual receiving $200,000 in dividend income each year. You used to pay about $78,000 in taxes on that money; now you pay only $30,000.

But, it's also not correct to make a blanket statement such as, "Dividends are taxed at 15%." The dividends that get taxed at 15% are called **qualified dividends**. These include dividends from GE, MSFT, or most any C-corporation. But there are **ordinary dividends**, which we'll get to in a second.

First, however, why are dividends now taxed at just 15%? This relates to our look at the income statement. Remember the phrase "net income after tax"? That reminds us that corporations such as GE and MSFT pay dividends after they've paid tax on their profit. Unlike bond interest, dividends are not deducted from a company's income to reduce their tax burden. Since GE or MSFT already paid tax on the profits before paying some of them to shareholders in the form of a dividend, why should shareholders get fully taxed on that money?

Turns out they shouldn't, and they don't. We pointed out that C-corporations subject the owners to the double taxation of income, but at least, the taxation on dividends is reduced for most investors. If your marginal tax rate is 25%, 33%, or 35%, you pay only 15% on qualified dividends. But, check this out—if your tax bracket is lower than 25%, the tax you pay on qualified dividends is zero percent.

Zero. But, again, not all dividends are qualified and taxed at the kinder, gentler rates. The dividends that don't qualify for this tax treatment include ordinary dividends, which are taxed at ordinary income rates. REITs pay out 90% of their earnings pre-tax to shareholders to act as a conduit to the investors. But, since the REIT receives a tax break on the dividend, the unit holders do not. REIT investors pay ordinary dividends taxed at ordinary income rates.

For investors who reach the 39.6% marginal bracket, qualified dividends and long-term capital gains are now taxed at 20%.

Finally, I am giving you the "real-world" tax rates on dividends. The exam will likely avoid the issue entirely and say something like, "If the tax on dividends is 20%, what is Joe's after-tax return?" The exam generally wants to see if the test taker can work with a concept rather than seeing if he has memorized endless tables of data.

Interest paid on corporate and government bonds is taxable at ordinary income rates. This explains why wealthier investors often try to hold their corporate bonds in tax-advantaged accounts, which we'll discuss in a few pages. Corporate bond interest is taxable at the federal, state, and local government levels, while US government bond interest is taxable at the federal level exclusively.

Corporate bond interest is taxable in states that have an income tax, and even a few cities tax the corporate bond interest that their residents earn. GNMA, FNMA, and FHLMC are taxable at the federal, state, and local levels, also, just like corporate bonds.

Taxation of municipal securities

The interest on general obligation bonds is tax-exempt at the federal level, but your state could tax the interest if you buy a bond from an out-of-state issuer. If you live in Georgia and buy a bond issued by the State of Alabama, Georgia can tax that interest. Plus, if you live in Atlanta, Georgia, and Atlanta has a tax on bond interest, your city could tax you as well.

How could you avoid being taxed by Georgia and the city of Atlanta? Buy a bond issued by Atlanta, Georgia. The state will give you a break, and so will Atlanta.

Finally, if you live in Atlanta and buy a bond issued by Valdosta, Georgia, the federal government will give you the tax break, and so will the State of Georgia, since both Valdosta and Atlanta are in that state. But, what about Atlanta—did you help them out? No, so they can tax you. How do you get Atlanta off your back? Buy one of their municipal securities. You help us finance our schools, we'll help you reduce your tax burden.

SITUATION	FEDERAL	STATE	LOCAL
Resident of Topeka, KS, buys a Toledo, OH, municipal bond	EXEMPT	TAXABLE	TAXABLE
Resident of Topeka, KS, buys a Wichita, KS, municipal bond	EXEMPT	EXEMPT	TAXABLE
Resident of Topeka, KS, buys a Topeka, KS, municipal bond	EXEMPT	EXEMPT	EXEMPT

Not all municipal securities pay tax-free interest. The ones used for public purpose/essential services do, but if the tax code says that the bond is a "private activity" bond, the interest is subject to **alternative minimum tax (AMT)**. Most municipal bond investors are subject to AMT, which would force them to add some of the interest received on a private activity bond back into their taxable income. For that reason, **private activity bonds** usually offer higher yields (before tax). An example of a private activity bond is a bond issued to finance a parking garage that will be operated by a private company, or bonds issued to build a sports stadium. If the exam says your customer wants a municipal bond but is concerned about AMT, put her into a general obligation bond, such as a school bond. Or look for the concept of "essential, public purpose."

And, some municipal bonds are taxable. For example, if a public university has already issued a certain amount of GO debt that is outstanding, additional bond issues could be taxable, requiring the issuer to offer much higher yields to investors. Or, if the bond issue is a refunding issue used to call bonds, there is no exemption for the interest paid to investors in that case, either.

So far, we have been discussing the income that securities provide to investors through interest and dividend payments.

Capital Gains

On the other hand, think of a **capital gain** as the profit you take when you sell a security for more than you bought it.

Back to our GE example. You bought 1,000 shares @$30 each. Let's say you sell 100 shares for $40 to take a vacation. If you held GE for more than 1 year, you'd realize a long-term gain of $1,000, since $10 times 100 shares = $1,000 in capital gains. Go ahead and take your vacation, and at the end of the year, you'll owe Uncle Sam 15% of that $1,000, or $150. Your state may tax the gain as well. And, if you're in the top tax bracket of 39.6%, you pay 20% to the U.S. Treasury.

If you had sold that stock within a year, the gain would be taxed at your ordinary income rate since it's a short-term capital gain. If your ordinary income rate is 25%, you owe the IRS $250. If it's 35%, you only kept $650 of that capital gain when the dust settles.

Cost Basis

A capital gain is the difference between your **proceeds** (what you sell it for) and your **cost basis** (what you paid for it). Think of your "cost basis" as all the money that has gone into an investment after being taxed. When you buy GE for $30 a share, you don't deduct that from taxable income, so $30 a share is your cost basis. You also pay a commission in most cases, so you add that to your cost basis. When you bought 1,000 shares of GE @$30, you paid a $50 commission. So, while we used round numbers above to introduce the concept, your cost basis is really $3,050 divided by 1,000 shares, or $30.05 per-share.

If an investor purchases shares of the same stock at different times and for different prices, there are different methods of determining the cost basis when he sells the stock someday. For example, if he bought 100 shares for $50, 100 shares for $60, and 100 shares for $75 over the past several years, which 100 did he just sell? The IRS assumes the method used is **first in first out (FIFO)**. That means, he just sold the shares with the $50 cost basis, leading to a much larger taxable capital gain vs. using the shares purchased for $75.

Could he use the $75 cost basis? Yes, but he and the broker-dealer would have to identify the shares with the **CUSIP number** when the sell order is placed. That method is called **share identification**.

The method many investors use is **average cost,** in which they total all the money spent on the shares and divide that by the current number of shares. This method is available only when a broker-dealer or other custodian holds the shares on the investor's behalf.

Proceeds

Broker-dealers charge commissions when customers buy and when they sell securities. So, when you buy shares of GE, you add the commission to the cost basis, and when you sell those shares of GE, you subtract the commission from your proceeds. If you sell 100 shares of GE @40 and pay a $50 commission, your proceeds would be $3,950, or $39.50 per-share. On your tax returns for the year in which you sell the stock, you would report that your proceeds were $3,950, while your cost basis on those 100 shares was $3,005. The capital gain on that sale is $945.

Holding Period

If you sell a security held for one year or less, that is a short-term gain or loss. If it's a gain, it is taxed at your marginal rate. If you hold a security for more than one year, that is considered a long-term gain or loss. If it's a gain, it is taxed at the same 15% currently used for qualified dividends for most investors (0% for low-bracket, 20% for top-bracket investors).

One advantage of a buy-and-hold investment strategy is that any gains will likely be taxed at the lower long-term capital gains rates. This helps portfolio performance.

How do you count your **holding period**? In Publication 564 the IRS explains:

> To find out how long you have held your shares, begin counting on the day after the trade date on which you bought the shares. (Do not count the trade date itself.) The trade date on which you dispose of the shares is counted as part of your holding period. If you bought shares on May 6th of last year (trade date), and sold them on May 6th of this year (trade date), your holding period would not be more than 1 year. If you sold them on May 7th of this year, your holding period would be more than 1 year (12 months plus 1 day).

As with qualified dividends, if the investor's marginal tax rate hits 25-35%, he pays no more than 15% tax on long-term capital gains, and if his marginal rate is lower than that, he could end up paying zero percent on capital gains. Zero percent.

Capital Losses

You don't pay the tax on the day you sell the stock. Rather, you figure it into your income taxes when you file for the year. But you'll want to keep track of the gain, because the IRS will want to know, and because when you sit down with your accountant at the end of the year, you might decide to sell some other stocks at a loss to balance out that gain. You took a $945 gain on GE. If you sell another stock at a $1,000 **capital loss**, you'd end up at zero capital gains for the year.

Congratulations, you made no money this year. And, therefore, you have no capital gains taxes to pay. You could sell even more stock at a loss. If you lost, say, $10,000 for the year, you could use $3,000 of your total or net loss to offset (reduce) your adjusted gross income for the year. So, if your AGI was going to be $53,000, now it's only $50,000. That reduces your tax bill.

But you really did lose money. See the relationship? If you're paying no tax, it's because you're making no money. If you're paying taxes, it's because you're making money. Personally, I prefer the latter, but that's not the point, and many would argue that it's better to reduce your tax burden than to have the misfortune of making money in the stock market.

Some will even purposely take a net loss for the year and continue to carry the excess that's over the $3,000 limit forward. I know a few investors who have enough capital losses to last the rest of their lives, $3,000 at a time. They took about $100,000 in capital losses in 2002, and it's going to take quite some time to use that up at three grand a year.

Lucky devils.

Offsetting Gains with Losses

In any case, if an investor only made a couple of sales during the year, figuring gains and losses would be extremely easy. An exam question, of course, could be anything but. Let's use possible exam questions to show you how to deal with the tricky process of matching up gains and losses to figure an investor's net gains and net losses.

Jarod Stevens had the following results on four stock sales last year:
$15,000 in long-term gains
$5,000 in long-term losses
$5,000 in short-term gains
$13,000 in short-term losses

Therefore, the tax implications were
A. short-term capital gain of $8,000
B. long-term capital gain of $2,000
C. short-term capital gain of $2,000
D. long-term capital gain of $15,000

Step one: line up the long-term gains and the long-term losses, then line up the short-term gains with the short-term losses. Matching up the long-term gain of $15,000 with the $5,000 long-term loss leaves Jarod with $10,000 in long-term capital gains. Subtract the $13,000 short-term loss from the $5,000 short-term gain, and Jarod has $8,000 in short-term losses. Now, here's the tricky part. You can take the $10,000 long-term gain and reduce it by the $8,000 short-term loss for a net long-term gain of $2,000.

Why is that $2,000 treated as a long-term capital gain? Because the IRS defines a net long-term capital gain as any long-term capital gain that remains after subtracting any short-term losses. Or think of it this way—it's the long-term net capital gain of $10,000 that triggered the capital gains tax. Regardless, the answer is…*B*. I know. I don't like taxation much myself, but it could easily make the difference between a pass and a no-pass on the exam, so let's keep plodding through this.

Jarod Stevens had the following results on four stock sales this year:
$15,000 in long-term gains
$23,000 in long-term losses
$15,000 in short-term gains
$5,000 in short-term losses

Therefore, the tax implications are

A. short-term capital gain taxed at a maximum of 15%
B. no net gains or losses
C. short-term capital gain of $2,000 taxed at ordinary income rates
D. long-term capital loss of $8,000, short-term capital gain of $8,000

Line up the long-term with long-term, and the short-term with short-term. You end up with a net long-term loss of $8,000 and a net short-term gain of $10,000. The $8,000 in losses brings the total capital gain down to $2,000, which will be taxed as a short-term capital gain. Why a short-term capital gain? Because it was the short-term net gain that triggered the tax. The answer is...*C.*

One last time.

Jarod Stevens had the following results on four stock sales last year:
$15,000 in long-term gains
$5,000 in long-term losses
$5,000 in short-term gains
$17,000 in short-term losses

Therefore, the tax implications will be
A. short-term capital gain of $2,000
B. long-term capital gain of $2,000
C. short-term capital gain of $5,000
D. short-term capital loss of $2,000, which offsets ordinary income

Match up long-term with long-term and short-term with short-term, then net out your results. There is a net long-term gain of $10,000 and a net short-term loss of $12,000. That makes it a net loss of $2,000, which can be used to offset ordinary income.

Too bad Jarod couldn't have lost another $1,000 on our stock picks to take full advantage of our services, huh? In any case, the answer is...*D.*

Wash Sale Rules

So, the "benefit" of selling securities at a loss is that you can offset your ordinary income by up to $3,000 per year. But, to use that loss, stay out of that stock for at least 30 days. If you sell MSFT at a loss, don't buy any Microsoft stock for 30 days. And, you could not have purchased any 30 days *before* you made the sale, either.

Also, don't get clever and buy warrants, convertible bonds, convertible preferred stock or call options that convert to Microsoft common stock. Just take your capital loss and stay out of Microsoft for 30 days both before and after the sale.

What if you promise not to buy any Microsoft common stock over the next 30 days but can't stop yourself? Then, you can't use the loss now to offset ordinary income on your taxes because of wash sale rules. Never fear, though, because if you took a $7-per-share loss on Microsoft, you would add

$7 per-share to your cost basis on the new purchase. If you were to repurchase MSFT @$40, your cost basis would be $47. In other words, you would eventually get the benefit of that loss you took, but not now. And, if you recall our discussion of the time value of money, now is always a better time to get those dollars rather than at some point in the future.

When you sell a bond at a loss, there is a similar rule. Either wait 30 days to buy a replacement, or, if you want to sell a GE bond at a loss and buy another GE bond, you'll need to substantially alter some features of the bond: interest rate, maturity, call feature, or some combination. Or, just buy a bond from a different issuer. The test might call this process a **bond swap**.

When an investor makes regular and frequent investments into a mutual fund, he would typically end up executing wash sales whenever selling shares for a loss. Why? Chances are he either bought or is about to buy more of the same shares with his automatic investments.

Unrealized Capital Gains

An **unrealized capital gain** is just an increase in value, a "paper gain," as some say. There is no tax to pay just because your asset has become more valuable. As with your house, you owe no capital gains tax on your securities just because they have gone up in value. Only if the investor sells the security or the house and realizes a profit would there be a capital gains tax to pay.

Capital Gain or Loss on a primary residence

Selling a house for a capital gain is usually more pleasant than doing the same with shares of stock. If a homeowner owns and lives in a primary residence any two of the previous five years leading up to the sale of the property, any capital gain taken when he sells his house is tax-free up to $250,000 for individuals and up to $500,000 for married couples. He must meet the "ownership and use tests" to claim up to those maximum amounts. But, even if he doesn't meet the two-year ownership and use tests, he may qualify for a reduced maximum amount if suffering a financial or health-related hardship.

If two people jointly own a house, each could claim up to $250,000 on his or her separate return. A married couple claiming up to $500,000 as a tax-free capital gain is required to file jointly for the year they take advantage of this maneuver. For more information look up IRS Publication 523.

What about a capital loss on a primary residence? What if you put on a $100,000 addition to your house but end up selling for less than your cost basis? That is always painful. If you wanted to take a capital loss on your primary residence, you would first need to convert it to a rental property. If you rent it out, you can take depreciation on the property as we did under our look at partnerships. And, now, if you end up selling for less than your cost basis, you do get to claim a capital loss to offset taxable capital gains for the year.

Then again, if you have no capital gains for the year, that loss doesn't help much.

Mutual Fund Taxation

The owner of the securities inside a mutual fund is the investment company itself. The fund sells pieces of this portfolio to investors in the form of common stock.

Income Dividends

So, like any common stockholder, a mutual fund holder will probably receive dividends. A stock mutual fund earns dividends from the stocks that they own. A bond fund receives regular interest payments on their fixed-income portfolio. A balanced fund earns both dividends and interest from the securities held in the portfolio. The funds pay expenses with that money and if there's a profit left over, they distribute it to the shareholders. The shareholders receive convenient **1099-DIV** statements that help keep track of this income, which will be taxable at some rate.

If it's a stock fund, the investor is taxed at ordinary or qualified dividend rates, depending on the composition of the fund.

If it's a bond fund, income checks will be taxed just like bond interest, because that's where the income is derived. If it's a government bond fund, the interest is only taxable at the federal level. If it's a corporate bond fund, the interest is taxable at all levels. And if it's a municipal bond fund, the interest is tax-exempt at the federal level, but the investor's state government often taxes the interest received on out-of-state municipal bonds. For that reason, there are many state-specific municipal bond mutual funds for residents of high-tax states such as California, Virginia, and Maryland.

Capital Gains in Mutual Funds

There are two ways that capital gains come into play for mutual funds, but before we get to that, remember that investors have no control over when the investment adviser for the fund sells a stock or bond. If the investment adviser realizes more gains than losses, the fund realizes a net gain for the year. They can either distribute this to the shareholders or not. Either way, investors are taxed on their proportional share of this capital gain. That's the trouble with investing in funds that buy low and sell high. It's called a capital gain, and the **capital gains distribution** is taxed at the investor's long-term capital gains rate.

Distributions to Shareholders

The first thing to remember is that a fund almost always makes sure that when it takes a capital gain, it's a long-term capital gain, since, as we saw, the difference to a high-tax-bracket investor could be significant. Assume it's a long-term gain on the exam. Could it be a short-term gain?

Sure, but that is the exception rather than the rule.

We've been saying that the interest on U.S. Treasury securities is exempt from state and local taxation, and it is. Notice we've said nothing about capital gains until now. Yes, capital gains (not interest payments) on U.S. Treasuries are taxable at the federal, state, and local levels.

And, on the tax-free front, even though the dividend checks received from tax-exempt municipal bond funds are usually tax-exempt at the federal level, any capital gains distributions are treated as capital gains.

Shareholder Sales

The second capital gains issue with mutual funds is within the investor's control, just as it is on a share of GE or MSFT. If she sells her mutual fund shares within a year, any gain is a short-term gain, taxed at her ordinary income rate. If she holds them for more than one year, it's a long-term gain, taxed at a maximum of 15% for most investors.

Unrealized Gains

If a mutual fund buys a stock at $10, and the stock now trades at $15, there is no tax to pay. Unrealized gains make the NAV of the fund go up, but that doesn't affect the investor unless or until A) the fund realizes a gain on the shares by selling for a profit, or B) the investor does by redeeming his shares at a higher value.

Cost Basis on Reinvestments

Many investors choose not to take the income and capital gains distributions as checks. Rather, they apply that money towards more shares of the fund, which they buy without a sales load (at the NAV). Since the distributions are taxed either way, the investor adds to her cost basis by the amount of the distribution.

Let's say she bought the ACE Equity Income Fund at $10 per-share. Last year, she received $1 in dividends and $1 in capital gains distributions per-share. If she reinvests the $2 per-share, she pays tax on that amount, and her cost basis rises by that amount, too.

Taxation of Annuities

Accumulation Period

During the accumulation phase of a deferred variable annuity, the investment grows tax-deferred. So, all the dividends and capital gains distributions from the subaccounts are reinvested into more units, just like most people reinvest distributions back into a mutual fund. If the individual dies, the death benefit is paid to the beneficiary. The death benefit is included in the annuitant's **estate** for estate tax purposes, and the beneficiary pays tax on anything above the cost basis. If the husband bought the annuity for $50,000, and it's now worth $60,000, she'll receive $60,000 and pay ordinary income rates on the $10,000 of earnings.

Sometimes people cash in their contract earlier than expected. If they're under 59½ and don't have a qualifying exemption, they will not only pay ordinary income tax on the earnings, but also a 10% penalty tax, too. So, if it's a $60,000 annuity, and a 49-year-old surrenders the contract that he bought for $50,000, he'd pay his ordinary income rate on the $10,000 of earnings and a 10% penalty of $1,000. You didn't think the IRS would, like, penalize him 10% and then take his ordinary income rate on what's left, did you? It's his ordinary income rate plus 10% of the excess over his cost basis.

Notice how only the excess over cost basis is taxed and/or penalized on a non-qualified annuity. The cost basis was taxed before it went into the account.

So, if he's not 59½ yet, the IRS is giving him all kinds of reasons not to surrender the contract. And, we already mentioned that the insurance company will keep a percentage on the back end if he surrenders during the early years of the contract. So, he can have his money if he wants to, but if he takes it out too soon, there will be penalties and taxes to deal with.

72(t) and Substantially Equal Periodic Payments

We've mentioned that the magic age for taking distributions is 59½ because, otherwise, the individual is hit with early withdrawal penalties. Remember that annuities are by nature retirement plans and are subject to the 10% penalty for early withdrawals made without a qualifying exemption. One exemption available is to utilize IRS rule "72(t)." A reference to "72t" relates to an individual taking a series of substantially equal periodic payments (SEPP). The IRS won't penalize the early withdrawal if the individual sets up a schedule whereby he or she withdraws the money by any of several IRS-approved methods.

Once he starts the SEPP program, he needs to stay on it. The IRS requires him to continue the SEPP program for five years or until he is 59½, whichever comes last. So, if the individual is 45, she'll have to keep taking periodic payments until she's 59½. If the individual is 56 when she starts, she'll have to continue for 5 years. Either that, or cut the IRS a check for the penalties she was trying to avoid.

Loans

Some insurance companies allow contract owners to take a loan against the value of the annuity during the accumulation period. Usually, the interest charge is handled by reducing the number of accumulation units owned. If the owner pays back the loan in full, the number of units goes up again. Unlike a loan against a life insurance policy, however, a loan from an annuity is treated as a distribution. In other words, it is not tax-free.

1035 Exchanges

Both annuities and insurance policies allow the contract owner to exchange their contract for another without paying taxes. That's fine, just don't forget the surrender period. If someone has a 6% surrender fee in effect, and an agent pushes them to do a 1035 exchange, the IRS won't have a problem with it, but FINRA almost certainly will.

Also, this isn't the same thing as a life insurance contract. With a life insurance policy, people often cash in part of their **cash value**. If they're only taking out what they put in—or less—the IRS treats it as part of their cost basis. In an annuity, however, if someone does a **random withdrawal** for, say, $10,000, the IRS considers that to be part of the taxable earnings first.

Most annuities are non-qualified, which means they are purchased with non-tax-deductible dollars. When you cut the check for, say, $50,000 for the annuity, you get no tax deduction from the IRS that year against adjusted gross income. In other words, that $50,000 was taxed that year, so the tax collectors won't tax that money again when you take it out someday. That $50,000 will be your cost basis. You will only pay taxes on the amount of earnings above that and only when you finally take out the money.

On the other hand, a "tax-qualified variable annuity" or "individual retirement annuity" is funded with pre-tax or tax-deductible contributions with the same maximums used for Traditional IRA accounts. Like the Traditional IRA—and unlike the non-qualified variable annuity—withdrawals from the IRA annuity account must begin at age 70½.

The IRS refers to these plans as "individual retirement annuities," and they are basically just IRAs funded with an investment into a variable annuity. Why do that? Probably for the death benefit during the accumulation phase that guarantees your beneficiaries will receive at least the amount you contributed. Or, some people like the idea of an annuity payout that lasts for as long as they live, perhaps longer.

So, most questions focus on non-qualified variable annuities funded with after-tax dollars. But, don't be shocked if you get a question about variable annuities funded with tax-deductible dollars.

Annuity Period

When the annuitant begins receiving monthly checks, part of each check is considered taxable ordinary income, and part of it is considered part of the cost basis. Once the annuitant has received all the cost basis back, each additional annuity payment will be fully taxable.

Also, if the beneficiary is receiving annuity payments through a "life with period certain" or a "joint with last survivor" settlement option, she will pay ordinary income tax on part of each monthly check, too—as always, on the "excess over cost basis."

Taxation of Life Insurance

When we pay life insurance premiums, we don't take a deduction against income, so they are made after-tax. They usually grow tax-deferred, however, which is nice. When the insured dies, the beneficiary receives the death benefit free and clear of federal income taxes. But the death benefit is added to the insured's estate to determine estate taxes. It's that simple when the beneficiary has the lump-sum settlement option, anyway. If we're talking about those periodic settlement options that generate interest, some of those payments could be taxed as interest income.

Rather than take a loan, the policyholder can also do a "partial surrender," whereby the policyholder takes out some of the cash value—not enough to make the policy lapse, of course. Depending on how much has been paid in premiums, taxes may be due on the amount withdrawn. Unlike for variable annuities, the IRS uses FIFO here, assuming the first thing coming out is the cost basis, not the earnings. Only the part taken out above the premiums paid would be taxed.

If a loan is taken out, there are no immediate tax consequences.

Transferred Securities

A securities issuer's transfer agent keeps track of the transfers of ownership among shareholders. Usually a transfer of ownership is the result of a sale, but there are other ways to transfer ownership of stock. Stock can be inherited, received as a gift, or received as a charitable donation.

Inherited Securities

What if your grandmother bought stock at $10 a share several decades ago and passed it to you through her will when she—you know? What is your cost basis? Whatever the stock was worth on the day your grandmother—you know. If it's worth $30 on the date of death, then that's your cost basis, $30. For an inherited stock the recipient steps up the cost basis to the fair market value on the date of death. If the recipient sells the stock for $30 when the stepped-up basis is $30, there are no capital gains taxes.

Also, if the recipient sells this stock for more than $30, the capital gain is treated as long-term no matter how long he holds it. Most estates close out within a few months. If they liquidate the securities for more than the cost basis, there is a capital gain, but it's treated as long-term, even if it all happened in a few months.

The heirs who inherit appreciated securities can either value them as of the date of death or six months after. Estates often close out within six months and would, therefore, find it easier to value the stocks and bonds as of the date they sell it to cut checks to all the beneficiaries named in the will and trigger no capital gains taxes.

If they want to value the securities as of six months after the date of death, they'll need to value all assets as of that date. That means the estate may need to pay a real estate appraiser to value the house as of the same date the securities are valued. When the house is sold, the buyer might not be willing to pay the appraised value, or even if the house is sold for the appraised value, there are generally seller's expenses. In either case, the estate could end up showing a loss on the sale of the deceased's primary residence, or on the securities for that matter.

Gifted Securities

What if Grandma decided to give you the stock while she's alive? In that case, you would take her original cost basis of $10. If the stock is worth $40 when you sell it, your gain is $30 a share. Not like when you inherited the shares. Then, your gain would have only been $10.

You would take over Grandma's holding period, and not necessarily have to hold it for 12 months plus one day to get the long-term capital gains treatment. If she has already held the stock for years, your holding period is also long-term.

Tax-deductible Charitable Donations

What if Grandma decided to donate the stock to a charity instead of giving it to her grandkids? If she does that, she deducts the fair market value of the stock on the date of the donation. If it's worth $30,000 when she donates it, she can deduct $30,000 when figuring her taxes--up to a maximum of 40% of her adjusted gross income for the year.

What should an investor do if he has a stock that has appreciated significantly and one that has gone down in value? A good tax move might be for him to donate the appreciated stock to a charity and sell the loser for a capital loss. This way he will avoid a capital gain on the appreciated stock while also getting the tax deduction. And, he can use the capital loss on the other position to offset other gains or even some of his ordinary income. From there, he can donate the cash to a charity, or, of course, find other uses for it.

AMT

If an investor is in a certain income bracket, he is subject to an "Alternative Minimum Tax," or "AMT." That means that even though people say that municipal bonds pay tax-free interest, he will report *some* municipal bond interest on his AMT form as a "tax preference item." Generally, municipal bonds that are considered "private purpose" by the tax code subject investors to reporting income on their AMT forms. That's why many tax-exempt mutual funds also buy bonds that are not subject to AMT taxes.

The following is from IRS Publication 556 – Alternative Minimum Tax.

> The tax laws give preferential treatment to certain kinds of income and allow special deductions and credits for certain kinds of expenses. The alternative minimum tax attempts to ensure that anyone who benefits from these tax advantages pays at least a minimum amount of tax. The alternative minimum tax is a separately figured tax that eliminates many deductions and credits, thus increasing tax liability for an individual who would otherwise pay less tax. The tentative minimum tax rates on ordinary income are percentages set by law. For capital gains, the capital gains rates for the regular tax are used. You may have to pay the alternative minimum tax if your taxable income for regular tax purposes plus any adjustments and preference items that apply to you are more than the exemption amount.

A test question might also bring up the fact that the owner of a limited partnership interest will need to consult the instructions to his K-1 and may have to add certain tax preference items such as "accelerated depreciation" to his AMT form. The test question might say that "straight-line depreciation" would not be a tax preference item.

Progressive and Regressive

Progressive taxes include income, estate, and gift taxes. The bigger the income, estate, or gift, the higher the percentage rate the IRS charges.

Estates that are large get taxed, too. So, when Bill Gates passes away, his heirs will receive a ton of money, but the IRS will take some first in the form of estate taxes. The bigger the estate, the higher the rate of taxation. Progressive.

A **regressive** tax, on the other hand, is a flat tax. A list of regressive taxes would include sales, gas, payroll, and excise taxes. Everyone pays the same rate there. When you check out your items at Walmart, the cashier doesn't ask you your marginal tax bracket before giving you your total, right? No, it's a flat tax. Just like gas taxes are applied equally to gallons of gas whether they're pumped into a clunker or a Cadillac.

Lower-income Americans put a higher percent of their incomes into buying gasoline than high-income Americans do. If the secretary and the CEO both drive to work, they consume a similar amount of gasoline and pay a similar amount of gas taxes. If the amount of tax is, say, $800, that represents a much higher percentage of the secretary's income than it does the CEO's.

Unlike with income taxes, as the income levels drop, a flat tax represents a larger percentage of income. So, while the secretary's income might be taxed at no more than 15%, the gas and sales taxes she pays represent a much higher percent of her income than they do for the CEO in this example.

Corporate Taxes

Corporate profits are taxed at corporate tax rates. On the income statement bond interest is deducted pre-tax, while profits are taxed before dividends are paid to shareholders. Corporate profits (net income after tax) are taxed at that corporation's tax rate.

On the other hand, some companies use the IRS's Subchapter M to set themselves up as a "conduit" to investors. REITs do this. Many mutual funds do it, too. If a mutual fund has $1,000,000 in net income, for example, they often send at least 90% of it (900K) to shareholders as a dividend or "income" distribution. That way, the mutual fund company only pays tax on the remaining $100,000. The shareholders pay tax on the money the fund sends them. The company must send at least 90% of its net income to qualify for this tax treatment, and they can send more if they want.

When a corporation invests in the stocks of other companies, they receive dividends like any other investor. Unlike ordinary investors, though, the corporation receiving these dividends from shares of other companies' stock gets to exclude the first 70% from tax. That means they only get taxed on 30% of what they receive. And, if they're really an owner of the other company because they own 20% or more of it, they can exclude 80% of the income from tax. Berkshire Hathaway purchases smaller companies outright. They typically receive preferred dividends from those acquired companies, and if the smaller entity is being taxed on the net income, why should the parent company be fully taxed, too?

On the other hand, if a corporation holds the bonds of another corporation, they do not get to deduct any of the interest. That's because the company who paid the interest already deducted it from their taxable income. Municipal bond interest is tax-exempt to a corporate owner just as it is to any other owner.

Retirement Plans

In a taxable account the principal is reduced each year when the investor is taxed on interest,

dividends, and capital gains. In a tax-deferred account the principal is not taxed unless and until the individual finally takes distributions. The account balance grows faster when it is growing on a tax-deferred basis.

Tax-deferral is an advantage offered by deferred annuities and through retirement accounts. Whether one's contribution is tax-deductible, the fact that the interest, dividends, and capital gains will not be taxed each year is an advantage to the investor. That's why so many individuals participate in at least one retirement plan. Some retirement plans are started by the individual, and some are offered through an employer.

Let's start with the plans an individual can open, provided he has **earned income**. Earned income includes salary, bonuses, tips, alimony, and any income derived from actively participating in a business. It does not include passive income such as rental income from an apartment building or portfolio income such as bond interest, dividends, or capital gains.

Retirement plans are for working people who need to save up for retirement. If someone's sole source of income is rent checks or dividends, he probably doesn't need to save for retirement. And, if he does, he'll just need to do it outside a retirement account.

Individual Plans

An **IRA** is an **Individual Retirement Account**, or an Individual Retirement Arrangement.

Traditional

To contribute to a **Traditional IRA** the individual must be younger than 70 ½ and have earned income for the year. If the individual's income consists solely of dividends and bond interest, he can't make an IRA contribution for that year.

Contributions to an IRA are tax-deductible. If he contributes $5,000 to his IRA this year, that $5,000 no longer counts as taxable income. If he was going to pay tax on $52,000, now it's only $47,000 of taxable income for the year.

If he does have earned income for the year, an individual can contribute 100% of that earned income up to the current maximum. So, if she earns $1,800, then $1,800 is her maximum IRA contribution for that year. People 50 years and older can add a **catch-up contribution**. That amount is currently an extra $1,000.

At the time of writing, the maximum contribution to a Traditional IRA is $5,500, $6,500 for those 50 or older.

Penalties

Over-funding an IRA results in a 6% penalty on the amount above the maximum contribution for the year and any earnings associated with it. If the individual realizes she has over-funded her IRA for the year, she can remove the excess by the tax filing deadline the following year, or re-characterize the excess as part of the following year's contributions. If it's March 17, 2017 when she realizes she has over-funded her IRA by $1,000 for 2016, she can remove the $1,000 to avoid a penalty or fill out a form to re-characterize it as part of her 2017 contributions. If she does nothing, she pays a 6% penalty.

While we can always pull the money out of a Traditional IRA, if we take it out before age 59½, we'll pay a 10% penalty on top of the ordinary income tax that we always pay on withdrawals from IRAs. However, the following are qualifying exemptions to the 10% penalty. Although the withdrawal is taxable, the 10% penalty is waived for withdrawals made pursuant to:

- Death
- Permanent disability
- First home purchase for residential purposes
- A series of substantially equal periodic payments under IRS Rule 72-t
- Medical expenses
- Higher education expenses

A withdrawal pursuant to death means that the IRA owner has died and someone else is receiving the account balance as a named beneficiary. The beneficiary will be taxed but will not be penalized because the account owner died before age 59 1/2.

So, an individual can't have the money until he's 59½ without paying a penalty unless he uses one of the exemptions above. That's on the front end.

On the back end, he also is required to start taking it out by the time he's 70½. If not, the IRS will impose a 50% insufficient distribution penalty. We're talking about RMDs here, or **required minimum distributions**. When someone turns 70½, he has until April 1st of the following year to take out at least the required minimum distribution. If not, the IRS will levy a 50% penalty.

That's 50% of what he should have taken out at this point, not half the account value.

The absolute latest date that an individual can take his first withdrawal from a Traditional IRA without penalty is April 1st following the year he turns 70 1/2 . However, if he does that, he must take *two* distributions that year, which can push him into a higher tax bracket and make more of his social security benefits taxable. So, it's easier to take the first distribution in the year the individual turns 70½.

Unlike the Roth IRA, no contributions can be made into the Traditional IRA after age 70½.

Roth

The **Roth IRA** is funded with non-deductible contributions. However, the money comes out tax-free in retirement if the individual is 59½ years old and has had the account at least 5 years.

In retirement, then, the withdrawals you take from a Traditional IRA are taxable income. If you withdraw $30,000, you might only keep $22,000 after-tax. A withdrawal of $30,000 from your Roth IRA, on the other hand, leaves you with $30,000 to spend.

Unlike the Traditional, for the Roth IRA there is no requirement to take a distribution by age 70½. Since the IRS isn't going to tax that money, they couldn't care less when or even if it is withdrawn. In fact, individuals can keep contributing if they have earned income. So, a 72-year-old can refrain from taking Roth IRA withdrawals and can keep making contributions into the account if she has earned income. Neither option is available, on the other hand, for her Traditional IRA.

If the individual or married couple have adjusted gross incomes above a certain amount, they cannot contribute to their Roth IRAs. Period. So, get those Roth IRA accounts started while you're young and before you strike it rich. The money you contribute in your 20s and 30s can compound for decades, even if the IRS cuts off new contributions by age 40 based on your income.

If an individual has both a Traditional and a Roth IRA, the contribution limit is the total allocated among the two accounts. As I said, that is currently either $5,500 or $6,500 depending on age.

Also, the Roth IRA allows the individual to remove her cost basis, or the amount she has contributed, after five years without penalty. So, if he has contributed $25,000 into a Roth IRA and seven years later the account is worth $40,000, he could take the $25,000 out without a penalty and keep the remainder of $15,000 in the account. He could not put that $25,000 back in, however, and would not earn the tax-deferred and tax-free returns going forward.

But, as always, it's his money.

Converting a Traditional to a Roth IRA

Some individuals start out with a Traditional IRA and then decide to convert it to a Roth IRA. This requires the individual to pay tax on the entire amount going into the new Roth IRA, since Roth IRAs are funded with after-tax dollars. Even if the individual makes too much money to contribute to his Roth IRA, he can convert a Traditional IRA to a Roth IRA.

Investment Restrictions

I'm not sure why they do it, but some people like to use their Traditional IRA to invest in collectible items such as artwork, Persian rugs, antiques, coins, gems, stamps, etc. Funds withdrawn from the IRA to buy such items are considered distributed, which means the individual would pay ordinary income rates, plus a 10% penalty if he is not yet 59½.

US-minted gold or silver bullion coins are allowed, as they have intrinsic value. Collectible coins, on the other hand, are not suitable. Municipal bonds typically make poor investments for a Traditional IRA. Municipal bonds pay tax-exempt interest, which is why their coupon payments are so low. All money coming out of the Traditional IRA is taxed, so the municipal bond's tax-advantage is destroyed and all the individual is left with is a lower coupon payment.

Rollovers and Transfers

To move an IRA from one custodian to another, the best bet is to do a **direct transfer**. Just have the custodian cut a check to the new custodian. The IRA owner can do as many of these direct transfers as he wants. If, however, he does a **rollover**, things get tricky. First, he can only do one per year, and, second, it must be completed within 60 days to avoid tax ramifications.

In a rollover, the custodian cuts a check in the individual's name. The account owner cashes it and then sends the money to the new custodian, but any shortfall is subject to taxes and a 10% penalty. If the individual withdrew $50,000 but could only come up with $10,000 sixty days later, that $40,000 difference is taxed as ordinary income, plus a penalty tax of $4,000.

Employer-Based Plans

Plans offered through an employer either define the benefit to be received when the employee retires or the contributions made into the account. Usually, it is only the contributions that are defined.

Defined Contribution Plans

A **defined contribution plan** only defines the contributions the employer and/or the employee can make into the plan. The employer is not defining or promising any benefit at retirement. We'll talk about **defined benefit pension plans** in a bit, but let's focus first on the more familiar defined contribution plans.

At many companies new employees receive paperwork to fill out concerning the **401(k) plan** sponsored by the employer as an employee benefit. The employees choose a few mutual funds, and tell the HR department to deduct X amount from their paychecks to go into the 401(k) account. This way, part of their salary goes straight into a retirement fund and is not taxable currently, just like the money that goes into a Traditional IRA. Pretty attractive, especially if the employer matches what the employees elect to defer from each paycheck.

The amount of the employee's contribution is known as an **elective deferral**. Employers generally match all or part of an employee's elective deferral up to a certain percentage of compensation, as stipulated in their plan literature. But, they are not required to make **matching contributions**. Why might someone choose to participate in a 401(k) even if the company was not matching contributions? Maybe he likes the higher maximum contribution limit vs. the IRA or Roth IRA.

The advantage to a business owner setting up a 401(k) plan is that a vesting schedule can be laid out over several years, meaning that the employer's contributions don't belong to the employee until he is fully vested. However, 401(k) plans come with complicated **top-heavy** rules, which means the plan cannot provide benefits to just the key, highly compensated employees. A plan in which 60% of the benefits go to key employees is a plan that shows signs of being "top-heavy," and will need to adjust things or deal with tax problems.

For-profit companies offer 401(k) plans to their employees. Non-profit organizations such as schools and hospitals offer **403(b) plans** to their employees. As with a 401(k) plan, the employee indicates how much of her paycheck should go into the 403(b) account, which simultaneously gives her a tax break now and helps her save up for retirement later. As with a 401(k) plan, the contributions go in pre-tax but come out fully taxable when the participant starts taking distributions.

While a 401(k) plan might offer participants the ability to purchase stocks and bonds a la carte, a 403(b) plan only offers annuities and mutual funds as investment vehicles. The 403(b) plans can also be referred to as **Tax-Sheltered Annuities** or **TSAs**.

Some states and cities have begun to shift the burden of funding retirement benefits to their employees. These so-called **457 plans** are for state and local government employees, e.g., police and fire workers. Contributions are tax-deductible, and the plans use the same maximum contribution limits used by 401(k) and 403(b) plans.

Profit sharing plans are also defined contribution plans, but the contributions are never required. If the company does contribute, it must be made for all eligible employees based on a predetermined formula. For example, maybe all workers receive up to 10% of their salaries when the company has a banner year. The profit-sharing plan uses much higher maximum annual contributions than the 401(k), 403(b) or Section 457 plans. Of course, that would only matter if you happened to work for a profitable and generous employer.

A **money purchase plan** is not flexible the way a profit sharing plan is. The money purchase plan requires the employer to make a mandatory contribution to each employee's account, based on his/her salary, whether the company feels like it or not. The exam might say something like "in a money purchase plan, contributions are mandatory on the part of the employer and discretionary on the part of the employee."

Keogh plans are for individuals with self-employment income or for those working for a sole proprietorship with a Keogh plan in place. They're not for S-corps, C-corps, LLCs, etc.—only sole proprietors. If the individual in the test question has side income or is self-employed, he or she can have a Keogh. They can contribute a certain percentage of their self-employment income into the Keogh.

How much? A lot. As with the SEP-IRA, the business owner can put 20% of her compensation into a Keogh, and she can put in 25% of her employees' compensation. Some readers find it shocking that there may be employees at a "sole" proprietorship. But, trust me, there can be. A "sole proprietorship" is just a business with one owner, a guy doing business as himself. The number of employees he has? Anybody's guess. Also, to avoid confusion, remember we said that Keogh plans are for sole proprietorships only; we did not say that sole proprietorships can only have a Keogh plan. A SEP-IRA or SIMPLE IRA would also be available to a sole proprietor, for example.

A small business can establish a **SEP-IRA**, which stands for "Simplified Employee Pension" IRA. This allows the business owner to make pre-tax contributions for herself and any eligible employees. Twenty-five percent of wages can be contributed to an employee's SEP, up to the current maximum. SEP contributions are not mandatory on the part of the business owner. It's just that if the business makes any contributions, they must be made to all eligible employees as stipulated in the plan agreement.

Notice how the business makes the contributions, not the employees. So, if you're self-employed, you can contribute to your own SEP-IRA, but if you're an employee at a company with a SEP-IRA, it's the company who will make the contributions on your behalf. To establish a SEP, the employer uses a model agreement put out by the IRS (download it from www.irs.gov) that they and the employees sign. It does not have to be filed with the IRS, which does not issue an opinion or approval.

Keep in mind that even though a large contribution can be made to a SEP-IRA, that amount must represent 25% of wages. In other words, we often focus on the maximum amounts that can be contributed, but to make contributions at all the small business owner must be making a profit, and when contributing for employees, the contributions are 25% of wages. That means that the only way to put a lot of money into a SEP-IRA is to earn a lot of money—since 25% of a $33,000 salary is not going to make for a large contribution.

In that case, maybe the small business owner decides to set up a **SIMPLE Plan** instead. A SIMPLE plan can be either an IRA or a 401(k). The SIMPLE plan is for businesses with no more than 100 employees and with no other retirement plan offered. In a SIMPLE plan, business owners choose to either match the employee's contributions up to 3% of compensation, or to contribute 2% of the employee's compensation if he does not make an elective deferral from his paycheck.

Unlike with a 401(k) plan, employees are immediately vested in a SEP-IRA or SIMPLE plan.

Many companies reward key employees by offering them **employee stock options.** These options do not trade among investors but are essentially free call options that allow employees to buy the company's stock at a set strike/exercise price. To keep the employee around a while, the company usually awards the options to buy the stock on a vesting schedule by which the employee gradually receives options. An **ESOP** or **employee stock ownership plan** is what it sounds like. Through these plans the company allows all workers to purchase company stock at a discount and through a payroll deduction. The stock and the dividends/cap gains generated on it grow tax-deferred, like a 401(k) plan.

Defined Benefit Plans

Defined benefit pension plans are the opposite of defined contribution plans. In a defined contribution plan the employer puts in some money and then wishes employees the best of luck with retirement. For a defined benefit plan, the employer bears all the risk and, therefore, must earn sufficient returns on their investments to pay a defined benefit to retirees and their survivors.

Maybe that defined benefit is 70% of average salary figured over the employee's last three years of service, paid out each year in retirement, plus maybe a benefit to a spouse or children if he dies within a certain time.

A defined benefit pension plan is established as a trust and does not pay tax on the income it generates. In fact, the company gets to deduct the contributions it makes into the pension fund from taxable income. Therefore, these plans do not typically invest in municipal securities, since they are already tax-advantaged accounts.

Because corporations typically try to fund these plans only as much as required, defined benefit plans require an actuary to certify that funding levels are sufficient to cover future pension fund obligations.

ERISA Issues

ERISA is a federal securities act enforced by the Department of Labor. It's a "securities law" in the sense that most retirement plans offered in the workplace offer investments in securities to the participants. ERISA is shorthand for the federal government's Employee Retirement Income Security Act. ERISA was passed in 1974 and was designed to protect employees (and their beneficiaries) who depend on pension funds for their retirement security.

A defined benefit pension plan promises to pay a predetermined amount of benefits to employees when they retire. The employer sets it up and takes on the responsibility of figuring out how to deduct X amount of company dollars now and put them into the stock and bond markets wisely enough to pay out Y amount of pension fund dollars to retirees. Generally, the pension fund hires investment advisers to manage the fund's assets. Large pension funds typically dole out portions of the plan's assets to different money management/investment advisory firms. The investment committee hires various investment advisers to manage portions of the pension fund assets, and frequently even hires advisers to help them pick the other advisers.

The 401(k), defined benefit pension, profit sharing, and Keogh plan are all plans covered by ERISA. The SIMPLE and SEP-IRA, on the other hand, are informal plans between employer and employee.

Starting a 401(k) requires IRS approval, while starting a SIMPLE IRA requires the business owner to print and fill out a form for their own records.

ERISA does not require companies to have retirement plans. Rather, it establishes rules for companies who happen to have them.

Fiduciaries

A defined benefit pension plan is managed for the benefit of retirees. As the US Department of Labor explains:

Each pension plan has at least one fiduciary. The fiduciaries of a plan usually include:

- Trustee
- Investment advisers
- All individuals exercising discretion
- All members of the plan's administrative committee
- Those who select committee officials

The key to determining whether someone is a fiduciary is whether they are exercising discretion or control over the plan. Attorneys, accountants, and actuaries are generally not fiduciaries when acting in their professional roles.

The investment manager of a pension fund uses discretion/control to invest the plan assets; therefore, the investment manager is a "fiduciary" with obligations to the participants and beneficiaries of the plan. As ERISA makes clear:

- a fiduciary shall discharge his duties with respect to a plan solely in the interest of the participants and beneficiaries
- and for the exclusive purpose of: (i) providing benefits to participants and their beneficiaries; and (ii) defraying reasonable expenses of administering the plan
- with the care, skill, prudence, and diligence under the circumstances then prevailing that a prudent man acting in a like capacity and familiar with such matters would use in the conduct of an enterprise of a like character and with like aims
- by diversifying the investments of the plan so as to minimize the risk of large losses, unless under the circumstances it is clearly prudent not to do so; and
- in accordance with the documents and instruments governing the plan insofar as such documents and instruments are consistent with the provisions of this subchapter and subchapter III of this chapter.

The "documents and instruments governing the plan" might be referred to on the exam as an investment policy statement. If the policy statement says that no more than 40% of the plan assets are to be invested in equities, guess what? Don't put more than 40% into equities. Even if you ended up having a good year because of your renegade stock picks, you'd be in trouble. The only time to override the policy statement is if it clearly violates ERISA.

Also, notice how diversification is presumed to be part of a prudent investment policy, "unless under the circumstances it is clearly prudent not to do so." This is a direct link to the Uniform Prudent

Investor Act, which mentions ERISA many times throughout the text. In fact, all those bullet points overlap with the Uniform Prudent Investor Act. It's just that the UPIA is talking more to the administrators of private trusts, while ERISA is concerned with the fiduciaries running pension trusts.

Either way, if you're an investment adviser managing assets on behalf of beneficiaries, you need to use skill, prudence, and absolute honesty-above-reproach. You need to keep the costs of administering the plan reasonable. Why? Well, among other reasons, as the Department of Labor explains on a helpful website, "Fiduciaries who do not follow the basic standards of conduct may be personally liable to restore any losses to the plan, or to restore any profits made through improper use of the plan's assets." The website goes on to suggest, "However, fiduciaries can limit their liability in certain situations. One way fiduciaries can demonstrate that they have carried out their responsibilities properly is by documenting the processes used to carry out their responsibilities." In other words, every time you make a decision, keep good notes and make a backup. This stock was purchased for this reason, these bonds were sold for that reason, we used this broker-dealer to execute the sale for these reasons, etc.

Safe Harbor, 404(c)

This heavy fiduciary duty implies that the plan is managing the assets on behalf of employees/participants/beneficiaries. If we're talking about a 401(k) or other defined contribution plan that lets the employee choose investments, now it's the employee's problem what happens in the stock and bond markets. As an employer, you would probably rather match your employees' contributions into a plan in which they choose all their own investment options. That way, whatever happens in the market is at their own risk.

To relieve yourself of the fiduciary duty over investment losses, your plan must make sure that participants have control, as defined by ERISA and the rules written under the Act. First, the plan needs to make a clear written statement to participants that it "intends to constitute a plan described in section 404(c) of ERISA, and that the fiduciaries of the plan may be relieved of liability for any losses which are the direct and necessary result of investment instructions given by the participant or beneficiary." Also, the plan must:

- Offer a selection of at least three investment choices with materially different risk and return characteristics
- Provide the ability to change investment allocations at least quarterly
- Provide sufficient education and information about the plan to allow participants to make informed investment decisions

To sail into these safe waters, the plan needs to provide the three bullet points above. Most plans provide at least three different investment choices, and participants can almost always change allocations among, say, the growth, income, and long-term bond funds quarterly, if not every single day. It's the third bullet point that is probably the hardest to satisfy. To make sure they have provided sufficient education to shield themselves from liability for the investment losses their employees may end up with, the company must provide detailed information on the fees and expenses charged on investments, the risk/reward nature of all the investment options, the most recent prospectus for each investment option, the name of the investment manager/adviser for the investment options, and other important information.

Unfortunately, if the company gives too much advice of a personally targeted nature, they might cross into the territory of providing investment advice—yikes! That's the fiduciary relationship they're trying to avoid. So, many companies hire third-party investment advisers or other financial service providers to educate employees sufficiently to allow them to make informed investment decisions. The act of hiring an investment adviser or a provider of investment education is itself a fiduciary action, so the parties they choose had better know what they're doing. Otherwise, the company could be liable for the losses that result from incompetent or dishonest advice.

Also, note that advisers themselves are fiduciaries when giving advice or managing assets for employees. When we're talking about relieving oneself of fiduciary duties, we're only talking about the employer, and even there we're only talking about relieving themselves of responsibility for investment losses that result from the participant's investment decisions. But, if the company provides a reputable investment adviser to participants, it is relieved of the fiduciary duty in terms of how well the investments pan out.

The employer has fiduciary duties connected to the 401(k) plan. For example, the employer must make sure that when the employees make an investment into the plan, that money is deposited promptly. Sure, it is more fun to let it all sit in the corporate money market account a few extra weeks earning interest, but that would not satisfy the fiduciary duty. Is it good for the company or for the participant? As a fiduciary, think about the participants first.

Again, the employer has other fiduciary obligations to the people participating in the plan. It's just that the employer would prefer to pass the investment risk off to the employees. And since so many employers have already passed off the investment decisions and risks to employees, the industry you're in or are entering is looking like it's on a growth path for about 20–30 years.

How do I know the employees might need your services some day? Research has shown that whatever the investment options are, employees will divide their money evenly among that number of funds. For example, if the company offers a stock fund and a balanced fund, most employees will choose to put half in each, thinking they have now "diversified." In fact, since the balanced fund usually holds about 60% stock, the employee is not nearly as "balanced" as she thinks and has a large percentage of her retirement money in the stock market. Also, if there are 10 different stock funds, most employees put 10% in each one, regardless of how redundant or risky some of them are.

Company Stock

If the company allows participants to invest in company stock, it should make sure that the following bulleted list is followed:

- The company stock is publicly traded
- The company stock is traded with enough frequency and volume so participants' instructions to buy or sell can be executed promptly
- Participants are provided information given to shareholders of company stock generally
- Voting, tendering, and similar rights are passed through to participants
- The plan designates a fiduciary to ensure information regarding the purchase, sale, and holding of company stock, and the exercise of voting, tendering, and similar rights is maintained with procedures to keep it confidential

190

- An independent fiduciary is appointed to address any situations where the fiduciary responsible for confidentiality determines there is a potential for undue influence on a participant's decision to vote or tender shares

A plan may not "acquire any employer security or real property, if immediately after such acquisition the aggregate fair market value of employer securities and employer real property held by the plan exceeds 10 percent of the fair market value of the assets of the plan." In other words, we don't want the pension fund for XYZ Corporation to invest more than 10% of the pension fund's assets into XYZ securities. It would be bad enough if XYZ goes down; no need to drag the pension fund with it, right? We also don't want the plan to devote an extreme percentage of assets toward buying property that is then leased to the employing corporation. Again, if the plan put 90% of its assets into buying property that the employer can't afford to make payment on, that would be a real mess.

Special Types of Accounts

These days there are two basic ways to save for education. One is to purchase tuition credits at today's prices, based on the belief that tuition will be much more expensive by the time the child goes to school. The other method is to invest the money in special accounts that allow for tax-free withdrawals when used for qualified education expenses.

529 Savings Plan

The **529 savings plan** allows investors to save/invest for education. Usually it is a family member putting money away for a child's education, but the beneficiary does not have to be a child, or even a blood relative of the donor. In fact, an individual can set up a 529 plan for him or herself. The person who opens the account is the owner. The beneficiary is the person who will use the money for education. For 529 savings plans, the owner controls the assets.

Contributions are made after-tax (non-deductible), but the withdrawals used for qualified education expenses are tax-free at the federal level. Notice how I said "federal level." The plans are state-specific, so some states may tax the withdrawals. That means that if Grandma lives in New Jersey and buys a Wisconsin plan, New Jersey could end up taxing the money that the grandkids use for college. Then again, New Jersey might allow Grandma to deduct her contributions for purposes of state income taxes. So, you don't want to buy into a 529 savings plan without first checking how it will be taxed by the state.

And, even with the federal taxation, the withdrawals for education must be qualified withdrawals that cover tuition, room & board, books, etc. The expenses need to be directly related to education; otherwise, you'll get hit on them just like you do for an early IRA distribution (10% penalty plus ordinary income tax). If the beneficiary decides he doesn't need the money, the account can name a second beneficiary without tax problems, if the second beneficiary is related to the first.

And there is one area that can lead to confusion. Remember that when setting up a 529 plan it makes no difference whether the account owner is related to the beneficiary. It's just that if you start a 529 plan for a beneficiary and then discover that the kid has no intention of going to college, then if you want to avoid tax implications, you can only change the beneficiary to a blood relative of the beneficiary. If you want to change beneficiaries to someone not related, you'll have to deal with the 10% penalty and ordinary income tax.

Don't forget that when the donor is putting money into a 529 savings plan on behalf of her granddaughter, she is making a gift. Gifts over a certain amount are taxable to the one making the gift. With a 529 savings plan, this grandmother can contribute up to the gift tax exclusion without incurring gift taxes, and can even do a lump-sum contribution for the first five years without incurring gift tax hassles. In other words, if the annual gift tax exclusion is $14,000, she can put in $70,000 for the next five years. If she and Grandpa are married-filing-separately, they could put in twice that amount, or $140,000, without any gift tax issues. Note that if someone uses the five-year-up-front method, they can't make any more gifts to the beneficiary for the next five years without dealing with gift taxes.

The owner of the plan maintains control over the assets, deciding when withdrawals will be made. The money can be withdrawn to cover higher education expenses, such as tuition, books, and room and board. Bear in mind that it doesn't have to be "college," necessarily—just any school higher than high school, basically. So, if the exam asks if you can use the assets to go to heating & air-conditioning school, tell it that as long as the school is an accredited post-secondary institution eligible to participate in a student aid program, the answer is yes.

Prepaid Tuition

If you're sure that Junior won't mind going to college in-state, you might want to lock him in as a future Boilermaker, Hoosier, or Sycamore through a plan whereby you pay for his tuition credits now for any public school in the fine state of Indiana. I didn't say you were locking him into being *accepted* at IU or Purdue, but he would get to go to a state school with a certain number of credits already paid for. Parents worried about the ever-rising cost of tuition, then, can pay today's prices and redeem the credits more than a decade into the future.

These tuition credits cover tuition and fees only. If the child gets a scholarship or doesn't need the money because of something tragic like death or disability, a refund is typically provided plus a modest rate of interest. The exam could refer to prepaid tuition plans as "defined benefit plans." You pay for the tuition credits now, and then you hope the state can afford to provide the benefit of education when your child needs it.

Coverdell Education Savings Account

A **Coverdell Education Savings Account** (CESA) also allows for after-tax contributions (non-deductible), but the current maximum is only a few thousand dollars per year per child. While the 529 Plan is for higher education only, the Coverdell plan can be used for elementary, secondary, and higher education expenses. The distributions are tax-free at the federal level if used according to the plan guidelines. As with the 529 plan, the Coverdell ESA account can be used for education expenses, including tuition, books, and room and board. In a Coverdell contributions must stop on the beneficiary's 18th birthday, and the assets must be used for education or distributed to him by age 30. Also, there are income limits on the donors of a CESA, similar to the limits placed on people trying to fund their Roth IRAs.

So, should you use a 529 plan or a CESA? Generally, it would come down to the amount of money you want to contribute. If you're going to contribute only a few thousand dollars, you might as well use the CESA. If you want to put large amounts of money away, you'll pretty much have to use the 529 plan. Either way, you'll get tax deferral and tax-free withdrawals at the federal level, assuming you do everything according to plan.

UGMA/UTMA Accounts

If a donor wants to donate money for the benefit of a minor, all she has to do is set up the account as either an **UGMA** or **UTMA** account. UGMA stands for "Uniform Gifts to Minors Act" and UTMA stands for "Uniform Transfers to Minors Act." All states except Vermont and South Carolina have now adopted UTMA laws, which supersede UGMA laws. Either way, the child is going to eventually be in control of the assets, either at age 18 in a few states or age 21 in most states. There are even a few states that allow the transfer to happen as late as age 25, but that is the maximum and also not typical. The state used is typically where the minor resides, although it could be where the custodian resides.

Setting up the account requires no supporting documentation. The donor needs the minor's social security number and also provides the tax ID number of the custodian. The donor often manages the account as the **custodian**, although the two could be different parties, as well. If the donor is trying to minimize the size of his estate to avoid estate taxes, he will typically appoint another party as the custodian. Otherwise, the assets would be counted under his estate.

Either way, the account is opened as either UGMA or UTMA, making sure there's just one adult custodian and one minor child per account. You can't have two adults as custodians, and you can't have more than one minor child per account. You also can't have a corporation or a partnership acting as the custodian. Only an adult human being can serve in that role. And, that adult is a fiduciary, meaning if he "invests" the money at the racetrack or tries to engage in naked options, he could be forced to refund any losses caused by his lack of prudence.

If the exam asks what happens if you want to establish an UTMA for your niece, whose parents "oppose the gift," tell it that if you have the minor's social security number, you can open the account. The minor's parents have no access to the account that you will set up and/or manage as custodian. In fact, one cold probably keep them in the dark entirely about the existence of the account.

A proper title for an UTMA account would look like this: Mark Michelson, as Custodian for Michael Michelson under the Illinois Uniform Transfers to Minors Act. The adult custodian is the "nominal owner" while the beneficiary is the "beneficial owner" of this account. The gifts are considered "irrevocable and indefeasible," which means they cannot be taken back or treated as loans to be repaid. When the beneficiary reaches the state's age of majority (adulthood), there is nothing the donor or custodian can do to stop him from selling off all the securities and buying a Corvette. In a formal trust account—which we'll discuss up ahead—that sort of thing can be avoided. But an UTMA/UGMA account is a "trust" whose terms are drawn up in state law, as opposed to a formal trust account in which the trust documents stipulate the terms.

Of course, there is no reason to assume all young adults would be foolish with the account assets. Parents might set up an UTMA account so that the child at age 21 has money to make a down payment on a house or start a business. But, what the parents intended as a down payment on a house could, again, be spent on anything the new adult wants, period.

Since the child won't be needing the money for, say, eight years, surely the adult custodian can sort of "borrow" from the account from time to time as needed, if she repays it eventually, with interest, right?

Wrong. These accounts receive special tax consideration, so if the custodian is pretending the account is an UTMA account, but uses it to get interest-free loans, the IRS might start talking about tax fraud, back taxes, and penalties-plus-interest.

If the question asks if room and board would be a legitimate expense to be covered by an UTMA account, the answer is no. Room and board is something parents are expected to provide to their children, and not through some tax-advantaged account. Approximately the first $1,000 of income is exempt from taxation no matter how old the beneficiary is. The next $1,000 or so of income is taxed at the child's income tax rate. Seriously. Then, if there is more than about $2,000 and the child is under age 18, it will be taxed at the higher of the child's or the parents' tax rate. Or, if the child is over 18, that income is taxed at his tax rate.

So, I don't expect that level of detail in a test question, but I would expect a question asking about whether this account is tax-deferred or not. No. Some of the income is taxed favorably, period. Another tax consideration is that the donor can reduce the size of his estate by transferring assets to an UTMA/UGMA; however, if he wants to be sure the assets are excluded from his estate, he should appoint someone else as custodian.

Setting up UTMA/UGMA accounts requires no legal work, making it much cheaper than establishing a formal trust account. These days, investors typically use 529 Plans to save for college rather than custodial accounts, because assets in an UTMA/UGMA count against the child's chances of receiving financial aid more so than assets in a 529 Savings Plan.

Calculating Educational Funding Needs

When a financial planner estimates the educational funding needs for a client, she uses the following five inputs:

- Current tuition cost per year
- Education inflation rate
- Number of years of college attendance
- Number of years before college begins
- Expected investment return

Because tuition has historically risen even faster than the general rate of inflation, the calculation uses a specific rate for education costs, above the rate of the CPI.

Estates

When someone dies, the IRS and state tax collectors may end up taxing the value of assets (house, farmland, bank account, stock, life insurance, etc.) owned at the time of death.

Wait, how can the IRS can tax a dead person?

They can't. A dead person is not a person. The dead person's possessions become part of a **legal person** known as an **estate**. The estate is what can be taxed.

An estate is a legal entity in the same way that a trust, a corporation, or a partnership is a legal entity. None of those entities is a human being, but all are "legal persons" in the eyes of the law.

Think of it this way: Otis Redding is not a legal person. However, the Estate of Otis Redding *is* a legal person. The estate is a legally recognized entity. Like a corporation, it has an FEIN (federal employee identification number) and pays taxes on all those royalties received from songs like "Dock of the Bay," "R-E-S-P-E-C-T," and "Hard to Handle."

Like a corporation, the assets of the estate are separate from the assets of the beneficiaries of the deceased person's will. So, if some bass player files a claim that Otis Redding owes him $8,000,000, what happens if all the estate assets are only worth $1,000,000?

The bassist should have tried to collect sooner. Maybe he'll get every dollar of that eight million claim through the courts, but the children do not have to make up the difference. The estate is a separate legal entity, just like a corporation.

When Grandma dies, her checking and savings accounts, CDs, real estate, life insurance, etc., all go into a new legal entity called an estate. If you were named the executor of the estate, it's your job to get several death certificates and do all the paperwork required to transfer her checking and savings to a new bank account entitled, say, Jason Miller, Executor for the Estate of Maude L. Miller, Deceased. If Grandma owned stocks and bonds, they need to be re-titled in the name of the estate, as well. This will require affidavits, signature guarantees, stock powers, letters of office; the whole nine yards. When you effect these transfers of ownership, make sure you have plenty of original death certificates and that the court appointment/letters of office are no more than 60 days old.

You've probably heard the phrase that the only certainties in life are death and taxes. When we talk about estates, we're talking about both. When someone dies, the assets go into his/her estate and taxation is a concern. We'll look at the strategy of establishing trusts to minimize estate taxes in a few minutes, but, first, let's make sure we understand how an estate is treated for the purposes of taxation.

Think of an estate account as a short-term account where safe, short-term debt securities are generally the only appropriate investments. T-Bills and other money market instruments are usually the right recommendation for an estate account. Assuming no huge tax or legal problems, the assets of the estate will soon be distributed to the heirs/beneficiaries. What happens if the stocks, bonds, CDs, etc., earn interest/dividends in the meantime? That income is taxable to the estate. But, the legal fees charged by the estate attorney may well cancel that income out. If, however, the estate earns $5,000 in dividend income when the legal bills are just $2,000, there is $3,000 of taxable income there. The estate will file a tax return (a 1041) for that income.

Will the value of the estate itself be taxed? First, we start with the gross estate—the value of the assets before taking deductions. The following are included in the value of the gross estate:

- house, farmland, savings account, checking account, investment accounts, clothing, oil paintings, Harley, etc.
- value of insurance and annuity contracts
- assets placed in revocable trusts
- does not include assets placed in irrevocable trusts (except certain property transferred within three years of death!)

So, we add those values and then start subtracting things to reduce the value of this estate. If we reduce the value enough, we might avoid paying any estate taxes. The following reduce the gross estate:

- Funeral and administrative expenses
- Debts owed at the time of death
- Any charitable gifts made after death
- The marital deduction

The "marital deduction" means that husbands and wives pass their property to one another at death without paying estate taxes, which seems fair enough. It's when the assets then go from the "second to die" to the heirs that things get dicey. So, after we've added up the value of all the assets (gross estate) and subtracted the first three bullet points above, maybe what's left is $1 million. Will we have to pay estate taxes?

No. Currently, there is a lifetime credit of $5 million for estates, indexed for inflation. Since the taxable estate is below that number, we avoid paying estate taxes on the estate itself, as an entity or "person."

How are the heirs taxed once they inherit their share? Remember that when Grandma died, we took the fair market value of her securities as our cost basis, which we enjoyed. When we sell the stocks and bonds for more than that fair market value, the excess is a long-term capital gain, even if we realize it two or three months from now.

Generally, the state only goes after estate taxes when the estate is large enough to be taxed at the federal level.

Gifts

What if several months ago Grandma had gone in for her regular checkup and found out from her doctor that she had maybe two months to live? To avoid estate taxes, couldn't she just start handing out envelopes of cash to all the kids and grandkids?

Sure. In fact, the IRS is fine with that. See, the gifts that Grandma gives to individuals while she is alive are also taxable if they are over a certain amount. That number is forever changing but is currently $14,000. Whatever the amount is, there is an "annual gift-tax exclusion," which means that if Grandma gives anyone other than her husband a gift worth more than that amount, she must start chipping away at her lifetime gift tax credit. The amount of the credit that was used up over her lifetime will reduce the amount of the credit you and the other beneficiaries can use when trying to reduce the size of the estate to avoid paying estate taxes.

The IRS defines a **gift** as "transferring property to someone else and expecting nothing in return." The IRS also points out that the following can be considered gifts:

- selling something at less than its value
- making an interest-free or reduced-interest loan

Wait, so when Grandma sold Uncle Bill the back forty for $70,000 below market value, this could have been considered a "gift" to Uncle Bill?

Absolutely. So, when Grandma goes around giving people things worth more than the current annual exclusion, she files a return and tells the IRS that she's using part of her lifetime credit. What if the gift is worth no more than the current exclusion of $14,000?

Then nobody needs to know anything. In the following cases, no gift taxes would be due and no returns would have to be filed:

- Gifts made to a spouse
- Gifts that do not exceed current exclusion amount
- Paying tuition costs for someone else—payable directly to educational institution
- Paying medical costs for someone else—payable directly to the care provider
- Political and charitable donations

Gift Splitting

The IRS is clear on the topic of **gift splitting**, so let's use their Publication 950 from www.irs.gov to make the point:

> Harold and his wife, Helen, agree to split the gifts that they made during the previous tax year. Harold gives his nephew, George, $24,000, and Helen gives her niece, Gina, $18,000. Although each gift is more than the annual exclusion ($14,000), by gift splitting they can make these gifts without making a taxable gift.

That means is that half of $24,000 ($12,000) and half of $18,000 ($9,000) would be less than the annual exclusion of $14,000, so they can treat each gift as half from Harold and half from Helen. No gift taxes would be due and none of the lifetime credits would have to be used up, but the IRS requires that they file a gift tax return.

There are many horrible ways to die, none of which needs to be mentioned for our purposes here. From a financial planning standpoint, however, the worst way to die would be to die without a will or trust. Folks who do this are said to have died **intestate**. If that happens, not only do the deceased's assets go through the probate process, but, first, an administrator of the estate has to be named by the probate court.

At least with a will the deceased's wishes are stated, and—if there are no challenges—the distribution of assets will be made according to the stated will of the now deceased individual. When someone dies with a will, an executor is named. Although that saves some time with the probate process, it puts the estate through that process.

What's the problem with probate? The probate process makes the estate assets and their distribution a public record. It delays the distribution of the assets. And, it can easily consume 4% of the estate's value, as the beneficiaries watch money that would have gone to them get eaten up in legal and accounting fees.

So, before we look at all the different types of trusts, remember that what they all have in common is avoiding the probate process. Like an estate or a corporation, a trust is a separate legal entity with its own FEIN. The trust holds assets, just as a corporation or an estate holds assets. The person who administers and oversees the investments of the trust is the "trustee." The one who grants the assets to the trust is called the "grantor." And the ones who benefit from the trust are called the "beneficiaries."

When an adult sets up an UTMA/UGMA account, the minor owns and controls the assets at the age of adulthood/majority, which is usually no later than age 21. If he sets up a trust, on the other hand, he can specify all types of things in the trust agreement about when the beneficiary is to receive distributions and how much he is to receive. The exam might point out other advantages of establishing trusts:

- Faster and less costly way to transfer property upon death, when compared to a will
- Avoids probate court process (time, expense), especially if property is owned in several different states
- Eliminates challenges to estate—just specifically disinherit anyone who poses a challenge to your wishes upon your death
- Keeps transfer of property private
- Reduces amount of estate taxable to heirs

Revocable, Irrevocable

Reducing the amount of the taxable estate can come down to the difference between revocable and irrevocable trusts. In general, assets placed in an irrevocable trust do not count as part of the estate, while assets placed in a revocable trust do count. What's the difference? If the trust is revocable, the person who set it up (grantor) can revoke the assets and change the terms of the trust documents. Therefore, not only are those assets taxable to the grantor while he/she is alive, but when he/she dies, those assets do count towards the value of the estate, even if the assets were never "taken back." If a grantor sets up an irrevocable trust, the assets cannot be revoked.

Remember that the assets placed in an irrevocable trust are no longer taxable to the grantor while he is alive, and when he dies, the assets do not count towards the value of the estate that the heirs are hoping to keep below the amount that triggers estate taxes.

The irrevocable trust will either distribute income to the beneficiaries, or it won't. Either way, the interest, dividends, and capital gains generated are taxable. If the income is distributed to the beneficiaries, they include it on their own income tax forms. If the income is not distributed, it is taxable to the trust.

In a revocable trust, or even in an irrevocable trust where the grantor or grantor's spouse benefits from the income, the grantor is subject to taxation while he is alive. In fact, because the IRS basically ignores the trust structure for revocable trusts, they are often called **grantor trusts,** because there is really no separation between the grantor and the trust at this point. Unlike with the simple and complex trusts we are about to discuss, a grantor trust is not treated as a separate entity.

Simple vs. Complex

For purposes of paying federal income taxes all trusts are either simple or complex. A **simple trust** is required to distribute all income to the beneficiaries annually. No charitable donations can be made from a simple trust, and distributions from the principal or **corpus** of the trust are not regularly made to the beneficiaries.

A **complex trust** can make charitable donations and make regular distributions to the beneficiaries from the corpus or principal of the account. A complex trust also routinely retains some of the income generated by the account rather than distributing it the way a simple trust is required to do. If the trust does any of the three things mentioned, it is treated as a complex trust (charitable donations, retain income for corpus, distribute from corpus). In either case, income that is distributed to the beneficiaries is taxable to them, while income retained by the trust is taxable to the trust itself.

Although we don't associate the simple trust with distributions from corpus, the trustee can use his discretion to make a distribution of, say, a capital gain on a large stock sale to the beneficiaries. In any year that the trustee does so the trust is treated as a complex trust under the tax code.

Inter Vivos, Testamentary

A trust can be established while the grantor is alive or through his will when he dies. A trust established while the grantor is alive is called an **inter vivos** trust, while a trust established upon the death of the grantor through the terms of a will is known as a **testamentary trust**. An inter vivos trust can be either revocable or irrevocable. A testamentary trust is an irrevocable trust. In fact, all revocable trusts become irrevocable upon the death of the grantor, who is no longer able to revoke.

Inter vivos trusts are sometimes called "living trusts" while testamentary trusts are sometimes called "will trusts."

Split Trusts

If a married couple wanted to leave money to their children and their favorite charity, rather than forming separate trusts, they could form a **split trust**. A split trust or "split-interest trust" is a type of trust account that names both charitable and non-charitable beneficiaries. The most common types of split trusts are **charitable remainder trusts** and **charitable lead trusts**. A charitable remainder trust is an irrevocable trust that can be set up in two ways. With both accounts the priority is to leave adequate funds to the non-charitable beneficiaries, while also leaving a donation to the named charitable organization. In a charitable remainder annuity trust the beneficiaries receive fixed payments for a stated period, after which the remaining assets are distributed to the charity.

In a charitable remainder unitrust the non-charitable beneficiaries receive a stated percentage of the account's fair market value for a set time period after which the remaining assets are distributed to the charitable beneficiary or beneficiaries. Typically, the grantor is also the income beneficiary of the charitable remainder trust. That means he gets to take a charitable deduction on the amount contributed to the trust immediately and then live off the prescribed income stream for the rest of his life, knowing the remainder goes to a charitable beneficiary.

A charitable lead trust is set up when the priority is to leave assets to the named charitable beneficiary/beneficiaries, while the non-charitable beneficiaries will wait for their distributions. A charitable lead trust can also be set up as either an annuity or a unitrust. Either way, the designated charitable beneficiaries receive regular distributions of assets from the trust at scheduled intervals for a stated time. Once the organizations have received the pre-set number of donations, the trust distributes the remaining assets to the non-charitable beneficiaries.

Pooled income funds are trusts that enable donors to pool their donations into an investment fund. Unlike the other split trusts, a pooled income fund is owned by the charitable organization that benefits from it. The donors themselves are the beneficiaries of the trust, receiving distributions from the income generated by the fund while alive. When the donors pass away, their share of the fund is then distributed to the charity. This type of trust allows donors to enjoy investment income throughout their lives while ultimately benefiting a charitable organization.

Totten Trusts

If you were to ask a banker how you can pass assets to your loved ones and avoid probate, chances are you would hear the term **Totten trust**. A Totten trust is really a payable-on-death (POD) bank account. If someone wants the assets in the account to pass upon his death to a named beneficiary, a Totten trust can be set up. All that is required is some paperwork establishing the account as a payable-on-death account, which the bank keeps on file. The POD beneficiary has no rights to the assets while the grantor is alive, and when the account owner passes away, the beneficiary typically needs to go to the bank with a death certificate and a photo ID. The bank could place a brief hold on the funds, but the transfer of assets does not go into the probate process.

A Totten trust is a bank account whose balance will pass to a named beneficiary. It is a revocable trust.

Bypass Trusts

For a wealthy couple avoiding estate taxes can be a challenge both when the first spouse dies and when the second spouse passes. A bypass trust transfers the maximum amount subject to the unified credit into a trust whose income can be used by the surviving spouse over his or her lifetime. The surviving spouse cannot demand a distribution from corpus, but the trustee could use his discretion to make such a distribution.

When the surviving spouse dies, the assets in the bypass trust do not count towards his or her estate. In other words, when set up correctly, the assets that pass to a bypass trust avoid estate taxes for both spouses.

AB Trusts

Although not as common today, spouses used to frequently create AB or "split" trusts to avoid estate taxes. In this rather complex scheme, when one spouse dies, two trusts are created. One trust is irrevocable, the other revocable. As with any irrevocable trust, the surviving spouse may not change the terms of Trust A. The surviving spouse typically only receives the income generated by the irrevocable trust. Trust B—the revocable living trust—would be under his or her control.

Unfortunately, the surviving spouse would have to hire a tax attorney to determine how best to divide the spouses' assets into the A and B trusts and would have to keep records for the irrevocable trust and file tax returns annually.

QPRT, Q-TIP

One way for a wealthy person to reduce estate tax liability while staying in his home for a while is to create a Qualified Personal Residence Trust (QPRT). This maneuver would allow him to transfer the property to the trust at today's value as opposed to the almost certainly higher value in the future. The grantor retains tenancy for 10 years, after which the property passes to the beneficiaries of the trust. The home could not be seized by creditors, as it would now be owned by a trust. Creditors could only claim the value of the remaining term of tenancy—the rental income, for example—but could not seize the property itself.

People who are in a second (or third, etc.) marriage often want to provide for their spouse's income needs after death but also provide for their children of a previous marriage. This is often done by establishing a Qualified Terminable Interest Property trust or Q-TIP. The Q-TIP provides that the surviving spouse will receive a prescribed lifetime income stream from the trust when the other spouse dies. The trust principal then passes to the children after the spouse dies or remarries. Q-TIPs are common with second marriages because they preserve assets for the benefit of the children from an earlier marriage, rather than the spouse's children or family. Q-TIPs can also protect a spouse when the grantor believes he or she may waste the assets during the spouse's lifetime.

To qualify for the marital deduction, income from the Q-TIP must be used only for the benefit of the surviving spouse during his or her lifetime. Estate taxes on the principal are then deferred until the surviving spouse dies. In other words, passing the income to the surviving spouse does not trigger estate tax liability. That happens when the assets transfer to the next generation.

Crummey Trusts

We talked about the annual gift tax exclusion amount earlier. And, we saw that the value of a life insurance policy is included in the gross estate, unless some fancy estate planning is performed, that is. A **Crummey Trust** is an irrevocable life insurance trust designed to pay the premiums on a life insurance policy owned by a trust and also get around the annual gift tax exclusion amount. In a Crummey Trust the beneficiaries have the stated right to withdraw the gifts made to the trust for a certain time. Because they never do that, the gifts are used to pay the premiums on the life insurance policy, which is owned by the trust to keep its value separate from the estate of the deceased.

Trustees are sometimes family members and sometimes financial institutions. Either way, a trustee is a **fiduciary** who can be sued for negligence or self-dealing by the beneficiaries of the trust. The **Uniform Prudent Investor Act** is a piece of model legislation that provides guidance to trustees interested in avoiding such lawsuits and regulatory actions. While in earlier times a "prudent investor" was expected to avoid risk, as the Uniform Prudent Investor Act (UPIA) clarifies, the trustee's job is to consider the risk-reward nature of a portfolio so that a risky security here might be balanced out by an uncorrelated and safer security over there. For example, junk bonds might fit into an overall portfolio if balanced out by US Treasury Notes. Therefore, there is no list of prohibited investments. Rather, the trustee needs to read the trust documents and manage the risk/reward nature of the portfolio in a way that best meets the needs of the beneficiary or beneficiaries of the trust.

Diversification is considered a major part of any prudent investment strategy, and a trustee would only choose not to diversify if he had a good reason. For example, maybe he needs to wait until a short-term capital gain can be turned into a long-term capital gain before selling and rebalancing.

Some executors and trustees are just family members who have no training or experience in financial matters. While they would be held liable for fraud or self-dealing at the expense of the beneficiaries, their level of skill and care would not be assumed to be as high as that of bank's trust department. So, the UPIA clarifies that amateur fiduciaries are not held to the same standard as professional fiduciaries in terms of exercising skill and care in financial matters. Again, though, a test question could have an amateur fiduciary spending the interest payments received on Treasury Bonds when that money should, instead, be going into the estate account and eventually distributed to the other beneficiaries. That is a matter of self-dealing and "breach of fiduciary duty" regardless of her knowledge of the securities industry. If the executor decides to just move into the house of the deceased rather than get it sold for the benefit of the estate, this would also be a breach of fiduciary duty, no matter how often it probably happens in the day-to-day world.

In olden days, no responsibilities could be passed off, but the UPIA points out that a trustee could manage the investments of a pension trust while an insurance company handles payouts and actuarial calculations, for example.

In the next chapter, we will look in depth at investment advisers, who are always in a fiduciary or trustee relationship with their clients. Among many other concerns, investment advisers and their representatives must adhere to prudent investor standards.

Disclaiming an Inheritance

You could see a test question presenting a situation in which the wife of a recently deceased husband does not want or need the assets she is set to receive from the husband's will or trust agreement. If she wants the assets to bypass her and go to the next generation, she needs to formally disclaim the inheritance without ever touching or benefiting from the assets. This means she must do it in writing and within 9 months of the death of the deceased individual. If she does it correctly according to federal and state law, the assets are treated as if she never touched them. However, the decision to disclaim the inheritance is irrevocable. She cannot come back later asking for help from the trust. Also, she does not get to designate who receives the assets. That is up to the probate court or the trust agreement.

As we have seen, when assets pass from parents to the next generation, estate taxes could be due. Therefore, if someone tries to bypass that generation and leave assets to a family member who is two generations younger, the transfer is subject to both a generation-skipping tax and the estate tax. The person who is two generations younger is known as a "skip person," and an unrelated person is a skip person if he or she is more than 37.5 years younger than the one transferring assets. But, skip persons end up being off the hook if the parent dies before the transfer is made. That's right, if the generation to whom assets would have otherwise been transferred is already deceased, there was no end-run around the tax code, eliminating the generation-skipping tax.

Individuals and married couples can pass a certain amount to a skip person that is exempted from the generation-skipping tax, both numbers indexed for inflation. To leave assets for a skip person and avoid tax liability, many wealthy people establish generation-skipping trusts, whose sole purpose is to receive the maximum amount exempt from the generation-skipping tax and then provide benefits from there to the named beneficiaries.

Qualified Domestic Relations Order

As the IRS explains on their website (www.irs.gov),

> *A qualified domestic relations order (QDRO) is a judgment, decree, or court order (including an approved property settlement agreement) issued under a state's domestic relations law that:*
>
> 1. *Recognizes someone other than a participant as having a right to receive benefits from a qualified retirement plan (such as most pension and profit-sharing plans) or a tax-sheltered annuity,*
>
> 2. *Relates to payment of child support, alimony, or marital property rights to a spouse, former spouse, child, or other dependent of the participant, and*
>
> 3. *Specifies certain information, including the amount or part of the participant's benefits to be paid to the participant's spouse, former spouse, child, or other dependent.*

The topic of **qualified domestic relations orders** typically comes up during a divorce proceeding. When an attorney works out a divorce settlement agreement that divides various assets among the two soon-to-be-divorced spouses, he or she needs to include a qualified domestic relations order (QDRO) related to pension/retirement accounts. As the IRS defined above, the QDRO recognizes someone other than the plan participant—whom he or she is divorcing—as having a right to receive benefits from a qualified retirement plan. The QDRO states the percentage and/or number of payments the ex-spouse is to receive, which in most cases is 50% of the value of assets that was gained while the two were married—up to the divorce.

The smart move for tax purposes is for the ex-spouse to roll the money received into his or her own Traditional IRA. If this is pursuant to the QDRO, the spouse whose retirement account is being depleted avoids any taxes, and the ex-spouse whose retirement account is being augmented can defer the taxes until he or she takes withdrawals.

On the other hand, a painful move would be for a spouse to give a former spouse money from his retirement account without a QDRO in place. If that happens, the distribution is taxable to the spouse whose retirement account is being depleted and subject to a 10% penalty if he's not over 59 ½ years of age.

According to a helpful website (www.divorcesupport.about.com/od/pensionfundsandbenefits/f/qdro.htm):

A QDRO as part of a divorce decree should state the following:

- Name and mailing address of the "plan participant" (you) and the "alternate payee" (your ex)
- Each retirement qualified plan account to be split up under your divorce.
- Name of each plan to which the order applies.
- Dollar amount or percentage of benefits to be paid from each account to the alternate payee.
- Number of payments or the benefits period covered by the QDRO.

Your papers should also specify that a qualified domestic relations order is being established under your state's domestic relations laws and Section 414(p) of the Internal Revenue Code.

Account Ownership Techniques

The accounts we'll look at here have one thing in common: the account owner is planning for what could go wrong in the future (incapacity) or what will go wrong in the future (death).

Pay-On-Death

A **transfer on death** or **pay-on-death account** provides a way to transfer assets without the hassle and cost of probate. If an investor sets up an account this way, the executor or administrator of the estate will not have to take any action to ensure that the securities transfer to the designated beneficiaries when the account owner passes away. With TOD registration the investor maintains complete control of the assets during his lifetime. The named beneficiaries have no access to or control over the assets while the account owner is alive. A "POD" or "payable on death" account is the same idea applied to a bank or credit union account. As we saw, a pay-on-death bank account can also be referred to as a "Totten trust."

A related idea is the **durable power of attorney** that an individual can grant to someone else. A durable power of attorney would stay in force even after the individual was declared mentally incompetent. The person granted this durable power of attorney can make healthcare, financial, and legal decisions for someone who is incapacitated.

So, if your customer were incapacitated due to dementia, an agent could accept orders from the person granted durable power of attorney, after verifying that the person has been granted that power by the customer.

The durable power of attorney goes into effect if the individual becomes incapacitated. The power ends when the individual dies.

Joint Accounts

When two or more individuals jointly own the assets in the account, we call it a joint account. All the owners sign a joint account agreement. We can accept orders from any of the parties, and we can send mail to any of the parties. But, when we cut a check or distribute securities, they must be made out to all names on the account. In other words, if the account is entitled Barbara Williams and JoAnne Stevens, **Joint Tenants in Common**, do not cut the check to Barbara and tell her to settle with JoAnne next time they have lunch. Cut the check to "Barbara Williams and JoAnne Stevens, as Joint Tenants in Common."

A **Joint Tenants with Rights of Survivorship** (JTWROS or JTROS) account gives the survivor rights to all the assets. When one account owner dies, the surviving owner owns all the assets.

However, if the account is a Joint Tenants in Common (JTIC) account, when one party dies, at least part of the assets go to that person's estate. For JTIC accounts, the account owners indicate what % each party owns in the account agreement. For JTWROS, that wouldn't matter, as all assets go to the survivor.

Married couples often use either joint tenants in common or joint tenants with rights of survivorship accounts. However, such accounts also do not require the account owners to be married and may have more than two owners. On the other hand, a **tenancy in the entirety** account can only be established by a married couple. What separates these accounts from the other two is that while they are alive neither spouse can sell or give away his interest in the property without the consent of the other spouse, and creditors of either spouse cannot attach and sell one debtor spouse's interest in the property--only creditors of the married couple can do that.

If a test question says that one of your customers has an individual account at your firm and is now deceased, know that in a "common law" state, his wife only has a claim on half the assets if she is listed as an account owner. On the other hand, if we're in a "community property" state, the wife owns half of whatever the customer earned while they were married, whether he thought to name her on the account or not. In a transfer-on-death account, the deceased customer would have named a beneficiary, but that is subject to challenge, especially in "community property" states. Assets the now deceased husband had before the marriage would generally not be subject to a claim by the wife.

Trading Securities

On the **primary market** underwriters raise capital for corporations by selling securities to investors. The investors would never buy those securities if they didn't have a **secondary market** where they could later turn the securities back into cash. Securities are issued on the primary market, where the issuer receives money from the investor. Securities are traded on the secondary market among investors, with no money going to the issuer.

Broker-dealers not only perform investment banking activities on the primary market, but also, they execute trades for their customers on the secondary market. The broker-dealers trade the securities through various exchanges or electronic systems.

First Market – NYSE, etc.

Within the secondary market, there are four separate components. Let's start with the **first market**, the New York Stock Exchange. There are also regional exchanges in Chicago, Philadelphia, Boston, and San Francisco that are based on the NYSE. They tend to focus on regional stocks, but they also fill orders for NYSE-listed securities, such as GE, GM, and IBM.

Big member firms have a commission house broker ready to fill orders on the exchange. He works for a brokerage house and fills their orders for a commission. The more orders he can fill, the more money he can make. Firms that don't have a commission house broker often have orders executed by an individual known as a two-dollar broker. As with all brokers, a two-dollar broker earns a commission on transactions executed rather than taking a position in securities and dealing them. Then, there are competitive floor traders who try to buy low and sell high as much as possible through the trading session.

The NYSE now uses both a manual auction and an electronic trading model. That means that even though most trading throughout the day is done electronically, the exchange also uses manual auctions at the opening, at the closing, and during times of extreme volatility. A manual auction involves human beings communicating face to face in real time, indicating their buying and selling interest in a security through open outcry.

The firms in charge of running manual auctions are known as Designated Market Makers or DMMs. As a helpful video on the NYSE website explains, DMMs are kind of like commercial airline pilots. They have to be there for the take-off and the landing, and they have to step in whenever there is turbulence. During the rest of the flight, they participate, but not in such a dominant role.

Like other market participants, DMMs trade electronically throughout the day using trading algorithms. Algorithms are computerized mathematical formulas designed to determine buying and selling opportunities and execute trades automatically. Replacing the old "specialist" model, Designated Market Makers are charged with the responsibility to maintain a fair and orderly market in particular exchange-listed securities. Their job is to provide liquidity, especially during times of market volatility.

To prevent panic, they step in ready to buy or sell securities to keep the flow of trading moving. The DMM is required to quote at the National Best Bid or Offer (NBBO) a required percentage of the time. The NBBO is what it sounds like—the best prices for the security nationwide.

Supplemental Liquidity Providers play a unique role in the trading of securities on the secondary market. Supplemental Liquidity Providers are off-floor market participants using sophisticated computerized trading strategies to create high volume on exchanges to add liquidity to the markets. As an incentive to provide liquidity, the exchange pays the Supplemental Liquidity Provider (SLP) a fee/rebate.

As we mentioned, if I place an electronic order to buy 1,000 shares of, say, GE, my order could be filled in New York, Philadelphia, Boston, San Francisco, or Chicago. That's because they're all part of the "first market."

When an NYSE-listed security is sold, it doesn't matter whether it's sold in New York, Chicago, San Francisco, or Boston—the prices are all reported to the consolidated tape. That means that the seller has to report the price he just sold a certain number of shares within 30 seconds, whether it was sold in Philly, Boston, or the floor of the security's primary exchange.

If you've ever seen the data streaming across the bottom of the TV monitor, you've seen the prices being reported to the "tape." Yes, all that "10s GE 35.55" stuff means something. It means that someone sold (and bought) 1,000 shares of GE for $35.55 per-share. The number of round lots comes first, then the stock symbol, and then the price at which the transaction took place. Let's look at some more trades as reported to the consolidated tape:

GE36.55...10s.IBM95.04... 99s.C.75.15...13,000s.GE.36.70

The first thing we see is the stock symbol GE. If there is no number before the symbol, we know that one round lot (100 shares) of GE just traded for $36.55 per-share. In the next case "10s" means 10 round lots, or 1,000 shares. So, 1,000 shares of IBM just traded at $95.04 per-share. Next, we see that 99 round lots, or 9,900 shares of "C" (for Citigroup) just traded at $75.15 per-share. But, when the number of shares gets up to 10,000 or more, they stop talking in round lots and just list the actual number of shares. In other words a trade for 10,000 shares would not be indicated as "100s." Rather, it would be "10,000s". Therefore, we read the tape to indicate that 13,000 shares of GE just traded for $36.70 per-share.

Also note that for stocks trading at $175 a share or higher, a round lot is now just one share. For these stocks, a transaction for less than 100 shares will no longer be reported as odd-lot transactions.

As usual, things get more complicated. What if you saw the following on your exam and were asked to interpret the report?

MCD12s35 .35

That means 1200 shares of McDonald's traded at $35, followed by a trade for 100 shares at $35. Remember, if there's no number before the price, that means one round lot or 100 shares traded at that price. And then we could see something like this:

MCD35 .15

That means 100 shares of McDonald's traded at $35, followed by another round lot that traded at $35.15. In other words, there is a world of difference between "35.15" and "35 .15." In the first case, 100 shares sold at $35.15. In the second case, 100 shares sold at $35, followed by 100 shares at $35.15.

For preferred stock, a round lot is just 10 shares, and they indicate that with an "s/s." Therefore, what does the following report mean?

ABC pr 7s/s.85.05

It means that 70 shares of ABC preferred stock traded for $85.05 per-share.

The following abbreviations are also used on the consolidated tape:

- SLD: the report is out-of-sequence or late
- Halt: sometimes trading in a stock is halted, usually when big news is about to come out
- OPD: the first trade that happens after a delayed opening or a trading halt
- Pr: preferred stock (also look for the s/s)
- R/T: rights
- W/S: warrants

I have been teaching in this industry for over 16 years now. When I first started, distinguishing the NYSE/1st Market from the OTC/2nd Market was getting more complicated but not too bad. The NYSE was an **exchange** that used "open outcry" like all **auction markets** did at the time. Teaching the class in Chicago, I could usually get the students to relate to the idea of the funny-colored jackets, the bad, disheveled ties and hairstyles, and the arcane hand gestures used by swearing, snarling, spitting traders down in the pits at the options exchange, the mercantile exchange or the board of trade.

Well, this industry changes faster than most. Even though the NYSE is an auction market and is an exchange, much of the trading is done electronically. And, electronic trading is what we used to safely associate with the "OTC/2nd market," which we will discuss next.

Back in the day, we would routinely hit students with questions that neatly sorted the words "listed" and "exchange" over on one side with the NYSE/1st Market, and then the OTC/2nd Market safely on the other side, where securities were "traded" or "quoted" but never "listed" because even NASDAQ, the cream of the OTC crop, at that time was not a true "exchange." It always made for awkward moments with the smartest-guy-in-the-room when I had to explain how a NASDAQ stock could be threatened with a "de-listing," if no stocks were never "listed" on NASDAQ to begin with.

NASDAQ has been an exchange for years now, and they have routinely used the terms "listed" and "de-listed" to describe the securities trading through their electronic trading facility. The term "listed" is usually thought of in terms of what it does *not* refer to. The term "listed" now accurately refers to NYSE securities and NASDAQ securities; however, the term should not be associated with securities trading over-the-counter but not on NASDAQ, e.g., the Over-the-Counter Bulletin Board, which we'll look at in a few pages.

Issuers who want to list their securities for trading on NYSE have to meet the exchange's rigid listing criteria. If s company lists its security on the NYSE (or NASDAQ), it will be monitored closely by the exchange, and if they do not meet all obligations under exchange rules and SEC rules, their security will suddenly not be trading.

For a company doing an IPO and getting authorized to list and trade on the NYSE, the total market value for the outstanding shares is a minimum of $40 million and $100 million for other companies. We're just talking about the shares of stock themselves. A company wanting to list and stay listed on the NYSE has to meet at least one of three financial tests. One is called the "earnings test" and is based on the profitability of the issuer, as its name implies. The next is the "valuation/revenue" test that is based both on the market value of the stock and the revenue of the company issuing it. And, there is an "assets/equity" test based on market valuation, assets, and stockholder's equity.

No matter which test is being used, not that many companies can meet it for an initial listing, let alone maintain it to avoid being de-listed. Sometimes the issuing company itself will decide to de-list their security. If so, all that is required for a voluntary delisting is for the company's board of directors to approve it and for the issuer to then file a form with the SEC certifying the board's approval of the resolution.

In addition to common stock, companies also list their debt securities on the NYSE, as we see at http://www1.nyse.com/bonds/nysebonds/1095449059236.html. To meet the requirements here, the issue has to have a principal value of at least $5 million.

If the bond is convertible, it can only be listed if the underlying common stock is subject to real-time last sale reports in the US, and the par value has to be $10 million or larger. Even if the issue of debt securities meets those minimum sizes and requirements, the NYSE will only list the issue if it meets one of several criteria that require that the issuer have its stock listed on the NYSE, or that an issuer with stock listed on the exchange is either a majority owner or in common control with the other issuer, or that any NYSE-listed issuer has guaranteed the issue. There is also a criteria based on the credit rating of the issue being at least "B", which, as you probably remember or know, is a junk rating.

As the website for NYSE Bonds indicates:

> NYSE Bonds operates the largest centralized corporate bond market in the U.S., providing an opportunity for participants to trade bonds in a fair, open environment. On NYSE Bonds, firm and executable orders entered by members or sponsored participants are displayed on the order book, and executed on a strict price/time priority.

Over-the-Counter

While the first market is an "auction market," the second or Over-the-Counter market is a **negotiated market**. Since traders do not gather together on the floor of an exchange, investors need big dealers to maintain inventories of over-the-counter stocks. We call these big buyers and sellers **market makers**, because they make a market in that security possible. A market maker is a broker-dealer who carries an inventory of a security and stands ready to either buy or sell it throughout the day.

Investors are able to trade shares of MSFT, ORCL, and CSCO only because there are broker-dealers who "make a market" in those securities. A "market" is a two-sided quote, allowing buyers to buy at the ask price and sellers to sell at the bid price.

Market makers electronically publish a **bid** and **ask** (or offer) price and stand ready to take either side of the trade, for at least one round lot. For stocks a round lot is 100 shares. So if a market maker says their quote is 20.00–20.11, they stand ready to buy 100 shares at $20.00 or sell 100 shares at $20.11. The difference between where they buy and where they sell is called the **spread**.

Broker-dealers can act as **brokers**, whereby they charge commissions, or they can act as **principals** in the transaction by selling stock from their own inventory, or buying stock for their inventory.

NASDAQ

Over-the-counter stocks that meet and maintain the listing criteria trade on an electronic exchange known as **NASDAQ**, which stands for National Association of Securities Dealers Automated Quotation system.

NASDAQ has three tiers. The NASDAQ Global Market Companies is a group of over 1,450 companies that have applied for listing after meeting and continuing to meet stringent financial and liquidity requirements and agreeing to meet specific corporate governance standards. And, there is the NASDAQ Global Select Market, with even higher listing standards. The former "NASDAQ SmallCap Market" has been renamed the "NASDAQ Capital Market Companies." This group of stocks consists of over 550 companies that benefit from access to the capital markets in spite of their smaller size and less proven track records. These companies have to stay current in all their SEC filings but do not have to meet the same financial standards of the Global and Global Select Companies.

Non-NASDAQ

Stocks that do not meet NASDAQ's financial, liquidity and corporate governance standards are referred to as **Non-NASDAQ OTC securities**. These securities trade on the OTC Bulletin Board and the OTC Markets, where spreads are wider and stock prices generally more volatile. When a company no longer meets NASDAQ's listing requirements, often the stock symbol changes, and the security begins to trade in the non-NASDAQ OTC market.

Securities trading here are not referred to as listed securities. The trading facilities have no regulatory relationship with the companies whose securities trade through them. Listed securities include those trading on NASDAQ and the NYSE, not here.

Third Market

The **third market** is a term used when an NYSE-listed security is traded over-the-counter. Maybe an institutional buyer can get a better, negotiated price for an order of 10,000 IBM, a listed security, so they decide to buy it over-the-counter. When a listed security trades OTC, we refer to that situation as the "third market." The Consolidated Quotation System (CQS) displays quotations on all common stock, preferred stock, warrants, and rights that are registered on the American Stock Exchange or the New York Stock Exchange and trading in the OTC market (third market). Although executed in the over-the-counter market, these transactions must be reported to the consolidated tape.

Fourth Market

The **fourth market** involves direct trading between institutional investors, completely bypassing brokers by using **Electronic Communications Networks (ECNs)**. Institutional investors include insurance companies, mutual funds, pension funds, big trust departments, broker-dealers, etc. They're professionals with millions/billions of dollars flowing in and out of the market. Basically, ECNs work like an eBay for securities transactions by matching up buyers and sellers. Some broker-dealers use a market maker to execute client transactions during normal business hours and then use an ECN to execute orders after normal business hours (after 4 p.m.). Well-known electronic communications networks include INSTINET and NYSE ARCA. Here are some essential facts on ECNs:

- If the ECN system cannot match a buyer and seller, a client's order can have a limited ability to be executed
- Some ECNs will only accept certain types of orders, such as limit orders
- Electronic communications networks allow market participants themselves to display quotes and execute transactions
- Participants are referred to as *subscribers* and pay a fee to the ECN to trade electronically through the system
- ECNs allow subscribers to trade after-hours, quote and trade anonymously
- ECNs act in an agency capacity and do not buy or sell for their own account (not a market maker)

Dark Pools, High-Frequency Trading

The term **dark pools of liquidity** refers to large institutional orders that are concealed from the public. As an example, imagine that a large pension fund wants to sell 1 million shares of GM to another large pension fund. Executing such a large order through the NYSE could be taken as a sign to the rest of the market to dump GM, meaning that the sale itself could depress the value of the stock. Therefore, the two pension funds decide to do the trade directly between themselves or possibly through a regional exchange. To execute the trade away from the NYSE is known as doing the trade "in a dark pool."

One side claims that dark pools provide more liquidity to the market and allow large trades to be executed without destabilizing the market for that security. The other side claims that such trades deprive all market participants from knowing the true prices at which specific securities are being traded.

We looked at Supplemental Liquidity Providers and saw that they receive a rebate as a financial incentive for providing liquidity to the NYSE market. Although the rebate might be a fraction of a penny, if the SLP can execute millions of trades per day, the incentive pays off. Therefore, a Supplemental Liquidity Provider often uses powerful computers to execute a huge number of trades powered by algorithms analyzing multiple markets and automatically executing trades based on spotting certain market conditions. Such trading is known as **high-frequency trading**.

It is estimated that more than half of all exchange volume comes in the form of high-frequency trading, where the traders with the fastest computers typically come out ahead. Proponents of high-frequency trading argue that it provides the most up-to-date pricing information, thereby facilitating price disco.

Some market participants and experts, however, are concerned that algorithms merely look for trends or momentum and exploit them. They are not designed to factor in war or economic news and, therefore can mindlessly exaggerate market factors. They also do not know when to stop or alter a trade and, therefore, often lead to a distortion in the buying or selling of a security far beyond what human traders would have done on their own.

Selling Short

You've probably heard that an investor should try to buy low and sell high, right? Well, some investors take that same principle and do it in reverse: they prefer selling high, then buying back low. We call these investors "short sellers."

It works like this. You go to your friend's house and see that she has a new mountain bike that she paid too much money for. Mind if I borrow your mountain bike, you ask, to which your friend agrees. On the way home you run into another friend, who admires the bike. She likes it so much, in fact, that she offers you two thousand dollars for it.

Sold! You take the $2,000 and put it in your pocket.

Wait a minute, that wasn't even your mountain bike! No problem. All you have to do is replace it with an identical machine. A few days later you go to the bike store to replace the borrowed bike, and—as predicted—the price has fallen to just $1,000. Perfect! You sold the bike for $2,000 and you can get out of your position by paying just $1,000, keeping the $1,000 difference as your profit. Just buy the bike for $1,000, wheel it over to your friend, and everybody's happy. Notice that you made money when the price went down. Therefore, you were "bearish" on the price of mountain bikes.

Short sellers don't sell bikes or search engines short, but they can sell the stock of companies who make bikes or search engines short. If you think Google is overpriced and headed for a drop, borrow the shares from your broker-dealer and sell them at what you think is the top. Sell Google for $700 and, you hope, buy it back later for $30, keeping $670 per-share as your profit.

However, many people tried that after Google went public at $85. When it got to $100, many were convinced the stock would only go down from there, so they sold it short at $100. Expecting to buy it back or "cover their short positions" for less than $100, these traders must have been really embarrassed to see the stock soon climb to $900 per-share.

Selling for $100 and buying for $900 is not a good business model. That's no different from buying for $900 and then selling for $100. It's just more dangerous. When you buy, you've already lost all you could ever lose. But when you sell stock short, there is no limit to how much you'll have to spend to get out of your position. I mean, reality would tell us that Google was never going to hit $10,000 a share, but, hypothetically, it could have. Higher even.

Short sellers are bearish. They profit when the stock goes down. But, they have limited upside and unlimited risk. If you sell a stock short for $5,000, $5,000 is the maximum you could make, and only if the stock went to zero. Your potential loss is unlimited, since no one can tell you for sure how high the stock could go up.

Stock is not the only thing that can be sold short. Treasury securities are frequently sold short, as are corporate bonds, ETFs (exchange-traded funds), and closed-end funds. Writers of options are "short the option" and complete the trade when they buy it back to close.

The SEC does not like it when short sellers sell shares that don't exist. Allowing them to do so would distort the downward (bearish) pressure on a stock by distorting the laws of supply & demand that determine the stock's market price. Therefore, broker-dealers must "locate" the shares their customers are selling short and document it before effecting the short sale—that means they reasonably believe the securities can be delivered by the settlement date (T + 3) as required.

In olden days, a short sale could only be executed at a price that was higher than the previous price for the security, or at the same price if the price before had been an "uptick." **Reg SHO** now requires that before executing a short sale, broker-dealers must locate the securities so that the laws of supply and demand are not distorted by "naked short selling," in which people sell stock that doesn't even exist short, artificially depressing its price. If the broker-dealer executes a short sale without reasonably believing the shares can be delivered by the lender, they have violated the rule.

In May 2010 Reg SHO was updated to impose a temporary version of the old uptick rule that applies when a "circuit breaker" is tripped for a security. Starting in May of that year if a security dropped during the day by 10% or more below its most recent closing price, short sellers would not be able to sell short at or below the current best bid price for the security. In other words, people "selling long," which means selling the shares they own, will have priority and will be able to liquidate their holdings before short sellers can jump onto the pile. As the SEC states in their unique brand of English:

> a targeted short sale price test restriction will apply the alternative uptick rule for the remainder of the day and the following day if the price of an individual security declines intra-day by 10% or more from the prior day's closing price for that security. By not allowing short sellers to sell at or below the current national best bid while the circuit breaker is in effect, the short sale price test restriction in Rule 201 will allow long sellers, who will be able to sell at the bid, to sell first in a declining market for a particular security. As the Commission has noted previously in connection with short sale price test restrictions, a goal of such restrictions is to allow long sellers to sell first in a declining market. In addition, by making such bids accessible only by long sellers when a security's price is undergoing significant downward price pressure, Rule 201 will help to facilitate and maintain stability in the markets and help ensure that they function efficiently. It will also help restore investor confidence during times of substantial uncertainty because, once the circuit breaker has been triggered for a particular security, long sellers will have preferred access to bids for the security, and the security's continued price decline will more likely be due to long selling and the underlying fundamentals of the issuer, rather than to other factors.

As we see from that passage, there is a big difference between a customer sell order marked "long" and a sell order marked "short." That is why Reg SHO requires all sell orders to be marked properly. When a customer "sells long," he is liquidating shares that he owns. To sell short, as we see, involves borrowing shares that will be sold and then replaced later by the customer. Short sales take place only in margin accounts, not cash accounts.

Bond Trading

Corporate bonds traded over-the-counter are reported to FINRA's **TRACE** system, which stands for **Trade Reporting and Compliance Engine**. Brokerage firms are now required to report price and volume data on all corporate bond transactions to TRACE, within 15 minutes. FINRA publicly disseminates that transaction data immediately on virtually 100 percent of over-the-counter corporate bond activity (approximately 22,000 transactions and $18 billion in volume every day). Recently, FINRA fined a firm $1.4 *million* for failing to report a percentage of their bond trades to TRACE. The purpose of the TRACE system is to provide transparency to the bond market, so by failing to report the trades, the firm deprived the market of the transparency it needs to remain effective. Several smaller fines have recently been levied for failing to report trades in "TRACE-eligible securities." FINRA insists that dealers provide the market with accurate and transparent data on securities transactions, and they are quite happy to remind them with disciplinary actions and fines.

The NYSE also provides a bond trading platform:

The NYSE Bonds trading platform provides a more efficient and transparent way to trade bonds. The platform incorporates the design of the current NYSE Arca all-electronic trading system. This system provides investors with the ability to readily obtain transparent pricing and trading information, enabling them to make better investment decisions. The system has also been expanded to include the bonds of all NYSE-listed companies and their subsidiaries without the companies having to list each bond issued. NYSE Bonds operates the largest centralized bond market of any US exchange or other self-regulatory organization. It offers investors a broad selection of bonds: corporate (including convertibles), agency and government bonds.

The majority of NYSE bond volume is in corporate debt, with some 94% in straight, or non-convertible bonds, and 6% in convertible debt issues. As of Monday, December 1, 2008 all NYSE Amex (formerly American Stock Exchange) listed bonds transferred to an electronic trading platform based on NYSE Bonds called NYSE Amex Bonds. Like NYSE Bonds, this electronic trading platform is based on the design of NYSE Arca's comprehensive matching technology allowing NYSE Members to enter orders to buy or sell bonds electronically.

MSRB Rule G-14 requires that transactions in municipal bonds be reported within 15 minutes of trade execution to the MSRB's Real-time Transaction Reporting System (RTRS). The MSRB disseminates trade data about all reported municipal securities transactions almost immediately at www.investinginbonds.com. You may have noticed that for both TRACE and RTRS, bond transactions are reported within 15 minutes, but when we're talking about stock transactions, the report is due within 30 seconds. Yet another indication of the increased volatility and faster pace of the stock—as opposed to the bond—market.

Types of Orders

Market Order

If a customer wants to buy 1,000 shares quickly, he places a **market order**. A market order is filled as fast as possible, at the best available market price for the security.

Limit Order

Sometimes customers name their price by placing a **limit order**. If a stock is at 43, maybe they're interested in selling it. They'd be more interested if they could sell it for $45, so they enter a **sell limit** order above the current market price. Sell limit @45 means the investor will take 45 or better (*more* is better for a seller). If he can get 45 or 45.15, or even higher, he'll sell his stock. If the bid never rises that high, he won't sell it.

Another investor is interested in buying a stock currently trading at 30. He'd be more interested in buying it at $25, so he places a **buy limit** order below the current price. That means he'll buy the stock if he can get it for $25 or better (*less* is better for a buyer). If the ask/offer price never drops to $25 or lower, he won't buy it.

Market orders guarantee a fill but not a price. Limit orders, on the other hand, guarantee a price, but they do not guarantee the order will be filled. Many times, the stock's price fails to perform like an investor wants it to. If it's entered as a day order, the limit order either gets executed that day or it goes away. If the investor is going on vacation for three weeks and doesn't want to look at his stocks while he's gone, he can leave the order open by entering it **GTC**, which stands for good 'til canceled. If it doesn't get filled and the investor doesn't cancel it, the order remains open.

Stop Order

A buy limit order is filled only if the ask/offer price drops to the limit price or lower. A sell limit order is filled only if the bid price rises to the limit price or higher. Stop orders, on the other hand, are not based on the buying and selling interest represented by the Bid and Ask prices. Stop orders are triggered only when an actual trade occurs between two other investors at the stop price or higher for a buy stop, or at the stop price or lower for a sell stop order.

So, if the test question shows the stop price on the consolidated tape, understand that, by definition, that cannot be the customer's trade. That is the trade that put the customer's order in play. It is the "last sale" that activates the stop order. Also, any trade reported with the abbreviation "SLD" is a late report and cannot trigger a stop order.

Let's start with a **buy stop** order. A technical analyst sees that a stock is trading in a narrow range, between 38 and 40. The technical analyst sees no reason to tie up his money in a stock that is stuck in a narrow trading range, known as **consolidation**. He decides if the stock can break through resistance

(40), it will continue to rise, which is why he'd like to buy it on the way up. So, he places a buy stop above the current market price.

Buy stop @41 means the market price first must reach 41 or higher, at which point the order is activated. It will be executed at the next available price, whatever that is. Stop orders have an activation or trigger price, at which point they become market orders. So, if the ticker came in like this:

40.90, 40.95, 40.99, 41.00...

his order would now be triggered or activated at 41.00. It would then be filled at the next available price, regardless. And, if the last two prices had been 40.99, 41.01, the order would have been triggered at 41.01, at which point the price has passed through the stop price of 41.

Stop orders don't guarantee a price for execution. The price named as the stop is the price that triggers or activates the order. The order—now a market order—is filled at the next available price. Again, the stop price is not the exact price, either. A "buy stop at 41" is activated at 41 or any price higher than that. It's then filled as soon as possible.

On the other hand, let's say a day trader takes a large position in a high-risk security but then decides to play it safe and limit his loss. He buys 1,000 shares at $50 a share and immediately enters a **sell stop** order at 49. This means if the stock stays above $49 he's in. As soon as it falls to 49 or lower, though, he's out. A sell stop at 49 is activated as soon as the stock's price hits 49 or lower, at which point it is sold at the next available price. The exam might tell you that a customer is bullish on a stock but fears a possible downturn in the short-term. What should she do?

Well, if she originally bought in at $20 and the stock is now at $50, she should make sure she doesn't lose too much of the $30 profit she has within her grasp. Many investors end up snatching defeat from the jaws of victory at this point, probably because they don't know how to use sell stops or "**stop loss**" orders. A sell stop at $48 or $49 would protect this paper gain, and also leave room for more upside.

If someone wants to also name the price for execution, he can enter a **stop-limit** order. Now his stop order also names the most he will pay or the least he will accept for a stock. A buy stop @50, limit 50 would start out just like a buy stop order. The stock must hit 50 or higher before it's triggered. But, by adding the limit to the order the investor is saying he won't pay more than $50 for it, period.

On the other hand, a sell stop @30, limit 30 is triggered if the stock hit 30 or lower, but the investor will not take less than $30 a share. If the order is triggered and then the bid falls lower than 30, this sell order won't get executed, and the investor will end up holding a loser that would have otherwise been sold with a sell stop (not a stop-limit) order.

Or, our technical analyst who wants to buy stock on the way up might want to place a cap on how much he pays. If so, he enters a **buy stop-limit** order. In other words, a "buy stop @41" could be filled at whatever price—probably near $41—while a "buy stop @41, limit 41" could only be filled at $41 or lower. Neither order, however, is activated unless and until the stock first trades one time at $41 or higher.

Investing "on **margin**" is a high-risk strategy that involves buying securities on credit, hoping to make more on the securities positions than the broker-dealer charges in interest on the margin loans. Broker-dealers love **margin accounts** because they open a whole new line of business. Suddenly they're credit card companies, and they don't even have to issue the little plastic cards. Plus, credit card companies have no collateral from their customers. In a margin account, customers pledge the assets they are buying on credit to the lender, the broker-dealer. If things turn south, the broker-dealer can sell the stock or bond to recover the money they lent. So, the interest rate they charge is lower than what we pay on a credit card, since they have collateral backing the loan.

People talk about the "equity" in their houses. Maybe they bought the house for $200,000 and borrowed $180,000 to do that. If so, their account starts out like this:

$200,000   Market Value

• $180,000   Money Owed
  _____
$20,000   Equity

Equity equals the difference between what someone owns (assets) and owes (liabilities). Let's say that this home's value increased 15% for three years running. At this point the value of the asset has risen while the amount owed has dropped. The account now looks like this:

$304,175   Market Value

• $170,000   Money Owed
  _____
$134,175   Equity

What can these homeowners do with that equity? They can borrow against it.

In a margin account, we don't buy houses on credit. Rather we buy stocks and bonds on credit. If their market value rises, we win. What if their market value starts to drop? we have a problem. This is, of course, where margin accounts get their bad name, but they're not all bad.

A "margin account" is a different type of account than a "cash account." In a **cash account**, customers must pay in full when they purchase securities, and they cannot sell short in a cash account. If the account is approved for margin trading, the customer can buy securities on credit and sell them short.

REG T

The Securities Exchange Act of 1934 gave the Federal Reserve Board the authority to regulate margin accounts. The "Fed" regulates credit, and one form of credit is the margin account, in which the broker-dealer fronts the customer half the purchase price of a security.

To purchase stock on margin, the broker-dealer follows **Regulation T (Reg T)**, which states that a listed stock can be pledged as collateral by the customer in exchange for a loan from the broker-dealer up to a maximum percentage of its value. Reg T tells broker-dealers how much credit they can extend to their customers—that percentage has been 50% for quite some time. The industry sometimes refers to the amount that a customer puts down as the "Fed call."

When a customer buys $200,000 of stock, he puts down ½ or $100,000. The other ½ or $100,000 is provided by the broker-dealer, who looks forward to charging interest on that $100,000 for as long as the customer would like to owe them. The amount that the customer puts down is referred to as "the margin." The "margin" refers to the amount of money the investor is required to deposit; the rest of the market value is extended on credit.

Regulation T requires 50% of the purchase price to be deposited by the customer within two business days after the settlement date of the transaction. Any market price change between the purchase of the security and the required payment would not affect the amount of the deposit the customer is required to make. If the stock purchased on margin rises from, say, $50 to $60, or drops from, say, $50 to $40, the margin call is based on $50 per-share; it is figured at the time of purchase.

Long Positions

Say a customer bought 1,000 shares @40 and made the required Reg T deposit of half or $20,000. At that point the customer's account looks like this:

LMV   –   Dr   =   Equity   Reg T Deposit

$40,000 – $20,000 = $20,000 $20,000

LMV stands for "long market value." It could be referred to as "market value" or "current market value." The "Dr" stands for "debit register," which can also be called the "debit balance." This is the amount the customer borrowed and owes his broker-dealer, like the mortgage balance that the homeowner owes the lender. So, the long market value of the stock he bought is $40,000. He made the required Reg T deposit of half—20K—the broker-dealer fronted him the other half. Do you suppose the broker-dealer wants that money back?

You bet, so it's a debit (Dr) to the client's account until he pays it off.

He "owns" an asset worth 40K and he owes 20K to the lender. That's why his equity is $20,000. Just like if you owed $80,000 on your mortgage when your house was worth $100,000—the difference of $20,000 is your equity.

Equity, Excess Equity

The investor has $20,000 of equity. What happens if the stock rises, to, say, $50 a share? The account looks like this:

LMV   –   Dr   =   Equity

$50,000 – $20,000 = $30,000

The amount owed to the broker-dealer (Dr) didn't change. The long market value of the stock went up, increasing the equity dollar-for-dollar. Now, let's compare the equity of $30,000 to Reg T, which is 50% of the market value or "LMV." Reg T wants to see 50% equity in the account. Does this customer have at least half his "LMV" as equity? Half of 50K is $25,000. The customer has $30,000 of equity. That's **excess equity** of $5,000. Like this:

$$\text{LMV} \ - \ \text{Dr} \ = \ \text{Equity} \ - \ \text{Reg T} \ = \text{Excess Equity}$$

$$\$50,000 - \$20,000 = \$30,000 - \$25,000 = \ \$5,000$$

Since this customer has excess equity of $5,000, $5,000 is credited to a special line item called "**SMA.**" SMA, which stands for **Special Memorandum Account,** is a line of credit that the customer can tap. I mean he can withdraw $5,000 of his cash, like it's in a savings account, right? Not at all. The $5,000 is just a number. But, if the customer wants to borrow that *amount* of money, he can. And whenever he borrows from SMA, that amount is added to the debit balance/debit register. See why customers love margin accounts, especially when the markets are moving in the proper direction? The customer can just tell the broker-dealer to cut him a check for $5,000, which will be added to his tab, like this:

$$\text{LMV} \ - \ \text{Dr} \ = \ \text{Equity}$$

$$\$50,000 - \$25,000 = \$25,000$$

Borrowing the cash didn't affect the long market value of the securities. We added the amount borrowed to the debit balance, which reduced equity and wiped out the SMA. SMA can be used as a cash advance that will be repaid with interest. Or, SMA can be used as an initial margin requirement for the purchase of more stock. So, instead of borrowing the cash, the customer could have used the $5,000 SMA credit to purchase $10,000 of stock. If so, the account would have looked like this:

LMV	Dr	Equity	SMA
$60,000	$30,000	$30,000	$0

If the customer buys more stock, that adds to the market value of securities held long in the account. Why did his Dr go up by $10,000? Because the customer in our example used his line of credit (SMA) as his margin deposit, and the broker-dealer fronted him the other half, or $5,000, which is also added to the Debit. So, he borrowed $5,000 from his line of credit (SMA), plus $5,000 that the broker-dealer fronted him for the additional stock purchase. In other words, when the stock moves your way, you can end up using borrowed money to borrow more money. When dividends, interest, or capital gains distributions from mutual funds come into the account, that income is applied to the debit balance. Therefore, SMA is affected by such income being applied to the debit.

Reg T demands that a customer put up 50% of the long market value initially. After that, what happens if the customer's equity dips below 50%?

Not much. Even though the account is called "restricted," there really aren't many restrictions. The customer is required to put up ½ to buy more stock. If the customer sells stock, he can withdraw/borrow ½ the proceeds.

Surprisingly, when the market value of a securities position drops, that does not affect SMA. It reduces the market value of the stock and, therefore, the equity, but SMA is just a line of credit. It does not get taken away. The customer can always use SMA so long as using it does not take him below the minimum maintenance requirement, which we're about to look at.

Minimum Maintenance

Reg T tells us what to put down on an initial transaction, and any excess above Reg T gives the customer "SMA." But, SMA and excess equity are terms used when the market is cooperating with the margin customer. What happens when the market goes the wrong way? Suddenly, the customer's equity is deficient, and he either must throw more cash on the fire or start liquidating securities.

Reg T requirements apply initially and then help us figure if the customer has SMA. The customer's larger concern is the SRO 25% minimum maintenance requirement. The regulators say that a customer's equity cannot go lower than 25% of the long market value. If it does, the customer gets a maintenance call to bring the equity up to the minimum 25%. If the customer can't deliver the cash, the firm sells securities equal to four times the amount of the maintenance call. The following numbers should help to clarify the concept of the minimum maintenance requirement:

LMV	Dr	Equity	Minimum	Call	Liquidate
40,000	20,000	20,000	10,000	0	0

At this point, the customer has twice as much equity as the minimum (25% of long market value).

If the stock goes from 40K down to 30K, we're okay:

LMV	Dr	Equity	Minimum	Call	Liquidate
30,000	20,000	10,000	7,500	0	0

But, if the long market value falls to 24K, we're in trouble:

LMV	Dr	Equity	Minimum	Call	Liquidate
24,000	20,000	4,000	6,000	2,000	8,000

The SROs demand $6,000 in equity, which is ¼ of $24,000, and the customer has only $4,000. So, the customer gets a maintenance call informing him that he needs to deliver $2,000. If the customer does that, the account looks like this:

LMV	Dr	Equity	Minimum	Call	Liquidate
24,000	18,000	6,000	6,000	0	0

He paid down the debit by $2,000 and now he has $6,000 in equity, the bare minimum of 25% of market value. If he didn't have the cash, the firm would have liquidated $8,000 worth of securities. If so, the account would have looked like this:

LMV	Dr	Equity	Minimum Maintenance
16,000	12,000	4,000	4,000

Whereas, it used to look like this:

LMV	Dr	Equity	Minimum Maintenance
24,000	20,000	4,000	6,000

Selling the $8,000 worth of securities reduced the LMV and the Dr by an equal amount, leaving the customer with exactly 25% equity. By the way, since the firm might have to sell a customer's stock in a hurry, they hold the customer's securities in "street name." That means the securities are registered in the name of the firm for the beneficial ownership (FBO) of the customer, who hasn't exactly paid for them yet.

Also, the 25% requirement is the minimum maintenance. Many broker-dealers require a higher minimum maintenance than just 25% to protect themselves. The regulators are just fine with that, so long as the firm does not let equity drop below 25%.

Short Positions

Remember that when a customer sells short, he is selling borrowed securities in anticipation that he can replace them at a lower price. So, if he wants to sell short $10,000 worth of securities, he must deposit half that value, or $5,000 to meet the Reg T requirement. If he did so, his account would look like this:

Cr	$15,000
SMV	– $10,000
Equity	$5,000

The "Cr" stands for the "credit" and the "SMV" stands for "short market value," or, perhaps, we could just call it the "market value." In any case, when the customer sells short $10,000 worth of securities, that $10,000 is credited to the customer's account. Remember, he sold some stock—someone paid him $10,000.

So, our investor gets the proceeds from the sale, and deposits another 50% of that to meet the Reg T requirement. The $10,000 he took in for selling the stock, plus a $5,000 cash deposit equals a total credit of $15,000.

If the "SMV" goes down, as the investor hopes, he'll have more equity. For example, if the SMV dropped to just $5,000, the customer's equity would increase by $5,000, like this:

Cr	$15,000

$$\frac{\text{SMV} \quad - \quad \$5,000}{\text{Equity} \quad \$10,000}$$

The credit didn't change. He started with a credit of $15,000, and that's all the credit he's going to have. It's the market value (SMV) that changed, dropping in the desired direction for our short seller.

And if the market value of the securities sold short were to increase, his equity would shrink, like this:

Cr $15,000

SMV   − $11,000

$$\frac{\qquad\qquad\qquad}{\text{Equity} \quad \$4,000}$$

How high can the SMV go before a customer gets one of those nasty maintenance calls? For short accounts, customers need 30% of their SMV as equity. If the customer's SMV is $11,000, he needs at least $3,300 in equity. You can find the highest SMV at maintenance by taking the "Cr" and dividing it by 1.3. Since the customer has a credit of $15,000, just divide that by 1.3, and you see that the highest SMV without a maintenance call is $11,538. If the securities' value doesn't exceed that number, his account will remain properly margined.

Combined Equity

To find combined equity, find the equity for the long positions and add it to the equity for the short positions. You can also remember that the formula for combined equity is:

$$\text{LMV} + \text{Cr} - \text{Dr} - \text{SMV}$$

Which is just another way of saying, "Add the two things that go on top and subtract the two things that go on the bottom." So, if a customer had an LMV of $20,000, a Cr of $20,000, a Dr of $10,000, and SMV of $10,000, his combined equity is $20,000:

$$\text{LMV} + \text{Cr} - \text{Dr} - \text{SMV}$$

$$20,000 + 20,000 - 10,000 - 10,000$$

In other words, he has $10,000 equity on the long positions, and $10,000 equity on the short positions. He must have 25% equity for the long, and 30% for the short. This customer is okay on both fronts. Each day the markets are open, the margin department recalculates requirements by marking to the market. If market values have gone the wrong way, the customer might receive a margin call. If market values have gone the right way, the customer might see SMA increase.

Marginable Securities, Accounts

Not everything can be purchased "on margin," but that doesn't mean it can't be purchased within a margin account. A "margin account" is an account that has been approved for margin. The following securities are "marginable," meaning they can be purchased using margin:

- NYSE, NASDAQ, AMEX stocks
- OTC securities on the FRB's approved list

The following can be purchased inside a margin account, but must be paid in full:

- Non-NASDAQ OTC securities
- Options
- IPOs or any new issue for 30 days
- Mutual fund shares

Performance Measures

There are many ways to measure the performance of an investment account.

Holding Period and Annualized Return

If it takes three years to achieve a 9% return, the investor's **holding period return** is 9%. If it takes five or seven years to achieve a 9% return, the investor's holding period return is 9%. Another name for holding period return is total profit. Based on what he invested, the investor's paper gain or loss represents a percentage of that, regardless of the holding period.

To measure the return on an annualized basis take the 9% holding period return and divide it by the number of years it took to achieve it. If the holding period is three years, divide 9% by 3 for a 3% **annualized rate of return.**

If the holding period is more than one year, divide the return by the number of years. If the period is less than one year, multiply. For example, a -3% return over Q1 is -12% annualized. Or, a 5% monthly return is 60% on an annualized basis.

Question: An investment's market value decreases from $10 to $8.50 over Q1. The investment's annualized rate of return is…?

Answer: if the market price drops from $10 to $8.50, take that $1.50 divided by the original $10. The investment just dropped 15% over one quarter. Since there are four quarters per year, multiply the 15% by four, a negative 60% annualized rate of return.

Yield and Total Return

The interest rate that a bond pays is called the **nominal yield**. If a bond has a nominal yield of 5%, it pays $50 a year per $1,000 par value, usually in two semiannual installments of $25. End of story.

For investors on the secondary market, however, the story goes on in the form of **current yield**. That $50 per year the issuer pays would be more attractive if we could get it for $500 rather than for, say, $1,000. In fact, it is exactly twice as nice. Yielding $50 of income from an investment of $1,000 represents a 5% current yield, but getting that same $50 from a $500 investment is a 10% current yield.

Also, when the bond matures, it pays out $1,000. If someone bought it for $1,000 and receives $1,000 at maturity, big deal. But, if he bought it for $500 and receives $1,000 at maturity, he gained $500, on top of all the interest payments received. Now we're talking about **yield to maturity**, which is the yield an investor would receive in the form of all the interest payments plus (or minus) the difference between what they paid for the bond, and the par value the bond pays out at maturity.

Question: One of your clients purchased a GE 5s debenture of '19 @96.375. What is the current yield?

Answer: the "5s" means that the coupon rate is 5% or $50 per year. Divide that $50 of annual interest by the market price of $963.75, and you've got the current yield of about 5.2%.

For **yield to call**, remember that a call can happen sooner than the maturity date. So, for people who bought the bond at a discount from par, their yield to call is even better than current yield or yield to maturity, since they would end up making their gain sooner. But, for people who bought the bond at a premium to par, their yield to call is even worse, since they realize their loss a lot sooner.

So, the yields go in this order: nominal yield, current yield, yield to maturity, and yield to call. For a **discount bond**, they go UP in that order; for a **premium bond**, they go DOWN in that order. That is the bond see-saw covered in the discussion of debt securities, and it's also a way of measuring returns on bonds.

There is a big difference between yield and **total return** for a mutual fund, UIT, or closed-end fund investor. If an investor pays $10 for a mutual fund share and receives $1 in an income or dividend distribution, the investor's yield is 10%.

But, what if the fund share dropped $2 in the meantime? That's a drop of 20% in value! Suddenly, who cares about the 10% yield? The total return is negative. If the value drops 20% and the dividend is only 10%, the total return is −10%. So, when selling mutual fund products to investors, agents must be sure to explain how yield and total return are different. And they should never quote one without quoting the other and explaining the difference.

Let's say an investor receives a dividend of $1 and the share price appreciates $2. That represents a return of $3. Three dollars on top of $10 is a 30% total return.

Doesn't have to be a mutual fund, either. Any stock or bond would have a total return because there are only two ways that an investment can help. Number one, it pays some income and, number two, it goes up in value. That's total return. It can be positive or negative depending on how things turn out.

Question: XYZ common stock pays a quarterly dividend of 75 cents. One of your investors purchased the stock at $50 at the beginning of Q3. If the stock trades for $49 at the end of Q3, what is your investor's annualized rate of return?

Answer: how much money did the investor make over the quarter and what happened to the value of his investment? He took in 75¢, but the stock dropped $1. I'd say he's down 25¢ on a $50 investment, which is a return of negative ½%. Multiply the negative ½% by 4 to get a total annualized rate of return of - 2%.

Inflation-Adjusted, Real Return

The trouble with being a fixed-income investor is that your income is fixed. If you own a 5% bond, what happens if inflation is > than 5%?

That's a risk of being a bond investor, and we don't completely escape it in the stock market, either. When we factor in the effects of inflation, we are talking about something called either **inflation-adjusted return** or **real return**. If we receive a 4% return from a bond, is that enough to help us pay bills in retirement? Not if the price of everything is rising by more than 4%. What if we're receiving 4%, but the price of everything is rising, say, 8%?

We are falling behind. So, if inflation is rising, investors need to calculate whether the return on their investments is rising even higher and faster than the rate of inflation. The number that takes this into account is called the inflation-adjusted return or real rate of return.

To calculate it we subtract the rate of inflation from a portfolio's return. If the investment returns 8% when inflation is 3%, we have an inflation-adjusted return of 5%. If the investment returns 3% when inflation is 8%, we have an inflation-adjusted return of −5%. We may not be losing money on paper, but we are losing purchasing power.

Question: Frank Dodd's investment appreciates 2% during a period in which the Consumer Price Index (CPI) increases 3%. What is Frank's real rate of return?

Answer: Frank's return is 1 point less than the CPI. Therefore, his real rate of return is -1%.

After-Tax Return

Bond interest is often taxable, and if so, it's taxed as ordinary income. Treasury securities are taxed at ordinary income rates by the federal government. Corporate bond interest is taxable by the federal, state, and local governments. Clearly, when we cut a check for taxes, this reduces the returns on our investment. The return on an investment after-tax is referred to as the investor's **after-tax return**.

When looking at municipal securities we take the comparable taxable bond yield and multiply it by the percentage the investor keeps. If he is in the 28% federal tax bracket, he gives up 28% of the return to taxes and keeps 72%. So, if a corporate bond pays $100 a year, he keeps 72% of that, or $72 per year.

The after-tax yield on a bond paying 10% is 7.2%. Not as impressive when we factor in the taxes. The formula to calculate after-tax yield is:

$$\text{Taxable yield} * (100\% - \text{tax bracket})$$

Question: An investor purchasing a corporate bond yielding 9.5% would find that a tax-free bond yielding _____ would be equivalent? The investor is in the 25% marginal tax bracket.

Answer: take 9.5% (.095) and multiply that by the percentage the investor keeps, which is 75% or .75. What is .095 times .75? 7.125%. That is all the tax-free municipal bond would have to yield to put the same dollars in the investor's pocket.

A municipal bond doesn't have to pay as much interest as a taxable bond, since investors don't pay federal income tax on the interest paid by most municipal bonds. Someone in a 30% marginal tax bracket would come out better with a 7% municipal bond than with a 9.5% corporate or Treasury bond.

With the municipal bond, the investor would keep $70. With the taxable bond, she would keep 70% of 9.5%, which is only $66.50. To figure a municipal bond's **tax-equivalent yield**, take the yield the bond pays and divide by (100% minus tax bracket). In other words, in our example, take the 7% and divide it by 70% (100% minus 30%) to see that the municipal bond's 7% yield is equivalent to a 10% taxable yield for this investor.

Rather than have you calculate here, the exam might ask, "What is the following formula used to calculate?"

$$\text{Tax-exempt yield} / (100\% - \text{tax bracket})$$

The formula is used to calculate "tax-equivalent yield."

Question: An investor in a 30% marginal tax bracket would find that a General Obligation bond of the State of New York paying 4% is equivalent to a taxable bond paying...?

Answer: take the 4% and turn it into .04. Divide that by 70% (100% minus tax bracket). This investor would find that a 4% tax-free yield is equivalent to a taxable yield of 5.7%.

Investors are generally **risk averse**, which means they don't like risk. Risk is measured by volatility or **standard deviation**. The more unpredictable the returns of an investment, the riskier that investment is. So, if your investment adviser/portfolio manager earns an 11% total return for the year, you can then adjust that number for the risk it took to achieve it.

The **Sharpe ratio** is the most common form of **risk-adjusted return** measures. Using the Sharpe ratio, the portfolio manager only gets credit for the return he got above the **riskless rate of return**. If the account grew 11% when 3-month U.S. Treasury Bills yielded 4%, we take the 11% minus the 4%, and we're down to 7%. We then divide that 7% by the standard deviation/risk over the period. If the standard deviation is high, the Sharpe ratio is weak; if the standard deviation is low, the Sharpe ratio is strong. The higher the Sharpe ratio, the better the risk-adjusted return of the portfolio.

Alpha is the risk-adjusted return of the portfolio compared to the benchmark. If the exam talks in terms of "positive alpha" or "negative alpha," it is referring to whether the portfolio manager is adding value (positive alpha) or not (negative alpha) with his active management. Because hedge funds try to extract big market returns in all environments, they are often marketed to investors with the phrase "alpha-driven results." How good is your portfolio manager? Alpha points to the answer of that important question.

An investor who puts his money into index funds and lets it ride is on the opposite side of the chart from investors hoping their hedge fund manager can extract gains in bull, bear, or any other type of market. The best portfolio managers turn in results that exceed the expected return on a risk-adjusted basis—positive alpha. If the expected return is 8%, and the portfolio grows 9%, this represents positive alpha of 1%.

Time- and Dollar-Weighted Return

Mutual fund prospectuses and sales literature show the total return of the fund both in bar charts and in statistical tables. While a mutual fund might have a 10% return over the past six years, the average investor in the fund might have a much different experience, depending on whether we're looking at the **time-weighted return** or the **dollar-weighted return** of the portfolio.

See, when a mutual fund has a good run, the buzz attracts a lot of new investors and new money into the fund. What happens if the fund has an amazing run for two years, attracting lots of new money, but then the fund goes flat for the next four years? What happens is this: the time-weighted return looks okay, while the dollar-weighted return does not. The time-weighted return is the average of the total return percentages. The dollar-weighted return weights the returns based on the dollars invested.

Say a growth fund with $100 million of assets has an average annual return of 20% over a three-year period. That performance attracts new assets of $1 billion. And, then, the fund goes flat for the next three years. The average return of the two three-year periods is 10%, which is the time-weighted return.

How did the average investor do? Not so well. Ten times as much money was invested into the fund after the three-year winning streak, so most of the money in the fund has made absolutely nothing while a small percentage has made a decent return. The dollar-weighted return is less than 2%.

Outside of mutual funds, an individual investor who continues to make contributions to his account would need to figure his dollar-weighted return, since some of the contributions have been invested for many years while some have been invested only a few months.

Expected Return

Modern Portfolio Theorists analyze data and figure out likely outcomes based on probability. One example of this is called **expected return**. If we feel an investment will most likely return 8% and has a 75% probability of doing so, we can say the investment has an expected return of 6%. In other words, 8% times the 75% probability of getting the 8% equals 6% (.75 x .08 = .06).

More likely, the exam would express three possible outcomes and say that that investment has a 75% chance of returning 8%, a 10% chance of returning 12%, and a 15% chance of returning −10%. What's the total expected return? Take 75% of 8% (6%), add it to 10% of 12% (1.2%), and add that to 15% of −10% (−1.5%). That's a total expected return of 5.7%.

What happens if we expect 5.7% and get −29.3%? That's why we don't guarantee results.

Rather than use numbers or calculations, the exam might want you to define expected return as "possible return on an investment weighted by the likelihood of the outcomes."

Sometimes expected return and standard deviation are lumped together to make vague predictions about an investment's results. For example, the expected return for the stock market (S&P 500) is, say, 10%, but the standard deviation is 15. What does that tell us about next year's stock market results? Not much, unfortunately. All it can tell us is that about two-thirds of the time, the market returns are somewhere between +25% and −5%, since we add and subtract 15 from the expected return of 10. Ninety-five percent of the time, the market is somewhere between +40% and −20% (two standard deviations). We could do "three standard deviations," but most people get scared out of stocks as soon as they see that the market can end up doing just about anything any given year. Which is, of course, what makes investing in stocks so much fun in the first place.

Question: PDQ common stock has a 40% chance of appreciating 10% and a 60% chance of appreciating 8%. Therefore, its expected return is…

Answer: just take 40% of 10 (4%) and add it to 60% of 8 (4.8%). The expected return is 8.8%.

Benchmarks

For evaluation purposes, portfolio managers compare the performance of their portfolios to some **benchmark**, like the S&P 500 index. The most helpful comparisons compare a portfolio to a benchmark that most accurately reflects the makeup of the portfolio. In other words, if the mutual fund owns mostly technology stocks, why compare the portfolio to a pharmaceutical industry index? More accurately and more usefully, we would compare it to a technology index.

If my client invests in blue-chip companies in various industries, maybe I use a "blue chip index" such as the **Dow Jones Industrial Average**. If I manage a small-cap portfolio, I'm trying to beat the **Russell 2000**, or the S&P SmallCap 600. If I'm the manager of a mid-cap portfolio, I'm hoping to beat the S&P MidCap 400. If I'm a bond fund manager, I'm being matched up against various bond indexes.

Weighting

Indexes generally assign more weight to stocks inside the index, based either on **market cap** or the share price itself. The Dow Jones Industrial Average gives more weighting to stocks priced around $100 than to those priced at, say, $25. So, the exam could say that the DJIA is a "price-weighted index of 30 large, mostly industrial stocks." S&P doesn't use the share price in and of itself to weight their indices; instead, they use **market capitalization**.

Of course, the concept of "weighting" is nothing new. In high school and college, you might have taken courses that made your mid-term worth 30% of the final grade, the homework 10%, class participation 10%, and the final exam 50%. In that case, the final exam was heavily "weighted" at five times the importance of either the homework or the class participation. Within the S&P 500 MSFT is weighted more heavily than many other stocks that comprise the large-cap index.

Possible Calculations

The exam might expect you to calculate a mortgage payment for a hypothetical client. Maybe you'll see something like this: Jennifer Myers is financing a $275,000 home with a 30-year fixed-rate mortgage of 6.5%. If she makes a down payment of 20%, her first monthly payment will be closest to which amount?

Okay, if Jennifer is putting down 20%, she's borrowing 80% of the purchase price. 80% of $275,000 is $220,000. The first year's interest payments will be 6.5% of $220,000 divided over 12 monthly payments. That's $14,300 in interest for the year, or about $1,191.66 per month. In interest. Is her mortgage an interest-only mortgage? If so, the answer is $1,191.66 per month. But, if it's a 30-year fixed-rate mortgage, there's no way to quickly figure how much principal is added to her payment to amortize/pay off the loan over a 30-year schedule. If the exam makes it a 30-year traditional mortgage, it must expect you to do the calculation we just did and then conclude that the payment is not all interest but is, rather, the interest plus a few hundred dollars of principal.

Therefore, you eliminate $1,191.66 and any answer that is lower than that. On the other end, if an answer is too high, like, say, $2,945.52, eliminate that one. Why? You know the interest component of the monthly payment is about $1,200—no way is $1,700 or so on top of that going toward the principal.

The monthly payment (without taxes and insurance) in this example is closest to $1,390.55.

The test might expect you to calculate how long a retiree's money will last if his IRA account earns X percent while he, meanwhile, is withdrawing Y amount. So, we need to go back to our formula for future value (FV). In our examples, we were assuming the investor would leave the money untouched so that if it compounds at 3% it's always the principal times 1.03. However, if the account is earning 3% while the account owner is withdrawing $12,000 a year, obviously, the account will be exhausted at some point. Which is, of course, the point of having a retirement account. The trick is to die before you run out of money rather than the other way around.

If the IRA is earning 3%, while the owner is withdrawing $12,000 a year from the account, how long before he runs out of retirement money? Let's say the IRA starts out at $100,000. The account grows 3% over the year, to $103,000. The client removes $12,000 at the end of the year, so the principal drops to $91,000. If that compounds at 3%, we get $93,700. The client removes $12,000, and now the account is down to $81,700. At this rate, the account will be exhausted in about 11 years.

Unfortunately, my assumptions there were extremely simple. To do a more realistic estimate of proper withdrawal rates, financial planners often use **Monte Carlo simulations** to estimate what would happen if inflation or interest rates went to this or that level. The Monte Carlo method is used in many different professions for decision making. The process uses multiple values for things like interest rates, stock market returns, inflation, etc. to come up with possible outcomes that should give the investor a more realistic plan for retirement.

Now What?

Securities agents are not tax professionals, so they can't give tax planning advice or tackle big problems related to estate planning. But, they have to talk about the tax implications of investing, accurately, and without harming the investor. Therefore, a possible question could be:

One of your customers has received a distribution from the ABCD All-American Tax-Exempt Bond Fund you recommended to her 37 months ago. If this is a distribution of net long-term capital gains, you would accurately inform the customer that
   A. The distribution is exempt from federal but not state taxation

B. The distribution is exempt from state but not federal taxation
C. The distribution is exempt from both federal and state taxation
D. The distribution is subject to both federal and state taxation

EXPLANATION: with the name "tax-exempt" right in the name of the fund, it sure is tempting to assume that all distributions from the fund are tax-exempt. Of course, nothing is ever that simple. First, even if this were a regular distribution from the interest payments received by the fund, it would be subject to state taxation. Right there, we can eliminate Choice B and Choice C. Again, if this were an income/dividend distribution coming from the bond interest received by the fund, then the answer would be A. However, this is a capital gains distribution, and, therefore, it is subject to taxation at both the federal and state levels. Eliminate Choice A, leaving us with

ANSWER: D

If the agent in the situation above gets in a hurry one day, he might accidentally tell this client to spend the distribution on a new Cadillac, thinking it is all tax-exempt. Later, when the customer finds out it was subject to her long-term capital gains rate of maybe 15 or even 20%, well, that's the kind of problem you and the regulators would rather avoid.

Registered representatives sell a lot of mutual funds. A test question might ask something like this:

A mutual fund investor receives a dividend distribution of $500 and a long-term capital gains distribution of $250. What is true if the investor reinvests both distributions into more shares of the fund?
A. She defers taxation until the new shares of the fund are ultimately sold
B. The full amount of the reinvestment is added to her cost basis
C. The amount of any taxes due is added to her cost basis
D. The dividend is added to the cost basis, while the capital gains distribution is subtracted

EXPLANATION: even though Choice A is tempting, remember that mutual funds offer no tax deferral. Tax-deferral is provided by various tax-advantaged accounts, which we will look at in the next chapter. Eliminate Choice A. Choice B kind of seems logical at first maybe—let's put in on the side. Choice C looks even more logical—again, put it on the side. Choice D makes no sense at all, so we can eliminate that one. Okay, so we know it's either B or C. Do we add the full amount of the reinvestment or just the amount of the taxes paid on the reinvestment? What is "cost basis"? Cost basis can be thought of as all the money that has gone into an investment and been taxed. What you pay for a stock or bond is your cost basis. What you pay for a mutual fund is your cost basis. And then, since your dividends and capital gains are taxable whether you reinvest or spend the check, you add the full amount of the distribution to your ever-rising cost basis any time you reinvest. Eliminate Choice C, leaving us with

ANSWER: B

It's time to do the online review exercises. After a break, take the chapter review quizzes. Then, watch the related training video lessons before moving onto the fourth and final chapter.

RIAs, IARs, Broker-Dealers, and Agents

Many investors know the importance of investing but have no idea how to approach it. Fortunately, there are financial services firms known as **investment advisers** happy to assist in exchange for a percentage of the client's account balance. The adviser might manage client accounts in exchange for 1% of assets. Under that arrangement if the client puts $1 million under the adviser's management, 1% would work out to $10,000 a year to the adviser, more as the account value increases or the client adds more funds.

That's a big difference from how a securities agent working for a broker-dealer gets paid. A securities salesperson gets paid for generating activity. The agent earns a commission when the customer buys a stock and then gets a commission when he sells the stock—regardless of whether the customer makes or loses money on the position. But an investment adviser acting as a portfolio manager charges a percentage of the assets in the account. The client's $1 million account balance pays the adviser $10,000 a year if they bill 1% of assets. But, if that account grows to $1.3 million, the adviser's fee rises to $13,000, and so on. On the other hand, if the account drops to $400,000, the investment adviser's paycheck drops right along with it, to $4,000. That's why many investors prefer to work with a fee-based investment adviser, knowing that their compensation is linked to the value of the account rather than the number of trades executed.

Most full-service financial firms can sign up clients either as brokerage customers or as advisory clients. If the client has a $10 million account and only likes to buy and sell a few times a year, she would almost certainly save money paying commissions in a brokerage account the few times she traded compared to 1% of $10 million a year—since that is $100,000 a year in management fees. But, if the client believes in active portfolio management anyway, the advisory side could set him up with a **wrap account**, which bills a flat fee as a percentage of the account value for a professional to manage the account, and that might make more sense.

Broker-dealers and the agents who work for them make money by executing buy and sell orders for securities. Investment advisers, on the other hand, don't get paid for executing securities transactions, and they don't sell securities to clients. Investment advisers are compensated for advising investors. It might seem strange that someone actively trading the client's account is "advising" the client. I mean, isn't he doing a little more than just giving advice if he's buying and selling stocks as he sees fit? Yes, but "investment advice" is a legal definition that covers different types of business models, all of which have one thing in common—the professional's compensation comes from telling investors how to invest in securities or investing on their behalf.

Another type of investment adviser is the **financial planner**. A financial planner doesn't trade the investor's securities portfolio. Rather, the planner puts together detailed financial plans that may concern insurance needs, reducing taxes, estate planning, education funding, retirement planning— the whole financial picture. With this business model, the adviser would usually meet with the client occasionally, charging an hourly rate or a flat fee. $300 an hour would not be unheard of for a financial planner, or maybe $3,000 for a complete financial plan. Many planners earn certifications, but the only legal requirement is to register as an investment adviser before offering and delivering financial plans to investors. Usually registration requires passing the Series 65 or Series 66 exam, but financial planners with their CFP certification are eligible for an exam waiver.

Quick question: did I just say that CFPs don't have to register as investment advisers or IARs? Not at all. They have to register. It's just that they usually receive a waiver from their state securities department to get out of taking the Series 65 exam.

The definition of investment adviser also includes professionals who issue reports or analyses on securities for compensation. Market-timing newsletter writers also typically meet the definition of investment adviser if the newsletter comes out based on market developments rather than on a fixed publication schedule.

A registered investment adviser could be owned as a sole proprietorship, a partnership, an LLC, etc. Regardless, the RIA is the business entity compensated for providing investment advice. On the other hand, an **investment adviser representative** is an individual who represents an investment adviser. If he's a portfolio manager or a salesman, he's probably an investment adviser representative (IAR) who needs to pass the exam and get registered.

Are all individuals working for an investment adviser required to register? No. But, if the individual working for an investment adviser helps to make recommendations to clients or sells the services of the firm, she must register as an investment adviser representative. Or, if she supervises people who do that, she must be a registered investment adviser representative.

On the other hand, the employees performing ministerial work are not defined as investment adviser representatives. So, the individual who makes the coffee, replaces the toner, and tells callers that Mr. Williams-is-at-lunch-would-you-like-to-go-to-voice-mail—that employee does not have to register unless he also gets involved with the investment side of the business.

Investment Adviser Representatives are registered employees of investment advisers who:

- manage accounts
- make recommendations
- determine recommendations
- sell services of firm
- supervise those who do any of the above

So, the investment adviser is the business that provides investment advisory services to its clients. It can be organized as a sole proprietor, an LLC, a corporation, etc. The individuals who represent investment advisers by soliciting or serving the firm's clients are called investment adviser representatives. Either way, investment advisers and investment adviser representatives are in the business of providing investment advice.

On the other hand, broker-dealers and agents are in the securities transaction business. Besides helping people trade securities on the secondary market, broker-dealers bring securities to investors for the first time on the primary market and raise money for their clients as investment bankers. You have probably heard the term "IPO" or "initial public offering." This involves investment bankers taking a privately-owned company and selling its shares to the public for the first time to raise millions or even billions of dollars for the issuer, and a few percentage points for the investment bankers as well.

Whether they're helping customers trade securities on the secondary market or raising capital for their investment banking clients on the primary market, broker-dealers and their agents are in the securities transaction business. They get paid to execute the trade. Their conduct is covered by the Securities Exchange Act of 1934, with its "know your customer" rule. Unlike investment advisers, broker-dealers don't have the **fiduciary duty** of loyalty spelled out in the Investment Advisers Act of 1940 and, therefore, don't have to provide as much disclosure of potential conflicts of interest.

Broker-dealers can also help people invest, of course. We just need to understand that their motivation is to get customers to buy and sell securities. Period. An investment adviser must put the clients' needs ahead of their own, since they're investing the client's money in a way that is supposed to benefit only the client.

There is really no way to invest in securities without broker-dealers because these are the firms who can buy and sell securities and clear/settle the transactions involving bazillions of dollars each day the markets are open. Many investors find the broker-dealer model to be all they need. When it comes time to buy or sell securities, the investor pays some extra fees whether we call them commissions, sales charges, or markups. Broker-dealers sit across the table from the customer either selling them investment products like mutual funds or talking them into buying or selling individual securities.

On the other hand, many investors want a professional to sit on the same side of the table with them and manage the portfolio on their behalf. Trades will be executed by the broker-dealer with custody of the account, but the investment adviser will enter them on the client's behalf, with the client's best interests in mind. To some, this extra layer of investment advice is overkill, but to many others it is essential to have an experienced professional managing the account for a reasonable fee.

The large full-service firms often have a broker-dealer and an investment advisory business set up under the same parent company. That's fine, but the two entities are separate from each other, with separate names, as well. Of course, whether the firm is an investment adviser or a broker-dealer, the securities regulators have the authority to crack down on those who violate securities laws and regulations to provide protection to investors.

State and Federal Securities Acts

We have referred to various federal securities Acts in earlier sections. Let's now turn our attention to state securities law.

Uniform Securities Act

Each state has its own securities law designed to protect investors in the state. While there are differences among the state laws, there are far more similarities. That is because the securities laws in each state typically follow the model legislation for state securities law called the **Uniform Securities Act**. The Uniform Securities Act announces its purpose as follows:

> Relating to securities; prohibiting fraudulent practices in relation thereto; requiring the registration of broker-dealers, agents, investment advisers, and securities; and making uniform the law with reference thereto.

The state securities regulators want the securities laws uniform from state to state, and they want to protect investors by requiring persons in the securities industry and offerings of securities to be registered. The states end up tweaking things, but, overall, the state securities laws all sound pretty much the same when they're defining key terms such as: agent, security, investment adviser, broker-dealer, offer, sale, fraud, etc. Some might call their state regulator the "Securities Commissioner," and others might refer to them as "The Bureau of Securities," but they all take their cue from the Uniform Securities Act and appoint an agency to provide necessary protection to investors.

Remedies and Administrative Provisions

The Uniform Securities Act calls the official in charge of securities regulation the [**Administrator**] and puts the term in brackets, encouraging each state to insert the appropriate title. Often the Secretary of State is the Administrator, with a specific "Division" or "Department of Securities" enforcing the state's securities act. For example, in Illinois one would apply for a driver's license with the same office with which he would file Form ADV for an advisory firm. Is that office called "The Administrator?" No. But that office is an administrative authority with the power to grant, deny, suspend, or revoke licenses to protect residents of the state.

We don't want dangerous, unlicensed drivers on the roads making things unsafe for everyone else. Similarly, we don't want dangerous people out there taking money from investors.

Under the Uniform Securities Act to provide necessary protection to investors, the Administrator can:

- Issue rules and orders
- Issue subpoenas to obtain evidence and testimony
- Issue subpoenas at the request of other regulators
- Cooperate with other regulators
- Apply to a court of law to issue a court order to compel persons to comply with subpoenas
- Administer oaths, take testimony
- Investigate both in and outside the state
- Publish results of investigations, actions

An Administrative rule is, for example, a requirement to file Form ADV Part 1 with the state if the firm is an investment adviser. An order is issued if someone breaks that rule by providing investment advice without bothering to get registered. If someone is violating the securities laws of the state, the Administrator can issue an order to suspend or revoke their license to sell securities or provide investment advice.

Or, if the person is not currently registered, the Administrator can issue a cease and desist order. Maybe the Administrator finds out a local farmer is about to issue certificates granting investors 4%

interests in payments from several windmill turbines going up on his property. Wait—stop! Those securities must be registered before they are even offered to investors. So, maybe the Administrator issues a ccase and desist order, ordering the farmer to stop offering the securities until the offer has been properly registered and cleared for sale.

How did the Administrator find out? Investors who lose money or realize they are about to be ripped off tend to find out which office of the state they can talk to. State securities Administrators provide investor complaint forms, and they have investigators on staff who talk to investors and gather evidence.

A subpoena is a demand for information. If the Administrator issues a subpoena or a cease and desist, and the affected party fails to respond or cooperate, that is known as **contumacy**. The Administrator would then have to apply to a court—or get the Attorney General's office to do it—and seek an injunction or restraining order from the court. If the affected party disregards a court order, they could be held in contempt of court, and that can lead to fines and even jail time.

In the bullet list above we saw that the Administrator of one state can issue a subpoena at the request of the Administrator of another state. The test might even point out that this can happen, even if the violation leading to the subpoena did not happen in the Administrator's state. Provided it would have been a violation of that Administrator's state's securities law/regulations, he can issue the subpoena.

On the other hand, the Administrator cannot:

- Issue injunctions
- Impose criminal penalties
- Impose fines
- Make arrests

The Administrator is not the police, nor a court of law. The Administrator is an administrative authority who registers securities professionals and offers of securities. They can petition a court to issue a judicial injunction or have someone fined and thrown in jail for fraud. But they have to ask first.

In other words, while an unruly agent can have a restraining order issued against him or have himself fined and thrown in jail, it's not the Administrator who makes it happen. It takes a court ruling, not just an Administrative order. Unfortunately, if the court does issue an injunction, the Administrator can then use that as a reason to issue an order that takes away or denies the person's license, or prevents him from ever getting one.

Administrative Orders

When the Administrator discovers that a person is harming investors, they can issue an order against that person. But, usually, they give the individual or firm a heads-up and show the reasons for the state's concern.

Punitive Orders

If it's an order to deny, suspend, or revoke a license, the Administrator must provide the affected parties with:

- Prior notice
- Opportunity for a hearing
- Written findings of fact, conclusions of law

They're usually nice enough to do that even before issuing a cease and desist order, but they don't have to be. It depends, of course, on what's going on. There are plenty of emergency cease and desist orders issued because what's happening or what's about to happen is so out of control that they need to take action now. But before issuing a "stop" order to deny, suspend, or revoke a registration, the Administrator will provide the three bullet points above.

After receiving the notice of hearing from the Administrator, the **respondent** usually must file an answer in writing by a certain deadline. If there is to be a hearing, it is open to the public, and the affected party can be represented by an attorney and can present evidence and witnesses in his favor. But this is not a trial. This is an Administrative hearing to determine if someone's license should be suspended, revoked, denied, etc.

The Administrator's office sends one of their attorneys to present their findings to the hearing officer, and the respondent's attorney—if he can afford one—puts on a defense. The hearing officer is like an arbitrator, a third party who listens to the testimony, examines the evidence, and can recommend that the person have his license denied, suspended, or revoked. Let's hope that this whole experience is only something you read about for your exam. You do not want to be referred to as the respondent in any documents or proceedings with the Administrator of any state.

If the respondent has his hearing and loses, he can file an appeal of the Administrator's order in a court of law if he does so within 60 days. The Administrator's order to suspend or revoke the license is in effect until the court is convinced and compelled to overturn the Administrative order. And, that is not something that happens often.

Why would the Administrator issue a stop order, in the first place? First, the order must be "in the public interest, providing necessary protection to investors," and, then, someone:

- has filed a false or misleading application
- has willfully violated or willfully failed to comply with any provision of this act
- was convicted within last 10 years of any securities-related misdemeanor or any felony
- is enjoined by any court from engaging in the securities business
- is the subject of an order of the Administrator denying, suspending, or revoking registration as a broker-dealer, agent, or investment adviser
- is the subject of an order entered within the past 5 years by the securities administrator of any other state or by the SEC denying or revoking registration as a broker-dealer, agent, or investment adviser
- is the subject of an order of the SEC suspending or expelling him from a national securities exchange or national securities association registered under the Securities Exchange Act of 1934

- has engaged in dishonest or unethical practices in the securities business
- is insolvent
- isn't qualified because they lack training, experience, and knowledge [Lack of experience isn't enough if the applicant does have training and knowledge]
- has failed reasonably to supervise his agents if he is a broker-dealer or his employees if he is an investment adviser
- has failed to pay the proper filing fee (denial only, and the order is vacated as soon as the fee is paid)

That might look like an intimidating list, but, really, it comes down to a few important concepts. Like, if any other regulator already has a problem with the applicant, we have a problem with that. If the agent is already misleading us on the application, we don't want to see how much he will try to mislead his investors. If a firm isn't supervising a bunch of rowdy agents, we can revoke the license. And—not surprisingly—if the person is a convicted felon, or convicted of a misdemeanor concerning forgery, counterfeiting, embezzlement, perjury, fraud, etc., we don't have to give them a license, and we can take the one we granted right back. After letting them tell their side of the story, of course. And letting them spend a fortune on attorney fees.

Speaking of attorney fees, an Administrative hearing over a license is not a trial in either a civil or criminal court, but respondents do generally hire an attorney to present their case and maybe convince the state to cut them some slack. Or, if they know their situation is hopeless, they can just not show up for the hearing, which the state takes as an admission of all their findings of fact. That's called a default decision. No matter what the respondent did, he just made it a lot worse by refusing to cooperate with the Administrator.

Again, the Administrator doesn't have authority to hand down criminal convictions, but if an applicant has been convicted of a felony or a securities-related misdemeanor, that would seem like a good reason to deny, suspend, or revoke the license to sell securities or provide investment advice, right?

Notice how a felony is a felony, but the misdemeanors that matter involve mishandling money or being deceptive. Shoplifting a small amount of merchandise is a misdemeanor—at least on one's first offense—but that would represent a major red flag for anyone now wanting to join a financial services firm, including broker-dealers and investment advisers. Jumping out of a cab and running away—theft of services—might seem a petty offense, but, again, it's relevant to the securities industry. Some charges start out as felonies, too. Reading the IL Criminal Code recently, I noticed that forgery is never a misdemeanor. But, even if it were, signing other people's names to documents without their consent is about as relevant to this industry as one could imagine.

Although regulators usually only hold felonies and securities-related misdemeanors against an applicant or registrant for 10 years, Form U4 asks if the individual has ever been convicted of, pled guilty or no contest to, or even been charged with any felony or securities-related misdemeanor. So, if you get a question about an applicant who answers "no" to the disclosure questions because a felony conviction occurred 12 years ago, remember that this will give FINRA and the state regulators grounds to deny or take away his license. On the other hand, if he had told the truth, there would have been no such action taken.

The Administrator can take two specific actions without first giving notice and an opportunity for a hearing. The cease & desist order can be issued without prior notice, because sometimes the thing that someone is doing or is planning to do is so outrageous that the state needs to stop him in his tracks. Also, the Administrator can "summarily suspend a registration pending final determination" of the matter. That means that until the hearing has been held and the decision has been reached, the license is "summarily suspended."

So, the Administrator can never issue an order to deny, suspend or revoke a license without prior notice, opportunity for a hearing, and written findings of fact and conclusions of law. On the other hand, a cease & desist or a summary suspension could be issued, with a hearing soon to follow.

Non-punitive Orders

Denial, suspension, and revocation orders are punitive orders, because they provide a form of punishment considered necessary to protect investors. On the other hand, there are two orders that are non-punitive: withdrawal and cancellation. If the firm or agent decides they no longer want a license in, say, the State of Tennessee, they can withdraw rather than pay a renewal fee. Fine.

Of course, if they think they can withdraw to avoid a suspension/revocation, I've got news for them. The Administrator can initiate a suspension or revocation proceeding for up to a year after their departure if he finds out that there was a reason they were in such a hurry to leave the state. And, that strike against them can knock the dominos over across all other states.

But a withdrawal in and of itself has nothing to do with punishment. The applicant or the registrant says thanks, but no thanks. Provided they haven't done anything wrong, the Administrator accepts the withdrawal.

A cancellation order happens because the party dies, goes out of business, is declared mentally incompetent, or can't be located. Canceled. The person, apparently, no longer needs the license, so it's canceled.

Like a driver's license, if the individual dies, the state cancels his securities license as opposed to revoking it. A revocation of a license is a punitive action taken when the individual becomes a danger to the residents of the state. A cancellation occurs because the person is no longer in need of the license.

Criminal Penalties

The criminal penalties for willful violations under the Uniform Securities Act are three years in prison, a $5,000 fine, or both, per violation. As the exam might say, "criminal liability attaches" when the person knew what he was doing—was not mentally incompetent—and did it anyway. Doesn't mean the guy had to know that what he was doing was against the law—he just had to be aware of what he was doing.

For example, he knew that his firm had custody of client assets but refused to indicate that on Form ADV. Did he or the firm read the rule prohibiting that? Doesn't matter. He knew the truth, and he put down a different answer, anyway. That's a willful violation. It's not as serious as printing up bogus stock certificates and selling them to investors, but it could lead to criminal prosecution.

The criminal prosecutors at the district attorney or attorney general's office must come after an offender within 5 years of the alleged misdeed. Otherwise, the statute of limitations expires.

Normally, you'd think ignorance of the law is no excuse. However, under the Uniform Securities Act, in the case of a false/misleading document being filed with the Administrator, if the respondent can prove that they did not mean to make a misleading filing, they cannot be imprisoned. They can be fined in this case, but not imprisoned. In a criminal case, the burden of proof is almost always on the prosecutors representing the state, but in this situation, the burden of proof would shift to the respondent who's claiming ignorance.

We're talking about the criminal penalties under the Uniform Securities Act only. There are other state and federal laws that someone can be tried under. I mean, if an agent breaks into a client's home and steals $500,000 from the wall safe, I think we can place all issues concerning his securities license at the bottom of the priority list. He is going to prison for breaking and entering, burglary/home invasion, maybe getting a mandatory minimum sentence of 20 years if he was also carrying a loaded gun, etc. The fact that he will lose his license as an agent is a foregone conclusion once he is convicted of a felony. The fact that it involved "misappropriation" of large sums of cash means that even if he pleads it down to a misdemeanor, it's the type of misdemeanor that regulators use to revoke licenses.

The Uniform Securities Act states:

> The Administrator may refer such evidence as is available concerning violations of this act or of any rule or order hereunder to the attorney general or the proper district attorney, who may institute the appropriate criminal proceedings under this act. Nothing in this act limits the power of the state to punish any person for any conduct which constitutes a crime by statute or at common law.

Civil Liabilities

If someone sold me shares of bogus stock in a non-existent company, what would happen when my $50,000 investment becomes worthless? I could sue to make them return my $50,000 plus interest, plus court costs/attorneys' fees.

Under the Uniform Securities Act the plaintiff can sue for and recover:

- Price paid for the security and/or advice
- Plus interest
- Plus court costs/attorneys' fees
- Minus any income received on the security

We're not talking about pain and suffering here or punitive damages. Just give the investor his money back, plus interest. And, the attorneys for the plaintiff may petition the court to make the defendant pay their legal fees and any filing costs.

If it's discovered that some type of deception took place, the buyer can sue if he initiates action within two years of discovery, or three years from the event. That means if the transaction occurred 4 years ago, it's too late to file suit. Or, if the buyer has known about the deception for more than 24 months, same thing. The statute of limitations expires two years from discovery or three years from the event—whichever comes first.

Sometimes the seller discovers himself that the security sold was unregistered. If so, he messed up, but he can make the buyer a formal offer of rescission. This is a legal "do-over," where he offers to buy back the security plus interest. The buyer now has 30 days to accept the offer. If they just sit on it for more than 30 days, it's too late.

The Uniform Securities Act states that, "Each cause of action under this statute survives the death of any person who might have been a plaintiff or defendant." That means if the defendant has died, his estate can be sued. Or if the plaintiff has died, her estate can file suit on the defendant who defrauded her, as long the suit is filed before the statute of limitations expires.

Regulations of Securities and Issuers

If an investment of money does not meet the definition of a security, the Uniform Securities Act has nothing to say about it. I mean, even the anti-fraud statute does not apply. A security involves an investment of money, but not every investment of money is a security. Under the Uniform Securities Act a security is not a:

- Fixed annuity
- Whole life insurance, term life insurance, universal life insurance, endowment policy

That means we could not possibly commit securities fraud selling those things deceptively. Why not? Because they are not securities. Similarly, baseball umpires don't call many clipping violations. Two different sports subject to different regulations.

The Uniform Securities Act defines a security as any:

- note
- stock
- treasury stock
- bond
- debenture
- evidence of indebtedness
- certificate of interest or participation in any profit-sharing agreement
- collateral-trust certificate
- pre-organization certificate or subscription
- transferable share
- option on commodity/futures contract
- investment contract
- voting-trust certificate
- certificate of deposit for a security

- certificate of interest or participation in an oil, gas, or mining title or lease or in payments out of production under such a title or lease
- in general, any interest or instrument commonly known as a "security"
- warrant, right, or option for a security
- variable annuity or variable life insurance policy

Why define the term with such precision? Because if the investment meets the definition of a security, it is at least subject to the Uniform Securities Act's anti-fraud provisions. And, if it is a security, it needs to be registered unless shown to be exempt, as do the people offering and selling it. The first example in our list is a "note," which means any promissory note issued by an entrepreneur is a security subject both to anti-fraud and registration requirements, even if it seems like no big deal when the two people sit down to talk about it over lunch.

Did you notice the bulleted item "in general, any interest or instrument commonly known as a 'security'"? That means that if court cases or securities regulators have already deemed something to be a security, it's a security.

You may also have noticed the investment contract above. That was what the **Howey Decision** defined for us. The Howey Decision says that an "investment contract" is:

- investment of money due to
- an expectation of profits arising from
- a common enterprise
- which depends solely on the efforts of a promoter or third party

The SEC uses a three-pronged approach to determine if someone is an investment adviser. The SEC and state securities regulators use the Supreme Court's four-pronged approach to determine if something is a security. The "depends solely on the efforts of a promoter or third party" above means that this person is providing money, not labor, to the enterprise. The fact that the seller had no pre-existing relationship with the buyer would factor in, as well. For example, if you have been a trusted farm hand for many years and the farmer then sells you a part-ownership of his dairy farming operation, you could just be a managing member of the LLC.

But, if a farmer is offering investors 10% ownership certificates in which they provide money in exchange for a share of the farm's profits, that is a security. It's an investment of money in a common enterprise in which the investor would expect to profit solely through the efforts of others. Since the investment being offered is a "security," the farmer could end up committing securities fraud. If he, for example, provided an offering document representing that he owns 300 head of cattle, when it's really only 35, that is deceptive.

And, since this investment fits the definition of a security, it probably needs to be registered.

Registering Securities

If the securities offering is required to be registered with the state, this is what the Administrator requires with the registration statement:

- Filing fee

- Total amount of the offering
- Amount of securities offered in their state
- Names of other states where securities will be offered
- Any adverse order, judgment, or decree entered by a court, the securities agency or Administrator in any state, or the Securities and Exchange Commission in connection with the offering.

Also, know that:

- Registrations are effective for one year
- Securities offered by coordination or qualification may require an escrow account whose proceeds are impounded by the Administrator and not released to the issuer/underwriters until they have raised the specified amount
- Securities offered by coordination or qualification may need to be sold through a specified form as stipulated by the Administrator
- The securities registration statement must include consent to service of process
- Underwriters can file the registration on behalf of the issuer

Securities registrations are effective for one year going forward from the effective date. On the other hand, if an agent gets registered on August 15th, her license is going to expire on December 31st unless properly renewed. But if a security's registration is declared effective on August 15th, it will be effective for one year going forward. Also, issuers often apply for a "shelf offering," in which they register the securities now and then sell them gradually over two years, or maybe longer.

Administrative Stop Orders

So, as long as they fill out a securities registration statement and pay the filing fee, the entity is allowed to issue the securities, right?

Maybe, maybe not. The Administrator gets nervous when some little company decides it wants to sell securities to people who don't know any better. When an issuer registers a securities offering, the state is going to want to see the sales literature and advertising to be used in connection with the offering. They'll probably want to see a specimen of the security and, of course, all the offering documents. They'll want to know if the security has been registered with the SEC and if any other regulator—including the courts—might have a problem with it. They'll want to see a copy of the agreement between the issuer and the underwriters, as well as the agreement among the underwriters. That point seems to shock many students, but, trust me, the regulators want to know if the underwriters and/or promoters of the whole scheme are planning to get rich taking money for nothing while everybody else is left holding some high-risk security not worth the paper it's printed on.

If so, no. Just as he can do with the registration of an agent, broker-dealer, or investment adviser, the Administrator can prevent a security from getting registered. Why would he do that?

Because it's in the public interest and:

- The registration statement contains any statement that is incomplete, misleading, or false

- Any provision of the Uniform Securities Act, or any rule or order by the Administrator, has been willfully violated in connection with the offering
- The security registered or sought to be registered is the subject of an administrative stop order or a court injunction entered under any other federal or state act applicable to the offering
- The issuer's enterprise includes or would include activities which are illegal where performed
- The offering has worked or tended to work a fraud upon purchasers (or would so operate)
- The offering has been or would be made with unreasonable underwriter compensation or excessive promoters' profits, or unreasonable amounts or kinds of options
- A security seeking to be registered by filing is not eligible for such registration
- A security seeking to be registered by coordination has failed to comply with the requirements of that process
- The proper filing fee has not been paid (but only a denial order can be entered and shall be vacated once the fee is paid)

As with registrations of persons, before a deny, suspend, or revoke order is entered, the issuer would get a prior notice of an opportunity for a hearing and all the written findings of fact and conclusions of law. As before, there are emergency cease & desist orders and there are also summary suspensions pending final determination of a proceeding.

Methods of Registration

There are three different ways to register securities with the state securities Administrator. Let's start with Registration by Coordination.

Registration by Coordination

Why would they call this method "registration by coordination"? Because the issuer must first register the securities with the SEC under the Securities Act of 1933, and then they can coordinate the process with the states where the securities will be offered for sale. What if the issuer is not going to register with the SEC? Then they can't use this method. Also, the securities can generally not already be declared effective by the SEC. The Administrator could allow that to happen, but the greater the interval between the SEC declaration of effectiveness and the filing with the state, the more likely the Administrator will deny the registration.

So, the issuer of an interstate offering is subject to registration with the SEC under the Securities Act of 1933, and, since the issuer is not big enough to be granted an exemption at the state level, they also have to register with the states.

That's registration by coordination. As the Uniform Securities Act indicates, "A registration statement under this section shall contain the following information and be accompanied by the following documents in addition to the [requirements of all registrations] and a consent to service of process."

And those documents are:

- Three copies of the prospectus and all amendments filed with the SEC under the Securities Act of 1933
- If the Administrator requires it, a copy of the articles of incorporation and bylaws currently in effect, a copy of any agreements with or among underwriters, a copy of any indenture, and a specimen/copy of the security

So, the issuer and its underwriters are sweating it out with the SEC and also showing the state regulators what they've shown the federal regulators. The state wants to see what the stock or bond looks like, and they'd like to see how much the underwriters are going to make by selling securities in their state. The effective or release date, which is the day that the underwriters can sell to investors, will be declared by the SEC. If the issuer meets the following conditions, the effective/release date at the state level will be whatever day the federal regulators (SEC) declare:

- No stop order is in effect and no proceeding is pending (deny, suspend, revoke)
- The registration statement has been on file with the Administrator for at least 10 days
- A statement of the maximum and minimum proposed offering prices and the maximum underwriting discounts/commissions has been on file for two full business days

Registration by Filing

Securities registered under this method also must be registered with the SEC, as with registration by coordination. If the issuer and any predecessors have been in continuous operation for at least five years, registration by filing for their additional offering is available if:

- There has been no default during the current fiscal year or within the three preceding fiscal years in the payment of principal, interest, or preferred dividend
- The issuer and any predecessors during the past three fiscal years have had average net earnings, in accordance with generally accepted accounting practices (GAAP), of 5% of either the maximum offering price or the market price within 30 days of filing, whichever is higher

As the Uniform Securities Act says, a registration statement under this section shall contain the following information and be accompanied by the following documents in addition to the [general requirements for all securities] and the consent to service of process:

- A statement demonstrating eligibility to use this method
- Name, address, form of organization, the state or foreign jurisdiction where the issuer is organized and the date of organization, and the general character and location of its business
- If the securities are being sold by someone other than the issuer (non-issuer distribution), the name and address of the person, the amount of securities held by him as of the date of filing, and a statement of his reasons for making the offering
- A description of the security being registered
- If the issuer has not been in business continuously for five years—a balance sheet as of a date within four months prior to filing and a summary of earnings for each of the two fiscal years preceding the date of the balance sheet

If no stop order is in effect and no proceeding is pending, a registration statement under this section automatically becomes effective at 3 o'clock Eastern Time in the afternoon of the second full business day after filing the registration statement or the last amendment, or at such earlier time as the Administrator determines.

Registration by Qualification

Any securities offering may be registered by qualification, but, as we'll see, this is the most arduous method of registering securities at the state level. In addition to the requirements for securities registration in general, a registration statement under qualification must contain:

- The following information on the issuer: name, address, form of organization, state/foreign jurisdiction where organized and date of organization, description of physical properties and equipment, and a statement of the general competitive conditions in the industry in which it is or will be engaged
- With respect to e director and officer of the issuer: name, address, principal occupation for the past five years, amount of securities of the issuer held by him as of a specified date within 30 days of filing, the amount of the securities covered by the registration statement to which he has indicated his intention to subscribe
- Remuneration paid during the past 12 months and estimated to be paid during the next 12 months by the issuer to the directors and officers mentioned above
- For the folks who own 10%+ of the issuer's securities, indicate the amount of securities of the issuer held by them as of a specified date within 30 days of filing and the amount of the securities covered by the registration statement to which they have indicated their intention to subscribe
- If anyone is doing a non-issuer distribution connected to this offering, give the same information asked for under registration by filing/notification
- Capitalization and long-term debt of the issuer
- Kind and amount of securities to be offered, proposed offering price, estimated underwriter compensation and finders' fees to be paid
- Estimated cash proceeds to be received by the issuer, purposes for which the proceeds will be used and the amounts to be used for each purpose, source of any proceeds to also be used to achieve the purposes listed
- Description of any stock options outstanding or to be created in connection with the offering together with the amount held or to be held by e person required to be listed above (officer, director, 10%+ owners)
- Copy of any prospectus, pamphlet, circular, form letter, advertisement, or other sales literature to be used
- Specimen/copy of the security being registered, copy of articles of incorporation and bylaws, and copy of the indenture if applicable
- Signed statement of a legal opinion
- Balance sheet as of a date within four months prior to filing, income statement for each of the three fiscal years preceding the date of the balance sheet, and if any part of the proceeds of the offering will be used to purchase another business, the same financial statements on that business

A test question might ask, "Which of the following methods requires a specific response from the Administrator?" The answer would be "registration by qualification." The other two methods—coordination and filing—lead to a release/effective date determined by the SEC.

Exempt Securities

An exempt security is excused from the registration requirements of the Uniform Securities Act. If the security is non-exempt, it is not excused from registration requirements.

The following are exempt securities whose offerings are automatically excused from registration under the Uniform Securities Act:

- any security issued/guaranteed by US Treasury/US Government
- municipal securities
- any security issued by any Canadian government
- any security issued by a foreign government with diplomatic relations
- bank, savings institution, trust company security
- savings & loan, building & loan securities, credit union securities
- debt securities issued by an insurance company
- securities issued by railroad or other common carrier, public utility, or holding company subject to Interstate Commerce Commission, or the Public Utility Holding Company Act of 1935
- a federal covered security
- non-profit securities
- promissory note maturing in 9 months/270 days or less, issued with denominations of $50,000+, and rated in top 3 credit tiers by a nationally recognized statistical rating agency
- investment contract issued in connection with pension/employee benefit program

Two of those securities could lose their exemption if they aren't careful. Those two are:

- investment contract issued in connection with pension/employee benefit program
- non-profit securities (e.g., religious, educational, fraternal, charitable, social, or trade/professional associations)

Why are the securities above exempt? Because the Uniform Securities Act says so. Many are either the direct obligation of a federal government, or covered by some federal act like the Public Utility Holding Company Act of 1935, or covered by some federal agency such as the now-defunct Interstate Commerce Commission, which had jurisdiction to set rates for services provided by railroads, trucking companies, bus lines, freight forwarders, water carriers, oil pipelines, transportation brokers, and express agencies.

Fine, the state regulators have enough trouble trying to stop all the shady characters selling promissory notes to investors who don't know any better. Let the federal regulators deal with federal government securities and securities covered by various federal laws.

Federal Covered Securities

So, all securities must be registered at the state level, unless they are exempt. If the Uniform Securities Act declares a security to be exempt, that means it does not have to be registered and is not subject to the filing of advertising materials, sales literature, the prospectus, etc. The security and the offer and sale of it are subject to anti-fraud rules, but not subject to registration requirements.

We saw above that one type of exempt security is a "federal covered security." Like a federal covered investment adviser, federal covered securities don't have to be registered with the states. As their name suggests, these securities are covered at the federal level. The National Securities Markets Improvement Act of 1996 (NSMIA) is what created this special class of security. This Act also reminds us that while the SEC plays the important role of providing necessary protection to investors, they also play the important roles of promoting capital formation and encouraging efficiency and competition in the securities markets.

So, whenever they make rules, they try to balance the need to provide investor protection with the need to help issuers raise capital and the need to make the markets as efficient and competitive as possible. With this in mind, the federal regulators decided that investors would be plenty protected and the markets would become more efficient if certain securities registered only with the SEC. So, registration of the following federal covered securities is covered at the federal level only:

- Securities listed, or authorized for listing, on the New York Stock Exchange or the American Stock Exchange, or listed on the Nasdaq Stock Market (or any successor to such entities)
- Securities listed, or authorized for listing, on a national securities exchange that has listing standards that the Commission determines are substantially similar to the listing standards applicable to securities described in subparagraph (A); or
- Securities of the same issuer that are equal in seniority or that are a senior security to a security described in subparagraph (A) or (B)
- Securities issued by an investment company that is registered, or that has filed a registration statement, under the Investment Company Act of 1940
- SALES TO QUALIFIED PURCHASERS—A security is a covered security with respect to the offer or sale of the security to qualified purchasers, as defined by the Commission by rule. In prescribing such rule, the Commission may define the term 'qualified purchaser' differently with respect to different categories of securities, consistent with the public interest and the protection of investors.

Why should these securities automatically be on the federal government's turf? Well, if the security is trading on a national exchange, first, we're talking about interstate commerce, which is the federal government's domain. Second, the issuer must provide full disclosure and meet all kinds of rigid criteria just to be have the security trading on this national exchange.

Notice the phrase "has listing standards that the Commission determines are substantially similar to the listing standards applicable to securities described in subparagraph (A)." The "Commission" (SEC) also reserves the right to determine that exchanges created in the future have similar criteria. If so, those securities are federal covered, too.

And, if the issuer's common stock is federal covered, so is their preferred stock and so are their bonds (senior securities). Investment company securities include open- and closed-end funds, UITs, ETFs, and variable contracts. Those are federal covered. They might do a notice filing, but that's just a filing of notice with the states.

So, nobody said that a federal covered security doesn't have to be registered. What we're saying is that a federal covered security doesn't have to be registered with the states. All these issuers need to worry about is the Securities and Exchange Commission (SEC), which is plenty to worry about, as it turns out.

Now, let's apply the concept. Since these securities such as IBM, Microsoft, or variable annuities are federal covered, the states have no power to enforce anti-fraud regulations on any offer or sale, right?

How does the fraud definition go again? Does it say that it's unlawful to employ any device, scheme, or artifice to defraud in connection with any security that has to be registered with the state?

No, it says "any security." IBM doesn't have to register with the states, but if anybody makes a fraudulent offer or sale of IBM, the states can enforce anti-fraud regulations against that prohibited activity. IBM common stock is a security.

Just like a fixed annuity, right? No—a fixed annuity is not a security. If the investment is not a security, it is not subject to anything under the Uniform Securities Act. But, if the investment of money is a security, it is always subject to at least the anti-fraud statutes.

So, whether the security is required to be registered is one concern. If the issuers can claim an exemption, the issuers are happy about avoiding paperwork, fees, and public disclosure of their business. But registration has nothing to do with the f-word, fraud. If the investment of money fits the definition of a "security," the anti-fraud statutes apply. And, if the investment isn't even a security, then the Uniform Securities Act has nothing to say about it.

Exempt Transactions

Federal covered securities are exempt from state-level registration. Other exempt securities such as bank securities and religious organization securities are excused from the requirements to register and file sales and advertising materials with the Administrator. If it is an exempt security, it is a security that does not have to be registered.

On the other hand, non-exempt securities must be registered, unless they are offered and sold through an **exempt transaction**. Just like federal law, the Uniform Securities Act lists securities that are exempt from registration requirements and calls them "exempt securities." Then, the Uniform Securities Act lists transactions that make the security exempt from registration and calls them exempt transactions. Why don't these non-exempt securities have to be registered? Because they're being offered and sold in an exempt transaction, such as:

- any sale or offer to a bank, savings institution, trust company, insurance company, investment company, pension or profit-sharing trust, or other financial or institutional buyer, or to a broker-dealer
- private placements

> No more than 10 non-institutional buyers in the state per 12-month period

> Seller believes that all non-institutional buyers hold for "investment purposes"

> No commissions paid for soliciting any non-institutional buyer

- transactions between issuers and their underwriters
- transactions by fiduciaries: executors, administrators, sheriffs, marshals, receivers/trustees
- pledges
- unsolicited non-issuer transactions effected through a broker-dealer
- isolated non-issuer transactions
- any transaction to existing security holders of the issuer, if no commission is paid for soliciting buyers
- offerings of pre-organization certificates

> No more than 10 buyers, period

> No commissions paid for soliciting any buyer

> No payment made by any subscriber

- any offer (but not a sale) of a security for which a registration statement has been filed under the Uniform Securities Act and the Securities Act of 1933 if no stop order is in effect. Sales may only take place after registration is effective
- any transaction in a bond secured by a real mortgage or deed of trust provided that the entire mortgage or deed of trust, together with the bonds, are offered and sold as a unit
- non-issuer transactions in securities subject to reporting requirements of the Exchange Act of 1934, or in securities registered under the Investment Company Act of 1940, or in securities where the issuer has filed with the Administrator information substantially the same as that required for registered issuers by the Securities Exchange Act of 1934 for a period of at least 180 days prior to the transaction

If we dig below the surface, we can see the logic to most of these exemptions. For example, we can easily see why the transactions by fiduciaries—executors, administrators, sheriffs, marshals of the court, receivers/trustees in a bankruptcy liquidation of assets—qualify for a more relaxed treatment by the Administrator. They're all being supervised by the courts, whether it's an executor disposing of the estate assets or an accounting firm liquidating the assets of a company. A receiver placed in charge of a bankrupt entity's assets might liquidate those assets, some of which could be unregistered, non-exempt securities. Oh, well, it's not like this receiver/trustee/marshal in a bankruptcy is a securities dealer trying to skirt the registration requirements. And, these are non-issuer transactions between one investor and another.

On the other hand, there are not many transactional exemptions available to an issuer of a security. If my company wanted to offer some of the shares our charter authorizes us to issue to investors, we could get around registration requirements if we offered only to institutional investors, e.g., insurance companies and broker-dealers. Or, we could offer to up to 10 individuals who live in the state and call that a private placement. In both cases the Administrator would require a notice that the transaction occurred, but we could file it after the fact and would not have to make our financial statements and material risks to the business public. Rather, we could provide our financial and risk disclosures just to the small group of carefully selected investors.

And, when we do, we would be as careful as possible, as the transaction is still subject to anti-fraud regulations concerning complete and accurate disclosure of all material facts related to the investment.

If a company publishes a website or a full-page ad in a magazine soliciting investors, the regulators had better find a registration statement on file for this offering. On the other hand, if the company is talking to a handful of institutional investors, the state securities department does not have to put up a wall of protection in that case. The regulators always have the anti-fraud statutes to use if the institutional investors end up being defrauded, and, chances are, that won't happen nearly as often as it happens among retail investors.

Another exemption is for an offer of a security that is in the process of registration. If the issuer has filed the registration statement, they can take indications of interest, providing investors with a preliminary prospectus. They just can't make a sale until the effective date. And, they can't start making offers before that registration statement is on file.

Offers and Sales

As the Uniform Securities Act states:

> *"Offer" or "offer to sell" includes every attempt or offer to dispose of, or solicitation of an offer to buy, a security or interest in a security for value.*

An offer is an attempt to sell someone a security, or an attempt to entice them to offer to buy a security.

A sale is defined this way:

> *"Sale" or "sell" includes every contract of sale of, contract to sell, or disposition of, a security or interest in a security for value.*

Why are these definitions important? Because the most important part of the Uniform Securities Act is:

> *It is unlawful for any person, in connection with the offer, sale, or purchase of any security...to employ any device, scheme, or artifice to defraud.*

So, the respondent who is the subject of an Administrative action might hire an attorney to argue that the conduct in question did not fit the definition of "offer" or "sale." Because, if the conduct in question does fit the definition of an offer and/or a sale of securities, it is subject to the anti-fraud statutes and might require some people to get registered.

Not Offers

Under the Uniform Securities Act the following are not considered offers of securities:

- any bona fide pledge or loan of a security
- any stock dividend if nothing of value is given by stockholders for the dividend
- any act incident to a class vote by stockholders…on a merger, consolidation, reclassification of securities, or sale of corporate assets in consideration of the issuance of securities of another corporation
- any act incident to a judicially approved reorganization in which a security is issued in exchange for one or more outstanding securities, claims, or property interests

First, if I am pledging securities as collateral, I am not making an offer to sell securities. So, I can pledge a security as collateral even if the security isn't registered. A stock dividend is really a non-event. The issuer used to cut the big earnings pie into 10 million slices; now they're going to give everybody more slices by cutting the pie into 15 million smaller slices and having everybody pretend they've gained something. That is not an offer—just a way of pushing down the market price for the stock to entice investors to buy more of it.

When a corporation merges with another corporation, the acquiring company is not really offering their securities to the other shareholders—the two companies are going to become one. And the last bullet point relates to a bankruptcy proceeding. The bankruptcy judge will approve the plan to wipe out the current shareholders and give the bondholders shares in the newly organized entity. So, that's a way of dealing with creditors, not an offer of securities.

For extra credit google "tombstone ad images" and open a few tombstone announcements. Notice the text at the top stating that this is just an announcement and neither an offer to sell nor a solicitation of an offer to buy the securities being announced. All offers, the caveat states, are made by prospectus. So, yes, if you send someone a prospectus, you are offering to sell those securities.

Offers: Directed, Originated, Accepted

The next question is, "When has an offer been made in a state?" Luckily the Uniform Securities Act tells us that:

> *…an offer to sell is made in this state when the offer originates from this state, or is directed by the offeror to this state.*

If you get a test question stating that an agent in State A calls an investor in State B trying to interest the investor in some securities, tell the exam that an offer to sell a security has been made in both states. The Uniform Securities Act also gives the Administrator authority when an offer has been accepted in the state. An offer to sell "is accepted in this state when acceptance is communicated to the offeror in this state and has not previously been communicated to the offeror outside this state." That communication could be by phone, text message, email, fax, etc., by the way.

This is much simpler than it first appears. If an agent in North Dakota calls a customer vacationing in South Dakota and asks if she'd like to buy a variable annuity, an offer to sell a security has been made in both states. If the buyer isn't sure, maybe she calls back a few days later while visiting her Aunt Lorraine in Lincoln, Nebraska. "Sure," she says, "I'd like to communicate my acceptance of said variable annuity to you, the offeror." Now the offer has been accepted in Nebraska. The offer was D-directed into South Dakota, O-originated in North Dakota, and A-accepted in Nebraska. Who's got jurisdiction if the agent is scamming the customer? Could be any or all three states involved.

What if the investor cuts a check in Branson, Missouri? Nobody cares where the check is cut. It's all about where the offeror and offeree were when they were communicating. Also, if the agent had been offering shares of General Electric, headquartered in New York, that would not imply that the New York Administrator is somehow involved. GE has nothing to do with this North Dakota agent.

In another section we'll be saying that the North Dakota agent can call an existing customer who's just visiting the state of South Dakota without having to register as an agent in South Dakota. Fine. The agent could also get into his pickup truck and drive to the other state without getting a South Dakota driver's license. But, in either case, if the agent starts violating the law, the State of South Dakota can take action. What if the agent doesn't like that fact?

Tell him to stay out of South Dakota.

Federal Securities Acts

The securities markets are regulated by a handful of highly detailed federal securities Acts of the United States Congress. The Securities and Exchange Commission (SEC) also makes rules under these federal securities acts. The exam is expected to touch on just the fundamentals of each law, but even that requires us to do some homework.

Securities Act of 1933

As the SEC explains on their website:

Often referred to as the "truth in securities" law, the Securities Act of 1933 has two basic objectives:

- require that investors receive financial and other significant information concerning securities being offered for public sale; and
- prohibit deceit, misrepresentations, and other fraud in the sale of securities.

The scope of this securities law is narrower than the more far-reaching Securities Exchange Act of 1934. The Securities Act of 1933 focuses solely on the offering of securities to public investors for the first time. The Act requires issuers to register an offering of securities with the SEC before the issuer can sell or "issue" their securities to the public. Because of this law an investor must be provided with a prospectus that discloses everything he might need to know about the company issuing the security before the issuer or underwriters take his money and close the deal. Investors can read about the issuer's history, its board of directors, its products and services, its chances for success, and its risks of failure. They can look at the balance sheet and the income statement. They'll be taking a risk if they buy—because all securities carry risk—but at least they'll be able to make an informed decision because of this full and fair disclosure.

When a corporation wants to raise capital by selling securities, they get a group of underwriters together and fill out paperwork for the federal government in the form of a registration statement. Part of this registration statement will become the prospectus, which is the disclosure document that investors will be provided with. An "underwriter" is just a broker-dealer that likes to take companies public, remember. Another name for an underwriter is investment banker.

Once the underwriters file the registration statement on behalf of the issuer, the process goes into a cooling-off period, which lasts a minimum of 20 days. This process can drag on and on as the SEC reviews the paperwork, but no matter how long it takes, the issuer and underwriters can only do certain things during this cooling-off period. Number one, they can't sell anything. They can't do any general advertising of the securities offering.

The underwriters can seek "indications of interest," but those aren't sales. Just names on a list. If someone gives an indication of interest, they must receive a preliminary prospectus, which contains everything that the final prospectus will contain except for the effective date and the final/public offering price or "POP." The registered rep may not send a research report along with the preliminary prospectus and may not highlight or alter it in any way. A research report is considered sales literature and, remember, during the cooling-off period no sales or advertising is allowed.

The preliminary prospectus is also referred to as a "red herring," due to the red-text warning that information may be added or altered. The release date and the final public offering price are two pieces of information yet to be added to what's in the red herring to make it a final prospectus. But, the preliminary prospectus has virtually all the material information a potential investor would need before deciding to invest or not.

The underwriters can announce that a sale is going to take place by publishing a tombstone ad in the financial press. That is because a tombstone ad only announces that a sale of securities will take place at a particular offering price (or yield) and informs the reader how to obtain a prospectus. But it is neither an offer nor a solicitation to buy the securities.

The issuer and the underwriters attend a due diligence meeting toward the end of the cooling-off period to try and make sure they provided the SEC and the public with accurate and full disclosure. Nothing gets sold until the SEC "releases" the security on the release date/effective date. Starting on that date, the prospectus must be delivered to all buyers of these new securities for a certain length of time.

And, even though the SEC makes issuers jump through all kinds of hoops, they do not approve or disapprove of the security. They don't guarantee accuracy or adequacy of the information provided by the issuer and its underwriters. In other words, if this whole thing goes horribly wrong, the liability rests squarely on the shoulders of the issuers and underwriters, not on the SEC. For that reason, there must be a disclaimer saying basically that on the prospectus. It usually looks like this:

So, how does the SEC feel about the investment merits of the security? No opinion whatsoever. They just want to make sure investors receive full and fair disclosure.

Exempt Securities

The Securities Act of 1933 is a piece of federal legislation, so it's not surprising that US government securities are exempt from this act. So are municipal securities. Charitable organization securities, such as church bonds, are exempt from the act. So are bank securities, which are already regulated by bank regulators. Securities that mature in 270 days or less—commercial paper, bankers' acceptances—are also exempt from this arduous registration process.

An exempt security is excused from the registration requirement, but it's a security. So, if anybody offers or sells it deceptively, that is considered securities fraud, which is always a bad idea. People can get sued and thrown in jail for fraudulent offers/sales of securities, and registered representatives have been known to lose their registration. Whether a security had to be registered or not has nothing to do with whether securities fraud transpired. Securities fraud can happen with *any* security, whether it's common stock or an exempt US Treasury Bond. If the seller gets the buyer's money through lies, tricks, and deceit, we're talking about securities fraud.

Exempt Transactions

There are exempt securities, and there are also transactions that qualify for exemptions. In other words, there's absolutely nothing special about the security being offered here—it's the way it's being offered and sold that makes it exempt from the typical registration process. Under a Reg A exemption, an issuer can sell a small offering of securities without going through the full registration process. Or, if the issuer agrees to sell the stock to residents of only one state, they will qualify for a Rule 147 exemption. This only works if the issuer's main business is located in that state and 80% of its assets are located there. Also, the buyers can't sell the security to a non-resident for 9 months after the close of the offering period. The issuer registers with the state, rather than the SEC, since it's all taking place in that one state. IntrAstate. All in A state. The issuer would most likely use "registration by qualification" to do the intra-state IPO. The SEC is federal, in charge of interstate commerce. So if it's all within a state, it's that state's concern.

Sometimes issuers offer their shares primarily to "accredited investors." These are sophisticated investors, often with millions of dollars at their disposal. If the individual has a certain amount of net worth or income, he/she is accredited, and presumed to be able to look after him- or herself. So, an issuer can place their securities under a Reg D transaction with as many of these folks as they want. This "private placement" is not being offered to the public, so the regulations are loser. Besides wealthy individuals, the issuer can place these unregistered securities with as many institutional investors as they want. They can also sell to insiders of the corporation, which would include officers, directors, and large shareholders. So, a Reg D/private placement transaction is exempt from the Act of 1933 because it is offered to an exclusive group of investors.

Crowdfunding

Even though we just looked at concerns for non-accredited purchasers in Reg D private placements, anyone can invest in a **crowdfunding** securities offering. Because of the risks involved with this type of investing, however, investors are limited in how much they can invest during any 12-month period.

The limitation depends on net worth and annual income. If either the investor's annual income or net worth is less than $100,000, then during any 12-month period, he can invest up to the greater of either $2,000 or 5% of the lesser of his annual income or net worth.

If both his annual income and net worth are equal to or more than $100,000, then during any 12-month period, an investor can commit up to 10% of annual income or net worth, whichever is less, but not to exceed $100,000.

As when determining who is and is not an accredited investor, the value of the investor's primary residence is not included in the net worth calculation. In addition, any mortgage or other loan on a primary residence does not count as a liability up to the fair market value of the home.

Companies may not offer crowdfunding investments to investors directly. Rather, they must use a broker-dealer or funding portal registered with the SEC and also a member of the Financial Industry Regulatory Authority (FINRA).

Investors open an account with the crowdfunding intermediary to make an investment, and all written communications relating to the crowdfunding investment will be electronic.

Before an investor can make a crowdfunding investment the broker-dealer or funding portal operating the crowdfunding platform must ensure that he reviews educational materials about this type of investing. In addition, the investor must positively affirm that he understands he can lose all of the investment, and that he can bear such a financial loss.

Investors also must demonstrate that they understand the risks of crowdfunded investing. The sharing of views by the crowd is considered by some to be an integral part of crowdfunding. Broker-dealers and funding portals, through their crowdfunding platforms, are required to have communication channels transparent to the public. For example, on an online forum—relating to each investment opportunity.

In these channels, the crowd of investors can weigh in on the pros and cons of an opportunity and ask the company questions. All persons representing the company must identify themselves.

Investors have up to 48 hours prior to the end of the offer period to change their mind and cancel their investment commitment for any reason. Once the offering period is within 48 hours of ending it is too late to pull out. However, if the company makes a material change to the offering terms or other information disclosed to investors, investors are given five business days to reconfirm the investment commitment.

Investors are limited in their ability to resell their investment for the first year and may need to hold for an indefinite period. Unlike investing in companies listed on a stock exchange where investors can quickly and easily trade securities on a market, crowdfunding is similar to holding a direct participation program interest. To sell the investment an interested buyer must be located.

Securities Exchange Act of 1934

As the SEC explains on the same page of their website:

> With this Act, Congress created the Securities and Exchange Commission. The Act empowers the SEC with broad authority over all aspects of the securities industry. This includes the power to register, regulate, and oversee brokerage firms, transfer agents, and clearing agencies as well as the nation's securities self-regulatory organizations (SROs). The various securities exchanges, such as the New York Stock Exchange, the NASDAQ Stock Market, and the Chicago Board of Options are SROs. The Financial Industry Regulatory Authority (FINRA) is also an SRO.
>
> The Act also identifies and prohibits certain types of conduct in the markets and provides the Commission with disciplinary powers over regulated entities and persons associated with them.
>
> The Act also empowers the SEC to require periodic reporting of information by companies with publicly traded securities.

The Securities Exchange Act of 1934 gave the SEC broad powers over the securities markets. The Act gave the Federal Reserve Board the power to regulate margin. It also requires public companies to file quarterly and annual reports with the SEC. If a material event occurs before the next regular report is due, the issuer files an 8-K. There are reports filed when the officers and members of the board sell their shares. Mergers and acquisitions must be announced through various filings. You get the idea.

The Securities Exchange Act of 1934 talked about insider trading, warning investors not to pass around or use non-public information. If you knew that your sister's company was going to be purchased by Google, it would be tempting to buy calls on her company's stock and tell your clients to do the same. Unfortunately, the SEC would sue you in civil court, where the maximum civil monetary fine is "treble damages," meaning they could fine you three times the amount of your benefit from using the information.

The Securities Exchange Act of 1934 gives federal prosecutors the authority to prosecute criminal violations. So, if the insider trading activity is handled in civil court, the SEC will try to extract three times your benefit. If they turn it over to the US Attorney's office for criminal prosecution, now we're talking about a potential prison term.

Although the Act of 1934 talked about insider trading, apparently it didn't quite get the message across. So, in 1988 Congress passed the **Insider Trading & Securities Fraud Enforcement Act** of 1988 and raised the penalties for insider trading, making it a criminal offense with stiff civil penalties as well. If an agent's brother-in-law happens to be the Chief Financial Officer of a public company and over a few too many martinis lets it slip that his company is going to miss earnings estimates badly this quarter, the agent is now in possession of material inside information.

Any material information the public doesn't have, that's inside information. Material inside information must not be circulated or used by those who know about it. If the agent told clients to sell their shares in his brother-in-law's company, or if bought puts on the stock for his wife's account, he would likely be pursued for insider trading by the SEC.

People who violate the act can be held liable to "contemporaneous traders." That means that if the agent is dumping shares based on an inside tip, and that hurts another trader, there could be grounds for civil action.

The investment banking arm of a broker-dealer has access to all kinds of material non-public information. To prevent that sensitive information from flowing to other areas of the firm, the broker-dealer is required to create a **Chinese wall** around departments that obtain such information. No, they don't build an actual wall. They just try to prevent the investment bankers working on a merger from revealing some good trading tips to the registered representatives working the telephones.

Trust Indenture Act of 1939

As the SEC states:

> This Act applies to debt securities such as bonds, debentures, and notes that are offered for public sale. Even though such securities may be registered under the Securities Act, they may not be offered for sale to the public unless a formal agreement between the issuer of bonds and the bondholder, known as the trust indenture, conforms to the standards of this Act.

The Trust Indenture Act of 1939 is all about protecting bondholders. If a corporation wants to sell $5,000,000 or more worth of bonds that mature outside of one year, they must do it under a contract or indenture with a trustee, who will enforce the terms of the indenture to the benefit of the bondholders. In other words, if the issuer stiffs the bondholders, the trustee can get a bankruptcy court to sell off the assets of the company so that bondholders can recover some of their hard-earned money. Sometimes corporations secure the bonds with specific assets like airplanes, securities, or real estate. If so, they pledge title of the assets to the trustee, who just might end up selling them off if the issuer gets behind on its interest payments.

Investment Company Act of 1940

The SEC summarizes this federal securities law like so:

> This Act regulates the organization of companies, including mutual funds, that engage primarily in investing, reinvesting, and trading in securities, and whose own securities are offered to the investing public. The regulation is designed to minimize conflicts of interest that arise in these complex operations. The Act requires these companies to disclose their financial condition and investment policies to investors when stock is initially sold and, subsequently, on a regular basis. The focus of this Act is on disclosure to the investing public of information about the fund and its investment objectives, as well as on investment company structure and operations. It is important to remember that the Act does not permit the SEC to directly supervise the investment decisions or activities of these companies or judge the merits of their investments.

So, mutual funds must register their securities and provide a prospectus to all investors under the Securities Act of 1933. The Investment Company Act of 1940 requires the investment company itself to register and then lays out an exhaustive array of dos and don'ts for their operations. The Investment Company Act of 1940 classified investment companies as face amount certificate companies, unit investment trusts, or management companies. As we saw in an earlier chapter, the management companies are either open-end or closed-end funds. The distinguishing factor is that the open-end funds are redeemable, while the closed-end shares trade on the secondary market among investors. The unit investment trust has no investment adviser managing the portfolio and is sometimes linked with "having no board of directors." Note that the separate account for a variable annuity is registered under this Act, too, either as an open-end fund or as a UIT.

To fit the definition of "investment company," the shares must be able to easily be sold and the number of shareholders must exceed 100. Hedge funds go the other way to avoid fitting the definition of "investment company." That is, they don't let people sell their investment freely and they keep the number of investors under 100, because if you can escape the definition of "investment company," you can escape the hassle of registering the investments and providing lots of disclosure to the SEC and the public markets. As usual, under the Act of 1940 the average investor is protected more than the sophisticated investor. Mutual funds and variable annuities are for the average investor; therefore, they need to be registered and watched closely by the SEC. Hedge funds are for the sophisticated investor primarily, so maybe things don't need to be watched so closely with them.

Investment Advisers Act of 1940

The SEC is *way* into the Investment Advisers Act of 1940, so let's let them explain it in their own words:

> This law regulates investment advisers. With certain exceptions, this Act requires that firms or sole practitioners compensated for advising others about securities investments must register with the SEC and conform to regulations designed to protect investors. Since

> the Act was amended in 1996 and 2010, generally only advisers who have at least $100 million of assets under management or advise a registered investment company must register with the Commission.

If you want to give people your expert advice on their specific investment situation and receive compensation for doing so, you must register under the Investment Advisers Act of 1940 or under your state securities law. Portfolio managers, financial planners, pension fund consultants, and even many sports and entertainment agents end up having to register to give investment advice to their clients. All open- and closed-end funds are managed by registered investment advisers, and pension funds typically farm out their assets to many different investment advisory firms. Because the role they play is so important and so potentially dangerous, all investment advisers must be registered unless they can qualify for some type of exemption.

Federal covered advisers (federally registered advisers) are subject to the provisions of the Investment Advisers Act of 1940. That's why we saw that the Administrator of a state cannot impose a higher net capital requirement on investment advisers in the state than what is established by the SEC under the Investment Advisers Act of 1940. A federal covered investment adviser with offices in various states only complies with the recordkeeping requirements and the net capital requirements set by the SEC.

The SEC doesn't care whether an investment adviser is subject to registration or not. Either way, if the person fits the definition of "investment adviser," he is at least subject to the anti-fraud section of the Investment Advisers Act of 1940. If the investment adviser qualifies for an exemption, he may get to skip various filing requirements. And, certain rules would not apply to this person, but he would be subject to the anti-fraud provisions of the Act if he meets the definition of an investment adviser.

That also means that if the person is not an investment adviser, he is not subject to the Investment Advisers Act of 1940, period. I doubt the exam would go there, but this represents a major difference between federal and state securities law. The Uniform Securities Act doesn't look to see if someone is or is not an investment adviser per se. Rather, it looks at the activity, as we see from this passage: "It is unlawful for any person who receives, directly or indirectly, any consideration from another person for advising the other person as to the value of securities or their purchase or sale…" Again, that would seem like an unlikely test question, but one never knows. Either way, remember that an investment adviser with an exemption is excused from some or all registration requirements; however, anyone who is an investment adviser or is acting like one is subject to the anti-fraud sections of federal and state securities law.

The SEC can discipline federal covered investment advisers through administrative hearings to determine if a license is to be denied, suspended, or revoked. They can also represent the U.S. Government in federal court and ask a judge to issue an injunction against an investment adviser violating various sections of the "Advisers Act."

Regulation of RIAs and IARs

The first thing an investment adviser registering with the regulators sees on Form ADV is this:

Then, after that, the four different ways an adviser could use the same form:

- Submit an initial application to register as an investment adviser with the SEC
- Submit an initial application to register as an investment adviser with one or more states
- Submit an annual updating amendment to your registration for your fiscal year ended __
- Submit an other-than-annual amendment to your registration

Whether the adviser registers with the SEC or with one or more state regulators, Form ADV is filed electronically through a system called the **Investment Adviser Registration Depository** (IARD). Setting up an IARD account is the first step in the registration process. Once an adviser establishes an IARD account, the adviser can access Form ADV (Part 1) on IARD, complete this part of Form ADV, and submit it electronically to the SEC.

To register with the SEC, the adviser must check at least one box showing the SEC why they're eligible. For example, if the assets under management are at least $100 million, or if the adviser manages registered investment company portfolios, they are eligible for federal registration. Within 45 days, the SEC will either grant the registration or—in rare, unfortunate cases—start proceedings to determine if the registration should be denied.

So, one use of Form ADV Part 1 is to file an initial application with the SEC. Another use is to update the registration on an annual basis. Within 90 days after the end of each fiscal year, the adviser must file what the SEC calls an annual updating amendment to renew the registration. They must update their responses to all items on Form ADV Part 1 when they do this. And—as always—they pay a fee. You're dealing with the federal government; they like fees.

A third use of Form ADV Part 1 is the "other-than-annual updating amendment" mentioned on Page 1 of the form. That means if something major changes at the firm—they move to a different state, their business structure changes, or management changes hands—they must file a new Form ADV to inform the SEC of the change promptly (within 30 days of the change).

See the difference? They update ADV Part 1 every year with the annual updating amendment. And, if something major changes at the firm, they update promptly, whenever this change occurs. Since the latter is used for a purpose other than the purpose of updating annually, it is called an "other-than-annual updating amendment."

Form ADV contains two parts. Part 1 contains the following information:

- the name and form of organization under which the investment adviser engages or intends to engage in business; the name of the state or other sovereign power under which such investment adviser is organized; the location of his or its principal business office and branch offices, if any; the names and addresses of his or its partners, officers, directors, and persons performing similar functions or, if such an investment adviser be an individual, of such individual; and the number of his or its employees;
- the education, the business affiliations for the past ten years, and the present business affiliations of such investment adviser and of his or its partners, officers, directors, and persons performing similar functions and of any controlling person thereof;
- the nature of the business of such investment adviser, including the manner of giving advice and rendering analyses or reports;
- the nature and scope of the authority of such investment adviser with respect to clients' funds and accounts;
- the basis or bases upon which such investment adviser is compensated;
- whether such investment adviser, or any person associated with such investment adviser, is subject to any disqualification which would be a basis for denial, suspension, or revocation of registration of such investment adviser under the provisions of subsection (e) of this section; and
- a statement as to whether the principal business of such investment adviser consists or is to consist of acting as investment adviser and a statement as to whether a substantial part of the business of such investment adviser consists or is to consist of rendering investment supervisory services

The regulators want some basic information about the investment advisory firm. What's the address? Is this a business address or a makeshift office above a garage? Yes, an adviser could be a sole proprietor. He could also work from home in his pajamas. I would assume he would shower, shave, and dress for any regulatory inspections, but I'll leave that to him.

In any case, the regulators want to know if this advisory business is a sole proprietorship, a partnership, a corporation, an LLC, etc. If it's a corporation, where is it incorporated? Tell us about the partners, officers, and directors of the firm.

What is the education and business background of the owners and principals of the business? How many employees does the RIA have? What kind of services does it offer to clients? How many and what types of clients does it serve? How are they compensated? Do they have discretion over the accounts, or custody over client assets? Do they act as a principal in client transactions? Do they get compensated from broker-dealers that have custody of client accounts? Et cetera, et cetera.

Investment Adviser Representatives

The investment adviser is a business that registers with either the SEC or one or more state securities regulators.

Individuals hired by the adviser are **investment adviser representatives** if they engage in:

- managing portfolios
- making determinations

- rendering advice
- selling the firm's services
- supervising anyone engaging in the activities above

Employees who are not involved with such activities are typically called "ministerial employees" and are not considered to be IARs subject to registration. Anyone who matches up with the bullet list above is a **supervised person.** The SEC requires advisers registered with them to "adopt and implement written policies and procedures reasonably designed to prevent violation, by the adviser and its supervised persons, of the Act and the rules that the Commission has adopted under the Act."

Investment advisers registered with the SEC must review no less frequently than annually their policies and procedures for adequacy and update and revise them as needed. The RIA also must designate a supervised person as the chief compliance officer responsible for administering the firm's written policies and procedures.

Federal Covered Advisers

The following are eligible to register exclusively with the SEC:

- Adviser with at least $100 million of assets under management
- Adviser to a registered investment company
- Mid-sized adviser ($25–100 million assets under management) to a business development company
- Pension consultants providing advice to employee benefit plans with assets of at least $200 million
- Adviser that would be required to register in 15 or more states
- Internet investment advisers
- Affiliates of federally registered adviser if the principal office and place of business of the affiliate is the same as that of the SEC-registered adviser
- Newly formed advisers that reasonably believe that they will become eligible for federal registration within 120 days
- Adviser with their principal place of business in the US Virgin Islands
- Adviser with their principal place of business outside the United States

An adviser with over $110 million of assets under management must register with the SEC, as must an adviser managing investment company assets or a mid-sized adviser managing business development company assets. The others are eligible to register with the SEC. Why would they even want to register with the SEC? Well, if they were an internet adviser in Colorado with clients in Montana, California, Oregon, and Washington, they might get tired of dealing with five different regulators; therefore, it is easier to register with the SEC exclusively.

Notice Filings

On Form ADV Part 1 the SEC asks which states need to receive a copy of the form. See, even though the investment advisory firm is registering with the SEC, they typically need to make a **notice filing** with any state where they have a place of business. Since the federal covered adviser is filing notice with various states, the regulators call this process a notice filing. For the privilege of having the SEC file a duplicate of the form with various state regulators, the adviser pays a notice-filing fee.

So, even though the firm is federal covered, they would perform a notice filing in the state(s) where they maintain an office. And, they would be subject to the state's anti-fraud authority. It was NSMIA (National Securities Markets Improvement Act) that created this concept of "federal covered advisers," but NSMIA made it clear that the state regulators have the authority to require and collect a fee for a notice filing, and have the authority to legally pursue even a federal covered adviser if they're defrauding investors in the state.

Withdrawal from Federal Registration

If the adviser wants to withdraw their registration, they file a Form **ADV-W**. They don't just stop showing up at the office. Maybe the firm is switching from federal to state-level registration. If so, the investment adviser would file their annual updating amendment reporting that they are no longer registering with the SEC. They would then file an ADV-W within 180 days after the close of their fiscal year. During this period while they are registered with both the Commission and one or more state securities authorities, the Investment Advisers Act of 1940 and applicable state laws apply to their advisory activities.

Although this next scenario is not a withdrawal, it makes sense to talk about the opposite case here, where the adviser is moving up from state-level registration to federal (SEC) registration. Why? Maybe their assets under management have grown to over $100 million, or they now advise registered investment companies. In this case, the IA must apply for SEC registration within 90 days of filing an annual updating amendment to Form ADV that showed why they're suddenly eligible.

Even if a firm has withdrawn its registration with the SEC, they can end up getting in trouble. In fact, although the ADV-W is considered effective when it's filed, the registration continues for 60 days in case the SEC needs to take regulatory action against a firm that is suddenly in a big hurry to flee from their watchful eyes. Up to and during this 60-day period, the SEC can suspend a firm's registration. A suspension is a strike against the firm, and the SEC can suspend a firm for up to 12 months. Why would the SEC take such an action against an investment adviser? Perhaps the adviser:

- Willfully made or caused to be made any false or misleading report or application regarding a material fact, or omitted a material fact
- Has been convicted within the previous 10 years of any felony or any securities-related misdemeanor
- Is enjoined by court order
- Has willfully violated any provision of federal securities law
- Has willfully aided another person's violation of federal securities law or has failed to supervise a person who commits a violation
- Is subject to an order of the SEC barring or suspending the person from being associated with an investment adviser

Wrap-Fee Programs

One of the problems with a brokerage account is that the client often wonders if the agent is executing trades to make commissions. Some clients prefer to pay a portfolio manager whose compensation is tied to the value of the account, while also knowing there are no extra charges for large numbers of trades.

The solution for these clients is the wrap account. A wrap account is an advisory account where portfolio management services, custody, and brokerage transactions are wrapped together into one flat fee called a wrap fee. Investment advisers sponsor these programs by getting custodial broker-dealers on board to charge a flat fee for all trades entered by the adviser's portfolio managers. This way the client receives portfolio management and pays nothing extra even if frequent trades are executed on his behalf. This eliminates the concern for churning. But, it also involves a high, built-in fee for trading that is only appropriate for clients interested in active management of their account.

If the adviser sponsors a wrap-fee program, the adviser must deliver a written disclosure statement or wrap fee brochure of how these fees work, pointing out that the client may pay more this way than if the services were purchased separately. Generally, clients who are comfortable with frequent trading do better under wrap-fee programs, while those who are more buy-and-hold types would probably save money paying for each transaction if/when it occurs.

If one adviser refers the client to another adviser who will provide the client with a wrap fee brochure, the first adviser does not need to do so.

State Registration

In general, large advisers register with the SEC, while smaller firms register with the states. If the firm has not been excluded from the definition of investment adviser and not granted an exemption from state registration, they'll have to register in the states where they have a place of business. The investment adviser files an application with the state securities Administrator, the same Form ADV used for SEC registration. The state securities Administrator might also require the applicant to publish an announcement in one or more specified newspapers published in the state.

The initial application is accompanied by a consent to service of process, which you can see at www.nasaa.org under "uniform forms." This authorizes the Administrator to receive legal papers known as "service of process" on the applicant's behalf in any non-criminal legal complaint, meaning that I wouldn't have to chase down the suddenly hard-to-locate adviser; instead, I'd just serve process on the Administrator, which would have the same validity of serving them on the party who doesn't seem to be returning voice or emails.

The consent to service of process is filed with the initial application for advisers, adviser reps, broker-dealers, agents, and securities subject to state registration. The consent to service of process is filed only initially; it does not have to be filed with each renewal application. Fees must also be paid to the state when the applicant registers. A federal covered adviser, still subject to the state's anti-fraud authority, typically files a consent to service of process with the Administrator, as well.

As the Uniform Securities Act stipulates:

> With respect to investment advisers, the [Administrator] may require that certain information be furnished or disseminated as necessary or appropriate in the public interest or for the protection of investors and advisory clients. To the extent determined by the [Administrator] in his discretion, information furnished to clients or prospective clients of an investment

adviser that would be in compliance with the Investment Advisers
Act of 1940 and the rules thereunder may be used in whole or
partial satisfaction of this requirement.

NASAA has a model rule that declares the minimum net capital for an adviser based on certain activities:

- Adviser with custody: $35,000
- Adviser with discretion but not custody: $10,000
- Adviser accepting prepayment > $500 six + months in advance: positive net worth

Because maintaining custody leads to higher net capital requirements and the expense of getting the books independently audited, many advisers avoid maintaining custody and use a qualified custodian instead. If the adviser has custody or accepts prepayment as indicated above, the adviser must submit an audited balance sheet to both the Administrator and the client.

State regulators may not require an adviser properly registered in its home state and meeting that state's net capital requirements to maintain a higher requirement. Federal covered advisers who provide notice filings in the state are subject to the SEC net capital requirements. The states could not make the adviser comply with a higher requirement than what's covered under the Investment Advisers Act of 1940. Similarly, the Administrator can't require a higher net capital for broker-dealers than what is required under the Securities Exchange Act of 1934.

Record Keeping
Investment advisers must keep all kinds of books and records on their business, such as:

- Receipts and Disbursements Journals (money and/or securities)
- General Ledger
- Order Memoranda
- Bank Records (for the firm)
- Bills and Statements (for the firm)
- Financial Statements (for the firm)
- Originals of all written communications received and copies of all written communications sent by the investment adviser relating to (A) recommendations/advice, (B) any receipt, disbursement or delivery of funds or securities, or (C) the placing or execution of any securities transaction
- List of Discretionary Accounts
- Advertising
- Personal Transactions of Representatives and Principals
- Powers Granted by Clients
- Disclosure Statements
- Solicitors' Disclosure Statements
- Performance Claims
- Customer Information Forms and Suitability Information

- Written Supervisory Procedures

If the adviser has custody of client funds or securities, the firm must also keep:

- Journals of Securities Transactions and Movements
- Separate Client Ledgers
- Copies of Confirmations
- Record by Security Showing Each Client's Interest and Location Thereof

Notice above that the adviser needs two separate and related lists: one is a list of each client and which securities he holds in his account, another list is by each security, e.g., MSFT common stock, and how many shares each advisory client owns of that total. You can imagine how those cross-referenced lists could help spot any discrepancies.

If the adviser actively manages client assets, the firm must maintain:

- Client Purchases and Sales History
- Current Client Securities Positions

These records (the two above bullet points) are required to be maintained in an easily accessible place for a period of five years from the end of the fiscal year during which the last entry was made and, for the first two years, the records must be maintained in the adviser's principal office. Electronic records are okay, provided the firm can verify that the records are accurate and complete and could not have been easily altered.

Maybe a test question will want you to say that a "read-only" file would work, since it would not allow anyone to make alterations to the records. In other words, electronic records must give the regulators confidence that certain transactions have not been accidentally deleted or altered to conceal some sort of violations. Record-keeping is a big responsibility and that deficient records lead to fines and sanctions by the state regulators.

Each year NASAA publishes data on the results of state securities regulatory examinations of advisers, and each year the main problem is a lack of record keeping. If the adviser has discretion but doesn't keep sufficient records on the transactions made using that discretion, it's a problem. If the adviser puts out advertising touting their stock picks, but can't seem to back it up with trade confirmations and account statements, it's a problem. If the adviser seems to have five or six more investment adviser reps working at the firm than they've indicated on Form ADV, well, you get the idea.

Finally, if a firm is deemed to have custody of client funds and securities, what sort of questions would the state regulators be trying to answer? Luckily, NASAA saw fit to tell us. As NASAA states on their website (www.nasaa.org):

    If an adviser has direct or indirect access to client funds or
    securities, it is considered to have custody of client funds and

is subject to additional scrutiny. State regulators will want to see how you handle those assets by asking the following:

Has the adviser complied with the rules relating to safeguarding client assets in the adviser's custody?

Does the Form ADV reflect that the adviser has custody?

Are these assets maintained in segregated accounts?

Does the adviser maintain the required records of client assets in its custody?

Does the client get an itemized statement at least e three months showing the assets in the adviser's custody and the activity in the account?

Has a surprise audit of client assets been conducted at least annually by an independent accountant?

If the adviser has discretionary authority over the client's account, is there any evidence of excessive trading, self-dealing, preferential treatment, unsuitable recommendations, unauthorized transactions, or incomplete disclosure?

NSMIA

The **National Securities Markets Improvement Act of 1996** decided that certain advisers should be "federal covered." These firms register with the SEC only. So, if the adviser had an office in Albany, New York, they would not register with the State of New York if they were a federal covered adviser. They would, instead, register with the SEC. Either way, the firm would fill out Form ADV, but they would indicate on it that they were registering with the SEC, and provide a notice filing to the State of New York. But a **notice filing** is a filing of notice, not a registration.

Federal covered advisers are subject to the state's anti-fraud authority. But if they don't plan on defrauding investors, they can have an office in the state without registering with the state. The firm just needs to have the SEC send the state regulators a copy of Form ADV and all required schedules and pay a notice filing fee. This is done through the convenient **IARD** system. The state can also demand a consent to service of process.

What about the investment adviser representatives working for a federal covered adviser? As with any IAR, these individuals register with the states. The investment advisory firm registers with the SEC if they're federal covered, but the individuals register with the states where they maintain a place of business.

The officers, partners, and directors of the adviser are automatically registered as investment adviser representatives when the firm registers. Similarly, partners, officers, and directors of a broker-dealer who will act as agents are automatically registered as agents when the broker-dealer registers. These individuals provide disclosure when the firms register; therefore, there would be nothing additional to disclose by filing a Form U4 required of an agent or IAR.

As the SEC explains, "Until 1996, most investment advisers were subject to regulation by both the SEC and one or more state regulatory agencies. The Act was amended in 1996 and again in 2010 to allocate regulatory responsibility between the SEC and the states. Today, most small advisers and 'mid-sized advisers' are subject to state regulation of advisers and are prohibited from registering with the SEC. Most large advisers (unless an exemption is available) must register with the SEC, and state adviser laws are preempted for these advisers."

Until 2010 the threshold to register with the SEC as a federal covered adviser was surprisingly low—just $25 million of assets under management. With the passage of Dodd-Frank, that threshold was raised to $100 million of assets under management (AUM). At $100 million of assets under its continuous management an investment adviser may register with the SEC—at $110 million they must register with the SEC. And, if an adviser was SEC-registered the previous year, they may remain so as long as their assets under management have not fallen below $90 million.

What we're talking about here is registration with either the SEC or a state securities regulator. Financial planners do not really have assets under management, so they register with the state securities Administrators as do portfolio managers with, say, $50 million of assets under management. Large advisers with, say, $100 billion of assets under management register with the Securities and Exchange Commission under the Investment Advisers Act of 1940, as do advisers to registered investment companies.

However, Dodd-Frank didn't make things quite so simple. Rather, it left a few types of investment advisers as exempt from registration with the SEC yet subject to filing certain reports and information with the SEC, anyway. An **exempt reporting adviser** is either claiming an exemption from SEC registration because it is solely an adviser to one or more venture capital funds or because it is an adviser solely to private funds with less than $150 million of assets. In neither case is the adviser subject to full registration with the SEC; however, both types of exempt reporting advisers are required to file annual reports with the SEC and to provide much of the information required on Form ADV.

And, while exempt reporting advisers are exempt from SEC registration, some are subject to registration and/or reporting with one or more state securities regulators.

The instructions to Form ADV provide several requirements for exempt reporting advisers. First, if the adviser is already registered with the SEC or one or more state securities Administrators, they must file a Form ADV-W and wait until the withdrawal is accepted by the appropriate securities regulator. Then, within 60 days of relying on one of two exemptions from registration, the exempt reporting adviser must file its first report with the SEC.

If the exempt reporting adviser is not subject to registration with any state securities authority, it only has to fill out prescribed parts of Form ADV. However, if the adviser is subject to state registration, it must complete Form ADV Part 1 in its entirety. Part 2A and Part 2B of Form ADV have to do with an investment adviser's brochure and supplements, neither of which apply to exempt reporting advisers.

Some advisers start out as exempt reporting advisers, but then things change. For example, an adviser relying on the exemption based on venture capital funds might later wish to take on a client that is not a venture capital fund. If so, it must file its final report as an exempt reporting adviser and also register with the SEC in the same filing. Same thing for an adviser whose total assets under management for their private-fund clients now exceeds $150 million.

SEC Release IA-1092

Some readers would probably think that after the regulators went to the trouble of spelling out all those details, it's now clear who is and is not an investment adviser and who does and does not have to register. Unfortunately, that is not the case. In fact, it is so unclear that the SEC is frequently responding to letters from attorneys of various clients trying to figure out if it's okay to do what they're proposing to do without registering as an investment adviser. Such requests are called "requests for no-action relief." That means the attorney for the client is seeking verification from the SEC or the securities Administrator that his client is okay to do what he proposes to do without registration, and the regulators will take no action. Sometimes the regulator can grant "no-action relief," sometimes they can't.

What kind of facts would the regulators use to determine if someone is acting as an investment adviser? All relevant facts, but there are three "prongs" that we need to look at, which help the regulators determine if someone meets the definition of "investment adviser."

Why is it so hard to make such a determination? Some professionals provide investment advice in connection with other financial services, and maybe they don't think of the advice as being an important part of the business. For example, a financial planner who focuses almost exclusively on insurance products could be considered to provide investment advice if he told clients to sell their mutual funds to buy his fixed annuity. Many sports and entertainment agents are attorneys who negotiate contracts for star athletes and performers. They also end up telling clients how to invest their money. A sports agent might not issue a detailed report on stocks, but if tells his client to put 1/3 in real estate, 1/3 in insurance, and 1/3 in mutual funds, he is giving investment advice. Pension funds hire consultants to help select the investment advisers for the fund. Are those people investment advisers or not? Usually, they are.

Since it's not always clear if a professional meets the definition of "investment adviser," the SEC issued a release in 1987 that attempts to explain their thought process when determining if someone is or is not an investment adviser. This release made clear that the "three-pronged" test to determine if someone is an investment adviser involves the following:

- Does the professional provide investment advice?
- Is he/she in the business of providing advice?
- Do they receive compensation for this advice?

If the answer to all three questions is "yes," then the person is an investment adviser and must register unless they can claim an exemption. So, first, does the professional provide investment advice? Generally, if someone is helping someone decide whether to invest in securities or how to allocate a portfolio based on the client's needs, that person is providing investment advice. The advice in this case doesn't have to be on a specific security. If a financial planner or sports agent is helping clients pick investments in securities in general as an alternative to an investment in real estate or insurance-based products, then he is an investment adviser. In fact, if we rewrote that sentence in the other direction—the professional is helping clients pick insurance-based products or real estate as an alternative to investing in securities—same deal.

Pension consultants who help pension plans decide either which securities to invest in or whether to invest in securities over some other asset are advisers. The consultants who help the funds determine which investment advisers to hire or retain are as well.

What does it mean to "be in the business of providing advice"? The SEC and NASAA determined that a person is in the business of providing advice if he or she gives advice on a regular basis and that advice "constitutes a business activity conducted with some regularity." The frequency is a factor, but not the only factor in determining if the person is "in the business" or not. In other words, the regulators take it all on a case-by-case basis. What are the relevant factors in the case of this adviser who claims they don't have to register? Does it look like something that's part of a regular business or not?

Providing advice doesn't have to be the main activity of the person, either. The person could be a CPA doing tax work and only providing investment advice if a client asks for it. That's close enough for the regulators. If the person "holds himself out to the public" as one who provides investment advice—via business cards, billboards, letterhead, office signage, etc.—then he is in the business and is an adviser.

What about the compensation question, the third prong? Some folks would like to think they're not advisers because they don't receive money for their advice. But regulators wouldn't leave a loophole that big. They use the broader term "compensation" to determine who is and isn't an investment adviser. Compensation is any economic benefit, not necessarily money. Even if someone other than the client pays the compensation, the person is an investment adviser. For example, if a firm advises Coca-Cola's employees on how to allocate their 401(k) investment dollars, and bills the company, they meet the definition of an investment adviser.

Some securities agents with a Series 6 or 7 function as financial planners, even if they don't call themselves that. Many of these planners figure they can put together a financial plan for free and only get paid off any resulting commissions to avoid being defined as investment advisers. Unfortunately, Release IA-1092 says they would likely be considered investment advisers because they receive an economic benefit as a result of their advice. The compensation might come directly or indirectly as the result of providing investment advice to clients. However it comes, the regulators will probably require such people to get registered.

Notice it's not about the language one uses. It doesn't matter whether the compensation is called a "commission" or a "fee." The compensation doesn't have to be listed as a separate item. The regulators, as always, look at how things function. If it were based on terminology, the folks who wanted to escape registration could just use different terms.

Soft Dollar Compensation

Compensation can come in the form of "soft dollars," such as receiving services from broker-dealers when advisers direct clients to have them maintain custody of assets. Benefits such as research reports, custodial and clearing services, and special software aiding in research are considered soft-dollar compensation, so if the adviser receives anything like that from a broker-dealer because of the advisory clients, the adviser must disclose this relationship to clients.

Most soft-dollar compensation is allowable, though it must be disclosed to clients. On the other hand, the regulators won't let investment advisers receive the following soft-dollar compensation arrangements at all, even with disclosure: furniture and office equipment, salaries or overhead, vacations, cell phones, etc. In other words, the only form of soft-dollar compensation that is allowed is a service that helps the clients of the adviser. Paying the advisory firm's overhead or sending them on lavish vacations, on the other hand, cannot be said to benefit clients.

Allowable:

- Research reports
- Custodial and clearing (trade processing) services
- Special software aiding in research

Non-allowable:

- Furniture and office equipment
- Salaries or overhead
- Vacations
- Cell phones

Regulation of Broker-Dealers and Agents

Broker-dealers and their agents, as well as investment advisers and their representatives, generally must be registered with the Administrator. These professionals can be firms or individuals. Either way they are persons. A person may include an individual, but the definition of "person" is not limited to that. Microsoft is a legal person. A Unit Investment Trust is a legal person. The estate of a dead person is a person, even if the dead person is not.

Since the definition of "person" includes corporations, partnerships, etc., when the regulators want to refer to an individual, they usually call him a natural person. When they use the word "person" or "any person," they're referring to any individual, partnership, corporation, etc. These are all "legal persons."

A person is not:

- Dead
- Declared mentally incompetent
- A minor child

So, if they're not dead, declared mentally incompetent, or a child, they're a person who can manage their own affairs, sign binding contracts, etc. A broker-dealer or investment adviser could be organized as either a sole proprietorship or a corporation. A sole proprietorship is considered a natural person, while the C-Corporation is a legal person.

The Uniform Securities Act defines a broker-dealer like this:

> *A broker-dealer is any person engaged in the business of effecting transactions in securities for the account of others or for its own account.*

So, the investment would have to be a security as defined by law, not a fixed annuity or a whole life insurance policy. But if any person is effecting transactions for the accounts of others in securities, they fit the definition of "broker-dealer." And, if the state discovers they're doing it without a license, they typically have a problem with that.

As the Uniform Securities Act says, "It is unlawful for any person to transact business in this state as a broker-dealer or agent unless he is registered under this act." The next sentence of the Uniform Securities Act says, "It is unlawful for any broker-dealer or issuer to employ an agent unless the agent is registered. The registration of an agent is not effective during any period when he is not associated with a broker-dealer registered under this act or a particular issuer. When an agent begins or terminates a connection with a broker-dealer or issuer, the agent as well as the broker-dealer or issuer shall promptly notify the [Administrator]."

A test question could ask what needs to happen when an agent terminates employment with one broker-dealer and signs up with another broker-dealer. Answer: both broker-dealers and the agent must notify the Administrator promptly. In practical terms, that means that the one firm completes the U5 to terminate the agent's employment, and the other firm completes the U4 to hire the agent. The agent is also filling out the information, so "both broker-dealers and the agent" are informing the Administrator.

Registration Procedure

The Uniform Securities Act grants the Administrator the power to make rules concerning what is required of broker-dealers, agents, investment advisers, and investment adviser representatives for purposes of registration. The application used must contain information such as:

- Applicant's form and place of organization
- Applicant's proposed method of doing business
- Qualifications and business history of the applicant
- For broker-dealers and investment advisers—qualifications and business history of any partner, officer, or director
- Any injunction or administrative order or conviction of a misdemeanor involving a security or any aspect of the securities business, and any conviction of a felony
- Applicant's financial condition and history

Before they start doing business in the securities industry within a state, they need to apply for a license, on which they tell the state about their background and how they propose to do business. Is the broker-dealer a partnership or a corporation? If a corporation, where is it incorporated and can we please see a copy of the articles of incorporation and the bylaws? Does a court or another state Administrator have a problem with them? Are they financially sound, or teetering on the verge of bankruptcy?

That sort of thing.

After they register, assuming the state sees no problem with the information provided, the license will be granted no later than noon of the 30th day after filing. When filing the initial application, the applicant must sign and attach a form called a consent to service of process. This document gives the Administrator the authority to receive "service of process" in any non-criminal suit against the applicant. In other words, should another state need to serve papers on an investment adviser, they don't have to chase them around and around. Instead, they can just serve the papers on the Administrator, which is the same thing as serving them on the person who has already signed his consent to let the Administrator receive the process on his behalf.

You wouldn't let a carpet cleaning company into your house unless they were bonded and insured. Although unlikely, their equipment or chemicals could destroy $10,000 worth of carpeting or send a child to the emergency room. Are they able to cover that damage?

Similarly, a firm with custody over client assets or an agent with discretion over an account could cause damages. Therefore, there usually needs to be a **surety bond** in place to cover potential losses to client accounts. Broker-dealers, investment advisers, and IARs and agents with discretion may be required to maintain surety bonds in amounts up to $10,000.

A test question may point out that this surety bond can be obtained by a cash deposit or a deposit of securities. While the Administrator can rule which type of securities can be used as a deposit, he cannot rule that the deposit has to be cash. And, if an individual or a firm has or ends up with a criminal conviction, he/they may find that no insurance company will issue a bond to back them up in the future. In which case, it's usually time for a new career.

Record Keeping Requirements

The Uniform Securities Act's "Post-Registration Provisions" state that:

> *Every registered broker-dealer and investment adviser shall make and keep such accounts, correspondence, memoranda, papers, books, and other records as the Administrator by rule prescribes.*

The Administrator generally requires that a broker-dealer keep the books and records required by the SEC under the Securities Exchange Act of 1934, with those requirements enforced by FINRA.

As it states in the Uniform Securities Act:

> *All the records referred to are subject at any time or from time to time to such reasonable periodic, special, or other examinations by representatives of the Administrator, within or without the state, as the Administrator deems necessary or appropriate in the public interest or for the protection of investors.*

The word "books" conjures an image of paper, but the "books and records" required by broker-dealers and investment advisers are typically kept electronically these days. Of course, that immediately brings up concerns about the ability to alter the records, lose them, or give access to them to people who shouldn't have it. NASAA published a model rule on recordkeeping requirements, which made the following points:

In the case of records created or maintained on electronic storage media, the investment adviser must establish and maintain procedures:

(A) To maintain and preserve the records, so as to reasonably safeguard them from loss, alteration, or destruction;

(B) To limit access to the records to properly authorized personnel and the [Administrator] (including its examiners and other representatives); and

(C) To reasonably ensure that any reproduction of a non-electronic original record on electronic storage media is complete, true, and legible when retrieved.

Net Capital Requirements

The Administrator may require a minimum net capital for a broker-dealer or investment adviser applying for or renewing their license. That means that, depending on their activities, the Administrator can rule that the firm's balance sheet must show a net worth of at least this amount. Remember here that agents/IARs don't have minimum net capital requirements, but broker-dealers and investment advisers must file financial reports as required by the Administrator to show that they're meeting the net capital requirements. "If the information contained in any document filed with the Administrator becomes inaccurate or incomplete in any material respect, the registrant shall promptly file a correcting amendment," says the Uniform Securities Act.

Seems reasonable enough. If the firm's net capital drops from, say, $5 million to $5,000, the Administrator needs to know about that. Broker-dealer net capital requirements are based on the types of activities the firm is involved with—the riskier the activities, the greater the minimum net capital requirement. The Administrator requires that broker-dealers meet a certain minimum financial requirement, but, really, it's the Securities and Exchange Commission that establishes broker-dealer net capital requirements.

Renewals and Other Registration Specifics

Not only must persons in the securities industry file an initial registration, but also they must renew their license each year. When do registrations of persons expire? On December 31st, unless properly renewed. How does one renew a license? Same way we renew our vehicle registrations—by paying the required fee. States send out a notice to renew a registration or license some time in advance of the end of the year, although that is not codified in the Uniform Securities Act. It surely does reduce the number of registrations that would otherwise lapse due to procrastination, though.

So, broker-dealers, agents, investment advisers, and investment adviser representatives need to apply for a license, need to renew that license every year, and need to keep whatever records the Administrator requires. The Administrator has the power to inspect the required records whenever it's necessary or appropriate in the public interest or for the protection of investors.

The exam may point out something from the Uniform Securities Act, which states:

> *When the Administrator finds that an applicant for initial or renewal registration as a broker-dealer is not qualified as an investment adviser, he may by order condition the applicant's registration as a broker-dealer upon his not transacting business in this state as an investment adviser.*

That means if a broker-dealer also wants to be an investment adviser, the state may say, "No. You can be a broker-dealer as long as you don't try to stretch and hurt yourself acting as an investment adviser, which you, apparently, have no business trying to do." In other words, they don't lose their broker-dealer license just because they also wanted to transact business as an adviser. They have to promise not to act as an adviser if they want to keep their broker-dealer license.

The Uniform Securities Act also stipulates that when the Administrator is determining the qualifications of broker-dealers and investment advisers, they can base their decision only on the firm and the agents themselves…not on the receptionist or the file clerk, for example. Or on the limited partners who invested in the firm and have nothing to do with its day-to-day operations. Note that I wrote "qualifications" of such LPs. If any of the owners has a criminal or regulatory history, that could cause the firm to have its licensed denied or revoked.

If you get a question about the registration of a successor firm, remember this passage from the Uniform Securities Act, "A registered broker-dealer or investment adviser may file an application for registration of a successor, whether or not the successor is then in existence, for the unexpired portion of the year. There shall be no filing fee."

In other words, if Able-Brooks Broker Dealers, LLC, is going to become Able-Brooks, Inc., in early spring, they can register the new entity, which can use the rest of the year's registration without paying a fee.

Exclusions and Exemptions for Persons

The other day I was visiting several state securities department websites and found an enforcement action taken by a large Midwestern state. Seems there was a successful insurance agent writing whole life insurance and indexed annuity business. He was a guy in his mid-50s who saw no reason to be securities licensed. He was only selling insurance products, after all.

The respondent in the enforcement action held dozens of free hot lunch seminars primarily for retired investors. He got all his marketing materials from an organization based in Portland, Oregon, which was lucky since he would not have been willing or able to create even one PowerPoint slide, let alone an entire presentation, himself. The marketing organization also issued a certificate attesting to his ethics and clean background, which looked like a good deal for just $150 plus an annual $50 renewal.

So, the respondent would pull in 20 or 30 affluent retirees, feed them a nice catered lunch, and then dim the lights for his PowerPoint presentation. As the state securities Administrator pointed out, some of the titles of the slides included:

- Why your $ isn't safe in the bank!
- FDIC's credit rating is D–
- Earn up to 25%, guaranteed!
- Heads you win—tails you win!

Clearly the message worked its magic by scaring several dozen investors into liquidating their savings accounts and fixed-income mutual funds to buy the indexed annuity product this gentleman was pitching. All told, he pulled in something like $14 million in annuity investments that year pocketing something like $725,000 in commissions.

Here were some of the problems that the state securities Administrator had:

- The respondent held himself out as an objective, impartial investment adviser when, in fact, he was an annuity salesman.
- The respondent held himself out as an investment adviser without being registered as such or shown to be exempt from registration.
- The respondent failed to disclose the 10-year surrender period on the annuity product that contradicted his many assurances to investors that the product provided "excellent liquidity."
- Several investors have faced financial emergencies leading to losses of up to 10% of their invested principal despite assurances from the respondent that this was a "can't-lose investment opportunity."
- The respondent's sales materials were deceptive and misleading.
- The respondent presented credentials issued by an organization with no objective criteria for certification other than payment of a fee.
- The respondent used high-pressure and misleading sales practices to intimidate and convince senior investors to sell securities to purchase his annuity product.

The state securities Administrator was stating this in the notice of hearing, where they have to explain what the respondent did and which sections of state law or securities rules he violated. The hearing would be held at the Administrator's office to determine if the state should issue an order preventing the respondent from ever applying for any type of securities license or offering/selling securities in the state. Also, they were considering filing a petition with the courts to order that restitution be paid to any investor who wanted his/her money back.

So did the annuity salesman end up, like, in jail?

Easy now. This is merely a state securities Administrator here. And, the respondent did not cash the investors' checks and buy himself crazy-expensive luxury toys. He just used some deceptive methods to move their money from perfectly safe bank accounts and fixed-income mutual funds into fixed annuities with steep surrender charges that were not disclosed.

But, the situation is not cut and dried, either. Securities regulators are lawyers, but the respondent's lawyers are going to attack and twist every definition involved with the case. The Uniform Securities Act's anti-fraud statute says it's unlawful for any person "connected with the offer, sale, or purchase of any security" to mislead or deceive the investor. But, we contend that our client did not, in fact, make an offer or sale of any security; therefore, no fraud occurred.

Maybe the state counters that the respondent in effect was connected to the sale of various bond and money market mutual funds—which are securities—required to free up money for investors to purchase his annuity products. But, his attorneys counter that he never advised them on any aspect of the sale, so it's not his problem where investors get the money to buy his insurance product.

On another note, the state is contending that the respondent acted as an investment adviser. They say he was deceptively holding himself out as an objective investment adviser, which is fraudulent, and that he was unregistered and not exempt from registration. Then again, the respondent's attorneys argue that since the product he offered and sold is not a security, he is not an "investment adviser."

Up to now we've been talking about the different "persons" in the securities industry: broker-dealers, agents, investment advisers, and investment adviser representatives. Now we need to drill down deeper into these definitions, focusing on the people who either do not meet the definition of broker-dealer, agent, investment adviser, or investment adviser representative or are excused from having to register as such.

As we've seen, a "broker-dealer" is defined by the Uniform Securities Act as "any person engaged in the business of effecting transactions in securities for the account of others or for his own account."

Not a Broker-Dealer

The Uniform Securities Act then states that a:

"Broker-dealer" does not include:

- agent
- issuer
- bank, savings institution, or trust company

That means that agents, issuers, banks, savings institutions, and trust companies do not meet the definition of "broker-dealer." They are excluded from the definition. So, if the question is looking for "broker-dealers," skip over any answer choice that's talking about agents, issuers, banks, savings institutions, or trust companies.

Why?

They're not broker-dealers.

Okay, but why are the regulators pointing this out? I mean, who thought that a bank or savings institution might be a broker-dealer in the first place? Turns out banks, broker-dealers, and investment advisers are all in the financial services industry. Many large firms have divisions that cover all the bases. The securities laws are trying to keep all those divisions separate.

When your grandmother used to go to the bank as a young woman, she would have never seen any signs about IRAs or mutual fund investing. But these days we see information on investing in securities while waiting for a teller or an open ATM. That's because the bank and the broker-dealer are related entities. They probably have the same parent company. But the securities regulators are pointing out that if a bank wants to get into the broker-dealer business, they need to establish a separate entity and register it as a broker-dealer.

Later we'll see that these full-service financial firms probably also have a registered investment adviser. In that case, there would probably be a public company in which we could own stock and underneath that public company we'd find a bank, a broker-dealer, and an investment adviser. It's like three children of the same parent—they're related but separate entities. For example, there is a public company that trades under the stock symbol WFC. That's "Wells Fargo" for short. Under that **bank holding company** we would also find a bank, a broker-dealer, and an investment adviser with similar but slightly different names.

Exemptions

The persons above are not broker-dealers. Now let's talk about broker-dealers who are excused from registration requirements. If the broker-dealer has no place of business in the state, they can engage in securities transactions with the following investors in the state without having to register:

- issuers of the securities involved in the transactions
- other broker-dealers
- banks, savings institutions, trust companies, insurance companies
- investment companies as defined in the Investment Company Act of 1940
- pension or profit-sharing trusts
- other financial institutions or institutional buyers

On the other hand, if the broker-dealer has any non-institutional customers residing in the state, they must register there.

Also, a broker-dealer is not required to register in a state if they're dealing with an existing customer who just happens to be visiting the other state temporarily. They can't solicit for new clients in that other state, but the broker-dealer and the agent can do securities business with an existing customer temporarily in another state. That means that if the existing customer stays so long he becomes a resident of that other state, then the broker-dealer and agent would have to register in that state. But, calling a customer who happens to be on vacation does not require the broker-dealer or agent to be licensed in that other state.

Not an Agent

The Uniform Securities Act defines an "agent" as "any individual other than a broker-dealer who represents a broker-dealer or issuer in effecting or attempting to effect purchases or sales of securities." The Uniform Securities Act also points out that if the individual represents the issuer of the securities involved, he would not be an agent if:

- the security is exempt (for specific exempt securities only!)
- the transaction is exempt

If he represents the U.S. Treasury selling T-Bonds, he is not an agent. Or, if he represents the issuer of commercial paper in a direct sale to a pension fund, he is not an agent.

The Uniform Securities Act also says that an individual can effect transactions with the issuer's employees, partners, or directors if no commission or other remuneration is paid. Maybe the individual works in the human resources department and helps employees buy their employer's stock for the 401(k) plan. Provided he receives no commission for the transactions, he is not an agent. But, clearly, if the company offered him, say, $50 for every sale of stock, he might start pressuring the employees to buy stock, and that is a different situation.

But the fact that the individual is representing the issuer of the securities is not the be-all and end-all. There are only five specific types of exempt securities that afford an exemption for the individual, and if the transaction does not qualify for an exemption, that individual is an agent of the issuer and must register.

The Uniform Securities Act says, "A partner, officer, or director of a broker-dealer or issuer, or a person occupying a similar status or performing similar functions, is an agent only if he otherwise comes within this definition."

In other words, if he's not functioning as an agent, he's not an agent. If the individual is on the board of directors for a broker-dealer, is he automatically an agent? No. Not unless he wants to start offering and selling securities. If he just wants to sit on the board, he's a board member. If he wants to act like an agent, he's an agent. And, if this person will act as an agent, his registration is effective when the firm's registration is effective. There is no need to register him or her as an agent separately.

Notice how the whole idea of avoiding the requirement to register as an agent is predicated on the fact that the individual represents the issuer of the securities. And, the issuer must be issuing exempt securities or issuing securities through an exempt transaction. That means that my company could hire an individual to sell our stock only to certain broker-dealers and banks within the state. Not only is that transaction exempt, but also the individual would not have to be registered as our agent.

What if the individual represents a broker-dealer? Then, he must register if:

- he and/or the broker-dealer have a place of business in the state
- the investors are individuals (not institutions)

An agent who sells municipal securities for a broker-dealer has to get either a Series 52 or a Series 7, even though he is offering and selling exempt securities. The municipal bonds don't have to be registered. The agent offering and selling them on behalf of a broker-dealer does.

Just like for the broker-dealer he represents, if the agent has no place of business in the state, and the customers are all institutional investors, he does not have to register in that state. Also, the agent can do business with an existing customer who is not a resident of the state without having to register. If you're an agent in Nebraska, one of your existing customers might go on vacation to Florida. If so, you can contact your customer without having to register in Florida. Same way you could drive your rental car in Florida without having to get licensed.

Of course, if your customer becomes a Florida resident, that's completely different.

Investment Adviser Exclusions

Here is the definition of "Investment Adviser" under the Uniform Securities Act:

> "Investment adviser" means any person who, for compensation, engages in the business of advising others, either directly or through publications or writings, as to the value of securities or as to the advisability of investing in, purchasing, or selling securities, or who, for compensation and as a part of a regular business, issues or promulgates analyses or reports concerning securities. "Investment adviser" also includes financial planners and other persons who, as an integral component of other financially related services, provide the foregoing investment advisory services to others for compensation and as part of a business or who hold themselves out as providing the foregoing investment advisory services to others for compensation.

The following are excluded from the definition of "investment adviser" by the Uniform Securities Act:

> "Investment adviser" does not include (1) an investment adviser representative; (2) a bank, savings institution, or trust company; (3) a lawyer, accountant, engineer, or teacher whose performance of these services is solely incidental to the practice of his profession; (4) a broker-dealer or its agent whose performance of these services is solely incidental to the conduct of its business as a broker-dealer and who receives no special compensation for them; (5) a publisher of any bona fide newspaper, news column, newsletter, news magazine, or business or financial publication or service, whether communicated in hard copy form, or by electronic means, or otherwise, that does not consist of the rendering of advice on the basis of the specific investment situation of each client; (6) any person that is a federal covered adviser; or (7) such other persons not within the intent of this subsection as the [Administrator] may by rule or order designate.

First, an investment adviser is not an investment adviser representative and vice versa. One is the firm, the other represents the firm. We saw the same relationship between the broker-dealer firm and the agent who represents it.

As with the definition of broker-dealer, the following entities are also excluded from the definition of investment adviser: banks, savings institutions, and trust companies. They may be related to the investment adviser, with the same parent company and everything, but the investment adviser is not the bank or the savings & loan and vice versa. If a bank or other savings institution wants to get into the managed funds business, they set up a separate entity and register that entity as an investment adviser, just as they must do if they want to set up a broker-dealership.

Since I own a few shares of Wells Fargo common stock, I decided to look up the Form ADV information on their investment adviser. As their registration information indicates, Wells Capital Management is the investment advisory subsidiary of Wells Fargo Bank. The bank is not an adviser. The adviser is not a bank. Related, sure. But separate entities.

Lawyers, accountants, teachers, and engineers could all end up talking about securities or the value of securities, or having conversations with investment implications. Lawyers could be doing estate planning and trying to determine the value of an oil & gas partnership that nobody knew anything about. An accountant could be "advising" someone to make a maximum 401(k) contribution. A teacher could be teaching about the value of IBM stock. And an engineer or geologist could be rendering his opinion that there is, in fact, oil or natural gas under a particular field with that opinion attached to a securities offering document. In none of those cases is the professional acting as an investment adviser.

For example, making a maximum 401(k) contribution could help a client's tax situation. As long as the accountant isn't helping the client select the investments, she's just acting as an accountant. So, if their advice is "solely incidental" to their profession, they escape the definition of "investment adviser." Be careful how you read the test question, though. If the lawyer or accountant is providing investment advice, then they are acting as investment advisers. It's just that their professions might require them to deal with securities' values to some extent. If it's within the scope of their profession, they're not acting as investment advisers. On the other hand, if the accountant in my example suggests the company offer index ETFs as investment vehicles, she has probably crossed the line.

Broker-dealers and their agents do advise clients on how to invest. But, as the above language states, if they don't get compensated for the advice itself, and only get paid by commissions or markups/markdowns on the sale of securities, then they are just acting as broker-dealers and/or agents. Now, that doesn't mean that because someone is an agent he is automatically not an investment adviser. If a securities agent starts providing financial planning services on the side, he is an investment adviser who needs to register and let the broker-dealer know what he's up to.

The Wall Street Journal and Forbes pass out general investment advice in exchange for the subscription or newsstand price. That doesn't make them an investment adviser. They would have to be rendering advice based on a specific situation and getting compensation for it before anyone would accuse them of being an investment adviser.

This point of distinction could lead to confusion, unfortunately. A publication of general and regular circulation does not meet the definition, but what if the circulation is irregular, based on market movements or market signals? In that case, the regulators usually consider the newsletter writer to fit the definition of "investment adviser." There is a big difference between, on the one hand, writing general articles on investing and, on the other, charging people to tell them when to buy and sell stock through email or text messaging, or even targeted mailings based on market conditions.

The definition of investment adviser includes this phrase, "any person who, for compensation, engages in the business of advising others, either directly or through publications or writings, as to the value of securities or as to the advisability of investing in, purchasing, or selling securities." That means if you have, say, 30 clients and rather than meet with them face-to-face you, instead, send them written recommendations, you are acting as their investment adviser. When the advice is specific to the client's needs, you're an adviser.

If you're writing a newsletter, newspaper, magazine, etc., that goes to a general audience on a regular publication schedule, you're not an adviser. Notice it's not the terminology we use that makes us an adviser or not. It's not whether you call the publication a "newsletter" that determines if you're an investment adviser. It's the function of that "newsletter" or "financial publication" or of your written recommendations that determines things. Are you publishing information on small-cap stocks in general to a general audience who receives the publication regularly? Or, are you dressing something up as a "newsletter" when, in fact, you're just charging people to tell them which securities to buy and sell and when to buy and sell them?

You don't have to meet with someone to "advise" them, remember. If your sophisticated website takes the financial data that visitors enter and delivers a personalized investment recommendation, you are an investment adviser if you get any sort of compensation as a result of this website. But, again, if you're just writing articles about investing, chances are you do not meet the definition of an investment adviser.

A federal covered adviser is defined as an adviser under the federal Investment Advisers Act of 1940 and, therefore, not defined under the state securities law as an investment adviser. Finally, the Administrator also has the authority to name other individuals and entities that he considers outside the scope of regulation as an "investment adviser."

Investment Adviser and IAR Exemptions

The persons above are excluded from the definition of "investment adviser." Whatever an investment adviser can or can't do does not apply to them. They are no investment advisers.

If they are granted an "exemption," on the other hand, that means they are an adviser, but are excused from having to go through the process of registration. In other words, a bank is not an investment adviser. On the other hand, an investment adviser registered in Wisconsin may be exempted from registration requirements in other states where they do not maintain a place of business.

The following persons might be investment advisers, but they don't have to register in the state:

- person who has *no place of business in this state* if his only clients in this state are other investment advisers, broker-dealers, banks, savings institutions, trust companies, insurance companies, investment companies as defined in the Investment Company Act of 1940, pension or profit-sharing trusts, or other financial institutions or institutional buyers

- person who has *no place of business in this state* if during any period of twelve consecutive months he does not direct business communications into this state to more than 5 clients other than those specified above

Notice how I put the phrase "no place of business in this state" in italics. If the firm has a place of business in the state, the firm will always have to register in the state unless it happens to be a federal covered adviser.

The same is true for IARs of state-registered advisers. If they have a place of business in a state, they must register there. If they have more than 5 non-institutional clients in a state, they must register there. But, as with their firm, the IAR is exempt from registration if he has no place of business in a state and his only clients are certain institutions and/or no > 5 non-institutional clients.

Use of Solicitors

If I formed an RIA, I would probably hire some licensed individuals as my investment adviser representatives. I'd send the state a U4 form with their information, pay a fee, and then tell my new sales force to bring in clients with lots of assets to manage.

Or, I could use the services of individuals or firms in an independent-contractor relationship. Since the individual or firm solicits new business, the regulators call such persons **solicitors**. To use a solicitor the adviser must be registered; there can be no outstanding order suspending, limiting, or barring the solicitor's activities; and there must be a written agreement between the solicitor and the adviser. Also, the following conditions must be met:

- The agreement between the adviser and the solicitor must describe the solicitation activities and the compensation arrangement.
- The solicitor must provide the client with the adviser's disclosure brochure and a separate solicitor disclosure document.
- The adviser must receive a signed acknowledgment from the client that he/she received both the
- RIA's and the solicitor's disclosure documents

The adviser needs a signed acknowledgment from the client that both disclosure brochures were received. Also, you can bet that if the solicitor were some shady character, the adviser would not be able to stand back shrugging off responsibility to the regulators.

The adviser is expected to do due diligence on the solicitors they use, and if an adviser knew the individual was a convicted felon and hired him anyway, the adviser would face regulatory action.

Is the solicitor required to be registered? Not by the SEC, and not by all the state securities Administrators. The important point is that the adviser must be registered, must oversee the solicitor, and the solicitor cannot be someone ineligible for registration because of criminal or regulatory events. Most states call a "solicitor" an "investment adviser representative" and make him register as such. But not all states feel that way.

Disclosures

Investment advisers and their IARs are required to provide many types of disclosures to prospects and clients.

ADV Part 2

Before prospects sign the agreement with the advisory firm they must receive the investment adviser's **disclosure brochure.** The brochure is typically a PDF copy that prospects and clients can download. If it is not a copy of the Form ADV Part 2 submitted to the regulators, the brochure must contain the same information as what was uploaded when the firm registered, and re-uploaded each year to reflect any material changes.

The test might ask when the brochure must be delivered to a prospect. The answer for a state-registered adviser is within 48 hours (before) of signing the contract, or at the time of signing the contract if the client has five days to cancel without penalty. A federal covered adviser—operating under SEC rules—can deliver the brochure before or at the time the client signs the advisory agreement.

If an investment adviser provides substantially different types of advisory services to different clients, any information required in the disclosure brochure may be omitted for a client if that information does not apply. For example, only wrap-fee clients would receive the wrap fee supplement to ADV Part 2.

Information in the disclosure brochure informs prospects and clients of the essential information on their investment adviser, such as:

- Types of securities about which advice is rendered and the types of analyses used to make such recommendations
- Services provided, fees charged
- Education and business background of all officers of the firm and any employee that determines advice
- Any compensation incentives to the adviser for placing trades through broker-dealers/affiliations with other securities professionals
- A balance sheet if the adviser has custody or requires prepayment of fees of >$500 six or more months in advance
- Criminal and regulatory disclosure (if any is required) over previous 10 years

Not all Registered Investment Advisers have to deliver this brochure. If the client is an investment company or a business development company defined under the Investment Company Act of 1940, the adviser is not required to deliver a brochure. For example, an investment adviser such as Janus Capital Management has a contract with the board of directors of the Janus Funds. The adviser does not send a disclosure brochure to each shareholder who buys into the mutual funds. Rather, those investors receive a prospectus or other disclosure document before buying into the fund, under the Securities Act of 1933, and can read the semi-annual and annual reports required under the Investment Company Act of 1940.

Also, if the advice is considered "impersonal," meaning it isn't tailored to specific client situations and costs less than $500 per year, the adviser is not required to deliver a brochure. The opposite of "impersonal" advice is "supervisory services," where the adviser purports to tailor advice to each client, rather than directing advice to a whole group of clients—retirees, teachers, day traders, small-cap value investors.

I'm not saying if someone charges less than $500 per year and doesn't meet regularly with investors he escapes the definition of "investment adviser." The amount of money does not determine whether someone is or is not an investment adviser. The activities performed by the professional determine this under the three-pronged approach used by the SEC. For example, I subscribe to a newsletter on value stocks in which regular recommendations are made to buy, hold, and sell particular stocks. Why do I read and pay for this monthly newsletter? Because it is written by people who know what they're doing, actual investment advisers. Do they have to deliver their ADV Part 2 to me and the thousands of other subscribers?

No, they never purport to have looked at our situations and tailored their recommendations based on their analysis. The advice is impersonal because of that and because the annual subscription is well south of $500. Are they investment advisers? Yes—they have managed other people's money for years as RIAs or IARs. If not, why would I read, let alone pay for, their advice?

On the other hand, when the SEC is using the three-pronged approach to determine if a newsletter writer is an investment adviser, they ask if he is providing advice based on the individual situations of the readers. If not, it doesn't matter what he charges; he is not an investment adviser, if that is all he does.

Now, before anyone shouts, "No fair—why doesn't he have to register?!" ask who would read, let alone pay for, some guy's advice if he has never been and is not currently an investment adviser? If some creative writer wants to publish a blog and entertain his readers while discussing securities investing, he is exercising his First Amendment rights under the U.S. Constitution. Provided he doesn't engage in fraud by, perhaps, taking money from OTC equity securities issuers to pump up their stock price, he's good to go.

Though, again, how he gets people to pay for investment advice without having any "street cred," I have no idea.

In the past Form ADV 2 was presented in a check-box format that many investors found hard to read. Now the SEC requires advisers to use a narrative, "Plain English" style when creating the disclosure brochure. As the SEC explains, advisers must:

- Use Plain English.
- Use a narrative form as opposed to the former check-box approach.
- Add a table of contents with the disclosure items listed in the same order as the items in the form.
- Provide a supplement (ADV Part 2B) about advisory personnel on whom clients rely for investment advice.

- Provide a copy of the current (updated) brochure annually to existing clients that includes or is accompanied by the summary of material changes; or provide existing clients a summary of material changes that includes an offer to provide a copy of the current brochure.
- Attach a cover page to the adviser's brochure (ADV Part 2) that states that the brochure has not been approved by the Commission or any state securities authority. Also, if an adviser refers to itself as a "registered investment adviser," it also must include a disclaimer that registration does not imply a certain level of skill or training.

Concerning ADV Part 2B, the SEC writes:

> Rule 204-3 also requires that each firm brochure be accompanied by brochure supplements providing information about the advisory personnel on whom the particular client receiving the brochure relies for investment advice. Among other things, the brochure supplements will contain information about the educational background, business experience, and disciplinary history (if any) of the supervised persons who provide advisory services to the client. The brochure supplement thus includes information that would not necessarily be included in the firm brochure about supervised persons of the adviser who actually provide the investment advice and interact with the client. We are requiring as proposed that a client be given a brochure supplement for each supervised person who: (i) formulates investment advice for that client and has direct client contact; or (ii) makes discretionary investment decisions for that client's assets, even if the supervised person has no direct client contact. We believe that clients are most interested in learning about the background and experience of these individuals from whom they receive investment advice. We are adopting as proposed, the requirement that advisers deliver an updated supplement to clients only when there is new disclosure of a disciplinary event, or a material change to disciplinary information already disclosed.

For existing clients, a federal covered adviser must deliver annually either the brochure or a summary of all material changes since their last annual updating amendment. Advisers now file ADV Part 2A electronically with the SEC. They create it in Adobe PDF format, and then upload it electronically.

Advisers provide ADV Part 1 when registering and renewing with the SEC and/or the state securities Administrators. As we've seen, they also deliver ADV Part 2 to prospects and offer to deliver it to existing clients annually. Through the SEC's Investment Adviser Disclosure Page (IAPD) both are also available to anyone interested in viewing the information. A good use of your time would be to look at an ADV Part 1 and ADV Part 2 for any registered investment adviser.

We will explore the many conflicts of interest that arise in the advisory industry up ahead. For now, let's note that because an investment adviser's investment advice must be disinterested and objective, any time that is not possible a conflict of interest exists and must be disclosed. If, for example, the adviser receives a management fee but also earns commissions on the amounts clients place in certain mutual funds, there is an added incentive to steer clients to those funds. The way to handle the conflict is to make it clear that the adviser receives extra financial benefits when clients invest in certain mutual fund products.

As with other conflicts of interest, the adviser should inform the client upfront orally, followed by a written statement that may need to be acknowledged by the client with his signature. And, the disclosure brochure should explain how this works under the section explaining compensation.

If the adviser receives soft-dollar compensation from the custodial broker-dealers that clients use, this is also a potential conflict that must be disclosed. Although it seems harmless for the RIA to receive services and benefits based on client assets under custody with the broker-dealer, remember that any benefit the adviser receives from client assets or transactions is a potential conflict of interest that must be disclosed.

Custody

If an investment adviser has direct or indirect control over client assets, it is deemed to maintain custody of those assets. We will look at the many details involved with this business practice up ahead. For now, let's note that certain disclosures are required when an RIA has custody of client assets. As the SEC explains, "When the investment adviser uses a qualified custodian, the adviser must notify the client immediately in writing of the qualified custodian's name, address, and manner in which the funds or securities are maintained when the account is opened. If the adviser opens accounts for a client with more than one custodian, the client must be notified of all qualified custodian locations. Prompt notification to the client in writing following any changes to the client's account information also is required."

If an adviser can deduct management fees from the client account by way of the custodian, this does equal custody. However, the rigid requirements associated with custody are waived if the adviser gets the client's permission to do this in writing and delivers a billing statement to the custodian and client explaining how their fee was calculated every time they receive it.

Unlawful Representations

Regulators register securities professionals. They never certify or approve them. A securities professional might earn credentials such as Chartered Financial Analyst or Certified Financial Planner, but that means an independent organization has issued that designation. To indicate that a firm or individual has been "certified" or "approved" by the securities regulators is a violation. Section 208 of the Investment Advisers Act of 1940 makes this clear:

> Representations of sponsorship by United States or agency thereof. It shall be unlawful for any person registered under section 203 to

represent or imply in any manner whatsoever that such person has been sponsored, recommended, or approved, or that his abilities or qualifications have in any respect been passed upon by the United States or any agency or any officer thereof.

This must be made clear to all prospects and clients. On the adviser's disclosure brochure (Form ADV Part 2) a statement such as the following is required at the beginning of the document, "This brochure provides information about the qualifications and business practices of ABC Advisers, a registered investment adviser. Registration does not imply a certain level of skill or training but only indicates that ABC Advisers has registered its business with state and federal regulatory authorities, including the United States Securities and Exchange Commission (our SEC number is ###-69766). The information in this Brochure has not been approved or verified by the United States Securities and Exchange Commission or by any state securities authority."

No matter how hard one works to pass the exam, if he implies that his registration sets him apart from other advisers or IARs, he is committing fraud. Some advisers must register, some are exempt. Neither status implies anything about the adviser's level of skill or training.

Supervisory services involve an ongoing relationship with the client in which the adviser oversees the investments and, perhaps, trades the account with discretion. Consulting and market-timing services would typically not be considered supervisory. Some advisers call themselves an **investment counsel**, but the title may only be used by those advisers performing "supervisory services." Also, to call itself an "investment counsel," the adviser's main business must be rendering investment advice.

Securities regulators have cracked down on financial services professionals who use special designations to mislead senior citizens. While some of the credentials are legitimate, many make the regulators nervous, including "Certified Financial Gerontologist." Regulators recently performed a survey that showed that one-quarter of all senior investors were told that the financial professionals they were talking to were specially certified or qualified to help senior citizens, and half of those investors said they were more likely to listen to the advice because of that. Unfortunately, designations are often obtained by paying a fee to the organization that prints an official-looking certificate without verifying anything about the professional receiving it.

Performance Guarantees

Investment advisers managing portfolios typically earn a percentage of assets. They do not, however, impose a management fee only if the portfolio value increases. Similarly, management fees are not refunded if the portfolio value fails to increase by a stated and "guaranteed" rate.

We looked at fixed annuities earlier in which annuitants are guaranteed a certain minimum rate of return. That is fine for an insurance product. But, neither the advisory nor the brokerage industry may issue such guarantees.

No one is saying the word "guaranteed" is prohibited. The U.S. Government guarantees U.S. Treasury securities as to payment of interest and principal. If we explain the limits of that guarantee to investors, we are doing our jobs correctly. A fixed annuity is guaranteed by the claims paying ability of the insurance/annuity company. If we explain the limits of that guarantee, we are not misleading investors.

So, while some products and securities come with guarantees, no investment adviser or broker-dealer may offer investors performance guarantees.

Client Contracts

The contract signed by the investment adviser and the advisory client is a big deal. The regulators require that all important terms of the contract be made clear to the client. For example, what are the advisory fees, how are they charged, does the adviser have discretion or custody, and what is the term of the agreement?

The Uniform Securities Act lays out three main concerns for advisory contracts: assignment, change in partnership composition, and compensation.

Assignment of Contract

The prohibition against **assignment of contract** means that an adviser cannot sell or transfer a customer's contract to another party without the client's consent. Not only would the investment adviser get in trouble for assigning the contract to another party without the client's consent, but if their contract with the client forgot to stipulate that this is not allowed, that would also be a violation, even if no contract was assigned. The Uniform Securities Act states:

> "...that no assignment of the contract may be made by the investment adviser without the consent of the other party to the contract."

Notification of Change in Partnership Structure

The Act also says:

> "...that the investment adviser, if a partnership, shall notify the other party to the contract of any change in the membership of the partnership within a reasonable time after the change."

If the advisory firm is organized as a partnership, whenever one of the partners withdraws or dies—or a new partner is admitted—the firm must inform all clients in a reasonable time that the partnership structure has changed. Why? Maybe some are clients because of Jenkins and never cared for Williams or Sonoma, so if Jenkins leaves Williams, Jenkins, and Sonoma Wealth Management Partners, LP, maybe it's time for them to go, too. It doesn't matter in this case if the change was due to a partner with a majority or minority interest. The adviser must disclose the change in ownership to clients promptly.

A related issue is assignment of contract as it relates to a change of ownership. If a minority partner is admitted, withdraws, or dies, even though the partnership must inform its clients of that fact in a timely manner, that is not considered to be an "assignment of contract." In other words, the investment adviser has not changed so drastically that the account is now being handled by another party. The contract didn't get assigned by ABC to XYZ, nor did ABC suddenly become XYZ. It's just that ABC has a slightly different partnership structure now.

On the other hand, if the change in partners involves a majority owner being admitted or withdrawing, that would require the clients to sign new advisory contracts. If the firm didn't do that, they would have assigned the clients' contracts in violation of securities law. The same applies to an adviser owned as an LLC—a change in the managing members must be announced to clients promptly, but there is no assignment unless a majority ownership stake were involved. Also, if an adviser organized as a corporation sells or even pledges a majority of the corporate stock to another party, that would also = assignment of contract. And, again, a client's advisory contract cannot be assigned; rather, a new contract would have to be executed between the client and the other adviser.

Compensation

The Uniform Securities Act is so concerned with how investment advisers are compensated that it states along with the other two requirements, "Except as may be permitted by rule or order of the Administrator, it is unlawful for any investment adviser to enter into, extend, or renew any investment advisory contract unless it provides in writing that the investment adviser shall not be compensated on the basis of a share of capital gains upon or capital appreciation of the funds or any portion of the funds of the client."

Investment advisers typically are compensated as a percentage of the account assets or as an hourly rate. They are not compensated based on how much an account rises over the financial quarter, let alone how one stock or group of stocks happened to rise.

To review, then, both state and federal securities laws require advisory contracts to provide at least three things in writing:

- The adviser shall not be compensated for performance (except in certain cases)
- No assignment of contract is allowed without client consent
- If the adviser is a partnership, clients will be notified of any change in the partnership structure

Correspondence and Advertising

Advertisements

The Securities and Exchange Commission defines an advertisement for an adviser as:

> any notice, circular, letter or other written communication addressed to more than one person, or any notice or other announcement in any publication or by radio or television, which offers (1) any analysis, report, or publication concerning securities, or which is to be used in making any determination as to when to buy or sell any security, or which security to buy or sell, or (2) any graph, chart, formula, or other device to be used in making any determination as to when to buy or sell any

security, or which security to buy or sell, or (3) any other
investment advisory service with regard to securities.

Whatever the media used, an adviser is creating an advertisement if the communication addresses more than one person concerning the firm's advisory services. Advertisements for investment advisers must be fair and accurate. An adviser may not use testimonials from satisfied clients. Having a client speak well of an IAR or the firm is misleading, because other clients may have quite different experiences. The adviser can list past performance or recommendations provided they don't imply that future results are somehow implied or guaranteed. And, if the adviser lists past stock picks, they must include all recommendations—winners and losers—over the same period, which must be at least one year. If the complete and detailed results aren't provided in the advertisement, it needs to be clear that a list will be provided upon written request without charge or obligation.

Also, if the adviser's stock picks are up 50%, how does that compare to the market in general? If the recommendations listed pertain only to a select group of the adviser's clients, this needs to be made clear. It also needs to be clear whether the performance figures are including the IA's management fees, and if not, there must be a caveat that if advisory fees and commissions were factored in, results would be lower.

The SEC stipulates, "If the advertisement claims that any graph, chart, formula or other device being offered will assist any person in making his own decisions, the advertisement must prominently disclose the limitations thereof and the difficulties with respect to its use." If the adviser offers "free services with no obligation," those services had better be free, with, sure enough, no obligation. In general, IA advertisements need to go to great lengths to avoid misleading prospects and clients. And, any performance claims made by the adviser need to be backed up by the "books and records" required to be kept by the firm.

To understand how much trouble improper advertising can be for an investment adviser let's look at an actual disciplinary action by the securities Administrator for the State of Illinois.

STATE OF ILLINOIS

SECRETARY OF STATE

SECURITIES DEPARTMENT

_____)

IN THE MATTER OF: ROBERT WILLIAM ESCH) No.

DBA WHITEMOUNTAIN FINANCIAL) 0300042

_____)

CONSENT ORDER

TO THE RESPONDENT: Robert William Esch

DBA WhiteMountain Financial

539 Troy Plaza

Troy, Illinois 62294

C/O Charles J. Northrup

Sorling, Northrup, Hanna,

Cullen & Cochran, Ltd

Attorneys at Law

607 East Adams Street, Suite 800

Springfield, Illinois 62705

WHEREAS, Robert William Esch DBA WhiteMountain Financial on January 12, 2005 executed a certain Stipulation To Entry Of Consent Order (the "Stipulation"), which hereby is incorporated by reference herein.

WHEREAS, by means of the Stipulation, the Respondent has admitted to the jurisdiction of the Secretary of State and service of the Notice of Hearing in this matter and the Respondent has consented to the entry of this Consent Order.

WHEREAS, the Secretary of State, by and through his designated representative, the Securities Director, has determined that the matter related to the aforesaid formal hearing may be dismissed without further proceeding.

WHEREAS, the Respondent has acknowledged that the allegations contained in paragraph seven (7) of the Stipulation shall be adopted as the Secretary of State's Findings of Fact as follows:

1. At all times relevant, the Respondent was an Illinois registered Investment Adviser and Investment Adviser Representative pursuant to Section 8 of the Illinois Securities Law of 1953, 815 ILCS 5/1 et seq. (the "Act").

2. That from on or about January 2003 to on or about July 15, 2004 the Respondent advertised, operated and managed an investment management system under the name of the Super T Asset Management System and had about 25 persons participating in the system including the Respondent and some of the Respondent's family members.

3. The Super T Asset Management System was advertised and described to clients and prospective clients ("clients") as an investment advisory program in which the client would invest a minimum of $25,000 to be managed by the Respondent for a management fee of .75% of assets under management or a minimum of $250 each half year. Additionally, clients were told that their investment would be invested all in cash or all in one stock of the Respondent's choice. In later contracts, the phrase "all one stock" was replaced with "all one security" or "all one investment."

4. As part of the Super T Asset Management System, clients entered into an investment advisory contract with the Respondent in which they agreed to open brokerage accounts with a third party discount brokerage firm and give authority to the Respondent to execute transactions in these accounts on their behalf. Pursuant to such authority the Respondent executed buy and sell transactions of the security SPY, an exchange traded fund in the form of a Unit Investment Trust listed on the American Stock Exchange.

5. The Respondent mailed, delivered or caused to be delivered to clients advertising material which included performance measurement figures and/or charts for the Super T Asset Management System.

6. The Respondent violated the Illinois Securities Act and its Rules and Regulations in the following matter.

7. The advertising material referenced in paragraph 5 above contained performance measurements without complying with United States Securities and Exchange Commission Rule 206(4)-1 of the Rules and Regulations Under the Investment Advisers Act of 1940.

8. Additionally, the advertising material was misleading or false because: (a) it did not disclose that the past performance measurements for the Super T Asset Management System were not based upon actual trades but were based solely upon hypothetical recommendations and transactions; (b) failed to disclose that the percentage returns quoted in the material were before any fees paid or transactions costs and that actual returns would be lower; (c) failed to disclose that a quoted annualized rate of return was hypothetical and based upon a projection of a rate of return from 3-4 months and not upon an actual annualized rate of return; and (d) falsely misrepresented that the Super T Asset Management System was a registered or trademarked system when in fact it was not.

9. Failed to disclose material information to clients by: (a) failing to disclose that management fees were negotiable and that some clients were paying a reduced fee or had their fees waived by the Respondent; (b) failing to disclose that the minimum investment amount of $25,000 in the Super T Asset Management System was negotiable and some clients had invested less; (c) failing to disclose that the security SPY was an Exchange Traded Fund and a Unit Investment Trust and not a stock; and (d) failing to disclose that some participants in the Super T Asset Management System were relatives of the Respondent and were not paying advisory fees and/or had invested less than the minimum investment amount of $25,000.

10. Respondent entered into some investment advisory contracts with clients which: (a) did not include terms stating that the contract could not be assigned without the consent of the other

party; (b) did not reflect that the minimum investment amount had been modified by previous agreement of the parties; and/or (c) identified the incorrect name of the client/party to the contract.

11. For some clients, the Respondent was accepting fees of over $500 and six or more months in advance but was not complying with Illinois Securities Department Rule 844 and in one case the Respondent billed the client an incorrect fee amount resulting in an overcharge to the client of 2.5 times the correct amount.

12. The Respondent provided to clients forms which he requested the client to fill out which stated at the bottom of the forms that: a) "This form is required by the Illinois Securities Department. Thank you for your cooperation."; or (b) "The information requested on this form is required by the Illinois Securities Department. Your cooperation is appreciated." When in fact neither the form nor the information was required by the Illinois Securities Department.

13. Filing a Form ADV with the Department which contained misleading or inaccurate information or omitted material information.

14. That Rule 130.844 of the Rules and Regulations under the Illinois Securities Act, 14 Admin Code 130.100 et seq., provides, inter alia, that each registered investment adviser which accepts prepayment of fees in excess of $500.00 per client and six (6) or more months in advance shall file [with the Department] a statement of financial condition (balance sheet) and interim financial statement, in such detail as will disclose the nature and amounts of assets and liabilities and net worth of the investment adviser.

15. Section 8.E.1(b) of the Act provides, inter alia, that subject to the provisions of subsection F of Section 11 of the Act, the registration of an investment adviser or investment adviser representative may be suspended or revoked if the Secretary of State finds that the investment adviser or investment adviser representative has engaged in any unethical practice in the offer or sale of securities or in any fraudulent business practice.

16. Section 8.E.1(m) of the Act provides, inter alia, that subject to the provisions of subsection F of Section 11 of the Act, the registration of an investment adviser or investment adviser representative may be suspended or revoked if the Secretary of State finds that the investment adviser or investment adviser representative has conducted a continuing course of dealing of such nature as to demonstrate an inability to properly conduct the business of the dealer, limited Canadian dealer, salesperson, investment adviser or investment adviser representative.

17. Section 8.E.1(q) of the Act provides, inter alia, that subject to the provisions of subsection F of Section 11 of the Act, the registration of an investment adviser or investment adviser representative may be suspended or revoked if the Secretary of State finds that the investment adviser or investment adviser representative has failed to maintain the books and records required under this Act or regulations under this Act or under any requirements established by the Securities and Exchange Commission or self-regulatory organization.

WHEREAS, the Respondent has acknowledged that the allegation contained in paragraph eight (8) of the Stipulation shall be adopted as the Secretary of State's Conclusion of Law as follows: By virtue of the foregoing, the Respondent is subject to the entry of an Order which revokes his investment adviser and investment adviser representative registrations in the State of Illinois pursuant to the authority provided under Section 8.E.1(b), (m) or (q) of the Act.

NOW THEREFORE IT IS HEREBY ORDERED THAT:

1. The allegations contained in paragraphs seven (7) and eight (8) of the Stipulation shall be and are hereby adopted as the Secretary of State's Findings of Fact and Conclusion of Law;

2. The Respondent's Investment Adviser and Investment Adviser Representative registrations in Illinois are revoked as of the last date that the registrations were effective;

3. The Respondent, Robert William Esch, shall pay a fine of $15,000 payable to the Secretary of State by certified check or money order within thirty days of the entry of the order;

4. The Respondent shall deliver a copy of this consent order, along with a cover letter stating that if the recipient has any questions regarding the consent order to contact the Illinois Securities Department, to all of his current and former investment advisory clients within 10 business days of the entry of the consent order;

5. The Respondent shall not reapply for any registration under the Illinois Securities Act for two years from the date of entry of the consent order; and

6. The formal hearing scheduled on this matter is hereby dismissed without further proceeding.

ENTERED: This day of , 2005.

_____

JESSE WHITE

Secretary of State

NOTICE: Failure to comply with the terms of this Order shall be a violation of Section 12.D of the Illinois Securities Law of 1953 [815 ILCS 5] (the "Act"). Any person or entity who fails to comply with the terms of this Order of the Secretary of State, having knowledge of the existence of this Order, shall be guilty of a Class 4 felony.

Attorney for the Secretary of State:

David Finnigan

Illinois Securities Department

Lincoln Tower, Suite 200

520 South Second Street

Springfield, Illinois 62701

Telephone: (217) 785-4947

First, it is not okay to enter advisory contracts with clients that state the minimum investment is $25,000 and the management fees are a set amount, when, in fact, some clients don't have to meet the minimum and don't have to pay any fee at all. If the minimum investment and the fees charged are negotiable, it is an unethical and fraudulent business practice to sign contracts with clients that state or imply otherwise.

Speaking of the advisory contracts, notice that the adviser accepted prepayment of fees in excess of $500 six or more months in advance but did not comply with the Administrator's rules governing this practice. Receiving that type of upfront fee creates custody, in other words, and he failed to comply with the requirements for investment advisers with custody of client assets. Also, his contracts failed to state that no assignment of contract was allowed without client consent. So, even though he didn't assign the contracts, he got dinged for forgetting to insert that clause into the contract itself.

Okay, so his advisory contracts had problems, and he accidentally billed someone 2.5 times the correct amount. Stuff happens, right? What really caught my attention was his advertising. I mean, come on, all I have to do is find the 10 best performing stocks of last year and put out an advertisement claiming that I invested in them. If I didn't mind getting in trouble, that is.

So, according to the order, not only did he not purchase the stocks he claimed to have picked, but the performance figures on the little pretend stock picks only covered a period of 3 or 4 months, which he then multiplied by 3 or 4 to get an annualized rate of return. Now, when we were calculating annualized rates of return in another section, we were just doing an academic exercise. No way can an investment adviser get a 10% return in one week and then advertise his 520% annualized rates of return.

When an investment adviser puts out an advertisement listing stock picks, the period covered must be at least one year. And, the regulators expect the adviser to have purchased the stocks he claims to have bought and that he can back it all up with the books and records required to be kept by the firm.

I mean, if you say you picked all those stocks, what's the problem with pulling out the trade confirmations and account statements backing up your claims?

Finally, not only did he apparently not pick any of the stocks he claimed to have bought; not only did the period used not cover a full year; but also, the performance figures he quoted failed to clarify that if management fees and transaction costs had been included, the numbers would have been lower.

To avoid problems like this, many independent RIAs use consulting firms to help with registration and compliance. Such firms would have red-flagged and helped fix the contracts and advertisements for this adviser. Whatever their fee, it would have been more attractive than having this disciplinary action taken and having to sit out a full two years before even attempting to re-enter the business.

Using the Internet

NASAA has a policy statement on the use of the internet for "general dissemination of information on products and services." Basically, it comes down to this: if you're putting up a website discussing your services and products, anyone with a web connection can see it, which might include people in states where you and the broker-dealer are not registered. If you are deemed to be transacting securities business in a state where you're not registered, your life is going to become complicated. So, NASAA is putting out the uniform idea for state regulators that an agent, broker-dealer, adviser or IAR using a website is not considered to be transacting business in states where they're not registered if the following bullet points are followed:

- The Internet Communication contains a legend in which it is clearly stated that the broker-dealer, investment adviser, BD agent or IA rep in question may only transact business in this state if first registered, excluded or exempted from registration requirements, and follow-up, individualized responses to persons in this state that involve either the effecting or attempting to effect transactions in securities, or the rendering of personalized investment advice for compensation, will not be made absent compliance with state registration requirements, or an applicable exemption or exclusion

In other words, your website needs some text clearly explaining that you're not trying to offer securities or investment advice through the website and would only do so if registered or excused from registration in the web visitor's state.

Also:

- The Internet Communication does not involve either effecting or attempting to effect transactions in securities, or the rendering of personalized investment advice for compensation in this state over the Internet, but is limited to the dissemination of general information on products and services

That means the website can not involve effecting or attempting to effect purchases/sales of securities or the delivery of personalized investment advice for compensation.

This NASAA policy statement applies to state-registered investment advisers and investment adviser representatives, whether working for a federal covered or state-registered advisory firm.

Investment advisers must develop and implement written policies and procedures reviewed at least annually for effectiveness. A few years ago, the SEC published a "risk alert" in which they remind RIAs using social media to adopt, implement, and periodically review the effectiveness of their policies and procedures concerning social media.

Why would social media rise to the level of a "risk alert"? As the SEC explains, social media "converts the traditional two-party, adviser-to-client communication into an interactive, multi-party dialogue among advisers, clients, and prospects, within an open architecture accessible to third-party observers. It also converts a static medium, such as a website, where viewers passively receive content, into a medium where users actively create content."

If you've ever piled onto one of those awful late-night Facebook free-for-alls that most participants regret in the morning, you can imagine how out of hand a discussion about a variable annuity or a wrap fee program could get on social media.

Whether it's a site that they operate themselves or a third-party venue such as Facebook, firms are now using social media for many different purposes: to communicate with existing and potential clients, promote services, educate investors and recruit new employees. It only makes sense that they need clear written policies on how IARs and solicitors can and cannot communicate through social media.

What does the SEC mean by the term "social media"?

> "Social media" is an umbrella term that encompasses various activities that integrate technology, social interaction and content creation. Social media may use many technologies, including, but not limited to, blogs, microblogs, wikis, photos and video sharing, podcasts, social networking, and virtual worlds. The terms "social media," "social media sites," "sites" and "social networking sites" are used interchangeably in this communication.

An RIA's use of social media must comply with various provisions of federal securities law, including antifraud, compliance, and recordkeeping provisions. The SEC lays out several concerns and makes suggestions as to how an adviser could evaluate the effectiveness of its compliance program. For example, the firm may want to create usage guidelines depending on the potential risks to itself and clients, possibly providing IARs and solicitors an exclusive list of approved social media sites and a list of prohibited functionalities on a site. The firm may want to develop clear content standards, especially content that includes investment recommendations or a recommendation of the adviser's services.

The SEC states, "A firm may also consider whether to articulate clear guidelines with respect to such content, and whether to prohibit specific content or impose other content restrictions." Some firms provide approved content for their IARs to use on social media, and their policies prohibit IARs from posting anything other than what the RIA provides them.

The SEC writes, "A firm may consider how to effectively monitor the firm's social media sites or firm use of third-party sites, taking into account that many third-party sites may not provide complete access to a supervisor or to compliance personnel." Since many social media sites protect their users' privacy, it may be impossible to monitor what IARs are posting, especially at a large firm. Therefore, the policy might need to include a list of prohibited sites, as we saw earlier.

To avoid violations of securities laws and rules, the RIA may need to consider pre-approval of content, since after-the-fact reviews would come after much damage had already been done.

An adviser may need to develop a training program for IARs and may require them to sign a certification that they are all adhering to the firm's policies on social media.

Testimonials are not allowed in an adviser's advertising because they are inherently misleading. The testimonial of any one client may not represent the experiences of other clients, so the testimonials used in many other industries become a special problem for RIAs and IARs. If the adviser runs a social media site that allows third parties to post and interact, they must make sure they aren't encouraging testimonials.

RIAs and IARs are not allowed to invite clients to write public commentary on the firm's social media site. However, if the public commentary comes from a truly independent third-party site such as Angie's List, things are different. Now, the testimonial rule would not apply if the following criteria are met:

- the independent social media site provides content that is independent of the investment adviser or IAR
- there is no material connection between the independent social media site and the investment adviser or IAR that would call into question the independence of the independent social media site or commentary
- the investment adviser or IAR publishes all of the unedited comments appearing on the independent social media site regarding the investment adviser or IAR

Commentary would not be independent if the investment adviser or IAR directly or indirectly authored the commentary, whether in their own name, a third party's name, or an alias, assumed or screen name. And, there is a material connection between the site and the RIA/IAR if either compensated a social media user for authoring the commentary, including with any product or service of value, or if they prioritized, removed or edited the commentary.

So, the comments from an independent site could be rebroadcast through the firm's social media site, if the RIA or IAR have no control over which comments are shown, and if no one was compensated for making the comments. Many readers might have already assumed that writing favorable reviews on Angie's List under a series of aliases and then feeding those to the top of your firm's social media site is a violation. But, apparently, it needed to be pointed out.

The SEC also explains that if a user hits a "like" button on an adviser's social media site, that could imply he is giving a testimonial on his experiences with the adviser. The SEC explains in a footnote that "Third-party use of the like feature on an investment adviser's social media site could be deemed to be a testimonial if it is an explicit or implicit statement of a client's or clients' experience with an investment adviser or IAR. If, for example, the public is invited to 'like' an IAR's biography posted on a social media site, that election could be viewed as a type of testimonial."

The SEC published guidance in 2014 on how to deal with the prohibition against testimonials in which they write, "The staff also has stated that an investment adviser's publication of an article by an unbiased third party regarding the adviser's investment performance is not a testimonial, unless it includes a statement of a client's experience with or endorsement of the adviser. The staff also has stated that an adviser's advertisement that includes a partial client list that does no more than identify certain clients of the adviser cannot be viewed either as a statement of a client's experience with, or endorsement of, the adviser and therefore is not a testimonial."

Recordkeeping requirements don't distinguish between types of media, so an RIA must manage the task of keeping records of social media communications. The SEC states, "A firm that intends to communicate, or permit its IARs to communicate, through social media sites may wish to determine that it can retain all required records related to social media communications and make them available for inspection." Because such recordkeeping could prove costly and difficult, many RIAs take the SEC's suggestion and limit how the IARs and solicitors use social media.

Research Reports

It is a violation for broker-dealers to compensate their research analysts, who publish reports on the merits of particular stocks, based on the amount of investment banking they can drum up by making certain companies happy with said research reports. In other words, a broker-dealer can't offer a bonus to the research analyst who just wrote a positive report on, say, GE when GE then hires the firm to help with a merger/acquisition as a thank-you for helping to push the price of the stock up, that inflated stock now being used to acquire the target company.

The investment banking division cannot set the compensation of research analysts, and there can be no link between the research analysts and the investment banking division. If you look at a research report these days, you'll see lots of disclosure on the front cover that the broker-dealer may do underwriting business for the issuer whose stock they are researching. Due to a settlement with the New York State Attorney General's office, the disclosure also mentions that readers should consult other sources before making decisions and can request free independent research reports from the broker-dealer.

Ethical Practices and Fiduciary Obligations

Under securities law investment advisers and investment adviser representatives are defined as **fiduciaries**. A fiduciary is in a trustee relationship with clients as opposed to an agency relationship. RIAs and IARs are not product salesmen. Rather, they are fiduciaries who must always place their clients' interests ahead of their own. Whenever the adviser's and the client's interests are in conflict, the actual or potential conflict must be disclosed to the client, often requiring the client's signature on a written acknowledgment.

Beyond conflicts of interest there are several other business practices that could be deemed unethical and therefore provide securities regulators a reason to take disciplinary action against an RIA and/or its IARs.

Investment advisers performing what the SEC calls "continuous, supervisory management services" typically receive a flat fee. Maybe they charge 1% of the assets, which provides incentive for the adviser. One percent of $150,000 is nice, but one percent of $200,000 is even nicer. So, the percentage stays flat and the adviser's compensation only grows if the customer's assets grow.

Some advisers would prefer to take a share of the paper gains or the actual profits made from trading. Every time the adviser buys at 10 and sells at 18, the adviser gets a piece of that capital gain. What about the rest of the stocks?

That, right there, is the problem. If a client were to pay an adviser with a share of capital gains, the adviser could make a profit on one lucky stock pick even if the rest of the account goes down to zero. Say a client invested $100,000 with an investment adviser who said he was not going to charge any ongoing fees. Rather, he would just take half of any trading profits. Sounds nice at first, but let's say he puts the client into 10 stocks with $10,000 invested in each. One stock goes up from $10,000 to $18,000, and the adviser sells it for an 80% profit. The client makes a short-term capital gain of $8,000, and the adviser takes $4,000.

The client's $4,000 could be taxed somewhere between 25% and 39.6% at the federal level, plus a few more percentage points at the state level. So, the after-tax gain is about $2,500.

Now, the adviser tells the client to be patient, just wait until those 9 other stocks go up. Only, they never do. The client waits and waits, and waits some more, but not only do the other stocks not begin to rise on cue, they also begin to spiral downward. The account drops from $90,000 to $60,000 in a hurry, then slowly drifts down to $36,000, at which point the client tells him to sell everything and send a check for what's left.

So, how did the client do in this case? He put down $100,000 and is left with $36,000 plus an after-tax profit of about $2,500. He is down close to 62%! How did the adviser do? He made a fast profit of $4,000 with absolutely no risk to himself. Maybe it's not such a great way to compensate an investment adviser after all!

Or, maybe dependable, blue chip growth and income stocks are perfectly suitable for a client's portfolio. Unfortunately, if the investment adviser gets paid on a share of capital gains/appreciation, why bother with the slow-and-steady stocks that might not go anywhere for a while? Regardless of the client's risk tolerance, why not pick 20 of the most speculative stocks trading on the OTC Bulletin Board?

Offering to share the gains or just the capital appreciation with an investment adviser entices the adviser to take on much bigger risks and often puts the adviser's interests in conflict with those of the client.

And that's why advisers cannot be compensated as a share of capital gains as a general rule. Advisers managing a portfolio, generally, should be compensated as a percentage of assets over a specified period.

The Uniform Securities Act then clarifies that this rule "does not prohibit an investment advisory contract which provides for compensation based upon the total value of a fund averaged over a definite period, or as of definite dates or taken as of a definite date." That means that while an adviser can't share the gains on individual stocks or take a percentage of the amount that the account "went up," the firm can bill the client based on the average account balance over a certain period or bill a percentage of assets as of, say, the end of each financial quarter, or on the last day the market is open for the calendar year.

Investment advisers explain how they charge for their services in detail in their disclosure brochure and in the contracts they and their clients sign. If they or the client cancel the contract, how are any prepaid fees returned, or unpaid fees collected? Such details must be explained clearly in client contracts with the adviser.

Financial planners typically charge an hourly rate for their services. Or, some might charge a flat fee to draw up a plan for retirement savings or estate planning techniques. Either way, if their compensation involves securities in any way, they are investment advisers subject to registration requirements.

A person can meet the definition whether his compensation is called a commission or a fee. We like to find neat categories in which the word "fee" makes someone an investment adviser while the word "commission" makes him a securities agent. Not quite. If a securities agent with a life and health insurance license provides financial plans for "free" but then receives commissions on all the products recommended in the "plan," she probably meets the definition of an investment adviser. In other words, she should be registered as an RIA or IAR, and as an agent this outside business needs to be disclosed to her employing broker-dealer.

Fraud

There are many ways an investment adviser or investment adviser representative could lose their securities license. Operating as an IAR without bothering to pass the exam and register first, for example, would lead to regulatory problems. But the state securities regulators are primarily out to protect their residents from activities that are deceptive, manipulative, or dishonest in the securities industry. We have looked in some detail at the model act known as "The Uniform Securities Act" throughout this chapter. This is how the model legislation announces its purpose from the start:

```
Relating to securities; prohibiting fraudulent practices in
relation thereto; requiring the registration of broker-dealers,
agents, investment advisers, and securities; and making uniform
the law with reference thereto
```

So, we see that the Uniform Securities Act relates only to securities and that its first objective is to prohibit "fraudulent practices in relation to [securities]."

The people who pose a potential threat to the residents of any state include agents, broker-dealers, investment advisers, investment adviser representatives, plus all the entrepreneurs trying to raise money for their little companies no one knows anything about. Whether registered in the industry or not, any person who is connected with the offer, sale, or purchase of any **security** is prohibited from making any misleading statement or leaving out important information in a way that is misleading.

We're talking about the f-word here: **fraud**. Securities fraud is a financial crime in which someone misrepresents the truth in a way that takes advantage of the other side in connection to an investment in securities. For example, if an investment adviser inflated client account balances to overcharge them, this would be fraudulent. If an adviser sent out bogus account statements to conceal the fact that all client funds had long ago been converted to a fleet of Cadillac Escalades™, this would also operate as a fraud. Fraud can cause a person to lose their securities license (administrative action), get themselves sued (civil liability) and maybe even thrown in prison (criminal liability).

Let's look at a real-world example of an investment adviser who apparently defrauded investors in New Jersey and ended up looking at prison time for her alleged misdeeds:

Office of The Attorney General, Anne Milgram, Attorney General

Division of Criminal Justice, Gregory Paw, Director

JACKSON WOMAN PLEADS GUILTY TO DEFRAUDING INVESTORS OF $641,000

TRENTON - Attorney General Anne Milgram and Criminal Justice Director Gregory A. Paw announced that an Ocean County woman pleaded guilty today to defrauding investors of more than $600,000 through a false investment scheme.

According to Director Paw, Zina A. Martin, 43, of Jackson, pleaded guilty today to second-degree securities fraud before Superior Court Judge James Den Uyl in Ocean County. Under the plea agreement, Martin faces a sentence of three to five years in state prison. In addition, Martin must pay restitution to her victims of $641,000.

During the plea hearing, Martin admitted that she represented to investors that their money would be placed within certain investment vehicles but, in fact, she used the funds for other purposes. An investigation by the New Jersey Bureau of Securities determined that Martin used the funds to pay business expenses, make payments to other investors, and pay personal expenses, including mortgage payments, monthly living expenses and the purchase of a Cadillac Escalade.

Martin solicited $641,000 from about 25 investors as sole owner and president of Kairos Financial Corporation, which had offices at 331 Newman Springs Road in Red Bank. The Bureau of Securities investigation determined that Martin distributed a brochure to investors describing six different investment funds called the "Kairos Funds," including average yearly returns for some of the funds. She also issued monthly statements informing investors of the amounts they purportedly held in each of the funds. In reality, the Kairos Funds were fictitious and investor monies were commingled in a brokerage account of Kairos Financial.

The case was investigated for the Bureau of Securities by Supervising Investigator Michael McElgunn, Investigator Richard Smullen and Chief of Enforcement Richard Barry. Deputy Attorney General Patrick Flor is prosecuting the case for the Division of Criminal Justice - Major Crimes Bureau and handled today's plea hearing.

In October 2007, the Bureau of Securities revoked the investment adviser registrations of both Martin and Kairos Financial.

You might have assumed it's a violation to create pretend mutual funds to misappropriate money from investors. It didn't involve guns or threats of violence, but property was wrongfully taken just the same. Then again, the securities regulators are not police officers. The regulators are administrative authorities concerned with granting, suspending, or revoking licenses to protect investors. When the activities go beyond unethical business practices and into the land of criminal offenses, the state securities regulators turn the case over to a criminal prosecutor. In the above press release, we see that the state securities department also took away this individual's license, but the larger story was that she was headed to prison after taking a plea bargain. That criminal case was handled by a different department than the one granting and revoking licenses to work in the securities investment industry.

And, I'm not implying that all acts of deception automatically lead to jail time. People in the brokerage and advisory industries make mistakes and suffer lapses of judgment. Funds that were siphoned from customer accounts by a rogue agent have been known to be promptly replaced by the employing broker-dealer, with that agent bounced from the business but nothing beyond that. In general, jail or prison time is for those who make off with customer funds, leaving a mess too big for an employer to fix by settling with just one customer. And, when someone is creating little pretend securities as a ruse to take investors' money, prosecutors usually have mail fraud and wire fraud charges to file, as well, since false documents and statements would have been sent through the mail or over some electronic medium.

So, chances are you will make a few mistakes over your career. But, chances are you will not try to complete an IPO in a company that doesn't exist. Agents who make mutual fund recommendations that were too aggressive are maybe suspended for a few weeks or months. Individuals who create bogus mutual fund investments designed to steal money from investors lose their licenses permanently, and then also may face criminal prosecution and lawsuits from those who were harmed.

Custody of Client Assets

If fraud is the f-word, **custody** is the c-word. Much of the fraud that takes place in the advisory business could be avoided if investors refused to give their investment adviser control of the account assets. I'm talking about small-time operators there, as opposed to large full-service financial firms that have a bank, a broker-dealer, an investment adviser, and maybe an insurance company all under the same roof. I'm saying, don't give your money to some guy you just met through a friend of a friend if you have any interest in getting it back.

On the other hand, if a large investment adviser is an affiliate of a large bank or broker-dealer, then custody is a natural thing for the adviser to have. In these cases, there must be an outside auditing firm providing the independent oversight I mentioned earlier, with a special report provided to the SEC.

Most small advisers avoid taking custody of client assets, while the large firms connected to broker-dealers and/or banks do it, but with much oversight. An investment adviser is considered to have custody of client assets if the adviser is either holding the funds/securities or has the ability to appropriate them. If the adviser can automatically deduct money from the client's account or write checks out of the account, the adviser is considered to have custody of client assets. Or, if the adviser has an ownership stake in the broker-dealer who maintains custody, the adviser is also considered to have custody of client assets. Or, if the adviser is the general partner in a limited partnership or a managing member of an investment LLC, the adviser is considered to have custody.

The Uniform Securities Act requires that before taking custody, the adviser first must check with the state securities Administrator to see if there is a rule prohibiting custody of client assets. If so, they don't take custody. If there is no rule against it, the adviser can take custody so long as they notify the Administrator in writing. So, what if there's no rule against taking custody, and the adviser, in fact, takes custody but fails to inform the Administrator?

The adviser messed up.

Maintaining custody is an awesome responsibility, and it requires the adviser to maintain higher minimum net worth, to provide an audited balance sheet to the regulators and to clients, and the adviser even has to pay a CPA to come in and audit the books once a year in a surprise audit. If the CPA can't make sense of all the securities and cash positions on the "books and records," they must notify the Administrator promptly to get the firm in trouble. So, the real point of "custody" is that most advisers avoid it like the plague. They're advisers, not banks, right?

The exam might ask what the adviser should do if he receives a check from a client payable to a third party and does not want to be considered to have custody of client assets. First, the third party must be an independent party and not an affiliate of the adviser. Second, to avoid being deemed to have custody, the check must be forwarded to the third party within three business days of receipt, and the adviser must keep records of what happened.

Also, if the adviser inadvertently receives client securities in the mail, they must be returned to the sender within three business days. As long as the adviser keeps records as to what happened with the check and/or the securities, they will avoid being deemed to have custody. Therefore, they don't need to maintain higher net worth, update their registration information, or have the expensive CPA audit.

Since few advisers want to keep books and records as accurate as a bank's, most use qualified custodians for their clients' funds and securities, including:

- Banks and Savings Associations
- Registered Broker-Dealers (Custodial Broker-Dealers)
- Registered Futures Commission Merchants
- Foreign Financial Institutions

And, if we're talking about mutual fund shares, the IA uses the transfer agent, which is the party holding custody of investors' mutual fund shares. That doesn't mean there are large stacks of paper certificates for all the shares of a large mutual fund, but the transfer agent must keep the ownership records electronically, which is just as large a responsibility.

The NASAA website also states:

> NOTE: because the qualified custodian needs to be independent, there should not be any affiliation between the investment adviser and the qualified custodian through any direct or indirect common control relationship.

> When the investment adviser uses a qualified custodian, the adviser must notify the client immediately in writing of the qualified custodian's name, address, and manner in which the funds or securities are maintained when the account is opened. If the adviser opens accounts for a client with more than one custodian, the client must be notified of all qualified custodian locations. Prompt notification to the client in writing following any changes to the client's account information also is required.

And then continues with:

> Advisers who automatically deduct management fees from the client account held by the custodian do have custody, but they can avoid maintaining higher net worth or having the CPA audit if they follow "certain safeguards."

This means that the adviser must get the client's written authorization to bill the custodian directly, and the adviser must provide both the custodian and the client with a **billing statement** showing how they arrived at their fee. Do they have custody? Yes. Do they have to deal with the higher minimum financial requirements? No.

Account statements will be sent from the custodian to the client and must be sent at least quarterly; however, it is up to the investment adviser to send billing statements to the client. Account statements show the securities positions in the account and their most recent market values, plus any dividends and interest received, purchases and sales of securities, deposits, and withdrawals of cash over the period. A billing statement, on the other hand, is just an invoice showing the adviser's management fee and how they arrived at it. Since the adviser has a fiduciary duty to the client to make sure that those account statements are being sent by the custodian, it's a good idea to ask the custodian to send a duplicate to the adviser.

For more information on custody, visit www.nasaa.org and read the Q & A as well as the NASAA Model Rule on Custody.

Conflicts of Interest

As mentioned, investment advisers and their IARs are fiduciaries who must disclose all material conflicts of interest to clients. The SEC explains:

> As an investment adviser, you are a "fiduciary" to your advisory clients. This means that you have a fundamental obligation to act in the best interests of your clients and to provide investment

308

advice in your clients' best interests. You owe your clients a duty of undivided loyalty and utmost good faith. You should not engage in any activity in conflict with the interest of any client, and you should take steps reasonably necessary to fulfill your obligations. You must employ reasonable care to avoid misleading clients and you must provide full and fair disclosure of all material facts to your clients and prospective clients. Generally, facts are "material" if a reasonable investor would consider them to be important. You must eliminate, or at least disclose, all conflicts of interest that might incline you — consciously or unconsciously — to render advice that is not disinterested. If you do not avoid a conflict of interest that could impact the impartiality of your advice, you must make full and frank disclosure of the conflict. You cannot use your clients' assets for your own benefit or the benefit of other clients, at least without client consent. Departure from this fiduciary standard may constitute "fraud" upon your clients.

The advice needs to be disinterested, so anything that could make it "not disinterested" must be disclosed. If I'm buying a mutual fund for my advisory client because of the suitability and the excellent track record of performance and low expenses, I'm probably acting as a fiduciary. If I'm buying the mutual funds that pay me the best compensation as an agent or broker-dealer on the side without disclosing that to the client, my advice is "not disinterested," and I may end up receiving registered mail from the regulators.

Also, notice the "consciously or unconsciously" phrase. An adviser may unconsciously favor advice and actions that benefit the adviser and must, therefore, be mindful of situations that may lead to that problem. He may be the most honest person in the world, but if he's getting a commission when putting his advisory clients' assets into certain securities, the advice is "not disinterested."

Clients of investment advisers have a right to expect all investment advice to be given objectively— the adviser doesn't stand to benefit when the client accepts the advice. Rather, the adviser is just giving the client the best advice they can and will charge the same amount whether the client buys a mutual fund, a stock, a bond, or even nothing. We demand that investment advisers remain impartial, disinterested, objective advisers. They get compensated for doing just that.

So, if a recommendation to a client would lead to a benefit to the adviser if the client accepts it, we have a potential conflict of interest. The regulators and the courts have determined long ago that a failure to disclose any conflict of interest to an advisory client is a fraud/deceit, period. Therefore, the following conflicts must be carefully and clearly disclosed to advisory clients. Notice I didn't say the investment adviser can't do it; just that they must clearly disclose the practice to advisory clients.

And that's why I'm presenting "conflicts of interest" as a separate but related section to "fraud" here rather than presenting the following actions as subheadings to "fraud," as if they are automatically fraudulent. They are not. The following actions are only fraudulent if advisers fail to properly disclose them to their advisory clients.

Acting as Principal

Full-service firms often have an investment advisory business and a broker-dealer business. So, when the investment advisory business is managing client accounts for a percentage of assets, should they buy the securities directly from the affiliated broker-dealer? Does that sound objective? Any chance some of the trades this month might have been executed to help the affiliated broker-dealer more than it helped the advisory clients? Whose interests is the adviser looking out for here? In other words, the interests of the client are to be placed ahead of the adviser's, but, suddenly, the adviser's and the client's interests may be in conflict. Therefore, this conflict of interest must be disclosed.

To execute a **principal transaction** the adviser must disclose this fact and get the client's written consent before "completion of the transaction," which is settlement of the trade. To act as a principal means the adviser will buy or sell the security on behalf of the client from or to the proprietary account of the related broker-dealer. It's okay to do it, if the potential conflict of interest is disclosed and the customer's written consent is given before the deal is completed.

This only applies when the investment adviser is recommending the security. If this is an "unsolicited" order, then it was the client's idea, and now we have a completely different situation. It's when the investment adviser is recommending that the client buy a security (or using discretion to buy it) that we need the disclosure. Note that recommending a security and using discretion to purchase it on behalf of the client is the same thing for the purposes of this rule.

Agency Cross Transactions

Another example of where the adviser will benefit because of the advice is called an **agency cross transaction**. Here, the firm is buying 1,000 shares of ABC for the client's account, and, as it turns out, their related/affiliated broker-dealer will act as a broker between the client and the seller.

So, should the client buy these 1,000 shares because they're a good investment, or because the adviser likes to help the affiliated broker-dealer pocket commissions in addition to the percentage-based advisory fee assessed on the account? That's what we mean by a conflict of interest—any situation where the adviser might be financially tempted to talk the client into something that benefits the adviser, as opposed to giving objective advice.

It might only be a potential conflict of interest, but the fact is that businesses like to make money, so there's just the chance the advice to buy or sell the security might be tainted by the adviser's financial incentive. The firm might not even charge the advisory client a commission, but if they're charging the brokerage client a commission, that could be the incentive that makes their advice less than objective.

So, as usual, the adviser must disclose the potential conflict of interest in such a case, get the advisory client's written consent by settlement of the trade, and at least once per year send a statement itemizing all the agency cross transactions effected on behalf of the client. And, the brokerage customer's transaction must be unsolicited. The adviser and broker-dealer cannot convince the brokerage customer to buy or sell to the advisory client. It's just that the transaction is suitable for the advisory client's account, and there is a customer of the broker-dealer who wants to buy or sell that security.

If the investment adviser charging an asset-based fee is also a broker-dealer, they might want to act as a dealer/principal when the customer takes the advice to buy or sell a security, or they might want to act as an agent/broker when the customer takes the advice. Many advisers are not broker-dealers, though. Rather, they manage the accounts but let a completely unaffiliated broker-dealer hold the clients' assets and execute all the trades.

Firms such as Charles Schwab and TD Ameritrade are two who reach out to such independent RIAs to provide custodial and clearing services. If I wanted to, I could take and pass the Series 65 again, then register as an investment adviser in Illinois or Colorado. If so, I would get my clients to grant me the authority to place trades in their account (discretion), but TD Ameritrade, the folks who currently have custody of my various IRAs and taxable accounts, would have custody of my client accounts, too. They would execute all the trades that I enter on my clients' behalf and would send account statements to the clients.

So, as a businessman, maybe I work out a deal with TD Ameritrade to provide some economic benefit to me or my firm in exchange for letting them have custody of my client assets. Illegal? Hardly. But if the investment adviser receives any economic benefit from the broker-dealer in exchange for maintaining custody and executing securities transactions for the advisory clients, this must be disclosed to clients. As the SEC told us, "You cannot use your clients' assets for your own benefit or the benefit of other clients, at least without client consent." If anyone can imagine how "client consent" could be obtained without first providing disclosure, I'm not sure I follow. Right? If the client doesn't even know about it, there is no way he or she could have consented.

Even if the economic benefit is considered soft-dollar compensation in the form of research services or computer software aiding the adviser, it would have to be disclosed to clients as a potential conflict of interest. Note that advisers can receive certain forms of soft-dollar compensation if they disclose the practice; however, the following forms of compensation are not allowed to be accepted by broker-dealers:

- Furniture and office equipment
- Salaries or overhead
- Vacations
- Cell phones

Investment advisers and their IARs often also have a Series 6 or 7 license, allowing them to be compensated for selling mutual funds and variable annuities. If an adviser or an IAR is recommending mutual funds and annuities to their clients, they need to disclose the conflict of interest here. Their advice is not objective if it leads to extra compensation, right? A 12b-1 fee is a form of regular compensation that the salesperson receives as long as the client stays invested in the mutual fund, and some funds pay upfront based on the sales charge on a front-end loaded fund (A-share). So, as NASAA indicates on their website, an investment adviser must disclose the fact that "the adviser is receiving transaction-based compensation, including 12b-1 or other marketing fees, related to securities recommended to its clients."

Again, did they recommend that you purchase a growth-and-income fund because it's an excellent investment opportunity, because it's an excellent opportunity for them to make 12b-1 fees, or maybe a little of both? When the adviser provides proper disclosure of potential conflicts of interest, the investor then has a chance to decide such important answers for herself.

Holds a Position in the Security Recommended

When a stock trades on the OTC market, it is called a NASDAQ stock if it's big and important enough to quote regularly over NASDAQ. The little, less important ones that aren't worth quoting all the time, trade on the "OTC Bulletin Board" or "Pink Sheets." These are often illiquid markets, which means that any large buy or sell order tends to shoot the stock price way up or way down. Therefore, if the investment adviser happens to own 10,000 shares of some thinly traded Bulletin Board stock, they would benefit if they could get about 100 clients to put in buy orders. In fact, that might be the main reason they recommend the stock, which would be in direct conflict to their "fiduciary duty" to the client—to put the client's needs first. The stock recommended should be recommended only because it benefits the client. If the purchase of the stock would also benefit the adviser, that potential conflict of interest needs to be disclosed ahead of time.

So, investment advisers must disclose that they may buy and sell the same securities that are bought and sold for client accounts.

Trade Allocations

Portfolio managers aren't generally buying different stocks for different clients. Generally, a portfolio manager has a portfolio model that all clients go into, and the adviser purchases what are called "bunched trades" and then allocates the big bunch of, say, ORCL or IBM shares to various accounts. As the SEC says, "An adviser may defraud its clients when it fails to use the average price paid when allocating securities to accounts participating in bunched trades and fails to adequately disclose its allocation policy. This practice violates the Advisers Act if securities that were purchased at the lowest price or sold at the highest price are allocated to favored clients without adequate disclosure." The SEC also says, "An adviser may defraud its clients by waiting to decide how to allocate a trade among its clients' accounts based on subsequent market movements. The concern is that the adviser could allocate the trade to favored clients if the price movement was favorable and allocate the trade to other accounts if the price movement was unfavorable. This practice is known as 'cherry-picking,' and violates the Advisers Act."

Also, there is nothing more exciting than an IPO of some company that most people are convinced is the new-new thing. But advisers need to make sure they have a policy on allocating IPO shares— especially "hot" ones, or those that are in great popular demand—and disclose any conflicts of interest here. As the SEC says, "An adviser may defraud its clients when it disproportionately allocates hot initial public offerings (IPOs) to favored accounts, and does not adequately disclose this practice to all clients. For example, allocations of IPOs may be inequitable when the following types of accounts are favored: proprietary accounts; accounts that pay performance-based fees; accounts that have relatively poor performance; and new investment companies (to boost performance to attract additional assets)."

Broker-dealers who underwrite municipal securities are prohibited from buying favor with mayors, school board members, governors, and the like to later reap their reward through lucrative underwriting deals for state and local municipal bonds. They cannot pay a third party with political clout to solicit business for the firm, and they cannot make or arrange to be made political contributions except by following a set of stringent rules.

First, neither the firm, a related political action committee (PAC), nor a municipal finance professional can contribute to political campaigns for officials they are not entitled to vote for. If the municipal finance professional is eligible to vote for a candidate, he or she can contribute up to a certain amount ($250) per elected official of the issuer without making the firm ineligible to do securities business with that issuer for two years. Of course, that means if a municipal finance professional contributed more than that amount, the firm would have to refrain from doing securities business with the issuer for two years. And, wouldn't you hate to be the guy who caused the firm to lose all that business by donating, say, $500 without informing your supervisor?

The firm and its municipal finance professionals are also prohibited from talking other firms, employees, individuals, or political action committees into making contributions to political campaigns for officials of an issuer that the firm is either engaged in securities business or seeks to be engaged in securities business with that issuer.

As you might expect, all political contributions related to the firm, its municipal finance professionals, and any related PACs are subject to record keeping by the broker-dealer following this MSRB rule.

So, that's for broker-dealers. Why would an investment adviser solicit business with a government entity? 529 Savings Plans are all run by the states, who then contract out to various investment advisers managing the portfolios. Or, maybe the adviser wants to manage a defined benefit pension plan for a state teachers' retirement fund, or the city police or fire department. Et cetera, et cetera.

The SEC states that it seeks to prevent "fraudulent, deceptive or manipulative acts, practices, or courses of business" with this rule. That means that advisers to government entities should be chosen based on their skills and services without any suggestion that they are being awarded business in return for helping officials with that government entity get elected.

Under a rule implemented under the Investment Advisers Act of 1940 the SEC prohibits virtually all investment advisers from providing any "investment advisory services for compensation to a government entity within two years after a contribution to an official of the government entity is made by the investment adviser or any covered associate of the investment adviser (including a person who becomes a covered associate within two years after the contribution is made)."

Advisers cannot compensate folks who happen to have political clout to land business with government entities, either. The rule prohibits the adviser from "providing or agreeing to provide, directly or indirectly, payment to any person to solicit a government entity for investment advisory services on behalf of such investment adviser unless such person is: A regulated person; or an executive officer, general partner, managing member (or, in each case, a person with a similar status or function), or employee of the investment adviser; and from coordinating, or soliciting any person or political action committee to make, any:

- Contribution to an official of a government entity to which the investment adviser is providing or seeking to provide investment advisory services
- Payment to a political party of a State or locality where the investment adviser is providing or seeking to provide investment advisory services to a government entity."

So, the firm cannot make payment to the brother-in-law of the governor in exchange for helping them land business with the State. They can solicit government entities only through registered investment advisers or broker-dealers who have not made political contributions to that entity over the previous two years.

The term "covered associate" includes the owners, officers, and/or directors of the firm, employees who solicit government entities for business on behalf of the adviser, or any PAC controlled by the adviser or any of the individuals mentioned as covered associates. These are all individuals whose contributions to political campaigns could trigger the firm having to cease or refrain from doing business with an issuer.

The exceptions are similar to the MSRB rule—if the covered associate is eligible to vote for an official, he or she can contribute up to $350 to the political campaign of any one official of the issuer, or up to $150 for a candidate for whom the covered associate is not entitle to vote but wanted to support.

Of course, records of political contributions are required, and the investment adviser would need to regularly review its policies, training, and supervisory system related to such contributions.

Disclose or Abstain

Usually, disclosing potential conflicts of interest ahead of time and obtaining the client's consent will take care of the problem; however, sometimes the conflict is so great that the IA must abstain from action. What is so bad that mere disclosure would not take care of the problem? How about if the portfolio manager manages the investment account (the proprietary accounts mentioned a few lines earlier) of the investment advisory business he works for? In this account there are 1 million shares of XYZ common stock. XYZ common stock has also been placed in many client accounts, based on the portfolio manager's discretion. Well, one morning the portfolio manager reads in *The Wall Street Journal* that XYZ's CEO is going to be indicted for fraud, and the company is also going to restate earnings for the past five years, so he unloads the 1 million shares the firm is holding before starting to sell the shares he's put in client portfolios.

Not a chance. Advisers are fiduciaries, who must put the needs of their clients first. This obvious conflict of interest is a no-no, and no amount of disclosure would make it okay. The adviser should have abstained from this self-serving activity. I mean, isn't the adviser the same genius who put XYZ stock in the client portfolios? Why should the captain of the ship get to be the one to bail out with the only lifeboat on board when the iceberg looms up out of the fog? You steered us into this mess, Captain, and you can go down with the rest of us.

Client Confidentiality

If an advisory firm is trying to land new clients, it would probably be tempting to show prospects what the firm has done for existing clients, disclosing the identity, affairs, or investments of their clients, especially the rich and famous ones.

Yes, well, the existing clients—as well as the securities regulators—would have a problem with that. The only way the firm can disclose the identity or the financial matters of its clients is if the clients give permission, or if the firm is forced to turn over the information by a court order or a subpoena.

Code of Ethics

Investment advisers are responsible for the activities of their employees and, therefore, the SEC requires that advisers "establish, maintain, and enforce a written code of ethics." If you are an investment adviser, your code of ethics needs to include:

- A standard of business conduct that you require of your supervised persons reflecting your fiduciary obligations and those of your supervised persons
- Provisions requiring your supervised persons to comply with applicable federal securities laws
- Provisions that require all of your access persons to report, and you to review, their personal securities transactions and holdings periodically
- Provisions requiring supervised persons to report any violations of your code of ethics promptly to your chief compliance officer
- Provisions requiring you to provide each of your supervised persons with a copy of your code of ethics and any amendments, and requiring your supervised persons to provide you with a written acknowledgment of their receipt of the code and any amendments

For purposes of this rule, the SEC uses the term "access persons" and then defines them as

```
any supervised person who has access to nonpublic information
regarding any clients' purchase or sale of securities, or
nonpublic information regarding the portfolio holdings of any
reportable fund, or who is involved in making securities
recommendations to clients, or who has access to such
recommendations that are nonpublic.
```

In other words, if you are making recommendations to clients, managing their portfolios, or know what securities are inside those client portfolios, you are an access person. If your firm manages mutual funds, and you know what they're buying before the public does, you are clearly an "access person." Directors, officers, and partners are presumed to be access persons, as well. Under this code of ethics, the adviser needs to keep records of their access persons' securities holdings (what they own) and transactions (what they buy and sell). The holding reports must include:

- The title and type of security, and as applicable the exchange ticker symbol or CUSIP number, number of shares, and principal amount of each reportable security in which the access person has any direct or indirect beneficial ownership

- The name of any broker, dealer or bank with which the access person maintains an account in which any securities are held for the access person's direct or indirect benefit; and
- The date the access person submits the report

These reports must be filed with the chief compliance officer no later than 10 days after becoming an "access person," and once a year an updated report must be filed. The information must be accurate as of no more than 45 days prior to filing the report.

The transaction reports that "access persons" must file with the chief compliance officer must include at a minimum:

- The date of the transaction, the title, and as applicable the exchange ticker symbol or CUSIP number, interest rate and maturity date, number of shares, and principal amount of each reportable security involved
- The nature of the transaction (e.g., purchase, sale or any other type of acquisition or disposition)
- The price of the security at which the transaction was effected
- The name of the broker, dealer or bank with or through which the transaction was effected; and
- The date the access person submits the report

These transaction reports need to be submitted for each financial quarter and no more than 30 days after the end of the quarter. The simplest way to comply with the code of ethics requirement is for the adviser to require their "access persons" to have copies of their brokerage statements and trade confirmations sent to the firm.

The rule also states that before an access person buys into an IPO or limited offering, he/she must receive pre-approval from the chief compliance officer. And, lest we think the SEC lacks a sense of humor, the rule states, "if you have only one access person (i.e., yourself), you are not required to submit reports to yourself or to obtain your own approval for investments in any security in an initial public offering or in a limited offering, if you maintain records of all of your holdings and transactions that this section would otherwise require you to report."

Since every rule has exceptions, an investment made through an "automatic investment plan" is not a transaction that has to be reported. In other words, if you are set up for a DRIP (dividend reinvestment program), in which your dividends regularly purchase more shares of stock, that is not a suspicious purchase of securities since it's happening on autopilot. Or, if you're doing a systematic withdrawal plan from of a mutual fund, same deal. Finally, investments in the following are not reportable:

- Direct obligations of the government of the United States
- Banker's acceptances, bank certificates of deposit, commercial paper and high-quality short-term debt instruments, including repurchase agreements
- Shares issued by money market funds

- Shares issued by open-end funds other than reportable funds (you're not an adviser to this fund, and neither is the firm that controls you)
- Shares issued by unit investment trusts that are invested exclusively in one or more open-end funds, none of which are reportable funds

NASAA Model Rule on Business Practices for Advisers

The organization of state and Canadian provincial securities regulators is called **NASAA**, which stands for the **North American Securities Administrators Association**. They're not a regulatory body themselves. Rather, they are the organization of state securities Administrators that attempts to keep all the regulators on top of important issues and working from the same page when writing and rewriting rules for their various jurisdictions. NASAA oversees the Series 63, 65, and 66 exams, so you can send them a thank-you note when you're done with your test. Either way, their model rules and statements of policy are important on the exam, so let's look at a few in detail.

The following is the actual model rule telling investment advisers, investment adviser representatives, and federal covered advisers what types of business practices are unethical and could, therefore, lead to regulatory action.

Model Rule 102(a)(4)-1

Adopted 4/27/97, amended 4/18/04, 9/11/05

Rule 102(a)(4)-1 Unethical Business Practices of Investment Advisers, Investment Adviser Representatives, And Federal Covered Advisers

[Introduction] A person who is an investment adviser, an investment adviser representative or a federal covered adviser is a fiduciary and has a duty to act primarily for the benefit of its clients. The provisions of this subsection apply to federal covered advisers to the extent that the conduct alleged is fraudulent, deceptive, or as otherwise permitted by the National Securities Markets Improvement Act of 1996 (Pub. L. No. 104-290). While the extent and nature of this duty varies according to the nature of the relationship between an investment adviser or an investment adviser representative and its clients and the circumstances of each case, an investment adviser, an investment adviser representative or a federal covered adviser shall not engage in unethical business practices, including the following:

(a) Recommending to a client to whom investment supervisory, management or consulting services are provided the purchase, sale or exchange of any security without reasonable grounds to believe that the recommendation is suitable for the client on the basis of information furnished by the client after reasonable inquiry concerning the client's investment objectives, financial situation and needs, and any other information known by the investment adviser.

(b) Exercising any discretionary power in placing an order for the purchase or sale of securities for a client without obtaining written discretionary authority from the client within ten (10) business days after the date of the first transaction placed pursuant to oral discretionary authority, unless the discretionary power relates solely to the price at which, or the time when, an order involving a definite amount of a specified security shall be executed, or both.

(c) Inducing trading in a client's account that is excessive in size or frequency in view of the financial resources, investment objectives and character of the account in light of the fact that an investment adviser or an investment adviser representative in such situations can directly benefit from the number of securities transactions effected in a client's account. The rule appropriately forbids an excessive number of transaction orders to be induced by an adviser for a "customer's account."

(d) Placing an order to purchase or sell a security for the account of a client without authority to do so.

(e) Placing an order to purchase or sell a security for the account of a client upon instruction of a third party without first having obtained a written third-party trading authorization from the client.

(f) Borrowing money or securities from a client unless the client is a broker-dealer, an affiliate of the investment adviser, or a financial institution engaged in the business of loaning funds.

(g) Loaning money to a client unless the investment adviser is a financial institution engaged in the business of loaning funds or the client is an affiliate of the investment adviser.

(h) Misrepresenting to any advisory client, or prospective advisory client, the qualifications of the investment adviser or any employee of the investment adviser, or misrepresenting the nature of the advisory services being offered or fees to be charged for such service, or to omit to state a material fact necessary to make the statements made regarding qualifications, services or fees, in light of the circumstances under which they are made, not misleading.

(i) Providing a report or recommendation to any advisory client prepared by someone other than the adviser without disclosing that fact. (This prohibition does not apply to a situation where the adviser uses published research reports or statistical analyses to render advice or where an adviser orders such a report in the normal course of providing service.)

(j) Charging a client an unreasonable advisory fee.

(k) Failing to disclose to clients in writing before any advice is rendered any material conflict of interest relating to the adviser, or any of its employees which could reasonably be expected to impair the rendering of unbiased and objective advice including:

(1.) Compensation arrangements connected with advisory services to clients which are in addition to compensation from such clients for such services; and

(2.) Charging a client an advisory fee for rendering advice when a commission for executing securities transactions pursuant to such advice will be received by the adviser or its employees.

(l) Guaranteeing a client that a specific result will be achieved (gain or no loss) with advice which will be rendered.

(m) [Alternative 1] Publishing, circulating or distributing any advertisement which does not comply with Rule 206(4)-1 under the Investment Advisers Act of 1940.

(m) [Alternative 2] (1.) Except as otherwise provided in subsection (2.), it shall constitute a dishonest or unethical practice within the meaning of [Uniform Act Sec. 102(a)(4)] for any investment adviser or investment adviser representative, directly or indirectly, to use any advertisement that does any one of the following:

(i.) Refers to any testimonial of any kind concerning the investment adviser or investment adviser representative or concerning any advice, analysis, report, or other service rendered by such investment adviser or investment adviser representative.

(ii.) Refers to past specific recommendations of the investment adviser or investment adviser representative that were or would have been profitable to any person; except that an investment adviser or investment adviser representative may furnish or offer to furnish a list of all recommendations made by the investment adviser or investment adviser representative within the immediately preceding period of not less than one year if the advertisement or list also includes both of the following:

(A) The name of each security recommended, the date and nature of each recommendation, the market price at that time, the price at which the recommendation was to be acted upon, and the most recently available market price of each such security.

(B) A legend on the first page in prominent print or type that states that the reader should not assume that recommendations made in the future will be profitable or will equal the performance of the securities in the list.

(iii.) Represents that any graph, chart, formula, or other device being offered can in and of itself be used to determine which securities to buy or sell, or when to buy or sell them; or which represents, directly or indirectly, that any graph, chart, formula, or other device being offered will assist any person in making that person's own decisions as to which securities to buy or sell, or when to buy or sell them, without prominently disclosing in such advertisement the limitations thereof and the difficulties with respect to its use.

(iv.) Represents that any report, analysis, or other service will be furnished for free or without charge, unless such report, analysis, or other service actually is or will be furnished entirely free and without any direct or indirect condition or obligation.

(v.) Represents that the [Administrator] has approved any advertisement.

(vi.) Contains any untrue statement of a material fact, or that is otherwise false or misleading.

(2.) With respect to federal covered advisers, the provisions of this section only apply to the extent permitted by Section 203A of the Investment Advisers Act of 1940.

(3.) For the purposes of this section, the term "advertisement" shall include any notice, circular, letter, or other written communication addressed to more than one person, or any notice or other announcement in any electronic or paper publication, by radio or television, or by any medium, that offers any one of the following:

(i.) Any analysis, report, or publication concerning securities.

(ii.) Any analysis, report, or publication that is to be used in making any determination as to when to buy or sell any security or which security to buy or sell.

(iii.) Any graph, chart, formula, or other device to be used in making any determination as to when to buy or sell any security, or which security to buy or sell.

(iv.) Any other investment advisory service with regard to securities.

(n) Disclosing the identity, affairs, or investments of any client unless required by law to do so, or unless consented to by the client.

(o) Taking any action, directly or indirectly, with respect to those securities or funds in which any client has any beneficial interest, where the investment adviser has custody or possession of such securities or funds when the advisor's action is subject to and does not comply with the requirements of Rule 102e(1)-1. and any subsequent amendments.

(p) Entering into, extending or renewing any investment advisory contract, unless such contract is in writing and discloses, in substance, the services to be provided, the term of the contract, the advisory fee, the formula for computing the fee, the amount of prepaid fee to be returned in the event of contract termination or non-performance, whether the contract grants discretionary power to the adviser and that no assignment of such contract shall be made by the investment adviser without the consent of the other party to the contract.

(q) Failing to establish, maintain, and enforce written policies and procedures reasonably designed to prevent the misuse of material nonpublic information contrary to the provisions of Section 204A of the Investment Advisers Act of 1940.

(r) Entering into, extending, or renewing any advisory contract contrary to the provisions of Section 205 of the Investment Advisers Act of 1940. This provision shall apply to all advisers and investment adviser representatives registered or required to be registered under this Act, notwithstanding whether such adviser or representative would be exempt from federal registration pursuant to Section 203(b) of the Investment Advisers Act of 1940.

(s) To indicate, in an advisory contract, any condition, stipulation, or provisions binding any person to waive compliance with any provision of this act or of the Investment Advisers Act of 1940, or any other practice contrary to the provisions of Section 215 of the Investment Advisers Act of 1940.

(t) Engaging in any act, practice, or course of business which is fraudulent, deceptive, or manipulative in contrary to the provisions of Section 206(4) of the Investment Advisers Act of 1940, notwithstanding the fact that such investment adviser or investment adviser representative is not registered or required to be registered under Section 203 of the Investment Advisers Act of 1940.

(u) Engaging in conduct or any act, indirectly or through or by any other person, which would be unlawful for such person to do directly under the provisions of this act or any rule or regulation thereunder. The conduct set forth above is not inclusive. Engaging in other conduct such as non-disclosure, incomplete disclosure, or deceptive practices shall be deemed an unethical business practice. The federal statutory and regulatory provisions referenced herein shall apply to investment advisers, investment adviser representatives and federal covered advisers to the extent permitted by the National Securities Markets Improvement Act of 1996 (Pub. L. No. 104-290).

EXPLANATION. The first point this model rule makes is that an investment adviser, investment adviser representative, or federal covered adviser is a fiduciary and has a duty to act primarily for the benefit of its clients. Of course, we've already mentioned that, but notice how NASAA mentions it right off the bat in this model rule. It's that important.

Also, by listing all three terms (investment adviser, investment adviser representative, federal covered adviser), the document reminds us that each term is related yet different. The investment adviser and federal covered adviser are business entities, while the investment adviser representative is the individual who represents one of those business entities. Also, there is a difference between an "investment adviser" and a "federal covered adviser." The difference is that the federal covered adviser is registered with the SEC, while the "investment adviser" is subject to the state's registration authority. Notice how the provisions laid out in this document (written by a group of state regulators) "apply to federal covered advisers to the extent that the conduct alleged is fraudulent, deceptive, or as otherwise permitted by [NSMIA]."

Okay, so that's the introduction. Let's now look at the specific items mentioned in the model rule. Item (a) reminds investment advisers not to recommend the purchase or sale of any security unless they have reasonable grounds to believe it's a suitable recommendation. Notice how the item specifically mentions clients "to whom supervisory, management or consulting services are provided." Another type of advisory service is called "impersonal advice," and this advice does not even claim to be specific to the individual client. There is a world of difference between delivering the same advice to a group that is generally interested in, say, value investing, and providing "supervisory, management or consulting services" to a specific client. If I'm supervising your investment activities, managing your portfolio, or getting paid as a consultant, the regulators expect me to know something about your unique financial situation before I start running my mouth or running the meter.

The second item is a little surprising to me. I would have figured the adviser needs written discretionary authority from the client before using discretionary power, but it turns out the client can give oral authorization to get the discretionary nature of the account going. The adviser then has 10 business days after the first discretionary order is placed to obtain written authorization.

Broker-dealers need written discretionary authority before making any discretionary trades because they get compensated per transaction and the temptation to just start buying stuff on their client's behalf would be overwhelming. But, an investment adviser is compensated as a percentage of the assets. So, if the adviser enters foolish trades, they'll not only not gain from it, but also their fee will start going down with the assets. One percent of $1,000,000 is better than 1% of $800,000, after all. Whatever percent the client account drops, so drops the adviser's compensation. They're not stockbrokers who collected a commission a long time ago and now have no skin in the game.

Discretion allows a broker-dealer or adviser to enter transactions on behalf of a client without first talking to the client. If they can choose which security is to be bought or sold and how many shares, they are using discretion.

However, if the client knows he wants to buy 300 shares of ORCL today, that order does not require written discretionary authority. Choosing what time of day to enter a specific order does not make the regulators nervous, in other words. Choosing which security to buy or sell, or how many shares to buy or sell—those are big decisions that the adviser can only make if granted discretionary authority by the client.

While portfolio managers usually have discretion and do not talk to clients before placing trades, there could be financial planners out there who might otherwise over-step their authority. If the financial planner wants to log into an online broker-dealer's trading platform and enter a trade where the customer fully named the important details, not a problem—even if the financial planner decided to wait until the close to place the trade that same day. But, a financial planner without discretionary authority can never fill in the important details of a trade or decide to place a trade without first discussing it with the client.

Item (c) says that advisers should not try to induce their clients to become frantic traders, especially if the adviser is getting compensated for those transactions. So, churning is always a bad idea, and an even worse idea if the adviser is also benefitting from the trades.

Item (d) reminds advisers and their IARs not to purchase or sell securities when they have no authorization from the client to do so. I can't imagine trying to manage a client's portfolio unless I had the discretion to make trades as I saw fit, but that doesn't mean all investment advisers have been granted that discretion. If the adviser or IAR is unauthorized to execute transactions without talking to the client, doing so is a violation known as an "unauthorized transaction."

Item (e) is saying that if your client's husband calls up and says his wife wants you to sell 1,000 shares of MSFT, you can only do so if the client has given her husband written trading authorization and you have that on file. Otherwise, you must talk to your client, the wife. Don't take orders from anybody but your client, unless the third party has been granted written third-party trading authorization. This includes lawyers, accountants, insurance agents, and even the executor of someone's estate while the individual is alive. Not one of those individuals has any inherent right to discuss the investor's account with your firm. Doing so is a breach of your fiduciary duty, since client confidentiality is part of that duty.

Items (f) and (g) address borrowing and lending. Borrowing assets from clients is a practice that makes regulators nervous. An investment adviser can only borrow money or securities from a client if the client is a broker-dealer, an affiliate of the adviser, or a financial institution in the business of making loans (Bank, Savings & Loan, Thrift, etc.).

Examples of "affiliates" of an investment adviser include other business entities connected to the adviser, the owners/principals of the advisory firm, and the investment adviser representatives who have been with the firm at least one year. The regulators aren't going to stop the advisory business from getting capital from related entities and those who run the firm. What they won't do is let the adviser borrow money from any client who is not an institution in the business of lending money. And, if an IAR has a client who works as a mortgage broker, the IAR can get a mortgage through that client's business. The IAR, however, had better not ask the client to personally lend him money.

Advisers and IARs also may not provide loans to clients. For example, if a wrap-fee program requires a minimum account balance of $1 million, neither the firm nor their IARs can lend clients any shortfalls. Clients of an investment adviser can borrow through the adviser's affiliated lending institution. And the firm can provide loans to its own affiliates. But lending to advisory clients is an unethical and prohibited business practice for investment advisers and IARs.

Item (h) reminds advisers not to mislead prospects or clients about their qualifications, the qualifications of employees, or the services provided, or the fees charged for performing those services. For example, if an adviser sells a software program designed to reduce volatility in a fixed-income portfolio, they are required to explain the difficulties and limitations to its use. If the program is described as something to "avoid risk" or "avoid investment losses," chances are the regulators will not be pleased.

Item (i) says that if an adviser provides a report or a recommendation to a client when, in fact, that report or recommendation was prepared by someone else, the adviser must disclose the fact and tell the client who provided it. However, if the adviser orders prepared reports or uses published research/statistical analyses to come up with their own recommendations, that's different. No disclosure there. The adviser in this case is just doing their homework. ADV Part 2 would also indicate that the adviser uses reports and statistical analyses prepared by outside parties to render advice to clients, providing plenty of disclosure to prospects and clients.

Item (j) prohibits advisers from gouging their clients. What would make the fee "unreasonable"? The regulators are indicating that you and your firm have two options here: 1) you can charge fees that are reasonable or 2) the state can schedule a disciplinary hearing.

The next item, (k), is saying that if the advice being given will also lead to the advisory firm or any of its employees receiving a commission or any other compensation should the client act on the advice, that potential conflict of interest must be disclosed in writing. In other words, wouldn't you feel better about paying for investment advice knowing that the advice is being given by an objective professional, rather than someone who will make a commission if you take the advice? For example, if the IAR or adviser receives 12b-1 fees on the mutual funds recommended or purchased for the client, this needs to be disclosed.

Item (l) is the familiar prohibition against guarantees. Don't guarantee a profit. Don't guarantee against a loss.

Now, nobody said the word "guaranteed" can't be used. We're saying that investment advisers and IARs don't offer guarantees. The US Treasury guarantees the timely payment of interest and principal on a US T-Bond, and there are even guaranteed corporate bonds where a third party promises to pay if the issuer cannot. But, people in the securities industry do not guarantee investors against a loss or guarantee they will make a certain level of profit.

Item (m) is a little confusing at first, what with the whole "[Alternative 1], [Alternative 2]" thing. Either way, the item is telling advisers to be careful about the advertisements they put out. If they list the performance of their stock picks, the period shown must be at least one year. If the entire list of stock picks is not provided, the advertisement must indicate how the reader can obtain the complete list free of charge.

Also, testimonials from clients are not allowed.

```
Investment Advisers Act of 1940, Rule 206(4)-1...It shall
constitute a fraudulent, deceptive, or manipulative act,
practice, or course of business for any investment adviser to
publish, circulate, or distribute any advertisement...which refers,
directly or indirectly, to any testimonial of any kind concerning
the investment adviser or concerning any advice, analysis, report
or other service rendered by such investment adviser...
```

Item (n) is about client confidentiality. RIAs and IARs may not divulge the identity, affairs, or investments of clients to anyone else without the client's written permission or some sort of legal order to turn the information over to a court or the police. It might be tempting to show prospects what they have done for, say, Oprah Winfrey's account, but both Ms. Winfrey and the state securities Administrator would probably have a problem with that. Note that advisers cannot divulge the financial affairs or the identity of advisory clients unless they have the clients' written permission or a legal demand to turn over the information.

Item (o) boils down to, "Be careful what you do with client funds/securities under custody." The Rule 102e(1)-1 referenced in this item is also currently viewable at the NASAA website.

Item (p) reminds us that all advisory contracts must be in writing and must stipulate all the terms of the contract: services provided, term of the contract, advisory fees, formula for computing the fees, the amount of prepaid fees that are refundable, whether the adviser has discretion, and that no assignment of contract can occur without client consent. Even if the adviser did not end up assigning a client's contract to another party without consent, the fact that their contract with the client failed to state that provision could lead to problems with the regulators. So, before an advisory firm can sell a majority ownership position to a new entity, all client contracts would have to be re-executed with the new entity. Otherwise, the contracts would have been improperly "assigned" without client consent.

Item (q) is talking about the adviser's code of ethics policy. Any "access person" or individual at the firm who could easily see what the portfolio managers are up to is required to report his/her holdings to the advisory firm. We cover this in more detail elsewhere. Item (r) reminds us that state regulators often use SEC rules as their own—if the advisory firm has contracts that conflict with SEC rules under the "Act of 1940," the state Administrator has a problem with that.

Item (s) reminds us that no waivers of any provision are allowed. So, if the adviser wants to charge a client in a way that's not allowed, he and the client cannot just draw up a waiver indicating that they both mutually agree to violate the laws and rules governing the industry. Any such "waiver of compliance" would be considered null and void in an Administrative or court proceeding, anyway, which means it would not be worth the paper it's printed on, much less the legal fees spent having it drawn up.

Item (t) points out that whether an adviser or IAR is subject to state registration, federal-only, or exempted from registration at the federal level, they can get in trouble for fraudulent, deceptive practices by the state Administrator. Item (u) points out that beyond fraudulent/manipulative practices, an investment adviser or IAR can get in trouble for engaging in any conduct that is a violation of the securities laws of the state and the rules thereunder.

And the final blurb reminds us that this list is "not inclusive," meaning it does not represent all the issues that can lead to regulatory problems for investment advisers and their IARs. The issues discussed in the model rule are common regulatory concerns for the advisory business.

Business Practices for Broker-Dealers and Agents

As we've mentioned, broker-dealers are in the business of "effecting transactions in securities for the account of others or for their own account." That means they can help someone buy or sell securities and charge a commission, or they can take the other side of the trade and make a profit. In the first case, they act as a broker for the account of others. In the second case, they act as a dealer for their own account.

We saw that investment advisers register with Form ADV. Not surprisingly, broker-dealers register with **Form BD**. On this form, the regulators request information on owners and executive officers of the firm, so if any of those individuals also wants to act as a securities agent, no separate registration is required. These individuals include the board of directors, the CEO, CFO, Chief Compliance Officer, and other executive officers, and anyone who has a certain level of ownership in the firm.

A broker-dealer hires principals to supervise the firm's operations: the registered representatives, the communications, and the written customer complaints, etc. It's important to know that if you're a registered representative/securities agent, you must consult with your principal on just about everything. , the principal doesn't have a magic pen that can make prohibited activities suddenly okay. If you get a test question that implies that violating the rules is somehow okay as long as you receive "prior principal approval," that could be a red flag. Yes, you do need prior principal approval to do many things in the industry, but getting a principal to sign off on something also doesn't make it automatically okay to do.

Written customer complaints must be forwarded immediately to a compliance principal, of course. A principal must review and accept each new customer account. A principal must review all the trade/order tickets placed by the firm that day. Retail communications delivered to > 25 retail investors first must be approved by a compliance principal, as well.

While the broker-dealer (the firm) registers with Form BD, principals and agents are registered as "associated persons" of the firm through a **Form U4**. Depending on who's filling it out, Form U4 can be painful and embarrassing. The form requires the applicant's residential history over the previous five years. Then, a detailed employment history over the previous 10 years. And then it wants to know about any felonies and certain misdemeanors—both charges and convictions.

And, unlike with the 5-year residential and 10-year employment history, the form asks if the individual has <u>ever</u> been charged with any felony or any misdemeanor involving "investments or an investment-related business or any fraud, false statements or omissions, wrongful taking of property, bribery, perjury, forgery, counterfeiting, extortion, or a conspiracy to commit any of these offenses?"

Even if the individual has never been charged with, convicted of, or pled guilty to a crime, there are sections asking about any regulatory actions by any state or federal regulator of virtually any financially based industry, any civil actions in which a court handed down a penalty, or even arbitration awards to customers over a certain amount. U4 asks if the applicant has "ever voluntarily resigned, been discharged or permitted to resign after allegations were made that accused [him] of:

(1) violating investment-related statutes, regulations, rules, or industry standards of conduct?
(2) fraud or the wrongful taking of property?
(3) failure to supervise in connection with investment-related statutes, regulations, rules or industry standards of conduct?"

And, in case that wasn't enough probing, the form then asks about creditors and bankruptcies over the previous 10 years. The regulators don't prevent someone from associating with a firm just because of a bankruptcy or short sale on a house, but they want the information disclosed. And, saying "no" when the real answer was "yes" is a career-ender. Filing a false report, application, or document with a securities regulator is grounds for disciplinary action. Usually, the individual or firm who filed it will lose their registration.

So, as you can see, there's the license exam phase of the registration process that takes out a certain percentage of applicants, but even after many applicants pass their exams, the U4 phase of the process can delay the registration and even end it outright. For example, you could get a 90% on your exam, but if you also have a recent conviction for shoplifting, the regulators can prevent you from getting licensed.

But, a misdemeanor involving the following would not be considered investment-related:

- Possession of a controlled substance
- Public intoxication
- DUI
- Assault, battery

If those charges were felony convictions, it could be a game-over situation, but if they were misdemeanors they would not even have to be disclosed on Form U4. Would the regulators even find out or hassle the applicant about them? Yes, but the true game-over situations involve any felony at all, or any misdemeanor that involves money or dishonesty.

While the state securities Administrator can establish minimum net capital requirements for broker-dealers, net capital requirements are set by the SEC and enforced by FINRA. So, the exam might have an answer choice such as, "The Administrator may establish minimum net capital requirements for broker-dealers subject to the limits of the Securities Exchange Act of 1934." And, they could make it a tough question by emphasizing that the broker-dealer has a principal office in State A and then another state has a higher net capital—what requirement is the BD required to meet? The answer would involve meeting the net capital established by the SEC under the Securities Exchange Act of 1934.

If the principal of a broker-dealer fudges on the firm's financial reports with FINRA, he is, thereby, causing the firm to fail to comply with this requirement from the "Exchange Act." Remember that broker-dealers typically hold customer assets, so, like a bank, their own balance sheet is important. Un-invested customer cash is not wrapped up and placed in a vault. Rather, the broker-dealer parks it in an interest-bearing account and must be able to pay it upon demand. Are they good for it? That's what minimum net capital requirements are all about. And the SEC has been establishing them since the passage of the Securities Exchange Act of 1934.

The state securities Administrator can perform routine inspections of broker-dealers doing business in the state, and they can inspect them subject to investor complaints or information that the securities laws are being violated. The Administrator can require books and records of broker-dealers, but, as a practical matter, they can just insist that the firms meet the requirements of FINRA, many of which are dictated by the SEC. Broker-dealers who have discretion over customer accounts or custody of customer assets are usually required to maintain a surety bond or meet a minimum net capital requirement. In other words, in case customers end up with claims of churning, unauthorized trading, or missing assets, there is something backing up the ability of the firm to make good.

Client Funds and Securities

Criminals pulling in large amounts of cash through illegal activities should be careful not to drive $85,000 automobiles while having no job or business to explain their good fortune. If not, no matter how carefully they run their criminal enterprise, they can end up being convicted of racketeering and tax evasion due to their inattention to financials.

Therefore, criminals often use elaborate schemes to take their "dirty" money and make it "clean." Maybe they buy a car wash and write up phony receipts for phantom customers to match that up with a few hundred thousand dollars of illegal profits that end up being "cleaned" in the wash so to speak.

Money laundering is the process of taking illegal profits and disguising them as clean money to avoid detection or proof of any criminal activity. The three phases of money laundering are:

- Placement
- Layering
- Integration

Placement is the first stage in the cycle in which illegally generated funds are placed into the financial system or are smuggled out of the country. The goals of the money launderer are to remove the cash from where it was acquired to avoid detection from the authorities, and to then transform it into other assets, e.g., travelers' checks, money orders, etc.

Layering is the first attempt at disguising the source of the ownership of the funds by creating complex layers of transactions. The purpose of layering is to disassociate the dirty money from the source of the crime through a complicated web of financial transactions. Typically, layers are created by moving money in and out of offshore bank accounts of shell companies, through electronic funds transfers (EFTs). Because there are over 500,000 wire transfers circling the globe e day, most of which are legitimate, there isn't enough information disclosed on any single wire transfer to know how clean or dirty the money is. This provides an excellent way for money launderers to move their dirty money. Other forms used by launderers are complex dealings with stock, commodity and futures brokers. Given the sheer volume of daily transactions, and the high degree of anonymity available, the chances of transactions being traced are insignificant. In other words, broker-dealers are great places to launder money, which is why broker-dealers need to help the federal government clamp down on terrorists and other criminals trying to layer dirty money through a flurry of trading activity.

Integration is the final stage in the process. In this stage the money is integrated into the legitimate financial system. Integration of the now-clean money into the economy is accomplished by making it appear to have been legally earned. By this stage, it is difficult to distinguish "clean" financial assets from "dirty."

The Bank Secrecy Act (BSA) authorizes the U.S. Treasury Department to require financial institutions such as banks and broker-dealers to maintain records of personal financial transactions that "have a high degree of usefulness in criminal, tax and regulatory investigations and proceedings." It also authorizes the Treasury Department to require any financial institution to report any "suspicious transaction relevant to a possible violation of law or regulation." These reports, called "Suspicious Activity Reports," are filed with the Treasury Department's Financial Crimes Enforcement Network ("FinCEN").

This is done secretly (thus the law's name), without the consent or knowledge of bank customers, any time a financial institution determines that a transaction is suspicious. The reports are made available electronically to e U.S. Attorney's Office and to 59 law enforcement agencies, including the FBI, Secret Service, and Customs Service.

Recently, the U.S. Treasury Department used the Bank Secrecy Act (BSA) to require that for transmittals of funds of $3,000 or more, broker-dealers are required to obtain and keep certain specified information concerning the parties sending and receiving those funds. In addition, broker-dealers must include this information on the actual transmittal order. Also, any cash transactions over $10,000 require the same type of record keeping. For these, broker-dealers must file a **Currency Transaction Report (CTR)** with FinCEN.

Why? Because terrorist and other criminal organizations fund their operations through money laundering. Since broker-dealers are financial institutions, they're lumped in with banks and other custodians, all of them required to do all kinds of record keeping to help the government prevent these operations.

With the passage of the USA Patriot Act broker-dealers and other financial institutions must help the government monitor suspicious activity that could be tied to money laundering. Broker-dealers now must report any transaction that involves at least $5,000 if the broker-dealer knows, suspects, or has reason to suspect that it doesn't pass the smell test. A suspicious activity report (SAR) would be filed if the transaction falls within one of four classes:

- the transaction involves funds derived from illegal activity or is intended or conducted to hide or disguise funds or assets derived from illegal activity;
- the transaction is designed to evade the requirements of the Bank Secrecy Act
- the transaction appears to serve no business or apparent lawful purpose or is not the sort of transaction in which the customer would be expected to engage and for which the broker/dealer knows of no reasonable explanation after examining the available facts; or
- the transaction involves the use of the broker/dealer to facilitate criminal activity

As a FINRA notice to members announces, "To help the government fight the funding of terrorism and money laundering activities, federal law requires financial institutions to obtain, verify and record information that identifies each person who opens an account." The notice explains obligations under the Customer Identification Program (CIP) for financial institutions including banks and broker-dealers. The first thing member firms must do is establish a written policy for establishing and documenting the identity of each customer for whom the firm opens an account.

As of publication, Anti-Money Laundering requirements under the Bank Secrecy Act do not (yet) apply to investment advisers. If FINCEN's proposed rule goes through, however, federal covered advisers will be subject to such requirements. State-registered investment advisers would typically have a broker-dealer provide custody, and that firm would be subject to the requirements above.

Under the Customer Identification Program broker-dealers must obtain an individual's name, date of birth, residential address, citizenship, and social security/taxpayer ID. If the customer is not a U.S. citizen, the firm will need:

- taxpayer identification number
- passport number and country of issuance
- alien identification card number or government-issued identification showing nationality, residence and a photograph of the customer.

Even the U.S. citizen may need to show a photo ID, just as you do when you take your exam. E time I have opened an online brokerage account, for example, I have had to scan my driver's license and email or fax that to the broker-dealer, who has the obligation to make sure I'm not opening up a bogus account through which I will launder money.

The broker-dealer also must inquire if the customer is an employee of a broker-dealer or a self-regulatory organization. If so, the employer must be notified (which was already a requirement under FINRA rules).

And, the broker-dealer must inquire if the customer is a "corporate insider" of a publicly traded company. That term includes corporate officers and members of the board of directors, as well as anyone who owns 10% or more of the common stock. For example, if Jeff Bezos opens an account with your firm, he is a "corporate insider" at Amazon as well as any of the companies for which he serves on the board of directors, or owns 10% or more of the outstanding shares. Corporate insiders are constrained under the Securities Act of 1933's Rule 144. Because Mr. Bezos knows more about what's about to happen at Amazon than ordinary shareholders, the SEC wants to monitor his trading activities on AMZN closely. First, he cannot sell any of his holdings in AMZN unless he has held the shares at least one year. A Form 144 must be filed for the proposed sale no later than at the time of sale, and he can sell only a limited amount over the next 90 days (1% of the outstanding stock or the most recent four-week average trading volume). The sale of securities also may not be advertised.

So, as you can see, it would be great to have a billionaire customer like Jeff Bezos, but your firm will have added obligations surrounding his holdings in AMZN or any company for which he either sits on the board of directors or owns 10% or more of the shares.

Some customers are human beings, others are legal entities. As the same notice to members explains, "A corporation, partnership, trust or other legal entity may need to provide other information, such as its principal place of business, local office, employer identification number, certified articles of incorporation, government-issued business license, a partnership agreement or a trust agreement."

The federal government now maintains an **Office of Foreign Asset Control (OFAC)** designed to protect against the threat of terrorism. This office maintains a list of individuals and organizations viewed as a threat to the U.S. Broker-dealers and other financial institutions now need to make sure they aren't setting up accounts for these organizations, or—if they are—they need to block/freeze the assets. As the Department of Treasury explains, "As part of its enforcement efforts, OFAC publishes a list of individuals and companies owned or controlled by, or acting for or on behalf of, targeted countries. It also lists individuals, groups, and entities, such as terrorists and narcotics traffickers designated under programs that are not country-specific. Collectively, such individuals and companies are called 'Specially Designated Nationals' or SDNs. The assets of such persons are blocked, and U.S. persons are generally prohibited from dealing with them."

NASAA Policy Statement on Dishonest or Unethical Business Practices of Broker-Dealers and Agents

```
NASAA      ADOPTED      STATEMENT      OF      POLICY      5/23/1983
DISHONEST  OR  UNETHICAL  BUSINESS  PRACTICES  OF  BROKER-DEALERS  AND
AGENTS

Each  broker-dealer  and  agent  shall  observe  high  standards  of
commercial  honor  and  just  and  equitable  principles  of  trade  in
the  conduct  of  their  business.  Acts  and  practices,  including  but
not  limited  to  the  following,  are  considered  contrary  to  such
```

standards and may constitute grounds for denial, suspension or revocation of registration or such other action authorized by statute.

1. BROKER-DEALERS

a. Engaging in a pattern of unreasonable and unjustifiable delays in the delivery of securities purchased by any of its customers and/or in the payment upon request of free credit balances reflecting completed transactions of any of its customers;

b. Inducing trading in a customer's account which is excessive in size or frequency in view of the financial resources and character of the account;

c. Recommending to a customer the purchase, sale or exchange of any security without reasonable grounds to believe that such transaction or recommendation is suitable for the customer based upon reasonable inquiry concerning the customer's investment objectives, financial situation and needs, and any other relevant information known by the broker-dealer;

d. Executing a transaction on behalf of a customer without authorization to do so;

e. Exercising any discretionary power in effecting a transaction for a customer's account without first obtaining written discretionary authority from the customer, unless the discretionary power relates solely to the time and/or price for the executing of orders;

f. Executing any transaction in a margin account without securing from the customer a properly executed written margin agreement promptly after the initial transaction in the account;

g. Failing to segregate customers' free securities or securities held in safekeeping;

h. Hypothecating a customer's securities without having a lien thereon unless the broker-dealer secures from the customer a properly executed written consent promptly after the initial transaction, except as permitted by Rules of the Securities and Exchange Commission;

i. Entering into a transaction with or for a customer at a price not reasonably related to the current market price of the security or receiving an unreasonable commission or profit;

j. Failing to furnish to a customer purchasing securities in an offering, no later than the due date of confirmation of the transaction, either a final prospectus or a preliminary prospectus and an additional document, which together include all information set forth in the final prospectus;

k. Charging unreasonable and inequitable fees for services performed, including miscellaneous services such as collection of monies due for principal, dividends or interest, exchange or transfer of securities, appraisals, safekeeping, or custody of securities and other services related to its securities business;

l. Offering to buy from or sell to any person any security at a stated price unless such broker-dealer is prepared to purchase or sell, as the case may be, at such price and under such conditions as are stated at the time of such offer to buy or sell;

m. Representing that a security is being offered to a customer "at the market" or a price relevant to the market price unless such broker-dealer knows or has reasonable grounds to believe that a market for such security exists other than that made, created or controlled by such broker-dealer;

n. Effecting any transaction in, or inducing the purchase or sale of, any security by means of any manipulative, deceptive or fraudulent device, practice, plan, program, design or contrivance, which may include but not be limited to;

(1) Effecting any transaction in a security which involves no change in the beneficial ownership thereof;

(2) Entering an order or orders for the purchase or sale of any security with the knowledge that an order or orders of substantially the same size, at substantially the same time and substantially the same price, for the sale of any such security, has been or will be entered by or for the same or different parties for the purpose of creating a false or misleading appearance of active trading in the security or a false or misleading appearance with respect to the market for the security;

(3) Effecting, alone or with one or more other persons, a series of transactions in any security creating actual or apparent active trading in such security or raising or depressing the price of such security, for the purpose of inducing the purchase or sale of such security by others;

o. Guaranteeing a customer against loss in any securities account of such customer carried by the broker-dealer or in any securities transaction effected by the broker-dealer or in any securities transaction effected by the broker-dealer with or for such customer;

p. Publishing or circulating, or causing to be published or circulated, any notice, circular, advertisement, newspaper article, investment service, or communication of any kind which purports to report any transaction as a purchase or sale of any security unless such broker-dealer believes that such transaction was a bona fide purchase or sale of such security; or which purports to quote the bid price or asked price for any security, unless such broker-dealer believes that such quotation represents a bona fide bid for, or offer of, such security;

q. Using any advertising or sales presentation in such a fashion as to be deceptive or misleading; or

r. Failing to disclose that the broker-dealer is controlled by, controlling, affiliated with or under common control with the issuer of any security before entering into any contract with or for a customer for the purchase or sale of such security, the existence of such control to such customer, and if such disclosure is not made in writing, it shall be supplemented by the giving or sending of written disclosure at or before the completion of the transaction;

s. Failing to make a bona fide public offering of all of the securities allotted to a broker-dealer for distribution, whether acquired as an underwriter, a selling group member, or from a member participating in the distribution as an underwriter or selling group member; or

t. Failure or refusal to furnish a customer, upon reasonable request, information to which he is entitled, or to respond to a formal written request or complaint.

2. AGENTS

a. Engaging in the practice of lending or borrowing money or securities from a customer, or acting as a custodian for money, securities or an executed stock power of a customer;

b. Effecting securities transactions not recorded on the regular books or records of the broker-dealer which the agent represents, unless the transactions are authorized in writing by the broker-dealer prior to execution of the transaction;

c. Establishing or maintaining an account containing fictitious information to execute transactions which would otherwise be prohibited;

d. Sharing directly or indirectly in profits or losses in the account of any customer without the written authorization of the customer and the broker-dealer which the agent represents;

e. Dividing or otherwise splitting the agent's commissions, profits or other compensation from the purchase or sale of securities with any person not also registered as an agent for the same broker-dealer, or for a broker-dealer under direct or indirect common control; or

f. Engaging in conduct specified in Subsection 1.b, c, d, e, f, i, j, n, o, p, or q.

[CONDUCT NOT INCLUSIVE.] The conduct set forth above is not inclusive. Engaging in other conduct such as forgery, embezzlement, nondisclosure, incomplete disclosure or misstatement of material facts, or manipulative or deceptive practices shall also be grounds for denial, suspension or revocation of registration.

EXPLANATION. The policy statement starts with the conduct of broker-dealers and then moves on to the agents who represent them. Item A prohibits unreasonable and unjustifiable delays in delivering securities or in paying out a request from a customer's cash balance. Broker-dealers earn interest on their clients' un-invested cash, so they would probably prefer to sit on that client cash for as long as possible. However, if the client has $2,000 of "cash" in her account, the firm must pay her promptly upon request.

Regular-way settlement is "T + 3," so once that trade is completed on the third business day, the customer can request a check for that amount. Also, stocks that pay dividends and bonds that pay interest will build up the cash balance in the investor's account. NASAA is reminding broker-dealers that if their customers want their cash paid out to them, the firms cannot unreasonably delay these requests.

Also, if the broker-dealer has custody of client securities, they must deliver them promptly to the buyer when the client executes a sell order.

Item B is about churning. Churning involves excessive size as well as frequency of trading.

Remember that suitability is the name of the game, and frequent trading is unsuitable for most investors working with a registered representative. Of course, frequent trading does seem to help the agent's paycheck, and broker-dealers do know who their "big producers" are, but NASAA is reminding broker-dealers not to let registered reps encourage frequent trading or the trading of large positions relative to the account balance.

The fact that the agent first discusses all the trades with a customer and talks him into it does not imply there was no churning. It only implies that the agent's recommendations are unsuitable.

Item C is a reminder that when the firm recommends the purchase, sale, or exchange of a security, they must have reasonable grounds to make the recommendation based on an investigation of the client's situation. This brings up many important concepts. First, if the customer calls the firm to place an order, that's an unsolicited transaction in which the broker-dealer has no suitability requirements. But, if the broker-dealer recommends a transaction, they must know that it's suitable. If the client is "unsophisticated," the firm must determine that the client understands the complexities or risks of products such as collateralized mortgage obligations, deferred variable annuities, or securitized viatical settlements.

Item D reminds the firm not to buy or sell securities for a customer if the customer hasn't authorized the broker-dealer to do so. You might be shocked to see how many firms seem to forget this idea, but if the customer hasn't talked to anyone about buying or selling securities, the customer should never see purchases or sales taking place in the account, right? I mean, unless it's an honest mistake or a computer glitch, the firm and the agent(s) will likely face disciplinary action.

Item E is closely related. Before a broker-dealer can choose to enter purchase or sale orders on behalf of a client, without first talking to the client and getting his okay, the customer must grant written discretionary authorization. So, if the firm does not have written discretionary authorization from the customer before making any of those choices, they've made a big mistake.

An exam question might ask what the broker-dealer can do once the client informs the firm that the discretionary authorization form is in the mail. Not much at this point. The broker-dealer needs it signed, in writing, and on file, before they choose the asset, the activity, or the number of shares. The time and price at which an order is executed is not considered a major aspect, so the firm could take a market order from a customer and then have the "time and price discretion" to enter it later, when they're convinced the customer can get a better price—those are called "market not held" orders, by the way. The firm does not need written discretionary authority to choose time/price for a customer order.

So, if the customer says, "Buy 1,000 shares of a software company this morning," the firm would need written discretionary authority to insert the name of a particular company into that order, e.g., Oracle, Microsoft, or Salesforce. But, if the customer said, "Buy 1,000 shares of MSFT at a good price today," the broker-dealer would not need written discretionary authority to execute that as a "market not held" order that will be executed when they think they can get the best price.

Investment advisers can place trades that they feel are suitable, without first talking to the client, after receiving oral authorization from the client for 10 days before getting the authorization in writing. On the other hand, broker-dealers need it in writing before placing any discretionary orders for the customer. Why? Broker-dealers get paid per transaction, regardless of how the trade works out for the client, while advisers have no such incentive.

Item F reminds the firm not to let a customer start trading on margin unless the firm gets a signed margin agreement promptly after the initial transaction. So, discretionary authorization must be received in writing before the first discretionary trade, while for margin accounts the signature can be obtained no later than promptly after the first trade done on margin.

Item G speaks to the bookkeeping requirements for broker-dealers holding customer securities, some of which have been pledged as collateral for the loan in a margin account. NASAA is reminding broker-dealers to keep the customers' fully paid securities separate from the firm's securities or securities pledged as collateral to secure margin loans.

Item H reminds broker-dealers not to pledge customer securities as collateral unless they have written authorization from the customer. In a margin account, the customer signs a hypothecation agreement, giving the broker-dealer the authority to pledge the securities as collateral. But, if a broker-dealer just started pledging the securities that customers thought were in safekeeping as collateral for loans to the firm, we would have an ugly situation on our hands. It would be like finding out that a neighbor just borrowed $300,000 and put your house up as collateral. Even funnier, he can't repay the loan, so the bank is foreclosing on your property. To protect customer assets, broker-dealers need to keep their books stringently so that it's clear that these shares belong to the firm's account, and those belong to the customers.

Item I is straightforward. Let's say that a municipal bond issued by a small school district seldom trades. A customer comes in and wants to liquidate 100 of these bonds. There isn't much of a secondary market for these things, but if the firm knows that the most recent transactions occurred yesterday at $1,100 per bond, they can't give this customer $900 apiece for those same bonds. That's not reasonably related to the market price. The firm also can't charge commissions that are out of line with the industry norms.

Item J requires underwriters to deliver a prospectus "no later than the due date for confirmation." Sometimes, rather than a final prospectus, a final statement is sent out that completes any information not already covered in the preliminary prospectus. Either way, NASAA is reminding firms to deliver a prospectus in a new offering.

Item K reminds firms not to charge unreasonable or inequitable fees for services performed, including a host of various services that broker-dealers provide. The regulators don't spell out maximum fees, but they expect firms to keep their charges reasonable and fair among their various customers. If not, the Administrator can always schedule a hearing.

Point L is talking about a violation called "backing away." If a broker-dealer puts out a firm quote, they had better be prepared to trade at the price they indicate.

Point M is admonishing broker-dealers not to mislead customers by saying that a security is being offered "at the market" if there is no secondary market out there for the security. I have seen several examples of investors getting duped into buying preferred stock in some shaky company and then finding out later that the stock isn't listed or traded anywhere. Maybe one of those investors wants to liquidate and get some of her money back. The broker-dealer can't say that they're offering to buy those shares "at the market" unless they know an actual secondary market for the security exists. If they're the only firm willing to buy that preferred stock, they need to be clear about that.

Item N goes into detail in explaining that market manipulation will get someone into all kinds of trouble. We can't just get together with another firm and buy a block of thinly traded stock, then start creating the illusion of an active market for it, so that we can later dump our stock at a much higher price, all based on our deception and manipulation of the market. Well, we can do it—just not legally.

Item O reminds the firm not to guarantee the customer against a loss. Broker-dealers make suitable recommendations, but they don't protect customers from market losses. If the word "guaranteed" is used, it must be explained clearly to the investor to avoid misleading him. A U.S. Treasury security is guaranteed as to interest and principal by the U.S. Treasury, but it has interest rate and market risk. A corporate bond could be "guaranteed" if a third party promised to pay interest and/or principal in the event of a default, but that also needs to be explained clearly to an investor.

A broker-dealer could sell someone a "put-able bond" or a bond with a "put option" that gives the investor the right to sell the bond back for a set price in exchange for a premium. In this case, there is a written agreement, and it is clear what the customer paid and what the customer would get. But a broker-dealer doesn't tell a customer that if the trade they're recommending goes sour, the broker-dealer will eat the losses for them. They're not insurance companies accepting premiums in exchange for protection against market loss.

Item P reminds broker-dealers not to publish that a transaction has occurred unless they know it occurred. Otherwise the firm might be engaging in market manipulation, trying to make it appear that a stock's price is moving a certain way when it's based on fictitious transactions.

Item Q reminds the firm not to circulate material that is misleading or deceptive. For example, it might be tempting to put out a flyer that shows how much Company XYZ would be worth if over the next 6 months they eliminated $5 billion in debt, increased revenues 10,000%, and slashed costs 89% without resorting to layoffs or pay cuts. You could even show graphs of this incredible turnaround effort. Trouble is, it's all based on wild conjecture, is so improbable as to be nearly impossible and, therefore, should not be circulated at all. It is "nonfactual," misleading, and probably deceptive.

If the broker-dealer is owned by the issuer of the stock that the firm is selling to investors, that's kind of an important detail that should be disclosed, as Point R reminds us. Right? The broker-dealer is recommending that someone buy stock, bonds, or commercial paper in the parent company? Doesn't that sort of directly benefit the broker-dealer even beyond the typical commissions earned?

Item S reminds underwriters not to get greedy when they realize that the stock they're bringing to the primary market is likely to take off like a rocket ship. Might be tempting to hang onto the stock for their own accounts and cancel all the indications of interest, but that would be "failure to make a bona fide offering" and would get the firm into trouble.

Item T is a reminder to give customers the information they are entitled to. Customers are entitled to trade confirmations, account statements, mutual fund prospectuses, etc. They are even entitled to independent research on companies generated by other firms. Broker-dealers must respond to written customer complaints, as well. And, they must keep detailed records on how the complaint was handled.

And then the policy statement addresses agents specifically.

Item A reminds agents not to borrow money from customers unless the customer happens to be a lending institution: bank, savings & loan, thrift, credit union, building & loan, etc. An agent cannot "act as a custodian for" customer money or securities because generally once the client's money goes into the agent's bank or brokerage account, it has no chance of coming out again.

Item B warns against executing transactions not recorded on the books and records of the firm unless the agent has obtained written authorization from the firm to do so. An official order to deny an agent's license in the State of Washington told the sad story of an agent who got an elderly investor to cut him three personal checks for $50,000, all of which ended up in his brokerage account. So, right there, he has "acted as a custodian for client money" and "commingled client funds with his own," which is, to say the least, ill-advised. But then when he started executing trades, the Administrator could also add item B to the list of allegations, since those transactions were certainly not recorded on the regular books or records of the broker-dealer, who knew nothing about the little scheme.

Item C is clear. If there is an offering of stock open only to accredited investors, and your customer isn't close to meeting the net worth and income requirements, would it be okay to indicate a higher net worth and income on the required paperwork to allow him to buy the limited offering?

No. Opening accounts based on fictitious information is a major violation. It also shows why convictions for forgery or perjury are relevant to the industry.

Item D reminds us that, typically, agents should not share profits and/or losses with a customer. The only exception is when they're in a joint account with the customer and they have received the customer's authorization as well as the broker-dealer's.

Item E makes it clear that an agent can only split commissions with registered agents at the firm or a firm directly related to the firm—such as a subsidiary, for example. So, agents can split commissions, if the agent is registered and works for the same firm directly or indirectly. Many agents' assistants get their licenses to take client orders and share commissions with their agents. That's fine. But it wouldn't be fine for an agent to tell 20 of his friends that he'll split commissions with them in exchange for referrals. Don't share commissions with unregistered persons.

The policy statement then tells the agent not to do most of the things it told broker-dealers not to do. And then it ends with a reminder that these prohibited activities are not inclusive, meaning there's plenty of other stuff that could get an agent or broker-dealer in hot water with the regulators. They just pointed out some of the things not to do in this policy statement.

Cybersecurity, Privacy, and Data Protection

As the SEC recently stated, "Cybersecurity threats know no boundaries. That's why assessing the readiness of market participants and providing investors with information on how to better protect their online investment accounts from cyber threats has been and will continue to be an important focus of the SEC. Through our engagement with other government agencies as well as with the industry and educating the investing public, we can all work together to reduce the risk of cyber-attacks."

As a guidance publication by the SEC recently pointed out, "The Division has identified the cybersecurity of registered investment companies ("funds") and registered investment advisers ("advisers") as an important issue. Both funds and advisers increasingly use technology to conduct their business activities and need to protect confidential and sensitive information related to these activities from third parties, including information concerning fund investors and advisory clients."

The SEC suggests that advisers:

> Conduct a periodic assessment of: (1) the nature, sensitivity and location of information that the firm collects, processes and/or stores, and the technology systems it uses; (2) internal and external cybersecurity threats to and vulnerabilities of the firm's information and technology systems; (3) security controls and processes currently in place; (4) the impact should the information or technology systems become compromised; and (5) the effectiveness of the governance structure for the management of cybersecurity risk. An effective assessment would assist in identifying potential cybersecurity threats and vulnerabilities so as to better prioritize and mitigate risk.

The SEC also suggests that advisers:

> Create a strategy that is designed to prevent, detect and respond to cybersecurity threats. Such a strategy could include: (1) controlling access to various systems and data via management of user credentials, authentication and authorization methods, firewalls and/or perimeter defenses, tiered access to sensitive information and network resources, network segregation, and system hardening; (2) data encryption; (3) protecting against the loss or exfiltration of sensitive data by restricting the use of removable storage media and deploying software that monitors technology systems for unauthorized intrusions, the loss or exfiltration of sensitive data, or other unusual events; (4) data backup and retrieval; and (5) the development of an incident response plan. Routine testing of strategies could also enhance the effectiveness of any strategy.

As the staff writes in the guidance document, advisers should, "Implement the strategy through written policies and procedures and training that provide guidance to officers and employees concerning applicable threats and measures to prevent, detect and respond to such threats, and that monitor compliance with cybersecurity policies and procedures. Firms may also wish to educate investors and clients about how to reduce their exposure to cyber security threats concerning their accounts."

Along with other important areas—such as the trading of its investment adviser representatives and the security of customer funds—investment advisers need to annually review their policies, procedures, and training related to these important matters.

Sharing customer information with law enforcement officials is one thing. Providing it to telemarketers and identity thieves is quite another. To fight identity theft and to protect customers from having too much of their information shared with people they've never met, the SEC enacted **Regulation S-P**. This regulation requires that:

a financial institution must provide its customers with a notice of its privacy policies and practices, and must not disclose nonpublic personal information about a consumer to nonaffiliated third parties unless the institution provides certain information to the consumer and the consumer has not elected to opt out of the disclosure.

A "**consumer**" is a prospect, someone interested in establishing some type of account. A "**customer**" is a consumer who has a continuing relationship with the firm. A client of an investment adviser is an example of a consumer with a customer relationship to the RIA. Unless all the investment adviser's clients are institutions, the RIA is subject to the same requirements that broker-dealers, banks, and insurance companies are subject to.

Broker-dealers and investment advisers must deliver initial and annual notices to customers explaining their privacy policies and practices, the types of information they share and with whom, and about the opportunity and methods to opt out of their institution's sharing of their nonpublic personal information with nonaffiliated third parties. The initial notice must be provided no later than when the firm establishes a customer relationship with the individual.

Under federal law consumers can only limit certain types of information sharing between a financial institution and another party. The other party is either an affiliate or a non-affiliate, as defined in the financial institution's privacy statement. Consumers can limit the sharing of information with an affiliate that involves the consumer's creditworthiness. The consumer can also limit the information shared to both affiliates and non-affiliates for the purpose of marketing to the consumer. This is why the privacy notice mailed to the consumer typically has a mail-in form allowing him to check any or all of three boxes to limit the types of sharing the financial institution can engage in.

On the other hand, consumers do not have the right under federal law to limit the sharing of information that the financial institution engages in for the following purposes:

- the financial institution's marketing purposes to the consumer (new products, services)
- joint marketing with other financial companies (as defined in privacy notice)
- affiliates' everyday business purposes (information involving transactions and experiences)

Broker-dealers and investment advisers also need written supervisory procedures dealing with the disposal of consumer credit report information. Since firms typically look at a consumer's credit history before opening accounts—especially margin accounts—selling annuities, or providing financial planning services, the firms need to safely dispose of the information rather than just setting it all in a big box out back.

Broker-dealers often must respond to requests for documents under disciplinary investigations. When providing such information through a portable media device (DVD, CD-ROM, flash drive), FINRA requires that the information be encrypted. As FINRA states:

> *the data must be encoded into a form in which meaning cannot be*
> *assigned without the use of a confidential process or key. To help*
> *ensure that encrypted information is secure, persons providing*
> *encrypted information to FINRA via a portable media device are*
> *required to use an encryption method that meets industry standards*
> *for strong encryption and to provide FINRA staff with the*
> *confidential process or key regarding the encryption in a*
> *communication separate from the encrypted information itself (e.g.,*
> *a separate email, fax or letter).*

Beyond responding to the regulators' requests, customer emails also need to be encrypted, and registered representatives should not go around sharing customer information with anyone who doesn't need to know it.

The **FACT Act** is short for the **Fair and Accurate Credit Transactions Act.** Under this federal legislation, the three major credit reporting agencies, in cooperation with the Federal Trade Commission (FTC) set up a website at www.AnnualCreditReport.com that allows consumers to monitor their credit reports. This Act also attempts to reduce identify theft by requiring firms who collect information on individuals to safely dispose of it and by allowing individuals to place alerts on their credit history if they suspect fraudulent transactions. Broker-dealers gather information from consumers through various sales and marketing efforts. The FACT Act requires that they don't toss thousands of post cards or computer hard drives containing personal and financial information about consumers out in a dumpster behind the branch office.

The FACT Act requires the various agencies charged with its implementation to "identify patterns, practices, and specific forms of activity that indicate the possible existence of identity theft." The guidelines must be updated as often as necessary and cannot be inconsistent with the requirement to verify a customer's identity when opening an account. Right? See how we have competing concerns there? On the one hand, we want to shield customers from unauthorized access to their identities; on the other hand, we can't be so secretive that we don't know who's who on our customer list.

The Federal Trade Commission (FTC) has implemented a red flags rule that requires broker-dealers and other financial institutions to create written "Identity Theft Protection Programs" or "ITPPs" designed to identify, detect, and respond to warning signs (red flags) that could indicate identity theft. The four elements of a firm's ITPP (Identity Theft Protection Program) require broker dealers and other financial institutions to:

- identify relevant red flags for the covered accounts that the firm offers or maintains, and incorporate those red flags into its ITPP
- detect red flags that have been incorporated into the ITPP of the financial institution or creditor
- respond appropriately to any red flags that are detected to prevent and mitigate identity theft
- update the ITPP and its red flags periodically to reflect changes in identity theft risks to customers and the firm

Broker-dealers must design their Identity Theft Protection Program and have it approved by the Board of Directors of the firm or a designated member of senior management. The principals who approve the program must be involved in its oversight, development, implementation and administration. The firm must train staff to implement the ITPP. If the broker-dealer utilizes any third-party providers to help them with their responsibilities under the red flag rules, the firm must oversee those arrangements carefully.

At the time of publication, the following URL provides an excellent example of how broker-dealers comply with the concerns above: www.corclearing.com/content/privacy-statement.

Business Continuity Plans

To avoid panic in the financial marketplace, broker-dealers are required to prepare for catastrophic events caused by natural disasters, terrorist attacks, cyberattacks, power outages, etc. As the FINRA rule states: Each member must create and maintain a written business continuity plan identifying procedures relating to an emergency or significant business disruption. Such procedures must be reasonably designed to enable the member to meet its existing obligations to customers. In addition, such procedures must address the member's existing relationships with other broker-dealers and counter-parties. The business continuity plan must be made available promptly upon request to FINRA staff. FINRA then states that firms should consider such issues as:

(1) Data back-up and reco (hard copy and electronic)

(2) All mission critical systems

(3) Financial and operational assessments

(4) Alternate communications between customers and the member

(5) Alternate communications between the member and its employees

(6) Alternate physical location of employees

(7) Critical business constituent, bank, and counter-party impact

(8) Regulatory reporting

(9) Communications with regulators

(10) How the member will assure customers' prompt access to their funds and securities in the event that the member determines that it is unable to continue its business.

Firms must also provide disclosure to their brokerage customers as to how the firm would implement a business continuity and disaster recovery plan in the event of a disaster related to weather, terror attack, or cyberattack, etc. This disclosure is provided when the customer opens the account, upon request, and on the firm's website.

Now What?

Questions from this chapter that I expect to see on the Series 66 exam involve business practices for investment advisers, IARs, broker-dealers, and agents, as well as many of the registration issues covered in our look at the Uniform Securities Act. For example:

An investment adviser representative must register in the State if she:
  A. Has a physical presence or place of business in the state
  B. Has more than 5 clients in the state
  C. Has any non-institutional clients in the state
  D. Has any financial planning clients in the state

EXPLANATION: as you can see, a test question like this is not answered based on some memorized number or factoid. This question tests your understanding of fundamental concepts surrounding the registration of IARs under the Uniform Securities Act. What is more important—the number/type of clients an IAR has, or whether she has a physical presence in the state? The first thing that the Administrator needs to know is if the IAR is operating within the state. If not, then we see if she has more than 5 clients in the state, and—if so—how many are non-institutional? In other words, as soon as we see the IAR has a place of business in the state, we know she is an IAR subject to registration in the state. Eliminate the three choices about clients, leaving us with

ANSWER: A

Of course, there is sometimes a big difference between registration requirements for an IAR and the type of firm he or she represents—an investment adviser. For example:

All of the following have investment advisory businesses operating within State A. Which one must register with the securities Administrator for State A?
  A. An adviser with discretion over $357 million of assets
  B. A financial planner with 4 individual clients in the state
  C. A sub-adviser for a registered investment company under the Investment Company Act of 1940
  D. All choices listed

EXPLANATION: again, there is the step in which you learn the information. Then, there is the step in which you learn to apply it. If you are imagining a trip to the testing center in which you quickly recall a lot of memorized numbers and familiar phrases, please stop that. The test questions look much like this one. Your job is to figure them out as opposed to already knowing the answer after reading the first few words.

If they have a place of business in the state, don't they always have to register in that state? Isn't that what we *just said*?! We did, but that is true for broker-dealers, agents, and investment adviser representatives. When it comes to an investment advisory business, some advisers are federal covered and, therefore, not considered investment advisers in the state at all. This question brings up the two most familiar reasons an adviser could be federal covered. If the assets under management are over $100 million, or if they advise a registered investment company, they are a federal covered adviser. That eliminates both Choices A and C, which, in turn, eliminates Choice D. The only adviser subject to state registration is the financial planner, who would have no assets to count towards the $100 million of AUM (assets under management) for purposes of eligibility for exclusive SEC registration. The number 4 was a distractor, remember, since the question said the financial planner has a place of business in the state, leaving us with

ANSWER: B

As I said, the business practices of securities industry professionals is extremely important on your exam. For example:

Meg Megley is a securities agent who occasionally logs into various friends' accounts to rebalance their mutual fund holdings. If Meg receives no special compensation for her activity,

    A. No violation has occurred
    B. No violation has occurred because he does not receive compensation
    C. She is violating securities industry regulations
    D. She is violating securities industry regulations because he is not receiving compensation

EXPLANATION: the exam doesn't just ask if something is allowed or not. It asks if it's allowed for this or that reason, or prohibited for this or that reason. When that happens, try to figure out, first, if the activity is prohibited or not. This activity sure seems innocent enough. I mean, Meg isn't receiving any compensation for executing these securities transactions. <u>Not</u> receiving compensation seems like an unlikely violation, making Choice D appear weak. But, for this question, we really just have to know the NASAA policy statement, which tells agents specifically not to do this unless they have the prior written consent of their employing broker-dealer. Compensation is not relevant here; Meg should not be engaging in this unethical activity, leaving us with

ANSWER: C

It's time to do the online review exercises within our Pass the 66 Online Practice Question Bank. After a 20-minute-or-longer break, come back and take both chapter review quizzes. Then, move onto the several lessons in our training videos.

At that point—no more chapters to read. At that point, start working on the practice exams, each one a new and unique batch of 100 questions.

Glossary

3-Pronged Approach: Test used by SEC to determine if an entity meets the definition of an investment adviser. Does the person provide "investment advice" relating to securities and based on the client's situation? Does the person receive compensation as a result of providing investment advice? Is the person in the business of providing investment advice?

8-K: SEC report required by the Securities Exchange Act of 1934 of public companies announcing unusual material events.

10-K: SEC report required by the Securities Exchange Act of 1934 annually of public companies.

10-Q: SEC report required by the Securities Exchange Act of 1934 quarterly of public companies.

12b-1 fee: Fee deducted from a mutual fund's assets to cover distribution costs, e.g., selling, mailing, printing, advertising. An operating expense, unlike the sales charge that is deducted from the investor's check.

72-t: Section of the tax code allowing individuals to make withdrawals prior to age 59 ½ from a Traditional IRA or variable annuity without penalty based on taking a series of substantially equal payments over a number of years.

75-5-10 Rule: Diversification formula for a fund advertising itself as "diversified." 75% of the portfolio must have no more than 5% of assets invested in any one security, and no more than 10% of a company's outstanding shares may be owned.

200-day Moving Average: Average closing price over the previous 200 days for a stock or an index.

401(k) Plan: Qualified defined contribution plan offering employer-matched contributions.

403(b): Qualified plan for tax-exempt, non-profit organizations.

404(c): ERISA safe-harbor provisions allowing employers to pass off risk to participants of defined contribution plans.

457 Plan: Tax-advantaged retirement account for state and municipal government employees. AKA "Section 457 Plan."

529 Savings Plans: Education savings plans offering tax-deferred growth and tax-free distributions at the federal level for qualified educational expenses.

1035 Contract Exchange: Tax-free exchange of one annuity contract for another, one life insurance policy for another, or one life insurance policy for an annuity. The contracts do not have to be issued by the same company.

1040: Tax form used by individuals and sole proprietors.

1041: Tax form used by trusts and estates.

1065: Tax form used by partnerships.

1099-DIV: Tax form sent to investors showing dividends and capital gains distributions from a mutual fund for the tax year.

1099-INT: Tax form sent to investors showing interest payments for the tax year.

1099-OID: Tax form used to pay annual accretion on a zero coupon or any taxable original issue discount (OID) bond.

1120: Tax form used by corporations.

A

A-Shares: Mutual fund shares sold with a front-end sales load/charge. Lower annual expenses than B- and C-shares.

Acid Test: a term more commonly known as the "quick ratio," a more stringent measure of a company's short-term liquidity than the current ratio, as it excludes inventory from current assets.

Account at Maintenance: The point at which a customer's equity in a margin account is just high enough to avoid a margin call.

Account Freeze: Temporary restrictions placed on a customer account for violations of Regulation T.

Accounts Payable: What a company owes its vendors in the short-term, a current liability.

Accounts Receivable: What customers owe a company in the short-term, a current asset.

Account Statement: Document sent to a broker-dealer customer showing the recent value of all cash and securities, plus all recent activity in the account.

Accredited Investors: Large institutional investors, and individuals meeting certain income or net worth requirements allowing them to participate in, for example, a private placement under Reg D of the Securities Act of 1933, or hedge funds.

Accretion: Increasing the cost basis of a discount bond for tax purposes.

Accrual Basis: The accounting method used by most large companies in which revenue and expenses are recorded when invoices and bills are presented.

Accrued Interest: The interest that the buyer of a debt security owes the seller. Bond interest is payable only twice a year, and the buyer will receive the next full interest payment. Therefore, the buyer owes the seller for e day of interest since the last payment up to the day before the transaction settles.

Accrued Taxes: Taxes that are owed by a company over the short-term, a current liability.

Accrued Wages: Wages that are owed by a company over the short-term, a current liability.

Accumulation Stage/Period: Period during which contributions are made to an annuity, during which the investor holds "accumulation units."

Accumulation Units: What the purchaser of an annuity receives in exchange for his purchase payments during the accumulation phase, an accounting measure representing a proportional share of the separate account.

Active Investor: Investor who feels markets are not perfectly efficient and, therefore, selects investments.

Ad Valorem: Property tax, relating to general obligation municipal bonds.

Additional Takedown: The piece of the spread that goes to the various members of the syndicate when the bonds they've been allotted are sold.

Adjustable Rate Preferred Stock: Preferred stock whose dividend is tied to another rate, often the rate paid on T-bills.

Adjusted Gross Income (AGI): Earned income plus passive income, portfolio income, and capital gains. The amount upon which we pay income tax.

Adjustment Bond: Another name for an "income bond," on which the issuer may miss interest payments without going into default.

Administrator: (1) The securities regulator of a state; (2) A person authorized by the courts to oversee and liquidate an estate.

ADR: Abbreviation for an American Depository Receipt. A foreign stock on a domestic market. Toyota and Nokia are two examples of foreign companies whose ADRs trade on American stock markets denominated in dollars.

Advance Refunding/Pre-refunding: Issuing new bonds and depositing part of the proceeds in escrow ahead of the first legal call date on the existing bond issue.

Advance/Decline Ratio: The number of stocks whose market prices increased versus the number of stocks whose market prices decreased during a trading session.

Advertising: For investment advisers, any written communication delivered to more than one person.

Affiliated Investor, Person: Person who is an officer or director of the issuer, or a 10%+ owner of its common stock.

Age-Based Portfolio: A mutual fund or other portfolio adjusting asset allocation to match the needs of a beneficiary in a 529 Plan or an adult in a retirement account. AKA "lifecycle" or "target" funds.

Agency Cross Transaction: A potential conflict of interest arising when an investment adviser enters a trade for a client that is filled by matching the order with an order placed by one of the affiliated broker-dealer's customers. Requires disclosure.

Agency Issue (Agency Bond): Debt security issued by an agency authorized by the federal government.

Agent: Individual representing a broker-dealer or issuer in effecting/completing transactions in securities for compensation.

Aggressive Growth: Equity investments that face a higher risk of loss but also a higher potential return, e.g. emerging market or sector funds.

Aggressive Investor: An investor willing to risk a large loss of principal to earn potentially large returns.

Agreement Among Underwriters: Document used by an underwriting syndicate bringing an issue of securities to the primary market. This document sets forth the terms under which each member of the syndicate will participate and details the duties and responsibilities of the syndicate manager.

AIR: Assumed Interest Rate. Rate used to determine the value of annuity units and death benefits for variable contracts.

All or None: Type of underwriting in which the syndicate will cancel the offering if a sufficient dollar amount is not raised as opposed to being responsible for the unsold shares (as in a "firm commitment"). Also a type of order on the secondary market in which the investor wants the order to be canceled if the broker cannot acquire the full number of shares on one attempt.

Alpha: an investment's performance compared to a benchmark beyond what would be predicted by beta; the risk-adjusted performance compared to the benchmark.

Alternative Investment: An investment generally open only to sophisticated investors and providing limited or no liquidity, e.g. direct participation programs or hedge funds.

AM Best: Entity that rates the credit strength of insurance companies, a key to evaluating fixed annuities and other pure insurance products backed by the claims paying ability of the insurance company.

American Style: An option that can be exercised at any time up to expiration, as opposed to "European style."

Amortization: Spreading the cost of an intangible item, e.g., a patent or trademark, over its useful life.

Amortized: Intangible assets that have been written down over the estimated useful life of the assets.

AMT (Alternative Minimum Tax): Tax computation that adds certain "tax preference items" back into adjusted gross income. Some municipal bond interest is treated as a "tax preference item" that can raise the investor's tax liability through the AMT.

Annualized Return: The rate of return adjusted for increments of one year. For example, a 5% return over 1 month represents a 60% annualized rate of return, while a 15% return over three years represents a 5% annualized rate of return.

Annual Shareholder Report: Formal statement issued by a corporation to the SEC and shareholders discussing the company's results of operations, challenges/risks facing the company, any lawsuits against the company, etc. Required by the Securities Exchange Act of 1934. Form 10K.

Annual Updating Amendment: Process of annually updating all answers to an investment adviser's Form ADV-1 filing.

Annuitant: The person who receives an annuity contract's payments.

Annuitize: Process of converting an annuity contract's value to a series of payments to the annuitant.

Annuity: Contract between an individual and an insurance company that provides income for the rest of the individual's life in return for a lump-sum or periodic payment to the insurance company.

Annuity Units: What the annuitant holds during the pay-out phase, with the value tied to AIR.

Anticipation Notes: Short-term debt obligations of a municipality, often held by tax-exempt money market mutual funds.

Anti-Fraud Statutes: Key sections of federal and state securities law designed to protect investors from fraudulent, deceptive, or manipulative activities in the securities industry.

Appreciation: The increase in an asset's value that is not subject to tax until realized.

Arbitrage: A trading tactic that involves taking advantage of the disparity of two things. If you think GE will buy a small company, you can make a bet that GE will temporarily drop and the small company's stock will skyrocket. Or, you can trade on the disparity between a convertible bond and its underlying common stock.

Arbitration: Settling a dispute without going to an actual court of law.

Arbitration Award: The decision rendered through FINRA Arbitration.

Ask, Asked: The higher price in a quote representing what the customer would have to pay/what the dealer is asking the customer to pay. Ask/asked is also called "offer/offered."

Assessed Value: The percentage of market value used to calculate property taxes owed.

Asset Allocation: Maintaining a percentage mix of equity, debt, and money market investments, based either on the investor's age (strategic) or market expectations (tactical).

Asset-Backed Security: Bonds or notes backed by financial assets. Typically these assets consist of receivables other than mortgage loans, such as credit card receivables, auto loans, manufactured-housing contracts and home-equity loans.

Assets: Something that a corporation or individual owns, e.g., cash, investments, accounts receivable, inventory, etc.

Asset Coverage: A measure of how strong a company's balance sheet is relative to its obligations to bond holders

Assignment of Contract: Transferring an investment advisory client's contract to another party by any means; not allowed without client consent.

Associated Person: A registered representative or principal of a FINRA member broker-dealer.

Assumed Interest Rate: The full name for AIR, used to calculate payments in a variable annuity.

At-The-Money: An option whose strike price is equal to the market price of the underlying instrument.

Auction Market: The NYSE, for example, where buyers and sellers simultaneously enter competitive prices. Sometimes called a "double auction" market because buying and selling occur at the same time.

Auction Rate Securities: Debt securities with a variable rate of interest or preferred stock with a variable dividend rate that is re-set at regular auctions.

Audited: Financial statements that have been reviewed and certified by an independent public accountant.

Auditor: An independent public accounting firm that verifies and signs off on a public company's financial statements or an investment adviser's books and records concerning assets under its custody. KPMG and Deloitte, for example.

Authorized Stock: The number of shares a company is allowed to issue by its corporate charter. Can be changed by a majority vote of the outstanding shares.

Automated Client Account Transfer (ACAT): System that provides instructions among broker-dealers for transfer and delivery of customer assets among firms.

Automatic Reinvestment: Feature offered by mutual funds allowing investors to automatically reinvest dividend and capital gains distributions into more shares of the fund, without paying a sales charge.

Average Cost Basis: Method of figuring cost basis on securities for purposes of reporting capital gains and/or losses. The investor averages the cost for all purchases made in the stock, as opposed to identifying shares to the IRS when selling.

B

B-Shares: Mutual fund shares charging a load only when the investor redeems/sells the shares. Associated with "contingent deferred sales charges." B-shares have higher operating expenses than A-shares.

Backdating: Pre-dating a letter of intent (LOI) for a mutual fund to include a prior purchase in the total amount stated in the letter of intent. LOIs may be backdated up to 90 calendar days.

Back-end Load: Commission/sales charge added when mutual fund or variable contracts are redeemed. The back-end load declines gradually, as described in the prospectus. Associated with "B-shares."

Backing Away: Violation in which a market maker fails to honor a published firm quote to buy or sell a security at a stated price.

Backup Withholding: Required withholding from an investment account that results when the customer refuses/fails to provide a tax identification number.

Balanced Fund: Mutual fund that maintains a mix of stocks and bonds at all times. Related term "core fund."

Balance of Payments: The total inflow or outflow of capital for imports/exports and investments/financial products.

Balance of Trade: The difference between a nation's imports and exports. See trade surplus, trade deficit.

Balance Sheet: Financial statement of a corporation or individual showing financial condition (assets vs. liabilities) at a moment in time.

Balance Sheet Equation: Assets – Liabilities = Shareholders' Equity, or Assets = Liabilities + Shareholders' Equity. Forms the "foundation for all of accounting."

Balloon Maturity: A bond issue in which only some of the principal is paid off in early years, with most coming due at the final maturity.

Bankers' Acceptance (BA): Money-market security that facilitates importing/exporting. Issued at a discount from face-value. A secured loan.

Bank Holding Company: Company that owns banks and often other financial services firms including broker-dealers and investment advisers. For example, the Wells Fargo & Company (WFC).

Bar: The most severe sanction that FINRA can impose on an individual, effectively ending his/her career.

Basis: Synonym for yield. Or, reference to cost basis for tax purposes.

Basis Points: A way of measuring bond yields or other percentages in the financial industry. Each basis point is 1% of 1%. Example: 2% = .0200 = 200 basis points. 20 basis points = .2% or 2/10ths of 1%.

Basis Quote: The price at which a debt security can be bought or sold, based on the yield. A bond purchased at a "5.50 basis" is trading at a price that makes the yield 5.5%.

Bear, Bearish: Investor who takes a position based on the belief that the market or a security will fall. Short sellers and buyers of puts are "bearish." They profit when stocks go down. Seriously.

Bear Market: A trading market for stock or bonds in which prices are falling and/or expected to fall. Characterized by a series of lower highs and lower lows.

Bear Spread: A call or put spread in which the investor benefits if the underlying instrument's value drops. For example, an investor who buys the ABC Aug 50 call and sells the ABC Aug 45 call establishes a bear spread. The spread would also happen to be a "credit spread" in this case.

Bearer Bond: An unregistered bond that pays principal to the bearer at maturity. Bonds have not been issued in this way for over two decades, but they exist on the secondary market.

Behavioral Finance: The theory that seeks to explain stock market bubbles and crashes as investors acting irrationally through biases and inexpert understanding of important market and financial information.

Benchmark: The index to which an investment manager's results are compared.

Beneficiary: The one who benefits. An insurance policy pays a benefit to the named beneficiary. IRAs and other retirement plans, including annuities, allow the owner to name a beneficiary who will receive the account value when the owner dies.

Best Efforts: Type of underwriting leaving the syndicate at no risk for unsold shares, and allowing them to keep the proceeds on the shares that were sold/subscribed to. Underwriters act as "agents," not principals, in a best efforts underwriting.

Best Execution: SEC requirement for advisers and broker-dealers to execute customer transactions at the best available market price.

Beta Coefficient: Another way of referring to "beta."

Beta: Risk measurement that compares the volatility of a security or portfolio to the volatility of the overall market. A beta of more than 1 is associated with an investment or portfolio that is more volatile than the overall market. A beta of less than 1 is associated with an investment or portfolio that is less volatile than the overall market.

Bid: What a dealer is willing to pay to a customer who wants to sell. Customers sell at the bid, buy at the ask.

Billing Statement: The document an investment adviser delivers in connection with an advisory fee deduction explaining how the fee was computed.

Blank Check Company: A company without a specific business plan.

Blend Fund: A fund that does not stick to just growth or just value stocks.

Blind Pool Offering: A direct participation program in which the sponsor does not identify the assets of the partnership.

Blue Chip: Stock in a well-established company with proven ability to pay dividends in good economic times and bad. Lower risk/reward ratio than other common stock.

Blue Sky: State securities law.

Board of Directors: The group elected by shareholders to run a mutual fund or a public company and establish corporate management policies.

Bond: A debt security issued by a corporation or governmental entity that promises to repay principal and pay interest either regularly or at maturity.

Bond Anticipation Note (BAN): A short-term municipal debt security backed by the proceeds of an upcoming bond issue. Often found in tax-exempt money market funds.

Bond Certificate: A paper or electronic document stating the details of the bond.

Bond Counsel: Law firm advising a municipal issuer on the legality and tax treatment of a bond issue.

Bond Fund: Mutual fund with an objective of providing income while minimizing capital risk through a portfolio of bonds.

Bond Point: 1% of a bond's par value. 1 bond point = $10.

Bond Rating: Evaluation of a bond issue's chance of default published by companies such as Moody's, S&P, and Fitch.

Bond Ratio: A measure of an issuer's long-term solvency, found by comparing long-term debt to total capitalization (long-term debt plus shareholder's equity).

Bond Resolution: Document that legally authorizes the process of issuing municipal bonds for a specific purpose.

Bond Swap or **Tax Swap:** Taking a loss on a bond and replacing it with a substantially different bond to avoid triggering a wash sale.

Bonus Annuities: Annuities with special riders/features attached.

Book Entry: A security maintained as a computer record rather than a physical certificate. All US Treasuries and m mutual funds are issued in this manner.

Book Value or **Book Value Per-Share:** The hard, tangible asset value associated with each share of common stock. Calculated by taking stockholder's equity minus preferred shares, divided by the number of shares outstanding.

Brady Bonds: Debt securities issued primarily by Latin American government and collateralized by US Treasuries.

Branch Office: Any location identified by any means to the public or customers as a location at which the member conducts an investment banking or securities business. The small Charles Schwab or E-Trade office at the nearby mall or office complex is a "branch office."

Bottom-Up Analysis: A type of fundamental analysis involving a look at companies rather than the overall economy.

Breakeven: The price at which the underlying security is above or below the strike price of the option by the amount of the premium paid or received. For example, an ABC Aug 50 call @2 has a "breakeven" of $52 for both the buyer and the seller.

Breaking the Buck: Jargon used for the extremely rare case in which a money market mutual fund is unable to maintain the NAV-per-share at $1.

Breakpoint: A discounted sales charge or "volume discount" on mutual fund purchases offered on A-shares at various levels of investment.

Breakpoint Selling: Preventing an investor from achieving a breakpoint. A violation.

Broad-Based Index: An index such as the S&P 500 or the Value Line Composite Index that represents many companies from many industries.

Broker: An individual or firm that charges a commission to execute securities buy and sell orders submitted by another individual or firm.

Broker Call Loan Rate: An interest rate relating to margin accounts.

Broker-Dealer: A person/firm in the business of completing transactions in securities for the accounts of others (broker) or its own account (dealer).

Broker's Broker: A municipal securities firm acting as a broker for other firms who are not active in the municipal securities market to obtain pricing superior to what the firm could obtain itself.

BrokerCheck: Public disclosure database provided by FINRA allowing the public to check the qualifications and disciplinary history of member firms, principals, and agents.

Bull, Bullish: An investor who takes a position based on the belief that the market or a security will rise. Buyers of stock and call options are bullish.

Bull Market: A trading environment for stocks or bonds in which prices are rising and/or expected to rise.

Bulletin Board: OTC stocks too volatile and low-priced for NASDAQ.

Business Cycle: A progression of expansions, peaks, contractions, troughs, and recoveries for the overall (macro) economy.

Business Risk: The risk that the company whose stock or bond you own will not be successful as a business. Competition, poor management, obsolete products/services are all examples of business risk.

Buy and Hold: Investment approach that involves holding securities long-term to reduce transaction costs and based on a belief that good companies, in general, rise in value over time.

Buy limit: An order to buy a security at a price below the current market price, executable at a specified price or lower/better.

Buy stop: An order to buy a security at a price above the current market price triggered only if the market price hits or passes through the stop price.

Buy-To-Cover: The trade entered by a trader who has sold short to buy and replace the securities borrowed or close out an options contract.

C

C-Shares: A type of mutual fund share often called "level load" because of the high 12b-1 fee. Appropriate for shorter-term investing only.

Call (n.): A contract that gives the holder the right to buy something at a stated exercise price.

Call (v.): To redeem a bond or preferred stock prior to the redemption date.

Callable: A security that may be purchased by the issuer as of a certain date, e.g., callable preferred stock, callable bonds.

Call Premium: The price paid and received on a call option. Or, the amount above the par value paid by the issuer to call/retire a bond.

Call Protection: Period during which a security may not be called or bought by the issuer, usually lasting 5+ years.

Call Provision: The agreement between the issuer and the bondholders or preferred stockholders that gives the issuer the ability to repurchase the bonds or preferred stock on a specified date or dates before maturity.

Call Risk: The risk that a callable bond or preferred stock will be forcibly called when interest rates fall.

Call Spread: Buying and selling a call on the same underlying instrument where the strike price, the expiration, or both are different.

Cap: The maximum appreciation that an indexed annuity can experience in any given year, as stated in the contract.

Capital Appreciation: The rise in an asset's market price. The objective of a "growth investor."

Capital Appreciation Bond: Another name for a zero coupon bond, where the principal rises over time.

Capital Gain: The amount by which the proceeds on the sale of a stock or bond exceed your cost basis. If you sell a stock for $22 and have a cost basis of $10, the capital gain or profit is $12.

Capital Gains Distribution: Distribution from fund to investor based on net capital gains realized by the fund portfolio. Holding period determined by the fund and assumed to be long-term.

Capital Loss: Loss incurred when selling an asset for less than the purchase price. Capital losses offset an investor's capital gains and can offset ordinary income to a certain amount.

Capital Risk: The risk that an investor could lose some or all of her investment principal. For securities investors avoided only by purchasing US Treasury Securities *and* holding to maturity.

Capital Structure: The make-up of a corporation's financing through equity (stock) and debt (bonds) securities.

CAPM or **Capital Asset Pricing Model:** Method of calculating expected return based on the riskless rate, expected market return, and beta. Based on idea that equity investors expect the time value of money *plus* a risk premium to compensate for the risk taken by investing in the stock market.

Capping: A form of market manipulation. A violation.

Cash Account: An investment account in which the investor must pay for all purchases no later than 2 business days following regular way settlement. Not a margin account.

Cash Basis: The method of accounting used by some small businesses in which revenue and expenses are recorded only when payments are received or made.

Cash Dividend: Money paid to shareholders from an issuer's current earnings or accumulated profits.

Cash Equivalent: A security that can readily be converted to cash, e.g., T-bills, CDs, and money market funds.

Cash Flow: Net income plus depreciation/amortization. Or, "cash flow from operations" as shown on the company's statement of cash flows.

Cash Flows from Financing Activities: Cash provided/used through issuing securities, paying interest/dividends, redeeming bonds, or repurchasing stock.

Cash Flows from Investing Activities: Cash provided/used by selling or purchasing assets.

Cash Flows from Operating Activities: Cash provided/used by running the business.

Cash Settlement: Same-day settlement of a trade requiring prior broker-dealer approval. Not the "regular way" of doing things.

Cash Value: The value of an insurance policy that may be "tapped" by the policyholder through a loan or a surrender.

Catastrophe Call Provision: A provision for a municipal revenue bond providing for a mandatory call of the bonds due to unforeseen circumstances, e.g. a weather disaster, or the bonds losing their tax-exempt status.

Catch-Up Contribution: The increased amount that a person 50+ can make to a retirement account.

CDO or Collateralized Debt Obligation: A complex security like a CMO only rather than underlying mortgages, the debt securities are backed by a variety of other debt securities/loans.

CEO: Chief Executive Officer. Individual ultimately responsible for a corporation's results.

Certificate of Deposit or CD: A longer-term bank deposit offering higher yields than savings accounts.

Certificate of Limited Partnership: Document filed by the general partner of a direct participation program with a state disclosing who the partnership is and what it does.

CFO: Chief Financial Officer. Individual in charge of a corporation's financial activities.

Charitable Lead Trust: A split trust that provides income to a charitable beneficiary for a prescribed period before distributing assets to the non-charitable beneficiaries.

Charitable Remainder Trust: A split trust that provides income to a non-charitable beneficiary for a stated time before distributing assets to a charitable beneficiary.

Charitable Trust: A trust established to minimize tax liability by making a donation to a charitable beneficiary.

Chart: Graphical representation of a stock's price and volume information.

Chartist: A technical analyst making trading decisions based on stock charts and patterns.

Check-writing Privileges: A privilege offered by mutual funds, especially money market funds, by which investors can automatically redeem shares by writing checks.

Chicago Board Options Exchange Market Volatility Index: VIX, a key measure of market expectations of near-term volatility conveyed by S&P 500 stock index option prices.

Chinese Wall: The separation that is supposed to exist between the investment banking department and the traders and registered representatives to prevent insider trading violations.

Churning: Excessive trading in terms of frequency and size of transactions designed to generate commissions without regard for the customer.

Clearance: Post-trade processing done by clearing agencies such as the NSCC.

Clearing Agency: An entity such as the NSCC that performs post-trade processing for the clearing and settlement of securities transactions.

Clearing Rate: The interest rate established by auction in connection with auction rate securities.

Closed-end Fund: An investment company that offers a fixed number of shares that are not redeemable. Shares are traded on the secondary market at a price that could be higher or lower than NAV (or even the same as NAV). Also "closed-end management company."

CMO or Collateralized Mortgage Obligation: A complicated debt security based on a pool of mortgages or a pool of mortgage-backed securities. Pays interest monthly but returns principal to one tranche at a time.

Code of Arbitration: FINRA method of resolving disputes (usually money) in the securities business. All decisions are final and binding on all parties.

Code of Procedure: FINRA system for enforcing member conduct rules.

Coincident Indicator: Economic indicator used to determine where the economy is currently, e.g. personal income, manufacturing & trade sales.

Collateral: Assets pledged to a lender to support the loan, e.g. the house in a mortgage loan.

Collateral Trust Certificate: A bond secured by a pledge of securities as collateral.

Collection Ratio: The amount of taxes collected by a municipality divided by the amount of taxes assessed.

Combination: A multiple options position that is neither a straddle nor a spread. For example, if an investor buys an ABC Aug 45 call and sells an ABC Aug 50 put, he has established a combination. AKA "Combo."

Combination Privilege: Feature that allows investors to combine purchases of many funds within the mutual fund family to reach a breakpoint/reduced sales charge.

Combined Equity: In a margin account with both long and short positions combined equity is found by adding the Credit and the Long Market Value and subtracting the Short Market Value and the Debit Balance.

Combined Offering: An offering of securities in which both the issuer and other large shareholders will be selling to the public.

Commercial Paper: Short-term unsecured loan. Issued at a discount from the face value. A money market security.

Commission House Broker: A broker who works for a member of the exchange filling orders for the firm and receiving a commission per-order.

Commissions: A service charge an agent earns for executing a security purchase or sale.

Commodity: A basic raw material used to produce value-added products. For example, wheat, corn oil, sugar, and salt are commodities used to make the value-added product known as bread.

Commodity Future: Futures contract in which the underlying instrument is a commodity such as corn, wheat, soy beans, crude oil, live cattle, etc.

Common Stock: An equity or ownership position that allows the owner to vote on major corporate issues such as stock splits, mergers, acquisitions, authorizing more shares, etc.

Competitive Floor Traders: Members of the NYSE who buy and sell exchange-listed securities for their own account.

Competitive, Sealed Bids: Process used for most general obligation bonds in which the underwriting business is awarded to the syndicate that turns in the lowest cost of borrowing to the issuer.

Compliance Department: The principals and supervisors of a broker-dealer responsible for making sure the firm adheres to SEC, exchange, and SRO rules.

Complex Trust: A trust that does any of these things during the year: makes a deductible contribution to a charity, returns some income for corpus, or makes a distribution from corpus.

Compound Interest: An interest rate applied to an ever-increasing principal to which interest is continuously added, e.g. the rate offered on a bank CD. As opposed to "simple interest," which is applied to a flat principal, e.g. a long-term bond.

Compound Returns: What investors hope to achieve by reinvesting interest and dividends.

Concession: The amount that the seller of a new issue of municipal bonds receives, whether a syndicate member or a selling group member.

Conduct Rules: An SRO's rules for member conduct that, if violated, may lead to sanctions and fines.

Conduit Theory (Tax Treatment): A favorable tax treatment achieved if a company (REIT, mutual fund) distributes 90%+ of net income to the shareholders.

Confirmation: Document stating the trade date, settlement date, and money due/owed for a securities purchase or sale. Delivered on or before the settlement date.

Conflict of Interest: Primarily a concern for investment advisers and officers/directors of public companies, who may find their own interests at odds with those of clients or shareholders to whom they owe a fiduciary duty.

Consolidated Tape: The reporting "ticker" showing last-sale information for NYSE-listed securities, wherever they are traded.

Consolidated Quotation System (CQS): System used for trading in the third market.

Consolidation: A stock trading sideways, in a narrow price range. Sometimes called "accumulation."

Constant Dollar Plan: A defensive investment strategy in which an investor tries to maintain a constant dollar amount in the account, meaning that securities are sold if the account value rises and purchased if it goes down.

Constructive Receipt: The date that the IRS considers an investor to have put his grubby little hands on a dividend, interest payment, retirement plan distribution, etc. For example, IRA funds are not taxable until "constructive receipt," which usually starts somewhere between age 59½ and 70½.

Consumer Price Index (CPI): A measure of inflation/deflation for basic consumer goods and services. A rising CPI represents the greatest risk to most fixed-income investors.

Consumer: For purposes of Regulation S-P, a consumer is someone considering a financial relationship with a firm.

Contemporaneous Trader: Any investor harmed by another's manipulative/deceptive actions in the securities markets, especially in insider trading cases.

Contingency Offer: An offer of securities that will be canceled if a minimum amount is not raised, with all investor payments placed in escrow.

Contingent Deferred Sales Charge or **CDSC:** Associated with B-shares, the sales charge is deducted from the investor's check when she redeems/sells her shares. The charge is deferred until she sells and is contingent upon when she sells—the sales charges decline over time, eventually disappearing after 7 years, at which point the B-shares become A-shares.

Continuing Commissions: The accepted practice of paying retired registered representatives and principals commissions on business written while employed with the firm, e.g., 12b-1 fees on mutual funds and annuities.

Contraction: Phase of the business cycle associated with general economic decline, recession or depression.

Contribution: The money put into a retirement plan subject to the limits imposed by the plan.

Control Relationship: A situation in which the broker-dealer is related to the issuer of the securities involved in a transaction, requiring disclosure.

Conversion Ratio: The number of shares of common stock that the holder of a convertible bond or preferred stock would receive upon conversion. A bond "convertible at $50" has a conversion ratio of 20 (20 shares of stock per $1,000 par value).

Conversion/Exchange Privilege: A feature offered by many loaded mutual funds whereby the investor may sell shares of one fund in the family and use the proceeds to buy another fund in the family at the NAV (avoiding the sales load). All gains/losses are recognized on the date of sale/conversion for tax purposes.

Convertible: A preferred stock or corporate bond allowing the investor to use the par value to "buy" shares of the company's common stock at a set price. Sometimes called "hybrid securities," as they start out as fixed income but convert to common stock.

Cooling-off Period: A minimum 20-day period that starts after the registration statement is filed with the SEC. No sales or advertising allowed during this period, which lasts until the effective or release date.

Core Fund: Mutual fund that combines growth and value investing, or both stock and bond investing to provide a solid, "core" holding for a conservative investor.

Core Inflation: The CPI after food and energy costs are excluded. Core inflation removes the more weather-related and volatile pricing associated with food, oil, natural gas, etc. when measuring the overall rise or drop in pricing.

Corporation: The most common form of business organization, in which the business's total value is divided among shares of stock, each representing an ownership interest or share of profits.

Corpus: The principal of a trust as opposed to the income it generates.

Correlation: The relationship between two securities or market sectors that ranges from 1 to -1.

Cost Basis: The amount that has gone into an investment and has been taxed already. For stock, includes the price paid plus commissions. For a variable annuity, equals the after-tax contributions into the account. Investors pay tax only on amounts above their cost basis, and only when they sell or take "constructive receipt."

Cost Of Goods Sold of **COGS:** The cost of materials and direct labor going into the production of a company's products or delivery of its services, as opposed to general operating expenses and other costs/expenses listed on the income statement. A company subtracts COGS from revenue to arrive at its gross profit.

Coterminous: Municipal issuers who overlap, e.g., a village and a school district.

Countercyclical: Industries that are negatively correlated to the overall economy, doing better during recessions and worse during expansions.

Counterparty Risk: The risk faced by parties to a forward contract or repurchase agreement that the other side will default.

Coupon Rate: a.k.a. "nominal yield." The interest rate stated on a bond representing the percentage of the par value received by the investor each year. For example, a bond with a 5% "coupon rate" or "nominal yield" pays $50 per bond to the holder per year. Period.

Coverdell Education Savings Account: Tax-advantaged account used for educational funding in which funds may be accessed without penalty for qualified education expenses even for junior high or high school.

Covered Call: A position in which an investor generates premium income by selling the right to buy stock the investor already owns, and at a set price.

CPI or **Consumer Price Index:** Measure of inflation/deflation for basic consumer goods and services. A rising CPI represents the greatest risk to most fixed-income investors.

CRD or **Central Registration Depository:** An automated database used by FINRA to store and maintain registration records of former and current associated persons of member firms.

Credit: In a margin account, the amount of the proceeds from the short sale plus the initial Reg T deposit. For example, a short sale of $20,000 of ABC creates a credit of that $20,000 plus $10,000 or $30,000 in total.

Credit Agreement: Document that must be signed by a margin customer in which all finance charges are explained in connection to the margin account.

Credit Risk: a.k.a. "default" or "financial" risk. The risk that the issuer's credit rating will be downgraded, or that the issuer will default on a debt security.

Credit Spread: the difference in yields between high- and low-quality bonds of similar maturities.

Crossover Point: The point at which a limited partnership has exhausted the tax shelter and is now beginning to show a profit.

Crowdfunding: Investments made in early-stage companies by any investor, with limits based on net worth and income of the investor.

Crummey Trust: An irrevocable life insurance trust designed to pay the premiums on a life insurance policy owned by a trust and also get around the annual gift tax exclusion amount.

Cumulative Preferred Stock: Preferred stock where missed dividends go into arrears and must be paid before the issuer may pay dividends to other preferred stock and/or common stock.

Cumulative Voting: Method of voting whereby the shareholder may take the total votes and split them up any way he chooses. Said to benefit minority over majority shareholders. Total votes are found by multiplying the number of shares owned by the number of seats up for election to the Board of Directors.

Currency Exchange Risk: The risk that the value of the US dollar versus another currency will have a negative impact on businesses and investors.

Currency Transaction Report (CTR): Report submitted to the US Treasury by a broker-dealer when a customer deposits more than $10,000 cash.

Current Account: The difference between a nation's imports and exports. A "current account deficit" is synonymous with a "trade deficit."

Current Asset: Cash or something to be converted to cash in the short-term, e.g. accounts receivable, inventory.

Current Liability: A debt to be paid in the short-term, usually one year or sooner.

Current Ratio: Short-term measure of a corporation's liquidity found by dividing current assets by current liabilities; the higher the number, the more liquid the corporation.

Current Yield: Annual interest divided by market price of the bond. For example, an 8% bond purchased at $800 has a CY of 10%. $80/$800 = 10%.

CUSIP Number: An identification code for a security. Lost securities may be re-issued by the transfer agent if the CUSIP numbers are available, among other required proof of ownership.

Custodial Account: Investment account in which a custodian enters trades on behalf of the beneficial owner, who is usually a minor child.

Custodian: Party that maintains custody of a mutual fund's securities and cash. Performs payable/receivable functions for portfolio purchases and sales. In an UGMA, the custodian is the adult named on the account who is responsible for the investment decisions and tax reporting.

Custody: Having possession/control of an investor's assets, or the ability to appropriate them.

Customer: A person who opens an investment account with a broker-dealer.

Cybersecurity: Requirements for broker-dealers, investment advisers, stock exchanges, etc. to protect customer data from intrusion, theft, etc.

Customer Complaint: Defined by FINRA as "any grievance by a customer or any person authorized to act on behalf of the customer involving the activities of the member or a person associated with the member in connection with the solicitation or execution of any transaction or the disposition of securities or funds of that customer."

Cyclical Industry: An industry sensitive to the business cycle, e.g., steel, automobiles, and construction equipment.

D

Dark Pools of Liquidity: Large institutional orders concealed from the public and usually executed on the fourth market.

Dated Date: The date on which interest begins to accrue on a new issue of municipal bonds.

Day Order: A limit or stop order that will be canceled if not executed on the day it is placed. As opposed to "GTC."

Day-trading: Purchasing and selling—or selling and purchasing—the same security on the same day in a margin account.

Dealer: A person who buys or sells securities for his/its own account, taking the other side of the trade.

Death Benefit: The amount payable to the beneficiary of a life insurance (or annuity) contract, minus any outstanding loans and/or unpaid premiums.

Debenture: An unsecured bond backed by the issuer's ability to pay. No collateral.

Debit Balance: The amount that a margin customer owes the broker-dealer in a margin account.

Debit Spread: Buying a more expensive call/put and selling a less expensive call/put on the same underlying instrument.

Debt Limit: A self-imposed restriction on the total amount of general obligation debt that an issuer may have outstanding at any one time.

Debt per Capita: A measure that shows a bond analyst how much general obligation debt is outstanding divided by the number of residents of the municipality.

Debt Ratio: Measure of a company's long-term solvency found by comparing total liabilities to total assets. The higher the percentage, the more leveraged the company.

Debt Security: A security representing a loan from an investor to an issuer. Offers a interest rate in return for the loan, not an ownership position.

Debt Service: The schedule for repayment of interest and principal on a debt security.

Debt Service Coverage: The projected ability of a project built with revenue bond proceeds to cover the debt service.

Debt Statement: A statement in which a municipal issuer lists all of its outstanding debts.

Debt-To-Equity Ratio: Measure of long-term solvency found by dividing a company's total liabilities by shareholder equity. The higher the ratio, the more leveraged the company.

Declaration Date: The date the Board declares a dividend.

Default: When the issuer of the bond is unable to pay interest and/or principal.

Default Hearing: A disciplinary hearing held by FINRA or a state regulator when the respondent fails to cooperate and in the respondent's absence after proper notice has been served.

Default Risk: The risk that the issuer of the bond will stiff you. Measured by S&P and Moody's.

Defensive: An industry or a company that can perform well even during bad economic times. For example, food and basic clothing represent two products purchased through both good and bad economic times; therefore, stocks of food and basic clothing companies would be "defensive" investments.

Deferred Annuity: An annuity that delays payments of income, installments, or a lump sum until the investor elects to receive it. Usually subject to surrender charges during the deferral period.

Deferred Compensation Plan: A non-qualified business plan that defers some of the employee's compensation until retirement. Usually for highly compensated employees.

Deficiency Letter: SEC notification of additions or corrections that an issuer must make to a registration statement before the offering can be cleared for distribution.

Defined Benefit Pension Plan: Qualified corporate pension plan that, literally, defines the benefit payable to the retiree. Involves annual actuarial certifications as to sufficient funding levels to meet future benefit claims.

Defined Contribution Plan: Qualified corporate plan that defines the contribution made on behalf of the employee, e.g., profit sharing, 401(k).

Deflation: A general drop in demand and the level of prices across the economy, usually connected to an economic slump.

Delivery: The change in ownership of a security that takes place when the transaction settles. The seller delivers the securities purchased to the buyer or to the clearing agency.

Demand Deposit: Any deposit at a bank where the funds may be withdrawn at any time, e.g. checking and savings accounts.

Depletion Allowance: A cost reco system for natural resources investment programs.

Depository Trust Company: A subsidiary of the DTCC, the holder of physical stock certificates.

Depreciation: A non-cash expense on the income statement listed to spread the cost of a fixed asset over its useful life. Depreciation is also shown on the balance sheet, usually as "accumulated depreciation" next to fixed or long-term assets.

Depreciation Recapture: A tax collected when an investor sells an asset that was providing depreciation for more than the adjusted cost basis.

Depression: A prolonged economic slump, more severe than a recession.

Derivative: An investment that derives its value from some other instrument, includes options, futures, and forwards.

Designated Examining Authority: Another name for an SRO or Self-Regulatory Organization, e.g., CBOE or FINRA.

Designated Market Maker: NYSE market participant charged with maintaining a fair and orderly market in the stocks they quote. DMMs must quote at the national best-bid-or-offer (NBBO) a specified percentage of the time, and facilitate price disco throughout the day as well as at the open, close and in periods of significant imbalances and high volatility.

Developed Market: An economy with mature financial systems and infrastructures, as opposed to an "emerging market."

Developmental Program: An oil or gas drilling program in an area in which reserves are known to exist.

Diluted Earnings per-share: A company's EPS calculated as if all convertible securities have been converted to shares of common stock.

Dilution of Equity: A reduction in the earnings per-share of common stock, often due to convertible bonds or preferred stock being converted to common stock.

Direct Debt: The general obligation debt of a municipal issuer for which it is solely responsible.

Direct Participation Program (DPP): A limited partnership or similar pass-through entity in which the investor receives a share of income and expenses.

Direct Transfer: The easiest method of moving funds from a qualified retirement account to a Traditional IRA, or among such accounts. In a direct transfer the existing custodian sends assets to the new custodian, bypassing the account owner.

Disclaim an inheritance: To give up all claims on an inheritance so that it passes to other heirs.

Disclosure Brochure: Required information of an investment adviser provided to prospects and offered to clients; either a copy of ADV PART 2 or a document containing the same information.

Discount (n.): The difference between the (lower) market price for a bond and the par value.

Discount (v.): To calculate the present value of future cash flows by some rate known as the "discount rate."

Discount Bond: A bond trading below par value.

Discounted Cash Flow Analysis: A method of valuing a project or income-producing security based on the net present value of all expected cash flows.

Discount Rate: Interest rate charged by the 12 Federal Reserve Banks to member banks who borrow from the FRB. Or, the rate used when performing "discounted cash flow analysis." See textbook for explanation on discounted cash flow analysis.

Discretion: Authority given to someone other than the account owner to make trading decisions for the account.

Discretionary Income: What an investor has to invest after all expenses are met.

Disintermediation: A situation in which money is being withdrawn from banks and savings & loans by depositors to reinvest the funds into higher yielding money market instruments (Treasury bills, certificates of deposit, money market funds).

Distribution Stage (Annuity): Period during which an individual receives payments from an annuity.

Distribution Expenses: The cost of distributing/marketing a mutual fund, including selling, printing prospectuses and sales literature, advertising, and mailing prospectuses to new/potential clients. Covered by sales charges/12b-1fees.

Distribution: The money taken out of a retirement plan or annuity.

Distributor: A FINRA member firm that bears distribution costs of a fund, profiting from the sales charges paid by the investors; a.k.a. "sponsor," "underwriter," "wholesaler."

Diversification: Purchasing securities from many different issuers, or industries, or geographic regions, to reduce "nonsystematic risk."

Diversifiable Risk: Another name for an un-systematic risk, e.g. regulatory or business risk.

Diversified Fund: An open- or closed-end fund that complies with an SEC rule so that no more than 5% of assets are invested in a stock or bond and so that the fund does not own more than 10% of any issuer's outstanding stock. Associated with the "75-5-10 rule."

Dividend: Money paid from profits to holders of common and preferred stock if and when the Board of Directors declares.

Dividend Discount Model: A method of valuing a common stock as the present value of the dividends it will pay to the investor.

Dividend Payout Ratio: The amount of dividends paid divided by the earnings per-share. Stocks with high dividend payout ratios are typically found in "equity income" funds.

Dividend Reinvestment Plan or **DRIP:** A program allowing investors to automatically reinvest cash dividends into more shares of fractional shares.

Dividend Yield: Annual dividends divided by market price of the stock. Equivalent to current yield for a debt security.

Dividend/Income Distributions: Distributions from a fund to the investors made from net investment income. Typically, may be reinvested at the NAV to avoid sales charge.

DK Notice: A notice sent to the other broker-dealer when a firm does not recognize a transaction.

Do Not Reduce (DNR): A buy limit or sell stop order that will not be reduced for the payment of a cash dividend.

Dollar Cost Averaging: Investing fixed dollar amounts regularly, regardless of share price. Usually results in a lower average cost compared to average of share prices, as investors' dollars buy majority of shares at lower prices. Also a way of figuring cost basis for income tax purposes, usually called "Average Cost Basis."

Dollar Weighted Return: The rate of return weighted by the dollars invested rather than taking a simple average of annual returns (time-weighted return).

Domestic Equity Fund: A mutual fund that focuses on stocks of American companies.

Donor: Person who makes a gift of money or securities to another.

Double Barreled: A municipal bond backed by both the issuer's full faith and credit and revenues.

Dow Jones Industrial Average (DJIA): An index comprised of 30 large-cap companies.

DRP or **Disclosure Reporting Page:** Disclosure provided on a Form U4, Form U5, or Form ADV of prior bad acts relevant to the securities industry.

Dual-Purpose Fund: A closed-end fund with two classes of stock: income shares and capital shares. The income shares receive dividends and interest, while the capital shares receive capital gains distributions.

Due Bill: Document sent by a broker-dealer when a dividend payment was sent to the wrong party and belongs to the broker-dealer's customer.

Due Diligence: Meeting between issuer and underwriters with the purpose of verifying information contained in a registration statement/prospectus.

Durable Goods: Expensive purchases including appliances that are intended to last a long time.

Durable Power of Attorney: Legal documents appointing a third party to make binding financial and legal decisions if/when the individual becomes incapacitated.

Duration: The weighted average of a bond's cash flows; a bond's price sensitivity to a small change in interest rates.

DVP: A form of settlement in which payment will be made when the securities involved in the transaction are delivered and accepted. AKA "Delivery Versus Payment."

E

Earned Income: Income derived from active participation in a business, including wages, salary, tips, commissions, and bonuses. Alimony received is also considered earned income. Earned income can be used toward an IRA contribution.

Earnings Available to Common: Net income minus any preferred stock dividends. Dividing this amount by the shares outstanding arrives at the EPS for the company's common stock.

Earnings per-share (EPS): The amount of earnings or "net income" available for each share of common stock. A major driver of the stock's price on the secondary market. Found by taking "earnings available to common" divided by the shares outstanding.

Eastern/Undivided Account: A syndicate account in which participants are responsible for a percentage of all bonds, even if they sell their allotment.

EBIT: Earnings Before Interest and Taxes. The profit that would be shown before interest and taxes are subtracted from revenue on the income statement.

EBITDA: Earnings Before Interest, Taxes, Depreciation and Amortization. The profit that would be shown before interest, taxes, depreciation and amortization are subtracted from revenue on the income statement. Or, revenue minus COGS and general operating expenses only,

Economic Indicator: Data providing economists with important information about the current state and possible future direction of the economy and various sectors of the economy.

EDGAR: Section of the SEC's website where various required filings are made by reporting companies and accessible by the public. To pull up a prospectus, 10Q, or 10K, for example, go to the "EDGAR" section of www.sec.gov. EDGAR is an acronym for "Electronic Data Gathering, Analysis, and Retrieval."

Education IRA: Former name for the Coverdell Education Savings Account in which after-tax contributions may be made to pay qualified education expenses for the beneficiary.

Effective Date: Date established by SEC as to when the underwriters may sell new securities to investors; a.k.a. "release date."

Efficient Frontier: Graph showing expected return on the vertical axis and standard deviation on the horizontal axis, with a curve known as the efficient frontier upon whose line optimal portfolios are constructed to balance maximum returns with any risk taken. Portfolios behind the line are inefficient, and portfolios above the line are not possible.

Efficient Market Hypothesis: Investing approach that assumes markets are efficient with information immediately priced into securities. See textbook for "weak, semi-strong, and strong-form" of this hypothesis.

Elective Deferral: The amount an employee elects to have deducted from his paycheck and deposited into an employer-based plan such as a 401(K) or SIMPLE IRA.

Electronic Communications Networks (ECNs): Electronic trading platforms that allow institutional investors to buy and sell securities directly. AKA "Fourth market."

Emerging Market: The financial markets of a developing country. Generally, a small market with a short operating history, not as efficient or stable as developed markets. For example, Brazil, China, India.

Employee Stock Options: An employment benefit allowing employees to purchase company stock at a set price once the options are vested.

Employee Stock Ownership Plan or **ESOP:** Retirement plan in which the company allows all workers to purchase company stock at a discount and through a payroll deduction. The stock and the dividends/cap gains generated on it grow tax-deferred, as in a 401(k) plan.

Employment Indicators: Economic indicators relating to employment, e.g., weekly unemployment claims, non-farm payroll.

Equipment Leasing Program: A direct participation program that leases computers, mining equipment, etc. Depreciation is a major tax-advantage of such a program.

Equipment Trust Certificate: Bond secured by a pledge of equipment, e.g., airplanes, railroad cars.

Equity: Ownership, e.g., common and preferred stock in a public company.

Equity Funds: Mutual funds that primarily invest in equity securities.

Equity Income Fund: A mutual fund that purchases common stocks whose issuers pay consistent and, perhaps, increasing dividends. The fund has less volatility than an equity fund with "growth" as an objective.

Equity-Indexed Annuity: An insurance product offering a minimum guaranteed rate and the opportunity to participate in some of the gains of a index, usually the S&P 500. AKA "indexed annuity."

Equity Options: Standardized derivatives giving the holder the right to buy or sell the underlying stock at a set price (strike/exercise price).

Equity REIT: A Real Estate Investment Trust that owns and operates a portfolio of real properties.

ERISA: The Employee Retirement Income Security Act of 1974 that governs the operation of most corporate pension plans.

Estate: A legal entity/person that represents all assets held by a deceased person before he died.

Estate Tax: A tax on estates over a certain amount, currently $5 million indexed for inflation.

ETF or **Exchange-Traded Fund**: A fund that trades on an exchange, typically an index fund tracking the S&P 500, the Dow Jones Industrial Average, etc. Unlike an open-end index fund, the ETF allows investors to sell short, trade throughout the day, and even purchase shares on margin.

ETN or **Exchange-Traded Note:** a type of unsecured debt security issued by a financial institution, e.g., Barclays Capital, in which returns are based upon the performance of an underlying benchmark minus fees.

European Style: An option that may be exercised at expiration only.

Excess Equity: The amount of equity above the Reg T requirement in a margin account.

Exchange-Listed Security: A security that has met listing requirements to trade on a exchange such as NYSE, or NASDAQ. Also a "federal covered security" by definition.

Exchange Rate: The relative value of two currencies, e.g. US dollars to Yen or Euro, impacting exports and imports.

Exchanges: Any electronic or physical marketplace where investors can buy and sell securities. For example, NASDAQ, NYSE.

Exclusion Ratio: Method of determining which part of an annuity payment is taxable, and which part represents the tax-free return of the annuitant's after-tax cost basis.

Ex-Date or **Ex-Dividend Date:** The date upon which the buyer is not entitled to the upcoming dividend.

Executor: The party charged with administering an estate.

Exempt: Not subject to registration requirements of a securities law or rule/regulation.

Exempt Reporting Adviser: An investment adviser that is not required to register with the SEC under the Investment Advisers Act of 1940 but is required to file initial and annual reports. Such an investment adviser is either claiming an exemption because it is solely an adviser to one or more venture capital funds or because it is an adviser solely to private funds with less than $150 million of assets.

Exempt Security: A security not required to be registered under the Securities Act of 1933. subject to anti-fraud rules; not subject to registration requirements, e.g., municipal bonds and bank stock.

Exempt Transaction: A transactional exemption from registration requirements based on the manner in which the security is offered and sold, e.g., private placements or offers to institutional investors only.

Exercise: The act of using an option to buy or sell the underlying instrument.

Exercise Price: The price at which the underlying security can be bought (call) or (sold) in an options contract. AKA "strike price."

Existing Properties: A direct participation program that purchases operating real estate.

Expansion: Phase of the business cycle associated with increased activity.

Expected Return: A calculation of the return hoped for based on probabilities of outcomes or the CAPM formula.

Expense Ratio: A fund's operating expenses divided by/compared to average net assets. Represents operating efficiency of a mutual fund, where the lower the number the more efficient the fund.

Expiration Date: The date after which an options contract ceases to exist.

Exploratory Programs: A direct participation program that drills for oil or natural gas.

Extension Risk: The risk that interest rates will rise, and the holder of a CMO or mortgage-backed security will have to wait longer than expected to receive principal.

F

Face Amount: The amount of principal to be repaid on a bond or other debt security, AKA "par value."

Face-Amount Certificate: A debt security bought in a lump-sum or through installments that promises to pay out the stated face amount, which is higher than the investor's purchase price.

Face-Amount Certificate Company: One of the three types of investment companies under the Investment Company Act of 1940. Issues face-amount certificates. Not a UIT or "management company."

Fair and Orderly Market: What the DMMs (Designated Market Makers) at the NYSE are charged with maintaining.

Fair and Accurate Credit Transactions Act: Federal legislation that attempts to reduce identify theft by requiring firms who collect information on individuals to safely dispose of it and by allowing individuals to place alerts on their credit history if they suspect fraudulent transactions.

FDIC (Federal Deposit Insurance Corporation): Federal government agency that provides deposit insurance for member banks and prevents bank and "thrift" failures. Bank deposits are currently insured up to $250,000.

Feasibility Study: A study put together by a consulting firm analyzing the economic merits of a facility to be financed by municipal revenue bonds.

Fed Funds Rate: Interest rate charged on bank-to-bank loans. Subject to daily fluctuation.

Federal Covered: A security or an investment adviser whose registration is handled exclusively by the federal government (SEC).

Federal Farm Credit System: Organization of privately owned banks providing credit to farmers and mortgages on farm property.

Federal Open Market Committee (FOMC): Council of Federal Reserve officials that sets monetary policy based on economic data. The money supply is tightened to fight inflation, loosened to provide stimulus to a faltering economy.

Federal Reserve Board: Seven-member board directing the operations of the Federal Reserve System.

Federal Reserve System: The central bank system of the United States, with a primary responsibility to manage the flow of money and credit in this country.

FEIN or Federal Employer Identification Number: A tax ID number assigned to an entity such as a corporation, trust, or estate.

FHLMC or Freddie Mac: Like Fannie Mae, a special purpose enterprise structured as a public company that purchases mortgages from lenders and sells mortgage-backed securities to investors. Stock is listed on NYSE.

Fiduciary: Someone responsible for the financial affairs of someone else, e.g., investment adviser, trustee, who owes the beneficiary a duty of loyalty and a duty of good faith.

FIFO or First-In-First-Out: First-in-first-out. An accounting method for valuing a company's inventory or for determining the capital gain/loss for an investor. Using FIFO, an investor indicates that, for example, the 100 shares of ABC that were sold at $55 are the first 100 shares that he purchased.

Filing Date: The date that an issuer files a registration statement with the SEC for a new issue of securities.

Final Prospectus: Disclosure document delivered with final confirmation of a new issue of securities detailing the price, delivery date, and underwriting spread.

Financial Futures: Futures contracts where the underlying instrument is a stock index, interest rate, etc.

Financial Planner: Professional who provides total financial strategies to clients involving insurance needs, retirement needs, estate planning, investing, tax reduction, etc. Usually required to register as an investment adviser, unless securities are never part of any plan.

Financial Risk: Another name for "credit risk," or the risk that the issuer of a bond could default.

Financial Statement: A balance sheet, income statement, statement of cash flows, or other document showing various aspects of a business's financial condition or results. Found in the 10K and other required reports of public companies.

FinCEN: US Treasury's "Financial Crimes Enforcement Network." Suspicious Activity Reports must be provided to FinCEN if a broker-dealer notices activity in accounts that appears suspicious or possibly related to fraud or money laundering activities.

FINRA (Financial Industry Regulatory Authority): The Self-Regulatory Organization formed when the NASD and the NYSE regulators merged.

Firm Commitment: An underwriting commitment in which the underwriters agree to purchase all securities from an issuer, even the ones they failed to sell to investors. Involves acting in a "principal" capacity, unlike in "best efforts," "all or none," and "mini-max" offerings.

Firm Quote: A quote by a dealer representing a price at which the dealer is prepared to trade.

First Market: Another name for the exchange market, where the NYSE is the model.

Fiscal Policy: The process of taxation and spending done by the US Congress.

Fixed Annuity: An insurance product in which the annuitant receives fixed payments, usually for the rest of his or her life.

Fixed Assets: Long-term assets that generate revenue but are not intended to be sold. For example, a printing press.

Fixed Exchange Rate: A system in which a nation ties the value of its currency to a commodity such as gold or to another currency, e.g. the former system of fixing the exchange rate between Swiss Francs and Euro.

Fixed-Income: Type of investor who seeks a stream of income, usually from bonds, but also from preferred stock.

Flat Yield Curve: When yields are similar for short, intermediate, and long-term bonds.

Flexible Premium: A premium that may be changed as time goes on, a characteristic of "universal" insurance.

Floating-Rate Currency: A system allowing the value of a nation's currency to rise and fall due to supply and demand.

Flow of Funds Statement: A statement connected to a revenue bond showing how revenues are to be allocated in terms of operations and maintenance, reserve account deposits, debt service, etc.

Flow Through: Term used for an entity that passes through a share of net income or net loss to the owners rather than being taxed as a business entity. Includes partnerships, LLCs and S-Corporations but not C-Corporations.

FNMA or Fannie Mae: Like little brother Freddie Mac, Fannie buys mortgages from lenders and sells mortgage-backed securities to investors. A quasi-agency, a public company listed for trading on the NYSE.

FOMC: The Federal Reserve Board's Federal Open Market Committee. Sets short-term interest rates by setting discount rate, reserve requirement and buying/selling T-bills to/from primary dealers.

Footnotes: Explanatory notes provided to explain financial statements more clearly. For example, accounting methods for inventory or one-time expenses might require further explanation after the numbers are presented in the company's 10K.

Foreign Currencies: the currencies of various industrialized nations, including the U.S. Dollar, the Euro, the Australian Dollar, the British Pound, and the Yen, etc. Speculators trade such currencies via FOREX.

Foreign Currency Options: Standardized options in which the underlying instrument is a foreign currency, e.g., the yen, the euro, etc.

Foreign Exchange Risk: The risk to an American ADR holder that the American dollar will strengthen versus the currency used by the foreign corporation. For example, an American holding the Toyota ADR is at risk that the US dollar will strengthen versus the yen. AKA "currency exchange risk."

FOREX: the term used for trading foreign currencies; short for "foreign exchange."

Form ADV: Registration form for an investment adviser.

Form ADV PART 2: The disclosure document for an investment adviser.

Form BD: Registration form for a broker-dealer.

Form N-1A: SEC form filed by an investment company to register under the Investment Company of 1940 and to register its securities under the Securities Act of 1933.

Form U4: Registration form for a securities agent or principal of a broker-dealer, or an investment adviser representative.

Form U5: The form filed when an IAR or agent/principal terminate employment for any reason.

Forward: An unregulated derivative security.

Forward Pricing: The method of valuing mutual fund shares, whereby a purchase or redemption order is executed at the next calculated price. Mutual fund shares are bought and sold at the next computed price, not yesterday's stale prices.

Fourth Market: Electronic Communications Networks used by institutional investors to trade directly through an electronic alternative display facility.

Fractional Share: A portion of a whole share of stock. Mutual fund shares typically are issued as whole and fractional shares, e.g., 101.45 shares.

Fraud: Using deceit or manipulation to wrongfully take money/property from someone under false pretenses.

Free Credit Balance: The cash in a customer account that can be withdrawn.

Free-Look: Period during which a contract or policyholder may cancel and receive all sales charges paid.

Freeriding: Under Regulation T, freeriding occurs when a customer buys stock and then uses the sales proceeds rather than sending funds to pay for the buy side. Leads to an account freeze.

Freeriding & Withholding: A violation in which underwriters fail to distribute all shares allocated in an offering of a "hot issue."

Front-end Load: A mutual fund commission or sales fee charged when shares are purchased (A-shares). The amount of the load is added to the NAV to determine the public offering price (POP).

Front-running: The violation of taking advantage of a customer order by purchasing securities before entering a customer's buy order or selling securities before entering a customer's sell order.

Frozen Account: Account in which purchase orders will be accepted only if the cash is in the account due to the customer's failure to comply with Reg T.

Full Faith and Credit: A phrase used to denote that there are no specific assets backing a bond issue, only the issuer's ability to repay the loan.

Fully Registered Bonds: Bonds whose principal and interest payments are tracked/registered for purposes of taxation. A physical certificate with the owner's name, and interest payable automatically by the paying agent (no coupons).

Fundamental Analysis: Studying companies in terms of their competitive position and financial strength to determine the advisability of investing in their securities.

Fundamental Analyst: an analyst who makes securities investment decision based on studying the fundamentals of the issuer, including financial statements.

Funded Debt: Another term for corporate bonds backed by a sinking fund as opposed to collateral.

Fund of Funds: A mutual fund comprised of many funds from the same family.

Futures Contract: A derivative contract where the underlying instrument is a commodity or a financial index.

Future Value: The amount to which an investment will grow by a future date given a compounded rate of return.

G

GDP: Total of goods and services being produced by the economy; economic output regardless of the nationality of the workers.

GTC or **Good-Til-Canceled:** A limit or stop order that is to remain open until executed or canceled by the investor, as opposed to a "day order."

General Account: Where an insurance company invests net premiums to fund guaranteed, fixed payouts.

General Obligation Bond: Municipal bond backed by the issuer's full faith and credit or full taxing authority.

General Partner: The owner of a General Partnership or the manager of a limited partnership with unlimited liability and a fiduciary obligation to the limited partners.

General Partnership: A pass-through entity that provides no protection to the owners against debts and lawsuits.

Generic Advertising: Investment company communications with the public that promote securities as investments but not securities.

Gift: Transferring property to someone else with nothing expected in return.

Gift Splitting: Claiming a gift among both husband-and-wife to avoid exceeding the annual gift tax exclusion.

Gift Tax: A tax liability triggered when a gift exceeds the current exclusion limit.

Global Fund: A mutual fund investing in companies located and doing business all across the globe, including the US.

GNMA or **Government National Mortgage Association**: A government agency (not a public company) that buys insured mortgages from lenders, selling pass-through certificates to investors. Monthly payments to investors pay interest and also pass through principal from a pool of mortgages.

GNP: The economic output of a nation's citizens, wherever they are located.

Good Faith Deposit: Deposit required by a municipal issuer for all syndicates submitting bids for an issue of bonds. Typically 1–2% of par value.

Goodwill: Intangible asset representing the price paid to acquire a company above its hard, tangible value.

Government-Assisted Housing: A type of DPP investment that typically receives tax credits from a government in exchange for providing low-income housing for the community.

Grantor: The party funding a trust with a transfer of assets.

Grantor Trust: Trust where the grantor receives an economic benefit and, therefore, is responsible for taxation of the trust.

Green Shoe Clause: Agreement allowing the underwriters to sell additional shares if demand is high for an offering of securities.

Gross Domestic Product: See GDP.

Gross Margin: Gross profit divided *into* revenue. For example, a company with $100 million in revenue and cost-of-goods-sold of $70 million has a gross margin of 30%.

Gross National Product: See GNP.

Gross Profit: A company's revenues minus their "cost of goods sold." For example, a company with $100 million in revenue and cost-of-goods-sold of $70 million has a gross profit of $30 million.

Gross Revenue Pledge: Less common method used by revenue bond issuers in which debt service is paid even before operations & maintenance.

Growth: Investment objective that seeks "capital appreciation." Achieved through common stock, primarily.

Growth & Income: A fund that purchases stocks for growth potential and also for dividend income. Less volatile than pure growth funds due to the income that calms investors down when the ride becomes turbulent. Or, the investment objective of an investor seeking both growth and income.

Growth Funds: Mutual funds investing in stocks expected to grow faster than the overall market and trading at high price-to-earnings multiples.

Growth Stock: A stock in a company expected to outperform the market and trading at a high valuation ratio, e.g. P/E.

GSE or **Government-Sponsored Enterprise:** A privately held financial services company created by the US Congress, e.g. FNMA.

Guaranteed Bond: A bond that is issued with a promise by a party other than the issuer to maintain payments of interest and principal if the issuer cannot.

Guardian: A fiduciary who manages the financial affairs of a minor or a person declared mentally incompetent.

H

Head and Shoulders: Chart pattern used by technical analysts to determine that a bull or bear trend is about to reverse.

Hedge, Hedging: To modify the risk taken on a stock position by buying or selling options, e.g., a covered call.

Hedge Fund: Private investment partnership open to accredited investors only. Illiquid investments that generally must be held one or two years before selling. Typically charge a management fee plus the first 20% of capital gains in most cases.

High-Yield: Investment whose income stream is high relative to its low market price. A high-yield bond is either issued by a shaky company or municipal government forced to offer high nominal yields, or it begins to trade at lower and lower prices on the secondary market as the credit quality or perceived credit strength of the issuer deteriorates.

Holding Company: Company organized to invest in other corporations, e.g., Berkshire-Hathaway, which holds large stakes in other companies such as Coca-Cola, See's Candy, Dairy Queen, and Wells Fargo.

Holding Period: Period during which a security was held for purposes of determining whether a capital gain or loss is long- or short-term.

HOLDRs: A structured product introduced by Merrill Lynch in which investors own groupings/baskets of stocks usually by industry group, e.g. pharmaceuticals or consumer staples. Similar to ETFs, only HOLDRs do not change their composition over time or track a index.

Howey Decision: US Supreme Court decision that defined an "investment contract" as "an investment of money in a common enterprise where the investor will profit solely through the efforts of others."

HR-10: A reference to a Keogh plan.

Hybrid REIT: A REIT that owns and operates a portfolio of real estate as well as provides financing for real estate projects.

Hybrid Securities: another name for convertible bonds and convertible preferred stock.

Hypothecate: To pledge securities purchased in a margin account as collateral to secure the loan.

Hypothecation Agreement: Document that gives a broker-dealer the legal authority to pledge a margin customer's securities as collateral to secure the margin loan.

I

IARD or **Investment Adviser Registration Depository:** Defined by the SEC as "an electronic filing system that facilitates investment adviser registration, exempt reporting adviser filing, regulatory review, and the public disclosure information of investment adviser firms." Serves a similar purpose for the advisory industry served by CRD for the brokerage industry.

IDR or **Industrial Development Revenue Bond**: A municipal revenue bond that builds a facility that the issuing municipality leases to a corporation. The lease payments from the corporation back the interest and principal payments on the bonds.

Immediate Annuity: Insurance contract purchased with a single purchase payment that starts to pay the annuitant immediately.

Immediate or Cancel Order: Order to buy or sell securities in which the customer will accept any part of the order that becomes available at a certain price, with the remainder of shares to be canceled.

Income: Investment objective that seeks current income, found by investing in fixed-income securities, e.g., bonds, money market, preferred stock.

Income Bond: A bond that will pay interest only if the issuer earns sufficient income and the board of directors declares the payment; a.k.a. "adjustment bond."

Income Program: A direct participation program that invests in existing producing oil and/or natural gas wells.

Income Statement: A financial statement showing a corporation's results of operations over the quarter or year. Shows revenue, all expenses/costs, and the profit or loss the company showed over the period.

Indenture: A contract that spells out the responsibilities and rights of an issuer in connection with a bond issue.

Index: A theoretical grouping of stocks, bonds, etc. The Consumer Price Index is a theoretical grouping or "basket" of things that consumers buy, used to track inflation. The Dow Jones Industrial Average is a theoretical grouping of 30 large-company stocks that analysts use to track the stock market.

Indexed Annuity: Insurance product offering a minimum guaranteed rate of return and some participation in an underlying index, usually the S&P 500.

Index Fund: A mutual fund or ETF designed to track a index.

Index Option: A call or put option based on the value of a index, e.g., the Dow Jones Industrial Average or the S&P 500.

Indication of Interest: An investor's expression of interest in purchasing a new issue of securities after reading the preliminary prospectus; not a commitment to buy.

Inflation: A loss of purchasing power as measured by the Consumer Price Index (CPI).

Inflation-Adjusted Return: An investment's return after the rate of inflation/deflation has been factored in. AKA "real rate of return."

Inflation Risk: Also called "constant dollar risk" or "purchasing power risk," it is the risk that inflation will erode the value of a fixed-income stream from a bond or preferred stock.

Initial Public Offering (IPO): A corporation's first sale of stock to public investors. By definition, a primary market transaction in which the issuer receives the proceeds.

Insider: For purpose of insider trading rules, an "insider" is anyone who has or has access to material non-public information. Officers (CEO ,CFO), members of the board of directors, and investors owning > 10% of the company's outstanding shares are assumed to possess and have access to inside information. As fiduciaries to the shareholders, insiders may not use inside information to their benefit.

Inside or **Insider Information:** Material information about a corporation that has not yet been released to the public and would likely affect the price of the corporation's stock and/or bonds. Insider information may not be "disseminated" or acted upon.

Insider Trading and Securities Fraud Enforcement Act (ITSFEA) of 1988: An Act of Congress that addresses insider trading and lists the penalties for violations of the Act. Insider traders may be penalized up to three times the amount of their profit or their loss avoided by using inside information.

Institutional Investor: Not an individual, but, for example, a pension fund, insurance company, or mutual fund.

Insurance: Protection against loss of income due to death, disability, long-term care needs, etc.

Insurance Covenant: Promise by a revenue bond issuer to keep the facility properly insured.

Intangible Asset: An asset not easily valued or converted to cash, e.g. goodwill.

Intangible Drilling Cost or **IDC:** A source of tax shelter for oil & gas exploratory programs; includes labor and geological surveys as opposed to equipment and other depreciated costs.

Integration: The final stage in the money laundering process.

Interest Rate: The charge for borrowing money. In a loan, the borrower pays some rate against the principal amount borrowed until the loan is retired. That rate is the interest rate on the loan.

Interest Rate Options: Options based on the price or yield of US Treasury securities.

Interest Rate Risk: The risk that interest rates will rise, pushing the market value of a fixed-income security down.

Interest-Rate Sensitive: a fixed-income security, or any common stock where the issuer's operations are directly affected by interest rate changes, e.g., financial firms.

Internal Rate of Return: In discounted cash flow analysis, the rate of return that makes the net present value of cash flows expected from a project equal to zero. AKA "discount rate."

Internal Revenue Code (IRC): Tax laws for the US written by Congress with all blame passed off conveniently to the IRS.

Internal Revenue Service (IRS): Agency for the federal government responsible for collecting federal taxes for the US Treasury and for administering tax rules and regulations.

International Fund: A mutual fund investing in companies established outside the US.

Inter-positioning: Unnecessarily inserting another party between the broker-dealer and the customer. A violation.

Interstate Offering: An offering of securities in several states, requiring registration with the SEC.

Inter Vivos: A trust established during the grantor's lifetime, as opposed to a testamentary trust.

Intestate: To die without a will.

In-the-money: A call option allowing an investor to buy the underlying stock for less than it is worth or a put option allowing an investor to sell the underlying stock for more than it is worth. For example, if ABC trades @50, both the ABC Oct 45 calls and the ABC Oct 55 puts are "in-the-money."

Intrastate Offering: An offering of securities completed in the issuer's home state with investors who reside in that state, and, therefore, eligible for the Rule 147 Exemption to registration with the SEC. Intrastate offerings generally register with the state Administrator—registration by qualification.

Intrinsic Value: The amount by which an option is in-the-money. For example, if ABC trades @50, an ABC Oct 45 call has $5 of intrinsic value, regardless of what the premium might be.

Inverted Yield Curve: an atypical situation in the bond market in which shorter-term debt securities yield more than longer-term.

Inventory: Finished goods that have not yet been sold by a corporation. A current asset that is included in the current ratio but excluded in the quick ratio.

Inventory Levels: Economic indicator showing finished goods not yet sold, a lagging indicator.

Inventory Turnover Ratio: A measure of how effectively a company deploys its capital, found by taking cost of goods sold from the income statement and dividing that amount by the average inventory over the period.

Inverse ETF: An ETF designed to move in the opposite direction of the underlying index, usually by a factor of 2X or 3X.

Inverse Relationship: When one goes up, the other goes down, and vice versa. Interest Rates and Yields are inversely related to Bond Prices. Your rate of speed is inversely related to your travel time to and from the office.

Inverted Head-and-Shoulders: AKA "head-and-shoulders bottom," a reversal of a down trend.

Investment Adviser: A business or professional compensated for advising others as to the value of or advisability of investing in securities.

Investment Adviser Representative: An individual representing an investment adviser by performing portfolio management services, financial planning services, or selling the services of the adviser.

Investment Banker: A firm that raises capital for issuers on the primary market. AKA "underwriter."

Investment Banking: The business of helping companies with mergers and acquisitions, performing IPOs and additional offerings. Investment bankers raise capital for issuers not by loaning money (like a traditional bank) but by finding investors willing to contribute to the cause.

Investment Company: A company engaged in the business of pooling investors' money and trading in securities on their behalf. Examples include unit investment trusts (UITs), face-amount certificate companies, and management companies.

Investment Company Act of 1940: The federal securities legislation that classified Investment Companies and set rules for registration and operation.

Investment Company Products: Packaged investment products in which the pooled capital of many investors is managed by an investment adviser according to stated objectives and policies. For example, mutual funds and UITs.

Investment Contract: An example of a "security," defined by the Supreme Court's Howey Decision.

Investment Counsel: Term that may be used by investment advisers providing continuous, supervisory management services only (not impersonal advice).

Investment Grade: A bond rated at least BBB by S&P or Baa by Moody's. The bond does not have severe default risk, so it is said to be appropriate for investors, as opposed to the speculators who buy non-investment grade bonds.

Investment Objective: Any goal that an investor has including current income, capital appreciation (growth), capital preservation (safety), or speculation.

Investment Risk: Factors that can have a negative effect on the value of an investment or the income it produces.

Investment Style: An approach to investing, such as active, passive, or buy-and-hold.

IRA or **Individual Retirement Account**: A retirement account/arrangement for an individual with earned income and no older than 70 ½. The Traditional IRA offers tax-deductible contributions while the Roth IRA is funded with non-deductible contributions.

Issued Shares: The number of shares that have been issued by a corporation, a number usually lower than the number of shares authorized by the charter.

Issuer: An individual or entity who issues or proposes to issue any security. For example, the issuer of Google common stock is Google.

Issuing Securities: Raising capital by offering securities to investors on the primary market.

J

Joint Account: Investment account owned by more than one individual.

JTIC or **Joint Tenants In Common:** Account where the assets of the deceased party pass to the deceased's estate, not the other account owner(s).

JTWROS or **Joint Tenants with Rights of Survivorship:** Account where the assets of the deceased party pass to the other account owner(s).

Jumbo: A bank CD of large denominations that can be traded on a secondary market though not usually backed by FDIC insurance.

Junk Bond: A bond backed by an issuer experiencing financial difficulties. AKA "high-yield" or "high-income" bond.

K

K-1: Tax form required of people who own direct participation interests (limited partnership, S-corp).

Keogh: Qualified retirement plan available to sole proprietorships. AKA "Qualified Plan for the Self-Employed."

Keynesian Economics: Economic school of thought that advocates government intervention through fiscal policy as a way to stimulate demand for goods and services.

L

Lagging Indicator: Economic indicator used to confirm a recent trend, e.g. duration of unemployment, inventory.

Large Cap: A stock where the total value of the outstanding shares is large, generally greater than $10 billion. For example, SBUX, MSFT, ORCL.

Last-In-First-Out (LIFO): Accounting method used for random withdrawals from an annuity. The IRS assumes that all withdrawals represent part of the taxable "excess over cost basis" first.

Layering: The phase of money laundering in which the first attempt at disguising the source of the ownership of the funds is made by creating complex layers of transactions.

Leading Indicator: Economic indicator used to predict future developments in the economy, e.g. new claims for unemployment, building permits.

LEAPS: A long-term standardized option.

Legal Opinion: The opinion of the bond counsel attesting to the municipality's legal authority to issue the bonds as well as the tax status of the bonds.

Legal Person: An entity rather than a human being/natural person. For example, a trust, estate, or corporation.

Legislative Risk: The risk to an investor that laws will change and have a negative impact on an investment. For example, if municipal bonds lose their tax-exempt interest, their value would plummet. AKA "regulatory risk."

Letter of Intent or **LOI:** Feature of many mutual funds whereby an investor may submit a letter or form expressing the intent to invest enough money over 13 months to achieve a breakpoint.

Level Load: Ongoing asset-based sales charge (12b-1 fee) associated with mutual fund C-shares.

Leverage: Using borrowed money to increase returns. Debt securities and margin accounts are associated with "leverage."

Leveraged Buy Out (LBO): A transaction in which a private equity group buys out a company with the proceeds of a bond issue or a syndicate of loans.

Leveraged ETF: An exchange-traded fund using derivatives to increase its exposure to the underlying index, usually by a factor of either 2X or 3X.

Liabilities: What an individual or a company owes, e.g., credit card debt, bonds, mortgage balance, accounts payable.

LIBOR: stands for London Interbank Offered Rate, a benchmark rate that many large international banks charge each other for short-term loans.

Life Insurance: Protection against a sudden loss of income due to the death of the "insured."

Life Only/Life Annuity: Payout option whereby the insurance/annuity company promises to make payments only for the rest of the annuitant's life.

Life with Joint and Last Survivor: Payout option whereby the insurance/annuity company promises to make payments to the annuitant for the rest of his life, then to the survivor for the rest of her life.

Life With Period Certain: Payout option whereby the insurance/annuity company promises to make payments to the annuitant for the rest of his life or a certain period of time, whichever is greater.

Life With Unit Refund: Payout option whereby the insurance/annuity company promises to make at least a certain number of payments to the annuitant or beneficiary.

Lifecycle Fund: An age-based or target portfolio automatically adjusting asset allocation to match the investor's needs based on the age of the beneficiary or retiree, for example.

Limit Orders: Orders to buy or sell a security at a specified price or better.

Limited Liability: An investor's ability to limit losses to no more than the amount invested. Holders of common stock and limited partnership interests enjoy "limited liability," which means they can only lose 100% of what they invest.

Limited Liability Company or **LLC:** Form of business ownership in which the owners, called members, receive their share of income/loss and receive protection against personal liability.

Limited Partner: A person who owns a limited partnership interest. Has no managerial responsibility and is shielded from debts of—and lawsuits against—the partnership.

Limited Partnership: Form of business ownership in which income and expenses flow through directly to the partners rather than to a separate business entity.

Limited Representative: what one would be after passing the Series 6 and getting registered to represent one's broker-dealer. One would be a "general securities representative" once one passes the Series 7 exam.

Limited Tax Bonds: General obligation bonds backed by a tax whose rate may not be increased above a certain limit.

Limited Trading Authorization: Authorization for someone other than the account owner to enter purchase and sale orders but make no withdrawals of cash or securities.

Liquidation Priority: The priority of claims on a bankrupt entity's assets that places creditors (bondholders) ahead of stockholders and preferred stockholders ahead of common stockholders.

Liquid Net Worth: Net worth figured without including hard-to-sell assets such as real estate or art work.

Liquidity: Ability to quickly convert an investment to cash and get a fair price.

Liquidity Risk: The risk of being unable to sell a security quickly for a fair price; a.k.a. "marketability risk."

Listed: Refers to a security trading on NYSE, Nasdaq, or any nationally-recognized exchange that monitors the issuers who list for trading there.

Loan Consent: Document giving the broker-dealer permission to lend a customer's securities to short sellers.

London Interbank Market: where large international banks go to get short-term loans at the most competitive rates possible. See LIBOR.

Long: To buy or own. To begin a securities transaction by making a purchase.

Long-Term Capital Gain: Profit realized when selling stock held for at least 12 months plus 1 day. Subject to lower capital gains tax rates than short-term gains.

Long-Term Capital Loss: A loss realized when selling stock held for at least 12 months plus 1 day. Used to offset long-term capital gains.

Long-Term Liability: A debt to be repaid in the long-run, e.g., the principal value of an outstanding bond issue.

Lump Sum Payment: A settlement/payout option for annuities or insurance where the annuitant or beneficiary receives one payment as opposed to a series of payments.

M

Maintenance Covenant: A promise of a revenue bond issuer to keep the facility properly maintained.

Maloney Act: Amendment to the Securities Exchange Act of 1934 creating the NASD as a self-regulatory organization (SRO) for the over-the-counter (OTC) market.

Management Company: One of the three types of Investment Companies, including both open-end and closed-end funds.

Management Fee: The % of assets charged to a mutual fund portfolio to cover the cost of portfolio management services provided by the investment adviser to the fund.

Manager's Fee: Typically the smallest piece of the spread, paid to the managing underwriter for e share sold by the syndicate.

Managing Underwriter: The broker-dealer who negotiates the underwriting with the issuer and manages the syndicate during the offering.

Margin: Amount of equity contributed by a customer as a percentage of the current market value of the securities held in a margin account.

Margin Account: As opposed to a cash account, allows investors to engage in short sales and investing borrowed money.

Marginal Tax Bracket: The range of adjusted gross incomes subject to a marginal tax rate.

Marginal Tax Rate: The tax rate applied to the last dollar of income earned.

Markdown: Difference between the highest bid price for a security and the price that a dealer pays an investor for her security.

Marketability: The ease or difficulty an investor has when trying to sell a security for cash without losing his shirt. More often called "liquidity."

Marketability Risk: Usually called "liquidity risk," the risk that a thinly-traded security cannot be converted to cash without experiencing a loss of principal.

Market Cap: The total value of an issuer's outstanding shares.

Market Maker: A dealer maintaining an inventory of a security and a firm Bid and Ask price good for a minimum of 100 shares. Acts as a "principal" on transactions, buying and selling for its/their own account.

Market Manipulation: The illegal process of using deception to move securities prices in favor of the conspirators. Includes terms such as "painting the tape" or "pegging."

Market Order: An order to buy or sell a security at the best available market price.

Market Risk: A type of "systematic risk," the risk inherent to the entire market rather than a specific security. The risk that the stock market may suffer violent upheavals due to unpredictable events including natural disaster, war, disease, famine, credit crises, etc.

Marking to the Market: Process of calculating margin requirements based on the most current market values for the securities in a margin account.

Markup: The difference between the lowest ask/offer price for a security and the price that a dealer charges.

Material Information: A fact that could reasonably affect an investor's decision to buy, sell, or hold a security. For example, profits and losses at the company, product liability lawsuits, the loss of key clients, etc.

Matching Contributions: What the employer contributes to the employee's account based on the elective deferral chosen and the make-up of the plan.

Maturity Date: The date that a bond pays out the principal, and interest payments cease. Also called "redemption."

Mean: A measure of central tendency, the average of a set of numbers.

Median: The middle value in a set of numbers.

Member Firm: A broker-dealer and/or underwriting firm that belongs to FINRA or other securities association (MSRB, CBOE).

Millage Rate: The property tax rate used to calculate a property owner's tax bill. The assessed value times the millage rate is the property tax owed, before any exemptions or other factors are included.

Mini-Max: A type of best efforts underwriting where the syndicate must sell a minimum amount and may sell up to a higher, maximum amount.

Minimum Death Benefit: The minimum death benefit payable to the insured, regardless of how lousy the separate account returns are in a variable policy.

Minimum Maintenance Requirement: The minimum amount of equity that a margin customer must maintain on either a short or a long position.

Mode: The number in a data set occurring most frequently.

Model Rule: Publication by NASAA stating accepted regulatory approaches to certain aspects of the securities industry faced by state and provincial regulators.

Modern Portfolio Theory: Investment approach using optimal portfolios to maximize returns for a given level of risk. Based on belief that uncorrelated investments can reduce the overall risk of a portfolio. Associated with "efficient frontier."

Monetarists: Those who advocate and/or implement monetary policy, e.g. The Federal Reserve.

Monetary Policy: What the FRB implements through the discount rate, reserve requirement, and FOMC open market operations. Monetary policy tightens or loosens credit to affect short-term interest rates and, therefore, the economy.

Money Laundering: The process of turning profits from illegal enterprises into seemingly legitimate assets, e.g. Saul Goodman of "Breaking Bad."

Money Market Mutual Fund: A highly liquid holding place for cash. Sometimes called "stable value" funds, as the share price is generally maintained at $1. The mutual funds invest in—surprisingly—money market securities.

Money Market Security: A short-term debt obligation, e.g., commercial paper, bankers' acceptance, T-Bill.

Money Purchase Plan: A retirement plan in which the employer must contribute a set percentage of the employee's salary, regardless of profitability.

Monte Carlo: Simulations used to predict the effects of various factors, e.g. bear markets, inflation, high interest rates, etc., often used to assist with estimating withdrawal rates from a retirement account.

Moody's Investors Service: One of the top three credit rating agencies for corporate and municipal bonds as well as stocks.

Moral Obligation Bond: Type of revenue bond with a provision to seek emergency funding from the state legislature should the issuer run into financial problems.

Mortality & Expense Risk Fees: Extra charges in addition to charges for investment services for variable contracts to cover the risks of rising expenses and payouts connected to death benefits.

Mortality Guarantee: A promise from an insurance company to pay out no matter how soon the insured dies, or to pay an annuitant no matter how long he lives.

Mortgage-Backed Security: A security in which the interest and principal payments are backed by a pool of mortgages.

Mortgage Bond: A corporate bond secured by a pledge of real estate as collateral.

Mortgage REIT: A Real Estate Investment Trust that buys and/or makes loans for real estate projects.

MSRB (Municipal Securities Rulemaking Board): The self-regulatory organization overseeing municipal securities dealers.

Multiplier Effect: the outsized effect that a change in the reserve requirement can have based on the percentage of deposits banks are required to hold on reserve.

Municipal Bond: A bond issued by a state, county, city, school district, etc., to build roads, schools, hospitals, etc., or to keep the government running long enough to hold another election.

Municipal Bond Fund: A mutual fund that invests in municipal bonds with an objective to maximize federally tax-exempt income.

Municipal Note: A short-term obligation of a city, state, school district, etc., backed by the anticipation of funds from revenues, taxes, or upcoming bond issues, e.g., TAN, RAN, BAN.

Mutual Fund: An investment company offering equity stakes in a portfolio that is usually managed actively and that always charges management fees and other expenses.

N

Naked Call: Selling a call against securities not yet owned, leading to unlimited risk.

Narrow-based Index: Index focusing on a industry or geographic region, e.g., a transportation index.

NASD (National Association of Securities Dealers): Former name of the SRO empowered with the passage of the Maloney Act of 1938. Regulates its own members and enforces SEC rules and regulations. Now called FINRA after a merger with the regulators from the NYSE.

NASDAQ: National Association of Securities Dealers Automated Quotation system. The main component of the OTC market. Stocks that meet certain criteria are quoted throughout the day on NASDAQ, e.g., MSFT, ORCL, and INTC.

NASDAQ 100: A large-cap index comprised of 100 non-financial companies trading on the NASDAQ.

NASAA or **North American Securities Administrators Association**: Organization of state and Canadian provincial securities regulators responsible for the Series 66, Series 66, and Series 63 exams.

National Adjudicatory Council: NAC, the first level of appeal for a party sanctioned by the DOE under FINRA's Code of Procedure.

Natural Event Risk: Risk that a weather-related event could have a negative effect on securities or securities markets.

NAV or **Net Asset Value:** The net asset value of a mutual fund share. Assets – Liabilities/Outstanding Shares.

Needs Analysis: The process of determining how much insurance an individual should buy based on mortgage and other debts, income, final expenses, etc.

Negotiable: The characteristic of a security that allows an investor to sell or transfer ownership to another party. For example, savings bonds are not negotiable, while Treasury Bills are negotiable.

Negotiable CD: A bank CD that can be traded on a secondary market, usually of large denominations.

Negotiated Market: Another name for the "second" or "over-the-counter" market.

Negotiated Underwriting: A municipal bond—usually a revenue bond—underwritten without a competitive, sealed bid.

Net Asset Value: NAV, the value of one share of a mutual fund or unit of a UIT.

Net Asset Value per Bond: A measure of an issuer's long-term solvency, found by dividing the net tangible assets of the company (not goodwill and other intangible assets) by the number of bonds issued.

Net Income After Tax: Revenue minus all expenses. Also known as a "profit" or a "loss," depending on whether it's a positive or negative number.

Net Interest Cost: A measure of a municipal issuer's total cost of borrowing money by issuing bonds.

Net Investment Income: The source of an investment company's dividend distributions to shareholders. It is calculated by taking the fund's dividends and interest collected on portfolio securities, minus the operating expenses. Funds using the "conduit tax theory" distribute at least 90% of net investment income to avoid paying taxes on the amount distributed to shareholders.

Net Overall Debt: A municipal issuer's direct debt plus their overlapping debt.

Net Present Value: The present value of a project's expected cash flows minus the costs associated with acquiring the asset.

Net Profit: Another name for net income after tax.

Net Profit Margin, Net Margin: A company's net income after tax divided by revenue, showing the percentage of each dollar of revenue making its way to the bottom line.

Net Revenue: Another name for revenue, accounting for any returns, refunds or discounting. AKA "net operating revenue" or "net sales."

Net Revenue Pledge: The more common method used by the issuer of a revenue bond in which operations & maintenance are covered before debt service.

Net Sales: AKA, "net revenue."

Networking Arrangement: A broker-dealer operating on the premises of a bank where retail deposits are taken.

Net Worth: The difference between assets and liabilities.

New Construction: A type of DPP in which the partnership builds and then sells housing units.

New Issue Market: The primary market, where securities are issued to investors with the proceeds going to the issuer of the securities. Initial public offerings (IPOs), for example, take place on the "new issue market."

NHA – New Housing Authority (bonds): Revenue bonds issued by a municipal government but ultimately backed by the United States Government, who guarantees rental payments for the residents of the housing project.

No-Action Relief: Letter to a securities regulator verifying that a action or course of business would require no registration and lead to no regulatory action on their part if performed as stated in the request.

No-load Fund: Mutual fund sold without a sales charge, but one which may charge an ongoing 12b-1fee or "asset-based sales charge" up to .25% of net assets.

Nolo Contendere: A "no contest" plea to a criminal charge subject to disclosure on Form ADV, BD, U4 and U5.

Nominal Quote: A quote in which a dealer is giving an estimate rather than a firm price at which he is ready to trade. Must be clearly identified as nominal to avoid backing away.

Nominal Yield: Interest rate paid by a bond or preferred stock. The investor receives this % of the par value each year, regardless of what the bond or preferred stock is trading for on the secondary market.

Non-accredited Purchaser: Investor who does not meet various SEC net worth and/or income requirements. For a Reg D private placement, accredited investors may participate, but only a limited number of non-accredited investors may purchase the issue.

Non-cumulative Preferred Stock: Preferred stock that does not have to pay missed dividends (dividends in arrears).

Nondiscrimination Covenant: A promise by a municipal revenue bond issuer that all users of a facility must pay to use it, including VIPs of the municipality.

Non-diversified Fund: A fund that doesn't meet the 75-5-10 rule, preferring to concentrate more heavily in certain issues.

Non-equity Options: Standardized options based on things other than equity securities, e.g., indexes or foreign currency options.

Non-NASDAQ OTC Securities: Over-the-counter securities that do not meet the requirements of NASDAQ. For example, Pink Market or OTCBB securities. By definition, "unlisted" securities.

Non-systematic Risk: The risk of holding any one stock or bond. Diversification spreads this risk among different issuers and different industries to minimize the impact of a bankruptcy or unexpected collapse of any one issuer.

Non-Punitive: An order issued by the state securities Administrator that is not a deny/suspend/revoke order, e.g., a withdrawal or a cancellation.

Non-Qualified Plan: Tax-deferred, employer-sponsored retirement plan that falls outside the guidelines of ERISA, e.g., a non-qualified deferred compensation plan.

Normal Yield Curve: the typical state of the bond market in which yields on debt securities rise as their maturities lengthen.

Not Held (Order): AKA "market not held." A market order in which the customer allows the broker-dealer to enter the trade when they feel the price is right, as opposed to a market order, which is filled as soon as possible.

Note: A short-term debt security.

Notice Filing: A requirement under NSMIA for a federal covered adviser to notify any state securities regulator where it maintains a place of business, or for investment companies to notify the states where there shares are offered and sold.

Numbered Account: Account identified with a number rather than a name. Allowed if the owner files a statement with the broker-dealer attesting to ownership.

NYSE: New York Stock Exchange, an auction market where buyers and sellers shout out competitive bid and asked/offered prices throughout the day.

NSMIA or **National Securities Markets Improvement Act:** Legislation creating a class of securities to be registered exclusively with the SEC.

O

Obsolescence Risk: The unsystematic risk that an issuer's products/services will become obsolete or no longer in demand due to changing times, technologies, and consumer behaviors.

Odd Lot: Order for less than the usual trading unit for a security, e.g. fewer than 100 shares of common stock.

Odd Lot Theory: Investment approach that does the opposite of what odd-lot investors are doing.

Offer: Another name for "ask," or the price an investor must pay if he wants to buy a security from a dealer/market maker.

Offer of Settlement: A respondent's offer to the disciplinary committee of FINRA to settle his or her recent rule violations.

Office of Foreign Asset Control or **OFAC:** federal government office that maintains a list of individuals and organizations viewed as a threat to the U.S. Such individuals and entities are known as "Specially Designated Nationals."

Officers: High-level executives at a public corporation, e.g., the Chief Executive Officer (CEO), Chief Financial Officer (CFO), and the Chief Operating Officer (COO).

Official Notice of Sale: Advertisement in the Bond Buyer in which a municipal issuer hopes to attract potential underwriters.

Official Statement: Document that discloses detailed information about a municipal bond issuer's financial condition.

OID or **Original Issue Discount**: A bond purchased for less than the par value on the primary market, e.g., a STRIP.

Omitting Prospectus: Advertisement for a mutual fund that typically shows performance figures without providing (omitting) the full disclosure contained in the prospectus. Therefore, it must present caveats and encourage readers to read the prospectus and consider all the risks before investing in the fund.

Open-end Fund: Investment company that sells an unlimited number of shares to an unlimited number of investors on a continuous basis. Shares are redeemed by the company rather than traded among investors.

Open Market Operations: What the FOMC engages in when buying or selling US Treasuries to achieve targets for short-term interest rates.

Operating Agreement: Document governing the structure and operation of an LLC.

Operating Expenses: Expenses that a mutual fund deducts from the assets of the fund, including board of director salaries, custodial and transfer agent services, management fees, 12b-1 fees, etc. More generally, operating expenses are shown on a company's income statement to indicate expenses beyond COGS, e.g. administrative salaries, office supplies, office rent.

Operating Income, Operating Profit: Measurement from a company's income statement, revenue minus COGS, operating expenses, and depreciation.

Operating Margin: Operating income divided by revenue.

Opportunity Cost: The return on an investment given up to pursue another opportunity.

Option: A derivative giving the holder the right to buy or sell something for a stated price up to expiration of the contract. Puts and calls.

Order Room: The department of a broker-dealer that places trades. AKA "wire room."

Order Ticket/Trade Ticket: Information filled out by a registered representative when placing an order to buy or sell securities.

Ordinary Dividend: A dividend payment that does not receive qualified-dividend tax treatment but is, rather, treated as ordinary income.

Ordinary Income: Most income received by a taxpayer, including salary, wages, bonuses, bond interest, ordinary dividends, etc.

Ordinary Income Rate: Tax rate paid on earned income and some forms of investment income.

OTC/Over-the-Counter: Not traded on NYSE, but through NASDAQ and also Bulletin Board and Pink Market stocks.

Out-of-The-Money: An option that gives the holder no benefit because it has no intrinsic value.

Outstanding Shares: Number of shares a corporation has outstanding. Used to calculate EPS.

Overbought: A technical analysis/chartist term for a security trading near resistance.

Oversold: A technical analysis/chartist term for a security trading near support.

Overlapping Debt: The debt that a municipal issuer is responsible for along with a coterminous issuer.

P

PAC or **Planned Amortization Class:** Type of CMO (collateralized mortgage obligation) that provides more protection against extension risk vs. a TAC.

Paid-In Surplus: Amount above the par value that investors paid when purchasing the company's initial public offering.

Painting the Tape: Form of market manipulation in which bogus trades are reported to affect the market price of a security. A violation.

Par: The face amount of a bond payable at maturity. Also, the face amount of a preferred stock. Preferred = $100, Bond = $1,000. AKA "principal."

Parity: When a convertible bond's or convertible preferred stock's market price is exactly equal to the value of the shares to which it converts.

Partial Surrender: When a life insurance policyholder cashes in part of the cash value. Excess over premiums is taxable.

Participating Preferred Stock: Preferred stock whose dividend is often raised above the stated rate.

Participation: Provision of ERISA requiring that all employees in a qualified retirement plan be covered within a reasonable length of time after being hired.

Participation Rate: The percentage of the index's increase credited to the value of an indexed annuity.

Partnership: A flow-through business entity established as either a general or limited partnership, in which the owners—not the business itself—are taxed on their share of any net income.

Partnership Agreement: Agreement governing the operation of a general or limited partnership.

Partnership Democracy: Term referring to a limited partner's right to vote in certain matters of major importance.

Passive Income: As opposed to "earned income," the income derived from rental properties, limited partnerships, or other enterprises in which the individual is not actively involved.

Passive Investor: Investor who feels markets are efficient and, therefore, does not actively select/trade investments. Associated with the exclusive use of index funds based on the goals of the investor rather than on anticipated market movements.

Passive Loss: A loss derived from rental properties, limited partnerships, or other enterprises in which the individual is not actively involved.

Pass-Through Certificate: A mortgage-backed security (usually GNMA) that takes a pool of mortgages and passes through interest and principal monthly to an investor.

Payable (or Payment) Date: Date that a dividend check is paid to investors.

Pay-On-Death: A bank account that will transfer to a named beneficiary upon death of the account owner.

Payroll Deduction: Non-qualified retirement plan offered by some businesses.

P/E Ratio: The market price of a stock compared to the earnings per-share. Stocks trading at high P/E ratios are "growth stocks," while those trading at low P/E ratios are "value stocks." See "price-to-earnings ratio."

Peak: Phase of the business cycle between expansion (good times) and contraction (bad times).

Pegging: A form of market manipulation. A violation.

Penny Stock: An OTC equity security trading below $5 per-share.

Penny Stock Cold Calling Rules: Rules to protect consumers receiving telemarketing pitches to buy risky stocks trading below $5 a share. Rules require special disclosure and investor signatures when selling penny stocks.

Pension Plan: Contract between an individual and an employer that provides for the distribution of benefits at retirement.

Per Capita: For an inheritance, per capita means if a beneficiary dies, his share is split by the other named beneficiaries.

Performance Figures: Total return for a mutual fund over 1, 5, and 10 years, and/or "life of fund." Only past performance may be indicated, and there must be a caveat that past performance does not guarantee future results.

Period Certain: A payout option on an annuity promising payments for a minimum number of years.

Periodic-Payment Deferred Annuity: Method of purchasing an annuity whereby the contract holder makes periodic payments into the contract. The pay-out phase must be deferred for all periodic payment plans.

Permanent Insurance: Life insurance other than "term."

Per Stirpes: For an inheritance, per stirpes means if a beneficiary dies, his share passes to his heirs and not the other named beneficiaries.

Pink Markets: A virtually unregulated part of the OTC market where thinly traded, volatile stocks change hands.

Placement: The first stage in the cycle of money laundering in which illegally generated funds are placed into the financial system or are smuggled out of the country.

Placement Ratio: A statistic published in the Bond Buyer showing the dollar amount of municipal securities sold on the primary market out of the dollar amount offered the previous week; a.k.a. the "acceptance ratio."

Policy Owner, Policy Holder: The person who owns a life insurance policy. Often, though not necessarily, also the insured

Political Risk: The risk that a country's government will radically change policies or that the political climate will become hostile or counterproductive to business and financial markets. Faced especially by emerging market investors.

Pooled Investments: Investment products that combine the capital of many investors, e.g., mutual funds and REITS.

POP or Public Offering Price: The price paid by an investor purchasing a new offering of securities. For an IPO, this includes the spread to the underwriters. For a mutual fund, this includes any sales loads that go to the underwriter/distributor.

Portfolio: The combination of investments that an investor owns.

Portfolio Income: Income earned through investing in securities; not to be used toward IRA contributions and not off-settable with passive income.

Portfolio Optimization: Using the efficient frontier to match an investor's risk tolerance and objectives with the most efficient portfolio possible on a risk-adjusted basis.

Position Limit: Maximum number of options contracts that a trader can have on the same side of the market (bull/bear) and/or may exercise over a five day period.

Power of Substitution: Document that when signed by the security owner authorizes transfer of the certificate to another party.

PPI or Producer Price Index: A family of indices showing the prices received by producers at various stages of the production cycle: commodity level, intermediate demand, and final demand.

Precious Metals: Gold, silver, platinum, and palladium.

Precious Metals Fund: a mutual fund that typically holds shares of mining companies (gold, silver, copper, etc.)

Pre-dispute Arbitration Agreement: Agreement signed by the customer of a broker-dealer in which the customer agrees to use arbitration rather than civil court to settle disputes.

Pre-emptive Right: The right of common stockholders to maintain their proportional ownership if the company offers more shares of stock.

Preferred Stock: A fixed-income equity security whose stated dividends must be paid before common stock can receive any dividend payment. Also gets preference ahead of common stock in a liquidation (but behind all bonds and general creditors).

Preliminary Official Statement: The official statement for a municipal bond issue subject to further additions and changes.

Preliminary Prospectus: A prospectus that lacks the POP and the effective date; a.k.a. "red herring." Used to solicit indications of interest.

Premium: 1) The amount by which a bond's price exceeds the par value. 2), the amount paid to acquire an options contract. 3), the amount paid to maintain an insurance contract.

Premium Bond: A bond purchased for more than the par value, usually due to a drop in interest rates.

Prepayment Risk: The risk that the mortgages underlying a mortgage-backed security/pass-through will be paid off sooner than expected due to a drop in interest rates. Investors reinvest the principal at a lower rate going forward.

Present Value: The value today of an amount of money in the future, discounted by some compounded rate of return.

Preservation of Capital: Investment objective placing the emphasis on making sure the principal is not lost.

Pre-Tax Contribution: A contribution made to a tax-advantaged plan for which the individual receives a current deduction for income tax purposes, e.g. contributions to a Traditional IRA or 401(k) plan.

Pre-Tax Margin: A company's pre-tax profit divided by revenue.

Pre-Tax Profit: A measure of profitability from a company's income statement accounting for all expenses other than taxes.

Price-To-Book Ratio: The market price of a common stock compared to the book value per-share.

Price-To-Cash Ratio: The market price of a common stock compared to the cash flow per-share.

Price-To-Earnings Ratio: The market price of a common stock compared to the EPS of that stock. AKA "P/E ratio."

Price-To-Sales Ratio: The market price of a common stock compared to the revenue per-share.

Primary Market: Where securities are issued to raise capital for the issuer. AKA "new-issue market."

Primary Offering: Offering of securities in which the proceeds go to the issuer, e.g., an IPO.

Prime Rate: Interest rate charged to corporations with high credit ratings for unsecured loans.

Principal: A word that can mean many different things in the securities industry. 1) The amount to be received upon maturity for a bond, 2) A supervisor of a broker-dealer or investment adviser, 3) To buy or sell from or to a customer in a securities transaction, 4) The amount borrowed when taking out a mortgage, against which an interest rate is to be charged.

Principal-Protected Fund: A mutual fund for people who want their principal protected. Involves holding the investment for several years, at which point the fund guarantees that the value of the investment will be equal to at least what the investor put in.

Principal Transaction: A potential conflict of interest arising when the investment adviser enters a transaction to buy or sell a security on behalf of a client with the transaction done on a principal basis by the affiliated broker-dealer. Requires disclosure and client consent.

Private Activity Bond: A municipal bond subjecting investors to AMT because the issuer does not qualify under the Internal Revenue Code as a municipal issuer. For example, a parking garage built with the proceeds of a revenue bond may benefit a corporate entity as opposed to a city government or subdivision.

Private Equity Fund: An alternative investment fund open to sophisticated investors only and specializing in buying out companies both public and private.

Private Foundations: Charitable organizations that receive their support from a few donors and are usually controlled by their founders or large contributors.

Private Placement: Exempt transaction under Reg D (Rule 506) of the Securities Act of 1933, allowing issuers to sell securities without registration to accredited investors, who agree to hold them for a required period that is subject to change by the SEC before selling them through Rule 144. Or, an exempt transaction under state securities law in which the security is offered to no more than 10 persons in the state.

Private Securities Transaction: Offering an investment opportunity not sponsored by the firm. Requires permission from the firm and any disclosure demanded; otherwise, a violation called "selling away."

Probate: The process of "proving" a will through the submission of various legal documents used to gather the assets of the deceased, pay off debts, and distribute assets to any named beneficiaries.

Proceeds: The amount an investor receives when selling a capital asset, less any commissions or fees to execute the sale.

Proceeds Transaction: Using the proceeds from a sale of securities to buy other securities on the same day.

Producer Price Index: An index measuring price changes at the wholesale or producer level. AKA "PPI."

Profit: The bottom line of a company's income statement, revenue minus all expenses. AKA "net income."

Profit-Sharing Arrangement: A security involving a share of profits from any source.

Profit Sharing Plan: A defined contribution plan whereby the company makes discretionary contributions to a tax-advantaged account on behalf of employees according to a prescribed allocation plan.

Progressive Tax: A tax that increases as a percentage as the thing being taxed increases, including gift, estate, and income taxes. Not a flat tax.

Prospectus: Disclosure document that details a company's plans, history, officers, and risks of investment. It's the red herring plus the POP and the effective date.

Protective Covenants: Promises from the issuer of a revenue bond to the bondholders designed to protect the bondholders against default.

Proxy: A form granting the power to vote according to a shareholder's instructions when the shareholder will not attend the meeting.

Prudent Investor Standards: Guidance provided to fiduciaries investing on behalf of a third party, e.g., trustees or custodians of UTMA accounts.

Public Housing Authority (PHA) Bonds: Revenue bonds backed by guaranteed rental payments from the US Treasury. See "NHA/New Housing Authority Bonds."

PSA Model: Method of estimating the speed of prepayments on a CMO investment.

Public Charities: Organizations that by their nature conduct public activities, and have broad public support.

Public Offering: The sale of an issue of common stock, either an IPO or an additional offer of shares.

Public Offering Price (POP): The price an investor pays for a mutual fund or an initial public offering. For a mutual fund, POP = NAV + the sales charge.

Punitive: An order by the state securities Administrator to deny, suspend, or revoke a registration.

Purchase Payment: What an annuitant pays into the annuity contract.

Purchasing Power: The ability of a dollar to buy the things one needs on an inflation-adjusted basis. Inflation erodes the purchasing power of the dollar, which is why investors allocate funds to equity investments, the best inflation-adjusted investment vehicle historically.

Purchasing Power Risk: The risk that a fixed payment will not be sufficient to keep up with rising inflation (as measured through the CPI). AKA "inflation risk," "constant-dollar risk."

Put (n.): A contract giving the owner the right to sell something at a stated exercise price.

Put (v.): To sell.

Put Feature: A feature of some bonds allowing investors to put/sell the securities back to the issuer or underwriters, usually for the par value.

Q

Qualification: A method of registering a securities offering with the Administrator when not registering with the SEC and performing—usually—an intra-state offering only.

Qualified Dividend: A dividend that qualifies for a lower tax rate vs. ordinary income.

Qualified Domestic Relations Order: A legal document that recognizes someone other than the plan participant—whom he or she is divorcing—as having a right to receive benefits from a qualified retirement plan.

Qualified Institutional Buyers: Investors meeting certain SEC criteria allowing them to participate in certain investment opportunities not open to the general public.

Qualified Opinion: Opinion by the bond counsel for a municipal issuer in which some doubt or reservations are expressed.

Qualified Plan: Retirement plan that qualifies for deductible contributions on behalf of employers and/or employees and covered by ERISA. For example, 401(k), defined benefit, Keogh.

Quick Assets: Current assets that are easily liquidated; cash & equivalents and accounts receivable *minus* inventory. Quick assets are used to calculate the company's quick ratio from the balance sheet.

Quick Ratio: More stringent measure of liquidity than the current ratio. Inventory is excluded from current assets before comparing them to the company's current liabilities. AKA "acid test." Seriously.

Quote, Quotation: A price that a dealer is willing to pay or accept for a security. A two-sided quote has both a bid and an asked/offer price.

R

Random Withdrawals: Settlement option in an annuity whereby the annuitant takes the value of the subaccounts in two or more withdrawals, rather than one lump sum.

Range: In a set of numbers, the difference between the largest and smallest value.

Rate Covenant: Promise that the issuer of a revenue bond will raise rates if necessary to cover the debt service.

Rating Service: Company that assigns credit ratings to corporate and municipal bonds, e.g., Moody's and S&P.

Raw Land: Unimproved real estate providing no cash flow and no depreciation. A speculative investment in land.

Realized Gain: Amount of the "profit" an investor earns when selling a security.

Real Rate of Return: An investment's return after inflation/deflation has been factored in. AKA "inflation-adjusted return."

Rebalance: To sell securities to return to the stated percentages/goals of a portfolio. Associated with strategic asset allocation.

Recession: A significant decline in economic activity spread across the economy, lasting more than a few months, normally visible in real GDP, real income, employment, industrial production, and wholesale-retail sales.

Reclamation: Document sent by a broker-dealer when delivery of securities is apparently in error.

Record Date: Date determined by the Board of Directors on which the investor must be the holder "of record" to receive the upcoming dividend. Settlement of a trade must occur by the record date for the buyer to receive the dividend.

Recourse Note: Obligation of a limited partnership for which a limited partner is responsible personally beyond any collateral pledged to secure the loan.

Red Herring: Disclosure document containing essentially the same information that the final prospectus will contain, minus the POP and effective date. AKA "preliminary prospectus."

Redeemable Security: Security that may be presented to the issuer for payment, e.g., open-end funds.

Redemption: For mutual funds, redemption involves the sale of mutual fund shares back to the fund at the NAV (less any redemption fees, back-end loads). For bonds, the date that principal is returned to the investor.

Redemption Fee: A charge to a mutual fund investor who sells her shares back to the fund within a certain time frame.

Refunding: Replacing an outstanding bond issue by issuing new bonds at a lower interest rate. Also known as "calling" a bond issue.

Reg A: An exempt transaction under the Securities Act of 1933 for small offerings of securities.

Reg D: An exempt transaction under the Securities Act of 1933 for private placements.

Reg FD: Legislation requiring that any material non-public information disclosed by a public corporation to analysts or other investors must be made public.

Reg SHO: Rules requiring broker-dealers to locate securities before executing short sales.

Reg T: Federal Reserve Board requirements for cash and margin accounts.

Reg U: Federal Reserve Board requirements for credit extended by banks to broker-dealers for margin accounts.

Registered as to Principal Only: Bond with only the principal registered. Interest coupons must be presented for payment.

Registered Representative: Associated person of an investment banker or broker-dealer who effects transactions in securities for compensation.

Registered Secondary: Offering of securities by persons other than the issuer. For example, the former CEO of a corporation may offer a large block of restricted (unregistered) stock to the public through a broker-dealer.

Registrar: Party that audits the transfer agent to make sure the number of authorized shares is never exceeded.

Registration by Coordination: Method of registering a securities offering with the states where they are to be offered, in addition to required SEC registration.

Registration by Filing: Method of registering a securities offering with the states where they are to be offered in an additional offering that is also registered with the SEC.

Registration by Qualification: Method of registering a securities offering with only the state securities Administrator.

Registration Statement: Legal document disclosing material information concerning an offering of a security and its issuer. Submitted to SEC under Securities Act of 1933.

Regressive Tax: A flat tax, e.g., gasoline, sales, excise taxes.

Regular Way Settlement: The typical time frame for purchasing and settling securities transactions, e.g. T +3 for common stock trades or T + 1 for trades in US Treasury securities.

Regulated Investment Company: An investment company using the conduit tax theory by distributing 90% or more of net investment income to shareholders.

Regulatory Risk: The unsystematic risk that changes to legislation/regulations will have a negative impact on an issuer's business. AKA "legislative risk."

Reinstatement Privilege: A feature of some mutual funds allowing investors to make withdrawals and then reinstate the money without paying another sales charge.

Reinvestment Risk: The risk that a fixed-income investor will not be able to reinvest interest payments or the par value at attractive interest rates. Happens when rates are falling.

REIT (Real Estate Investment Trust): A corporation or trust that uses the pooled capital of investors to invest in ownership of either income property or mortgage loans. 90% of net income is paid out to shareholders.

Release Date: Date established by the SEC as to when the underwriters may sell new securities to the buyers; a.k.a. "effective date."

REMIC: another name for a CMO, stands for a Real Estate Mortgage Investment Conduit.

Repurchase Agreement: Agreement in which one party sells something to the other and agrees to repurchase it for a higher price over the short-term.

Required Minimum Distribution (RMD): The required minimum amount that must be taken from a retirement plan to avoid IRS penalties. Usually must occur by April 1st of the year following the individual's 70½th birthday.

Reserve Requirement: The % of deposits that a bank must lock up in reserve, established by the FRB.

Residual Claim: The right of common stockholders to claim assets after the claims of all creditors and preferred stockholders have been satisfied.

Respondent: The party named in a disciplinary proceeding or arbitration.

Restricted Person: Person who is ineligible to purchase an equity IPO, including members of the brokerage industry and their immediate family members.

Restricted Stock: Stock whose transfer is subject to restrictions, e.g., a holding period. Stock purchased in private placements is an example of restricted stock.

Retained Earnings: A balance sheet account showing accumulated net income, from which any dividends are first declared. Can be thought of as all the profits of the business that have not been paid out as dividends but, rather, reinvested into the business as reflected by other balance sheet accounts, e.g. capital equipment, new stores, etc.

Return on Equity: A measure showing how much in profits each dollar of common stockholder's equity generates for the company, net income / shareholder equity.

Revenue: The proceeds a company receives when selling products and services, the top line of the income statement. AKA "sales."

Revenue Anticipation Note (RAN): A short-term debt obligation of a municipal issuer backed by upcoming revenues.

Revenue Bond: Municipal bond whose interest and principal payments are backed by the revenues generated from the project being built by the proceeds of the bonds. Toll roads, for example, are usually built with revenue bonds backed by the tolls collected.

Reverse Repurchase Agreements: Repurchase agreement from the buyer's perspective.

Rights: Short-term equity securities that allow the holder to buy new shares below the current market price.

Rights of Accumulation: Feature of many mutual funds whereby a rise in account value is counted the same as new money for purposes of achieving a breakpoint.

Rights Offering: Additional offer of stock accompanied by the opportunity for each shareholder to maintain his/her proportionate ownership in the company.

Risk: The variability/volatility involved with investing, typically measured by standard deviation.

Risk-Adjusted Return: Returns adjusted for risk, most commonly through the Sharpe ratio.

Risk Premium: The higher yield offered on corporate bonds versus Treasury bonds of the same maturity.

Riskless Principal Transaction: Transaction in which a broker-dealer chooses to act as a principal when they could have acted as an agent for the customer.

Risk Modification Techniques: Using options and other strategies to reduce the risks presented by current holdings, e.g. buying a put to protect against a large loss on a stock holding.

Risk Tolerance: The ability to withstand fluctuations in principal value due to the investor's time horizon, financial stability, etc.

Rollover: Moving retirement funds from a 401(k) to an IRA, or from one IRA to another. In a "60-day rollover," the check is cut to the individual, who must then send a check to the new custodian within 60 days to avoid early distribution penalties.

Roll-up Transaction: The combination of business units with, for example, a DPP investment.

Roth IRA: Individual retirement account funded with non-deductible (after-tax) contributions. All distributions are tax-free provided the individual is 59½ and has had the account at least five years.

Round Lot: The usual or normal unit of trading. 100 shares for common stock.

R-Squared: A risk measure showing how closely the movement of a portfolio is due to the movement of the benchmark index.

RTRS: Trade reporting system used for transactions in municipal securities on the secondary market. AKA "Real-Time Transaction Reporting System."

Rule of 72: Not a regulation but, rather, a shortcut for figuring compounded returns. For example, if the compounded rate is 8%, 8 divided into 72 tells us the investment will double in approximately 9 years.

Rule (and Form) 144: Regulates the sale of "control stock" by requiring board members, officers, and large shareholders to report sales of their corporation's stock and to adhere to volume limits. The form is filed as often as quarterly—no later than concurrently with the sale.

Rule 144a: Rule that allows restricted securities to be re-sold to institutional investors including banks, insurance companies, broke5r-dealers, investment advisers, pension plans, and investment companies without violating holding period requirements.

Rule 145: Rule that requires corporations in a proposed merger/acquisition to solicit the vote of the shareholders of both the purchasing and the acquired corporation.

Rule 147: Transactional exemption under the Securities Act of 1933 for intra-state offerings of securities.

Russell 2,000: A small-cap index.

RVP: Receipt versus payment, a method of settlement whereby payment on the transaction is made when delivery of the securities is received and accepted.

S

Safe Harbor: Provisions under Section 404(c) of ERISA allowing employers to pass off investment risk to employees in retirement plans, e.g. a 401(k).

Safety: Investment objective that seeks to avoid loss of principal first and foremost. Bank CDs, Treasury securities, and fixed annuities are generally suitable. AKA "capital preservation."

SAI: Detailed and long-form disclosure document for a mutual fund. AKA "Statement of Additional Information."

Sale, Sell: To dispose of a security for something of value.

Sales: The top line of the income statement, usually called "revenue."

Sales Charge, Sales Load: One-time deduction from an investor's check that goes to the distributors/sellers of the fund. Deducted from investor's check, either when she buys (A-shares) or sells (B-shares).

Savings Bond: US Government debt security that is not "negotiable," meaning it can't be traded or pledged as collateral for a loan. Includes series I, EE and HH bonds.

Scheduled Premium: Life insurance with established, scheduled premium payments, e.g., whole life, variable life. As opposed to "universal" insurance, which is "flexible premium."

S-Corporation or **S-Corp:** A form of business ownership with a maximum # of shareholders who receive a share of income/loss and also protection of personal assets.

SEC Release IA-1092: Document explaining the SEC's approach to defining investment advisers based on a so-called "three-pronged approach."

Secondary Market: Where investors trade securities among themselves and proceeds do not go to the issuer.

Secondary Offering/Distribution: Distribution of securities owned by major stockholders—not the issuer of the securities. Not the same as an additional primary offer of securities.

Sector Fund: Fund that concentrates heavily in a particular industry, e.g., the "Technology Fund." Higher risk/reward than funds invested in many industries.

Sector Rotating: Portfolio management technique that involves selling or underweighting securities of companies in certain areas of the economy and buying or overweighting securities in other areas. For example, reducing holdings in pharmaceutical stocks to buy more stocks in the telecommunications sector.

Secured Bond: Corporate bond secured by collateral, e.g., mortgage bond, collateral trust certificate, equipment trust certificate.

Securities Act of 1933: Securities legislation requiring non-exempt issuers to register securities and provide full disclosure.

Securities and Exchange Commission or **SEC:** Federal government regulator of broad aspects of securities markets, empowered by passage of Securities Exchange Act of 1934.

Securities Exchange Act of 1934: Legislation that prevents fraud in the securities markets. No person and no security exempt from anti-fraud regulations. Created/empowered the SEC. Requires broker-dealers, exchanges and securities associations to register with SEC. Requires public companies to report quarterly and annually to SEC.

Security: An investment of money subject to fluctuation in value and negotiable/marketable to other investors. Other than an insurance policy or fixed annuity, a security is any piece of securitized "paper" that can be traded for value.

Self-Regulatory Organization: SRO, e.g., FINRA. An organization given the power to regulate its members. Not government bodies like the SEC, which oversees the SROs.

Sell Limit: Order to sell placed above the current market price that may be executed only if the bid price rises to the limit price or higher.

Sell Stop: Order to sell placed below the current market price, activated only if the market price hits or passes below the stop price.

Selling Away: Violation that occurs when a registered representative offers investment opportunities not sponsored by the firm.

Selling Concession: Typically, the largest piece of the underwriting spread going to the firm credited with making the sale.

Selling Dividends: Violation where an investor is deceived into thinking that she needs to purchase a stock to receive an upcoming dividend.

Selling Group: Certain broker-dealers with an agreement to act as selling agents for the syndicate (underwriters) with no capital at risk.

Selling, General, and Administrative: General operating expenses listed on the company's income statement. Expenses not directly related to the production of the company's product or delivery of its services. AKA "operating expenses."

Semi-Annual: Twice per year, or "at the half year," literally. Bond interest is paid semi-annually, for example.

Semi-Strong: Strain of Efficient Market Hypothesis that contends all published information is already priced into a security, making excess returns impossible through fundamental analysis.

Senior Security: Security that grants the holder a higher claim on the issuer's assets in the event of a liquidation/bankruptcy.

Separate Account: Account maintained by an insurance/annuity company that is separate from the company's general account. Used to invest clients' money for variable annuities and variable insurance contracts. Registered as an investment company under Investment Company Act of 1940.

SEP-IRA: Pre-tax retirement plan available to small businesses. Favors high-income employees (compared to SIMPLE). Only employ-er contributes.

Serial Maturity: An issue of bonds in which the principal is paid off gradually, usually each year until final maturity.

Series EE Bond: Nonmarketable, interest-bearing US Government savings bond issued at a discount from the par value. Interest is exempt from state and local taxation.

Series HH Bond: Nonmarketable, interest-bearing US Government savings bond issued at par and purchased only by trading in Series EE bonds at maturity. Interest is exempt from state and local taxation.

Series I Bond: Savings bond issued by the US Treasury that protects investors from inflation or purchasing power risk.

Settlement: Final completion of a securities transaction wherein payment has been made by the buyer and delivery of the securities has been made by the seller.

Settlement Options: Payout options on annuities and life insurance including life-only, life with period certain, and joint and last survivorship.

Share Identification: Method of calculating capital gains and losses by which the investor identifies which shares were sold, as opposed to using FIFO or average cost.

Sharpe Ratio: The most commonly used method of calculating risk-adjusted return.

Shelf Registration: Registering securities that will be sold gradually on the primary market.

Short: To begin a securities transaction by selling.

Short Interest Theory: Theory that a high level of short sales is a bullish indicator, as it creates potential buying pressure on a security.

Short Sale: Method of attempting to profit from a security whose price is expected to fall. Trader borrows certificates through a broker-dealer and sells them, with the obligation to replace them at a later date, hopefully at a lower price. Bearish position.

Short-Term Capital Gain: Profit realized on a security held for 12 months or less.

Short-Term Capital Loss: Loss realized on a security held for 12 months or less, deductible against Short-Term Capital Gains.

Signature Guarantee: Official stamp/medallion that officers of a bank affix to a stock power to attest to its validity.

SIMPLE IRA: Retirement plan for businesses with no more than 100 employees that have no other retirement plan in place. Pre-tax contributions, fully taxable distributions. Both employer and employees may contribute.

Simple Trust: Trust that accumulates income and distributes it to the beneficiaries annually.

Simplified Arbitration: FIINRA method of resolving disputes involving a small amount of money (currently $50,000).

Single-Payment Deferred Annuity: Annuity purchased with a single payment wherein the individual defers the payout or "annuity" phase of the contract.

Single-Payment Immediate Annuity: Annuity purchased with a single payment wherein the individual goes immediately into the payout or "annuity" phase of the contract.

Sinking Fund: Account established by an issuing corporation or municipality to provide funds required to redeem a bond issue.

SIPC: Stands for the Securities Investor Protection Corporation, a non-profit, non-government, industry-funded insurance corporation protecting investors against broker-dealer failure.

SMA: A line of credit in a margin account. AKA "Special Memorandum Account."

Small Cap: A stock where the total value of all outstanding shares is considered "small," typically between $50 million and $2 billion.

Soft-Dollar Compensation: Economic benefits provided to an investment adviser by a broker-dealer in exchange for using the broker-dealer's custodial and/or execution services.

Sole Proprietor: A business owned as a natural person.

Solicitor: An individual or entity who does not provide investment advice but, rather, sells the services of an investment adviser in exchange for compensation. In most states requires registration as an IAR.

Solvency: Ability of a corporation or municipality to meet its obligations as they come due.

Sovereign Debt: Bonds issued by a national government payable in a foreign currency.

S&P 500: A large-cap index comprised of the 500 largest-company stocks.

Special Assessment Bond: Revenue bond backed by an assessment on only those properties benefiting from the project.

Special Memorandum Account (SMA): Line of credit in a margin account.

Special Tax: A tax on gasoline, hotel and motel, liquor, tobacco, etc.

Special Tax Bond: A revenue bond backed by taxes on gasoline, hotel and motel, liquor, tobacco, etc.

Specialized Fund: A type of mutual fund devoted to a strategy or tactic, e.g. sector funds, asset allocation funds.

Specified Program: Direct participation program in which the assets of the partnership are identified.

Speculation: High-risk investment objective for investors willing to bet on a large price-change in an asset, irrespective of any income it might produce. Short-term speculators trade options and futures, while long-term speculation is evidenced by holding warrants or raw land.

Split Trust: A trust with both charitable and non-charitable beneficiaries, e.g. a charitable lead trust.

Sponsor: The party who puts together a direct participation program.

Spousal Account: IRA established for a non-working spouse.

Spread: Generally, the difference between a dealer's purchase price and selling price, both for new offerings (underwriting spread) and secondary market quotes. For underwritings the spread is the difference between the proceeds to the issuer and the POP.

Stabilizing/Stabilization: Surprising practice by which an underwriting syndicate bids up the price of an IPO whose price is dropping in the secondary market.

Stagflation: a rare economic climate in which inflation and stagnation occur simultaneously.

Standby Underwriting: Commitment by an underwriter to purchase any shares that are not subscribed to in a rights offering.

Standard Deviation: The dispersion of results from their mean, the standard unit of risk.

Statement of Cash Flows: one of three financial statements included in a 10Q or 10K filing along with the balance sheet and income statement, showing how much cash was provided/used through operations, investing, and financing.

Statute of Limitations: A time limit that, once reached, prevents criminal or civil action from being filed.

Statutory Disqualification: Prohibiting a person from associating with an SRO due to disciplinary or criminal actions within the past 10 years, or due to filing a false or misleading application or report with a regulator.

Statutory Prospectus: The prospectus for a mutual fund, as opposed to just the summary prospectus.

Statutory Voting: Method of voting whereby the shareholder may cast no more than the number of shares owned per candidate/item.

Step-Up Bond: A bond that makes higher interest payments in the future compared to the initial payment.

Stock: Ownership or equity position in a public company whose value is tied to the company's profits (if any) and dividend payouts (if any).

Stock Dividend: Payment of a dividend in the form of more shares of stock; not a taxable event.

Stockholders' Equity: The difference between a company's assets and liabilities. AKA "net worth."

Stock Power: Document used to transfer ownership of a stock.

Stock Split: A change in the number of outstanding shares designed to change the price-per-share; not a taxable event.

Stop Loss: Another name for a sell stop order. So named because an investor's losses are stopped once the stock trades at a certain price or lower.

Stop Order: A securities buy or sell order that is activated only if the market price hits or passes through the stop price. Does not name a price for execution. Or, a disciplinary order by the Administrator of denial, suspension, or revocation.

Stop-limit Order: A stop order that once triggered must be filled at an exact price (or better).

Straddle: Buying a call and a put on the same underlying instrument with the same strike price and expiration...or selling a call and a put on the same underlying instrument with the same strike price and expiration.

Straight Life Annuity: Settlement option in which the annuity company pays the annuitant only as long as he or she is alive. Also called "straight life" or "life only."

Straight Preferred Stock: Preferred stock whose missed dividends do not go into arrears, a.k.a. "non-cumulative preferred."

Strategic Asset Allocation: Allocating a portfolio according to the needs of the investor rather than on the expected direction of the stock and bond markets, e.g. any age-based portfolio for retirement or educational funding.

Street Name: Securities held in the name of a broker-dealer on behalf of customers.

Strike Price: Price at which a call or put option allows the holder to buy or sell the underlying security. AKA "exercise price."

STRIPS: Acronym for "Separate Trading of Registered Interest and Principal of Securities." A zero coupon bond issued by the US Treasury in which all interest income is received at maturity in the form of a higher (accreted) principal value. Avoids "reinvestment risk."

Strong Form: Strain of Efficient Market Hypothesis that assumes all information—public and private—is already priced into a security.

Structured Products: Investment products created and sold by a financial intermediary with terms agreed to by both parties to the contract, e.g., an Exchange Traded Note.

Student Loan Marketing Association or **Sallie Mae:** A government-sponsored enterprise providing liquidity to institutions making student loans.

Subaccount: Investment options available within the separate account for variable contract holders. Basically, these are mutual funds that grow tax-deferred.

Subchapter M: Section of the Internal Revenue Code providing the "conduit tax treatment" used by REITs and mutual funds distributing 90% or more of net income to shareholders. A mutual fund using this method is technically a Regulated Investment Company under IRC Subchapter M.

Subject Quotes: Quotes in which the dealer/market maker is sharing information and not yet ready to trade at those prices.

Subordinated Debenture: Corporate bond with a claim that is subordinated or "junior" to a debenture and/or general creditor.

Subscription Agreement: Document signed by a potential limited partner in a DPP.

Subscription Price: Price that all buyers of a new issue will pay to buy the security being offered on the primary market.

Suitability: Determination by a registered representative that a security matches a customer's stated objectives and financial situation.

Summary Prospectus: The most concise disclosure document used to offer and sell mutual fund shares.

Supervised Person: Another name for employees of an RIA required to register as IARs.

Supervision: System implemented by a broker-dealer to ensure that its employees and associated persons comply with federal and state securities law, and the rules and regulations of the SEC, exchanges, and SROs.

Surrender: To cash out an annuity or life insurance policy for its surrender value.

Surrender Charge: The percentage of the contract value retained by the insurance company when an annuity is cashed in during the surrender period.

Surrender Period: The period during which surrender charges apply in a deferred annuity.

Surety Bond: Insurance providing protection to a broker-dealer, investment adviser, or agent against actions related to losses in client accounts.

Swap: an agreement between two parties to exchange cash flows on a notional value over a stated time frame.

Syndicate: Group of underwriters bringing a new issue to the primary market.

Syndicate Letter: Another name for the agreement among underwriters. The document detailing the terms of operation for an underwriting syndicate.

Systematic Risk: Another name for "market risk," or the risk that an investment's value could plummet due to an overall market panic or collapse. Other "systematic risks" include inflation, interest rate, and natural event risk.

Swaps: private arrangements between financial institutions in which, for example, one side pays a fixed rate of interest while the other pays a floating rate on a notional sum.

T

T + 3: Trade date plus three business days.

TAC – Targeted Amortization Class: Type of CMO (collateralized mortgage obligation) that leaves the investor with greater extension risk as compared to a PAC (planned amortization class).

Tactical Asset Allocation: Changing the allocation of a portfolio based on anticipated market movements. Associated with active management and market timing.

Target Fund: An age-based mutual fund that shifts asset allocation in line with the retirement target date of the investors in the fund. AKA "lifecycle" or "age-based" fund.

Tax and Revenue Anticipation Note (TRAN): Short-term debt obligation of a municipal issuer backed by future tax and revenue receipts.

Tax Anticipation Note (TAN): Short-term debt obligation of a municipal issuer backed by future tax receipts.

Tax Credit: Amount that can be subtracted from the amount of taxes owed.

Tax-Deferral: The ability to delay taxation on investment income within a tax-deferred account until constructive receipt.

Tax-Deferred: Account where all earnings remain untaxed until "constructive receipt."

Tax-Equivalent Yield: Rate of return that a taxable bond must offer to equal the tax-exempt yield on a municipal bond. To calculate, take the municipal yield and divide that by (100% – investor's tax bracket).

Tax-Exempt Bonds: Municipal bonds whose interest is not subject to taxation by the federal government.

Tax Preference Item: Certain items that must be added back to an investor's income for purposes of AMT, including interest on certain municipal bonds.

Tax-Sheltered Annuity (TSA): Annuity funded with pre-tax (tax-deductible) contributions. Available to employees of non-profit organizations such as schools, hospitals, and church organizations. a.k.a. "403(b) Plan."

T-Bills: Direct obligation of US Government. Sold at discount, mature at face amount. Maximum maturity is 1 year.

T-Bonds: Direct obligation of US Government. Pay semi-annual interest. Quoted as % of par value plus 32nds. 10–30-year maturities.

Technical Analysts: Stock traders who rely on market data to spot buying and selling opportunities rather than information on the companies who issue stocks.

Telemarketing: To market by telephone, assuming you can get past the caller ID.

Telephone Consumer Protection Act of 1991: Federal legislation restricting the activities of telemarketers, who generally may only call prospects between 8 a.m. and 9 p.m. in the prospect's time zone and must maintain a do-not-call list, also checking the national registry.

Tenancy in the Entirety: Ownership method in which while they are alive neither spouse can sell or give away his interest in the property without the consent of the other spouse, and creditors of either spouse cannot attach and sell one debtor spouse's interest in the property--only creditors of the married couple can do that.

Tenants in Common: Joint account wherein the interest of the deceased owner reverts to his/her estate. AKA "joint tenants in common" or "JTIC."

Tender Offer: Offer to purchase the securities currently held by investors if the investors care to "tender" their securities for payment.

Term Life Insurance: Temporary insurance that builds no cash value and must be renewed at a higher premium at the end of the term. Renting rather than buying insurance.

Term Maturity: An issue of bonds that all mature on the same date in the future.

Testamentary: A trust established upon death of the grantor upon presentation of the will to the probate court.

The Insured: The person upon whose death a life insurance policy will pay out. Though usually also the policy owner, the insured could be a business partner whose death would require the other partners to do a buyout and, therefore, need the death benefit payable to the business.

Third Market: NYSE exchange-listed stock traded OTC primarily by institutional investors.

Third-party Account: Account managed on behalf of a third party, e.g., trust or UGMA.

Time Horizon: The anticipated holding period for an investment.

Times Interest Earned: Measurement from the income statement showing an issuer's ability to pay bond interest, EBIT divided by interest.

Time Value: The value of an option above its intrinsic value. For example, if XYZ trades @50, an XYZ Oct 50 call @1 has no intrinsic value but has $1 of time value.

Time Value of Money: The fact that a sum of money is worth more now than at some point in the future due to its earning potential.

Time Weighted Return: The average of returns over the time period.

Timing Risk: The risk of purchasing an investment at a peak price not likely to be sustained or seen again. Timing risk can be reduced through dollar cost averaging, rather than investing in a stock with one purchase.

Tippee: The guy who listened to the insider information.

Tipper: The guy who told him.

T-Notes: Direct obligation of US Government. Pay semi-annual interest. Quoted as % of par value plus 32nds. 2–10-year maturities.

Tombstone: Communication allowed during the cooling-off period to announce an offer of securities, listing the issuer, the type of security, the underwriters, and directions for obtaining a prospectus.

Top-Down Analysis: A type of fundamental analysis starting with overall economic trends and then moving down to industry sectors and companies.

Top-Heavy: A tax problem incurred by 401(k) plans providing too much benefit to key employees.

Total Assets: Current assets plus fixed assets plus intangible assets.

Total Liabilities: Current liabilities plus long-term liabilities.

Total Return: Measuring growth in share price plus dividend and capital gains distributions.

Total Takedown: The additional takedown plus the concession.

Totten Trust: A pay-on-death bank account.

Trade Confirmation: Document containing details of a securities transaction, e.g., price of the security, commissions, stock symbol, number of shares, registered rep code, trade date and settlement date, etc.

Trade Date: Date that a trade is executed.

Trade Deficit: Excess of imports over exports in a nation's balance of trade with a trading partner.

Trade Reporting and Compliance Engine (TRACE): System used to report corporate bond transactions in the secondary market.

Trade Surplus: Excess of exports over imports in a nation's balance of trade with a trading partner.

Trading Authorization: Form granting another individual the authority to trade on behalf of the account owner.

Traditional IRA: Individual retirement account funded typically with tax-deductible contributions.

Tranche: Class of CMO. Principal is returned to one tranche at a time in a CMO.

Transfer Agent: Party that maintains an issuer's shareholder records.

Transfer and Hold in Safekeeping: Buy order for securities in which securities are bought and transferred to the customer's name, but held by the broker-dealer.

Transfer and Ship: Buy order for securities in which securities are purchased and transferred to the customer's name, with the certificates sent to the customer.

Transfer on Death (TOD): Individual securities account with a named beneficiary—assets transferred directly to the named beneficiary upon death of the account holder.

Treasury Bill: see T-Bills.

Treasury Bond: see T-Bonds.

Treasury Note: see T-Notes.

Treasury Receipts: Zero coupon bonds created by broker-dealers backed by Treasury securities held in escrow. Not a direct obligation of US Government.

Treasury Securities: Securities guaranteed by US Treasury, including T-bills, T-notes, T-bonds, and STRIPS.

Treasury Stock: Shares that have been issued and repurchased by the corporation. Has nothing to do with the US Treasury.

Trendline: The overall upward, downward, or sideways pricing trend of a stock or index as revealed by a chart.

Trough: Phase of the business cycle representing the "bottoming out" of a contraction, just before the next expansion/reco.

True Interest Cost: Measure of a municipal issuer's total cost of borrowing money by issuing bonds. Unlike net interest cost, true interest cost factors in the time value of money.

Trust Indenture: Written agreement between an issuer and creditors wherein the terms of a debt security issue are set forth, e.g., interest rate, means of payment, maturity date, name of the trustee, etc.

Trust Indenture Act of 1939: Federal legislation requiring that corporate bond issues in excess of $5 million with maturities greater than 1 year must be issued with an indenture.

Trustee: Person legally appointed to act on a beneficiary's behalf.

Turnover Ratio: The frequency of trading that a mutual fund portfolio engages in.

TSA: Tax-sheltered annuity. A retirement vehicle for 403(b) and 501c3 organizations.

Two-dollar Broker: Independent broker on the floor of the NYSE.

U

UGMA or **Uniform Gifts to Minors Act**: Account set up for the benefit of a minor, managed by a custodian.

UIT or **Unit Investment Trust**: Type of investment company where investments are selected, not traded/managed. No management fee is charged. Shares are redeemable.

Unaudited: Financial statements that have been reviewed but not certified by an independent public accountant, e.g. a 10Q as opposed to a 10K report.

Underwriter: Broker-dealer that distributes shares on the primary market. AKA "investment banker."

Underwriting Spread: The profit to the syndicate. The difference between the proceeds to the issuer and the POP.

Unearned Income: Income derived from investments and other sources not related to employment, e.g., savings account interest, dividends from stock, capital gains, and rental income. Not eligible for an IRA contribution.

Unfunded Pension Liabilities: Obligations to retiring municipal workers that outweigh the funds set aside to pay them. A negative factor when analyzing general obligation municipal bonds.

Uniform Prudent Investor Act: A model Act providing guidance to fiduciaries interested in avoiding lawsuits for breach of fiduciary duty in terms of suitability/prudence in investment selection.

Uniform Securities Act: Model act that state securities laws are based on. Designed to prevent fraud and maintain faith in capital markets through registration of securities, agents, broker-dealers, and investment advisers. Main purpose is to provide necessary protection to investors.

Unit of Beneficial Interest: What an investor in a Unit Investment Trust (UIT) owns.

Universal Life Insurance: Form of permanent insurance that offers flexibility in death benefit and both the amount of, and method of paying, premiums.

Unlisted Security: A security that does not meet the listing requirements of a nationally recognized exchange such as NYSE or NASDAQ.

Unrealized Capital Gain: The increase in the value of a security that has not yet been sold. Unrealized gains are not taxable.

Unsecured Bond: A bond issued without specific collateral. AKA "debenture."

Unsolicited: A transaction placed by the investor at no prompting from an agent/broker-dealer.

Unsystematic Risk: A risk that affects only a issuer or industry space, e.g. regulatory risk.

User Fee: Source of revenue used to retire a revenue bond, e.g., park entrance fees, tolls, skybox rentals, etc.

UTMA or **Uniform Transfers to Minors Act:** A custodial account, like an UGMA. Some states allow the transfer to happen as late as age 25, while in most states this occurs at age 21.

V

Valuation Ratio: A comparison of a stock's market price to the EPS, book value, cash flow, or revenue associated with one share of that stock.

Value Funds: Mutual funds investing in stocks currently out of favor with investors trading at low multiples.

Value Stock: As opposed to a "growth stock," a value stock trades at a low P/E or price-to-book ratio.

Variable Annuity: Annuity whose payment varies. Investments allocated to separate account as instructed by annuitant. Similar to investing in mutual funds, except that annuities offer tax deferral. No taxation until excess over cost basis is withdrawn.

Variable Life Insurance: Form of insurance where death benefit and cash value fluctuate according to fluctuations of the separate account.

Variable Universal Life Insurance: Flexible-premium insurance with cash value and death benefit tied to the performance of the separate account.

Vesting Schedule: A time-table for determining at what point the employer's contributions become the property of the employee in a pension plan.

Viatical Settlement: The sale and purchase of a life insurance policy wherein the investor buys the death benefit at a discount and profits when the insured dies. AKA "life settlement."

Visible Supply: Total par value of municipal bonds to be issued over the next 30 days, published in the Bond Buyer.

VIX: a key measure of market expectations of near-term volatility conveyed by S&P 500 stock index option prices. There are both options and futures contracts based on the VIX or "fear index." Full name is the Chicago Board Options Exchange Market Volatility Index.

Volatility: Up and down movements of an investment that make investors dizzy and occasionally nauseated.

Volume: Total number of shares traded over a given period (daily, weekly, etc.).

Voluntary Accumulation Plan: Mutual fund account into which the investor commits to depositing amounts of money on a regular basis.

Voter Approval: Process of approving the issuance of a general obligation bond by referendum.

VRDO – Variable Rate Demand Obligation: Debt security whose interest rate is regularly re-set and which can be "put" or sold back to the issuer or a designated third party for the par value plus accrued interest.

W

Warrant: Long-term derivative security giving the owner the right to purchase stock at a set price. Often attached as a "sweetener" that makes the other security more attractive.

Wash Sale: Selling a security at a loss but then messing up by repurchasing it within 30 days and, therefore, not being able to use it to offset capital gains for that year.

Weak Form: The strain of the Efficient Market Hypothesis that contends technical analysis is of no value.

Western/Divided Account: Syndicate account in which each participant is responsible for their share of the bonds only.

When-issued Confirmations: Confirmations of a purchase on the primary market delivered before the bonds have been issued.

Whole Life Insurance: Form of permanent insurance with a guaranteed death benefit and minimum guaranteed cash value.

Withdrawal Plan: Feature of most mutual funds that allows investors to liquidate their accounts over a fixed time period, or using a fixed-share or fixed-dollar amount.

Working Capital: Difference between a company's current assets and current liabilities measuring short-term liquidity. Related term "current ratio."

Wrap Account or **Wrap Fee Program:** Account in which the customer pays one fee to cover the costs of investment advisory services, execution of transactions, etc.

Wrap Fee: Fee charged in a wrap account covering execution, custodial, and portfolio management services.

Wrap Fee Brochure: Required supplement to an investment adviser's ADV 2 if sponsoring a wrap program.

Y

Yield: The income a security produces.

Yield Curve: A graph representing the yields of debt securities of similar credit quality across various maturities.

Yield Spread: The difference in yields between two types of debt securities, e.g. junk bonds vs. investment-grade, or junk bonds vs. US Treasury's. AKA, credit spread.

Yield to Call: The yield received on a bond if held to the date it is called.

Yield to Maturity: Calculation of all interest payments plus/minus gain/loss on a bond if held to maturity. Or, the discount rate at which the sum of all future cash flows from the bond is equal to the price of the bond.

Z

Zero Coupon Bond: Bond sold at a deep discount to its gradually increasing par value.

Z-Tranche: The last tranche to receive principal in a CMO.

Made in the USA
Lexington, KY
12 February 2017